COMMUNIPAW.

HISTORY

OF THE

COUNTY OF HUDSON,

NEW JERSEY,

FROM ITS EARLIEST SETTLEMENT TO THE PRESENT TIME.

BY CHARLES H. WINFIELD,

COUNSELLOR-AT-LAW, AUTHOR OF "HISTORY OF THE LAND TITLES IN HUDSON COUNTY."

"Ask now of the days that are past."—*Bible.*

"Forsan et hæc olim meminisse juvabit."—*Virgil.*

"'Gainst the tooth of time
And razure of oblivion."—*Shakespeare.*

NEW YORK:

KENNARD & HAY STATIONERY M'FG AND PRINTING CO.,

No. 89 LIBERTY STREET.

1874.

PREFACE.

In the summer of 1869, while the author was investigating the title to the land now owned by the National Storage Company, near Communipaw, he had occasion to examine some old records. These awakened an interest in the past of this vicinity, which has increased with the subsequent years of research and toil. The following pages are the result. Whatever may be its imperfections, the candid reader may safely credit the author with considerable "work and labor done and performed," as the lawyers say, and an honest endeavor truthfully and impartially to reproduce the past and perpetuate the present, for the pleasure or profit of the future.

Not a statement has been made without authority for its justification; not a fact which could throw light upon or add interest to whatever has happened within the County has been omitted, so far as the same came to his knowledge.

The records at Albany, Trenton, Hackensack, Amboy and New York, besides many books, papers and private manuscripts, have been consulted. These have been depended on in preference to memories approaching the "forgetfulness of all things." The County was no inconsiderable part of New Netherland, and its history is contemporary and its government one with New Amsterdam. This suggested the starting point for investigation. It has been carried from that point until the present time. There cannot be much doubt but many interesting facts have escaped discovery; yet, it is believed, somewhat has been found and recorded new and interesting to the reader.

As, until a few years ago, the residents in the County were mostly comprised in a few families, the genealogies of these families are here inserted. In their preparation much assistance has been obtained from the records of the old churches. These in that early day were kept in a manner which should make the keepers of modern church records ashamed of their carelessness.

The sketches of some of the churches would have been more complete, had not persons who might be supposed to be interested therein been quite so indifferent.

To those who have by their subscriptions encouraged the author to publish this work he is profoundly grateful, and trusts they may have no cause to regret their part in its publication.

C. H. W.

JERSEY CITY, *February*, 1874.

TABLE OF CONTENTS.

CHAPTER V.—1664-1673.

CHAPTER VI.—1673-1764.

CHAPTER VII.

CHAPTER VIII.

CHAPTER IX.—FERRIES.

CHAPTER X.

HISTORY OF HUDSON COUNTY.

CHAPTER I.—1609—1638.

Claims of the early Discoverers—Arrival of Henry Hudson—The object of his expedition—Discovery of Newark Bay—Its several names—Attacked by the Indians—Names of Hudson's river—He Anchors in Weehawken Cove—Description of the country—The Dutch West India Company chartered—Plans of the Company to settle the country—Michael Pauw purchases of the natives, Hoboken, Ahasimus, Aressick and Staten Island—Names the colonie, Pavonia—First settlement in the County—Arrival of Bout—Arrival of Van Voorst—Feast at his house in Harsimus—Contest betwęen Pauw and the Directors—He sells Pavonia.

CONCERNING the discovery of the harbor of New York and the adjacent country much has been written, and different conclusions reached. It may, however, be safely asserted that the honor of its discovery does not belong to the distinguished commander of "de Halve Maan." In 1497, Jean and Sebastian Cabot, under commission of Henry VII. of England, sailed along the coast of North America, and claimed for their master the entire country, the shore of which they occasionally saw at a distance.[1]

In 1524, Jean de Verrazzano, a Florentine, in the service of Francis I., King of France, is supposed to have visited the bay of New York.[2] Governor Stuyvesant, in his "Manifesto" to the Governor of Maryland, says: "The French were, in the year of our Lord God Almighty 1524, the second followers of the discovery in these northern parts of this America by Johan de Verrazzano."[3]

---

[1] *O'Cal., N. N., i.,* 26.

[2] *Bancroft, U. S., i.,* 17.

[3] *Col. Hist. of N. Y., i.,* 149.

In 1525, Estevan Gomez, a Portuguese in the service of the Emperor, Charles V., who had fitted out the expedition for the purpose of discovering a shorter passage to the Moluccas,[1] visited the bay of New York. How thorough his explorations were is not known. As late as 1679 there was a tradition among the Indians that the Spanish were here before the Dutch, and that from them the natives obtained the maize or Spanish wheat.[2] On Ribero's map, which embodies the outlines of the map of Gomez, the whole country, from New Jersey to Rhode Island, is called *the land of Estevan Gomez.*[3]

In 1598, some Dutch in the employ of the Greenland Company came into the bay of New York, and, intending to use it for winter shelter, erected a "little fort" against the incursions of the Indians.[4]

By virtue of the discoveries of Verrazzano, Henry IV. of France, in 1603, gave to Des Monts that portion of the country lying between the fortieth and forty-sixth degrees of north latitude. This included the greater part of New Jersey. But the

---

1 *Biddle's Life of Cabot,* 271.

2 *Long Isl. Hist. Soc., i.,* 273.

3 *Hudson's Sailing Directions,* 45.

4 *Col. Hist. of N. Y., i.,* 149. In a letter (now in my possession) written by Robert Morris of New York to Abraham Ogden of New Jersey, dated Nov. 4, 1785, occurs the following passage: "The only valuable property at Pavonia was within a fort which continued necessary for its original purposes, to wit: a defence against the Indians," etc. Where Mr. Morris obtained his authority for the statement it would be difficult to tell.

It is proper to bear in mind that the Dutch generally denied all discoveries of the Hudson river prior to 1609; at least they denied that the natives recollected, or even had a tradition, that the bay had ever been visited by white men. Van Der Donck, who arrived in New Amsterdam in 1642 and wrote a description of the country in 1653, says: "The Indians, many of whom are still living, and with whom I have conversed, declare freely that before the arrival of the Low Land ship, the Half Moon, in the year 1609, they did not know that there were any other people in the world than those who were like themselves, much less any people who differed so much in appearance from them as we did." *N. Y. Hist. Soc., N. S.,* 137. The poetical account of the first arrival of Europeans at York Island which the Rev. John Heckewelder, a Moravian missionary in Pennsylvania, received from the Indians, bears out the same belief, that Hudson was the first white arrival. *Ibid,* 71. The weight of evidence, however, seems to be against the position.

grant of the French King was ignored by James I. of England, who, in 1606, granted to Edward Maria Wingfield[1] and his associates, under the name of the *South Virginia* or *London Company*, the land between the thirty-fourth and forty-first degrees of north latitude, and to the *North Virginia Company* he gave the land lying between the thirty-eighth and forty-fifth degrees of north latitude.[2]

While these bold navigators were facing the dangers of unknown seas, and monarchs were elated at the prospect of extending their sway over a new and wonderful land, events were transpiring in Europe which were destined to plant an empire on the banks of the Hudson. Notwithstanding the severe measures adopted by Charles V. and Philip II. to destroy the freedom and enterprise of Holland, that indomitable people not only baffled their foes in the field, but, in the midst of their cruel oppressions and the fires of long years of wars, kept alive a keen appetite for trade and adventure, and extended their commerce to every sea. The Spaniards had attempted to destroy the Dutch trade to the Indies, and the Netherland merchants now boldly sought a route to that El Dorado by the way of the northwest. To accomplish this, Henry Hudson, whom the Dutch writers call "the bold Englishman," was induced to enter the service of the Dutch East India Company. He was an experienced navigator, had already, under the patronage of some London merchants, made two attempts (in 1607 and 1608) to discover his favorite passage, and still had unshaken faith in final success. The Company put him in command of a yacht or "Vlie boat"[3] called the Half Moon,[4] of thirty lasts[5] burden, and manned by a

[1] Wingfield was one of the Councillors of the Virginia Company of London, and chosen its first president. He was a grandson of Sir Robert Wingfield of Huntingdonshire, and son of Thomas Maria Wingfield, so christened by Queen Mary and Cardinal Pole. *Camden Soc. Pub., No.* 43. He invested £88 in the venture. *Force's Coll., iii.*

[2] It will be observed that the two grants lap between the 38th and 41st degrees. Why this was so, unless to reduce the prior grant, I do not know.

[3] So called from being built to navigate the Vlie, or Texel. The name is now corrupted into "Fly Boat."

[4] De Halve Maan.

[5] A last is nearly two tons—*zwaarte van* 4,000 *pond*.

crew of twenty, partly Dutch and partly English. By his agreement with the Company, dated January 8, 1609, he was to sail about the first of April in search of a passage by the north side of Nova Zembla, and to continue along that parallel until he was able to sail south to the latitude of sixty degrees, and then hasten back to report to his employers. For this service he was to receive eight hundred guilders, and in case he did not come back within a year, then they were to give his wife two hundred guilders more. In case he found the passage, then the Company were to reward him "for his dangers, trouble and knowledge in their discretion." He was ordered "to think of discovering no other routes or passages except the route around by the north and northeast above Nova Zembla;" but if this could not be accomplished at that time, "another route would be the subject of consideration for another voyage."[1] Bound by his instructions not to go south of the sixtieth degree of north latitude, he sailed from the Texel, April 6, 1609. Disregarding his instructions, however, in his anxiety to discover his favorite object, he coasted along from Newfoundland as far south as the Chesapeake, and, returning, cast anchor inside of Sandy Hook,[2] on the third of September. Before him rose the Highlands of the Navesinck, while upon his left lay the shores of Monmouth. He pronounced the surrounding country "a very good land to fall in with, and a pleasant land to see." Here he lay for a few days, cultivating an acquaintance with the Indians, who seemed highly pleased with the pale face. "The people of the country came aboard of us, seeming very glad of our coming, and brought green tobacco, and gave us of it for knives and beads. They go in deer-skins loose, well dressed. They have yellow copper. They desire clothes, and are very civil."[3] On the morning of the sixth, John Colman, with four men, was sent to sound the river opening to the north. Passing through the Narrows, they found

---

[1] *Henry Hudson in Holland,* by H. C. Murphy.

[2] Called by the Indians, *Naosh, i. e.,* a point surpassing all others.

[3] *Juet's Journal of Hudson's Voyage. N. Y. Hist. Coll., N. S., i.,* 323.

" a very good riding for ships,"[1] and " a narrow river to the westward between two islands."[2] They found the shores on both sides " as pleasant with Grasse, and Flowers, and goodly Trees, as ever they had seene, and very sweet smells came from them. So they went in two leagues and saw an open sea."[3] On their return they were attacked by twenty-six Indians in two canoes, and Colman was killed.[4] His remains were interred at Sandy Hook, and the spot was named Colman's Point.[5] On the eleventh Hudson passed through the Narrows and anchored near the mouth of the Kill Van Kull, "and saw that it was a very good harbor for all winds." The next afternoon he went up the bay six miles —about opposite Communipaw. The surrounding country impressed him with being " as pleasant a land as one need tread upon." At seven o'clock the next morning he hoisted anchor for the exploration of the lordly river, which he hoped would lead him to the Indies; but which, instead of bearing his trusty ship to the shores of the Orient, will, as long as its waters roll on

---

1 *Hudson's Journal.* This was the upper bay, or " Great Bay," as Van Der Donck calls it, *Moulton, i.*, 214, or quasi per excellentiam, " The Bay." *N. Y. Hist. Soc., N. S., i.*, 140.

2 This was the Kill van Kull, or *Het Kill van het Cull, i. e.*, the creek of the bay. A *kill* may be either an inlet or an outlet. The name is now applied to the outlet of Newark Bay. At one time the same name was applied to Pinhorne's Creek, which is an inlet. At times it has been called *After Skull River* and *Kill van Corle.*

This was Newark Bay, afterward called *Het Achter Cull, i. e.*, the back bay, to distinguish it from " The Bay," or New York Bay. By the Dutch it was also written *Aghter* and *Achter Coll, N. Y. Hist. Soc., 2d, S., i.*, 93; and by the English *After Coll, Col. Hist. of N. Y., ii.*, 576, and applied to the territory bordering on the Kills, between Elizabeth and Amboy, as well as to the bay itself. It was afterward corrupted into *Arthur Cull* and *After Kull.*

4 This attack was probably made at the mouth of the Kill van Kull. It is also probable that the canoes were from Manhattan, for the Indians on the Jersey shore visited the ship the next day, and seemed to be ignorant of what had happened. This, I think, would not have been the case had the attack been made by any of their neighbors on the west side of the bay. It must also be borne in mind that there was no intercourse between the tribes on the opposite sides of the river. They were *infessissimi hostes. Moulton, i.*, 219.

5 *O'Cal., N. N., i.*, 36; *N. Y. Hist. Col*, *i.*, 324.

to the sea, bear his name down to posterity.[1] He did not return until the second of October, when, having been attacked by the Indians at the head of Manhattan Island, he bore gradually across the river, and anchored in Weehawken Cove, just above Castle Point.[2] On the fourth, with fair weather and a northwest wind, he weighed anchor, and, bidding a final adieu to the river he had explored, passed through the Kills to Amboy, and thence stood out to sea.[3]

---

[1] The Hudson River has had many names, some of them striking and beautiful. The Iroquois called it *Cohohatatea, i. e.,* "the great river having mountains beyond the Cohoh." The Mohegans called it the *Shatemuc, i. e.,* "the place of the pelicans." The Delawares named it *Mahican-ittuck, i. e.,* "the River of the Mohegans." By the Spaniards it was named *Rio St. Antonio,* in honor of St. Anthony; *Rio de Montaigne,* from the mountains through which it flows. Dr. Asher thinks they also called it *Rio de Gomez,* in honor of the navigator. *Hudson's Sailing Directions,* 47. The French called it *Reviere des Montaignes.* The Dutch named it *De Groote Rivier*, because of its magnitude; *Noordt Rivier, i. e.,* North River, to distinguish it from *De Zuydt Rivier, i. e.,* South River, or Delaware; *De Groote Noordt Rivier van Nieuw Nederlandt, i. e.,* The Great North River of New Netherland; *Mauritius,* in honor of Prince Maurice (Watson, *Historic Tales,* 21, and Schoolcraft, *Proc. N. Y. Hist. Soc.,* 1844, 94, say that this last name was not applied until 1623, but *Broadhead, i.,* 45., says it was already thus known in 1611); *Riviere van den Vorst Mauritius. Col. Hist. of N. Y., i.,* 13. It was also called *The River of Pavonia, Ibid,* 151, and *The River of Manahata.* The people of New England called it *The Mohegan River.* It was reserved for the English to honor their brave countryman by naming it *Hudson's Riv r.*

[2] Juet's language is this: "Within a while after we got down two leagues beyond that place, and anchored in a bay clear from all danger of them on the other side of the river, where we saw a very good piece of ground; and hard by it there was a cliff that looked of the color of white green, as though it were either a copper or silver mine; and I think it to be one of them by the trees that grow upon it; for they be all burned, and the other places are as green as grass." *N. Y. Hist. Col., N. S., i.,* 331. The description answers to Hoboken in every particular. The only difficulty about it is, he says, "It is on that side of the river that is called *Manna-hata.*" One of two things I think is certain, either he intended this last remark to apply to the place where the Indians attacked the vessel, or the translator is in error.

[3] It was during this visit that the whites introduced to the Indians the most deadly enemy of their race. They were not slow to learn that wine tastes better than water., and the wild joy of one debauch gave strong invitation to another. While they were a free people, unaccustomed to servitude, and therefore

Although Hudson failed in the direct object of his ambition, to him must be accorded the honor of making known to Europe the finest harbor of the western world and the great river which is an enduring monument to his memory. He had incidentally opened to the old world the loveliest and richest part of the new, where nature seemed to have scattered her gifts from a full hand. The forests abounded in all kinds of useful and ornamental trees, many of them bearing delicious fruit. Vines grew everywhere, yielding in abundance. Plants of nearly every variety grew in great profusion, useful for food and for medicine. Through the forests roamed innumerable buffaloes, panthers, bears, deer, elk, foxes, wildcats, wolves, raccoons, beavers, otters, musks, hares, rabbits, squirrels and ground-hogs. These invited the Indian to the chase, for they supplied him with both food and clothing. The fowls of the air were numerous and of great variety. In the waters of the bay and river life was not less active and varied. At times the bay appeared to be alive with water fowl. The swans, similar to those in the Netherlands and "full as large," were so numerous that the water and shores where they resorted appeared "as if dressed in white drapery."[1] There were three kinds of wild geese, so numerous that sixteen were killed at a shot; ducks, widgeons, teal, brant, blue-bills, whistlers, coots, eel-shovelers, and pelicans,[2] with many strange fowls, some

---

had not in their language a word to express "subjection," so, being a temperate people, unused to "hot and rebellious liquors," they had no word in their language to express "drunkenness." It was left to the pale face to name the monster they had brought to the red man.

[1] *N. Y. Hist. Col., N. S., i.*, 174. The upland which lay in the vicinity of the intersection of Grand street and Hudson avenue was known by the Dutch from the earliest times as *Swane Punt, i. e.*, Swan's Point. It is probable that the place received its name from the fact that it was the resort of the swans in the brooding season.

[2] Watson, in his *Historic Tales of the Olden Times*, and Schoolcraft, *Proc. N. Y. Hist. Soc.*, 1844, 94, say it is not known that pelicans ever visited the waters of New York. Van Der Donck speaks of them as common. The Mohegans who lived on the banks of the Hudson named the river *Shatemuc*, from *Shaita*, a pelican, and *uc*, denoting locality or place, hence the name showed it to be *the place of the pelican*. From the fact that they imposed their name upon the river which they frequented, I conclude that they must have been very numerous.

of which were nameless. Many of these have long since forsaken the neighboring waters. The river and bay were rich in many kinds of fish, among which were whales.[1] Among the shell-fish were lobsters, some of them "being from five to six feet in length," and oysters, some of which were "fit to be eaten raw," others were "proper for roasting and stewing," each of which would "fill a spoon and make a good bite."[2]

It was natural that such an abundance and variety of food should have attracted to the neighboring shores numerous tribes of Indians. Many were settled in the vicinity at the time of Hudson's visit. Those inhabiting the present State of New Jersey and the neighboring parts of New York were of the general stock of the Delawares, or Lenni Lennape,[3] but were divided into two branches, called by the English *Mohegans* and *Mincees*, or *Monseys*, and by the Dutch *Manhikans* and *Sanhikans*.[4] The Mohegans dwelt on the east side of the river, and were the hereditary enemies of the Mincees or Sanhikans, who dwelt on the west side.[5] These were divided into numerous tribes, and these again into clans. On New York Island dwelt the fierce Manhattans.[6] De Laet says they were "a wicked nation," "a bad race of sav-

---

[1] In 1647 two whales ascended the Hudson as far as Cohoh, *N. Y. Hist. Soc., N. S., i.*, 143, possibly, like their enterprising predecessor, seeking a northwest passage to the Indies! In the Weekly Post Boy of Dec. 11, 1752, is the following item: "Last Saturday a whale 45 feet long run ashore at Van Buskirk's Point, at the entrance of the *Kills* from our Bay; where, being discovered by people from Staten Island, a number of them went off and killed him, and may now be seen at Mr. John Watson's, at the ferry house on Staten Island."

[2] Van Der Donck's "New Netherlands." *N. Y. Hist. Col., N. S., i.*, 177.

[3] Original or unmixed race; manly men.

[4] This word, according to Heckewelder, is derived from "sankhican," which signifies *fire works*, and means *the fire workers*, or *fire work people*.

[5] *Broadhead, i.*, 73. The *Sanhikans* were sometimes also known as the *Wabingi*, or *Wappinges*. This latter name is derived from the Delaware word *Waping*, signifying *Opossum*. They inhabited the western shore from the mouth of the river to the Catskill. They were divided into tribes, which hereabouts were the Raritans, Hackingsacks, Pomptons, and Tappaens.

[6] *Mon-ah-tun-uk, place of the dangerous river, i. e.*, Hell Gate, and applied to the inhabitants of the adjoining island. They were the *people of the whirlpool*.

ages," "enemies of the Dutch." On Long Island[1] were the savage *Metouwacks*, subdivided into numerous tribes. The Indians on the west side of the Hudson were a better people than the Manhattans. They carried on considerable traffic with the Dutch, exchanging corn, beans and squashes[2] for trifles. Among the Sanhikans some have supposed Hudson landed.[3] If he landed at all during his stay in the upper bay, of which, however, there is no record, it was, beyond a doubt, on the west shore. There the natives were friendly, while on the opposite shore they were positive enemies. Every inducement which could have persuaded him to land existed in favor of the Jersey shore. The natives between Bergen Point and Weehawken had extended to him many acts of kindness, and were neighbors and relatives of those in the vicinity of Sandy Hook, with whom Hudson held intercourse for some days.

The report of Hudson's voyage, on his return in the summer of 1610, awakened among the merchants of Holland a great de-

---

[1] Called by the natives *Sewan-hacky, i. e.,* "the land of shells"—the place where the Indians coined their money.

[2] *Astutasquash, i. e.,*"vine apple." *N. Y. Hist. Soc., N. S., i.*, 186. Van Der Donck speaking of the pumpkin, says: "It grows here with little or no labor, and need not yield to the apple for sweetness, so that the English, who generally love whatever tastes *sweet,* use it in their pies."

[3] Rev. Mr. Abeel, whose MS. is quoted in *Moulton, i.,* 218, says that on the point where New York is now built, Hudson found "a very hostile people. But those living on the western shore from the Kills upward came daily on board the vessel while she lay at anchor in the river, bringing with them to barter, furs, the largest and finest oysters, Indian corn, beans, pumpkins, squashes, grapes, and some apples, all which they exchanged for trifles: *Here Hudson landed.*"

At the time of Hudson's visit there were four islands near the Jersey shore, viz.: Ellis Island, or Bucking Island, called by the Indians *Kioshk,* "Gull Island;" Bedlow's or Kennedy's Island (from its owners, Isaac Bedlow and Archibald Kennedy, also known as Love Island before its conveyance to Bedlow, *N. Y. Hist. Soc. Proc.*, 1844, 98), named by the Indians *Minnisais,* "The Lesser Island" (from which it would appear that at one time it was smaller than Ellis Island); Oyster Island, which lay a short distance southwest, and Robin's Reef, or Robyn's Rift, that is, "seal reef," for in the Dutch robyn signifies a seal. In 1669, by request of Mr. Bedlow, the island now bearing his name was made a place of privilege from warrant of arrest. *Dunlap's N. Y., ii., cxvii.*

sire to engage in and even to secure a monopoly of the trade thus suddenly opened to their enterprise. A new vessel was fitted out and freighted for *De Groote Rivier*. The venture was successful, but whether any settlement was made is not known. It has been said, however, on the authority of Heckewelder, that the Dutch made a settlement on the Jersey shore in that year.[1] Of this fact there does not exist the slightest proof, and it may well be doubted, when we reflect that there were but four huts on Manhattan Island in 1614. In that year Sir Samuel Argall, of Virginia, sailed into the harbor, subjugated the "settlement," and placed it under tribute to the Governor of Virginia.[2] This subjection was, however, soon thrown off, fortifications were projected, and the Dutch were supreme for the next half century.

The merchants who had sent out vessels had been so successful that they sought, and in October, 1614, obtained from the States General of the United Netherlands a monopoly of the trade of the country between New France and (now for the first time called) New Netherland for four voyages within three years from January 1, 1615.[3] This monopoly was protected by threats of confiscation of vessel and cargo, "besides a fine of fifty thousand Netherland ducats," upon any intruder. The merchants thus secured for three years assumed the name of "The United New Netherland Company,"[4] and made preparations to reap all the advantages now placed exclusively in their hands. Ealkins established a trading post near Albany; Block, in the "Restless," explored the coast of *Scheyichbi*[5] and the *Lennapewihittuck*[6] as far as the Schuylkill. Treaties were made with the Indians, trading posts established at several points,[7] and wealth poured into the treasury of the Company.

---

[1] *O'Cal., N. N., i.,* 68, *n.* [2] *Ibid,* 335.

[3] *Col. Hist. of N. Y., i.,* 10.

[4] Beekman's address, *N. Y. Hist. Soc. Proc.,* 1847, 88 ; *Broadhead, i.,* 137.

[5] The Indian name of what is now New Jersey.

[6] Signifying the *Indian River,* now Delaware.

[7] There is no evidence that at this time a trading post was established within this county. Such probably was the fact, for two reasons : *First,* the Indians on this side of the river were friendly ; *Second,* Harsimus was looked upon as the natural outlet for the commerce of the interior. The subsequent purchase

This exclusive charter expired by its own limitation on the first of January, 1618. Its renewal was refused, and on the third of June, 1621, the "great armed commercial association," the Dutch West India Company, was chartered.[1] The charter gave them exclusive jurisdiction over New Netherland for twenty-one years, power to make contracts with the native princes, build forts, administer justice and appoint Governors. The government of the Company was vested in five chambers, and the executive powers in a board of nineteen delegates from the five chambers, including one to represent the States General. The nineteen gave to the Amsterdam chamber the management of the affairs of New Netherland, which, in June, 1623, was erected into a province.[2] Among the members of that chamber was Michael Pauw.

In the spring of this year an expedition was fitted out and thirty families sent over in the ship "New Netherland," to begin a permanent settlement. It was placed in charge of Cornelis Jacobsen May (or Mey), who was to be the first director of the colony. His administration over this infant colony was a very simple affair, and lasted but one year. He was succeeded by William Verhulst, as the second Director of New Netherland, in 1624, and he by Peter Minuit, in 1626.

It having been determined to establish the colonial headquarters on Manhattan Island, Minuit purchased it of the natives for sixty guilders,[3] and staked out a fort.[4] While this fort was being built a crime was committed, the result of which a few years afterward bore heavily on the settlements within the territory now comprising Hudson County. A Weckquaesgeck[5] Indian, with his nephew, then a small boy, and another

---

of Pauw was opposed by his associates, on the ground that to this point came all the native commerce, which ought not to be controlled by one man. The high commercial importance of our shore put upon it thus early has not in the least depreciated.

[1] A copy of this charter, *in extenso,* may be found in *O'Cal., N. N., i.*, 399.

[2] *Broadhead, i.*, 148.

[3] *Ibid*, 164.

[4] *Valentine's Hist. of N. Y.*, 25.

[5] Now Westchester County in the State of New York.

relative, came from his home to sell beaver skins to the Dutch. Before he reached the fort he was met by three of Minuit's servants, who robbed him of his peltries and murdered him. The nephew, who witnessed the outrage, swore to revenge his uncle's murder, and most terribly did he keep his word.[1]

In 1629 the condition of New Netherland did not meet the expectations of the Company. The population around Fort Amsterdam was small and dependent; the trading at Fort Orange and on the South River was very insignificant. No land was cultivated, save enough to supply the scanty wants of those attached to the Forts, and the only exports were furs and peltries. Plans were now devised to improve the condition of the Province. The Assembly of the XIX, on the 7th of June, 1629, granted "to all such as should plant any colonies in New Netherland" certain "freedoms and exemptions," consisting of thirty-one articles. Concerning them Mr. Broadhead remarks: "Reserving to themselves the Island of Manhattan, which the Company declared it was their intention to people first, they designated it as the emporium of their trade, and required all fruits and wares 'that arise on the North River and lands lying thereabouts,' should be first brought there. To private persons, disposed to settle themselves in any other part of New Netherland, the Company offered the absolute property of as much land as the emigrants might be able 'properly to improve.' To tempt the ambition of capitalists, peculiar privileges were offered to them. These privileges, nevertheless, were carefully confined to members of the West India Company."[2] Any member who should, within four years, plant a colony of fifty adults, in any part of New Netherland, excepting the Island of Manhattan, should be acknowledged as a "Patroon," or feudal chief of the territory thus colonized. Each colony might have lands sixteen miles in length on one side of a navigable river, or, if both banks were occupied, eight miles on each side, extending as far back into the country "as the situation of the occupiers will permit." Each patroon was promised a full title, upon con-

---

[1] *O'Cal., N. N., i.,* 105.

[2] *Broadhead, i.,* 194.

dition that he should satisfy the Indians for the land taken by him. If he established a city, he was to have "power and authority to establish officers and magistrates there." The Company were to protect and defend the colonists, finish the fort on Manhattan, and import "as many blacks as they conveniently could."[1]

The members of the Company were not slow to avail themselves of the "privileges." Godyn and Blommaert took a tract of land on the "South corner of the Bay of South River," and Van Rensselaer seized upon the regions adjacent to Fort Orange, called by the Indians, SEMMESSECK. Michael Pauw, Burgomaster of Amsterdam, and Lord of Achtienhoven, near Utrecht, finding the region on the west shore, opposite Manhattan Island, yet unappropriated, obtained, through the Director and Councillors of New Netherland, on the 12th of July and 22d of November, 1630, the following deeds from the Indians for land lying within this county. They are the first conveyances, by deed, of any land in East Jersey, and the following deed is the first of record in New Netherland:

"**We, Director** and **Council** of **New Netherland**, residing on the **Island** of **Manahatas** and the Fort Amsterdam, under the authority of their **High Mightinesses** the Lords States-General of this **United Netherlands** and the **Incorporated West India Company**, at their Chambers at Amsterdam, do hereby witness and declare that on this day, the date hereof underwritten, before us in their proper persons appeared and showed themselves, to wit: **Arommeauw**, **Tekwappo**, and **Sackwomeck**, inhabitants and joint owners of the land called **Hobocan Hackingh**, lying over against (opposite) the aforesaid **Island Manahatas**, who both for themselves and, *rato cavern*, for the remaining joint owners of the same land, declared that for and in consideration of a certain quantity of merchandize, which they acknowledged to have received into their own hands, power and possession, before the passing of these presents in a right, true, and free ownership, have sold, transported, ceded, conveyed, and made over, and by

---

[1] *Vide* Charter of Freedom and Exemptions at length in *O'Cal., N. N., i.*, 112.

these presents they do transport, cede, and convey to and for the behoof of **Mr. Michiel Pauw**, absent, and for whom we, *ex-officio*, accept under suitable stipulations, viz.: the aforesaid lands by us named **Hoboken Hacking**, extending on the South side, Ahasimus; Eastward, the **River Mauritius**, and on the West side surrounded by a valley (marsh) and morass, through which the boundaries of said land can be seen with sufficient clearness, and be distinguished; and that, with all the jurisdiction, right, and equity, to them, the grantors, in their quality aforesaid, belonging: Constituting and putting in their place and stead the already mentioned **Mr. Pauw**, in the real and actual possession thereof, and at the same time giving full and irrevocable power, authority, and special command to the said Mr. Pauw peaceably to enjoy, occupy, cultivate, have and hold the aforesaid land *tanquam actor et procurator in rem suam acpropriam;* and also to do with and dispose of the same as he might do with his own lands to which he has a good and lawful title; without their, the grantors, in their quality aforesaid, saving or reserving any part, right, action, or authority thereto in the least, either of ownership or jurisdiction; but altogether to the behoof as aforesaid, henceforth, forever, wholly and finally desisting, renouncing, and quit-claiming; promising hereby, moreover, not only to keep, maintain, and fulfill this, their grant, and whatever shall be done by virtue thereof, inviolable and irrevocable forever, but also to keep and maintain the same land against all persons free from any claim, challenge, or incumbrance to be made thereon by any person; as also to cause this sale and grant to be approved of and held valid by the remaining joint owners as they are by right obligated to do; all in good faith without fraud or deceit.

In witness whereof these presents are confirmed with our usual signature and with our seal thereto affixed.

Done at the aforesaid Island of Manahatas, in Fort Amsterdam, this 12th July, 1630."[1]

"**We**, the **Director** and **Council** of **New Netherland**, residing on

---

[1] *Land Papers (Albany), G. G.*, 1; *Winfield's Land Titles,* 3. This is the

the **Island** of **Manahatas**, under the jurisdiction of their High Mightinesses the Lords, the States-General of the **United Netherlands**, and the **General Incorporated West India Company**, do, by these presents, publish and declare, that on this day, the date underwritten, before us in their own proper persons, came and appeared, **Kikitoauw** and **Aiarouw**, **Virginians**, Inhabitants and joint owners of the land named **Ahasimus** and the peninsula **Aressick**, as well for themselves as, *rato caverende*, for **Mingm**, **Wathkath** and **Cauwins**, joint proprietors of the same parcels of land, and declared in the same quality that for and in consideration of certain parcels of goods, which they, the appearers, acknowledged before the passing of these presents to their full gratitude and satisfaction to have received into their possession, hands, and power in their right and free (unincumbered) ownership, and by virtue of the title and article of sale, they have sold, transported, ceded, and delivered, and by these presents they do transport, cede, and deliver to and for the behoof of the **Noble Lord Michiel Pauw** (absent), and for whom we, *ex-officio*, accept the same with suitable stipulations, namely, the aforesaid land **Ahasimus**[1]

---

first time the name of Hoboken is met with. It is an Indian word, and is said to mean *tobacco pipe*. The name, as given in the above deed, with its suffix, "Hackingh," signifying *land*, gives us *the land of the tobacco pipe*. Here the natives were accustomed to procure a stone, out of which they carved pipes. "As tobacco was a natural production of the country, the natives were great smokers. Tobacco pouches hung at their backs, and pipes were their inseparable companions." *Trumbull's Hist. U. S., i.*, 24. Judge Benson thought that Hoboken was a Dutch name. *N. Y. Hist. Soc., 2d Series, ii.*, 112. The name is spelled in various ways, as: *Hobocan-Hacking, Hobocan, Hoboken, Hobocken, Hobucken, Hobokina, Hoboquin, Hobuk, Hoebuck, Hobock, Howbuck, Hoobock, Hoobook, Hooboocken.*

[1] This name is probably Indian. It was applied to that portion of the upland of Jersey City which lies east of the hill, excepting Paulus Hoeck, which was separated from Ahasimus by the salt marsh extending from Communipaw Cove to Harsimus Cove, and generally from Warren to near Grove street. The name has received many spellings, viz.: *Ahasemus, Ahasymus, Ahassimus, Ahasymes, Ahsymes, Achassemes, Harsimus, Horsemus, Horsimus, Horsumus, Hassems, Hasimus, Hassimis, Hassemes, Haassemus, Hossemus, Horressimese.*

and **Aressick**,[1] by us named the **Whores Corner**,[2] extending along the river **Mauritius** and the **Island** of the **Manahatas** on the east side, and the **Island Hoboken Hackingh** on the north side, surrounded by swamps, which are sufficiently distinct boundaries, and that with all the action, right, and equity to them in their quality aforesaid appertaining, constituting and substituting the said grantee as the attorney for the said **Mr. Pauw**, in their stead and state, in the real and actual possession of the same, and at the same time giving him full and irrevocable power, authority, and special license, to the said **Mr. Pauw**; and to his successors, *tanquam in rem suam*, the aforesaid land and its appurtenances peaceably to enter upon, possess, inhabit, farm, occupy, use, and to do therewith and thereon, trade and dispose as he the cedentee may do with his own lands and domains honestly and legally obtained, without their, the **Grantors**, in their aforesaid quality, having thereto or any part thereof, any part, right, action, or jurisdiction in the least, without reserving or saving any ownership, command, or jurisdiction, but to the behoof aforesaid from henceforth and forever, wholly and absolutely desisting, relinquishing, and renouncing by these **Presents**. Promoting, moreover, not only this their conveyance, and all that may be done by virtue thereof, to keep forever firm, inviolable, and irrevocable, but also the said land to deliver and keep from all demands, challenge, or incumbrances, any and every one that may thereto make any pretense; and, moreover, this purchase and conveyance to cause to be approved and made valid by the other joint owners, as in equity they are bound to do, standing thereto in all good faith without fraud or deceit. **Witness** our several signatures and confirmed by our seal appended thereto.

---

[1] This was the Indian name of Paulus Hoeck, and is said to signify *burying ground*. It was applied to the circular piece of upland lying east of Warren street, on which Jersey City had its beginning in 1804.

[2] *Hoeren Hoeck*, so called from a well-known custom of the natives in entertaining strangers, and with which they welcomed the Dutch when they first came to this vicinity. *N. Y. Hist. Soc., 2d Series, ii.*, 281, *n.*; *Col. Hist. of N. Y., iii.*, 342.

Done at **Manahattas** in the **Fort Amsterdam** this 22d day of Nov., in the year 1630."[1]

Preceding this last deed, and on August 10th, 1630, Pauw obtained a deed from the Indians for Staten Island, "on the west shore of Hamel's Hooftden."[2]

The purchase of November 22d, 1630, was one of vast importance. Then, as now, the shore between Communipaw and Weehawken was of great commercial value. The Indians held it in high estimation as a place of resort, from which they conveyed their peltries directly across to the fort. Pauw, latinizing his name, bestowed it upon the district, and thenceforth it was called Pavonia.[3] The purchase was unpopular with the Company. Pauw's ownership of the tract "occasioned much quarreling and jealousy, and prevented the colonies prospering as they would have done." Those of the Directors of the Dutch West India Company who had failed to obtain a share of the newly acquired spoils looked with a jealous eye upon those who, by reason of their large and well selected possessions, had become patroons. This strife between the "ins and outs" waxed warm and warmer, until finally the fortunate Directors (except the patroon of Pavonia), preferring peace to their wild acres in New Netherland, divided with their clamorous associates.

Up to this time there is no evidence that a settlement had been made on the west side of the river. Some writers have supposed that buildings were erected within this county as early as 1618.[4] It is, however, mere supposition. It will be borne in mind that in 1623 there were only a few bark huts erected on the lower end of Manhattan Island, and it is not at all likely that the very few whites then in the country would have weakened their power of defence by separate settlements.

---

[1] *Land Papers (Albany), G. G.*, 8; *Winfield's Land Titles*, 8.

[2] *Land Papers (Albany), G. G.*, 6. Thus the first civilized ownership of Staten Island connects it with New Jersey. Carteret once made an unsuccessful claim for it.

[3] Pauwonia. *N. Y. Hist. Soc., N. S., i.*, 264; *Broadhead, i.*, 202. Pauw in the Dutch, as pavo in the Latin, signifies a peacock.

[4] *Broadhead, i*, 89; *Whitehead's East Jersey*, 16.

After the arrival of the immigrants, consisting of thirty families, possessed of domestic animals and other conveniences for a permanent settlement, who in this year came out from the fatherland with Captain May, it is very probable that the inviting shore on this side of "De Groote Rivier" would not long escape the eye of such practical agriculturists.[1] The attention of traders being attracted to our shore by its many advantages for traffic with the Indians, and the farmer invited hither by the fertility of the soil, it may well be, when the number of the colonists permitted, that some venturesome pioneer erected his cabin within the bounds of this county. But where, when, and by whom such first cabin was erected it is now impossible to tell. Yet it is certain that before 1633 some sort of settlement had been made in Pavonia. How much of a settlement this may have been is not known. Pauw made his purchase in the summer and fall of 1630. By the third article of the "Freedoms and Exemptions" he was obliged, within four years next after he gave notice to any Chamber of the Company in Holland, or to the Commander or Council here, that he had taken up any land, to plant a Colony of fifty souls, upward of fifteen years old, within the bounds of his purchase, one fourth part within one year, and the balance within the three remaining years.[2] If the patroon of Pavonia complied with this requirement, there must have been within the bounds of this county, in 1633, at least thirteen persons above the age of fifteen years. But the patroon did not comply with the law respecting the settlement of his colonie, and this, as will be shown hereafter, was one of the causes of difference between him and the Directors, and finally forced him to transfer to the Company all of his interest in Pavonia.[3] Whether he failed to comply with the conditions the first year or afterward is not known. Hence the impossibility of ascertaining the extent of the settlement. But whatever it was, and whether established by himself in pursuance of some regular plan in compliance with the "Freedoms and Exemp-

[1] *Broadhead, i.*, 150.
[2] *O'Cal, N. N., i.*, 112.
[3] *Winfield's Land Titles*, 5.

tions," or by individuals attracted hither for private gain or convenience, Michael Paulusen, an officer of the Company, was in charge of the colonie in 1633. On the afternoon of the twentieth of May in that year, Captain De Vries visited him, and has left this entry in his journal: "Coming to the boat on Long Island, night came on and the tide began to turn, so that we rowed to Pavonia. We were there received by Michiel Poulaz, *an officer in the service of the Company.*"[1] The latter part of this entry seems to indicate that Paulussen, or Pauluszoon, was not in charge at Pavonia as an officer of the patroon. Being in the employ of the Company, he probably occupied a hut on Paulus Hoeck, and, for his employers, purchased peltries from the Indians. In the latter part of this year the Company gave orders for the erection of two houses in Pavonia.[2] This, so far as evidence can be found, was the first step taken to erect regular buildings within this county. They were shortly afterward built. They were constructed and paid for by the Company, although Pauw may have furnished the means. One was built at Communipaw, afterward owned by Jan Evertse Bout, and the other at Ahasimus, afterward occupied by Cornelis Van Voorst.

---

[1] *N. Y. Hist. Soc., N, S., i.,* 257. It is probable that Poulaz was the first Dutch resident in Paulus Hoeck, and left his name to the place. *Broadhead, i.,* 223. Judge Benson intimates that this place received its name from Paulus Schrick, who at one time lived in the "Town of Bergen." *N. Y. Hist. Soc., 2d Series, ii.,* 111. It is true there was such a man, and he may have lived in Bergen, but what has his residence in one place to do with the name of another? It was called "Pouwels Hoeck" before May, 1638. I have not been able to find Schrick's name in the records prior to 1652. The following are the different ways of spelling this name, adding in each instance its suffix of Hoeck, or Hook, viz.: *Paulus, Paules, Poules, Poulus, Powels, Powlas, Powlass's, Powles, Powless, Powlis, Powley's.* Dr. O'Callaghan, *New Neth. Reg.,* 118, puts Poulusen down as a clergyman of the Reformed Church, residing in Pavonia in 1633. I very much doubt that he was a clergyman. After 1633 no more is heard of him in Pavonia. He returned to New Amsterdam, where he received a grant for a piece of land, Jan. 21, 1647. *Land Papers (Albany), G. G.,* 163. He was admitted to the rights of a small burgher April 13, 1657. *New Neth. Reg.,* 177. He made his mark thus:

[2] *O'Cal., N. N., i.,* 156. *Broadhead, i.,* 244. *N. Y. Col. MSS., i.,* 81.

Paulusen was succeeded by Jan Evertse Bout, who arrived in New Netherland June 17, 1634, commissioned by Pauw to be his superintendent. He established his headquarters at Communipaw, which thus became the capital of the colonie of Pavonia.[1] He was succeeded in June, 1636, by Cornelis Van Vorst, who came out as Pauw's "head commander," and took up his residence at Ahasimus, in one of the two houses erected in 1633.[2] He had no sooner become settled in his new "mansion,"

---

[1] Bout was a man of considerable importance in the early history of New Netherland. He was born in 1601, *Valentine's Manual,* 1863, 611, came from Barneveldt, *N. Y. Col. MSS., iii.,* 58, and arrived here in the ship "Eendracht" in 1634. He was in the employ of the Dutch West India Company in Holland, whence he was sent by patroon Pauw to superintend his colonie at Pavonia. *Valentine's Hist. of N. Y.,* 94; *O'Cal., N. N., i.,* 167. His wife's name was Tryntje Simons De Witt. *N. Y. Col. MSS., iii.,* 58. He held the position of superintendent at Pavonia until the summer of 1636, when he was succeeded by Cornelis Van Vorst. *Broadhead, i.,* 263; *N. Y. Hist. Soc., N. S., i.,* 259. He continued, however, to reside at Communipaw. In 1638 his wayward affections brought him into more than doubtful relations with a daughter of Ham, in his service. This coming to the notice of the authorities in New Amsterdam, Schout Lupolt, in his official capacity, visited the jolly Jan to remonstrate with him about the cause of the *scandalum magnatum.* But Bout was in no humor to endure foreign intermeddling with the internal economy of the sovereignty of Pavonia. He flew into a passion, told the Schout in plain Dutch that he was *een hond, een dief, een schobbejak* (a dog, a thief, a rascal), snapped his defiant fingers in the face of the official, and said, "If you or any one belonging to you come to Pavonia, I will shoot you or them." *N. Y. Col. MSS., i.,* 41. This blast was sufficient; the Schout beat a hasty retreat, and for the first time "State's Rights" were vindicated in New Jersey! Bout was probably the first white settler at Communipaw, and was presented with the Bouwerie there after Pauw had parted with his interest in Pavonia. *Col. Hist. of N.Y., i.,* 432. In 1641 he was one of the "Twelve," one of the "Eight" in 1643, and one of the "Nine" in 1647 and 1650. Shortly after the war of 1643 he became a resident in "Breucklen," where he was appointed Schepen in 1646. *N. Y. Col. MSS., iv.,* 259; *New Neth. Reg.,* 73. He soon arrayed himself in opposition to the government, and signed the "bold memorial to the government of the fatherland." *Col. Hist. of N. Y., i.,* 271. In 1654 he was reappointed Schepen. He refused to accept, whereupon he was "directed to hold himself in readiness to return to Holland by the ship 'King Solomon.'" *Alb. Rec. ix.,* 118. Threats of banishment are no longer necessary to induce men to hold office! He died at Gowanus in 1670. *Valentine's Hist. of N. Y.,* 95.

[2] For the history of Van Vorst, *vide* "Van Vorst Family."

which was a frame house thatched with cat-tail, than the dignitaries of New Amsterdam, representing both church and state, resolved to pay him a visit, as well to assure him of their distinguished consideration as to "sample" his newly arrived Bordeaux. On the 25th of June, 1636, Wouter Van Twiller, who was always "glad to taste good wine," but on whose shoulders rested the weighty cares of the New Netherland state, and Dominie Everardus Bogardus, the bold Dutch preacher and husband of Anneke Jans, accompanied by Captain De Vries, came over to Pavonia. Van Vorst entertained them with princely hospitality from his newly filled wine cellar. As time passed on and the sampling of the wine was repeated, the Governor and the Dominie grew warm and disputatious, if not angry with their host. The modest entry in De Vries' journal, that they "had some words with the Patroon's Commissary," plainly means that they quarreled with him. The subject of the dispute was a murder which had been recently committed in Pavonia. Although the discussion ran high and bad blood for a while threatened the peace of the occasion, yet another bumper or two was like oil on the troubled waters, for "they eventually parted good friends." Leaving their host and his good *Vrouwtje*, they entered their boat and started for Fort Amsterdam. Van Vorst, determined to deepen their impression how royally the representative of the patroon of Pavonia could entertain such distinguished guests, fired a salute from a swivel[1] mounted on a pile[2] in front of his house. How the reverberations of that primal salute must have rolled over the hills of Ahasimus! and what a brilliant illumination followed to light the way of his parting guests. "A spark unfortunately flying on the roof, which was thatched with reeds, set it in a blaze, and in half an hour the whole building was burned down."[3] Thus ended the first recorded entertainment in Pavonia.

In the mean time the dissatisfaction existing among the direc-

---

[1] *Steen-stuk*, a stone gun.

[2] "Stood on a pillar" is the language of De Vries.

[3] *N. Y. Hist. Soc., N. S., i.*, 259. *Broadhead, i.*, 263.

tors of the Company that a few of their associates had seized upon the best and most desirable portions of the country was increasing, and they became divided into two parties. They were at variance as to the interpretation to be given to the articles of the "Freedoms and Exemptions." The Company, through those directors who had not become patroons, claimed a monopoly of the fur trade, and would restrict the patroons and their retainers to agricultural pursuits. On the other hand, the patroons claimed an unrestricted trade along the coast and in the rivers, and exclusive commerce and jurisdiction within their colonies, within which they would not suffer any exercise of authority by the officers of the Company. This condition of affairs could not long exist without producing trouble.

On the 17th of December, 1633, the Assembly of the XIX resolved that Pauw, with the other patroons, should give to that body an account of their purchases. On Monday, the nineteenth of the same month, the patroons appeared according to the resolution and defended their rights. It was easy enough to satisfy themselves that their position was impregnable, but to satisfy those who felt themselves aggrieved by the condition of things in New Netherland, and especially in Pavonia, was no light task. These were not convinced, and therefore appointed a committee of five to negotiate with the patroons and to defend the claims of the Company; and in case no agreement concerning the points in dispute could be arrived at between them, then they resolved that the subject should be referred to a "Committee of their high Mightinesses, or one of the high courts of Justice."[1] The committee and patroons failed to agree upon a compromise, and the whole matter in dispute was, by resolution of the Assembly of the XIX, adopted March 27, 1634,[2] referred to their High Mightinesses, who appointed a committee of six to examine carefully into the cause of the dispute, and at the same time issued the following summons to Pauw, and, *mutatis mutandis*, to the other patroons:

---

[1] *Moulton, i.*, 421.

[2] *N. Y. Col. Hist., i.*, 90.

"*To Mr. Michiel Pauw, Lord of Achtienhoven, Co-Patroon in New Netherland, the 13th May*, 1634.

THE STATES.

"Whereas we have this day deputed some Lords from our Assembly, to hear and examine you and the other interested patroons, planters in the Colonies in New Netherland, on the one part, and the delegated Directors of the West India Company and the authorized stockholders on the other part, relative to the differences which have arisen, with power afterwards to determine the said differences, as by plurality of votes they shall find equitable; and the 22d instant having been fixed and appointed by the said Lords, our Deputies, as the day for the business; we have therefore resolved to notify you thereof, commanding you to attend here at the Hague, duly provided in all things, as the case requires, on the evening of the 21st instant, in order to appear on the next day, for the purposes aforesaid, before the above mentioned Lords, our Deputies, who will then proceed to business. Wherein fail not; giving notice hereof to the other patroons, planters who are also interested in the aforesaid differences. Done 13 May, 1634."[1]

The investigation was postponed until the 14th of June. On the sixteenth the patroons put in their defence. It was in writing, of considerable length, and its demands for themselves and charges against the Company of an extraordinary character.[2] Neither their claims nor their charges could be passed in silence by the Company. On the twenty-second of the same month they exhibited their replication "to and against the pretension and claim of Michael Pauw, Kiliaen Van Rensselaar, and Samuel Blommaert, Patroons in New Netherland, handed in and delivered to their High Mightinesses' deputies," in which they protested against the joint action of the patroons and claimed that as the right of each depended on its own peculiar merits,

---

[1] *Col. Hist. of N. Y.*, *i.*, 70.

[2] *Ibid*, *i.*, 83. Here also may be found a copy *in extenso* of their points of defence.

their defence should be several.[1] The patroons forthwith rejoined, asking their High Mightinesses to construe the "Freedoms and Exemptions" that it might be known which party was in fault, and declared that the continuation or abandonment of their colonies depended on their Lordships' judgment.[2] On the 24th of June the deputies resolved to postpone their decision for twelve days, in order that the parties might amicably settle their differences.[3] In August following the Assembly of the XIX commissioned some of their directors "to treat and transact with all the Patroons and colonists in New Netherland" for the purchase of their rights.[4] Shortly afterward (in either 1634 or 1635, for the same is without date), a new "project of Freedoms and Exemptions" was promulgated by the States General.[5] The fifth article contained the following language: "But every one is notified that the Company reserves unto itself the Island of Manhates, Fort Orange, with the lands and islands appertaining thereto, *Staten Island, the land of Achassemes, Arasick and Hobokina.*" The domains of Pauw were included in this reservation, on condition that the Company should make the reservation good. The Company continued the negotiations with the patroon, and finally succeeded in purchasing the colonie. They paid Pauw 26,000 florins[6] for his interest in Pavonia. Thus he ceased to be a patroon in New Netherland, and the annoyance which his colonie had caused no longer existed.[7]

During these long and bitter contentions between the Com-

---

[1] *Col. Hist. of N. Y.*, *i.*, 89. [2] *Ibid, i.*, 90. [3] *Ibid, i.*, 91.

[4] *Broadhead, i.*, 249. [5] *Col. Hist. of N. Y.*, *i.*, 96.

[6] *Ibid, i.*, 423. A florin is equivalent to forty cents.

[7] Dr. Koenen says the colony was in Pauw's name at the time of his death, and that his son, Dr. Isaac Pauw, having removed his residence in 1652, and thereby lost the privileges of citizenship in Amsterdam, *afterward lost his interest in the colony of his father*. *N. Y. Hist. Soc. Proc.*, 1860, 35. This is a great error.

In accordance with the "Freedoms," etc., Harsimus (in part) was reserved, and became known as the West India Company's Farm, but Aressick and Hoboken were disposed of at an early date, without regard to the reservation.

pany and patroons, Pavonia, in common with the rest of the country, was retrograding instead of advancing. Dissensions within had been productive of difficulties without. The character of those who had come hither to seek their fortunes was not in all cases of the best. Disregarding the exclusive privileges of the Company, many of them, prompted by a desire of gain, had unlawfully entered into trade with the Indians, exchanging guns, powder and lead for peltries. The savages were not slow to learn that these weapons were more deadly than the bow and arrow, and a general feeling of uneasiness and alarm began to spread among the settlers.

CHAPTER II.—1638-1646.

Arrival of Kieft—Settlement in the County—Difficulties with the Indians—Murder of Smitz—The people assemble—The twelve chosen—Van Vorst killed by an Indian Chief—The river Indians flee to Manhattan—Thence to Pavonia—Description of the settlements in the County—The Indians encamp near Communipaw—Kieft orders their destruction—Attacked and slain by the Dutch—Communipaw Massacre—Terrible revenge—Pavonia a desolation—Treaty of Peace—Savages again on the Warpath—Van Vorst taken prisoner—Peace declared.

William Kieft arrived here as Director-General on the 28th of March, 1638. At that time there were in all New Netherland only seven bouweries and two or three plantations.[1] This backward state of the province may be attributed to the unfortunate disagreements between the Company and the patroons, and the many irregularities which in consequence grew up among the settlers. Kieft reformed the government in many respects, and put a stop to certain wrongs which some of the Dutch were practising toward each other and toward the Indians.[2] Under the new order of things prosperity seemed to revive. Abraham Isaacsen Planck purchased Paulus Hoeck on the first of May, 1638, for two hundred and fifty guilders.[3] Jan Evertsen Bout took a lease of the " Company's farm in Pavonia,"[4] and De Vries took Staten Island and established a colonie there. Other parts of New Netherland were active and thriving. And yet of all men who ever ruled over the country Kieft knew the least of Indian character, or how to tame the wild natures of the sons of

---

[1] A *bouwerie* was the home farm on which the farmer resided; a *plantation* was an out-farm, tilled, but not occupied.

[2] *O'Cal., N. N., i.*, 183 ; *Broadhead, i.*, 277.

[3] *N. Y. Col. MSS., i.*, 13, 14, 22.

[4] *N. Y. Col. MSS., i.*, 53 ; *Winfield's Land Titles*, 48. Afterward known as "Gamoenepaen."

the forest. They beheld the thrift and enterprise of the whites with jealousy, looked upon their growing power with dread, and hoped for the time when they might glut their revenge for the wrongs they had endured. This feeling was not without cause. For in their social intercourse they had been scorned, in their commercial transactions they had been cheated, and without law or justice they had been plundered and slain by the hated Swannekins.[1] Well might they live in fear of the coming time when, unless they defended themselves now, while their enemies were yet few, they should be driven from their homes and the graves of their fathers. Regardless of the situation of affairs, Kieft put a match to the train and hastened the explosion. On the 15th of September, 1639, he resolved to exact a tribute of maize, furs, and wampum from the Indians, and in case of their unwillingness to pay, he proposed to employ all necessary force to remove their reluctance.[2] These wild men of the forest, who were born freemen and had never been taught in the school of subjection, were filled with indignation at such an unjust measure. "He must be a mean fellow," said they, for "he has not invited us to live here, that he should take away our corn."[3] They had extended freely their simple, yet hearty hospitality to the strangers who had come from an unknown land, and now their guests would impose upon them a degrading tribute. They had endured many rebuffs, and suffered many inexcusable encroachments from the domineering and grasping disposition of the whites, and now they were to be forced to contribute what before they had willingly given or sold.

To meet the impending danger and resist the threatened imposition, the Indians were not wholly unprepared. Commercial intercourse, social familiarity, and domestic service among the settlers had acquainted them with the habits, dispositions, and numbers of the whites. Their skill in the use of the guns they

---

[1] From *Schwonnack*, "the salt people," because they came across the salt water. *Moulton, i.*, 255. At first the Indians called the Dutch *Woapsid Lennappe*, that is, "the white people."

[2] *N. Y. Col. MSS., iv.*, 49.

[3] *Valentine's Hist. of N. Y.*, 41.

had obtained in exchange for peltries made them confident in their strength, and their sense of right convinced them of the justice of their cause.[1] Hence they were not in a mood to submit to every indignity and outrage which the impolitic Kieft would heap upon them.

Added to the general sense of wrongs endured, the Weckquaesgeck boy, whose uncle had been robbed and murdered by Minuit's servants in 1626, had now (1641) become a man. The great outrage done to his relative had not been forgotten. During all these long years he had kept the fire alive in his heart. The time had come for it to burst forth with the destructiveness of a "consuming fire." "An eye for an eye and a tooth for a tooth" was the law of his race. The deep damnation of his uncle's taking off demanded a just and full atonement. Its obligations could not be avoided, neither could it be satisfied with a slight retaliation. In the execution of this law he was "right resolute to die."

"What doth the Indian love? Revenge.
What doth he fight for? Revenge.
What doth he pray for? Revenge.
It is sweet as the flesh of a young bear;
For this he goes hungry, roaming the desert,
Living on berries, or chewing the rough bark
Of the oak, and drinking the slimy pool."

The perturbed spirit of the slain was not at rest, for his murder was unavenged. The voice of the dead was heard in the moaning of the sea, in the rattling of the thunder, in the roaring of the storm, in the rustle of the leaves, in the sighing of the wind, chiding the tardy soul of the living. Many moons had come and gone since the old man was sent to join his fathers; many winters had whitened and springs and summers adorned his rude resting place, and yet the heaven that he had hoped for was not his, for his nephew's duty was unperformed. The one must satisfy vengeance, or the other could never enter the hunting grounds which lie in the Hereafter. Urged onward by this feeling, the young man sought his victim, indifferent as

[1] *Broadhead, i.*, 308.

to whom it might be. It happened to be an inoffensive old man, Claes Cornelisz Smits, a "Raadmaker," living in the vicinity of Canal street. Pretending a desire to barter some beavers for duffels,[1] he watched his opportunity, killed Smits, robbed the house, and escaped with the booty.[2] Satisfaction and the surrender of the savage were promptly demanded. But as he had only acted in accordance with the custom of his race, the Sachem refused to surrender him. Kieft wished to seize upon this occasion to punish the natives, but feared the people, whose interest lay in maintaining peace with the savages. He called them together for consultation. After deliberation they came to the conclusion that the murderer should be punished, "but subject to God and opportunity," after making all necessary preparations.[3] They then chose "Twelve Select Men," and "empowered them to resolve on everything with the Director and Council." This was the first representative body in New Netherland. In it were Maryn Adriaensen, Jacob Stoffelsen, and Abraham Isaacsen Planck, three men who were prominent in the early history of Pavonia. The "Twelve" were true to the views of their constituents, and counseled delay.[4] They gave their opinions separately, but were unanimous in advising the Director to consult "time and opportunity" in executing any measure that might be resolved upon, and that before any action should be begun the Twelve were to be notified. Thus peace was for the present maintained, but confidence was not restored. Yet a little longer the fires which were soon to burst forth in a consuming conflagration smouldered.

The year 1642 closed gloomily. Universal uneasiness manifested itself. Wild stories were circulated and believed. Captain De Vries, who had established a new colonie called Vriesendael, at Tappaen, in passing through the woods toward "Ackensack,"[5]

---

1 A coarse kind of cloth.

2 *Broadhead, i.*, 316.

3 *N. Y. Hist. Soc., N. S., i.*, 277.

4 *Broadhead, i.*, 329.

5 An Indian word and said to signify *low land. Hist. Magazine, iii.*, 85. It is written in many ways: *Ackensack, Ackingsack, Ackinghsack, Akkingsakke, Ackenkeshacky, Ackinkeshacky, Hagensack, Haghkinsack, Hackensacky, Hack-*

met an Indian who said the whites had "sold to him brandy mixed with water" and had stolen his beaverskin coat. He said he was going home for his bow and arrows, and would shoot one of the "roguish Swannekins."[1] He kept his word and shot Garret Jansen Van Vorst, who was roofing a house in "Achter Col."[2] Another account is, that one of the "Hacquinsacq" chiefs, a sort of shiftless fellow, being drunk, was taunted by the Dutch and asked if he could make good use of his bow and arrows when in that condition. He answered the question by killing Van Vorst with his arrow, and then asked if he was able or not.[3] The chiefs were alarmed at what had been done, and hastened to their friend De Vries for advice. They offered to pay two hundred fathoms of wampum to Van Vorst's widow, in order to purchase their peace.[4] Kieft would accept of nothing less than the murderer. Him the chiefs could not, or would not surrender. Their excuse was that he had gone two days' journey off among the Tankitekes, "and besides, he was the son of a chief."[5]

The year 1643 opened as the last year had closed—full of doubt and gloom. In the depths of the winter the fierce Mohawks came down upon the Weckquaesgecks, Tankitekes and

---

ingkeshacky, Hackinkasacky, Hackensack, Hackinsack, Hackquinsack, Hacquinsacq, Hackinsagh, Hachingsack, Haghkingsack, Hakkensak.

[1] *N. Y. Hist. Soc., N. S., i.*, 266.

[2] The name here seems to be applied to the country lying between Newark Bay and Tappaen. It was the colonie of Myndert Myndertsen van der Horst the headquarters of which were at Hackensack, "an hour's walk from Vries endael." *Broadhead, i.*, 313.

[3] *Breden Raedt, Doc. Hist. of N. Y. iv.*, 102. *Vide* Van Vorst Family.

[4] *O'Cal., N. N., i.*, 264. The Greeks and Indians seem to have entertained similar ideas of atonement.

"A son's or brother's death,
By payment of a fine, may be atoned;
The slayer may remain in peace at home,
The debt discharg'd ; the other will forego,
The forfeiture receiv'd, his just revenge."

Derby's Iliad, Book IX., lines 731–5.

[5] *O'Cal., N. N., i.*, 263. The Tankitekes were the Haverstraw Indians, of whom Pacham was chief.

Tappaens, whom they wished to place under tribute.[1] Seventeen of them were slain, and many women and children made prisoners, "the remainder fled through a deep snow to the christians' houses on and around the Island of Manhattan. They were humanely received, being half dead of cold and hunger, and supported for fourteen days; even some of the Directors' corn was sent to them." Soon another panic seized them, and again they fled, part of them to Pavonia, where the Hackingsacks bivouacked one thousand strong.[2] They came over to this side of the river on the 23d of February, 1643, and encamped on the westerly edge of Jan de Lacher's Hoeck,[3] behind the settlement of Egbert Woutersssen[4] and adjoining the bouwerie of Jan Evertsen Bout.[5] Here it may be proper to let the poor frightened savages rest for two days, and in the mean while take a glance at the condition of Pavonia, and learn what was taking place in New Amsterdam.

Up to this time, February, 1643, no settlement had been made north of Hoboken. At this place a farm-house and brew-house had been built and a bouwerie cleared and planted. Here Aert Teunissen Van Putten and his family resided.[6]

---

1 *N. Y. Hist. Soc., N. S., i.*, 267.

2 *O'Cal., N. N., i.*, 265.

3 The encampment was a few blocks east of the Lafayette Reformed Church, and near the corner of Pine and Walnut streets, in Jersey City.

4 *Col. Hist. of N. Y., i.*, 209; *Broadhead, i.*, 351. Wouterssen, from Yselstein, was the first occupant of the present Mill Creek Point, or Jan de Lacher's Hoeck. He held it under a lease from Bout, June 20, 1640. *N. Y. Col. MSS., i.*, 201. On September 1, 1641, he married Engeltje Jans van Bresteede, widow. *Valentine's Manual*, 1862, 650. On May 10, 1647, he obtained a patent for a "tract of land called in the Indian Apopcalyck, extending from Dirck Straatmaker's Kil to Gemoenepaen or Jan Evertz Kil, northeast by east and southwest by west, behind the kil which runs through betwixt the upland and the marsh, extending west northwest to the woods." *Land Papers (Albany), G. G.*, 216. This included all the land south of the Abattoir and east of Sycan's Creek. *Winfield's Land Titles*, 56. He was an *Adelborster*, or gentleman soldier, in the army in 1653. He removed from Pavonia and went to New Amsterdam, where he died in 1680.

5 Bout's farm included all of the upland lying between Communipaw Creek, where the Abattoir now stands, on the south, and the meadow where the engine house of the Central Railroad now stands, or Maple street, on the north.

6 Van Putten was the first white resident of Hoboken. He leased the farm

At Ahasimus was the family of Cornelis Van Vorst, now deceased, at the head of which was Jacob Stoffelsen, who had married Van Vorst's widow.

At Paulus Hoeck were Abraham Isaacsen Planck[1] and his tenants, Gerrit Dircksen Blauw,[2] Claes Jansen Van Purmerendt *alias* Jan Potagie,[3] and Cornelis Arissen.[4]

At Jan de Lacher's Hoeck, or Mill Creek Point, as an under tenant of Bout, resided Egbert Wouterssen with his family.

At Communipaw lived Jan Evertsen Bout. After his arrival in 1634, he held this land as Pauw's representative until the patroon sold to the Company. Then, July 20, 1638, he leased the bouwerie for a term of six years for one quarter of the crops.[5] He afterward received, as a gift, a patent for the farm. The following is a copy of this grant:

February 15, 1640, for twelve years from January 1, 1641. *N. Y. Col. MSS., i.,* 187. Kieft was to erect a small house, and Van Putten was to give as rent "the fourth sheaf with which God Almighty shall favor the field." He cleared the land, fenced the fields, erected the first brew-house in the county, stocked the place with twenty-eight head of large cattle, besides hogs, goats, and sheep, and planted a number of fruit trees. *Col. Hist. of N. Y., i.,* 328.

[1] *Ibid, i.,* 194, 195.

[2] Blauw occupied one morgen of land for a "tobacco plantation," under lease dated October 21, 1638, for twelve years from the first of the month, at twenty-five carolus guilders annually, "with express condition that Gerrit Dircksen shall not keep for himself more than six goats and hogs for slaughter, and one sow big with young." *N. Y. Col. MSS., i.,* 55.

[3] Jan Potagie, or "Soup Johnny," also occupied one morgen for the raising of tobacco. *Ibid,* 60. *Vide* Van Vorst Family.

[4] Lease dated April 20, 1643, to run for six years from May 1, 1644, for the whole of Paulus Hoeck, with house and garden of Planck; "on which Paulus Hoeck Abraham Planck shall cause a barn to be built at his expense, which barn and house Cornelis Arissen must keep water tight; said lessee shall pay as rent for the first year 100 guilders, for the remaining five years 160 guilders annually, if Jan Potagie continues to reside on the Hoeck, but if said Potagie shall leave, the lessee shall pay for the aforesaid five years 180 guilders." *N. Y. Col. MSS., ii.,* 53.

[5] This land must have been very productive. Van Der Donck says that Bout laid a wager that he could raise a crop of barley on a field containing seven morgens, which would grow so tall in every part of the field that the ears could easily be tied together above his head. Van Der Donck went to see the field of barley, and found that the straw was from six to seven feet high, and very little of it any shorter. *N. Y. Hist. Soc., N. S., i.,* 159.

"We, Willem Kieft, Governor General, and Council under the high and Mighty Lords States General of the United Netherlands, High Mightiness of Orange and the Honorable Directors of the authorized West India Company, residing in New Netherland, make known and declare that on this day hereunder written, we have given and granted to Jan Everse Bout a piece of land lying on the North River, westward from Fort Amsterdam, before these pastured and tilled by Jan Everse, named Gamoenepaen[1] and Jan de Lacher's Hoeck,[2] with the meadows, as the same lay within the post and rail fence, containing eighty-four morgens.[3]

"In testimony whereof are these presents by us signed, and with our seal confirmed, in Fort Amsterdam, in New Netherland, the which land Jan Everse took possession of in Anno 1638, and began then to plough and sow it.

WILLEM KIEFT.

"By order of the Honorable Governor General and Council of New Netherland.

"CORNELIS VAN TIENHOVEN, Sec'y."[4]

---

[1] This is the first time the names of these two places are met with. It has been said that "Gamoenepaen" received its name from being the *settlement of Pauw. Dunlap's Hist. of N. Y., i.*, 50. *Gemeente*, "community or commons." It is a possible origin rendered plausible by the modern orthography of the word, which is not older than the present century. But Pauw had sold out his interest some time previous, and it was the *land*, not the *settlement*, that was so named. Up to this time the place had been included in the general name of Pavonia. Now it was applied to the upland east of the hill and south of the meadow between Communipaw avenue and Walnut street. The orthography, and especially the final syllable of the word, precludes the idea of its being derived from Pauw. It is, I think, beyond doubt an Indian word. It has been written in many ways, *e. g.: Gemeene Pas* (common way ?), *Gamoenepaen, Gamoenipan, Gemoenapa, Gamoenepa, Gemoenepa, Gemeenapa, Gemoenepaen, Ghmoenepaen, Gemeenepaen, Gmoenepaen, Commanepa, Commenapa, Communepah, Communipaw.*

[2] That is, *John the Laugher's Point.* It was a circular piece of upland at the mouth of Mill Creek, surrounded on three sides by salt marsh and on the east by Communipaw Cove. It is probable that this name immortalizes the jovial disposition of Jan Evertsen Bout, who was its first occupant, and, after Pauw parted with his interest therein, held it under a lease (dated July 20, 1638) from the Company.

[3] For an explanation of this measure, *vide Winfield's Land Titles*, 26.

[4] The original is now in possession of John C. Van Horn, in good preserva-

On the bluff immediately in the rear of Cavan Point, and just where the Central Railroad crosses the Morris Canal, lived Dirck Straatmaker.[1] It is possible there might have been a few other families than those above named, living along the shore between Hoboken and Cavan Point, but if so the fact has not survived. There was no building on the Heights, and, as far as known, none other in the county.

As soon as the Indians had fled to the Dutch for protection from the wild warriors of the north, Kieft saw the opportunity for which he had waited since the murder of the "Raadmaker," and intimated the same to De Vries. He had dissolved the representative "Twelve," and yet he feared the people, should he attack the Indians. Well he might, for besides the retaliation which would fall upon the scattered whites and outlying plantations, the savages were the guests of the Dutch, "strong both against the deed." Violent and unscrupulous men, however, soon opened a way for the slaughter of the savages. Among the former "Twelve" were Jan Jansen Dam (or Damen), Maryn Adriaensen, and Abraham Isaacsen Planck, "three inconsiderate boors."[2] Kieft's secretary, Cornelis Van Tienhoven, was a crafty, subtle, intelligent, sharp-witted man. "He was an adept in dissembling. Where he laughed heartiest, he bit worst; where he hated most, he pretended the warmest friendship. In words and dealings he was loose, false, deceitful and lying; promising every one, but when they came to the point 'he was not at home.'" He and Planck were brothers-in-law, and sons-in-law of Dam. Planck, Dam and Adriaensen were the cronies of Kieft. As Kieft was dining with Dam at Shrovetide, on the night of February 24, 1643, and had become mellow with drinking "mysterious toasts," and so open to the approach of evil counsel, the host, with Planck and Adriaensen, assuming to

---

tion. It is without date, but Van Tienhoven says the farm was given to Bout "long after the house was burnt." *Col. Hist. of N. Y.*, *i.*, 432. The house was destroyed in 1643.

[1] *Winfield's Land Titles*, 58. This bluff took the name of Straatmaker's Point.

[2] *Breeden Raedt, Doc. Hist. of N. Y., iv.*, 102.

speak for the people, presented to Kieft the following cruel petition drawn up by Van Tienhoven, for the immediate slaughter of the unsuspecting Indians:[1]

"*To the Honorable William Kieft, Director General of New Netherland, and his Honorable Council.*

"The whole of the freemen respectfully represent, that though heretofore much innocent blood was spilled by the savages without having had any reason or cause therefor, yet your Honors made peace on condition that the Chiefs should deliver the murderer into your hands (either dead or alive), wherein they have failed, up to the present time; the reputation of which our nation hath in other countries, has thus been diminished, even, notwithstanding innocent blood calleth aloud to God for vengeance: we therefore request your Honors to be pleased to authorize us to attack the Indians as enemies, whilst God hath fully delivered them into our hands, for which purpose we offer our persons. This can be effected, at the one place by the freemen, and at the other by the soldiers.

Your Hono[rs]' subjects,
MARYN ADRIAENSEN,
JAN JANSEN DAMES,
ABRAHAM PLANCK.

By their authority,
CORNELIS VAN TIENHOVEN,
Secretary."[2]

Although the "Twelve" had been dissolved by Kieft himself, and he therefore well knew that no one could speak for them, he was weak enough to heed the voice of three men who falsely spoke in the name of "the whole of the freemen." In his anxiety to perform what he thought a great and heroic deed, he yielded to their counsel, and resolved to "make the savages wipe their chops."[3] On the following day Van Tienhoven and Hans Stein, at one time a deputy jailor in New Amsterdam, came

---

[1] *Col. Hist. of N. Y.*, *i.*, 345.
[2] *Ibid*, *i.*, 193.
[3] *N. Y. Hist. Soc.*, *N. S.*, *i.*, 269.

over to Pavonia to reconnoitre the camp of the Indians.[1] Captain De Vries and Dominie Bogardus, having been informed of what was going on, remonstrated against the whole proceeding, but in vain. Kieft was ambitious "to perform a feat worthy of the ancient heroes of Rome."[2] He immediately issued the following order:

"Sergeant Rodolf is commanded and authorized to take under his command a troop of soldiers and lead them to Pavonia, and drive away and destroy the savages being behind Jan Evertsen's,[3] but to spare as much as it is possible their wives and children, and to take the savages prisoners. He may watch there for the proper opportunity to make his assault successful; for which end Hans Stein, who is well acquainted with every spot on which the savages are skulking, accompanies him. He, therefore, shall consult with the aforesaid Hans Stein and the corporals. The exploit ought to be executed at night, with the greatest caution and prudence. *Our God may bless the expedition.*

"Done 25 February, 1643."[4]

With such revolting blasphemy did the weak Director end such a cruel order! A similar order was given to Adriaensen to attack the Indians at Corlaer's Hoeck. Most wicked and inopportune were both. The settlers were scattered and entirely without notice of the impending blow. Their position and want of preparation for defence rendered them an easy prey to the savage. Under these circumstances the Dutch authorities were entering upon a course the end of which was destruction.

The light of the 25th of February, 1643, was fading, and the shadows of the black winter night were drawing over the beau-

---

1 *N. Y. Hist. Soc., N. S., i.*, 345; *Doc. Hist. of N. Y., iv.*, 103.

2 *N. Y. Hist. Soc., N. S., i.*, 269.

3 De Vries says they encamped at Pavonia, "near the Oyster Bank." *Ibid, i.*, 268. "On Jan de Lacher's Hoeck, near Jan Evertsen's bouwerie." *Col. Hist. of N. Y., i.*, 209. "By the bouwerie of Jan Evertzoon." *Ibid, i.*, 195. "Near Jan Evertsen Bout's bouwerie." *Ibid, i.*, 199. "Behind the settlement of Egbert Wouterssen, and adjoining the bouwerie of Jan Evertsen Bout." *O'Cal., N. N., i.*, 267.

4 *N. Y. Hist. Soc., N. S., i.*, 278.

JAN DE LACHER'S HOECK, OR MILL CREEK POINT.

tiful bay. Huddled and shivering on the western slope of Jan de Lacher's Hoeck, under the protection of the Dutch, the unsuspecting Indians thought themselves safe from the fierce Mohawks. But while they drew around the camp fires and talked or dreamed of their forsaken wigwams, Manhattan was all astir with the movement of troops and citizens. The noble-hearted De Vries stood beside the Director as the soldiers under Sergeant Rodolf passed by the fort on their way to Pavonia. "Let this work alone," said he; "you will go to break the Indians' heads, but it is our nation you are going to murder." "The order has gone forth; it shall not be recalled," was Kieft's dogged reply.[1] The sergeant, with his eighty soldiers armed for the slaughter, marched down to the river, and, embarking in boats prepared for the purpose, silently rowed toward the shores of Pavonia. Rounding the southerly point of Paulus Hoeck, under the guidance of Hans Stein, they pulled for the high point at the mouth of Mill Creek. Here they landed. Climbing the bank, they passed close to the house of Egbert Wouterssen, and cautiously approached their sleeping victims. Suddenly the sound of musketry and the wild shrieks of the Indians rang out in the midnight. Even at this distance of time, "the horrors of that night cause the flesh to creep as we ponder over them." Captain De Vries, who, in contemplating the consequences of the expedition, could not sleep, says, "I remained that night at the Governor's, and took a seat in the kitchen near the fire, and at midnight I heard loud shrieks. I went out to the parapets of the fort and looked toward Pavonia. I saw nothing but the flash of the guns, and heard nothing more of the yells and clamor of the Indians, who were butchered during their sleep."[2] Neither age nor sex could stay the hand of the unrelenting Dutch. Sucklings were torn from their mothers' breasts, butchered in the presence of their parents, and their mangled limbs thrown into the fire or water. Others, "while fastened to little boards"—the rude cradle of the papoose—were cut through, stabbed, and miserably massacred. Some were thrown alive into the river, and

---

[1] *O'Cal., N. N., i.*, 267.

[2] *N. Y. Hist. Soc., N. S., i.*, 269.

when their fathers, obeying the promptings of nature, rushed in to save them, the soldiers prevented their coming to shore, and thus parents and children perished. The babe and the decrepid old man shared the same fate. Some succeeded in hiding among the bushes from their destroyers, but the next morning, driven out by hunger to beg for bread, were cut down in cold blood and thrown into the fire or river. De Vries says, "Some came running to us from the country having their hands off, some, who had their legs cut off, were supporting their entrails with their arms, while others were mangled in other horrid ways, in part too shocking to be conceived; and these miserable wretches did not know, as well as some of our people did not know, but they had been attacked by the Mohawks." Isaac Abrahamsen, a captain of one of the vessels which had brought over the soldiers, and was waiting for their return, saved a little boy and hid him under the sails; but toward morning the poor child, overcome with cold and hunger, made some noise. Instantly he was "heard by the soldiers; eighteen Dutch tigers dragged him from under the sails in spite of the endeavors of the skipper, who was alone against eighteen, cut in two and thrown overboard."[1] Eighty Indians were slaughtered at Pavonia during that night, and this, says De Vries, was "the feat worthy of the heroes of old Rome."

Great was the rejoicing on Manhattan when the soldiers returned bearing the ghastly heads of some of the victims as the trophies of their brilliant exploit. Planck's mother-in-law went so far as to kick these heads in her yet unappeased rage! But, closer than they knew, sorrow and mourning were following upon the heels of their unhallowed rejoicing. How could it be otherwise? What though the slayers were "Christians" and the slain savages? "Hath not a Jew eyes? hath not a Jew hands, organs, dimensions, senses, affections, passions? fed with the same food, hurt with the same weapons, subject to the same diseases, healed by the same means, warmed and cooled by the

[1] Breeden Raedt, *Doc. Hist. of N. Y.*, *iv.*, 104.

[2] *O'Cal., N. N.*, *i.*, 269.

same winter and summer, as a Christian is? If a Jew wrong a Christian, what is his humility? revenge; if a Christian wrong a Jew, what should his sufferance be by Christian example? why, revenge. *The villainy you teach me I will execute; and it shall go hard but I will better the instruction.*"

How suddenly had briars sprung up in the trail![1] While yet the fiendish orgies were being enacted, the work of retaliation had begun. Dirck Straatmaker, in company with some Englishmen and his wife, who had a baby[2] in her arms, came at an early hour upon the bloody field for the purpose of plunder. The surviving Indians, who now saw the soldiers filing off toward their boats, while the others tarried, fired upon Straatmaker's party, with what result the following certificate will show:

"We, the undersigned, sergeant, corporal, and soldiers, at the request of the Attorney-General, attest that on the — February, 1643, in the morning, after we had beaten a party of savages at Pavonia, behind Egbert Wouterssen's, the wife of Dirck Straatmaker, with a few Englishmen, arrived on the spot where the slain were lying, with a view to plunder maize or any other article. We declare solemnly we warned said Dirck Straatmaker and his wife and told them to go home, to which Dirck replied, 'There is no danger. If there were a hundred savages, none of them would hurt us.' Upon which the undersigned left the spot, according to their orders, to go to the house of Egbert. When they arrived there they heard a shriek; then the sergeant ordered some of his soldiers toward the spot, where they found

---

1 "There are briars in the trail between us." An Indian proverb, signifying that trouble exists between the tribes.

2 This child was saved. He was named Jan Dircksen Straatmaker. Shortly afterward he was bound by the authorities in New Amsterdam to Claes Teunissen, with whom he had, on Feb. 28, 1659, been living for sixteen years. He was then in his seventeenth year. *Minutes of the Orphan's Court, New Amst.*, 96. He must, therefore, have been very young at the time of the massacre. It is probable that from him came the family of that name which for a long time lived in Hoboken. He married Geesje Gerrits, Jan. 14, 1665. *Winfield's Land Titles*, 58.

Dirck, aforesaid, wounded (who died a while after of his wounds), and his wife dead. The soldiers saved the English, who had only one gun amongst them all.

"Thomas Willet declared that Dirck aforesaid, being asked, 'Why did you not come with us when we warned?' answered, 'I might have well escaped by running, but I did not wish to leave my poor wife.'

"All which the undersigned declare to be true. Done 18th May, 1643, in New Netherlands.

"JURIAEN RODOLF, Sergeant,
"PETER PETERSEN, Corporal,
"THOMAS WILLET."[1]

So unsuspecting were the Indians of the treachery of the Dutch, that some of them fled from Pavonia to the fort in New Amsterdam for protection, believing for a time that they had been attacked by the Mohawks.[2] They were soon undeceived, however, and forthwith entered upon a relentless war. Eleven tribes resolved upon the work of destruction. They murdered all the men they could find, dragged the women and children into captivity, burnt houses, barns, grain, haystacks, and laid waste the farms of the whites. From the Raritan to the Connecticut not a white person was safe from the tomahawk and scalping knife, except those who clustered around Fort Amsterdam. Says Roger Williams, "Mine eyes saw the flames of their towns, the flights and hurries of men, women, and children, and the present removal of all that could to Holland."[3]

The people laid the fearful responsibility of their present calamities upon Kieft. He tried to shift it upon the shoulders of the three who had urged him to the great wrong. "I have," said he to Bout, "wherewith to defend my conscience, namely, Maryn Adriaensen, Jan Damen, and the man over there, your neighbor," meaning Planck. "You have done fine work," said Jacob Stoffelsen. "You must blame the freemen," responded Kieft. "You have now done fine work, in causing the murder of

---

[1] *Valentine's Manual*, 1863, 541.
[2] *N. Y. Hist. Soc., N. S., i.*, 269.
[3] *Rhode Island Hist. Soc., iii.*, 159.

Christian blood," said Blauw of Paulus Hoeck, alluding to his stepson, who had been killed. "You must put the blame on the freemen, of whom your neighbor, Abraham Planck, is one," replied the Director.[1] Adriaensen became indignant at the attempt to place the responsibility of the war upon him and his associates. It was more than he chose to bear. Rushing upon the Director with cutlass and pistol, he demanded, "What devilish lies are these you have been telling of me?" He was seized, disarmed, and committed to prison. His attack was the signal for a general rising, which was, however, readily subdued, and Adriaensen was shortly after sent in chains to Holland for trial.

Kieft, goaded by the stings of conscience and the taunts of those who had suffered, attempted to conquer a peace, but was unsuccessful. He then turned with suppliant voice to the same God whom he had mocked in his infamous order to Sergeant Rodolf: "Whereas, we continue to suffer much trouble and loss from these heathen, and many of the inhabitants find their lives and property in jeopardy, which no doubt is the consequence of our manifold sins; therefore the Director and Council have deemed it proper that next Wednesday, being the fourth of March, shall be holden a general fast and prayer, for which every individual is solicited to prepare himself, that we may all, with true and incessant prayer, seek God's blessed mercy, and not give occasion through our iniquities that God's holy name may be contemned by the heathen."[2] Neither his attempt to lay the blame upon others, nor his attempt to force the natives into submission, nor his humbling himself before God could screen him from the tempest of indignation that burst upon him. To such a pitch were the people aroused that the proposition was made to depose him from his office and ship him to Holland.[3]

---

[1] *Col. Hist. of N. Y.*, *i.*, 195.

[2] *Valentine's Manual*, 1863, 540.

[3] Hendrick Kip was heard to say: "The Kivit (meaning the director) ought to be packed off to Holland in the Peacock, with a letter of recommendation to Master Gerrit (the public executioner) and a pound flemish, so that he may give him a nobleman's death." *N. Y. Col. MSS.*, *ii.*, 53.

It was now approaching the latter part of March. The season of the year was near when the Indians must prepare for the maintenance of themselves and families by planting. This could not be done in the midst of a war. Advances were therefore made by Pennawitz, chief of the Canarsees, for the re-establishment of peace. This resulted in a "talk" on Long Island, followed by a treaty of "solid peace" on the 25th of March.[1] Some of the Long Island sachems then went to Hackensack and Tappaen to persuade those tribes to send to the fort and make peace with the Dutch. Nearly a month passed before they could be induced to put any faith in the Director. At length Oritany, sachem of the Hackensacks, invested with full power by the neighboring tribes, repaired to Fort Amsterdam, and entered into the following compact:

"This day, the twenty-second of April, 1643, between Willem Kieft, Director-General, and the Council of the New Netherlands, on the one side, and Oratatin, Sachem of the savages residing at Ack-kin-kas-hacky,[2] who declared that he was delegated by and for those at Tappaen, Reckgawawanc, Kictawanc, and Sintsinck, on the other side, is a PEACE concluded in the following manner, to wit:

"All injustices committed by said nations against the Netherlanders, or by the Netherlanders against said nations, shall be forgiven and forgotten forever; reciprocally promising, one the other, to cause no trouble, the one the other; but whenever the savages understand that any nation, not mentioned in this treaty, may be plotting mischief against the Christians, then they will give to them a timely warning, and not admit such a nation within their own limits."[3]

To impress the savages with the solemnity and honesty of this compact, presents were mutually exchanged. But these savages, untutored in the elaborate deceptions of diplomacy, did not feel that the presents received were commensurate with the great

---

[1] *Valentine's Manual,* 1863, 540. [2] Hackensack.

[3] *Alb. Rec., ii.,* 220; *O'Cal., N. N., i.,* 277.

wrongs they had suffered, and they went away grumbling. Hence the peace thus concluded was only apparent and did not last long. The river tribes were not at ease. The great injuries inflicted upon them by the hated Swannekins were unavenged or unatoned, and nothing but blood or a full satisfaction could extinguish the fierce hatred which they nursed. Early in August the war whoop was sounded above the Highlands, and thence rolled southward. In some instances by stealth, in others by open violence, the savages waged a relentless war. Seven different tribes joined the coalition, which spread terror on every side. In this hour of peril Kieft called upon the people whom he had previously slighted to come to his assistance. They selected EIGHT representatives to confer and advise with the Director and Council. In this body was Jan Jansen Damen, but, for the part he had taken in bringing about the February massacre, he was expelled, and Jan Evertsen Bout of Communipaw chosen in his stead. The EIGHT resolved on war, and Kieft proceeded to arm the people, and stationed them in small companies to protect the outlying settlements. But the savages were alert and gave the Dutch but little time for preparation. The force detailed to defend Lord Nederhorst's colonie were routed on the night of September 17th, and the house in which they took refuge was burned. Jacob Stoffelsen, then living near the present corner of Henderson and Third streets in Jersey City, fearing his place might be injured, had three or four soldiers detailed for its protection. On the 1st of October nine Indians came to his house. They were kindly disposed toward him, and did not desire to injure his person. Under some pretence they induced him to cross over to the fort. They then approached the soldiers as friends. These, being thrown off their guard by this show of friendship, gave no attention to their muskets, were attacked and killed, and the buildings burned. The savages took young Ide Van Vorst prisoner and carried him off to Tappaen.[1] Aert Teunissen of Hoboken, out on a trading excursion, was killed

[1] *N. Y. Hist. Soc., N. S., i.,* 272. The next day, at the request of Kieft and Stoffelsen, De Vries went to Tappaen and ransomed the "boy."

near Sandy Hook,[1] and afterward his farm was laid waste and his cattle were destroyed. The four bouweries in Pavonia—Bout's at Gamoenepaen, Wouterssen's at Jan de Lacher's Hoeck, Stoffelsen's at Ahasimus, and Teunissen's at Hoboken—were laid waste and the buildings destroyed, not generally by open force, but by creeping through the bush and setting fire to the roofs, which were constructed either of reeds or straw.[2] Before leaving, they burned every house in Pavonia, except the brew house in Hoboken,[3] and destroyed every bouwerie and plantation, with twenty-five lasts[4] of corn and other produce, and killed or drove away the cattle.[5] Pavonia and adjoining districts suffered more than any other section. So thoroughly was their destruction accomplished that from Tappaen to the Highlands of the Navesinck the country was once more in possession of its original masters.[6] All was desolation. In the language of the Eight to the States General: " Every place almost is abandoned. We, wretched people, must skulk, with wives and little ones, that still are left, in poverty together, by and around the fort on the Manhattes, where we are not one hour safe. . . . These heathen are strong in might. They have formed an alliance with seven other nations; are well provided with guns, powder, and ball, in exchange for beaver by private traders, who have had for a long time free course here. The rest they take from our brethren whom they murder."[7]

These troubles produced much discontent among the colonists. Poverty followed in the wake of the war. The company's treasury was depleted, and Kieft attempted to replenish it by heavier taxation. This, added to the war, kept the country in an almost disorganized condition until the spring of 1645. Then a number of tribes concluded a treaty of peace with the Dutch. In honor of this event, a " grand salute of three guns" was fired by Jacob Jacobsen Roy, gunner in Fort Amsterdam. Unfortunately, one of the pieces—a brass six-pounder—exploded, and poor Roy was

---

1 *Valentine's Hist. of N. Y.*, 47.
2 *Ibid*, 46; *Col. Hist. of N. Y.*, i., 185.
3 *Col. Hist. of N. Y.*, i., 329.
4 *Ibid*, i., 190.
5 *Broadhead*, i., 369.
6 *O'Cal., N. N.*, i., 389.
7 *Ibid*, i., 393.

badly wounded in the right arm.[1] It was not, however, until the thirtieth of August, that the river Indians consented to lay down their arms, and enter into the following treaty:

"This day, being the 30th of August, 1645, appeared in the Fort Amsterdam, before the Director and Council, in the presence of the whole Commonalty, the sachems or chiefs of the savages, as well in their own behalf as being authorized by the neighboring savages, namely: ORATANEY, Chief of *Ackinkes-hacky;* SESSEKENICK and WILLIAM, Chiefs of *Tappaen* and *Reckgawawank;* PACHAM and PENNEWINK (who were here yesterday and gave their power of attorney to the former, and also took upon themselves to answer for those of *Onaney* and the vicinity of *Majanwetinnemin*, of *Marechowick*, of *Nyack* and its neighborhood), and AEPJEN, who personally appeared, speaking in behalf of *Wappinx*, *Wiquaeskecks*, *Sintsnicks* and *Kichtawons.*

"FIRST. They agree to conclude with us a solid and durable peace, which they promise to keep faithfully, as we also obligate ourselves to do on our part.

"SECOND. If it happen (which God in his mercy avert) that there arise some difficulty between us and them, no warfare shall ensue in consequence, but they shall complain to our Governor, and we shall complain to their sachems.

"If any person shall be killed or murdered, justice shall be directly administered upon the murderer, that we may henceforth live in peace and amity.

"THIRD. They are not to come on Manhattan Island, nor in the neighborhood of Christian dwellings with their arms; neither will we approach their villages with our guns, except we are conducted thither by a savage to give them warning.

"FOURTH. And whereas, there is yet among them an English girl, whom they promised to conduct to the English at Stamford, they still engage, if she is not already conducted there, to bring her there in safety, and we promise in return to pay them the ransom which has been promised by the English.

---

[1] *N. Y. Col. MSS., iv.*, 221.

"All which is promised to be religiously performed throughout the whole of New Netherlands.

"Done in Fort Amsterdam, in the open air, by the Director and Council in New Netherland, and the whole commonalty, called together for this purpose, in the presence of the MAQUAS ambassadors, who are solicited to assist in this negotiation as arbitrators, and Cornelius Anthonissen, their interpreter, and an arbitrator with them in this solemn affair. Done as above."

This treaty was signed by Sisendogo, Claes Norman, Oratanev, Sessekemis, William of Tappaen, Jacob Stoffelsen, Aepjen, sachem of the Mohicans, and Cornelis Teunissen, all of whom affixed their mark; and by Willem Kieft, La Montagne, Jan Underhill, Francis Doughty, George Baxter, Richard Smith, Gysbert Opdyke, Jan Evertsen Bout, Oloff Stevensen and Cornelis Haykens.[1]

Thus closed the first Indian war. It had been carried on for eighteen months with but slight intermission. On the return of peace, the owners and tenants of farms on the west side of the river came back to and rebuilt their desolated bouweries.[2]

---

[1] *Valentine's Manual*, 1863, 544.

[2] Bout was among the number who returned. Before he had reconstructed his dwelling, however, he sold the "farm and a poor, unfinished house, with some few cattle, for 8,000 florins," to Michael Jansen. *Col. Hist. of N. Y., i.*, 432. *Vide Vreeland Family*. It is probable that Jansen purchased this farm in 1646. Certainly he was residing there in September, 1647. The farm sold to Jansen was only part of the tract given to Bout by the Company. The other part he sold to Claes Comptah, *alias* Claes Pietersen Cos, for 1,444 florins, 3 stivers. *New Amst. Rec., iii.*, 143. *Winfield's Land Titles*, 48.

CHAPTER III.—1646—1658.

Arrival of Stuyvesant—Murder of Simon Walinges at Paulus Hoeck—Conference with the Indians—Tracts of land taken up in the County—War again breaks out—Pavonia destroyed—All the settlers flee—Indians return their prisoners to Paulus Hoeck—Detached settlements forbidden—Persecution of the Quakers.

On the 28th of July, 1646, Petrus Stuyvesant was commissioned Director General, and arrived at Manhattan on the 11th of May, 1647. Shortly after his arrival the Indians began to complain that the presents promised to them when they entered into the treaty of peace had not been received. Being without money and without goods, he was unable to satisfy their demands, and yet knew that if a war should break out, he would be censured by the fickle multitude. In this dilemma the commonalty were called upon to select eighteen representatives, from whom the Director and Council selected Nine to advise the Government when requested. Manhattan, Breuckelen, Amersfoort and Pavonia made the necessary selections from their best citizens.[1] From Pavonia appeared Michiel Jansen, the farmer,

[1] The merchants, burghers and farmers were represented in this Board. Its duties were—*First*. To promote the honor of God, the welfare of the country, and the preservation of the Reformed Religion, according to the discipline of the Dutch Church. *Second*. To give their opinion on matters submitted to them by the Director and Council. *Third*. Three of the nine, viz.: One merchant, one burgher, and one farmer, were to attend for a month in rotation on the weekly court, as long as civil cases were before it, and to act subsequently as referees or arbitrators on cases referred to them. If, in case of sickness or absence, either of these three could not attend, his place was to be filled by another of the Nine of the same class. Six retired from office annually, to be replaced by an equal number selected from twelve names sent in by the whole board. They held their sessions in David Provoost's school room, and were the immediate precursors of the Burgomasters and Schepens, and of a municipal form of government in the city of New Amsterdam. *New Neth. Reg.*, 55.

who held a seat in the same body in the years 1649 and 1650.[1]

Stuyvesant profited by the experience of his predecessor in his intercourse with the Indians. His manner toward them was conciliatory, and it was nearly two years after his arrival before any difficulty arose on this side of the Hudson, and even this was seized upon by the Director to prove the mildness of his government toward the natives. The following resolution of the Council, passed March 11, 1649, and the subsequent conference with the Indians, throw all the light upon this incident which can now be obtained:

"*Whereas*, on the 9th of March last, at Pavonia, about Paulus Hoeck, one Simon Walinges[2] was found dead, having been, as is supposed from the arrows and wounds in his head, killed by the Indians, although it cannot be ascertained to what tribe they belonged; yet thus far it is the general opinion that it was done by strangers, either from the Raritan or from the south, lured to this crime by their avarice, because they took from the house in which the murdered man resided about three hundred guilders in strung sewant, four beavers and five otters, with some cloth and friezes, which theft, no doubt, drew the man from his house, as he was discovered a pistol shot from the door in the path, lying dead on the ground, with a small ladder in his hand,[3] and as the murdered man, without knowledge of the court, and against common usage, was carried, by some individuals, away from the spot where he was killed, and brought to this side of the river on the Manhattans before this city; so the transaction has occasioned much commotion among the inhabitants and Indians —more so as some of our people took hold of the Indians and denounced them as guilty of the crime, which was then followed

[1] *New Neth. Reg.*, 56.

[2] His surname was Van der Bilt. *Broadhead, i.*, 509. He came to this country in 1636, and settled in Rensselaerwyck.

[3] The meaning of this I do not comprehend, unless he lived in a sort of block-house, which rendered a ladder necessary for entrance and exit, and which, in the excitement of the moment, he carried with him after emerging from the house in pursuit of the thieves.

by a general flight of the Indians from the Manhattans, and accounts of the transaction were spread far and wide.

"Wherefore, to prevent its spreading further, the Director General and Council have deemed it advisable—first, to make no further stir about this murder, and do our best to appease both Christians and Indians, and reconcile them again to one another, to bury the corpse, and urge the Christians carefully to abstain from betraying any desire of revenge."[1]

The Indians, fearing that the Director would seek revenge after the manner of his predecessor, sent some of their leading men to New Amsterdam to ask forgiveness and renew the covenant of friendship. On the 19th of July the Sachems Seysegekkunes, Oratamus (Orataney?), Willem of Tappaen, and Pennekek of Achter Col (Elizabethtown), met the Council at the fort. Pennekek made a speech to the effect that the Minquas of the south desired to live with the Dutch in friendship, and, to signify their wish, he laid down a present for the Director; that one Indian of Meckgackhanic had lately, without the knowledge of his people, done some mischief at Paulus Hoeck, and asked that it might be excused; that the Raritans, residing formerly at Wickquakeck, had a sachem, and wished him to intercede for them; that Meyternack, Sachem of Nyack, with his tribe, was desirous to be included in the treaty, and would continue and remain friends to the Dutch; that he proclaimed the same for the Indians of Remahennonk; that their heart was upright, and they wished to live with the Dutch in friendship, and that all the past might be forgotten, and said: "Could you see my heart, then you would be convinced that my words are sincere and true."

Governor Stuyvesant replied in a conciliatory speech, and presented the Indians with about twenty florins, and some tobacco and a gun to Oratamus. The Indians were delighted, reaffirmed the treaty of peace, and returned to their homes.[2]

From this time until the year 1655 the settlers on the west side of the Hudson pursued the even tenor of their way without

[1] *N. Y. Col. MSS.*, *iv.*, 428.

[2] *Valentine's Manual*, 1863, 548.

much disturbance from any source. They joined in the general crusade against the hard-headed Peter, very much as the masses now do against officials, but beyond this they were occupied in improving their farms. The favorable situation of the land had attracted notice, and numerous grants had been made by the company to individuals since the devastating war of 1643. The wounds of that terrible contest were healed, and health and prosperity were everywhere visible. Jacob Jacobsen Roy, the gunner of Fort Amsterdam, had received a grant for one hundred and fifteen morgens of land at Constapel's Hoeck.[1] Claas Carstensen, the Norman, sometimes called Van Sandt, had taken up fifty morgens, extending from bay to bay, and including the central part of the recent township of Greenville, then called Minkakwa.[2] Maryn Adriaensen had received a plantation of

[1] *Land Papers* (*Albany*), *G. G.*, 141. *Winfield's Land Titles*, 73. The Dutch word for gunner is *konstapel;* hence Konstapel's Hoeck, or Gunner's Point. It derived its name from the occupation of its first European owner. It lies east of Bergen Point, at the mouth of the Kill van Kull. It is a rolling piece of sandy land, separated from the main by salt marsh. Different parts of it are known as Bird's Point, Van Buskirk's Point, and Mitchell's Point. On account of its distance from populous settlements, it is being extensively devoted to those kinds of pursuits which require isolation. Its Indian name was *Nipnichsen*. Roy received the patent in March, 1646. His wife's name was Fokeltje Willems. *N. Y. Col. MSS., ii.*, 29.

[2] *Land Papers* (*Albany*), *G. G.*, 197. *Winfield's Land Titles*, 59. The map of the county will show that Cavan Point is about opposite Droyer's Point—the former in New York bay, the latter in Newark bay. The two points stretch out like wings. Above them are meadows, below them is a good shore, and only about one-half the distance across. By rowing around either of these points the natives had a short and easy portage from one bay to the other, and a good landing upon either side. Hence they named the place *Minkakwa* (corrupted by the Dutch into *Mingackque*), "the place of the good crossing"—from *mino*, or *min*, "good," and *kakiwe*, "to cross over a point of land on foot." It included that part of the county which lies between the Morris canal, or Fiddler's Elbow, on the south, and the bluff where the Central Railroad crosses the Morris canal on the north.

Prior to 1644 Carstensen lived on Long Island. He married Hilletje Hendricks, April 15, 1646; was admitted to the rights of a small burgher, April 13, 1657, *New Neth. Reg.*, 172, and appointed interpreter of the Algonquin language in 1658. *Ibid*, 133.

fifty morgens at Awiehaken.[1] Dirck Zieken (or Sycan) had obtained a patent for a plantation below Gemoenepaen, and back of Kewan.[2] Sycan's Creek, winding through the meadows, between Cavan Point and the upland, still perpetuates the name of

---

Winfield's Land Titles, 36. Adriaensen was born in 1600. *N. Y. Col. MSS.*, *i.*, 249. Came from Vere to this country in 1631, and settled in Rensselaerwyck. *O'Cal., N. N.*, *i.*, 434. He shortly afterward came to New Amsterdam, was chosen one of the "Twelve," August 29, 1641, and bore a prominent part in the troubles of 1643. He was a bad man, a noted freebooter; *O'Cal., N. N.*, *i.*, 434; a drunkard, *N. Y. Col. MSS.*, *i.*, 200, and a slanderer. *Ibid*, *iv.*, 94. His wife's name was Lysbet Tysen. She survived him, and married Geerlief Michielsen, May 3, 1654. *New Amst. Rec.*, *i.*, 448.

The name of this place is now corrupted into *Weehawken*, formerly also written *Whehocken*, *Weehawk* and *Weehauk*, but the true name is as given in the text.

It still retains much of its primitive attractiveness. Halleck has sung its beauty:

> Weehawken! In thy mountain scenery yet,
> All we adore of nature, in her wild
> And frolic hour of infancy, is met;
> And never has a summer's morning smiled
> Upon a lovelier scene. * * *
> Tall spire, and glittering roof, and battlement;
> And banners floating in the sunny air,
> And white sails o'er the calm blue waters bend,
> Green isle and circling shore—are blended there,
> In wild reality. When life is old
> And many a scene forgot, the heart will hold
> Its memory of this.

The word is Indian, and several attempts have been made at its definition. Weeh-ruh-ink, the termination in *auk*, meaning "tree," suspected to apply to the rock which in its structure resembles trees. *N. Y. Hist. Soc. Proc.*, 1844. 106. The modern orthography gives a sound similar to *Ye-haw-kans*, signifying "houses." *Macauly's N. Y.*, *ii.*, 267. In a letter received from Hon. J. Hammond Trumbull, of Connecticut, he says: "The last syllable of *Weehawken* appears to represent the location affix, *ing* or *ink*. I am inclined to believe that *Wehoak* denotes 'the end' (of the Palisades), corresponding to the Massachusetts *Wehque*, 'ending at,' or wôhk-ôew (Eliot), 'at the end of.' This definition seems to me to be the most probable."

[2] The upland along the shore, between the Abattoir and Cavan Point, was granted to Egbert Wouterssen, May 10, 1647, by the Indian name of Apopcalyck. *Winfield's Land Titles*, 36. The northerly part is known as *Raccocas*, formerly *Regpokes*, *Rightpokus*, *Right-pocques* and *Right-Coakkus*. The lower part was Kewan, now known as Cavan Point, sometimes as Great Kaywan. Kewan is Indian, and signifies a *point of land*. On a map in *Marshall's Wash-*

this owner of the land on its western bank.[1] In 1654 patents were issued for land in the southerly part of Jersey City and in Bayonne, down to near the present First Reformed Church. The tracts were designated by this general description, "between Gemoenepaen and the Kil van Kol." Most of them lie within the district afterward known as Pembrepogh, but as that name is not mentioned in the patents, it would seem fair to infer that the same was not then known to the Dutch, or, at least, not applied to this portion of the county. The grants were as follows:

October	23, to Jacob Wallingen, from Hoorn,[2] -	25	morgens.
December	4, to Jan Cornelissen Buys,[3] - - -	25	"
"	5, to Jan Lubbertsen,[4] - - -	25	"
"	5, to Jan Gerritsen Van Immen,[5] - -	25	"
"	5, to Jan Cornelissen Schoenmaker,[6] -	25	"
"	5, to Gerrit Pietersen,[7] - - - -	25	"
"	5, to Lubbert Gysbertsen,[8] - -	50	"

ington, Vol. V., dated August 27, 1776, Kewan is named "Gallows Point." In the olden time this point extended into New York bay much further than it now does. In the last seventy years the water has encroached upon it at least two hundred feet. A cherry orchard once stood where fishermen now stake their nets.

1 This is the creek through which the water of the Off-fall (which stream took its rise in Tuers' pond, near the Bergen Reformed Church) forced its way to the bay. From Straatmaker's Point to the bay it is yet in existence; above that point it was destroyed by the construction of the Morris canal.

2 *Winfield's Land Titles,* 71. It is probable he came to this country with Captain De Vries in 1635 or 1636. *N. Y. Col. MSS., i.,* 64.

3 *Winfield's Land Titles,* 64. Buys was admitted to the rights of a small burgher, April 14, 1657. He was living in Midwout in 1663. He was known as "Jan, the Soldier."

4 *Ibid,* 65. Lubbertsen was appointed clerk of the Company, September 8, 1654, but on the 19th of March, 1658, the same position was refused him. On the 13th of August, 1658, he was licensed to keep school in New Amsterdam, "to teach reading and cyphering;" was admitted to the rights of a small burgher, April 14, 1657, and appointed one of the commissioners to fortify Bergen in 1663.

5 *Ibid,* 66.

6 *Ibid,* 66.

7 *Ibid,* 65. Pietersen was admitted to the rights of a small burgher in 1657.

8 *Ibid,* 62. Gysbertsen was a wheelwright by trade; came over in 1634, and settled in Rensselaerswyck.

December 5, to Jan Cornelissen Crynnen,[1] - - 25 morgens.
" 5, to Gysbert Lubbertsen,[2] - - 25 "
" 5, to Hendrick Jansen Van Schalckwyck,[3] 25 "

Michiel Jansen had also received a patent for twenty-six and a half morgens, and his brother-in-law, Claes Jansen, the baker, a patent for forty morgens lying at and near Communipaw. At Hoboken, Ahasimus, Paulus Hoeck,[4] and Communipaw were flourishing farms.[5]

Ten years had passed since the treaty with Kieft had secured peace to the country. We have now reached the month of September, 1655. Stuyvesant, in command of a squadron of seven vessels, having on board between six and seven hundred men, had departed on the fifth for the South river to expel the Swedes, who had made a settlement there.[6] In his absence troubles arose which bore disastrously upon the settlements on the west side of the river. They grew out of such a trifling fact that one almost fails to appreciate the wonderful stupidity which precipitated them.

Hendrick Van Dyck, the schout-fiscal, had a farm in New Amsterdam south of Trinity Church, extending from Broadway to the North river. He had with much care planted a peach orchard with trees imported from Holland. This fruit was a rarity in those days, and to the Indians it was a novelty. The sight of the blushing peach was a sore temptation to the poor savages, so irresistible, indeed, that they were not loth to venture their lives in the dark nights to sail around in their canoes, and, by a stealthy march and scaling of fences, to appropriate the fruit. The wrath of Van Dyck's wife upon discovering these raids upon

---

[1] *Winfield's Land Titles*, 68. [2] *Ibid*, 69.

[3] *Ibid*, 70. The most of these patentees were soldiers.

[4] This place was, during this year, called on to furnish its quota of troops to exterminate the pirates on Long Island Sound. It furnished one man of the forty required for that purpose. *O'Cal., N. N., ii.*, 258.

[5] Mr. Whitehead, a scholar of accurate learning, says that the several plantations on this side of the river were abandoned in 1651. *Whitehead's East Jersey*, 20. This is a mistake. They were not abandoned until 1655.

[6] *Broadhead, i.*, 604.

her orchard knew no bounds. A watch was set for the thieving savage, but in the chase the wild rover was too nimble for the heavy-bottomed Dutchmen. As capture was impossible, nothing remained but to give the rogues a dose of shot, and Van Dyck was assigned to the duty. At midnight he secreted himself in the orchard and waited for the intruder. A dim figure soon scaled the fence and began to pluck the forbidden fruit. Van Dyck fired; the victim fell. It was an Indian girl, and she was dead. The news of the outrage soon spread, and the Indians deliberately resolved upon signal vengeance. Giving no warning of their purpose, on the night of the 15th of September sixty-four canoes, carrying five hundred warriors, all armed,[1] landed at New Amsterdam and scattered themselves through the streets. Van Dyck, for whom they were searching, fled to the house of his neighbor, Vandiegrist.[2] They attacked the house, and in the affray Van Dyck was wounded in the breast by an arrow, and Vandiegrist was cut down with a tomahawk. The town was quickly aroused; the guard attacked the savages and drove them to their canoes. They then crossed over to the west side of the river, and "in the twinkle of an eye" a house at Hoboken[3] was in flames, and all Pavonia was soon on fire. From one end of the settlement to the other the torch and the tomahawk did their work. Excepting the family of Michiel Jansen at Communipaw, every man who did not seek safety in flight was killed. All the cattle were destroyed, and everything burned. From Pavonia they passed over to Staten Island, and laid that waste.[4] The at-

1 Fourteen hundred men belonging to the same expedition arrived shortly afterward. *Valentine's Manual*, 1863, 552.

2 This Vandiegrist was subsequently one of the owners of Slaugh's Meadow. *Winfield's Land Titles*, 128.

3 Vanderkemp translates this "Harbol." *Alb. Rec.*, *xiii.*, 327.

4 Captain Adrian Post, his wife, five children, one servant and one girl, were saved, *Alb. Rec.*, *viii.*, 158, but captured. *O'Cal.*, *N. N.*, *ii.*, 293. He afterward acted for the Dutch Government in redeeming captives taken by the Indians. He settled in Bergen, where he became ensign, Sept. 6, 1665; representative, June 10, 1673; the first prison-keeper in East Jersey, July 19, 1673, and lieutenant, July 15, 1675. He was a man of considerable influence, and the founder of the Post family. He resided in the town on lot 164; *Winfield's Land Titles*, 81; and died Feb. 28, 1677.

tack raged for three days with all the fury of savage warfare. The Dutch lost one hundred in killed, one hundred and fifty were carried into captivity, and over three hundred were deprived of their homes. Twenty-eight bouweries and a number of plantations were destroyed, besides a large amount of grain and a number of cattle.[1] The savages of Ahasimus, Ackinkeshacky, Tappaen, and others were present in this conflict, and were guilty of shocking cruelties, against their solemn promise, confirmed by an oath, *which they never took before*, viz.: "May God, who resides above, take vengeance on us if we do not keep our engagements and promises."[2]

For the second time Pavonia was a desolation. The settlers on this side of the river, in common with those of other places, took wing and fled to New Amsterdam for protection.[3] Here the most of them remained for the next five years, until better days returned. As soon as Stuyvesant, then on the Delaware, heard of the attack by the savages, he hastened his return. Immediately on his arrival he adopted plans for the defence of the Province. The Indians, being encumbered with the prisoners they had taken, sent in Captain Post with a proposal of ransom. On the 13th of October Pieter Kock[4] conducted Captain Post back to Paulus Hoeck, where he met the Indians. They were displeased that the captain had not returned at the time specified, and gave expression to their feelings by saying, "Ye Dutchmen lie so fast that we cannot trust you." They promised, however, that all the prisoners should be at Paulus Hoeck within two days. "Come and see it."[5]

Although they had invited negotiation and accused the Dutch of falsehood, they prevaricated and delayed to release the captives. Stuyvesant soon lost all patience with them, and issued the following order:

---

[1] *O'Cal., N. N., ii.*, 291.

[2] *Alb. Rec., x.*, 165.

[3] *Valentine's Manual*, 1860, 616.

[4] Pieter was accustomed to come to the shores of Pavonia under more favorable circumstances. It was here, but a few years before, that he wooed but failed to win Annetje Van Vorst.

[5] *Alb. Rec., xiii.*, 65.

"CAPTAIN POST.—Whereas, the savages appear studiously to delay the pending negotiations, which were begun with mutual consent, and with a prospect of satisfactory arrangement, and as they appear, by their repeated excursions, to endeavor to discourage our soldiers, by keeping them constantly on the move, and being ferried over time and time again, meantime no decision is come to respecting the prisoners in their hands;

"Therefore, we desire you, or any other person familiar with the Indian language, to demand in our name of the Sachems Pennekek, Oratanev, and others, what is their final intention, and whether they have concluded to deliver over our prisoners or not, and if so, when. And we also require that they will not keep us longer in suspense or tell us lies.

"Done in Fort Amsterdam, October 16, 1655."[1]

On the following day the Sachem of Achter Col brought to Paulus Hoeck a number of his captives, as appears by the following action of October 18th:

"WHEREAS, Pennekek, a chief of the savages, did yesterday, being the 17th of October, bring in fourteen persons of the Dutch nation, males and females, who had been taken captive by his nation, and placed them again under the protection of the Dutch government, and at the same time, as a further token of his good will, brought in Captain Post, he also a prisoner, and thereupon solicited the Director to reciprocate his courtesy in presenting him with some powder and balls;

"The Director-General and Council judge the request of Pennekek a matter of considerable importance, and having maturely considered it, resolved to send him, as a proof of their good will, two Indians who were taken captive by our men, as a free gift of the Director-General, with a small quantity of powder and ball, in the hope that by these means the remaining Christians may obtain their liberty."[2]

The fact that a body of savages with prisoners were gathered at Paulus Hoeck caused quite a commotion in New Amsterdam

---

[1] *N. Y. Col. MSS., vi.*, 153.

[2] *Valentine's **Manual***, 1863, 557.

The curious rowed over to Pavonia and prowled around the camp. Those who were indignant over the captivity of relatives insulted the Indians if they landed on Manhattan. The authorities, fearing the natural result of such conduct, made a general order on the 18th of October that no person should presume to go over to Paulus Hoeck, by boat, canoe, or other vessel, nor should any one converse with the Indians, under penalty of correction. No person, whoever he might be, should, on the arrival or departure of any boat, or when the Indians should arrive, crowd to the landing, or indulge in clamor or noise, under penalty of imprisonment, whether young or old. If any person crossed the river without showing a token (or permit) from the authorities, the Indians were authorized to arrest and hold him for ransom.[1] On the 19th Post, Claes Jansen de Ruyter, and Peter Wolfertsen van Couwenhoven brought over the above views of the government, with some presents for the Indians, and returned on the 21st with twenty-eight ransomed captives. The savages also sent a message that twenty or twenty-four others would be sent in on receipt of a proper quantity of friezes, guns, wampum, and ammunition. The Director then wished to know how much they would take for the "prisoners *en masse*, or for each." They replied, seventy-eight pounds of powder and forty staves of lead for twenty-eight persons.[2] The offer was accepted, and additional presents made. This seems to have ended the second general Indian war.

At this time it does not appear that there was one white resident remaining within the limits of this county. The savage was again the undisturbed lord of the soil. Even Michiel Jansen, who escaped the slaughter of September, had fled to New Amsterdam with his numerous family. Stuyvesant, being a practical man, attempted not only to conciliate the Indians for the present, but to provide for the safety of settlers in the future. He had long before this, and on several occasions, made known his views as to the impropriety of detached or isolated settlements, which exposed the people to destruction. He now

---

[1] *N. Y. Col. MSS., vi.*, 107.

[2] *O'Cal., N. N., ii.*, 294.

put those views into definite and authoritative shape by the following

"ORDINANCE

Of the Director-General and Council of New Netherland for the formation of villages, and prohibiting straw roofs and wooden chimneys. *Passed January 18th*, 1656.

"WHEREAS, sad experience hath from time to time proved that, in consequence of the separate dwellings of the country people located on the Flatland in divers hooks and places, in complete opposition to the Order and good intention of the Honble Company and its government here, many murders of People, killing and destruction of Cattle, and burning of Houses, have been committed and perpetrated by the Indians, natives of this Country, the most of which might have been, with God's help, prevented and avoided, if the good Inhabitants of this Province had settled themselves together in the form of Towns, Villages, and Hamlets, like our neighbors of *New England*, who, because of their combination and compact residences, have never been subject to such, at least not to so many and such general disasters, which have been caused, next to God's righteous chastisement, on account of our sins, by tempting the Savage Barbarians thereto by the separate residences of the Country people; the one not being able, in time of need, to come to the assistance of the other, in consequence of the distance of the places, and the impossibility of the Director-General and Council to provide each separate country house with a guard. To this, then, besides the Murders, Damages, and destruction of divers People, Bouweries, and Plantations already suffered, is owing also the last, to the serious loss and hindrance of this country and the people thereof, the recurrence of which is to be apprehended and expected hereafter no less than now and heretofore, unless the good Inhabitants are taught by their losses and those of others to be wiser and more prudent, and to allow themselves to be influenced by good law, as they are bound to be, to form compact dwellings in suitable places in form and manner as will be laid down to the Inhabitants by the Director-General and Council, or their Commissioners, when the Director-General and Council will be able to assist and maintain their subjects, with the power intrusted to them by God and the Supreme government.

"In order that this may be the better executed and obeyed in future, the Director-General and Council aforesaid do hereby not only warn their good subjects, but likewise charge and command them to concentrate themselves, by next Spring, in the form of Towns, Villages and Hamlets, so that they may be the more effectually protected, maintained and defended against all assaults and attacks of the Barbarians, by each other and by the military intrusted to the Director-General and Council; Warning all those who will, contrary hereunto, remain hereafter on their isolated plantations, that they will do so at their peril, without obtaining, in time of need, any assistance from the Director-General and Council. They shall, moreover, be fined annually in the sum of 25 guilders for the behoof of the public.[1]

"Furthermore, the Director-General and Council, in order to prevent a too sudden conflagration, do Ordain that from now henceforth no Houses shall be covered with Straw or Reed, nor any more Chimneys be constructed of Clapboards or Wood.

"Thus done, resolved, resumed and enacted in the Assembly of the Director-General and Council, holden in *Fort Amsterdam* in *New Netherland*. Dated as above."[2]

During the following summer the authorities, on information

---

[1] In the latter part of this year Jacob Stoffelsen asked for permission to return to his farm at Harsimus. In his petition he set forth that he had been twice driven away by the Indians, that he was an old man, and was willing to build a small house and barn. The authorities insisted upon their placard of January 18th. They claimed that imperious necessity required that separated settlements should be discouraged. Yet they permitted Stoffelsen to continue the cultivation of his farm at his own risk during the following year. This on December 21, 1656. *N. Y. Col. MSS., viii.*, 313.

[2] *N. Y. Col. MSS., vi.*, 226. On the subject of the preceding ordinance, the Directors in Amsterdam wrote as follows, December 19, 1656:

"We are well pleased with the Edict your Honors have enacted respecting the separate habitations of the outside people, provided it apply to the Builders of new dwellings, and not to those whose houses are already erected and constructed, for we do not think it fair to constrain the latter thereto." *N. Y. Col MSS., xii.*, 45.

that a few Tappaen Indians were contemplating mischief against the whites, reaffirmed the above ordinance, and commanded the people to concentrate in villages.[1]

This ordinance was perhaps the principal cause which prevented the repeopling of Pavonia for several years. The people could not make up their minds to abandon their separate settlements and concentrate in villages. Therefore they quietly remained in exile upon the Island of Manhattan. Neither they nor the authorities would abandon their positions; hence the fields of Pavonia remained desolate.

During the next two years the attention of the authorities and people was largely engrossed with religious matters. A persecution of "Non-Conformists" began, and Dominies Megapolensis and Drisius held the garments of those who stoned the saints. Whatever doctrine they preached, they practiced this: "Stand by thyself, come not near to me; for I am holier than thou." They demanded that Dominie Goetwater, a Lutheran minister, who had presumed to come to New Amsterdam to instruct the people in his way of belief, should be sent back in the same ship in which he came. The "Friends," who had been expelled from Boston, came within the bounds of New Netherland, and proclaimed their simple, comprehensive creed. They were immediately pursued with pains and penalties. If they demanded to be informed what law they had broken, and called for their accusers, that they might know their transgression, tortures followed, such as would rival those of the Inquisition. Even those who entertained the persecuted, or showed them sympathy, were accused of treating with contempt all ecclesiastical and political authority. If one whose soul thirsted for the water of life waited upon the ministrations of any other than a duly authorized expounder of Heidelburgh, he or she was instantly accused of being absent from worship and profaning the Lord's Day. So soon and so completely had Netherlanders forgotten the great lesson of the Low Land War, in which William the Silent laid his life upon the altar, and whole hecatombs of their countrymen had

---

[1] *N. Y. Col. MSS., viii.*, 56.

been sacrificed, that every man might pray to God in his own language and worship Him in what form he might, personally responsible to Him only for the honesty and genuineness of that prayer and worship. Alas, for human weakness which naturalizes tyranny in every heart; which makes every man's *credo* a Procrustean bed upon which he would lengthen or shorten every other man's *credo* until it fitted with exactness.

> "Alas for the rarity
> Of Christian charity
> Under the sun."

It is some satisfaction, however, to know that these persecutions were mostly confined to the east side of Hudson's river. It is very doubtful if any such cruelties for opinion's sake were indulged in within the bounds of this county. On Monday, the 23d of September, 1658, three persons—Tomas Christen, Tomas Chapman and John Cook—were carried before the Council, suspected "to be of the sect called Quakers, which they unquestionably proved, entering the room without paying any mark of respect their heads covered." They had come from "Gemeene Pas" (Communipaw), and requested permission to pass on to New England. This was denied. The sheriff conducted them back to Communipaw, and they were warned not to come again, under the penalty of corporal punishment.[1]

[1] *N. Y. Col. MSS., viii.*, 991.

CHAPTER IV.—1658—1664.

Deed from the Indians for all the land in the County, between Hackensack and Hudson—The Refugees desire to return to Pavonia—Forced to concentrate—Petition to found a village on the Hill—The village of Bergen begun—Its Founders and Name—Its manner of settlement and defence—Its first Charter and Court—Names of Officers—Lot owners ordered to take out Patents—A Well ordered to be dug in the Village—Communipaw fortified.

WE have now reached a state of peace in the history of Hudson County which is not again to be broken in upon by an Indian war. With considerable accuracy Stuyvesant comprehended the policy to be pursued toward the savages, and skillfully seized every occasion to temper their wild dispositions. Feeling that possibly their title to the land in Pavonia had not been satisfactorily extinguished, and that this might be one cause of complaint with them, and urged thereto by the great desire of the refugees to return, he entered into negotiations for its purchase. On the 30th of January, 1658, he received from them a deed, of which the following is a translation:

"This day, the date hereunder written, appeared before the Honorable Director-General, Petrus Stuyvesant, and the gentlemen of the Council of New Netherlandt, at the Council Chamber, in the Fort Amsterdam, in New Netherlandt, Therincques, Wawapehack, Saghkins, Kogkhennigh, Bomokan, Memiwokan, Sames, Wewenatokwee, for themselves and in the name of Moikopes, Pepoghon, Parsoihques, and others, partners of the lands hereafter mentioned. Who declare to be the right owners of the lands lying on the West side of the North River, in New Netherlandt, beginning by the great Rock above Wiehacken, and from thence across through the lands, till above the Islandt Siskakes,[1]

[1] Siskakes, Sikakes, Secaucus, is an Indian word, and signifies *the place where the snake hides.* It must have retained its peculiarity down to the times of the

and from thence along the Channel side till Constable's Hook. And from Constable's Hook again, till the aforementioned Rock, above Wiehacken, with all the lands, islands, channels, valleys, therein comprehended, in such manner as the aforementioned parcel of lands are surrounded and encompassed by the North River, the Kill van Koll,[1] and the aforesaid direct line from the Rock above Wiehacken, till above Siskakes, where it is divided by the Channel. Which lands they offer absolutely to sell unto the Director-General and Council, upon which the General and Council on the one side, and the aforesaid Indians, for themselves and them that are absent, have accorded and agreed in the manner following, in the presence of the hereinafter mentioned Christian and Indian witnesses: The aforesaid Indians do acknowledge to have sold, resigned, and transported, as they do by these presents, all the lands heretofore mentioned, to the aforesaid Director-General and Council and their successors, for eighty fathom of wampum, twenty fathom of cloth, twelve kettles, six guns, two blankets, one double kettle, and one half-barrel of strong beer. Which effects they hereby acknowledge to have enjoyed and received before the passing and signing of this.

"Wherefore they do declare, for themselves and them which are absent, to resign and transport the lands before mentioned, to the abovementioned General and Council, in full, free and perfect property, desisting of all actions and claims which they could or might pretend to the lands before mentioned—the transporters promise now or hereafter, not to make any pretensions thereon; but to keep and hold this transport firm, sure, and inviolable. Promising also to the said Director and Council, to free and warrant the said lands against all claims any other Indians might pretend to, and if it should happen that in future times any of

---

Dutch, for they named it "Slanghenbergh," which in English is *Snake Hill.* It is a high rock rising out of the salt marsh on the east side of the Hackensack river. Its name was transferred to all of the upland lying between the river and Pinhorne creek.

[1] The Kill van Kull included Pinhorne creek as well as the channel between Bergen Point and Staten Island.

the Dutch, by any Indians, should be damaged on pretension they were not fully paid for the lands aforesaid, they, the sellers, do promise to repair and satisfy the damages. It is also stipulated and agreed, the aforesaid Indians shall depart and remove by the first convenient opportunity, off the lands aforesaid; and that none of their nation shall come and continue to dwell upon it, without knowledge and consent of the Director-General and Council. Thus done at the fort Amsterdam, and signed with the marks of the Indians, after the cargoes were delivered to their hands, on the 30th day of January, Anno Domini 1658.

T, the mark of Therincques made by himself.

t, the mark of Seghkow.

J, the mark of Sames.

t, the mark of Koghkenningh. Wairimus Couwee.

J, the mark of Wawapehack.

J, the mark of Bomokan.

t, the mark of Wewenatokwee.

J, the mark of Memirvokan.

J, the mark of Sames, as witness, otherwise called Job.

"We, the Subscribers, witnesses hereunto, desired by the Director-General and Council, do certifye and declare, by this present, that the above bargain for the lands before mentioned, is so made before us, and the lands, by the sellers transported to the Director-General and Council; on the conditions and terms comprehended in the bill of sale, the conditions and substance plainly told, acquainted and declared to the sellers by the interpreters Govert Loocquermans, Peter Wolphertson van Cowenhoven, and Claas Carstensen, and also by Wharimes van Couwe, formerly an owner of the lands aforesaid; and whereupon, the sellers have consented to the bargain, transported the lands, and received the mentioned cargoes and wampum, signed the conditions, with the above marks.

"In witness hereof, have we subscribed this, the day and year aforesaid, at the fort Amsterdam, in New Netherland, in the Council Chamber.

" JOH. MEGAPOLENSIS,	PETRUS STUYVESANT,
" SAMUEL DRISIUS,	NICASIUS DE SILLE,
" OLOFF HERENSIN,	PITER TOUNEMAN,
" GOVERT LOOCQUERMANS,	PIETER COWENHOVEN,
" MACHIEL YANSEN,	JAN EVERTSEN BOUT,
" *J*, the mark of CLAAS,	
" CARSTENSEN NOORMAN,	

" T' Present,

" CORNELIUS VAN RUYVEN, *Secr.*"[1]

This deed conveyed all that part of Hudson County which lies east of the Hackensack river and Newark Bay, and comprised the territory of the old township of Bergen. The farmers of " Gomoenepa," who had been driven from their homes in 1655, had, on the 22d of the same January (1658), expressed a desire to return to their deserted bouweries. For this purpose they petitioned as follows:

"*To the Director-General and Council in New Netherland:*

" Shows with all due reverence the interested farmers, who have been driven away by the Savages from their farms in Pavonia, Gemoenepaen, and other neighboring places, how that they, supplicants, should incline to reoccupy their former spots

[1] *N. Y. Col. MSS.*, *viii.*, 707; *Taylor's Annals*, 46. It may be well to note here that the Indians, in the conference held at Easton, October 23, 1758, gave to Governor Bernard two deeds, by which they released all their right and title to the soil of New Jersey, for which they received £1,000. *Smith's Hist. of N. J.*, 479. These deeds were, at the request of Governor Franklin, ratified by the Six Nations at a conference held at Fort Stanwix (Rome), October 24, 1768. *Col. Hist. of N. Y.*, *viii.*, 112. Not only the Dutch, but also the English, always dealt with the New Jersey Indians with great fairness, and extinguished their titles by acceptable compensation. This fair treatment was traditional among them; and to show their appreciation of it, at the latter conference, after a special meeting upon the subject, the Six Nations conferred upon the governor, as representative of the people, the euphonius name of SAGORIGHWEYOGHSTA—" The Great Arbiter, or Doer of Justice." *Ibid*, *viii.*, 117. I am quite sure the reader will be delighted with such a pet name, and beguile his leisure hours with its frequent repetition.

of residence, to restore their buildings, and cultivate their former fields; but as they have been greatly injured and suffered immense losses by the incursions of said savages, by which it will be highly difficult for them to renew their former business of farming, so they now, in their present situation, should earnestly solicit that they might be favored by your Hon. with some privileges, to assist them in this arduous task, so as by an exemption of tithes and other similar burthens, during a few years, as your Hon. in their discretion may deem proper for their relief. Expecting your favorable apostil,[1] they remain,

"Your Hon. humble Servants,

"MICHIEL JANSEN,[2]
"CLAES JANSEN BACKER,[3]
"CLAES PETERSEN VOS (COS),[4]
"JANS CAPTAIN,
"DIRCK SEIKEN,[5]
"DIRCK CLAESEN,[6]
"LYSBET TYSEN."[7]

Upon this petition the following order was made on the same day:

"The supplicants are permitted, in consideration of the reasons explained in their petition, the privilege of exemption from the payment of tithes and the burthens attached to these during six years, provided that they, in conformity to the orders and placards of the Director-General and Council, concentrate themselves in the form of a village, at least of ten or twelve families together, to become in future more secure and easier to receive aid for their defence in similar disastrous occurrences; without which the Director-General and Council deem the reoccupation of the deserted fields too perilous, which, if it might nevertheless happen, contrary to their order and placard, the Director-

[1] A note in the margin of a book or writing; *hic*, an order.
[2] *Vide* VREELAND FAMILY.
[3] *Winfield's Land Titles*, 50.
[4] *Ibid*, 47. *Vide* GARRABRANT FAMILY.
[5] *Ibid*, 65.
[6] *Vide* VREELAND FAMILY, *note*.
[7] She was the widow of Adriaensen, patentee of Weehawken.

General and Council consider themselves not only excused, but declare that the aforesaid concession or exemption during six years shall be null and void."[1]

The petitioners accepted the conditions imposed and returned to their farms, for they longed to escape from the city and the pursuits they were obliged to follow there.[2] They were reluctant, however, to forsake their bouweries or to erect a village for the protection it might afford. Nearly two years passed after they received permission to return,[3] and yet no village was formed, no provision made against the attacks of the Indians. This delay obliged the authorities to enforce penalties for disobedience of previous orders upon the subject of detached settlements. On the 9th of February, 1660, they did ordain, *inter alias*, as follows:

"In order to prevent, and in future put a stop, as much as possible, to such Massacres, Murders, and Burnings, by cruel Barbarians, at the separate dwellings, the Director-General and Council of *New Netherland* do, therefore, hereby notify and Order all isolated Farmers in general, and each in particular, wherever they may reside, without any distinction of persons, to remove their houses, goods, and cattle before the last of March, or at latest the middle of April, and convey them to the Village or settlement, nearest and most convenient to them; or, with the previous knowledge and approval of the Director-General and Council, to a favorably situated and defensible spot in a new palisaded Village to be hereafter formed, where all those who apply shall be shown and granted suitable lots, by the Director-General and Council or their Agents, so that the Director-General and Council, in case of any difficulty with the cruel Barbarians, would be better able to assist, maintain, and protect their good Subjects with the force intrusted to them by God and the Supreme authority. Expressly warning and commanding all

[1] *Alb. Rec., xiv.*, 27.

[2] Many of the Pavonians, including Michael Jansen and Casper Steinmets, kept tap-rooms in the city during their exile. *New Amst. Rec., ii.*, 133.

[3] The exact date of their return is not known.

and every whom these may concern, to transport their property, previous to the time aforesaid, into Villages or Hamlets, on pain of confiscation of all such goods as shall be found, after the aforesaid time, in separate dwelling and farm-houses."[1]

Following closely upon the promulgation of this enactment, and on March 1, 1660, Tielman Van Vleck[2]

and Peter Rudolphus, with the commendable ambition to be the founders of a village, sought permission "to settle on the maize land behind Gemoenepaen."[3] They were unsuccessful; why, is not now known. Undiscouraged, however, Van Vleck, on April 12, 1660, sent in another petition, numerously signed, for permission to settle a village and some bouweries "on the maize land behind Gemoenepaen."[4] This request was also refused.[5] This second refusal put a stop to all efforts to found a village in this county until the 16th of August following, when several "inhabitants of this province," that is, of New Netherland, whose names, unfortunately, have not been preserved, petitioned for permission to "begin" to cultivate farms and plantations on the west side of the river, "behind Communepah," and "to make there a village or concentration." On the same day the authorities gave the following decision upon the subject:

"The petition is granted to the supplicants, provided that the village shall be formed and placed on a convenient spot, which may be defended with ease, which shall be selected by the Director-General and Council or their commissioners.

"Secondly. That all persons who apply and shall share with

---

[1] *N. Y. Col. MSS., ix.*, 53.

[2] Van Vleck may justly be regarded as the founder of Bergen. He came originally from Bremen, studied under a notary in Amsterdam, came to this country about 1658, and was admitted to practice the same year. *N. Y. Col. MSS., viii.*, 932. He was made the first Schout and President of the Court at Bergen, September 5, 1661. *New Neth. Reg.*, 100. After the capture of the country by the English he returned to New York and resided there in 1671.

[3] *N. Y. Col. MSS., ix.*, 117. [4] *Ibid, ix.*, 143. [5] *Ibid, ix.*, 146.

others by lot, shall be obliged to make a beginning within the time of six weeks after the drawing of lots, and to send hither at least one person able to bear and handle arms, and to keep him there upon a penalty of forfeiting their right, besides an amende of 20 florins, in behalf of the village, and to pay besides others his share in all the village taxes, which, during his absence, have been decreed and levied."

The requirements and directions of the above apostille are sufficiently plain. Whoever will look at the topography of the village, which was shortly afterward begun on the "Hill," will come to the conclusion that it must have been laid out in strict conformity to these requirements, and it is highly probable that it was laid out by Governor Stuyvesant himself. When the village should be located, the lots within its bounds were to be distributed among settlers by lottery, without charge, and within six weeks thereafter the erection of buildings upon the lots was to be begun.

Up to the date of the above petition it is manifest that the present "Jersey City Heights" were without a name and without a white inhabitant. The place was described as "behind Gemoenepaen." There was a small clearing about where Montgomery street crosses Bergen avenue, but it is probable that it had been made by the savages, as it was known as the "Indian corn field," or "Maize land," and, after the village was established, as the "old Maize land." If the reader will keep in mind the date of the petition and permission to form a village—August 16, 1660—we will get very close to the date of the foundation of the village of Bergen. In a survey of a lot for Douwe Harmensen in November, 1660 (the day of the month is not given in the return of the survey), the land is described as being "omtrent het dorp Berghen in't nieuwe maiz Lant"—*near the village of Bergen in the new Maize land.*[1] This particular lot, in the description of which the name first occurs, lay "in the rear of Christian Pieterse's land, in breadth twenty rods along from the

---

[1] *N. Y. Col. MSS., iii.*, 142. As late as August 4, 1661, it was called *Nieuwe dorp op't maislant.*

creupple bush to the Kill," and is lot numbered seventy-nine on the Field Map, and is now, in part at least, owned by the Marion Building Company at West End.[1] This survey is conclusive proof that the village then existed and had a name, and beyond all doubt its position was selected, the village surveyed and laid out, and a name given to it between the sixteenth of August and some time in November, 1660.[2] Beautiful for situation,

---

[1] *Winfield's Land Titles*, 110.

[2] Many conjectures have been indulged in and somewhat has been written as to when and by whom Bergen was founded, and as to the origin of the name. Writers have generally followed Smith in his suppositions. This author thought the Danes had assisted the Dutch in its settlement, and that its name was in honor of the capital of Norway. *Smith's N. J.*, 61. Mr. Whitehead, *East Jersey*, 16, says it was commenced about 1618, and endorses Smith's origin of the name. Dr. Taylor, in his *Annals*, 45, holds the same opinion, except as to the derivation of the name. Being more of a Dutchman than a Dane, he holds to the probability that the name comes from Bergen op Zoom, a town in Holland. In the *N. J. Historical Collection*, 226, it is said that Bergen is the oldest village in New Jersey, "presumed to have been founded about 1616," and to have "received its name from Bergen in Norway." Gordon, in his *History of New Jersey*, 7, presumes that between 1617 and 1620 a settlement was made at Bergen, and the name taken from the capital of Norway. *Mulford's History of New Jersey*, 41, endorses this view. Sypher and Apgar, *History of New Jersey*, 10, with a bold if not ingenious originality, say that Hudson's men (!) made small settlements at Bergen as early as 1617, clearly showing that the authors did not know what they were writing about. Yet this work is designed for a text-book in our schools! Now,

1st. By whom was it settled? From a careful examination of the names of the original settlers, not only of the village of Bergen, but of the Colonie of Pavonia, and after an earnest endeavor to ascertain whence they came, I have concluded that the settlement was made by Hollanders (or perhaps more properly speaking, Netherlanders), Danes, Swedes and Norwegians. Of these there were more Netherlanders than of all the others combined. Oldmixon, while intimating a probability that the Danes settled it, admits that "the Dutch, always industrious in trade, worked them so far out of it that Berghen, the northern part of New Jersey, was almost entirely planted by Hollanders." *British Empire*, i., 283.

It may be proper to mention here a statement which I find in *Pictures of New York*, 10: "It was the custom of the Dutch West India Company to grant land to those who had served out the time they had contracted for with the Company. Hence Bergen and Communipaw and several other places were settled by disbanded soldiers; and it is remarkable that the inhabitants of those places retain their ancient manner of living, and the very disposition

easily defended, and surrounded by good farm lands, the new village was soon in a flourishing condition. It was laid out in a square, the sides of which were eight hundred feet long, with two streets crossing each other at right angles in the centre,[1] and a street around the whole plot. Along the exterior of this surrounding street palisades were erected before April, 1661, to secure the place from the attacks of the Indians. In the centre of the plot where the streets intersected was a public plot of about one hundred and sixty by two hundred and twenty-five

---

of soldiers, especially the old men still living and their descendants, seem most of them to follow their footsteps." Carrying the idea of the military settlement still further, it is said that among the soldiers of Stuyvesant, who were transplanted to Bergen, were some of the Moorish race, whose peculiar complexion, physiognomy and characteristics are, it is alleged, yet to be traced in their descendants—the swarthy complexion, the sharp, dark eye and curling black hair, so opposite to the ruddy color, the light eye and fair hair of the Hollander. *N. J. Hist. Soc. Proc.*, 1845–6, 48.

2d. As to the name. *Bergen* in Norway received its name from the hills which almost surrounded it. *Bergen op Zoom*, eighteen miles north of Antwerp, stands on a hill surrounded by low marshy ground, which, with its fortifications, afforded great security. Thus it will be seen that the two supposed godfathers of our Bergen received their names from local circumstances. Are not the same circumstances existing here to give the same name to the new village? On two sides of the hill was marsh, and the only other place for settlement was along the river. To the eye of the Hollander, accustomed to look upon marshes or low land redeemed from the sea, the ridge growing in height as it extended north from the Kill van Kull, was no mean affair. To him it was *Bergen*, the *Hill*, and, like the places of the same name in Europe, it took its name from the hill on which it was built. This I believe to be the true origin of the name.

There is another *possible* derivation, which it is proper to mention, without adopting it. Stuyvesant directed the village to be located on some spot easy of defence. The motive—in fact, the primary thought—which necessity suggested in the formation of the village, was *safety*. The settlers were driven to it as to a city of refuge from the savage foe. In the Dutch language, the verb *bergen* means "to save," probably derived from *berg*, a hill, which in case of attack is a place of safety. If the verb be used as a substantive, we would then have *Bergen*, a "place of safety." Very appropriate and very beautiful!

3d. When Bergen was settled is sufficiently shown in the text.

[1] These streets were originally straight, but owing to encroachments by adjoining property owners, at least the one running north and south is quite crooked.

feet. These streets quartered the town, and each quarter was divided into eight building plots.[1] On the sides of the town, where the cross streets came to the palisades, were gates, called

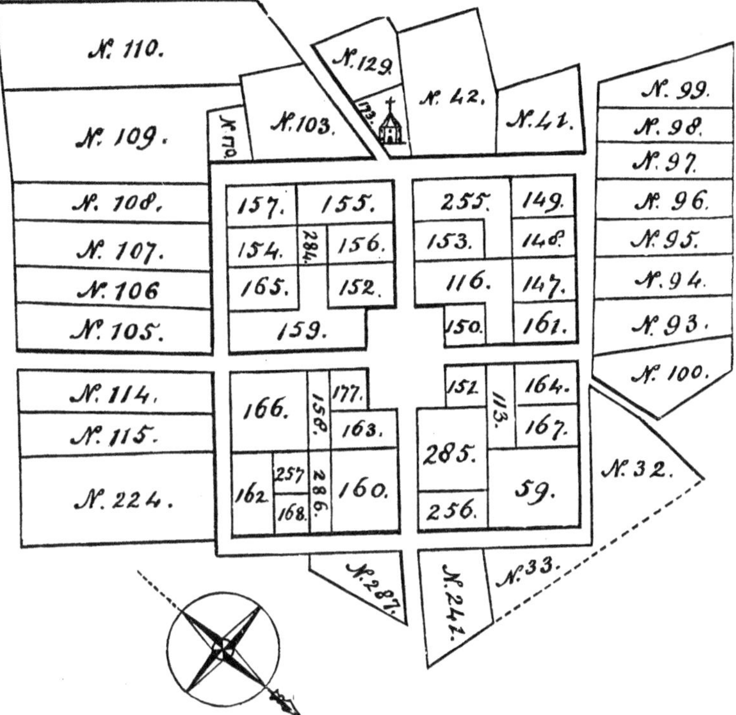

BERGEN AND BUYTEN TUYN IN 1660.

the northeast gate, northwest gate, etc., through which were roads leading into the woods.

The beauty and general desirableness of its situation, the fear of the Indians, the stringent orders of the Director-General, and the advantages of the new settlement, caused the village to grow so rapidly that in May, 1661, not an unoccupied lot remained

[1] By some manipulation the southwest quarter is made to contain, in 1764, nine lots, and the southeast quarter only seven lots. The map inserted in the text is copied from the Field Map made in 1764. I have no doubt that it correctly shows the town plot, as originally laid out, the shape of the lots and the general features of Buyten Tuyn.

inside of the fortifications.[1] The buildings first erected were of logs, and, at least the barns, covered with reeds, in spite of the Director's order.[2] The land within the village plot was laid out in lots by Jacques Cortelyou, the sworn surveyor,[3] and numbered. In the same manner the land surrounding the town was laid out in larger plots, to be used as plantations by those whose house lots were within the village. These lots adjoining the town were called "Buyten Tuyn," *Outside Gardens*, a name which they retain to this day. In like manner the salt meadow on the Hackensack, when it did not pass with the upland as one lot, was mapped and numbered. But few of these numbers have been discovered, yet enough to make one regret that the map, the distribution and ownership of the lots in Bergen and Buyten Tuyn, have not been found. An old historian says, "The manner of laying out originally is singular, but small lots where their dwellings are, and these contiguous in the town of Bergen. Their plantations, which they occupy for a livelihood, are at a distance; the reason of fixing thus is said to

---

[1] *N. Y. Col. MSS*, *ix.*, 599.

[2] *Powers of Atty. New Amst.*, 65. In a lease here recorded, dated April 1, 1661, from Guert Coerten to Jacob Luby, of a "lot at Gweykonck, otherwise called the maize land, being No. 16," we learn that the town had already passed an ordinance or made an order that the lots should be fenced. The lease provided for the construction of a house thirty feet long and a barn fifty feet long, to be built along the palisades of the village. The lessee was to cut and smooth the timber and haul it, as also the *reeds to cover it.* In March the lessor was to deliver on the land a plow and "a wagon against the harvest following," for their joint use. He was also to provide the lessee on halves with two young cows, and two three-year old oxen on half risk, and in the following spring two more young cows and two oxen. The lease was for six years. Rent for the first two years, fifteen pounds of butter from each cow; for the last four years, two hundred guilders in coin or good wampum. This was the first lease of a lot within the town of Bergen, and it shows the currency then in use. Cornelius C. Van Rypen now resides upon this lot.

[3] Cortelyou was the first surveyor in New Amsterdam, and made the first map of that city in 1656. I have no doubt that he laid out the town of Bergen and surveyed the adjoining plantations. He was the town surveyor after the country was in possession of the English. He died in 1693, leaving three sons and two daughters. His descendants are quite numerous, some of them living in New Jersey.

be through fear of the numerous Indians in the early times of their settlement."[1]

The village grew rapidly. In one year it became of sufficient importance to merit a local government. Up to this time the court of Burgomasters and Schepens in New Amsterdam had, since its organization in 1652, exercised legal jurisdiction on the west side of the river. Henceforward matters in controversy here were to be decided by a local court, subject to the right of appeal to the Director-General and Council. On the 4th of August, 1661, Tielman Van Vleck, at his own request, was appointed Schout of the *Nieuw dorp op't maislant*,[2] though he was not commissioned until the 5th of the following month.[3] On this latter date was adopted the following

"ORDINANCE

of the Director-General and Council of New Netherland erecting a Court of Justice at Bergen:

"PETRUS STUYVESANT, on behalf of the High and Mighty Lords States General of the *United Netherlands*, the Honble Directors

---

1 *Smith's Hist. of N. J.*, 61.

2 *N. Y. Col. MSS.*, *ix.*, 705.

3 *Ibid*, *ix.*, 763. The following is a copy of his commission, as translated by Vanderkemp:

" *Whereas*, it is requisite to preserve justice in the village of Bergen, situated to the west side of the North River, in New Netherland, that a well qualified person officiates there as sheriff, for which office being recommended to us the person of Tielman Van Vleck, Notary Publick within this city; So is it that we, having a full confidence in his abilities, virtue and talents, commissioned and appointed him, so as we do by this, as sheriff of the aforesaid village, to officiate in that capacity in the aforesaid place and its districts, in conformity with the instruction which he has already received, or which he may receive in future, and in consequence of it to bring to justice every transgressor of any political, civil or criminal laws, ordinances and placards, and to have them mulcted, executed and punished with the penalty comprehended in these, to promote that by his directions and denunciations all criminal cases and misconducts may be brought to light, decided with speed, and all judgments executed without delay; and further, to act in this respect in such manner as a good and faithful sheriff is in duty bound to do on the oath which he hath taken. We therefore command the Schepens and all the inhabitants within the district of the aforesaid village to acknowledge the aforesaid Tielman Van Vleck for our officer and sheriff, and to procure him in the exercise of his office all possible aid whenever

of the Incorporated West India Company, Director-General of *New Netherland*, *Curacao*, *Bonaire*, *Aruba* and their dependencies, together with the Council,

"To all those who shall see these Presents, or hear them read, Greeting, make known:

"That their Honors do not hope or wish for anything else than the prosperity and welfare of their good Inhabitants in general, and in particular of the People residing in the Village of Bergen, situate on the West side of the North River, and in order that such may be effected and preserved with greater love, peace and unity, and to manifest and to prove in deed to every Inhabitant of the above-mentioned Village the effect thereof, the Director-General and Council aforesaid, considering the increase and population of said Village, have therefore resolved to favor its Inhabitants with an Inferior Court of Justice, and to constitute it as much as possible, and as the circumstances of the Country permit, according to the laudable custom of the city of *Amsterdam* in *Holland*, but so that all judgments shall be subject to reversal by and an appeal to the Director-General and Council of *New Netherland*, to be by their Honors finally disposed of.

"In order that all things there may be performed with proper Order and respect, it is necessary to choose, as Judges, honest, intelligent persons, owners of real estate, who are lovers of peace and well affected subjects of their Lords and Patroons, and of their Supreme government established here, promoters and professors of the Reformed Religion, as it is at present taught in the Churches of the *United Netherlands*, in conformity to the Word of God and the Order of the Synod of Dordrecht. Which Court of Justice, for the present time, until it shall be herein otherwise Ordained by the said Lords Patroons, or their Deputy, shall consist of one Schout,[1] being on the spot, who shall, in the name of

---

it is required, as we deem this beneficial to the service of the country and serviceable to the promotion of justice." *Alb. Rec., xix.*, 221.

This commission was issued September 5, 1661, the same day that the village government and court were organized.

[1] Schout or Sheriff. The word is derived from *Schuld*. According to Grotius the name is an abreviation of "Schuld-rechter," or criminal judge. His func-

the Director-General and Council, convoke the appointed Schepens[1] and preside at the Meeting; and with him, of three Schepens, to which Office are, for the present time and ensuing year, commencing the 20th of this month, elected by the Director-General and Council, *Michael Jansen*, *Harman Smeeman*,[2] and *Caspar Stynmets*.[3]

---

tions were somewhat analogous to those of bailiff or county sheriff; combining, however, with them the duties of a prosecuting attorney. *Broadhead, i.*, 453. The "Schout-Fiscal" instituted all suits before the Council. *O'Cal., N. N., i.*, 101.

[1] Magistrates, somewhat like justices or aldermen.

[2] Smeeman was born in 1624 at Iserlow, a town in the county of Mark, Westphalia. His arrival here was at an early date. In 1645 he married Elizabeth Everts, and she dying, he married Barent Dircksen's widow. In 1657 he purchased of Michael Jansen a farm at "Gemoenepa" for 900 florins, but where the same was situated has not been ascertained. In the same year he was admitted to the rights of a small burgher. When the settlers were permitted to return to Pavonia, he settled on his farm. In 1663 he was one of three commissioners to fortify "Gemoenepa," and received fifty pounds of powder for its defence. When, in 1664, Governor Stuyvesant summoned a "Landtag" to consider the state of the Provinces, Smeeman and Englebert Steenhuysen were selected to represent Bergen. He was reappointed Schepen in December, 1663. He seems to have been fond of the sports of the day, and with but little reverence for Sunday. For on that day, February 8, 1654, he engaged in the sport of *Pulling the Goose*. *N. Y. Col. MSS., v.*, 217. Vanderkemp says that this was a game among the farmers in Gelderland and on the borders of the Rhine. A goose was fastened by a rope between two poles, the neck and head greased with oil or soap. They who entered the lists drove on a full gallop, and usually fell when they missed their aim. He who carried off the goose was called king for that festival. *Alb. Rec., ix.*, 84.

[3] At what time Steinmets came to this country does not appear. In the spring of 1652, having lost his first wife, he married Jannekin Gerrits, of Zutphen, probably living at Harsimus at that time. For his third wife he married Tryntje, the widow of Jacob Stoffelsen, and former widow of Jacob Walingen Van Horn. *Winfield's Land Titles*, 71. He resided at Harsimus, and was driven out by the Indians in 1655. He went to New Amsterdam, where, on February 22, 1656, he was licensed to tap beer and wine for the "accommodation of the Burghery and Strangers." *New Amst. Rec., ii.*, 85. He was admitted to the rights of a small burgher, April 11, 1657. *New Neth. Reg.*, 175. On the 21st of June he was appointed lieutenant of the Bergen militia. *N. Y. Col. MSS., x.*, 149; and on the 4th of September, 1673, was made captain. *Col. Hist.* of *N. Y., ii.*, 597. In 1674 he was a deputy from Bergen in the Council of New Orange, *Ibid*, 702; and a representative from Bergen in the first and second General Assembly in New Jersey. *Leaming & Spicer*, 77, 85. After his marriage with Stoffelsen's widow he took possession of the West India Company's

"Before whom all matters touching civil affairs, security and peace of the Inhabitants of *Bergen*, also justice between Man and Man, shall be brought, heard and examined, and determined by definitive Judgment to the amount of Fifty guilders and under, without appeal; when the sum is larger, the aggrieved party shall be at liberty to appeal to the Director-General and Council aforesaid, provided that he enters the appeal within the proper time, and gives security, according to law, for the principal and costs of suit.

"In case of disparity of votes and opinions on any occurring cases, the minority shall coincide with the majority, without any contradiction. But those who are of a different advice and opinion can cause their advice and opinion to be entered on the roll or record; but in no wise make public their rendered advice outside the court, nor make it known to parties, under arbitrary correction, at the discretion of the court itself.

"The Schout shall, pursuant to the first Article, preside at the meeting and collect the Votes; also act as Secretary until further Order and increase of population. But if he have to act for himself as a party, or in behalf of the right of the Lords Patroons, or in behalf of justice for the right of the Fiscal, in such case he shall rise up and absent himself from the Bench, and then have no advisory, much less a casting vote; but one of the senior Schepens shall, in such case, preside in his place.

"What is set forth in the preceding Article of the Schout shall also apply to the Schepens, whenever any cases or questions arise in the aforesaid Court between themselves as parties, or between others related by consanguinity to the appointed Schepens, such as brothers, brothers-in-law and cousins in the first or direct line.

"All Inhabitants of *Bergen* shall, until further Order, either of

---

farm at Harsimus, and, as was always the case with the possessors of that farm, became involved in trouble with his neighbors, Van Vorst and others. *Col. Hist. of N. Y., ii.*, 704, 716. He died in 1702. His descendants, at one time, were quite numerous in this county, but they have long since died out.

the Lords Patroons or their Supreme government, be amenable to and subject to be cited before said Schout and Commissaries, who shall hold their Session and Court meeting in the Village aforesaid every 14 days, harvest time excepted, unless necessity and circumstances require.

"In order to provide the good Inhabitants of *Bergen* with cheap and inoppressive justice, the Schout, as president, and the Schepens of the Court must, for the convenience of parties, appear on the Court day, and at the place appointed, on pain of forfeiting Twenty stivers, at the disposition of the Board; they being notified, at least twenty-four hours before the Court day, to appear, by the Court messenger to be appointed by the Director-General and Council; and double as much for the President, unless excused by sickness or absence. If appearing too late, and after the appointed hour, the fine to be Six stivers.

"No extraordinary Court shall be Ordered at the cost and charges of parties, except on the application of both parties, under submission to costs on loss of suit, which costs shall previously be deposited by the applicant or appellant, to wit: For each Schepen, Fifty stivers; for the President, Three guilders, besides the fee for the Clerk and Court messenger to be hereafter appointed, and other Ordinary costs according to law.

"All cases of Crime shall be referred to the Director-General and Council of *New Netherland;* saving that those of the Court may and are bound to apprehend, arrest, and to detain and hold in confinement all Criminal delinquents until they can send them under proper guard to the Supreme government, and, in the mean time, take good and correct Information touching the crime committed, at the cost of the Criminal, or the Treasury, and such transmit at the same time with the delinquent.

"Minor offences, such as Brawls, Slanders, Scolding, Striking with the fist, Threats, simple Drawing of a knife or sword without assault or bloodshed, are left to the adjudication and decision of the Court aforesaid, in which cases the Schout there shall have power to act before the Court as Prosecutor, saving, nevertheless, the clause of Appeal, in case the condemned may find himself aggrieved by the sentence of the Court.

"All cases of Major crimes and Delinquents charged with Wounding and Bloodshedding, Whoredom, Adultery, public and notorious Theft, Robberies, Smuggling of contraband articles, Blasphemy and Profanation of God's Holy name and religion, Slandering and Calumniating the Supreme Government or its Representatives, shall, after the information, affidavits and testimony have been taken, be referred to the Director-General and Council of *New Netherland.*

"Should the situation of affairs so require that the President and Schepens consider it necessary, for the greater security of the peace and quiet of the Inhabitants, to enact, in the absence of the Director-General and Council, some Ordinances for the greater advantage and contentment of the aforesaid Village and Court in the above-named District, respecting Surveys, Highways, Outlets, Posts and Fences of lands, laying out of Gardens, Orchards, and such like matters, that may most concern the Flat country and agriculture; also in regard to the building of Churches, Schools and similar public Works, and the means how and by which the same are to be effected, they are to commit to writing their opinions thereupon, and deliver them to the Director-General and Council, with the reasons upon which they are founded annexed, in order, if such be deemed necessary and useful, that they may be confirmed, approved and ordered by the Director-General and Council.

"Said Schout and appointed Schepens shall also be particularly careful, and be bound strictly to observe, and cause to be observed, the Law of our Fatherland, and the Ordinances and Edicts of the Honble Director-General and Council heretofore Ordained and published, or hereafter to be ordained and published, and not to suffer anything to be done contrary thereto, but to see that the contraveners may be proceeded against according to Law.

"Said Schout and Court shall not have power to enact, publish, much less to post up, any Ordinances, Edicts, or such like Acts, except with the previous knowledge and consent of the Director-General and Council.

"The Schout and Schepens shall also be particularly careful, and be bound to assist the Honble Directors, as Lords and Patroons of this Province of *New Netherland*, under the Sovereignty of their High Mightinesses, the Lords States General of the *United Netherlands*, and them to help to maintain in their Supreme Jurisdiction, Right and Domains, and all other their Prerogatives.

"Whereas, it is customary in our Fatherland and other well regulated Governments that some change be made annually in the Magistracy, so that some new come in, and a few continue, in order to inform the new, the Schepens now appointed shall pay due attention to the Conversation, Demeanor and Fitness of honest persons, inhabitants of their respective Villages, in order to be able, about the time of changing or election, to furnish the Director-General and Council with correct information as to who may be found fit, so that some may be then elected by the Director-General and Council.

"Thus done and given at the Meeting of the Honble Director-General and Council, holden in *Fort Amsterdam*, in *New Netherland*, the 5 September, 1661."[1]

The magistrates, before they could enter upon the duties of their office, were obliged to take the following oath: "We promise and swear, in the presence of Almighty God, that we will be faithful to the sovereignty of the high and mighty Lords, the States General, the Lords Directors of the privileged West India Company, Department of Amsterdam, as our Lords and Patroons, the Director-General and Council now placed over us or hereafter to be appointed, that we will respect and execute their commands, that we will exercise good justice to our best knowledge, repell all mutiny, troubles and disorders to our best abilities, maintain the Reformed Religion, and no other, and support the same, and conduct ourselves punctually in conformity to the instruction which we already received or may yet receive, and further act as good and faithful magistrates are in duty bound to do. So help us God Almighty."[2]

---

[1] *N. Y. Col. MSS., ix.*, 765.

[2] *Alb. Rec. xix.*, 282.

Thus was established the first municipal government and the first court within the present State of New Jersey, unless "the existence of the somewhat apocryphal tribunal of Hospating, near Hackensack, be admitted."[1] And it may not be inappropriate to insert here the names of the members of this court while under the Dutch rule, so far as the existing records reveal them.

SCHOUTS, PRESIDENT.

Names.	Date of Appointment.
Tielman Van Vleck, - - - -	September 5, 1661.
Balthazar Bayard,[2] - - - - -	March 17, 1664.
Claes Arentse Toers,[3] - - - -	August 18, 1673.

---

[1] *O'Cal., N. N., ii*, 428. Hospating, Espatingh, Espatin, "a hill." In 1657, Van de Capellen, through his agent Van Dincklagen, concluded with the Indians a treaty "with submission to the courts of justice at Hospating, near Hackinsack, on Waerkimins-Connie, in New Netherlands." *Broadhead, i.*, 641. Mattenow was chief at this place. *O'Cal., N. N., ii.*, 575. In 1674 it was decided to be without the bounds of the Indian grant to Stuyvesant, *Col. Hist. of N. Y., ii.*, 707; and therefore not within Hudson County, though it must be close to the northern boundary.

[2] Bayard's grandfather was a professor of theology in Paris, whence he was driven by religious persecution to Holland. Here his son Samuel married Anna, a sister of Governor Stuyvesant, by whom he had three children—Balthazar, Nicholas and Petues. Balthazar was a brewer; in 1664 married Maritje, daughter of Govert Loockermans; was clerk in the Secretary's office from 1654 to 1660; represented Bergen in the first and second General Assembly in East Jersey in 1668. Shortly after this he returned to New York. He was appointed schepen in New Orange, August 16, 1673, assistant alderman in 1686-87, and alderman in 1691.

[3] *Winfield's Land Titles*, 91. It was at Toers' house in Bergen that Knatsciosan, an Indian, attempted to murder his brother, Jan Arentse Toers, by "giving him several dangerous wounds," on the 11th of April, 1678. The Governor and Council met at Bergen on the 24th, with the Sakamakers of the Hackensacks, viz.: Manoky, Mandenark, Hamahem, Tanteguas and Capeteham. They acknowledged that the offender deserved "corporall punishment," but, as Toers was mending, asked for his release, and promised that if he ever again attempted the like, they would deliver him up "for justice without mercy to be done upon him." The Indians bound themselves to pay one hundred fathoms of white wampum, or an equivalent in skins, within twenty days. *Book 3 of Deeds* (*Trenton*) 144. Claes was the second coroner for the county of Bergen, appointed December 6, 1683.

Town Clerks.

Names.	Date of Appointment.
The Schout,	September 5, 1661.
Balthazar Bayard,	March 17, 1664.
Claes Arentse Toers,	August 18, 1673.

Schepens.

Names.	Date of Appointment.
Michiel Jansen, Harman Smeeman, Caspar Steinmets,	September 5, 1661.
Caspar Steinmets, Engelbert Steenhuysen,[1] Gerrit Gerritsen,	October 16, 1662.

[1] Steenhuysen was a tailor by trade, and came from Soest, the second city in Westphalia; arrived at New Amsterdam in the ship *Moesman*, of which Jacob Jansen was skipper, April 25, 1659, paying for his fare and freight 36 florins. *Alb. Rec., viii.*, 434. With Herman Smeeman he represented Bergen in the "Landtag" in 1664. *Broadhead, i.*, 729. He has the honor of being the first schoolmaster in Bergen, having been licensed October 6, 1662. *New Neth. Reg.*, 133. The following memorial of the authorities of Bergen, dated December 17, 1663, reveals some unpleasantness in that relation: "Shew reverently the sheriff and commissaries of the village of Bergen, which they presume is known to your Honors, that before the election of the new commissaries ye were solicited for Michael Jansen, deceased, to be favored with the appointment of a clerk (voorleser) who should at the same time keep school, to instruct the youth, the person of Engelbert Steenhuysen, who possessed the required abilities, so is that the sheriff and commissaries, now a year past, proposed it to the community, who then approved it, and resolved to engage him not only as clerk (voorleser), but with the express stipulation that he, besides this function, was to keep school, which the aforesaid Steenhuysen agreed to do, and did so during five quarters of a year, for which was allowed him *f*250 in seawant annually, besides some other stipulations besides the school money, so as reason and equity shall demand. Now, so it is that the aforesaid Engelbert Steenhuysen, whereas he has a lot and house and a double farm, situated in the jurisdiction of the village of Bergen, is, by the complaints of a majority of the community, obliged, with the other inhabitants, to provide for the sustenance of a soldier, by which the aforesaid Engelbert Steenhuysen considers himself highly aggrieved, and so resigned his office, pretending that a schoolmaster and clerk ought to be exempt-

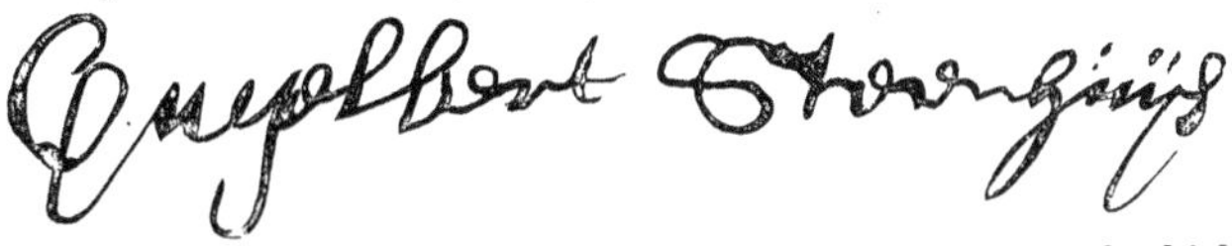

Names.	Date of Appointment.
Balthazar Bayard, Adolph Hardenbrook, Harman Smeeman,	December 17, 1663.

ed from all taxes and burthens of the village, which he says is the common practice through the whole christian world, which by the sheriff and commissaries is understood that only that can take place when such a clerk or schoolmaster does not possess anything else but the school-wharf, but by no means when a schoolmaster is in possession of a house and lot and double farm, that he in such a case should pay nothing from his lot and lands, and the community at large is of the same opinion, as he receives his salary as clerk, and not only is obliged to act well in his capacity as clerk (voorleser), but even to look out and procure himself a proper and convenient place to keep school, which he thus far neglected, and pretends that the community must effect this, so that he may keep his school in it. They cannot perceive how Engelbert Steenhuysen can be permitted to resign his office when he neglected to notify his intention a half a year before; wherefore the supplicants address themselves to your Honors, humbly soliciting them to insinuate to the aforesaid Engelbert Steenhuysen to continue in his service this second year, and to declare if the aforesaid Engelbert Steenhuysen is or is not obliged by his possession of a lot and farm to provide in the maintenance of a soldier, so well as the other inhabitants." *Alb. Rec.*, *xxi.*, 439.

COLUMBIA ACADEMY.

Names.		Date of Appointment.
Gerrit Gerritse, Thomas Fredericks,[1] Elias Michielse,[2] Peter Marcellissen,[3] Cornelis Abramse,		August 18, 1673.
Walinck Jacobse,[4] Engelbert Steenhuys, *Bergen*, Enoch Michielse, *Gemoenepas*,[2] Claes Jansen, *Ahasymus*,[5]		August 31, 1674.[6]

The parties interested in the above memorial were summoned before the Council and heard at length, and Steenhuysen was commanded to serve his time according to his contract.

From this communication it appears that the school house was not yet built. One was, however, shortly afterward constructed on the lot where the school house now is. It was built of logs. The Columbia Academy was erected on the same lot in 1790, and taken down in 1857 to make room for the present structure.

[1] Thomas Frederick De Cuyper. *Winfield's Land Titles*, 94. He is said to have been a woodsawyer, and was admitted to the rights of a small burgher, April 12, 1657.

[2] *Vide* VREELAND FAMILY.

[3] He came from Brest in the ship *Beaver;* arrived May 9, 1661, with his wife, four children and two servants. His children were aged respectively 13, 6, 4 and 2 years. His servants were male and female. The passage cost him as follows: For self, 36 florins; wife, 36 florins; children, 90 florins; servants, 70 florins. He was the founder of the Merseles family in this county and vicinity.

[4] *Vide* VAN WINKLE FAMILY. [5] *Vide* VAN VORST FAMILY.

[6] The appointments for this year were selected by the authorities from the following nominations by the people of Bergen, on the 15th of August, as appears by the following extract from the Court Register in Bergen, which is preserved:

"To the meeting a nomination of Schepens was made to be presented to the Director-General and Council, by a majority of the votes, as follows:

"For the Village of Bergen, Adrian Post, Walinck Jacobze, Engelbert Steenhuys, Douwe Hartmanse.

"For Gemoenepa, Enoch Michielse, Hartman Michielse.

Names.	Date of Appointment.
Jan Dircksen Seicken, *Minckaque and Pemerpoch*,[1]	August 31, 1674.

COURT MESSENGERS.[2]

Jan Tibout, - - - - - - -	1661.
Claes Arentse Toers, - - - - - -	1663.

Under the necessity laid upon them, as before observed, the people had flocked to the new village and taken lots (for they were free) in the general distribution, but had neglected to take patents for them. This neglect made confusion and caused the enactment of the following ordinance:

"All Inhabitants of *New Netherland*, and especially those of the Village of *Bergen*, on the West side of the North River; also all others who have or claim any Lands thereabout, are Ordered and commanded that they, within the space of three months after the date hereof, at latest, before the first of January next, shall have all the cultivated and uncultivated Lands which they claim, surveyed by the sworn Surveyor, and set off and designated by

" For Ahasymus, { Ide Cornelisse Van Vorst, Claes Jansen.

" For Minckaque and Pemrepock, { Jan Dirckse Seicken, Hessel Weigertsen.

" From which nominations his Hon. shall be pleased to make the election.

" Agrees with the Register. Quod attestor.

" CLAES ARENTSE TOERS,
" Secretary."
Alb. Rec. xxii., 440.

This was in accordance with the practice in Holland, where the Stadtholder appointed the magistrates out of double their number presented to him.

[1] This name was applied to that part of the county which lies between the Morris canal and the First Reformed Church in Bayonne. The following are some of the ways of writing the word: Pembrepogh, Pembrepock, Pemerpogh, Pemrepogh, Pemerapogh, Pemmerapugh, Pemmerapock, Pemmarepocq, Pemmerpogh, Pemrepogh, Pamrepogh, Pamropogh, Pamrepock, Pamrapaw, Pamarapogh, Pamperpogh, Pimbrepow.

[2] The duties of court messenger seem to have been to read in the church on Sunday, to sing with the school, to assist in burying the dead, to attend to the tolling of the bell, and to summon parties to court.

proper marks, and on exhibition of the Return of survey thereof, apply for and obtain a regular Patent as proof of property, on pain of being deprived of their right, to the end that the Director-General and Council may dispose, as they may deem proper, of the remaining Lands which, after the survey, may happen to fall outside the Patents, for the accommodation of others. All are hereby warned against loss and after complaints.

"Thus done in *Fort Amsterdam* in *New Netherland*, the 15 September, 1661."[1]

As the village had been palisaded for protection from outside attack, the people were anxious to get the full benefit of these fortifications. But the cattle must be watered, and since there were no means within the defences for that purpose, the gates must be opened and the cattle driven to water. While thus engaged, both cattle and people were liable to annoyance from the Indians. To obviate this danger, the court of Bergen ordained as follows:

"Whereas, the Schout and Schepens have reflected and duly considered that some persons drive their Cattle to water outside the Land gate and Fence now provided and erected, they have deemed it advisable and highly necessary that a Public Well be constructed for the public accommodation, on the Square, to water the Cattle,

"They hereby Ordain, on the ratification of the Honble Director-General and Council of *New Netherland*, that every one of the Inhabitants of *Bergen*, after having been notified by *Jan Tibout*, the messenger, shall be and appear, on the day prefixed, personally, or by substitute, on pain of arbitrary correction by the Officer.

"Done at the Court of the Village of *Bergen*, and signed by the Schout and Schepens, the 28 January, 1662.

"TIELMAN VAN VLECK, president,
"HERMAN SMEEMAN,
"CASPAR STEYNMETS,
"MICHAEL JANS."

---

[1] *N.Y. Col. MSS.*, *ix.*, 788. Several of the lots were abandoned and passed

RATIFICATION.

"The Director-General and Council of *New Netherland* approve and ratify the above resolution of the Schout and Commissaries of *Bergen*; they, therefore, Order all and every whom it may concern, on notification of the messenger, to appear, or to send a proper person in their stead, at the appointed time and place, on a penalty of 5 guilders for each day, to be forfeited by such as absents himself, to be applied for the benefit of the Village in general. Dated 9 February, 1662."[1]

Under this law a well was dug in the centre of the square. Troughs were placed around it for the cattle, and a long sweep used for raising the water. The well continued in use until within the present century, when it was covered over and a liberty pole placed in it. This pole was taken down in the fall of 1870, when the square was paved and all traces of the well destroyed.[2]

Among other annoyances which arose in the government of the village, was the lack of men necessary for its protection. It was laid out in the woods and surrounded by unreliable Indians. Several of the lots in the town had been taken by people living in New Amsterdam, who neither came here to reside, nor sent men to do their part in the defence of the place, as was required by the charter. In all communities where one member shirks a duty, the other members are forced to bear unjust burdens. Those who resided in the town were obliged to contribute to its defence for their own safety, and thus protected the property of non-residents while securing their own. They felt this to be unjust, and their complaints to the authorities called forth the following ordinance, passed November 15, 1663:

"On the repeated complaints of the majority of the Inhabit-

---

in Carteret's grant to the freeholders, and became common property. These abandoned lots may be seen on the Field Map, and were allotted as common land.

[1] *N. Y. Col. MSS*, *x.*, 50.

[2] The destruction of this well was almost a sacrilege. Its associations and its memories should have pleaded "like angels trumpet-tongued against the deep damnation of its" filling up. Perhaps in no other country would such an outrage have been attempted.

ants of the Village of *Bergen*, that some continue to neglect to occupy the Lots they obtained in said Village and to keep thereon a man fit to bear arms; also, that some absent themselves without providing their Watch, whereby the people of said Village are so much fatigued that they cannot any longer stand at their posts, and are unwilling to go any longer on guard, unless the others who have vacant Lots keep for the guard one man with them for each Lot; the Director-General and Council, in order to prevent this confusion, resolve that all those who claim any Lots in the aforesaid Village shall, within 24 hours after the service hereof, furnish and continually maintain for each Lot, one man able to bear arms and to keep watch and ward, on pain of having the Lots with the Lands thereunto appertaining, as surveyed by the Surveyor, immediately given and granted in propriety to others. Let every one be hereby warned for the last time."[1]

Communipaw was exempt from the general order that the people should remove to the new village of Bergen. It was the intention to establish a village at that place also. On the eighth of September, 1660, Jacques Cortelyou was ordered to survey "Gemeenepa" and lay it out into village lots.[2] The lots thus surveyed fronted on the bay and had a depth of about 200 feet. They extended from Communipaw avenue on the north to the Bay Shore House on the south. Within this small territory the village was erected and defences set up against the attack of the Indians. But the settlers did not all lend a willing hand to erect these defences. Some of them were too willing that the others should do all the work and bear all the expense, satisfied that their individual interests would be secured in the general protection. To this those who were willing to perform their duty would not submit, and on the tenth of February, 1661, Tielman Van Vleck, for himself and in the name of Michiel Jansen, Caspar Steinmets, and Harman Smeeman, presented a petition "that it might please the Director-General and Council to issue their

---

[1] *N. Y. Col. MSS., x., Part ii.*, 389.

[2] *Alb. Rec., xxiv.*, 398. *Winfield's Land Titles*, 54.

PRYOR'S MILL, NEAR POINT OF ROCKS.

orders with regard to the palisadoing of the new village on Gemoenepa, so that it may be unanimously undertaken;" and that all persons be commanded to make use of the newly laid out wagon road, and not of any other.

On this petition the apostille was: "The persons named in this petition are authorized to promote as well the palisadoing of the village as that of the land, so, as they considered the situation of the place and time, shall deem proper, carefully observing that the palisades which are used are of a due length and thickness, viz.: between six and seven feet above the ground, and to communicate this to the inhabitants of the village by affixed billets, commanding them, upon an amende of two £ flanders, to be paid in behalf of the village by each one who, at the determined day, shall be found to have neglected the one or the other part of his duty. What regards the waggon road,[1] this may be delayed to a more favorable opportunity. On the day as above."[2]

---

[1] The road referred to in this proceeding was the way from Communipaw to Bergen, running by the "Off-fall."

[2] *N. Y. Col. MSS., ix.*, 521. Such proceedings, looking to a mutual protection, seem to have encouraged settlers. On the 9th of May following Egbert Sanderson and Jan Theunissen, inhabitants of Midwout and Amersfoort, Long Island, petitioned for leave to erect a saw-mill on a stream at "Gemoenepae," and move their families there, and for a lot of land for each. The request was granted. *N. Y. Col. MSS., ix.*, 599. I have no doubt that they proceeded to erect a mill, probably on the site where Prior's mill subsequently stood, near Point of Rocks. In the patent to Claes Pietersen Cos, dated June 3, 1671, the "Mill of Hossemus" is mentioned. *Winfield's Land Titles*, 48. It was a landmark at that early date. From this mill the stream took its name of "Mill Creek." It was also called "Creek of the Woods" and "Creek of the Highwoodlands," from the fact that it wound around the foot of the hill then crowned with trees.

Sandersen, in company with one Bartel Lott, on October 20th, 1661, petitioned again for permission to erect a saw-mill in "the newly commenced village of Bergen," and, inasmuch as there were no unoccupied lots, they asked for permission to negotiate with Jan Everse Karseboom for one. They were referred to the schepens of Bergen. This points to Showhank brook as the stream on which they desired to erect the mill. Karseboom owned the land there. *Winfield's Land Titles*, 127.

This stream took its rise in an Indian spring in West Hoboken, and ran south till it came to where New York avenue crosses Palisade avenue. There it turned down the hill through a wild ravine and emptied into Mill Creek. After

The good work of palisading the village does not seem to have been well done, if it was done at all, for on the 18th of June, 1663, Gerrit Gerritsen, Harman Smeeman and Dirck Claessen were appointed commissioners to fortify Gemoenepa.[1] All this precaution was necessary, for the savages yet prowled hereabouts, though their depredations were not so frequent as formerly. Yet in a journal of the Esopus war (1663), kept by Martin Krygier, it is reported that two Dutchmen were killed between "Gemoenapa" and the "Maize Land" (Bergen), but who they were or why they were killed is not known.

---

this land came into the possession of the Van Vorst family there was a saw-mill on this stream at the foot of the hill. It was destroyed by fire, December 13th, 1835.

[1] *N. Y. Col. MSS., x., Part ii.*, 133.

CHAPTER V.—1664-1673.

New Netherland captured by the English—Sir Edmund Ployden's claim to New Jersey—Governor Carteret reorganizes the court at Bergen—Specimens of suits in this court—Names of officers—People of Bergen take the oath of allegiance—First tavern license—Assemblymen elected—Carteret's charter to Bergen—Why he granted the land to the Freeholders.

We now approach the downfall of the Dutch power in New Netherland. Events pass rapidly, and soon bring about the closing scenes. For more than fifty years the industrious Dutch had labored to establish a colony which would insure wealth to individual enterprise and be a source of strength and glory to the Fatherland. Nature, in its untamed wildness, had been to a laudable extent subdued; the savage, reluctant to forsake his old hunting-grounds and the graves of his fathers, had yielded to purchase, or been mollified by judicious treatment. In the midst of the unfavorable circumstances of their brief possession, they had succeeded in planting the seeds of what may now be considered a grand empire. The city which they founded has become the commercial centre of the continent, and after the lapse of two centuries since they yielded to another power, bears yet upon its face many of the features of the original settlement. In this county the language is still used among the old inhabitants, and in a few cosy nooks and quaint old families the customs of the Fatherland are still held in reverence. *Kerstijd* (Christmas), with its merrymakings, good dinners and many gifts, still makes its annual visit to gladden the hearts of old and young; *Nieuw Jar* (New Year), with its cakes, wine and punch, yet opens the door of almost every house, and all day long visitors come and go, smiling and greeting. *Paas* (Easter) ever brings abundance of eggs, which, like Joseph's coat, are "of many colors," and wonderfully mysterious to the youngsters. Santa Claas, laden with gifts, makes his regular calls upon all devout believers. The footprints of his tiny reindeers are still seen in the snow, and the chimney shows marks of his descent. He comes, however, only to those who sleep in the faith that he will come, and who have called upon him in the following devout prayer:

Sint Nicholaas, good heilig man,
Trekt uw' besten Tabbard an,
En reist daarmee naar Amsterdam,
Van Amsterdam naar Spanje,
Waar appellen van Oranje,
En appèllen van Granaten,
Rollen door de straten.
Sint Nicholaas, myn goden vriend,
Ik heb u altyd wel gediend,
Als gy my nu wat wilt geben
Fal ik u dienen als myn leven.[1]

On the 12th of March, 1664, Charles II. granted to his brother James, Duke of York, *inter alias*, all that part of New Netherland lying east of Delaware bay. On the 25th of May an expedition sailed from Portsmouth, England, to perfect the Duke's parchment title by reducing the country to his possession. Stuyvesant seems to have been informed of the intended expedition.[2] Seeing the danger approaching, the people of Bergen took measures to put their village in a better state of defence. At their request, on the 21st of February, 1664, Arent Laurens, Jacob Luby, Harman Edwards, Laurens Andriessen, Paulus Pietersen, Jan Swaen and Jan Lubbertsen were appointed commissioners to erect block-houses for the protection of the town.[3] Whether they

---

[1] Saint Nicholas, good holy man,
Put your best tabbard on you can,
And in it go to Amsterdam,
From Amsterdam to Hispanie,
Where apples bright of Oranje,
And likewise those pomegranates named,
Roll through the streets all unreclaimed.
Saint Nicholas, my dear good friend,
To serve you ever was my end;
If something you will now me give
Serve you I will long as I live.

[2] *Broadhead, ii.*, 21.

[3] *N. Y. Col. MSS., x., Part iii.*, 73. *New Neth. Reg.*, 158.

were ever begun or completed before the capture by the English, or where located, is not known.

The Duke's squadron was yet on the Atlantic, and the country yet in possession of the Dutch, when he, by deeds of lease and release, dated the 23d and 24th of June, conveyed to John, Lord Berkeley, a brother of the Governor of Virginia, and Sir George Carteret,[1] the tract of land lying between the Hudson and Delaware rivers; "which said Tract of Land is hereafter to be called by the Name or Names of *New Cæsarea* or *New Jersey*."[2] On the 8th of September his forces, under command of Colonel Richard Nicolls, captured New Amsterdam. This was done without a pretence of England and Holland being at war, but simply by way of reclaiming his own! Ignorant of the fact that his master had already conveyed and named the territory included in the grant to Berkeley and Carteret, Colonel Nicolls gave it the name of *Albania*, in honor of the Duke.[3]

---

[1] *Leaming and Spicer*, 10. Berkley is described as a "bold and insolent man, weak, not incorrupt, and very arbitrary." Carteret was "the most passionate man in the world." *Broadhead, ii.*, 81.

[2] This is the first time the name was applied to this State. It was given in honor of Sir George Carteret, who was born in the Island of Jersey in 1599. In 1626 he was appointed Governor of Jersey, in 1640 comptroller of His Majesty's ships, and in 1645 was created a baronet. He stood by the King in the civil war, followed the Prince of Wales to France in 1652, was thrown into the Bastile in 1657, and afterward banished from France. He entered London with Charles II., in 1660, was appointed Vice-Chamberlain, member of the Privy Council, and Treasurer of the Navy. In 1668 he was appointed one of the Board of Trade, and in 1669 expelled the House of Commons on a charge of embezzlement. In 1673 he became one of the Lords of the Admiralty, and died January 14, 1679. His remains were interred at Hawnes, in the county of Bedford. *Col. Hist. of N. Y., ii.*. 410.

[3] *Broadhead, i.*, 745. *Col. Hist. of N. Y., iii.*, 103. It is said that for some time the territory was called *New Canary*. These are not the only names which the State has borne. Sir Edmund Ployden, an impecunious dignitary, while in prison for debt, applied to Charles I. for a patent to settle the river Delaware. Being unsuccessful, he appealed to Stafford, Viceroy of Ireland, and obtained the patent of June 21, 1634. The extent of the grant was "four hundred and four score miles in compass or circuit of the mainland and country of America adjoining and lying near Delaware Bay, between Virginia and New England." This included New Jersey. The territory was erected into a "free county pala-

Articles of capitulation were agreed upon between Stuyvesant and Nicolls, two of which were as follows:

"III. All people shall continue free denizens, and shall enjoy their lands, houses, goods, wheresoever they are within this country, and dispose of them as they please.

"XI. The Dutch here shall enjoy their own customs concerning their inheritances."[1]

On the 10th of February, 1664-5, Berkeley and Carteret commissioned Philip Carteret, a brother of Sir George, to be Governor.[2] He arrived in the latter part of July, 1665, and early in August assumed control of the Province. A few days afterward he reorganized the court at Bergen, and issued the following commission:

"By Virtue of the Power and Authority Given to me by the Lords Proprietors of New Jersey, I doe hereby Nominate and appoint you, Cap't Nicholas Verlett, to constitute and appoint a Court of Judicature for the Inhabitants of Bergen, Gemoenepaen, Ahasymes and Hooboocken, to be held and kept as often as Occasion shall Require in the aforesaid towne of Bergen, where you, the said Captn Verlett, Is by Vertue of these P^r^sents to be President of the said court, And there to hear and Determine all Causes of Difference between party and party according to Jus-

---

tine," named *New Albion*, over which Sir Edmund became Earl palatine. For the settlement of this province a company was formed of forty-four lords, barons, baronets, knights, gentlemen and adventurers, in the name of "The Albion Knights for the conversion of the twenty-three Kings" of Charles River. In 1643 the Earl came to New Amsterdam and claimed his rights, but soon retired, "for he would not quarrel with the Dutch." He esteemed the province a paradise, and when speaking of it in England said: "The spring waters there are as good as small beere heere." This Irish patent seems to have been given without the royal authority or consent, and was void. By his will, dated July 29, 1655, proved July 27, 1659, he gave *New Albion* to his son Thomas for life, and then to his heirs male, with the income of certain lands in England for the "planting, fortifying, peopling and stocking" of New Albion. Andrew Wall, son-in-law of Thomas, afterward obtained possession of the letters patent and refused to surrender them. Thomas willed them to his son Francis, May 16, 1698, but it is doubtful if the devisee ever obtained them.

[1] These articles may be found *in extenso* in *O'Cal., N. N., ii.*, 532.

[2] *Leaming and Spicer*, 26. *Whitehead's East Jersey*, 36.

tice and Right. W[t] the advice and Assistance of Herman Smeeman, Casper Steynmets of Bergen and Elyas Michiels of Gemoenepaen, Whoe are hereby appointed Magistrates to sett in the said Court as yo[r] Assistants, And you have hereby Likewise Power to apoint a Register or Clark of the said Court, Whoe is to keepe a Recorde of all Actions and causes that are brought before you, And a Serjant or Statesboade to Execute all Such Acts and Warrants as shall proceed from you as occasion shall Require, Provided that all Writs, Warrants and Sutes are to be in his Ma[ties] Name, And what you w[t] the advice of your Assistants shall act by Vertue of this Power given you, shall be Effectuall and good in Lawe, And that Noe Apeale shall be made to the Governor and his Councill, Und[r] the some of tenn Pounds sterling, And this Commission to continue till Wee shall otherwise provide for the settlement of those affaires and no Longer.

"Given und[r] my hand and seale of the Province of New Jersey aforesaid the thirtieth day of August, 1665, and in the 17th yeare of his Ma[ties] Raigne."[1]

---

[1] *Liber* 3 *Deeds* (*Trenton*) 1. The records of this court which would have thrown so much light on the early history of Bergen and the manners and customs of the people, unfortunately are lost. After diligent search I have found the record of only two suits, both of which were appealed, and, strange to say, both were about hogs. I will here insert them for the curious reader:

Extract from the Register of the Minutes of the Court of Bergen, dated 11 November, 1673:

The Schout, CLAES ARENTSE TOERS, *Pl't'ff*,
contra
Captain JOHN BERRY, *Deft.*

"Pl't'ff proceeds against the Deft on a complaint made by Capt. Sandford to the Rt. Hon[ble] the Governor-General in regard to the removal from Major Kingsland of some hogs without the knowledge of any officer. Whereupon the Schout prosecutes for the value thereof. Deft. acknowledges having carried off the hogs to his house, but on the Statement of Sandford's negro, Tjick * * * Deft. claims that they were his.

"The Schout, acting on behalf of justice, maintains that no one can be his own judge on the naked saying of a negro. He proceeds therefore on a charge of Theft.

The judges of this court under the English rule were as follows:

Nicholas Verlet, President.

Commissioned.

Judges			Commissioned
Harman Smeeman, Casper Steinmets, Elias Michielse, Ide Van Vorst,	Assistants,	- -	August 30, 1665.

"The magistrates demand of deft. if he hath anything further to produce as his answer.

"Deft. answers—Nothing else than that I claim that they are my own hogs.

"The Schout demands that deft. be condemned criminally, and demands a fine of 500 guilders, and that the hogs be put back in the place from which they were taken.

"The magistrates condemn the deft. in a fine of 250 guilders, one-half for the officer, one-third of the other half for the church, and one-third for the poor, and one-third for the Court of Bergen, and in case the Deft. cannot furnish further proof that they are his own hogs, he is ordered to deliver up the hogs into the hands of the officer of the jurisdiction of Bergen, and pay, moreover, the costs incurred herein.

"Agrees with the aforesaid Register, quod attestor." *N. Y. Col. MSS., xiii.,* 286.

The appeal from this judgment is unique, and throws additional light upon several customs of that day:

"Capt. John Berry humbly informs your Honor that, on the 11th January, 1670, new style, I departed hence from my plantation (situate a short English mile from Captain Sandford), leaving 13 sows, one boar and 2 barrow hogs. I returned here again in July, 1670, expecting to have found at least 100 hogs, but instead of an increase they were diminished (according to Captain Sandford's statement) to one sow and six barrows, which were not forthcoming. But very early on the subsequent morning my upper servant brought me word that some of the hogs had come back from Milfort, whereupon I answered him they may carry them back there; and about an hour after that Capt. Sandford's negro came there. So seeing the aforesaid hogs, he said to me, 'Here is a sow belonging to my master, and the old sow.' I asked him, 'What old sow?' He answered, 'One of the sows which you left here when you went to Barbadoes.' I asked him if she had had no increase, to which he gave me a vague reply, only saying that they had last winter 7 shoats. Whereupon I said: 'There are six young pigs with her about the same age, and for the most part of the color of the sow, according to all appearance they are six of the seven.'

		Commissioned.
Tynament (Tielman ?) Van Vleck, Town Clerk,		March 8, 1669
William Sandford, President,		
Samuel Edsall, Lourens Andriesen,	either to act as President,	February 15, 1674.

To which he answered, 'I believe so.' Then I said to him, 'Let us go near by and see if they do not belong to your master.' Which we did, and when we had taken a good look at them, he said, 'No, they are not my master's; they have not any holes in their ears' (which was the distinctive mark betweene Capt. Sandford and Mr. Kingsland's). Then said I to him, 'One of the young pigs has a lame foot,' whereupon he answered that one of my sows had a broken knee. Then said I again, 'Beyond a doubt these six barrows are the product of my sow.' The negro replied, 'I think so.' He earnestly requested me not to let it be known that he had disclosed to me, for if his master came to know it, he should be very angry with him. 'Well,' I said, 'from all appearance they justly belong to me; I shall provisionally convey them to my plantation.' But two or three days after I had reached home, I went to the plantation. Shortly afterward I had some conversation with Captain Sandford respecting these hogs. I said to him, 'They do not belong to you, for you have told myself that all your hogs had holes cut in their ears, but to all appearance they belong to me.' He answered, 'All do not belong to me; there is one at the plantation to which I shall lay claim, as it appears.' For when I returned to my plantation, my upper servant told me that Captain Sandford's housekeeper had been there to look them up, saying that they belonged to them, inasmuch as the aforesaid sow did not belong to me, but that I had given her to Capt. Sandford, as well as the Boar, for the wintering of 2 oxen; which is untrue. (These words are in tacit acknowledgment that they were the progeny of the sow.) But that pretense is now out of doors, for he recovered 120 from me for the wintering of the aforesaid oxen, and he has been allowed by the arbitrators between us as much as is customary for the wintering of oxen, and the sow and Boar remain mine. But I should trust and hope more, had I to do with people who professed the fear of the Lord and had an upright heart.

"When the aforesaid hogs came back to the house I had them caught, and went immediately to Capt. Sandford, but he not being at home, the housekeeper and I had some sharp talk on this matter. She said to me that she had had the greatest trouble to bring them up, and therefore ought to have them in preference to any other person. I answered they were not hers on that account, but to all appearance they were the increase of my sow, and therefore belonged to me. She replied that they belonged to her. Then said I, 'How; if all your hogs have holes in their ears?' 'See well to it,' she said, 'you will find holes in the ears of some, and I warn you, sir, that you will not meet with success.' 'Well,' said I, 'send one of your Negroes with me; they are now in the Stone house, and let him see; if there are holes in the ears, I shall let them go, unless such are of recent date.' But she refused to send any one. Next morning

		Commissioned.
John Berry, President. Samuel Edsall, Lourens Andriesen, Elias Michielsen, Engelbert Steenhuysen,	- - - - -	March 13, 1676.

when we examined the hogs by daylight we found that they had holes in the ears, but the scab was yet on the holes, and matter under the scab, and they had a stinking smell, whence it clearly appears that the holes were recently made, but the mark of the plantation was of old, and I congratulate her thereon, and believe it was done when they were shoats, long before they strayed away. Whence it is clearly manifest that such was done to deceive the Honble Governor or me. For they do not belong to me. If they are of the plantation it is mine. The cause being small, I carried only four away from there, and left two to run at large there until my return ; but where they landed I believe Capt. Sandford or his housekeeper knows best, for they could not have any previous knowledge of my journey. Thereupon Captain Sandford craftily made his complaint to the Honble Governor that I had carried off from there some hogs which belonged to him or some one else ; for he knows that they are neither his nor his housekeeper's.

"On this complaint the Schout came to me and asked me if I had taken any hogs away from there. I answered him right out, 'Yes.' He inquired how many. I said, 'Four.' 'Why did you do so?' I answered, 'Because they apparently belonged to me.' Then said he to me I must appear before the next court at Bergen to justify such act. I said to him, 'It shall be done, and very effectually.' I repaired thither, as your honor can see by the copy of their judgment hereunto annexed.

"1st. And in case I am blamed for having done so without the knowledge of the Schout, I answer thereto, had I known, as I did not, that the Dutch law required me to do so, I had justly deserved censure ; but not knowing that, I knew no better than that I might carry these hogs home, as I presumed they justly belonged to me, finding them so near my land and the place to which I had carried so many, communicating my intention therein to the person who set up a claim to them.

"2d. Had I let them run about, they would have perhaps fared no better than the other two which I left loose, as well as my sow that has not turned up, but apparently has gone the same road as the rest of my hogs and their offspring have gone ; there being some people in the world who consider all as fish that comes into their net.

"Right Honorable, this is the real truth of this matter, whereby I hope your honor will clearly see my innocence in this instance. That I carried them silently away, without informing any one ; and when the Schout questioned me thereupon, denied the deed, or acted evasively, which I could have done had I had a dishonest intention, it might have created some presumption, and had I

These same persons were reappointed, February 16, 1677.

The following were appointed, June 13, 1673, members of the Special Court of Oyer and Terminer, to be held at Bergen, June 24, 1673, with power to try all causes brought before them: William Sandford, President; John Pike, John Bishop, Samuel Edsall and Gabriel Minvielle. The General Assembly having provided for holding a semi-annual court in each county, the following persons were appointed, February 16, 1676, to hold a court in Bergen on the first Tuesday in the following

---

an intention to perpetrate dirty actions, there were opportunities enough without any one being knowing of them, before the hogs had been driven away and their number known. But, on the contrary, I strictly charged my negroes not to touch anything, but it is evident that they did not violate my order therein, insomuch that Capt. Sandford himself said that he thought the occurrence took place lately.

"My most earnest desire is that your Honor would please to take these points into consideration and to annul the aforesaid judgment, so that such an undeserved stain may not remain on me and my posterity. I pray forgiveness for having troubled your Honor with this long narrative. The highly prized pledge of an honorable name, which I esteem far more than all riches, hath caused me to do so. I conclude it with my prayer that the Divine Wisdom may be pleased to endue your Honor with intelligence and understanding not to justify the guilty and not to condemn the innocent, both of which are an abomination in the eyes of a righteous God. 17 *Proverbs, v.* 15.

"I would only inform your Honor that, according to the English law, it is usual to do as I have done in this case, and by that law I might take these hogs away with me, and in case any one lay claim to them, he should summon me before the public court of Justice and the Jury of 12 men had to decide thereupon, and if the ownership was found in me, then the Plaintiff is condemned to pay all my costs; and in case they found for the Plaintiff, then I was condemned to restore the property and to make good his costs and damage; that is, what the Defendant hath appropriated and converted to his own use. This is called an action of Trover and Conversion. But were an accusation of Theft made, a serious action would be against the complainant. Had I been aware that the Dutch Law demanded otherwise, I would have conformed thereto. The Word of God declares that where there is no law there is no Transgression. At least, a misconception ought not to be viewed through a magnifying glass, as the Schout of Bergen tried to do in the avaricious craving for a fine.

"Your honor will please to reflect that Theft is a deed of darkness and silence and shuns the light, and confesses only on compulsion; whereas my actions in this case were in every step the contrary."

It is proper to state that the penalty in this case was, on appeal, reduced to

March, viz.: John Berry, President; Samuel Edsall, Lourens Andriesen, Elias Michielsen and Engelbert Steenhuysen. To hold the same court at the same place on the first Tuesday in March, 1679, the following persons were appointed February 18, 1679, viz.: John Berry, President; Lourens Andriesen, Elias Michielsen, and Epke Jacobs. Ide Cornelisen Van Vorst, Gerrit Gerritse (Van Wagenen), Dirck Claes Braecke, and Elias Michielse (Vreeland) were chosen July 27, 1680. Lourens An-

---

100 guilders, on condition that defendant return the hogs, or prove them to be his within six months. *Col. Hist. of N. Y., ii.*, 729.

The following record may be found in *N. Y. Col. MSS., xxix.*, 218:

"At a Court of Sessions held at Berghen, in New Jersey, Sept. 15, 1680.

"The Court opened by Harry Newton.

"A Jury empannelled & sworne.

"The Triale betweene Mr. William Lawrence, Pltff.

"Mr. Michael Smith, Deft.

"The Decl. upon an action of trespasse upon the case about a parcell of Hoggs said to be stolen by the defts. negroes from the pltff. The deft. offers to come to agreemt.

"The Court adjourned.

"Afternoone.

"The negroes of Mr. Smith examined. Righto confest that hee and his 2 comrads had killed 11 hoggs in the woods and brought two home on Saturday night, and told his mr. of it in the morning, who was very angry, and told them they would bee hanged, &c. The rest were brought home after to the num. of 9.

"Harman Roeloff relates his finding 2 hoggs dead in the woods the sunday morning, & went and acquainted Mr. Smith.

"The two were wounded, small holes like swan shot.

"The negroes deny to have had any gun. The negro Jeremy confesses, also doth Harman. Mr. Baker's negroe confesses to have killed one hog unmarked, about the same time.

"Ordered all 4 to bee secured by the court. Their masters engaging they should bee forthcoming, were sett at liberty.

"Afterwards the arbitrators employed to reconcile the matter in difference between Mr. Lawrence & Mr. Smith being sent to, returning answer that they could not bring in their report conveniently till the morning. Court adjourned till morning.

"Thursday, Sept. 16, 1680.

"In the morning

"Mr. William Lawrence

"Mr. Michael Smith

"The Arbitrators, come into Cort & declare their incapacity of ending their

driesen, President; Samuel Edsall, Enoch Michielse and Gerrit Gerritse, August 31, 1681; and Lourens Andriesen, President; Samuel Edsall, Enoch Michielse and Gerrit Gerritsen, August 31, 1682; Claes Arentse Toers, Hans Diedricks and Enoch Michielse, December 5, 1683. William Douglas was appointed Clerk, March 28, 1683.[1]

---

arbitration, having not liberty to chuse an Umpire. The cort allow them liberty & gave them three hours time.

"The court in meane time adjourned.

"Afternoone.

"The Arbitrators with their umpire bring in their report.

"Mr. Lourens Andries, } named by ye pltff.
"Mr. Claes Arents, the Clarke, }

"Mr. John Baker, } by ye deft.
"Mr. William Douglas, }

"John Ward, Umpire.

"The award £32 10s 0d Losse of Stock; £2 19s. 0d towards his bill of charges, to be pd in 6 m. One halfe in good winter Wheate & halfe in specie of the produce of ye country.

"Judgment according to ye award, & upon default at the time, Execution.

"Two of Mr. Smith's Negroes, vizt., Jeremy and Harman, condemned to be whipt 20 Lashes apiece, & Will, Mr. Baker's Negroe, the like, Righto, for his engagement for the future to amend, & reveale his knowledge of any thieving or &c., done by other Negroes, & to be Executioner to the above three, is remitted.

"Execution was done accordingly in sight of the court.

"After which the court dissolved."

Mr. Smith was a son-in-law of Capt. John Berry, and probably the ancestor of the Smith family at Secaucus. He was sheriff of Bergen county in 1683, and hence was the first sheriff of the county.

[1] The following commission (*Book* 3 *of Deeds, Trenton*) was sent to the court one week after Sandford's appointment:

"*Whereas*, Emanuell, a Negro belonging to the family of Capt. Nicolas Verlett, deceased, hath Maliciously and by the Instigation of the divill sett on fire a barne in the towne of Berggen belonging to the said family, and being proved against him by General Circumstances, and more perticularly by his owne Confession to the Consumation of the said barne and divers cattle that were therein, to ye Great loss and Impoverishing of the said family, which Is death accord-to the Lawes for any person that shall comit wilfully any such abominable Crime, These are therefore to give full power and Authority to the Justice and Magistrates of the said towne and corporation of Bergen to bring the said Emanuel to a tryall before them, and according to the Lawes of England iff he

In due time, after the surrender, the oath of allegiance to the British crown was administered to the inhabitants of Bergen. The following is a true copy of the oath, to which is added the names of those who subscribed to it:

"The Oath of A Legeance taken by the Inhabitants Bergen alias and in the Jurisdiction thereof, Beginning the 20 November, 1665:

"You doe sware by the holy Evangelists Contayned in this book to bare true faith and A Legeance to our Govr Lord King Charles the Second and his lawfull Successors, and to be true and faithful to the Lords Propryeto^{rs} and their Successors and the Government of this Province of New Jersey as long as you shall continue a freeholder and Inhabitant Vnd^{r} the same Without any Equivocation or mentall reseruation Whatsoeuer, and so helpe you God.

"Captt. Nicholas Ver Let, Justice,
"Herman Smeeman, Magis^{tr},
"Gasper Steinmets, ditto
"Elyas Michielsen, ditto
"Ider Cornellissen, ditto
"Hans Diedrect, Constable,[1]
"Tynemant Van Vlickt, towne Clarke,
"Captt. Adrian Post, Ensigne,

Paulus Pietersen,
Hendrick Tunisen,
Adolph Hardenbrook,
Geurt Garetsen,
Barthel Lott,
Christian Pietersen,
Thomas Fredericksen,
Cornelis Abrahams,
Herman Edwarts,

---

be found Guilty by a Jury of the fact to passe Sentence of death upon him, which they are to execute in such forme and manner as they in theire Judgments and Wisdomes shall think fitt for the terror and Example of others, and for their so doing this shall be to them and Every of them a sufficient Authority, provided that this Commission shall be of no longer power and force but for this present occasion. Given under my hand and seal of the province the 15th day of March, 1669."

How long Bergen continued to be the seat of the principal courts of the county I am unable, with the information at hand, to state. But on the 20th of August, 1703, the courts for Bergen county were appointed to be held at Bergen. Perhaps the facts upon this subject will be more fully known when the records now being obtained from the colonial office in England shall have been published.

[1] Diedricks was a representative of Bergen in the General Assembly in 1686.

" Jacob Luby,	Herman Court,
" Arent Lawrence,	Renier Van Giesen,
" Jan Tibout,	Jan Euersen Casabon,
" Engelbert Steenhuis,	Joas Vand^{e} Lynde,
" Pieter Jansen,	Garret Garretsen,
" Laurence Andries,	Claes Arentsen,
" Derrick Tunisen,	Laurence Arentsen,
" Douwe Harmensen,	Isaak Van Vleck."

The village of Bergen was now four years old, and it is altogether likely contained within its bounds many droughty burghers to whom a tavern could administer great consolation. There is no evidence that such an institution existed in the village by permission of the Dutch authorities. Hence it is probable that the following is the first license to keep a hotel in that place:

" *Whereas*, the inhabitants of Bergen have thought fitt to have an Ordinary or publick Victualing House settled in their towne for the accommodation of Strangers and passengers and to Retaile all sorts of drink and other Licquers, for the Effecting Whereof the Magistrates have pitched upon Christian Pietersen, an inhabitant of the said towne, as the most fittest p^{r}son for that Employment, and for Which they have requested my Lycence: These are therefore to permitt and Lycence the aforesaid Christian Pietersen to sett up and keep the aforesaid Ordinary or Victualling hows for Entertainment of all Strangers and passeng^{rs} and to Retaile all sorts of drink and Other Licq^{rs} to all p^{r}sons Excepting Indians, provided he keep good Ord^{r} in his hows and fitt accommodation for strangers and not to exceed the rates that shall be appointed upon all sorts of drink and liquers[1] by the Magistrates of the said towne, hereby prohibiting all other p^{r}sons whomsoever to sell any sorts of drink or Licquers by way of retaile in their howses upon the penalty of paying to the use of the publick fiftie shillings for Every such offence for their contempt, Which said Lycence is to continue for one Whole yeare from the

[1] Until quite a recent date the Judges fixed the rate of charges which might

first day of January next Insuing the date hereof, and so to be renewed by the Secretary yearly.[1]

---

be demanded by tavern-keepers. The following were the rates at one time established in this county:

"A LIST of rates to be taken by every Licensed Innkeeper, as settled by the Judges of the Court of Common Pleas, for the County aforesaid, assembled June Term, 1844:

FOR MAN.	$	cts.
For Breakfast,		37
Dinner in Common,		37
Ditto extraordinary,		50
Supper,		37
Lodging per night,		25
Madeira Wine per quart,	1	50
Claret per ditto,		75
Lisbon, Fayal and Teneriffe Wine per ditto,	1	00
Fresh Lime Punch per quart,		75
Toddy per ditto,		37
Grog per ditto,		25
West India Rum per gill,		12
Geneva per ditto,		12
Brandy per ditto,		12
Whiskey and Cider Spirits per ditto,		12
Cider per quart,		8
Cider Royal or Bottle Cider per quart,		25
Strong Beer per ditto,		8
Ship Beer per ditto,		4
Porter per bottle,		37
Metheglin,		37
Champaigne Wine per bottle,	2	00

And so in proportion for a larger or smaller quantity.

FOR HORSE.		
For Oats per quart,		3
Indian Corn per ditto,		4
Stabling a Horse per night on English Hay,		25
Ditto for twenty-four hours,		37
Stabling a Horse per night on Salt Hay,		12
Ditto for twenty-four hours,		18
Pasture per night,		12
Ditto for twenty-four hours,		16

And so in proportion for a longer or shorter time."

[1] Christian and his good wife, Tryntje, continued to pass the pewter mug to him that was athirst, until Feb. 13, 1670, when his license was revoked, and Hans Diedricks reigned in his stead. Hendrick Cornelisen seems to have received a license March 10, 1669.

"Given Undr my hand and seal of the province, 14 Xbr, 1666, and in 18 yeare of his Maties Raigne."[1]

On the 7th of April, 1668, the people were called upon to elect representatives to an assembly to be held at Elizabethtown on the 25th of May following. For Bergen, Caspar Steinmets and Balthazar Bayard were chosen.[2]

From this time until the recapture of the country by the Dutch, the only thing of importance which occurred within the bounds of this county, save a few grants of land, was a charter to the town.[3] This charter was granted by Carteret. The following is a copy:

"This Deede Witnesseth of Charter granted to the Towne and Freeholders of Bergen, and to the Villages and Plantations thereunto belonging, cituated and being in the province of New Cesarea or New Jersey: By Honble Capt. Phillip Carteret, Esqr., Governour of the said Province, and his Counsil, under the Right Honble John Lord Berkley, Barron of Stratton, and Sr. George Carteret, Knt. and Baronet, the absolute Lords Proprietors of the same, Containing the Limitts and bounds of the Jurisdiction of the said Towne, together with the immunities and Priviledges thereunto belonging and appertaining, as followeth: Imprms. The Bounds and Limitts of the aforesaid Towne and Corporation of Bergen is to begin at the North end thereof, from a place called Mordavis Meadow, lying upon the west side of Hudson's river, from thence to run upon a N. W. lyne by a Three rail fence that is now standing to a place called Espatin, and from thence to a little Creek surrounding N. N. W., till it comes into Hackinsack river, containing in Bredth from the top of the Hill, 1½ miles or 120 chains, from thence it runs along the said Hackinsack river upon S. S. W. lyne till it comes to the point or neck of Land that is over against Statten Island and Shooter's Island in Arthur Cull Bay, containing in length about twelve miles,

---

[1] *Liber* 3 *of Deeds* (*Trenton*), 10.

[2] *Leaming and Spicer*, 77, 85.

[3] For information concerning these grants see *Winfield's Land Titles*.

from thence to run Eastward along the River called Kill van Cull that parts Statten Island from the Maine to a point or neck of Land called Constable's Point or Constable's houck, and from thence to run up Northward all along the Bay up into Hudson's river till it comes to Mordavis Meadow aforesaid; So that the whole tract of upland and Meadow property belonging to the Jurisdiction of the said Town and Corporation of Bergen is bounded at the North end by a tract of Land belonging to Captn. Nichs. Verlett and Mr. Samuel Edsall. On the East side by Hudson's river, on the South end by the Kill van Cull, that parts Statten Island and the Maine, and on the West by Arthur Cull Bay and Hackensack river, as it is more plainer demonstrated by a draught thereof, made by the Surveyor-General, hereunto annexed: The whole, both of upland and Meadows and Waist land, containing according to the survey 11,520 Acres English measure: Which said Limitts and bounds, together with all the Rivers, Ponds, Creeks, Islands, Inlets, Bays, Fishing, Hawking, Hunting, and all other appurtenances whatsoever thereunto belonging and appertaining. The half part of Golde and Silver Mynes, and the Royaltie of the Lords Proprietors only Excepted, to continue and remain within the Jurisdiction, Corporation or Township of the said Towne of Bergen, from the day of the date hereof and forever: The said Corporation submitting themselves to the Authority of the Lords Proprietors and the Government of this Province. To be holden by them, the said Corporation or Township, their heirs and Successors, as of the manner of East Greenwich, in free and common Socage.

"2dly. That all the Freeholders of the said Corporation or Township are hereby jointly and severally obliged to Pay or Cause to be paid to the said Lords Proprietors, their heirs and Successors, or to their Receivers-General, within the said Province, on every 25th day of March,[1] according to the English Accompt, the sum of fifteen Pounds Sterling, of good and Law-

[1] The beginning of the new year, *old style*. In 1752 the *new style* was adopted. That year began on the first of January, and on the third of September following, the old style ended, the next day being considered the 14th, *new style*.

ful money of England, or the Value thereof, in good and Current pay of the Country, as a Quit rent due to them, the whole said tract of Land above mentioned, in lieu of the ½d. Pr. acre, mentioned in the Concessions, which Payment is to begin on the 25th day of March, which shall be in the Year of Lord 1670, and so to continue forever, without any change to the said Lords Proprietors or their Agent; and that all Pattents for land herebefore Granted, or to be Granted within the said Limitts, are to be accompted upon the aforesaid Rent of Fifteen Pounds Sterling pr. annum.

"3dly. That all Freeholders living and Inhabiting within the said Jurisdiction, Corporation or Towneship, wether within the said Towne of Bergen, Comunipaw, Ahassimus, Minkacque, Pembrepock, or upon any other Plantation within the said Limitts, shall be deemed and accompted for Freemen of the said Corporation or Township, and having taken the oath of Aleagance to the King, and Fidelity to the Lords Proprietors, are to have a Free Voice in Election, and to enjoy All the Rights, Imunities and Privileges hereby Granted unto the said Corporation or Towneship.

"4thly. That the Freeholders aforesaid, or the Major Part of them, are upon the Governor's Summons to make Choice of two Deputies to Join with the General Assembly for the making of Laws and Carrying on the Public Affairs of the whole Province.

"5thly. That the Freeholders aforesaid, or the Major part of them, have Power to chuse their own Magistrates to be assistants to the President or Judge of the Court, and for the ordering of all Public Affaires within the said Jurisdiction. Provided that one of the said Magistrates is to be chosen out of the Freeholders of Minkacque or Pembrepock. They have Power likewise to nominate their Justice or Justices of the Peace and their Military Officers, Provided that the Justices of the Peace and the Military Officers are to be approved of and commissioned by the Governor.

"6thly. That the Freeholders aforesaid, or the Major part of them, have Power to chuse their own Minister for the preaching of the word of God, and the Administering His Holy Sacraments, and being so chosen, all persons, as well the Freeholders as the Inhabitants, are to contribute according to their estates and proportions of Land for his maintenance, or Lay out such a proportion of Land for the Minister, and the keeping of a Free School for the Education of Youth, as they shall think fit, which land being once laid out is not to be alienated, but to Remaine and continue forever from one incombant to another, Free from Paying of any hye Rent, or any other Rate or Taxes whatsoever, notwithstanding it shall and may be lawful for any particular person or persones to keep and Maintain any other Minister at their own Proper Cost and Charges.

"7thly. That in Religious Concerns and the Way of Worshipping of God there is liberty of conscience Granted to all Persons in Generall, as well to the freeholders as to others that are or shall be admitted Inhabitants within the said Corporation or Towneship, they taking or Subscribing the Oath of Allegiance to the King, and fidelity to the Lords Proprietors and their Successors, and that no Person whatsoever shall be Injured, Molested or Troubled for his or her difference in opinion in matters of Religion. Provided that this Liberty Granted shall not extend to Licentiousness or the Disturbance of others and the Public Peace.

"8thly. That the Freeholders aforesaid, or the Major part of them, have power to admit of their own Inhabitants, and to divide all Proportions of Land as are within their Bounds and Limitts aforesaid, that are not already appropriated and Pattented by particular persons before the day of the date hereof, According to their Allotments and estates, as the Justices and Magistrates shall in their Wisdoms and Discretions think fit, which Lands being so divided, every man's proportion is to be surveyed, butted and bounded by the Surveyor, and the same to be recorded by the Secretarie and Recorder-General of the Province, or by Eyther of them, which Propositions and Allotments being so Surveyed and Recorded after two years In possession, shall not be subject to any resurvey nor Alterations of Bounds, but shall remain according to the first survey for ever. And for the better avoiding of all Frauds and Sutes at Law, all Mortages, Transports, Sales and Leases for above the Terme of

One Yeare, and all other concerning Houses and Lands are to be recorded by the Secretary as aforesaid, for the Neglecting thereof all such contracts as aforesaid, are to be void, and of no effect in Law.

"9thly. That all Lands and Meadows that are appropriated and pattented by particular persons before the day of ye date of these presents shall continue and remain unto them without any alteration, unless the Proprietors thereof will give their Consent to the Contrary.

"10thly. That the Freeholders and Inhabitants of the said Corporation shall have a Free Trade allowed them, and that no tax of Custome, Excise or any Imposition whatever shall be imposed on them but such as shall be levied by the Governor and Council and General Assembly, for the defraying of the Public Charges and the Maintenance of the Government.[1] And that all Rates and Assessments relating to the said Corporation or Towneship shall be rated and levied by their Justices and Magistrates or whom they shall appoint.

"11thly. That in case of Invasion or Insurrection by the Indians or others, they are mutually, as well the Freeholders as all other Inhabitants, to Join with all other Townes and Plantations within the said Province, for the defence an safety of the same, but no Warr to be levied without the consent of the Governor, Councill and General Assembly.

"12thly. That all Freeholders aforesaid, or the Major part of them, have power annually on every first day of January, or at any other set tyme as they shall appoint, to chuse one or more

---

[1] This privilege (extended also to East Jersey) was the source of much uneasiness on the part of New York, and the cause of many efforts for the annexation of East Jersey to that province. The following extract will show the general argument used by New York: "East Jersey is scituate on Hudson's River over against Long Island, Staten Island and New Yorke, and they pretend by the aforementioned grant to be a free place and to have free ports to trade as they please, which if admitted must certainly destroy yor Maj^{ties} interest and revenue here; for what merchant will come to New York and trade and pay to Yo^{r} Maj^{ty} 2 and 10 p^{r} cent with the excise and Yo^{r} Maj^{ties} dutys settled here, if they can at 2 or 3 miles distance over against the same place go and be free from any duty or imposition whatever." *Col. Hist. of N.Y., iii.*, 798.

Constables for the Public Service, which said Constable or Constables are to be sworne in their office by the Justice of the Peace according to the oath prescribed.

"13thly. That all the Freeholders and others, the Inhabitants aforesaid, are to submit themselves to the Laws and Government of the Province, and to swear or subscribe to the Oath of Aleagence to the King and Fidelity to the Lords Proprietors. And in case they or any of them have a desire to remove or Transport themselves to any other place, they have liberty so to do, and to dispose of their Lands and Estates to their best Advantages.

"14thly. That the said Corporation or Towneship have power to Errect and Ordaine a Court of judicature within their own Jurisdiction, and for the Limitts thereof for the Tryall of all causes Actionable between party and party, from whence there shall be no Appeal under the sum of Five Pounds Sterling, and also for the Tryall of all Criminal and causes of Misdemeanor, and to inflict such Fines and Punishments as the Meritt of the cause shall require, as by Imprisonment, Stocking, Piloring, Ducking, Branding, Whipping[1] not exceeding twenty stripes, and the like, Which Court is to consist of a President, who is to be a Justice of the Peace, and the Magistrates, or any two of them at the least, a Clarke, and such other officers as they shall appoint, which said Magistrates and Clarke are to be sworne in their offices, and the Clarke to be approved of by the Secretary General of the Province, who is to keep an Exact Record of all actions that shall be brought in and tryed in said Court, and to give an account thereof unto him when thereunto required by the Governor and his Councill. No Freeholder is to be arrested or detained a Prisoner for debt until Judgment be passed and Execution granted, unless it can be made to appear that the party has an Intent to defraud his Creditors by running out of the

[1] In the olden time there was a lock-up on the easterly side of the Square, near the site of the present school-house. Within the last fifty years the stocks were in use on the westerly side of the Square, and but one generation has passed since the whipping-post was a wholesome antidote to petty offences and a terror to evil doers. Many an old person still living has seen the victim writhe under the lash, laid on with a skillful flourish by the old constable.

Country. That all persons, as well Freeholders as other Inhabitants, in Case of Appeal, the Appellant shall give in security to prosecute his Appeal, or stand to the Judgment of the Court. All causes according to the Laws of England shall be tried by a Jury of six or twelve men, and whomsoever shall trouble and molest his neighbor, being of the same Corporation, by arresting of him and going to Law in another Jurisdiction, shall be liable to a Fine according to the discretion of the Court. The Justice or Justices of the Peace being Commissioned and sworne in their office, have power to Administer the oath of Aleagance and Fidelitie, and all other Oaths that are required by the law, and to issue out in His Majestie's name, or in whose name or names It shall or may hereafter be appointed by the Lawes, their Warrants of Summons, and arrest within the limitts and Jurisdiction of the said Corporation or Towneship, directing the same to the Constable, Marshall, or what other Officer or Officers the said Corporation shall in their discretion think fit to appoint for that Service, who are to put the same in Execution accordingly, and also to Issue out their Warrants for the apprehending of all Malefactors and Runaways, and to prosecute them by way of Hugh and Cry, and to do all such thing and things by their authority according toLaw and Justice as may conduce to the Peace and well Government of the said Province, Corporation and Towneship. Provided that all Fynes are to be disposed of for Charitable or public uses. It is to be noted that whereas it is said in the Eight articles[1] that all Mortgages, Transports, Sales and Leases of Land are to be recorded by the Secretary, they are first to be acknowledged before the Governor or a Justice of the Peace by the Granter, or by two good Sufficient Witnesses, Attested on the backside of the aforesaid deed, which is a Warrant for the Secretary to record the same.

"In Confirmation of the premises, Wee the said Governor and the Councill have hereunto set our hands the 22d day of September, 1668, and the 20th year of the Reign of our Sovn. Lord Charles the Second of England, Scotland, France and Ireland,

---

[1] The eighth article of this Charter.

King, Defender of the Faith, &c.: and the Seale was placed by consent before signing.

"PH. CARTERET.

"Robert Vanguellen, Ni. Varlett, Samuel Edsall, Robert Bond, "William Pardon.

"James Bollen, Secretary and of the Councill."

What caused the granting of this Charter is not now known. The following certificate of Governor Stuyvesant may throw some light upon it:

"We, underwritten, the late Director-General and Council of New Netherlandt, hereby certify and declare that in the year one thousand six hundred and sixty-one, by us underwritten, in quality as aforesaid, have given and granted to the inhabitants of the village of Bergen, the lands with the meadows thereunto annexed, situate on the West side of the North River in Pavonia, in the same manner as the same was by us underwritten, purchased of the Indians, and as the same was to us delivered, by the said Indians, pursuant to an instrument of sale and delivery thereof, being under the date of the 30th of January, A. D. one thousand six hundred and fifty-eight; with this express condition and promise, that the aforesaid inhabitants of the before named village shall not be prejudiced in their outdrift, by means of any private collective dwellings (saving only the right of the then already cultivated farms at Gemoenepan). But that all such who have any lands within the district of the before named village, and especially at Pemrepogh, and Mingackque, all such owners shall be obliged to remove their dwellings and place them in the village or town of Bergen, or by or about the neighborhood of Gemoenepan before named. Conditioned, however, that the aforesaid owners (in case they should desire the same) should be permitted to share and divide with the inhabitants of the before named village or town, in the common lands of the said town, and in the place and stead of their lands lying at Pemrepogh and Mingackquie before named. (And especially that the meadows laying near the village or town of Bergen, where the same begins, at the West side along Kill van Kol, should be and belong to and for the use of the before named inhabitants of Bergen).

"And further, we the underwritten, certify and declare, that Michael Jansen, deceased (before or about the time that the aforesaid village or town was laid out), for himself, as also for and in behalf of his brother-in-law, Nicholas Jansen Barker,[1] did in our presence, renounce all the right they had to the pasture ground laying behind Gemoenepan, for a common outdrift and pasture between the aforesaid village or town, and the neighborhood of Gemoenepan, before named.

"And lastly, that no more lands were given or granted to Dirck Clausen, than Rightpocques, with the meadows thereunto belonging, as by the ground-brief thereof may further appear.

"In testimony of the truth, we have signed these with our own hands, in New York, the 26th of October, A. D.

"P. STUYVESANT,
"NICASIUS DE SILLE."[2]

By what instrument the lands herein referred to were granted

---

[1] Backer. *Winfield's Land Titles,* 50.

[2] *Taylor's Annals,* 50. "The year when this certificate was given is not intelligible in the original instrument. But as they certify as former Governor and Council, it must have been after August, 1664, when the English conquered the country. New York, February 20th, 1764. Translated from the Dutch, by Abm. Lott, Jun'r."

The last two paragraphs of the certificate seem to refer to the meadow through which the Morris canal now passes, between the Cavan Point road and Hudson avenue. There was a fierce controversy between the village of Bergen and the people of Communipaw, Raccocas and Minkakwa, relating to some land and the fences thereon, which was referred to arbitrators, and finally carried before the Governor of New Orange in July, 1674. *N. Y. Col MSS., xxiii.,* 364, 5, 9. In their appeal the inhabitants of Bergen show that their deputies —Hans Diedricks and Engelbert Steenhuysen—had yielded their claim, by which they were "cut off from the lowermost meadow," and a fence was erected by which they were "separated from Gemonepa so that we cannot have access to the water side except by a roundabout way." This leaves but little doubt as to the land in controversy, and it is the same referred to by Governor Stuyvesant as having been renounced by Michael Jansen. Jansen died in 1663, the Dutch surrendered in 1664, Stuyvesant died in 1671; hence the above certificate must have been dated between 1664 and 1671. It is quite probable that it was dated prior to Carteret's charter of Bergen.

to the inhabitants of Bergen we do not know. Such grant is not to be found in the Ordinance of September 5, 1661, and it is worthy of notice that many grants from the Dutch Government to individuals are to be found bearing a later date; yet the Governor must have understood the Ordinance of 1661 to contain such a grant, or else the grant to which he refers has been lost. Whatever the fact about the grant may be, it is quite probable that this certificate went far toward satisfying Governor Carteret that the freeholders of Bergen were entitled to all the unpatented lands. In this light the Charter of 1668 was only a confirmation of the rights which the "Freeholders, Inhabitants of Bergen," possessed under the Dutch Government.

CHAPTER VI.—1673-1764.

The country recaptured by the Dutch—Bergen summoned to surrender—The people comply and take oath of allegiance—The military power of Bergen organized—Controversy between Bergen and its dependent hamlets, Pembrepogh and Minkakwa—Bergen sends her soldiers to New Orange—The country surrendered to the English—Condition of the country in 1680—Its villages and farms—Provision for the care of the common land—Its final partition.

THE war which followed the seizure of New Netherland ended in the treaty of Breda, July 31, 1667, by which each party was to hold what had been captured during the contest. This confirmed New Netherland to the English. In March, 1672, war again broke out between England and the States. The Dutch despatched a small squadron to cruise on the American coast and destroy the English shipping. Cornelis Evertsen and Jacob Binckes, joining their forces at Martinico, sailed with their five vessels for the Chesapeake. Capturing some vessels there and obtaining information as to the state of the defences at New York, they sailed for that place. On the 29th of July, 1673, the fleet, now consisting of twenty-three vessels, carrying sixteen hundred men, anchored in the bay. The land forces of the Dutch were under Captain Anthony Colve, who took possession of the city on the following day.[1] Three days afterward (August 12th, N. S.) the following summons was sent to Bergen, one of the villages in the "Province of New Yarsey," which had not yet sent delegates to the Dutch commanders to treat concerning surrender:

"*To the Inhabitants of the Village of Bergen, and the Hamlets and Bouweries thereon depending:*

"You are hereby ordered and instructed to despatch Delegates from your Village here to us, to treat with us on next Tuesday, respecting the surrender of your town to the obedience of their

[1] *Broadhead, ii.*, 207. *Valentine's Hist. of N. Y.*, 170.

High Mightinesses, the Lords States-General of the United Netherlands, his Serene Highness the Prince of Orange, or on refusal so to do, we shall be obliged to constrain you thereunto by force of arms.

"Dated at the City Hall of the city of New Orange, the 12th of August, Anno 1673.

"CORNELIS EVERTSE, Junior,
"JACOB BENCKES.

"By their order.
"N. BAYARD, Secret^{y}."[1]

The good burghers of Bergen did not wait to be "constrained thereunto," but, influenced by a national sympathy, surrendered most graciously. On the 18th they sent in a list of the names of some of their most prominent citizens, from which the authorities in New York, now called New Orange, might make selection of magistrates. This being done, as hereinbefore stated, a certificate of their election was sent to them, and they were required to appear in New Orange to be sworn into office.[2] On the 21st they appeared, in accordance with the requisition, and took the following oath:

"We, the Schout, Schepens and Secretary of the Village of Bergen, qualified by the Honble Council of War, do promise and swear, in the presence of Almighty God, that we, each in his quality, will, according to the best of our knowledge and without passion, administer good law and justice between parties in cases brought before us; that we will promote the welfare of this village and its inhabitants; in all things defend the upright and true Christian Religion agreeably to the Word of God and the order of the Synod of Dordrecht taught in the Netherland church; in all circumstances obey, maintain and help to maintain the Supreme Government placed, or hereafter yet to be appointed over us, in the name of their High Mightinesses the Lords States-General of the United Netherlands and his Highness of Orange,

[1] *Col. Hist. of N. Y.*, ii., 571.

[2] *Ibid*, ii., 571.

and prevent, as far as in our power lies, everything that may conflict with it. So truly help us God."[1]

At the time of taking the oath the magistrates were notified that the commanders would visit Bergen on the following "Sunday after the sermon, in order to administer the oath of allegiance to all their people." On the 27th the commanders and Council of War of New Orange came over as they had promised. They found the number of the burghers of Bergen and surrounding dependencies to be *seventy-eight*,[2] sixty-nine of whom appeared at the tap of the drum and took the oath of allegiance. The magistrates were ordered to forward the oaths of those who were absent. The oath taken by the Dutch inhabitants was different from that taken by the English, and was as follows: "We do promise and swear, in the presence of the Almighty God, to be loyal and faithful to their High Mightinesses the Lords States-General of the United Netherlands, and his Serene Highness the Prince of Orange, and their governor, already, or hereafter to be, appointed here, and to comport ourselves on all occasions as loyal and faithful subjects are bound to do. So truly help me Almighty God."[3] On the 4th of September, the town of Bergen having sent in names for that purpose, the authorities in New Orange selected the following militia officers:

CASPAR STEYNMETS, *Captain.*

HANS DIEDERICKS, *Lieutenant.*[4] ADRIAEN POST, *Ensign.*

---

[1] *Col. Hist. of N. Y.*, *ii.*, 574, 578, 580. The Schout was afterward authorized "to fill and execute the office of Auctioneer." This position gave him the power to sell property on judgments pronounced by the court. Ordinarily, this right belonged, *ex-officio*, to the Provincial Secretary. *New Neth. Reg.*, 114. This court had power not only to hear and determine causes brought before them, but to pass ordinances for the government of the people. In October, 1673, this court passed an ordinance respecting the observance of Sunday, etc., which was approved by the council in New Orange. *Col. Hist. of N. Y.*, *ii.*, 643. *N. Y. Col. MSS.*, *xxiii.*, 133. This ordinance is missing.

[2] This I presume shows the number of white males above the age of twenty-one years.

[3] *Col. Hist. of N. Y.*, *ii.*, 589. Mr. Whitehead, *East Jersey*, 61, says the inhabitants of Bergen were "probably considered too much in their interest to require the binding influence of an oath."

[4] *Ibid*, *ii.*, 597. Diedricks was one of the grantees of "Haquequenunck,"

This provision for military organization was but keeping up what had been practised before the English took possession of the country, and what they continued when the Dutch rule had passed away. In less than two years after the foundation of Bergen, officers were appointed to marshall the growing powers of the ambitious village and its belligerent dependencies.

For Bergen. { Adriaen Post, *Ensign*, John Swaen, *Sergeant*. } Appointed June 30, 1663.

For Gemoenepa. { Harman Smeeman, *Ensign*, Gerrit Gerritsen, *Sergeant*. } " " "[1]

As officers of a foot company to be enlisted in Bergen, Gemoenepaen, Ahasymus and Hooboocken, the following appointments were made:

Nicholas Verlett, *Captain*,
Caspar Steinmets, *Lieutenant*,
Adrian Post, *Ensign*. } Appointed September 6, 1665.[2]

John Berry,[3] *Captain*,
Adrian Post, *Lieutenant*,
Elias Michielsen, *Ensign*. } Appointed July 15, 1675.[4]

William Laurence, *Captain*,
Jacob Lubert, *Lieutenant*,
Enoch Michielsen, *Ensign*. } Appointed July 4, 1681.[5]

Gerbrand Claesen, *Captain*,
Gerrit Gerritsen, *Lieutenant*,
Jan Adrianse Sip, *Ensign*. } Appointed Nov. 10, 1692.

March 28, 1679. *Whitehead's East Jersey*, 49. It is doubtful, however, if he ever settled there, for on " Thursday, the 2nd off May, 1689, the Justices off the peace off Bergen County and East Yarsey came and mett the Governor, vizt., Coll. Hamilton, Coll. Townly, Capt. Berry, Capt. Bowne, and Magistrates of Bergen, all promising that they would be aiding and assisting to reprias any comon enemy, and because there are noe militairy officers in commission in the County or Corporation off Bergen, Hans Diedrick was appointed Capt., Juriaen Thomas Leftenant, and Claes Teers (Toers) Ensigne of said Corporation, and Commissions given accordingly." *N. Y. Hist. Soc.*, 1868, 247.

[1] *N. Y. Col. MSS.*, *x.*, *Part ii.*, 168. [2] *Liber* 3 *of Deeds* (*Trenton*), 1.

[3] Berry's house in Bergen was, on the 19th of July, 1673, made the "prison for ye province," until a house could be built for that purpose, and Adrian Post, constable, was made keeper. *Book* 3 *of Deeds* (*Trenton*), 93.

[4] *Ibid*, 117. Michael Smith was appointed *Lieutenant* in this company June 2, 1677. *Ibid*, 134. [5] *Ibid*, 189.

Shortly previous to the re-occupation by the Dutch, a controversy arose between the authorities of the town of Bergen and the people residing in the "Villages of Pemrepogh and Mingagque," then considered as dependent hamlets. It seems to have been the rule that all the inhabitants should, without regard to creed, contribute to the support of the Precentor[1] and Schoolmaster at Bergen. To this the independent citizens objected. Thereupon, on the 18th of December, 1672, the Schout and Magistrates of Bergen ordered that all should pay. This being disregarded, they called upon the authorities in New Orange to compel the inhabitants of all the settlements, of what religious persuasion soever they might be, to pay their share toward the support of the Precentor and Schoolmaster.[2] Upon this appeal, it was, upon the 24th of December, 1673, ordered: "That all the said inhabitants, without exception, shall, pursuant to the resolution of the Magistrates of the town of Bergen, dated 18th Xber, 1672, and subsequent confirmation, pay their share for the support of said Precentor and Schoolmaster." Over this decision there was doubtless great rejoicing in Bergen and *Buyten Tuyn*. The Schoolmaster confided to his whip a more artistic flourish, and the Precentor chanted with a clearer voice. But his triumphant cadences were soon turned into the doleful minor by the unregenerate stubbornness of "Mingagque and Pemrepogh." These "uncircumcised in heart" thought Old Hundred and Windham, piping out from under the pulpit, very good music for those who were educated up to that standard, and were willing to pay for the luxury. The Schoolmaster, "with eyes severe," piloting the bewildered urchin through the mazes of the

[1] The precentor, or chorister, was generally the voorleezer or reader of the service preceding the sermon. Dr. Taylor says he was also for many years the schoolmaster, duly appointed by the consistory of the church. *Taylor's Annals*, 111. When, therefore, as in the text, precentor and schoolmaster are spoken of, it is highly probable that they refer to one and the same person. In the case of Steenhuysen, hereinbefore spoken of, he seems to have been appointed by the Governor and Council, after approval by the *people*, his name having been submitted to the "community" by the town authorities, the consistory having nothing to do with him.

[2] *Col. Hist. of N. Y., ii.*, 672.

multiplication table by the aid of the birch, was very good in his way to those who lived near enough to enjoy the blessing of his wisdom. But they resolutely refused to be thus edified or instructed, and declined to contribute to the general expense of such benefactions. On the 24th of May, 1674, the Schout and Schepens again complained that some of the inhabitants of those "independent hamlets," in utter contempt of the previous order, obstinately refused to pay their quota to the support of the Precentor and Schoolmaster. This persistent disobedience aroused the representatives of their High Mightinesses. They resolved to adhere to their previous order, and, to give it force by wielding over the heads of the disobedient direful threats of pains and penalties, ordered the "Schout to proceed to immediate execution against all unwilling debtors."[1] Thus circumstanced, the "unwilling debtors" must either fight or remonstrate against what they considered an oppression. They wisely chose the latter course. Lourens Andriesen, of Mingagque, and Joost van der Linde, of Pemrepogh, were appointed agents to submit the cause of the people to the authorities in New Orange. This was faithfully done, but, alas, "after due enquiry," it was formally adjudged, "that the inhabitants of Pemrepogh and Mingaghquy, shall promptly pay their share for the support aforesaid, on pain of proceeding against them with immediate execution."[2]

This was the end of the controversy. Judgment had been entered for Bergen in the court of final resort, and nothing remained better than submission. But contention upon one subject soon produced difference in views, and controversy upon another. The lands in the township that were not covered by grants were considered common for the use of all. A certain common fence had been constructed to separate the heifers and steers from the milch cows and oxen. A question then arose between the town of Bergen and the "dependent hamlets" Gemoenepa, Mingagque and Pemrepogh, respecting the making and maintenance of this fence. The cause of dispute was an old one, and had been referred by Governor Carteret and Council to four arbitrators cho-

[1] *Col. Hist. of N. Y., ii.*, 716.

[2] *Ibid, ii.*, 730.

sen by both sides. These arbitrators, on the 10th of April, 1672, submitted their award, which the people of Bergen were willing to obey, but it was rejected by the others. Bergen now appealed to the Governor and council of war to compel the other parties to perform the award. On the 24th of May, 1674, the inhabitants of the three "dependent hamlets" were ordered to regulate themselves according to the decision of the arbitrators, or within fourteen days to submit any objection which they could produce against the award.[1] It does not appear that any objections were ever filed or that they obtained any modification of the award.

From the first of the Dutch reoccupation it had been the care of the authorities in New Orange to prepare for the return of the English. The fortifications in the city were enlarged and strengthened. The people of the neighboring towns promised to repair to the city on the approach of the enemy. On the 22d of December, 1673, the people of Bergen were ordered to repair to New Orange, according to their plighted duty. A literal compliance with the order was at first dispensed with, and the same was modified so as to permit some men to remain at home. The captain, lieutenant and ensign were ordered to appear with their company fully armed, on Friday, the 29th of December, 1673, in front of Fort William Hendrick, leaving *six men in the town*. This being done, one-third of the company was furloughed and permitted to return home, there to remain until they were relieved on the third day. The officers and magistrates were authorized to give orders respecting the threshing the grain and the "foddering the cattle," but above all to keep proper guard day and night, so as not to be surprised and cut off from the city.[2] Afterward, on the 13th of March, 1674, a positive order was issued, commanding " all out people of the Dutch Na-

---

[1] *Col. Hist. of N. Y., ii.*, 714. From the above it would seem that Minkakwa was the abode of strife and contention at a very early day. If the antiquary will inform himself as to the present locality of that ancient district, he will be somewhat impressed with the theory that localities have much to do in the formation of certain traits of character.

[2] *Ibid, ii.*, 673.

tion" to repair to New Orange without delay, with their arms, on the first news of the enemy's approach, or on the coming of more than one ship at the same time. All who failed to obey this order were to be declared traitors and perjurers, and were to be proceeded against as enemies, or punished with death and confiscation. This order was to be made known by the proper officers, that none might plead ignorance.[1] On March 22d, 1674, the Schout of Bergen was notified to request the people to commission a militia officer and magistrate, with whom he was to attend a general conference at Fort William Hendrick on the 26th. The Schout, Claas Arentse Toers and Captain Caspar Steinmets appeared in the assembly as deputies from Bergen. They pledged themselves for the loyalty of their constituents, and promised that on the first notice of danger the people of Bergen would "observe their honor and oath" in repairing to New Orange. They only asked that some boats be sent over to convey the people thither.[2] All these precautions, however, went for nothing, for on the 9th of February, 1674, peace was established between England and Holland by the treaty of Westminster. By the sixth article of that treaty the country was restored to the English.[3] It was not, however, until the 10th of November following that the final surrender took place, when the Dutch rule in New Netherland passed away forever, and the English entered into possession, which they held for the next century.

While the war was in progress, and on March 18, 1673, Lord Berkley sold his interest in the Province to John Fenwick, in trust for Edward Billinge, for £1,000. Billinge had failed in business; Berkley was his particular friend and advised him to invest in New Jersey lands for the purpose of retrieving his fortune. He was pleased with the proposition, borrowed the money from his friends, and purchased the land in the name of John Fenwick, who was to have one-tenth of the same. Fenwick managed the purchase so well that, it is said, he would soon have stripped the other of all, but means were employed to compel him

---

1 *Col. Hist. of N. Y., ii.*, 696.

2 *Ibid, ii.*, 702.

3 *Whitehead's East Jersey*, 62.

to be satisfied with his tenth.[1] Billinge assigned his interest, less Fenwick's tenth, to William Penn, Gawn Laurie and Nicholas Lucas, February 9 and 10, 1674, in trust for his creditors. Fenwick sold his interest to John Eldridge and Edmund Warren, who sold to Penn, Laurie and Lucas.[2]

To clear up any shadow which the recent occupation by the Dutch might have cast upon former grants, Charles II. made a second grant to the Duke, June 29, 1674.[3] This was followed by the Duke, July 29, 1674, with a grant to Sir George Carteret of what was afterward known as East Jersey. On July 1, 1676, by the "Quintipartite Deed," the State was divided and Sir George received the eastern portion in severalty.[4] Sir George, by will dated December 5, 1678, appointed his wife, Elizabeth, sole executrix, and Earl Sandwich, Earl Bath, Lord Grenville, Sir Thomas Crew, Sir Robert Atkins and Edward Atkins trustees, to whom he devised his interest in New Jersey, to be sold for the payment of his debts.[5] On the 5th and 6th of March, 1680, East Jersey was conveyed to Thomas Cremer and Thomas Pocock, but the transfer does not seem to have been completed. On the 6th of the following August, the Duke indulged in a second grant to Penn and his associates of West Jersey, and Gordon says he also gave one to the representatives of Carteret on March 14, 1682. This has not been discovered, but the following warrant therefor exists:

"These are to direct and require you to prepare for my signature a Deed or fitting Instrument (agreeable to yt I have already executed unto Edward Billing and others) whereby I may release and confirm unto Sir George Carteret, ye heire of Sir George Carteret, (lately deceased,) his moyty of New Jersey (called East New Jersey) in America. For wch y^s^ shal be yor Warr^t^, Provided it be entred w^t^ my Auditor Gen^ll^ w^th^in two months of its date. Given und^r^ my hand at Windsor ye 6th day of September (80).

---

[1] *Long Isl. Hist. Soc.*, *i.*, 243. [2] *Gordon's Hist. of N. J.*, 72. [3] *Ibid*, 41.

[4] *Leaming and Spicer*, 61. This division was confirmed by the General Assembly in 1719. For a history of this line see *Whitehead's East Jersey*, 67. *Gordon's N. J.*, 71–5. *Smith's N. J.*, 195, 546–557.

[5] *Vide Will, Perth Amboy, Liber C* 3, 17.

"To Sir John Churchill Kn[t] my Atturney Gen[ll] or to S[ir] George Jeffreys Kn[t] my Sollict[e] Gen[ll]."[1]

These releases were given in consequence of an opinion of Sir William Jones, dated July 28, 1680. The Duke's Governor of New York had claimed jurisdiction over both of the Jerseys, and insisted on his right, in behalf of the Duke, to collect duties upon importations therein. These pretensions were resisted with much spirit, until finally the Duke referred the subject to Sir William Jones for an opinion. His decision was that the Duke could not legally demand any duty from the inhabitants of the Jerseys. The Duke gracefully yielded, and gave his third and final release of East Jersey.

On the 20th of February, 1681, Earl Sandwich released his interest in East Jersey to his associate trustees, and they again sought to negotiate a sale of the province. Failing to find a purchaser at even the sum of five or six thousand pounds, it was sold at public sale to William Penn, Robert West, Thomas Rudyard, Samuel Broome, Thomas Hart, Richard Mew, Ambrose Riggs, John Haywood, Hugh Hartshorne, Clement Plumstead, and Thomas Cooper, all Quakers. The lease and release were dated February 1 and 2, 1682, and the consideration was £3,400. To avoid any doubt which might arise by reason of the prior sale to Cremer and Pocock, they joined in the conveyance. The associates then (June 1, 1682) executed a declaration that there should be no benefit of survivorship among themselves. They held the Province for nearly a year, but they were Quakers, and therefore unpopular. To quiet opposition on this ground, they severally conveyed, in 1683, an undivided moiety of their respective interest to twelve others, viz.: Robert Barclay, Edward Billinge, Robert Turner, James Braine, Arent Sonmans, William Gibson, Gawn Laurie, Thomas Barker, Thomas Warne, James, Earl of Perth, Robert Gordon and John Drummond. These associates were afterward known as the "Twenty-four Proprietors."[2] On the 14th of March, 1683, the Duke confirmed the

---

[1] *Col. Hist. of N. Y.*, *iii.*, 285.

[2] *Leaming and Spicer*, 73. For a sketch of these proprietors, *vide Whitehead's East Jersey*, 199, &c.

sale of the Province to the twenty-four proprietors.[1] Under all of these different owners of the soil of the Province, the rights and powers of Government had always attached to the ownership.

Many patents for land in this county, east of the Hackensack, had been taken out before the fall of the Dutch power. By the third article in the capitulation, "all people were permitted to enjoy their lands, houses and goods, and dispose of them at pleasure." Under this article they felt secure until the treaty of Breda, dated July 25, 1667. Then the freeholders in this county took out confirmatory grants from the proprietors, subject to a quit-rent of half-penny per acre.[2] To this burden much of the lands in East Jersey is yet subject, though years have gone by since its collection was enforced. Whether it was to avoid the granting of particular tracts to individuals, or because the Dutch government had already granted to the town and freeholders all of the unappropriated lands in the old township, we do not know, but it is worthy of notice that the proprietors never gave to an individual an original patent for land in the township of Bergen.

By the second article of Carteret's Charter the quit-rent of half-penny per acre, so far as the township of Bergen was concerned, was compounded for £15 sterling per annum. In the course of time the payment of this was neglected, and finally refused. Hereupon a controversy arose between the proprietors and the freeholders of Bergen. Finally, Cornelius Van Ripen, a freeholder in the township, was arrested for the debt. A compromise was then agreed upon, and the freeholders of Bergen received a general release upon paying $1,500. This release was dated October 5, 1809.

The condition of this county in 1680 is minutely, though not in all respects accurately, described by George Scott[3] in a *bre-*

---

[1] *Leaming and Spicer*, 88.

[2] The fact that all of the water front from Weehawken to the Kill van Kull had been granted by the Dutch before the laws of England applied, may be interesting to those who grow disputatious over riparian rights. Should not these rights be construed by Dutch law rather than by English law?

[3] Colonel Nicols says that Captain Scott "was borne to worke mischiefe as farre as he is credited or his parts serve him." It is also said that he aimed to

chure entitled "The Model of the Government of the Province of East Jersey in America," published in Edinburgh in 1685, and reprinted in *East Jersey under the Proprietors.* He says: "Near unto *Snake hill* is a brave Plantation, on a piece of Land almost an Island, containing 1,000 or 1,200 Acres, belonging to Mr. Pinhorne,[1] a Merchant at New York, and one Edward

---

get from the Duke the territory which Berkeley and Carteret obtained. *Col. Hist. of N. Y., iii.*, 105. *Quaere:* was he related to Thomas Scott, who m. Caroline, dau. of Sir George Carteret?

[1] William Pinhorne left England in the ship *Blossom*, May 27th, and arrived at New York August 7th, 1678. *Col. Hist. of N. Y., ii.*, 741. He was a merchant, and a man of more than ordinary ability. On the 26th of March, 1679, he purchased of Edward Earle, Jr., one-half of the Secaucus tract and "one-half of the Stock, christian and negro servants." *Liber* 1 *of Deeds* (*Trenton*), 144. *Winfield's Land Titles*, 130. On the 15th of September, 1683, he was placed on a commission "to inquire into any piracies, felonies, &c., committed by Capt. Nicholas Clough." *N. Y. Col. MSS., xxxiv.*, 3. He was commissioned Alderman of New York by Governor Dongan on the 24th of November, 1683, *Ibid*, 9; received a captain's commission on the 16th of September, 1684; was chosen Speaker of the New York Assembly in October, 1685, *Col. Hist. of N. Y., iii.*, 716; appointed one of the Council of Governor Sloughter on the 31st of January, 1689. *Ibid*, 685. He remained in this position under Governors Ingoldsby and Fletcher. *Valentine's Manual*, 1864, 541. In the troubles of the period he took a prominent part, and finally became one of Leisler's judges. *Col. Hist. of N. Y., iv.*, 325. In March, 1691, he was at his own request appointed Recorder of New York City, *Ibid, iii.*, 767, which position he held until September, 1692, *Valentine's Manual*, 1864, 560, and on the 5th of the following May Fourth Justice of the Supreme Court of New York. *Col. Hist. of N.Y., iii.*, 716. On the 10th of September, 1692, having removed to his plantation in New Jersey, he lost the Recordership and his place in the Council of Governor Fletcher, in whose "humble thoughts those who bear no part burthen should eat no share of our bread." *Ibid*, 847. Early in 1693 he returned to New York, was restored to the Council and raised to the position of second Justice of the Supreme Court, with a salary of £100 per annum. *Ibid, iv.*, 25, 37. Governor Bellomont afterward charged him with having secured these positions by presenting Governor Fletcher "with some plate." *Ibid, iv.*, 321. On the 17th of July, 1693, he was appointed on a special commission to determine the propriety of establishing a permanent Court of Exchequer in New York. *N. Y. Col. MSS., xxxix.*, 39, 79. The anti-Leisler party coming into power, June 7, 1698, he was suspended from his official positions, *Col. Hist. of N. Y., iv.*, 321, and charged with being a "scandalous character," and with having cheated a wool merchant in London out of £4,000, with a part of which he purchased his farm in New Jersey. He now retired to Secaucus. But by direction of the Queen he

Eickbe.[1] Its well improved and Stockt.[2] Mr. *Pinhorne payed* for his half 500 lib. * * *

"To goe back to the South part of *Berghen neck*, that is oppo-

---

was in 1702 taken into the Council of Lord Cornbury. *Leaming and Spicer*, 619. Then the following commissions came to him in quick succession:

October 2, 1704, Second Judge of the Supreme Court of New Jersey.

May 22, 1705, Judge of the Bergen Common Pleas.

November 6, 1705, Second Judge and Assistant to the Chief Justice.

" 6, 1705, Judge of the Bergen Common Pleas jointly with Edward Earle.

June 8, 1708, Second Judge of the Supreme Court.

January 23, 1709, Judge of the Bergen Common Pleas.

" " Judge of the Bergen Oyer and Terminer. *Book of Commissions* (*Trenton*), *AAA*. On the removal of Lieutenant Governor Ingoldsby, Judge Pinhorne, who had married Ingoldsby's daughter Mary, as President of the Council, became Commander-in-Chief of New Jersey. This position he held until Governor Hunter, who arrived May 7, 1711, demanded his removal and claimed that without it there could be "noe hopes of peace or quiet." *Col. Hist of N. Y.*, *v.*, 204. He was dismissed from all official position in the early part of 1715. *Ibid*, *v.*, 361. He is described as "a very sensible, honest gentleman, who is a true member of the Church of England." *Ibid*, *v.*, 335. He died in the latter part of the year 1719. *Ibid*, *iii.*, 716. Pinhorne's creek (now written by Jersey City officials Pen Horn), on the easterly bounds of his old plantation, still perpetuates his name. He left a widow and four children: *John*, who was appointed clerk of Bergen county November 6, 1705, and admitted to the bar June 6, 1707; *Mary*, who married Edward Kingsland, of New Barbadoes Neck; *Martha*, who married Roger Mompesson, *Ibid*, *v.*, 423, who at one time was Chief Justice of New York, New Jersey and Pennsylvania, *Valentine's Manual*, 1864, 597 (after his death she married Richard Warman), and *Elizabeth*, who married Timothy Bagley. *Winfield's Land Titles*, 131.

[1] This is an error. *Edward Earle, Junior*, was the name. He came from Maryland, and on the 13th February, 1688, married Elsje Vreeland, of Gemoenepa. He purchased the island of Secaucus April 24, 1676, and sold to Pinhorne one undivided half of it. In 1693 he was appointed tax commissioner for Bergen, and in 1694 a commissioner of the highways. *Leaming and Spicer*, 335, 346. He was a member of the House of Deputies in 1695. *Record of Gov. and Council, East Jersey*, *i.*, 176. He was the founder of the Earle family in Hudson and Bergen counties, and was yet living in 1716.

[2] The following schedule will give some idea how the place was "stockt": "One dwelling house containing two lower rooms and a lean-to below stairs and a loft above, five tobacco houses, one hors, one mare and two coults, eight oxen, ten cows, one bull, foure yearlings and seven calves; between thirty and forty hoggs, foure negro men, five christian Servants." *Liber* 1 *Deeds* (*Trenton*), 144.

site *Staten Island*, where is but a narrow passage of water, which ebbs and flows between the said Island and *Berghen Point*, called *Constable's Hook.*[1] There is a considerable Plantation on that side of *Constable Hook*, *Extending* in Land above a mile over, from the Bay on the *East side* of the neck that leads to *New York*, to that on the west that goes to *Hackensack* and *Snake-hill;* the neck *running* up between both from the South to the north of *Hudson's River* to the outmost extent of their bounds. There belongs to that *Plantation* about 12 or 1500 Acres, and its well stockt and improved: it was settled first by *Samuel Edsall* in *Colonel Nicolls'* time, and by him sold 3 years ago for 600: lib.

"There are other small Plantations along that *neck* to the *East* between it and a Little village of 20 families called by the Indians ——— or Penelipe,[2] —— then further one to another cottage.[3] There are more where *Laurence* the *Draper* lives, a Dutchman;[4] there may be 16 or 18 Families; then one [on ?] to *George Umpane* [*Gemoeunepan?*] which is over against *New York*, where there is about 40 *Families*, within which, about the middle of the neck, which is here about 3 myles over, stands the Town of Berghen, which gives its name to that neck; then again Northward to the water side going up *Hudson's River*, there lyes out a point of Land, wherein is a *Plantation and a water* [mill ?] *belonging* to a merchant in *New York.*[5]

---

[1] This place seems to have been a port of piratical enterprises. In the *Post Boy, August* 8, 1757, I find the following commercial advertisement:

"TO BE SOLD

At Van Buskirk's, at Kil van Kull, A Parcel of likely Negro *Slaves*, Men, Women, Boys and Girls, just arrived from GUINEA in the Sloop Williams, DAVID GRIFFITHS, Commander. Apply to RICE WILLIAMS, or the said DAVID GRIFFITHS."

[2] The place here referred to, I have no doubt, is Pembrepogh. But as to there being twenty families there I have grave doubts. The author must have drawn heavily on his imagination, as he did in the population of Communipaw.

[3] Probably the present homestead of the Currie family.

[4] This was Laurens Andriesen, the founder of the Van Buskirk family. *Winfield's Land Titles*, 60. He lived on the shore about where Linden avenue strikes New York bay, in (late) Greenville.

[5] This I take to be Weehawken. On the 10th of June, 1678, Nicholas Bay-

"*Southward* there is a *small village* about 5 or 6 *Families*, which is *commonly* called the *Duke's Farme*,[1] and hath always paid a small annual rent to the Governor of New York, who first granted it out for two lives, but is leased out now for some years, yet is under the Jurisdiction of *New Jersey* for Government; further up is a good Plantation in a neck of Land almost an Island, called *Hobuk*. It did belong to a *Dutch Merchant*, *who formerly in the* Indian *war had his Wife*, *Children and Servants murdered by the* Indians, *and his house*, *cattle and stock destroyed by them*.[2] *Its now settled again and a mill erected there by one dwelling at* New York."

As to Bergen he says: "Here is a Town *Court* held by *Select Men* or *Overseers*, who used to be 4 or more as they please to choose *annually to try small causes*, *as in all the rest of the Towns; and two Courts of Sessions in the year*, *from which if the Cause exceed* 20 *lib*, *they may appeal to the Governor and Council*, *and Court of deputies in their Assembly*, *who meet once a year*. The Town is compact and hath been fortified against the *Indians*. There are not above 70 Families in it.[3] The acres taken up by the Town may be about 10,000, and for the *Out Plantations* 50,000, and the number of Inhabitants are computed to be 350,[4] but many more abroad. The greatest part of the Inhabitants which are in this Jurisdiction are Dutch, of which some have settled here upwards of 40 years agoe."[5]

---

ard had obtained the Proprietors' consent to use the water run at Wiehaken for a saw and corn mill. The Corporation of Bergen had given consent before this.

[1] Known also as the West India Company's Farm and Harsimus. *Winfield's Land Titles*, 132.

[2] This was Aert Teunisen.

[3] There were only thirty-two lots in the town, some of which were common land and not occupied. It is quite certain that not more than one family was upon any one lot. His several estimates are overestimated in about the same proportion.

[4] According to these figures and the number of families previously given, he makes the number in each family average but a fraction over two!

[5] It will be noticed that the above extract is a little confused and in some places greatly exaggerated. But it is well to remember that Scott was writing what we call a *puff*, for which he received his reward. *Whitehead's East*

From the final surrender to the English until the Revolutionary War—a whole century—but few incidents appear in the history of this county requiring notice. The people were quiet, domestic, unambitious, passed along through life adhering to truth, honesty and fair dealing, cultivating their farms and rearing their families in the fear of God and the doctrines of the old church of their fathers. The most of their troubles grew out of their lands, two-thirds of which lay in common.

As might have been expected, the Government of the Proprietors was a failure. In the year 1700 the inhabitants of the Province represented to King William "that there did not remain among them the shadow of law and Government," and requested him to take from the Proprietors a power of which they were unworthy. The colonie, in fact, became reduced to such a deplorable state by factions that it was represented "as being without law or gospel, having neither judge nor priest."[1] The Proprietors surrendered the Government of New Jersey to the crown on the 15th, and the Queen accepted the same on the 17th of April, 1702. They were glad to lay off a burden which was pecuniarily unprofitable and very productive of discord.

By this time the people of Bergen began to feel that the Charter of 1668 was not sufficiently comprehensive for the government of themselves and the protection of their property. They soon after this petitioned for a new Charter. On the 14th of January, 1714, the Queen granted what has since been known as

Queen Anne's Charter.

"Anne, by ye Grace of God of Great Britain, France & Ireland, Queen Defender of ye Faith &c. To all to whome these presents shall come or may in any wise concern, Greeting: Whereas our loving Subjects, Andreas Van Buskirk, Barnett Christian, Enoch Freeland, Rutt Van Horne, Frederick Culper, Wonder Dedericks and John Dedericks, Freeholders, Inhabitants of ye town of

Jersey, 236. The work was written from *what was told him,* what he had of his *own knowledge,* and what he *guessed at. Ibid,* 277.

[1] *Chalmer's Hist. Am. Colonies, i.,* 293, 376.

Bergen in ye County of Bergen, In our Province of New Jersey, on behalfe of themselves & ye rest of ye Freeholders of the s^{d} town, by their Humble Petition to our trusty and well Beloved Robert Hunter, Esqr, our Capt Generall and Governour in Chiefe of our Province of New Jersey, have sett forth that their Ancestors & Predecessors, Freeholders of ye s^{d} town, have possessed, held & enjoyed divers lands, tenem^{ts} & Hereditam^{ts}, & used & received Divers Privileges & Immunities by virtue of a Grant or Pattent sealed with ye seal of ye Province of New Jersey & signed by Phillip Cartaret, Esqr, Late Governour of this Province, & his Councill, under ye Right Honorable John, Lord Berkley, Barron of Stratton, & Sr George Carterett, Knight & Baronett, then absolute Lords Proprietors of ye s^{d} Province, bearing date ye twenty-second day of Sep^{t} Anno Dom. one thousand six hundred sixty & Eight, wch s^{d} Lands were butted & bounded as Followeth, viz." (*here follows the description as in Carteret's Charter*), "& whereas divers of ye s^{d} lands remain in common & undivided for ye generall good & Benefitt of ye Freeholders & Inhabitants of s^{d} town, on wch s^{d} Lands ye neighbouring townes & settled Do committ great waste and spoils in Cutting Down & carrying away great Quantities of their timber, who cannot be relieved In ye premises in ye ordinary course of Law or Equity through some Defects in ye Grant of Incorporation afores^{d}, wch to Prevent for ye Future they have prayed our Charter or Pattent of Incorporation, wch request we being willing to grant, know ye that of our Especiall Grace, certain knowledge & mere motion, we have given, granted, Ratified & confirmed, and Do by these presents for us, our heirs & successors forever, Give, Grant, ratifie & confirme unto Andreas Van Buskirk, Barnett Christian, Enoch Freeland, Rutt Van Horne, Henry Culper, Wender Dedreicks, John Dedreicks, in trust to & for themselves & ye rest of ye Freeholders, Inhabitants of ye s^{d} town and their successors forever within ye Limits & bounds afores^{d} ye Free Liberty & Privilidge of being a township, & they & their successors forever hereafter are & shall be by virtue Hereof a comunity or township, or body Corporate, or Politick in deed & in name by ye name of ye Trustees of the Freeholders inhabitants of ye township of Bergen,

& that they & their successors forever hereafter shall & may have a perpetuall succession of ye numBer of seven of ye principall freeholders & inhabitants of ye sd township of Bergen, who shall be ye trustees of ye Freeholders inhabitants of ye township of Bergen, that is to say, that upon ye Death or other avoidance of any one or more of ye sd trustees, it shall & may be lawfull for ye Freeholders of ye sd township for ye time being, being thereunto Sumoned or Warned by ye Constable or Constables of ye sd township for ye time being by order of ye surviving trustees of ye sd township of Bergen, or ye major part of them to assemble & meet together at such time & place within ye sd township as ye sd surviving trustees for ye time Being or ye major part of them, from time to time as need shall be, shall think fitt to nominate & appoint & there by majority of votes of ye sd Freeholders to Elect & chuse so many of ye Principal Freeholders of ye sd township residing within ye bounds of ye sd township as may make ye number of ye sd trustees to be seaven[1] wch trustees so chosen & elected as aforesd together with ye surviving trustees for ye time being shall be trustees of ye sd township to all intents and purposes as much as if they had been particularly nominated & expressed in this our sd Grant, & we do further Give & Grant unto ye sd trustees of ye Freeholders inhabitants of ye town of Bergen & their successors forever that it shall & may be lawfull to & for ye sd trustees & their Successors forever by ye name of ye trustees of ye Freeholders Inhabitants of ye Township of Bergen in any of our Courts within our sd province of New Jersey to Sue and be Sued, answer & be Answered unto, Implead & be Impleaded, Defend & be Defended. And we do further Give & Grant unto ye sd trustees of ye Freeholders Inhabitants of ye township of Bergen & their Successors forever Hereafter full Power and Lawfull Authority as Often as there shall be occasion at their Discretion or ye Discretion of the Major Part of them to Sumons & call together ye Freeholders of ye sd township & for ye sd Freeholders & their Successors so sumoned and called to-

---

1 *Vide Pamphlet Laws*, 1804, *p.* 419. This charter was amended so as to make the office of trustee annual.

gether to Assemble & meet together at such certain Days & at such Place as ye s^{d} trustees for ye time being, or the major part of them shall appoint to make & Enter in a Book for that purpose to be kept all such prudentiall rules and orders for ye Improvem^{t} preservation & Defence of their s^{d} Comons as they or ye Major part of them shall agree upon, as also to appoint a Clerk & Register for ye Doing thereof, & to contribute & Beg amongs themselves such sum or sums as are absolutely necessary for ye doing thereof from time to time as need shall be & not otherwise, & further, We do for us, ourselves & Successors Give & Grant unto ye s^{d} trustees of ye Freeholders Inhabitants of ye township of Bergen & their Successors forever, that they & their Successors by ye name afores^{d} be forever hereafter one body corporate & Politickall & Capable in ye Law to Purchase, have, take & receive & enjoy to them & their Successors forever ye use of ye Freeholders Inhabitants of ye township of Bergen, Lands, Tenem^{ts}, Messuages, Rents, Privilidges & other Hereditam^{ts} whatsoever, of whatsoever Nature, Kind & Quality they be in fee & perpetuity as also to Give, Grant, Bargain, allott, Lett, Dispose of any of the Land belonging or appertaining to ye s^{d} Comunity & as yett unappropriated, either for one, two or three Lives, for term of years, or in fee, & also that ye s^{d} Corporation shall & may forever hereafter have & Use a comon seal for ye Business of them & their Successors wth full power to alter, break & unmake ye same at their Discretion, & we do further Give & Grant to ye s^{d} trustees of ye Freeholders Inhabitants of ye township of Bergen & their Successors forever, that it shall & may be Lawfull for ye Freeholders Inhabitants of ye s^{d} town Annually & once in Every Year to Assemble & meet together on ye first Tuesday in May annually to choose two Constables, one Overseer of ye poor, and two Overseers of ye Highways by ye Majority of ye Voters of ye s^{d} Freeholders Inhabitants of ye town of Bergen, wch Constables & Overseers so chosen as afores^{d} shall serve in their Respective Offices in ye s^{d} town untill ye next Anuall Election If they so Long shall Live or pay ye sum of two pounds each Person refusing to serve for ye Use of the poor of ye s^{d} Town & That in case of ye Death or

Refusall of any of ye s^d Officers; As often as ye same shall happen out of ye Usuall anniversary Time of Election that it shall & may be Lawfull for ye Freeholders Inhabitants at any other time & place to Assemble & meet together to Chuse others in their Room & place & that it shall & may be Lawfull for any Trustees of ye place w^{th}in The s^d Township to administer an Oath to ye s^d Officers of ye s^d Town for ye true & Faithful Discharge of their Respective Offices to have, hold & enjoy all and singular ye s^d privilidges, Rights, Liberties & immunities afores^d to ye s^d Andreas Van Buskirk, Barnett Christian, Enoch Freeland, Rutt Van Hoover, Hendrick Culper, Wonder Dedericks, John Dedericks, Freeholders Inhabitants of ye township of Bergen & their Successors forever, yielding, Rendering & paying unto us, ourselves & Successors, or to our or their Collector & Receiver Generall of our s^d province for ye time being yearly & every Year Five Shillings in Lieu & stead of all other Rents, Services, Dues, Duties & Demands whatsoever for ye same.

"In Testimony whereof we have Caused these our Letters to be made Pattent & ye Seal of our Province of New Jersey to be affixed, & ye same to be Entered of Record in our Secretary's Office of Our s^d province. Witness our trusty & well beloved Robert Hunter, Esqr., our Capt Generall & Governor in Chiefe in & over our Province of New Jersey, New Yorke &c. This Fourteenth Day of January in ye twelfth year of our Reigne &c.

"BASS, *Secretary*."[1]

This charter was confirmed by the Council on the 13th of March, 1714.

The principal motive in requesting this Charter was to get power to protect and take care of the common lands. These comprised about two-thirds of all the lands in the township of Bergen, and were used by the freeholders for common pasture. To avoid the difficulty and confusion which would naturally arise from the cattle running together in the commons, the Legis-

[1] *Book of Commissions* (*Trenton*), 154.

lature, on the 7th of November, 1668, provided for the marking of cattle,[1] and directed a description of such marks to be entered in a book to be kept for that purpose. Laurens Andriesen was made recorder and marker, April 6th, 1670. This practice of marking thus instituted outlived the common lands and came down even into the present century. The following entries, taken from a fragment of the old town book now preserved in the county clerk's office, will give a good idea of the way such entries were made, and of the novelty of some of the marks:

"Hendrick van Winkel seyn merk Een gaffel uÿt het ent van het slinken oor en seyn brant op de slinken bil. H."

"Meyndert ger brantse seyn merk Een gaffel uyt het slinken oor En Een slip in het ent van het righter oor en seyn brant op de hooren, M. G."

"Pieter Boskerck syn merk Een half maentie onder uyt het slinken oor."

The law also provided that whenever an estray came upon one's premises it was a duty to record a description of the same with the Town Clerk, to enable the owner to recover his property.[2] The following are a few specimens of such recorded notices, literally copied, and they afford ample proof that the Town Clerk and the Schoolmaster were not the same person at that day:

"Strayed on the premises of John Stevens Hoboken a brown horse supposed to be three years old no artificial mark with a star in the forehead and left hind foot white about twelve hands high."

"A stray Muel at the House of Garret van Derhoof Being a Dark Brown Couller Marked on the left shoulder with the Letters N. A."

"A Red Bull with a Wite Streek on the Buttok with no mark at the House of Moses van Amen at Bergin Point the Creator will Be two years old this Spring."

With all the precaution the authorities could take, peace and

---

[1] *Leaming and Spicer*, 86. [2] *Nevill's Laws*, i. 357.

harmony were but uncertain tenants in the township. Some encroached upon the common lands, cleared and fenced beyond the bounds of their respective patents. Others imposed upon them undue burdens, cut and carried away the timber.[1] To settle all these difficulties the freeholders mutually entered into an agreement that they would employ a surveyor to run out the bounds of their respective land, and that each one would abandon whatever of the commons might have been appropriated, until the same should be properly and fairly partitioned.[2]

It is not now known that this agreement was ever carried out. The probabilities are that it was not; at all events it did not prevent the difficulties which it was intended to provide against. Matters continued to grow worse until, finally, on the 7th of December, 1763, the Legislature passed the act providing for a survey of the patented lands and allotment of the commons among the freeholders.[3] This act was of vast importance in the history of this county.[4]

The commissioners named in it appointed George Clinton of New York and Jonathan Hampton of Elizabeth surveyors (the latter did not act), and entered upon their work on the 6th of March, 1764, at the house of Stephen Bourdett at "Wiehaken," to which place all land owners were requested to bring their patents and title papers. Notwithstanding the extent and accuracy of their labors, the work was finished on the first day of March, 1765. Owing to uncertainty in the ownership of Secaucus, the commons allotted to that tract was not finally allotted until the 15th of June, 1785.

---

[1] *Nevill's Laws, i.*, 285.

[2] A copy of this agreement may be found, *in extenso*, in *Winfield's Land Titles*, 16.

[3] *Alinson's Laws*, 263.

[4] The reader who may be interested in looking at this act and at the survey and map made in pursuance thereof, is respectfully referred to *Winfield's History of the Land Titles in Hudson County, New Jersey*. In that work has been inserted many facts which throw light upon the titles to land in the county from 1609 to 1871. The publication of that work relieves me from tracing out the history of the land in this volume.

CHAPTER VII.

The Revolutionary War—How it affected Hudson County—Incidents of the war in this County—Fort Delancey—Capture of Paulus Hoeck—Block House Point—The Cow-Chase—Desertion of Sergeant Champe, &c., &c.

During the Revolutionary war that portion of Bergen County now known as Hudson County was important territory. Early in that contest it became manifest that whichever party held the city of New York must greatly depend on Bergen as the gate to New Jersey. Hence, each party while in possession was careful to strengthen it against the assaults of the other.

As soon as it was understood that the British were preparing to leave Boston for New York, Lord Sterling, then in command of the American forces in this vicinity, took measures to place Bergen in a condition of defence, and to open means of communication with the interior of the State. On the 18th of March, 1776, he proposed, *first*, to make a good and broad road from Brown's ferry to Paulus Hoeck ferry, which he considered of great importance to the city of New York; *second*, to make a good road from Weehawken to the Hackensack ferry.[1] He designed to place the Bergen militia at these works; two hundred men on the former, and one hundred men on the latter.[2] He devised the works on Paulus Hoeck and Bergen Neck; the former to prevent approach from the city of New York, and the latter to prevent inroads from Staten Island. For the location and design of them, he personally examined the ground on the 23d of March, and proposed to have them constructed by the militia of Bergen, Essex and Middlesex counties.[3] On the arrival of Washington orders were given for the immediate construction of the works at Paulus Hoeck, as they were considered "of im-

[1] This was afterward known as Dow's (or Douw's) ferry.

[2] *Am. Archives, 4th Series, v.*, 402.

[3] *Life of Lord Sterling*, 157.

portance."[1] These works were soon completed, and troops stationed in them. Of such importance were the works on Paulus Hoeck considered, that one of the objects of the great Hickey conspiracy was to seize and hold them in the name of the King.[2]

On the 29th of June the look-out on Staten Island announced the approach of forty sail. It proved to be the advance of Admiral Howe's fleet, bringing a portion of the British forces under General Howe. In two days other arrivals swelled the number of men-of-war and transports to one hundred and thirty. The troops landed on Staten Island, and the fleet cast anchor off the mouth of the Kill Van Kull. The tories in the vicinity now hastened to take sides against the colonies and for the king. The people of Staten Island led off and took the oath of allegiance to the British crown. On both sides of the Hudson the anti-revolutionists in great numbers repudiated further resistance to his majesty.[3] Many who had taken an active part with the patriots, now, looking upon the freedom of the colonies as a "lost cause," forsook their first love and, with the apostate's zeal, joined their former foes. Prominent among such were William Bayard, the owner of Hoboken, and Abraham Van Buskirk of Saddle River, who afterward became lieutenant-colonel in the British service.[4]

At this time General Hugh Mercer, the veteran of Culloden

---

[1] *Am. Archives, 4th Series, vi.,* 534. [2] *Irving's Washington, ii.,* 246.

[3] *Knight's Hist. of England, i.,* 271.

[4] The following sworn statement, found at Albany among the papers of the Committee on Conspiracies, is worthy of insertion here:

"[Miscel. Pap. 34 : 430.]

"To Coll° William Allison.

"Whereas it is represented to us that David Baulding of Bergen County in New Jersey, but now in the City of New York, can give very useful and important intelligence respecting the late discovered Conspiracy against the Rights and Liberties of America,

"We do therefore in Pursuance of a Resolve of the Congress of this Colony, authorize and request you to bring the said David Baulding forthwith before us, That he may be examined touching the said Conspiracy.

"Given under our Hand this 29 June 1776.

"PHIL LIVINGSTON,
"JOHN JAY."

and Du Quesne, who afterward fell, covered with glory, at Princeton, was in command in New Jersey, with his flying camp at Bergen. He had been sent by Washington to Paulus Hoeck to make arrangements for the Pennsylvania militia as they should come in. Fearing an attack from Staten Island, General Mercer was ordered on the 4th of July to place a guard of five hundred men at Bergen Neck. He was also recommended by the commander-in-chief to place a guard at the ferries over the Hackensack and Passaic rivers, and was promised that on the next day an engineer should be sent over from New York to erect some works for the security of those places.[1] After making an examination of the Neck and the general condition of things there, he reported that the cattle had not all been removed, that some families on the Point held intercourse with the enemy (at that time between eight and nine thousand strong on the Island), that Colonel Ford's force there amounted to not more than three hundred and fifty men, and that he could not reinforce them to

---

"[Miscel. Pap. 34 : 402.]

"The Information of Mr David Baldin, Saith he has had Reasons for some time past to believe there was a Correspondance kept up by the people of Rampo and the men of war as well from the temper of the people as from many Words Dropt from time to time he says that about the 17th Inst he told that Lawrence Van Bushkirk the Miller at Rampo, abraham Van boskerk and a Schoolmaster & Thomas Van Boskirk at Saddle River was going on Board the Man of War that something prevented all but the School Master who he veryly Beleives did go & that there is one Peter Van Bushkirk Living at or near the hook or mouth of the Kills in Bargain County who its frequently said has followed trading with the men of war who he has Reason to believe Carrys people on Board when Ever Requested, and has a sufficient Craft for that purpose, and that this Informant Came to New York on purpose to let it be known that on his way he stoped at Erlses in Bargain woods where he was Drinking toddy in Company with Francis Steephens Late a Resident of this City who took him the said baldin to be freindly to the tory side when said Stephens told Baldin that there was 50 Sale of Kings Ships near the hook and that there would soon be 150 Sail to New York that Erls said that knews Came from on board the Man of War this Week that Stephens Charged the Informant not to mention it to some certain freind of his in New York.

"Sworn the 29 June 1776 Before us:

"PHIL LIVINGSTON,
"JOHN JAY."

[1] *Am. Archives, 4th Series, vi.*, 1263.

five hundred after placing proper guards at the ferries. He proposed, therefore, to send the Pennsylvania militia to Bergen Neck as they arrived.[1] The different "passes in Bergen Neck" and on the Jersey shore opposite Staten Island were to be fortified by the chief engineer of the American forces to prevent the enemy

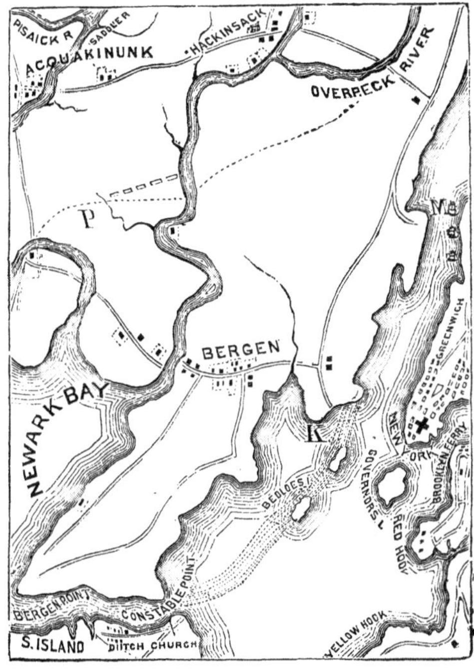

coming over.[2] To meet the crisis that was approaching, in the early part of July General Wadsworth's brigade was sent over to Bergen, where it was joined by a battalion of Jersey troops.[3]

General Mercer now feeling that he was in a fair state of preparation for the enemy, who showed no disposition to enter New

[1] *Am. Archives, 5th Series, i.,* 120. This post, afterward known as Fort Delancey, was situated on the rising ground, bounded by Forty-fourth and Forty-fifth streets and Avenues B and C, in Bayonne, about a quarter of a mile below the canal. It was held by the refugees under Captain Tom Ward for some years.

[2] *Ibid, 5th Series, i.,* 174.

[3] *Ibid, 5th Series, i.,* 328.

Jersey, formed a plan to attack him on Staten Island. His plans were all laid for the evening of the 18th of July. Great caution was required in his movements, for Bergen was filled with tories.[1] The sixth point in his plan of attack was as follows:

"Sixth. A party to attempt to surprise the enemy's guard on *Buskirk's Point*,[2] which is on the southeast corner of Bergen *Point*; this party, or guard, does not seem to be large, but it is said they are possessed of two six-pounders. The party that makes the attack must not attempt to go over the causeway or road over the meadow, the cannon being in all probability appointed to command that pass, but should be provided with some boards, and proceed in two or three columns over the meadow, where they will meet with no other obstruction than a small creek or ditch, which they will easily pass with the help of the boards. If this place is carried, a cannonade and bombardment should, as soon as possible, commence on the ships, a great number of which now lie within reach of the place. A cannonade should also commence on *Bergen Point*, opposite the church and *Decker's*, where it is said about six hundred men are posted; this cannonade, with round and grape shot, would confuse the troops in forming, and prevent their succoring the guard at *Elizabethtown Point*, or opposing our party who make their descent near *Shutter's Island*. The cannonade should also be kept up on such parts of the shore of *Staten Island* where any boats are collected or may assemble. The party for these several matters on *Bergen Neck* should be about seven hundred men, besides the riflemen."[3] His plans failed, however, on account of the bad weather, which prevented his forces crossing the Kill Van Kull.

Carrying out the instructions he had received, General Mercer stationed at the ferries over the Hackensack and Passaic rivers

---

[1] To show how alarmingly disaffection had spread among the people of Bergen, I have been told by old people that only fourteen whigs could be found in the whole township.

[2] A part of Constapel's Hoeck, on which the enemy had landed shortly after his arrival in the harbor. It was the first landing place of the British forces in New Jersey.

[3] *Am. Archives, 5th Series*, 1, 443.

two captains and one hundred and twenty-two rank and file.[1] About this time the troops on Bergen Point practiced occasionally on the fleet of the enemy. The following shows how ill-naturedly these little attentions were received:

"NEW YORK, *July* 25, 1776.

"Our troops stationed on Bergen Point give the Ministerial fleet and army some uneasiness, by firing at the tenders, boats, &c. It so galls and provokes them, that they return the fire with great fury, but have not done the least damage to our people. Last Lord's Day a great many shot were heard in this city and at *Bergen Point*. The occasion was this: A barge from the fleet, full of men, landed on the Point, but were opposed and driven off with precipitation by our troops; a smart fire ensued from a tender for a considerable time, without doing any injury."[2]

While General Mercer had been putting the shore of East Jersey in a state of defence, the forces of the enemy had been augmented by arrivals, until, in the harbor and on Staten Island, they numbered thirty thousand men.[3] The harbor was filled with their shipping. On the afternoon of the 12th of July—eight days after the Declaration of Independence—the Phœnix, carrying forty guns, under command of Captain Parker, and the Rose, carrying twenty guns, under command of Captain Wallace, came sweeping up the bay, having the advantage of both wind and tide. Then for the first time the thunders of civilized warfare burst from the sand-hills of Paulus Hoeck; then for the first time its batteries were trained upon an enemy. They opened on the ships with a spirited fire, which was returned with broadsides as they passed. The vessels suffered but little damage, their decks being protected by ramparts of sand-bags.[4] On the same evening Lord Howe sailed up the harbor, greeted by the booming of cannon and the huzzas of the British.

On the first of August Colonel Bradley's regiment was at

[1] *Am. Archives, 5th Series, i.*, 575.
[2] *Ibid, 5th Series, i.*, 578.
[3] *Irving's Washington, ii.*, 300.
[4] *Ibid, ii.*, 260.

Bergen, while the enemy still held Constapels Hoeck.[1] With Bradley's force, General Mercer had in East Jersey a considerable body of men. Washington was anxious for reinforcements in New York, and made known his wants to General Mercer. That officer replied as follows:

"POWLES HOOK, *August* 15, 1776.

"SIR: I was at Elizabethtown when your letters of the 13th and 14th reached me. The men who had been prepared to join the army at *New York* lay at *Newark*. The posts along the *Jersey* shore opposite to *Staten Island* are sufficiently guarded, and more troops are daily arriving. If you approve of it, a body of four hundred men, well accoutred, from the *Delaware* counties, may be stationed at *Powles Hook*, and four hundred of the *Jersey* men for the Flying-Camp at *Bergen-Town*, besides what we may spare to be ready in case of emergency at *Newark*. Eight hundred men will cross to-day to join you. If more are necessary, please to inform me. I shall be to-night at *Newark*.

"I have the honor to be, Sir, your Excellency's most obedient servant, H. MERCER."[2]

Again upon this subject he wrote to the President of Congress:

"NEWARK, *August* 28, 1776, 5 *o'clock A. M.*

"SIR: General Washington had wrote me that some reinforcements would be necessary at *New York* and *Powles Hook*. * * On the way yesterday evening, General *Wooster's* Aid-de-Camp met me, with a few lines from the General, signifying that it was General *Washington's* orders that I should march, with all our army under my command, immediately to *Powles Hook*. The necessary orders were sent to *Amboy*, *Woodbridge* and *Eliza-beth-Town*, last night, and I hope to have on Bergen, ready to pass over to *New York*, if required, from three to four thousand men. Our whole force, including the *New Jersey* militia, from *Powles Hook* to *Shrewsbury*, amounts to eight thousand and three hundred. * * * * General Washington, with the greater part of the Army, was on *Long Island* yesterday; and the ac-

[1]*Am. Archives, 5th Series, i.*, 713. [2]*Ibid, 5th Series, i.*, 964.

tion was continued at two o'clock. * * Considerable firing has been heard this morning, which still continues. What troops are here I am pushing on to *Bergen*, and shall be with them immediately."[1]

At the time he wrote this letter, the battle of Long Island was raging, and the patriots were being driven before the veterans of Europe. General Mercer promised assistance, and the following extract of a letter will show how well he kept his promise.

"In obedience to those orders from General Washington, between three and four thousand of the militia of *Pennsylvania* and *New Jersey* assembled at Bergen, ready to pass on to *New York*, but were countermanded on the retreat of the Army from *Long Island*. We have, however, strengthened the posts at *Powles's Hook* and *Bergen Neck* to the complement of twenty-five hundred men."[2]

The post at Paulus Hoeck was shortly afterward treated to another little skirmish with the enemy. On the 15th of September the British captured New York City. In the morning of that day three ships-of-war—the Roebuck and Phœnix, each of forty guns, and the Tartar, of twenty guns—stood up the Hudson, "causing a most tremendous firing."[3] The raw troops on the Jersey shore were little prepared for the peltings of such a pitiless storm. In a letter dated September 17, 1776, to Washington, General Mercer says:

"SIR: I received just now the favor of Colonel *Grayson's* letter of yesterday, and in consequence shall send off a detachment of the men inlisted for the Flying Camp to *Paulus Hook*. The militia of *Pennsylvania* and *New Jersey*, stationed on *Bergen* and at *Paulus Hook*, have behaved in a scandalous manner, running off from their posts on the first cannonade from the ships of the enemy."[4]

It is, however, stated in the *Freeman's Journal* of October 5th,

---

[1] *Am. Archives, 5th Series, i.*, 1193.
[2] *Ibid, 5th Series, ii.*, 158.
[3] *Irving's Washington, ii.*, 352, 367.
[4] *Am. Archives, 5th Series, ii.*, 367.

1776, that the vessels "were roughly greeted by the American battery at Paulus Hook." This certainly makes an issue of veracity between the old soldier and the newspaper. One cannot hesitate, however, in coming to a decision on such an issue.

For a short time after the capture of New York, Paulus Hoeck remained in possession of the Americans under command of Colonel Durkie.[1] During this time Washington would occasionally leave his camp at Harlaem, cross over to the Jersey shore, and, in company with General Greene, who had succeeded General Mercer in command on the Jersey shore, reconnoitre, sometimes as far down as Paulus Hoeck, to observe what was going on in the city and among the shipping.[2] It was manifest, however, that this position could not be held, New York being in possession of the enemy. Preparations were made for its evacuation. The following is General Greene's report of this event:

"CAMP FORT CONSTITUTION,[3] *September* 23, 1776.

"DEAR SIR: The enemy are landed at *Powley's Hook;* they came up this afternoon and began a cannonade on the batteries, and after cannonading for half an hour or a little more, they landed a party from the ships. General Mercer had ordered off from the *Hook* all the troops except a small guard, who had orders to evacuate the place from the first approach of the enemy. General Mercer mentions no troops but those landed from the ships; but Colonel *Bull*, and many others that were along the river upon the heights, saw twenty boats go over from *York* to *Powley's Hook*. This movement must have happened since General *Mercer* wrote. I purpose to visit *Bergen* to-night, as General *Mercer* thinks of going to his post at *Amboy* to-morrow."[4]

This fixes the date when the place was captured. Two days

---

[1] *Valentine's Manual*, 1866, 768. [2] *Irving's Washington, ii.*, 367.

[3] Changed to Fort Lee, in honor of General Charles Lee, who arrived in camp at Harlaem, October 14, 1776.

[4] *Am. Archives, 5th Series, ii.*, 494.

afterward in a letter from headquarters is a further account of the event:

"Gen. *Greene* informs us that General *Mercer*, seeing the enemy were determined to possess themselves by a stronger force of ships and men than we could oppose, removed all the stores and useful cannon, so that nothing fell into the enemy's hands but the guns that had been rendered unfit for further service. Our Army is posted at the town of Bergen, and our advanced party has possession of the mill just back of Powle's Hook."[1]

The Americans remained in possession of Bergen until Washington found it necessary to collect his forces preparatory to his retreat to the Delaware. By an extract from a letter dated October 4, 1776, written at headquarters, which was then at Bergen, we learn the time when and reason for its evacuation: "To-morrow we evacuate Bergen, a measure which will at first be condemned, and afterwards be approved of. For my own part, I am sorry that the enemy should possess another inch of *American* ground, but prudence requires another sacrifice. The reasons of leaving this place I take to be these: Bergen is a narrow neck of land, accessible on three sides by water, and exposed to a variety of attacks in different places at one and the same time. A large body of the enemy might infallibly take possession of the place whenever they pleased, unless we kept a stronger force than our numbers will allow. The spot itself is not an object of our arms: if they attacked, it would be to cut off those who defended it, and secure the grain and military stores. These have been removed; and when we are gone, a naked spot is all they will find. No other damage will follow, except a depression of some people's spirits, who, unacquainted with places, circumstances, and the secret reasons of such relinquishments, are apt to despond as if everything was lost. We go

[1]*Am. Archives, 5th Series, ii.*, 523. The mill here spoken of was Jacob Prior's mill, near the point of rocks. It was frequently visited by both parties during the war, and on one occasion from its window a British picket at Fort Putnam (now Putnam street) was shot.

to Fort Constitution as soon as we have seen the troops marched off. We shall leave a guard of observation behind us: this may prevent the enemy's discovering our removal for a day or two."[1] The design of General Greene was to "keep a good, intelligent officer at Bergen, to watch the motions of the ships."[2] As outguards at Bergen, Hoebuck, Bull's Ferry, Hackensack and opposite Spyt-den-Duivel, he had posted one hundred and sixty-eight officers and men.[3]

On the 20th of November, Fort Lee was evacuated, the army retreated to Hackensack and on through to the Delaware, and East Jersey was abandoned to the enemy. While, in 1777, the conflict was raging above the Highlands, among the hills of Saratoga and on the banks of the Brandywine, Bergen was left in the undisputed possession of the British. They stationed a considerable body of troops at Paulus Hoeck and strengthened the works. In command of this post they placed Lieutenant-Colonel Abraham Van Buskirk of Saddle River, who had deserted the patriot cause and gone over to the enemy. They also occupied the works on Bergen Neck, which they named Fort Delancey, in honor of Oliver Delancey, the great tory of Westchester. These two places were garrisoned principally by tories, or "refugees," as they called themselves. These partisans were active and unscrupulous in the cause of the king. Their zeal, however, exhibited itself more in plundering and murdering their old neighbors than in honorable warfare. The following extracts from newspapers, both whig and tory, will show how the people of the county suffered from friend and foe, and what generally was going on hereabouts during the greater part of the war:

"A party of 300 or 400 rebels, returning to New England from Morristown to Capt. Kennedy's House at Newark, plundered it."—*New York Mercury, Jan.* 20, 1777.[4]

"The Rebels came down to Secaucus last Wednesday, and

---

[1] *Am. Archives*, 5*th Series, ii.*, 867. [2] *Ibid*, 5*th Series, iii.*, 630.

[3] *Ibid*, 5*th Series, iii.*, 663.

[4] This house was on the east bank of the Passaic, at East Newark.

carried away all the grain, horses, cows and sheep they could get together, which they were obliged to swim over the Hackensack River, for want of Boats."—*Ibid*, *April* 7, 1777.

"On Monday, May 12th, 300 British under command of Lt.-Cols. Barton and Dougan marched from Bergen Town *via* Paramus, to attack some rebels under Gen. Heard at Pompton." —*Ibid*, *May* 19, 1777.

"A party of about 40 Rebels came down to Col. Bayard's Mills last Friday morning near Hoebuck Ferry and carried off some cattle, but being pursued by a few of the 57th Regiment, now stationed at Powles Hook, they took to their heels and made off."—*Ibid*, *June* 30, 1777.

"The rebels were as low down in Bergen last Friday night as Mr. Van Ripen's, the Blacksmith, and carried off from thence some horses."—*Ibid*, *Nov* 24, 1777.

About this time the sufferings of the troops for want of clothing were very severe, and created much comment. Among the suggestions for relief was the following by Governor Livingston, which, while it points out a novel store-house of relief for the Valley Forge sufferers, also incidentally describes an old time custom among the women in this vicinity at that period:

"I am afraid that while we are employed in furnishing our battalions with clothing, we forget the county of Bergen, which alone is sufficient amply to provide them with winter waistcoats and breeches, from the redundance and superfluity of certain woollen habits, which are at present applied to no kind of use whatsoever. It is well known that the rural ladies in that part of New Jersey pride themselves in an incredible number of petticoats; which, like house furniture, are displayed by way of ostentation for many years before they are decreed to invest the fair bodies of the proprietors. Till that period they are never worn, but neatly piled up on each side of an immense escritoire, the top of which is decorated with a most capacious brass-clasped Bible, seldom read. What I would, therefore, humbly propose to our superiors, is to make prize of these future female habiliments, and, after proper transformation, immediately apply them to screen from the inclemencies of the weather those gallant males who are now fighting for the liberties of their country. And to clear this measure from every imputation of injustice, I have only to observe that the generality of the women in that county, having for above a century *worn the breeches*, it is highly reasonable that the men should now, and especially upon so important an occasion, make booty of the petticoats."—*N. J. Gazette, Dec.* 21, 1777.

"On Thursday afternoon Captain John Richards, of New Barbadoes Neck, on his way to see some member of his family who was sick of the small-pox, was captured on the road between 'Three Pidgeons' and Bergen by two professed patriots, and was shot dead by one (Brouwer) as he was preventing the other (Lozier) robbing him of his watch."[1]—*Ibid, Feb.* 2, 1778.

"On Sunday, the 22d of March, 1778, a party of rebels came as near Powles Hook as Prior's Mill, and attempted to carry off some cattle. They are under command of one Johnson, and act on their own hook."—*Ibid, March* 30, 1778.

"On Sunday night, May 10th, a small party of rebels were as far down as Prior's Mills, and carried off two Negro men who were coming to Market with eggs and butter."—*Ibid, May* 18, 1778.

The daring patriots went as far as the same place on Friday and Saturday nights (May 15th and 16th) and carried off more negroes. A detachment from the Paulus Hoeck garrison gave them chase, but they escaped.

In September, 1777, Sir Henry Clinton, then in command at New York, planned a raid into New Jersey. He divided his force into four columns. The general point of rendezvous was the New Bridge, above Hackensack. One column, under General Campbell, entered New Jersey by the way of Elizabethtown; one, under Captain Drummond, by way of Schuyler's ferry;[2] one,

---

[1] Brouwer was arrested by the British, Feb. 15, 1778, and locked up in New York. Lozier was caught at the English Neighborhood, March 27, 1778, at the house of one De Groote. Richard's watch was found in his pocket.—*N. Y. Mercury, March* 30, 1778.

[2] This was afterward known as Dow's ferry. It was on the Hackensack

under General Vaughn, by way of Fort Lee, and the other, under Lieutenant-Colonel Campbell, by way of Tappaen. On the 12th the expedition set out. Clinton himself followed, passing up Newark bay to Schuyler's landing on the Hackensack (Dow's ferry). From this point he marched over the Belleville turnpike to Schuyler's House, where he found Captain Drummond with two hundred and fifty men. During the night General Campbell arrived with his detachment and the cattle he had collected *en route*. The different columns met as designed on the 15th. On the following day General Campbell marched his force from English Neighborhood to Bergen Point, whence he passed over to Staten Island. The result of the raid was the capture of four hundred cattle, four hundred sheep and a few horses, taken from the people of Essex and Bergen. In exchange, they had eight men killed, eighteen wounded, ten missing, and five taken prisoners.[1] As an offset to this raid, we find the following account of an expedition by the opposite party over part of the same ground:

"A party of rebel light Horse came down as far as Bergen Point last Tuesday night (July 28th), and returned next morning toward Hackensack. They visited Hoebuck on their way and carried off a great number of Cattle from the Inhabitants."—*N. Y. Mercury, Aug.* 3, 1778.

Smythe, in his diary, November 8th, says: "This afternoon a party of our horse brought in two rebel privates from Powles Hook. One of them is very intelligent and communicative; but the other is the most whimsical tony I ever have seen. Wherever he goes he carries with him a large gray cat, which he says came into the rebel camp on the night after the battle at Freehold Meeting House, and which he first discovered lapping a spot of dry blood on his sleeve, as he lay on his arms expecting another dash at the British. His affection for the cat is wonderful, as hers is for him, for they are inseparable. He says if we don't allow him extra rations for his cat he shall be obliged to allow them out of his own."[2]

---

river at the foot of Cherry Lane, a little above the bridge of the New Jersey Railroad.

[1] *Remembrancer*, 1777, *v.*, 420.

[2] *Carver, ii.,* 31, *cited in Moore's Diary, ii.,* 70.

In 1777 Lieut.-Colonel Van Buskirk, the tory, had his headquarters at Paulus Hoeck. From the time of his defection in 1776 until near the close of the war, when he sailed for Nova Scotia, he had used this post as a base for his predatory excursions. During the days of his patriotic impulses he had been intimate with John Fell, of Paramus, the chairman of the Bergen Committee of Safety, and by him entrusted with many important messages and duties. In the year 1777 Judge Fell was arrested at his home and brought to Paulus Hoeck as a prisoner. He was recognized by the tory Colonel.

"Times are altered since we last met," said the Colonel.

"So I perceive," the Judge coolly replied, looking at the Colonel's uniform.

"Well, you are a prisoner and going over to New York, where you will be presented to General Robertson, with whom I have the honor to be acquainted. I will give you a letter of introduction to him," said the Colonel.

The Judge thanked him and accepted the letter, which he afterward presented to Gen. Robertson. It so happened that the Judge and General were friends at Pensacola after the old French war in 1763. The purport of Van Buskirk's letter of introduction was that *John Fell was a notorious rebel and rascal!* and advising that due care should be taken of him. General Robertson handed the letter to the Judge and said: "My old friend, John Fell, you must be a very altered man and a very great rascal, indeed, if you equal this Colonel Buskirk."[1]

It is said in the *New Jersey Gazette* of October 28, 1778, that the only place then held by the British in the State of New Jersey was Paulus Hoeck. It is probable, therefore, that up to this time the post at Bergen Neck had not been occupied since its abandonment by the Americans. The exact date of the occu-

---

[1] *Onderdonk's Prison Ships.* Notwithstanding this expression of friendship, Fell was treated with such severity during his captivity that the Council of Safety in New Jersey, *Minutes, p.* 161, on Nov. 17, 1777, ordered James Parker and Walter Rutherfurd to be confined in the jail at Morristown until Fell and Wynant Van Zant should be exchanged or released from confinement in New York.

pancy of the latter post by the British is not known, but probably during the winter of 1778–9. The post at Paulus Hoeck was held by them with great tenacity. It was the only point at which they could with safety land their troops for incursions. Here, on the night of February 24, 1779, landed portions of the Thirty-third and Thirty-fourth Regiments of the British, under Lieut.-Colonel Sterling, on their way to attempt the capture of Governor Livingston at Elizabethtown. They marched across the hill to Brown's ferry, whence they were taken in boats sent for that purpose from New York around by the Kill van Kull.[1]

"On Sunday morning, March 14th, 1779, Colonel Van Buskirk received intelligence that a Captain and Lieutenant, with a party of Carolina troops, were at the Three Pigeons in Bergen Woods.[2] He despatched Lieutenant Haselop, of the Fourth Battalion of N. J. Volunteers, and a party of Refugees, in quest of them; but the Rebels, being apprized of his approach, took to their Heels, when, after pursuing them twelve miles into the country, came up with the party, and firing a few shot, made two of them prisoners, one of whom was wounded; the rest, with the advantage of sleighs and their wonted precipitancy, escaped." —*Rivington's Gazette, March* 17, 1779.

"On Friday night, April 2d, 1779, Lieut. Paul, of Colonel Shreve's Regiment, with twelve privates, were captured on Bergen Neck by a detachment of the 64th Regiment, which lay at Powles Hook."—*Ibid, April* 7, 1779.[3]

"On Saturday (April 17th, 1779), two of the Bergen County Militia, who with others had been out reconnoitering, suspecting, from the conduct of a boy they saw running in great haste towards a house on the bank of the Hudson River, about a mile above Wiehawk, that some of the infamous gang of robbers that have for some time infested this and neighboring parts of the

[1] *Hatfield's History of Elizabeth*, 472.

[2] Bergen Woods extended from the Fort Lee road on the north to the Hackensack turnpike at Union Hill on the south.

[3] Israel Shreve at this time commanded the Second New Jersey Regiment. He was commissioned Lieutenant Colonel, November 8, 1775, and Colonel January 1, 1777. *Liber C* 3 *of Commissions* (*Trenton*), 16.

State of New York, were concealed there, advanced as fast as possible to the house; one of them entered immediately and discovered five or six in the house, several of whom had arms, and with admirable presence of mind calling aloud to his companion as if a large party had accompanied him, discharged his musket and killed the chief of the gang on the spot. Retiring to load his piece, the rest of the villains took to their heels."—*New Jersey Gazette, April* 28, 1779.

"On Sunday night, 28th ult., a party of about thirty men belonging to Lieut.-Col. Van Buskirk's corps of tories and embodied Refugees stationed at Hoebuck, in the County of Bergen, went out as far as Closter on a horse stealing and thieving expedition."—*Same Paper*.

"Last Wednesday (Jan. 13th) a Mr. Allen, ensign in the rebel Army, with three Jersey militiamen, were apprehended on Bergen Point, by a party from Capt. Anstruther's company of the 26th Regiment."—*Rivington's Gazette, January* 20, 1779.

"Last Saturday, four privates of the Rebel Army were brought to Hoebuck by a detachment of Col. Buskirk's Regiment. They consisted of one of Bayler's Light-Horse, one continental, and two militiamen."—*Rivington's Gazette, March* 31, 1779.

"Early yesterday morning a party of the 4th Battalion, N. J. volunteers, were ordered out by their Lieut.-Col. Buskirk, under Capt. Van Allen, to intercept a gang of Rebels who paint themselves black and commit *murders and thefts* in Bergen County. Three of them were met a small distance from the Town of Bergen, carrying off an inhabitant, but being briskly pursued, one named David Ritzema Bogert, the other, the noted John Loshier, who was concerned in the murder of honest Capt. John Richards, and whose repeated instances of villainy had rendered him among the Rebels deserving their earliest attention for exchange, when lately taken by a party of the same Battalion, who have a *second time spared his life*."—*Rivington's Gazette, July* 24, 1779.

"A party of Rebels came down last Thursday as far as Prior's Mills, within a mile of Powlis Hook, and fired some shot at the sentry at that post, but a few men being ordered out after them, they soon took to their heels and made the best of their Way into the Bush."—*N. Y. Mercury, June* 21, 1779.

We now come to a brilliant episode in the history of Paulus Hoeck. Major Henry Lee—Light Horse Harry—an active and dashing officer, had frequently been employed by Washington in scouring the west bank of the Hudson and collecting information. In the course of his reconnoitering, and from information derived from other sources, he had discovered that the British post at Paulus Hoeck was negligently guarded. General Wayne's recent brilliant exploit at Stony Point had piqued his emulation, and he intimated to the commander-in-chief that an opportunity offered for an enterprise quite as daring. When first proposed, Washington did not favor the project. Writing on August 10th, 1779, he says that, considering the position of the enemy, he deems the attempt too hazardous, and unwarranted by the magnitude of the object. He thought the cause would lose more in case of failure than it could gain in case of success. He thought it best, therefore, to postpone the attempt.[1] Major Lee, however, was so sanguine of success that he had a personal interview with Washington, and received the desired consent and verbal instructions. These enjoined upon him to lose no time, in case of success, in attempting to bring off cannon, stores, or any other articles, as a few moments' delay might expose the party to great risk from the enemy on York Island; and if the post could not be carried by surprise the attempt was to be abandoned.[2] The position was a strong one, and it was almost rashness to attempt to carry it. Yet its very strength favored its capture by rendering its garrison negligent and unwatchful. On the north was Harsimus cove, on the east the North River, on the south Communipaw cove, and on the west a marsh in which was a creek running near the westerly edge of the upland from near Montgomery street southwesterly into the southerly cove near the foot of Van Vorst street. This creek had been connected with the Harsimus cove by a ditch about on the line of Warren street, made a few years previously by Major David

[1] *Spark's Washington, vi.*, 317. [2] *Ibid, vi.*, 3.

Hunt. Over this ditch, on the line of Newark avenue, was a drawbridge with a barred gate. Thirty paces inside of the ditch and creek was a row of abattis extending into the river. On the Hoeck were strong military works, first constructed by the Americans, and afterward strengthened by the British.[1] The main works were in the line of Sussex street, extending from about St. Matthew's church easterly to Greene street. The barracks were at the intersection of Essex and Warren streets. From the main fort a redoubt extended southerly along Washington street to a half-moon fort on the southerly side of Essex street. There was one fort on the northwest corner of Washington and Grand streets. Some block-houses had been constructed north of the main works, and one of them north of the road leading to the ferry. The burying-ground was on the west of Washington street, extending from Sussex street to a short distance south of Morris street.[2] The accompanying illustration from Lossing's Field Book, though not entirely accurate, will give a general idea of the situation of the works. One (A) redoubt was circular in form, and mounted six heavy guns. It had a ditch and abattis. The other (B), a little southeast of it, was of oblong form, and had three twelve-pounders and one eighteen-pounder; *a a* were block-houses; *b b b b b*, breastworks fronting the bay; *c*, part of the 57th regiment, of five hundred men, under Major Sutherland; *d*, pioneers; *e*, carpenters; *f f f*, barracks; *g*, bridge built by the British.[3] Lee was stationed near the New Bridge, about fourteen miles from the Hoeck. Fearing the treachery of the inhabitants, he carefully kept his own counsel, but gave out that he was about to go with a few troops

[1] *Col. Hist. of N.Y.*, *viii.*, 792.

[2] When Washington street was graded many bones and a few military relics were dug up. Mr. George Dummer placed the bones in a hogshead and buried them at the intersection of Morris and Washington streets.

[3] Marshall, in his *Life of Washington*, *iv.*, 136, says there were one fort, three block-houses, and some redoubts.

on a foraging expedition. This effectually disarmed suspicion, for such parties were frequent, and occasionally quite as large as his proposed force. He had taken the precaution to provide boats, which for the purpose had been brought from Pluckimin, and which were to be at Dow's Ferry at a certain hour in the night, under the command of Captain Peyton, for the purpose of taking his troops over the Hackensack; for it was his intention after the attack to retreat by this ferry and the Belleville turnpike across the meadows to the high ground on the east bank of the Passaic, on his way to the New Bridge. To hold the place with the enemy in New York was impossible, and did not enter into the plans of Washington or Lee. The object was to swoop down upon the post, strike an unexpected blow, and retreat, thus giving *éclat* to the continental arms. He had four hundred infantry and a troop of dismounted dragoons for the enterprise. Lord Sterling moved down to the New Bridge, to be in a position to cover the retreat if necessary. Lee moved from his encampment about four o'clock in the afternoon of August 18, 1779. He detached patrols of horse to watch the communication with the North River, and stationed parties of infantry at the different roads leading to Paulus Hoeck. He followed what was known as the lower road, which came into the present Hackensack road near the English Neighborhood church. When reaching the vicinity of Union Hill he filed into the woods. Here the guide, through timidity or treachery, prolonged the march to three hours; the troops became harassed and discouraged, and in endeavoring to regain the proper route some parties in the rear became separated from the main body. As singular as it may seem, with all this marching and floundering in the woods, with detachments stationed at different points and patrols along the river, they were not discovered. This is the more wonderful since it is well known that at about the time Major Lee started for Paulus Hoeck, Colonel Van Buskirk left that place, with a force of one hundred and thirty men, on a raid to the English Neighborhood,[1] and

---

[1] *Rivington's Gazette, August* 21, 1779.

yet the two forces missed each other in the darkness. A collision between them would have put an end to the enterpise upon which Lee had set his heart, and which for its extent ránges among the most heroic actions of the war.[1]

Notwithstanding all the delays incident to a night march and ignorance or treachery of the guide, Major Lee reached Prior's Mill at three o'clock on the morning of the 19th. The day was near at hand, and the tide, which would fill the ditch and overflow the road between Warren and Grove streets, was rising. Not a moment was to be lost. The punctilios of rank and honor were disregarded, and the troops ordered to advance in the positions they then held. Lieutenant Rudolph, who had been sent forward to reconnoitre the passages of the ditch, now reported to Major Lee that all was silent within the works, that he had fathomed the canal and found the passage possible. This intelligence was passed along the lines, and the troops pushed forward with resolution, order and coolness. Lieutenants M'Callister and Rudolph led the forlorn hope, who marched, with trailed arms, in silence. They reached the ditch at the intersection of Newark avenue and Warren street at half-past three o'clock on Thursday morning. The guards were either asleep or took the approaching force to be Colonel Van Buskirk's men returning from their raid. They were not undeceived until the advance plunged into the ditch. Immediately a firing began. The blockhouse guards ran out to see what was the matter and were seized. The forlorn hope, supported by Major Clarke, broke through all opposition, and soon became masters of the main work, with the cannon, &c. So rapid were they in their movements that the fort was gained before a piece of artillery was fired. The troops came pouring through the abattis, and in a few moments were victorious. Unfortunately, in crossing the ditch the ammunition was destroyed, and thus their firearms were useless. As soon as Major Sutherland, then in command of this post, comprehended the situation, he threw himself into a small redoubt, with a captain, subaltern and forty Hes-

[1] *Gordon's Hist. Am. Revolution, iii.,* 283.

sians. Major Lee had no time to dislodge him or remove or destroy property. Daylight was at hand, and he had some anxiety about the boats at Dow's Ferry. Besides this, the firing had aroused the British in New York, who could in a few minutes throw a large body of troops across the river. He therefore ordered an immediate retreat, and sent Captain Forsyth to Prior's Mill to collect such men as were most fit for action, and take a position on Bergen Heights to cover the retreat. Major Clarke was in the advance, with most of the prisoners; Lieutenants Armstrong and Reed formed the rear guard. Lee now rode forward to look after the boats at the ferry. To his dismay, not a boat was there to receive them. Captain Peyton, owing to the lateness of the hour, had removed them to Newark. He immediately countermarched his troops to the Bergen road *en route* for the New Bridge, communicated with Lord Sterling, and returned to the rear guard at Prior's Mill. His prospects were now discouraging. With troops worn down, ammunition destroyed, encumbered with prisoners, fourteen miles of retreat before him, on a route liable to be intercepted by troops from New York, with no way of escape to the left, he could only depend on the invincible courage of his men. On reaching the heights opposite "Weehock," Captain Handy moved on the mountain road to facilitate the retreat. Here Captain Catlett came up, with fifty men and good ammunition. One party was then detached in the rear of Major Clarke on the Bergen road, and one to move along the bank of the river. In this manner a sudden attack was prevented. At the Fort Lee road Colonel Ball, who had been forwarded to Lee's assistance, met him with two hundred fresh men. Shortly afterward a body of the enemy appeared upon the right and opened fire on the retreating Americans. Lieutenant Reed immediately faced them, and Lieutenant Rudolph threw himself into a stone house which commanded the road. This disposition checked the enemy, and gave the force time to cross the English Neighborhood creek, at the Liberty Pole, now Englewood. Just at that moment, Major Sutherland, who had followed Lee, came up, but halted, and finally fell back without venturing an attack. Major Lee arrived safely at New Bridge about one o'clock in the afternoon. He had captured one hundred and fifty-nine of the garrison, including officers, and lost two killed and three wounded.

In his report of the enterprise, he says: "Among the many unfortunate circumstances which crossed our wishes, none was more so than the accidental absence of Colonel Buskirk, and the greatest part of his regiment. * * A company of vigilant Hessians had taken their place in the fort, which rendered the secrecy of approach more precarious, and, at the same time, diminished the object of the enterprise by a reduction of the number of the garrison. Major Sutherland fortunately saved himself by a soldier's counterfeiting his person. This imposition was not discovered until too late.

"I intended to have burnt the barracks; but on finding a number of sick soldiers and women with young children in them, humanity forbade the execution of my intention. The key of the magazine[1] could not be found, nor could it be broken open in the little time we had to spare, many attempts having been made to that purpose by the Lieutenants M'Callister and Reed."[2]

---

[1] The location of this magazine was in the vicinity of the present almshouse, at the foot of Washington street, near the canal.

[2] In the *Anecdotes of the Revolution, ii.*, 413, may be found a curious story concerning this attack. It appears that one Van Skiver, a native of New York, and a private in Col. Van Buskirk's regiment, was an unexceptionable example of original sin. For some cause, then unknown to the Americans, he deserted the tories He then joined the Americans, and showed so much zeal and such inveterate and deadly animosity against his former friends, and spoke with such confidence of the feasibility of injuring them by an attack on their outposts, that Major Lee listened to his plans and finally acceded to the proposal to attempt the capture of Paulus Hoeck. Entire confidence, however, was not placed in Van Skiver. Armed with an axe, he was placed at the head of the advancing column, a file of men with fixed bayonets following immediately in his rear to do speedy execution upon him should he either falter or show the slightest symptoms of treachery. He was equal to the emergency, and ready to boldly attempt what he had proposed. With steady step and undaunted resolution he advanced and actually cut down two barriers in succession, giving free admission to the troops into the body of the place.

It might naturally be supposed that such a display of hostility to the British would have caused Van Skiver to be ranked among the most determined of the

This brilliant affair under the guns of New York was very galling to the British and tories. Sir Henry Clinton, in a letter to Lord Germaine, dated August 21, 1779, says: "On the 19th instant, the garrison at Powle's Hook being reinforced, Lieutenant-Colonel Buskirk was detached with part of the troops to cut off some small parties who interrupted the supplies of provision; a considerable body of rebels availed themselves of that opportunity to attempt the post. At three in the morning they advanced to the gate of the works, and being taken for Buskirk's corps returning, entered without opposition. I fear they found the garrison so scandalously absorbed, in consequence of their security, that they made themselves masters of a block-house and two redoubts with scarcely any difficulty."

The tory newspapers in New York say that "early in the morning a detachment from the Brigade of the Guards, under command of Colonel Gordon, and the Hessians landed at Paulus Hoeck, and with the light infantry under Captain Maynard pursued Lee. The pursuit was continued for fifteen miles, and two of the prisoners recaptured. Ensign Barrett of the Seventieth Regiment, with a small detachment, captured Captain Meals at the Three Pigeons. Upon his person were found the orders and dispositions of Lee, relating to the march and attack on Paulus Hoeck. Barrett also destroyed at the English Neighborhood a rebel armory, gunsmith's implements, and a great quantity of musket locks, bayonets, &c."[1]

While the British and tories were galled, the Americans were overjoyed at the *coup de main*. Washington sent his congratulations to Lord Sterling, and, in a letter to Congress, said: "The Major displayed a remarkable degree of prudence, address

---

king's enemies. But even at that moment his appearance of zeal was merely intended as a lure to gain respect and confidence, for he had scarcely returned to camp when it was discovered that he was in treaty, and actually far advanced in a plan, to deliver Lee and his Legion into the hands of the enemy. Severe was the penalty which he paid. Sentenced to five hundred lashes, he had the greater part of them inflicted, and was then drummed out of the army. He returned to New York, and was heard of no more.

[1] *Rivington's Gazette, August* 21, 1779.

and bravery upon this occasion, which does the highest honor to himself and to all the officers and men under his command. The situation of the post rendered the attempt critical and the success brilliant."

Under date of September 10, 1779, James Duane, in a letter to Alexander Hamilton, speaks of it as "One of the most daring and insolent assaults that is to be found in the records of chivalry; an achievement so brilliant in itself, so romantic in the scale of British admiration, that none but a hero, inspired by the fortitude, instructed by the wisdom, and guided by the planet of Washington, could, by the exploit at Paulus Hook, have furnished materials in the page of history to give it a parallel."[1]

On the 24th of September Congress passed the following resolutions respecting the affair:

"*Resolved*, That the thanks of Congress be given to his Excellency General Washington for ordering, with so much wisdom, the late attack on the enemy's fort and works at Powles Hook.

"*Resolved*, That the thanks of Congress be given to Major-General Lord Sterling for the judicious measures taken by him to forward the enterprise and to secure the retreat of the party.

"*Resolved*, That the thanks of Congress be given to Major Lee for the remarkable prudence, address and bravery displayed by him on the occasion; and that they approve the humanity shown in circumstances prompting to severity as honorable to the arms of the United States, and correspondent to the noble principles on which they were assumed.

"*Resolved*, That Congress entertain a high sense of the discipline, fortitude and spirit manifested by the officers and soldiers under the command of Major Lee in the march, action and retreat; and while with singular satisfaction they acknowledge the merit of these gallant men, they feel an additional pleasure by considering them as part of an army in which very many brave officers and soldiers have proved, by their cheerful performance of every duty under every difficulty, that they ardently wish to give the truly glorious examples they now receive.

[1] *Hamilton's Works*, i., 86, 87.

"*Resolved*, That Congress justly esteem the military caution so happily combined with daring activity by Lieutenants M'Callister and Rudolph, in leading on the forlorn hope.

"*Resolved*, That a medal of gold, emblematical of this affair, be struck, under the direction of the Board of Treasury, and presented to Major Lee.

"*Resolved*, That the brevet and the pay and subsistence of Captain be given to Lieutenant M'Callister and to Lieutenant Rudolph respectively."

Congress also placed in the hands of Major Lee $15,000 to be distributed among the soldiers engaged in the attack.[1]

MEDAL AWARDED TO LEE.

On one side is a bust of the hero, with the words HENRICO LEE, LEGIONIS EQUIT. PRÆFECTO. COMITIA AMERICANA. "The American Congress to Henry Lee, Colonel of Cavalry." On the reverse: NON OBSTANTIB. FLUMINIBUS VALLIS ASTUTIA & VIRTUTE BELLICA PARVA MANU HOSTES VICIT VICTOSQ. ARMIS HUMANITATE DEVINXIT. IN MEM. PUGN. AD PAULUS HOOK, DIE XIX AUG., 1779. "Notwithstanding rivers and intrenchments, he with a small band conquered the foe by warlike skill and prowess, and firmly bound by his humanity those who had been conquered by his arms. In memory of the conflict at Paulus Hook, nineteenth of August, 1779."[2]

[1] *Journal of Congress*, v., 368.

[2] The joy does not seem, however, to have been universal. There is and al-

From this time until the opening of the campaign in the spring of 1780, but little of a general character transpired in Bergen. In December following the attack on Paulus Hoeck, General Wayne moved down from the vicinity of Tappaen and encamped at Bergen. For a short time he kept a vigilant eye on Paulus Hoeck, and then moved back to Westfield into winter quarters.[1] The raids by both parties were kept up on the people of this vicinity. Money and valuables were buried and hidden, but now and then

---

ways will be an undertow continually working to destroy great reputations. Jealousy is all-sufficient in small minds to justify the meanest action. The following letter indicates an undertow to the popular wave:

"CAMP NORTH OF SMITH'S CLOVE,
"August 22, 1779.

"DEAR SIR:

"I suppose you have had a variety of accounts of the sacking of Powel's Hook, which was taken by surprise about 3 o'clock the morning of the 19th inst., and instantly evacuated again by us, after doing no greater damage than taking 7 officers and about 160 Rank and File prisoners, and killing about 20 in the Garrison. We have about 7 privates missing. Had not the officer who commanded —Major Lee—been in so great a hurry from the Garrison, much more execution might have been done, as they did not take time to carry off all the prisoners, or even to take a Major and party of men who were then in their power. Not the least damage whatever was done to the Garrison. The Magazine was not blown up, the Barricks not sett on fire, the Cannon not spiked, no article of Stores, Clothing, &c., &c., of which a great plenty were there, was the least damaged; in fact, nothing further was done than rushing into the Garrison in confusion and driving out the prisoners, mostly without their clothes. Perhaps there will be an inquiry into the reason of the confusion and great haste the party made to get out of the fort without destroying so many valuable stores as were in their possession. Several officers have been much injured in the Virginia line, on account of giving Major Lee the command of 300 of our men to reduce Powel's Hook, and unjust methods taken by him to have the command, by telling one of our Majors, who marched with the 300 men, that his commission was older than it really is—otherwise he would not have had the command over him. I believe Major Lee will be arrested. I marched with a covering party, but did not go near the garrison. Lord Sterling, who commands here, is very uneasy at our complaints on this affair. Several letters have passed between his lordship and the officers of our line concerning his ordering 300 of our men under Major Lee. * * *

"W. CROGHAN.

"Mr. Barnard Gratz, Phila."

Hist. Mag., 180.

[1] *N. Y. Mercury, Jan.* 10, 1780.

the secret places of these treasures would be revealed by the tory neighbors. In the house of the late Captain Howe, near Cavan Point, lived George and Garret Vreeland, father and son. One night the tories came to the house, locked them in the kitchen cellar (the kitchen is yet standing), and robbed the house of a large number of silver dollars. The next morning they were set free by their faithful old slave.

In these times, for the accommodation of the British, the people of Bergen were permitted to take provisions over the river. On these occasions they would take the opportunity to purchase what things were needed by their families. This fact was soon found out by the tories, who, whenever they could, would rob these Bergen merchants of their return cargoes. The strategists of Communipaw were equal to the emergency. There was a barn just south of Communipaw avenue, the doors of which they used for a code of signals. These doors were then made in two parts, and if, on the return of the skiffs from New York, the men in them saw the upper part of the door open, then they knew that all was right and their freight safe. But if, on the contrary, it was closed, then they might know that the tories were about, and they must tarry at Ellis Island. The tories finally found out the secret, but were uncertain if the door should be open or shut to signify a "welcome home" to the voyagers across the river. At one time, when they were waiting for the return of the richly laden argosies, a contention arose among them whether the door should be open or shut to signify that the coast was clear. Between the two the door was opened and shut and shut and opened in such rapid succession that the men in the boats, doubting as to the condition of things on shore, gave themselves the benefit of the doubt, pulled back to the island, and left the "gude vrouws" to fight it out with the tories.

It is said that one day the British sent a flag from Paulus Hoeck to General Wayne, then on New. Barbadoes Neck, which "Hop" Jerolamon, of the latter place, in his mistaken zeal, captured, and took the saddle and bridle as lawful prize. Mad Anthony, in turn, captured the indiscreet "Hop," put the saddle on his back (tradition puts the bridle in his mouth, *vide* Proverbs, xxvi., 3), and sent him to Paulus Hoeck to be punished at the discretion of the British. "Hop" keenly felt the mortification, but a "military necessity" pushed him along over the meadows and hill until he came to Prior's Mill. Here he encountered the enemy's pickets and wished to lay down his burden, thinking he had carried the joke far enough. Not so thought his captors, and he was forced to trudge along to headquarters "accoutred as he was."

Jacob Van Wagenen, living at Bergen, had everything stolen from him by the tories and British. One day they were driving off twelve of his cattle toward their barge, which lay in the Hackensack, just above the present bridge of the New Jersey Railroad. One of his faithful negroes endeavored to prevent them. They seized the courageous fellow, and hung him to a tree until he was willing to withdraw all opposition to the departure of his master's property.

The winter of 1779–80 was of unusual severity.[1] The British in New York were in great want of fuel. It became so scarce

---

[1] The river between Paulus Hoeck and New York was frozen over. Six persons, in attempting to cross over, were carried into the East river, "and providentially got on shore by the ice lodging on Blackwell's Island."—*Riv. Gaz., Jan.* 15, 1780. Governor Tryon caused the river between Paulus Hoeck and New York to be measured, and found it to be 2,000 yards wide.—*Valentine's Manual,* 1853, 464. The river has since been filled in to some extent on both sides. Imitating Governor Tryon, two inhabitants of Communipaw measured the distance from that place to Ellis Island, and found it to be 82 chains. They left the following record of their exploit:

"JANUARY 24th, 1780.

"De winter heel hart zynde die Rivier all over Gevrosen Wy die personen Genamt Cornelius Garrabrants en Giliam Outwater had der Gedocht om te meeten hoe veer het was van de oost hoeck van Hendrick Blinkerhoff een huys tot het Klin Ilant is 82 Kettings." A ketting is one chain.

It is worthy of notice that during the last 130 years the river has been passable on the ice only four times, viz., 1740–1, 1764–5, 1779–80, and 1820–1. In January of the latter year an enterprising vender of whiskey opened shop in the middle of the river. A "drouty crony," going from Jersey City for a glass, broke through the ice. A wag standing at the door of the saloon said to the proprietor: "Sir, there has a man just *slipped down cellar*—you had better look after him, or your liquors will be in danger." *Centinel of Freedom, Jan.* 30, 1821.

that the commandant was obliged to limit the maximum price to *four pounds sterling per cord!* The high price for wood was a great temptation to the tories. At that time the hill from Fort Lee to Bergen Point, except what had been cleared for the farms, was covered with a fine growth of thrifty timber. This they determined to cut off and sell to the shivering British. To make it safe for them to enter upon the business, it was necessary to have redoubts, breastworks or block-houses into which they could retire at night, and to which they might fly in case of attack by day. They therefore constructed the block-house at a place since called Block-House Point, near Bull's Ferry. They also threw up earthworks on the old Bergen road, just below Woodlawn avenue. They also had earthworks at Bergen, east of the town, near Blakeley Wilson's residence. Besides these, they had the fortifications on Paulus Hoeck, and at Fort Delancey, on Bergen Neck. At the latter place Captain Tom Ward held command.[1] His force consisted of negroes and vile characters of his own race. They became as notorious as himself. They were a band of plunderers, thieving and raiding by night over to Elizabethtown, Newark, New Barbadoes Neck, and along Bergen Hill as far up as Closter and New Bridge. He is represented as having been a terrible wretch. It is said that he once hired three negroes to kill a man in Bergen to whom he was indebted. "Little Will," owned by Van Ripen, was one of the three. Tom Cadmus, another tory, was sergeant, and ordered the fire. The negroes were afterward caught and hung in the swamp north of Brown's Ferry road, near the present Glendale House, and the bodies left hanging for weeks.

The block-house near Bull's Ferry was occupied by refugees

---

[1] He is said to have been a native of Newark, and a deserter. *Remembrancer*, *xi.*, 165. The latter part of the assertion may be true; the former part is not only denied, but met by the avowal that Tom Ward of Newark was a well known and active patriot. In the *N. Y. Mercury, August* 4, 1760, I find a paragraph that Thomas Ward, of Bergen County, had lost a son, who became mad from the bite of a wild cat. It is very probable that the father of that boy is identical with the notorious Captain Tom Ward, of Fort Delancey, and imitated Colonel Van Buskirk in deserting the cause of his country.

and wood-cutters, under command of Colonel Cuyler. It was located on the high point above the ravine which extends back from the river, on the north side of Guttenberg. It was protected on two sides by perpendicular rocks which rise from the shore and the ravine, and surrounded on the other sides by abattis and stockades, with a ditch and parapet. The only entrance to the block-house was a covered way large enough to admit but a single person.[1] Colonel Cuyler being temporarily absent from this post, Captain Tom Ward was in command of the seventy men stationed there. Washington, then near Sufferns, having been informed that there were a number of cattle on Bergen Neck exposed to the enemy, sent General Wayne to bring them off, and destroy the block-house at the same time. In the afternoon of the 20th of July, 1780, the first and second Pennsylvania regiments, with four pieces of Proctor's artillery and Moylan's dragoons, in all about one thousand men, started from their camp on the expedition. They arrived at New Bridge about nine o'clock in the evening. Here they rested four or five hours, and then pushed forward for Bull's Ferry. Major Lee, the hero of Paulus Hoeck, was sent to Bergen with his cavalry to bring off the cattle, while the remainder of the force marched against the block-house. General Irvine with a part of his brigade proceeded along the summit of the ridge, and the first brigade, under Colonel Hampton, with the artillery of Moylan's horse, by the direct road. About ten o'clock on the morning of the 21st, part of the first brigade reached the post. Moylan's horse and part of the infantry remained at the fork of the roads leading to Paulus Hoeck and Bergen, prepared to receive the enemy should he approach from that quarter. General Irvine was posted so as to prevent the enemy landing, should he approach by vessel. Near Fort Lee two regiments were concealed, prepared for the enemy. One regiment was posted in a hollow way on the north side of the block-house, and another on the south side, with orders to keep up a constant fire into the port-holes to favor the advance of the artillery. When the field-

[1] *Pennsylvania Packet, July* 25, 1780.

pieces arrived they were placed sixty yards distant, and a cannonade commenced, which continued from eleven o'clock until noon, without intermission. Up to that time but little impression had been made on the block-house, and orders were given to retire. Just at that moment one regiment burst through the abattis, and advanced to the stockades. They were received with such a galling fire from the tories that they were compelled to withdraw.[1] Boats were now beginning to move up and down the river, but no attempt was made to land. The sloops and wood-boats at the landing were destroyed, and three or four prisoners taken. The cattle were driven off as originally intended, but the other part of the expedition was a failure. General Wayne says that he lost fifteen killed and fifteen wounded.[2] The enemy claimed that "the brave Captain Ward pursued the rear upwards of four miles, retook twenty cattle, killed one rebel and took two prisoners." The refugees admitted the loss of four killed and eight wounded.[3] Among the latter were George and Absalom Bull, residents of the immediate neighborhood. General Wayne was chagrined at his failure, and on witnessing the slaughter of his men, shed tears. Washington deeply regretted the misfortune, and hastened to explain away the bad effect which the failure of the attack upon the Block-House might have upon Congress. Among other things he said, "Wayne for some time tried the effect of his field-pieces upon it, but though the fire was kept up for an hour, they were found too light to penetrate the logs of which it was constructed. The troops during this time being galled by a constant fire from the loop-holes of the house, and seeing no chance of making a breach with cannon, those of the first and second regiments—notwithstanding the utmost efforts of the officers to restrain them—rushed through the abattis to the foot of the stockade, with a view of forcing an entrance, which was found impracticable. This act of intemperate valor was the cause of the loss we

[1] Tradition says when the attacking party withdrew the tories had but one round of ammunition left.

[2] *Sparks' Washington, vii.*, 110.

[3] *Rivington's Gazette, July* 22, 1780.

sustained, and which amounted in the whole to 3 officers wounded, 15 non-commissioned officers and privates killed, and 46 non-commissioned officers and privates wounded."

To add a keener pang to the mortification of failure, the enemy indulged in great exultation. Sir Henry Clinton complimented the refugees in the following terms:

"SIR: The Commander-in-chief, admiring the gallantry of the Refugees, who in such small numbers defended their post against so very considerable a corps, and withstood both their cannonade and assault, desires his very particular acknowledgment of their merit may be testified to them.

"His Excellency requests that you will give in a return of the numbers present at this spirited defence, that he may give directions for uniform, clothing and hats being given them from the Inspector General's office.

"In future *your* requisition of ammunition will be valid with the Ordinance.

"I have the honor to be,
"Sir, your most obedient
"and most humble servant,
"JOHN ANDRÉ, D. A. D."[1]

The following sarcastic suggestion appeared in print:

"A lady presents her compliments to the Sir Clement of the Philadelphia Ball Room, and desires the next country dances may commence with a new movement, called,

A TRIP TO THE BLOCK-HOUSE;
OR, THE
WOODCUTTER'S TRIUMPH;

in compliment to a certain General, who (emulating his brother *Arnold*) was lately checked on the North River, by a *malheureuse* event, and his glories (now on the *Wane*) threatened with an insuperable mortification."[2]

---

[1] *Rivington's Gazette, July* 22, 1780.

[2] *Ibid, July* 28, 1780.

Even the King of Great Britain sang the praises of the block-house defenders in the following strains:

"The very extraordinary instance of courage shown by the Loyal Refugees, in the affair of Bull's Ferry, of which you make such honorable mention, is a pleasing proof of the spirit and resolution with which men in their circumstances will act against their oppressors, and how great advantages the King's troops may derive from employing those of approved fidelity. And his Majesty, to encourage such exertions, commands me to desire that you will acquaint the survivors of the brave *Seventy* that their behavior is approved of by their Sovereign."[1]

The expedition was very neatly caricatured in a mock heroic poem written by Major André, on the model of Chevy Chase. The whole is in three cantos. The first was published in *Rivington's Gazette*, August 16, 1780; the second, August 30, and the third, September 23. The last canto was sent to the paper the day before André left New York to meet Arnold, and published the very day he was captured at Tarrytown. Its composition may have been suggested by the fact that André had boarded with John Thompson, the Wood-cutting Agent at New York. It was written at headquarters, number one Broadway, except the first canto, which was written at Elizabeth-Town. Its title was "The Cow Chase, in three Cantos; Published on occasion of the Rebel General Wayne's attack of the Refugees' Block-house on Hudson's River, on Friday, the 21st of July, 1780." The following is an exact copy of the poem as it appeared in the *Gazette*:

---

[1] *Rivington's Gazette, Dec.* 13, 1780.

ELIZABETH-TOWN, *Aug.* 1, 1780.

THE COW CHASE.

BY

Major André.

CANTO I.

To drive the Kine one summer's morn,
The Tanner[1] took his way,
The Calf shall rue that is unborn
The jumbling of that day.

And Wayne descending Steers shall know,
And tauntingly deride,
And call to mind in ev'ry Low,
The tanning of his hide.

Yet Bergen Cows shall ruminate
Unconscious in the stall,
What mighty means were used to get,
And lose them after all.

For many Heroes bold and brave
From New-Bridge and Tapaan
And those that drink Passaick's wave,
And those that eat Soupaan,[2]

---

[1] Wayne's occupation.

[2] An Indian dish of ground corn boiled in water—written *sapaen*. Irving says: "The Van Brummels were the first inventors of suppawn, or mush and milk." It has had many names.

> "Thee the soft nations round the warm Levant
> *Polanta* call; the French, of course, *Polante*.
> E'en in thy native regions how I blush
> To hear the Pennsylvanians call thee *Mush!*"
> —*Harper's Magazine*, *July*, 1856, 145.

Modern fastidiousness dubs it *hasty pudding!*

And Sons of distant Delaware
  And still remoter Shannon,[1]
And Major Lee with Horses rare,
  And Proctor with his cannon.

All wond'rous proud in arms they came
  What hero could refuse?
To tread the rugged path to fame
  Who had a pair of shoes.

At six the Host with sweating buff,
  Arriv'd at Freedom's Pole,[2]
When Wayne who thought he'd time enough
  Thus spechified the whole.

O ye whom glory doth unite
  Who Freedom's cause espouse
Whether the wing that's doom'd to fight
  Or that to drive the cows.

Ere yet you tempt your further way
  Or into action come,
Hear soldiers what I have to say
  And take a pint of Rum.

Intemp'rate valor then will string,
  Each nervous arm the better
So all the land shall IO sing
  And read the Gen'ral's letter.[3]

---

[1] The number of Irish in the Pennsylvania line often caused it to be called the line of Ireland.

[2] Liberty Pole, a small hamlet, now the beautiful village of Englewood, where stood a hickory pole.

[3] The letter here referred to is probably the same printed in *Almon's Remembrancer*, *x.*, 290. It is from Washington to the President of Congress, July 26, 1780. After narrating the story of the expedition, the failure of the attack on the block-house by reason of the cannon being "too light to penetrate the logs of which it was constructed," and the "intemperate valor" of the men causing such great loss to themselves, he concludes: "I have been thus particular lest the account of this affair should have reached Philadelphia much exaggerated, as is commonly the case upon such occasions." *Supra.*

Know that some paltry Refugees
  Whom I've a mind to fight,
Are playing H—l amongst the trees,
  That grow on yonder height.[1]

Their Fort and Block-Houses we'll level,
  And deal a horrid slaughter;
We'll drive the Scoundrels to the Devil,
  And ravish wife and daughter.

I under cover of th' attack
  Whilst you are all at blows,
From English Neighb'rhood and Tinack
  Will drive away the Cows.

For well you know the latter is
  The serious operation
And fighting with the Refugees
  Is only demonstration.

---

[1] More truth than poetry, for to such an extent did the woodcutters play "h—l among the trees" in this county that, it is said, from Bull's Ferry to Bergen Point, they did not leave a stick large enough for a whipstock. At one time the growth of timber on the ridge was fine and heavy. In the early days New York city depended upon our forests for the defence of the city. When Cornbury feared the approach of the French, he wrote as follows:

"NEW YORK, May the 16th, 1706.

"GENTLEMEN:

"Having had intelligence lately from the West Indies that a French Squadron of Men-of-Warr, with Land forces on board them, intend to attack this place, I am taking the best methods I can to put the place into a posture of defence, for which purpose I shall want a considerable number of Stockades, and being informed that there are a great number of trees growing upon bergen point fit for that purpose, I send this therefore to desire that you will allow some persons who shall be sent from hence to cut the Stockades we want, and likewise that some of your people may help with their Carts to bring them to the water side, for which they shall be paid.

"I am,
"Gentlemen,
"Your assured friend,
"CORNBURY.

"To the Inhabitants of the Town of Bergen, in the Eastern Division of New Jersey."—*Proc. of N. J. Hist. Soc.*, *i.*, 124.

His daring words from all the crowd
  Such great applause did gain
That every man declar'd aloud
  For serious work with Wayne.

Then from the cask of Rum once more
  They took a heady jill,
When one and all they loudly swore
  They'd fight upon the hill.

But here—the Muse has not a strain
  Befitting such great deeds,
Huzza they cried, huzza for Wayne
  And shouting—did their Needs.

Canto II.

Near his meridian pomp, the Sun
  Had journey'd from the horz'n,
When fierce the dusky Tribe mov'd on
  Of Heroes drunk as poison.

The sounds confus'd of boasting Oaths,
  Re-echoed thro' the Wood,
Some vow'd to sleep in dead Men's Cloaths,
  And some to swim in blood.

At Irvine's Nod, 'twas fine to see,
  The left prepare to fight,
The while the Drovers, Wayne and Lee,
  Drew off upon the Right.

Which Irvine 'twas, Fame don't relate,
  Nor can the Muse assist her,
Whether 'twas he that cocks a Hat,
  Or he that gives a Glister.

For greatly one was signaliz'd,
  That fought at Chesnut-Hill,
And Canada immortaliz'd,
  The Vender of the Pill.

Yet the Attendance upon Proctor,
  They both might have to boast of;
For there was Business for the Doctor,
  And hatts to be disposed of.[1]

Let none uncandidly infer,
  That Stirling wanted Spunk,
The self-made Peer had sure been there,
  But that the Peer was drunk.

But turn we to the Hudson's Banks,
  Where stood the modest Train,
With Purpose firm, tho' slender Ranks,
  Nor car'd a Pin for Wayne.

For then the unrelenting Hand
  Of rebel Fury drove,
And tore from ev'ry genial Band,
  Of Friendship and of Love.

And some within a Dungeon's Gloom,
  By mock Tribunals laid,
Had waited long a cruel Doom,
  Impending o'er their heads.

Here one bewails a Brother's Fate,
  There one a Sire demands,
Cut off alas! before their Date
  By ignominious Hand.

And silver'd Grandsires here appear'd,
  In deep Distress serene,
Of reverend Manners that declared,
  The better days they'd seen.

---

[1] One of the Irvines was a hatter, the other a physician. Dr. Wm. Irvine,

Oh curs'd Rebellion these are thine,
Thine are these Tales of Woe,
Shall at thy dire insatiate Shrine
Blood never cease to flow?

And now the Foe began to lead,
His Forces to th' Attack;
Ball whistling unto balls succeed,
And make the Block-House crack.

No shot could pass, if you will take
The Gen'ral's Word for true;
But 'tis a d—ble Mistake,
For every Shot went thro'.[1]

The firmer as the Rebels pressed,
The royal Heroes stand;
Virtue had nerv'd each honest Breast,
And Industry each Hand,

" In Valour's Phrenzy,[2] Hamilton
" Rode like a Soldier big,
" And Secretary Harrison,
" With Pen stuck in his Wig."

after two years' captivity in Canada, now commanded the Second Pennsylvania Regiment. He died August 2, 1804. Brigadier James Irvine, of the militia, was taken prisoner at Chestnut Hill, near Germantown, in December, 1777.

[1] Wayne attributed his failure to the lightness of his guns, which he thought made no impression on the walls of the house. In this he was mistaken. *Sparks' Washington, vii.*, 117.

[2] *Vide* Lee's trial. " When General Washington asked me if I would remain in front and retain the command, or he should take it, and I had answered that I undoubtedly would, and that he would see that I myself should be of the last to leave the field; Colonel Hamilton, flourishing his sword, immediately exclaimed: 'That's right, my dear General, and I will stay, and we will all die here in this spot.' * * * I could not but be surprised at his expression, but observing him much flustered and in a sort of *phrenzy of valor*, I calmly requested him," &c., &c. Harrison, mentioned in this verse, had met André at Amboy.

"But lest the Chieftain Washington,
  "Should mourn them in the Mumps,[1]
"The Fate of Withrington to shun,
  "They fought behind the Stumps."[2]

But ah, Thadaeus Posset, why
  Should thy Poor Soul elope,
And why should Titus Hooper[3] die,
  Ah die—without a rope.

Apostate Murphy, thou to whom
  Fair Shela ne'er was cruel,
In death, shal't hear her mourn thy Doom,
  Auch wou'd you die, my Jewel?[4]

---

[1] A disorder prevalent in the American lines.

[2] For Witherington needs must I wayle,
  As one in doleful dumps;
For when his leggs were smitten off
  He fought upon his stumps.

The battle of Chevy Chase, or Otterbourne, on the borders of Scotland, was fought August 5, 1388, between the families of Percy and Douglass. The song was probably written much after that time, though long before 1588, as Hearne supposes. In the old copy of the ballad the lines run thus:

For Wetharryngton my harte was wo
  That ever he slayne shulde be,
For when both his leggis weare hewyne in to
  He knyled and fought upon his kne.

[3] This name should be written Hopper. His house was at Wagraw, above Aquackanonck, on the east side of the Passaic, near Hopper's mill. He was a miller, and the tories under John Van de Roder, a neighbor, one night took possession of the mill. Hopper's wife, hearing the noise, awoke her husband, and told him that some persons were in the mill. He arose, went to the door and demanded to know who was there, and was shot through the hand. They then rushed into the house, seized him, and compelled his wife to hold a candle while they thrust nineteen bayonets into him. At the time of this cruel murder Van de Roder exclaimed, "This is for an old grudge."

[4] *Vide* Irish song, "Smollett's Rehearsal."

Thee Nathan Pumpkin I lament,
Of melancholy Fate,
The Grey Goose stolen as he went,
In his Heart's Blood was wet.[1]

Now as the Fight was further fought,
And Balls began to thicken,
The Fray. assum'd, the Gen'ral's thought,
The Colour of a licking.

Yet undismay'd the Chiefs Command,
And, to redeem the Day,
Cry, SOLDIERS CHARGE! they hear, they stand,
They turn and run away.

CANTO III.

Not all delights the bloody spear,
Or horrid din of battle,
There are, I'm sure, who'd like to hear
A word about the Cattle.

The Chief whom we beheld of late,
Near Schralenberg haranguing,
At Yan Van Poop's[2] unconscious sat,
Of Irving's hearty banging,

Whilst valiant Lee, with courage wild,
Most bravely did oppose
The tears of woman and of child,
Who begg'd he'd leave the Cows.

---

[1]Against Sir Hugh Montgomery
So right the shaft he sett,
The gray goose wing that was thereon
In his heart's blood was wett.

[2] He kept a dram-shop.

But Wayne, of sympathizing heart,
  Required a relief
Not all the blessings could impart
  Of battle or of beef;

For now a prey to female charms,
  His soul took more delight in
A lovely Hamadryad's[1] arms,
  Than cow driving or fighting:

A nymph, the Refugees had drove
  Far from her native tree,
Just happen'd to be on the move,
  When up came Wayne and Lee.

She in mad Anthony's fierce eye
  The hero saw pourtray'd,
And all in tears she took him by
  ——The bridle of his Jade.

Hear, said the nymph, O great Commander!
  No human lamentations;
The trees you see them cutting yonder
  Are all my near relations,

And I, forlorn! implore thine aid,
  To free the sacred grove;
So shall thy prowess be repaid
  With an immortal's love.

Now some, to prove she was a Goddess,
  Said this enchanting Fair
Had late retired from the *Bodies*,[2]
  In all the pomp of war;

[1] A deity of the woods.

[2] A cant appellation given among the soldiery to the corps that had the honor to guard his majesty's person.

That drums and merry fifes had play'd
  To honour her retreat,
And Cunningham[1] himself convey'd
  The lady thro' the street.

Great Wayne, by soft compassion sway'd,
  To no inquiry stoops,
But takes the fair afflicted maid
  Right into Yan Van Poop's.

So Roman Anthony, they say,
  Disgrac'd th' imperial banner,
And for a gipsy lost a day,
  Like Anthony the Tanner.

The Hamadryad had but half
  Received redress from Wayne,
When drums and Colours cow and calf,
  Came down the road amain.

All in a cloud of dust were seen
  The sheep, the horse, the goat,
The gentle heifer, ass obscene;
  The Yearling and the shoat,

The pack-horses with fowls came by,
  Befeather'd on each side,
Like Pegasus, the horse that I
  And other poets ride.

Sublime upon his stirrups rose
  The mighty Lee behind,
And drove the terror-smitten cows,
  Like chaff before the wind.

But sudden see the woods above
  Pour down another corps,
All helter skelter in a drove,
  Like that I sung before.

---

[1] Cunningham was Provost-Marshal in New York.

Irving and terror in the van,
Came flying all abroad,
And cannon, colours, horse and man
Ran tumbling to the road.

Still as he fled, 'twas Irving's cry,
And his example too,
"Run on, my merry men all—For why?"
The shot will not go thro'.[1]

As when two kennels in the street,
Swell'd with a recent rain,
In gushing streams together meet,
And seek the neighbouring drain,

So meet these dung-born tribes[2] in one,
As swift in their career,
And so to Newbridge they ran on,—
But all the cows got clear.

Poor Parson Caldwell,[3] all in wonder,
Saw the returning train,
And mourn'd to Wayne the lack of plunder,
For them to steal again.

---

[1] Five Refugees ('tis true) were found
Stiff on the block-house floor,
But then 'tis thought the shot went round
And in at the back door.

[2] Under André's signature to a MS. copy of "The Cow Chase" are endorsed these lines:

"When the epic strain was sung
The poet by the neck was hung,
And to his cost he finds too late
The dung-born tribes decide his fate."

[3] Rev. James Caldwell, of New Jersey. His wife was shot by one of Knyphausen's men. When Knyphausen made his excursion to Springfield, Mr. C. collected the hymn books of his church for wadding. "Put a little Watts into them," said he to the soldiers. He was shot by James Morgan, one of the twelve months men, at Elizabethtown Point, on the 24th of November, 1781 He had gone down to the Point to meet a Miss Murray, who had come up from New York. He had placed her in his carriage, and returned to the boat for a

For 'twas his right to seize the spoil, and
To share with each commander
As he had done at Staten Island
With frost-bit Alexander.[1]

In his dismay the frantic priest
Began to grow prophetic,
You had swore, to see his lab'ring breast,
He'd taken an emetic.

I view a future day, said he,
Brighter than this day dark is,
And you shall see what you shall see,
Ha! ha! one pretty Marquis;[2]

And he shall come to Paulus Hook,
And great atchievements think on,
And make a bow and take a look,
Like Satan over Lincoln.

And all the land around shall glory
To see the Frenchman caper,
And pretty Susan tell the story
In the next Chatham paper.[3]

---

parcel containing tea, pins and mustard, when the shooting occurred. Morgan was not on duty at the time, and was supposed to have been bribed to do the act. He had previously threatened to "pop him over." Morgan was arrested and handed over to the civil authorities. The coroner's jury rendered a verdict against him, and he was committed by Mayor Isaac Woodruff, of Elizabethtown. He was tried at Westfield, in the January term, 1782, John Cleves Symmes, presiding Judge, found guilty, and executed by Noah Marsh, sheriff of Essex county, January 29, 1782. The trial was had in the church, and Colonel De Hart, of Morristown, was assigned to defend him.

[1] Lord Sterling. He led a foray into Staten Island, in January, 1780, in which 500 of his men were frost-bitten.

[2] La Fayette.

[3] The *New Jersey Gazette* was published at that place during the war. Susannah, the daughter of Gov. Livingston, wrote occasionally for that paper. She married John Cleaves Symmes, and became the mother of President Harrison's wife.

This solemn prophecy, of course,
  Gave all much consolation,
Except to Wayne, who lost his horse
  Upon the great occasion.

His horse that carried all his prog,
  His military speeches,
His corn-stalk whiskey for his grog,
  Blue stockings, and brown breeches.

And now I've clos'd my epic strain,
  I tremble as I show it,
Lest this same warrio-drover, Wayne,
  Should ever catch the poet.

In the following November the Block-house at Bull's Ferry was deserted, and its tory inmates went to Fort Delancey on Bergen Neck.[1] But the wood cutters did not cease their work. A good story is told of Garret Vreeland, who had a fine growth of timber where the New York Bay Cemetery now is. In this the wood-cutters were fiercely at work. One day he went to New York and obtained an order from the proper authorities, that no more of his trees should be cut. This order was duly presented to a burly knight of the axe, just as he was about felling a stately white oak. He leaned upon his helve, looked at the order and then at the tree. He was obliged to obey the one, yet greatly coveted the other. "Well," said he, "we can't *cut* any more, that's sure, but we can *girdle them and get them ready for next year!*" And so he did.

On the 24th of August, 1780, the light camp, under command of La Fayette, marched from the vicinity of Fort Lee down the road toward Bergen. About one o'clock the next morning they arrived near the town, where they halted, and threw out pickets and patrols. Colonel Stuart, with his regiment, took post within musket shot of Paulus Hoeck. In the morning the whole camp was on the brow of the hill, east of the town, in full view of the

---

[1] *Rivington's Gazette, Nov.* 25, 1780.

enemy.[1] The infantry spent the whole of that day in foraging, as low down as Bergen Point. Here they were fired upon by the enemy on Staten Island. But they unconcernedly loaded their wagons with grain, and drove off the cattle. The people, who were thus deprived of their property, received therefor certificates, which might "procure for them, at some future day, compensation." Besides this, they were reminded that they had "contributed heretofore very little to the support of this war, and that what was taken * * * * does not amount to the value of their taxes, * * * * * which they could have paid in no other manner, owing to their particular situation." But the party did not confine themselves to foraging for the use of the army. They used the occasion to pilfer from the people. For this one of the soldiers was hung. This bold appearance, in sight of the enemy, was considered by the Americans as an offer of battle to the enemy, and they taunted him for not accepting it. "We have done the same thing, precisely, as a man in private life who has been injured, and who twits the fellow by the nose, or shakes a cudgel over his shoulders, who abused him. Clinton has behaved like the fellow who quietly submits to the chastisement."[2]

The following *jeu d'esprit*, supposed to have been written by Susannah Livingston, daughter of the Governor, shortly afterward appeared. It refers to this expedition of La Fayette, and is a fair offset to André's "Cow Chase":

"To the Printer.

"Sir:

"As the inclosed letter, which was intercepted coming from New York, may possibly entertain some of your readers, it is sent to you for publication. The writer will perceive that proper care has been taken to conceal her name. I have only to ask the lady's pardon for the few comments that are added. —*August* 30, 1780."

---

[1] The exact position was on the hill, immediately over the Jersey City cemetery, and around the "oude boom," or old tree, which stood between Magnolia avenue and Henry street. This tree was cut down Dec. 20, 1871.

[2] *N. J. Gazette, Sept.* 6, 1780.

"New York, *August* 27, 1780.

"We've almost, sweet sister, been frightened to death,
Nor have we, as yet, quite recovered our breath.
An Army of rebels came down t'other night,
Expecting no doubt that the British would fight.
Next morning we saw them parade at the Hook,[1]
And thought, to be sure, this was too much to brook;
That soon would the river be crowded with boats,
With Hessian and English, to cut all their throats:
So we dress'd in high taste to see them embark,
Not thinking Sir Harry would go in the dark;
To light a retreat, as seen in his letter,[2]
He once used the moon—for want of a better;
Much less, having sworn, that the rebels he'd maul,
Could it enter our heads,—he'd not go at all.
Tho' now I think on't, ere since Greene beat old Knyp,[3]
Not one of his heroes have opened a lip,
Except to abuse them for fighting so well
With Greene at their head—to find quarters in h—ll.
—Ah! Tabitha, these men can swear with such grace,
One can't be offended, tho' done to one's face.
All day I was hurried without knowing why,
Each moment expecting to see them pass by,
The officers bowing, the drums in a clatter,
Their heads rising up, like ducks out of water,
Then glancing on me with a passionate air,
Turn round to their men & most charmingly swear.
But why should they thus our soft bosoms alarm,
Should they do like their masters—where is the harm?

[1] Paulus Hoeck.

[2] The battle of Monmouth, where Sir Harry Clinton says that he *took advantage of the moon.* I suppose that is what the lady alludes to. It may be well enough, however, to set her right by saying that he did not begin his retreat till the moon had gone down, which, vulgarly speaking, was really to take advantage of the moon.

[3] Knyphausen, commander of the Hessians at the battle of Springfield, near Newark, June 23, 1780.

But this was all vision, Tabitha, to me,
Not an officer came, so much as to tea.
The Major himself, who has always some story
To lessen the worth of American glory,
Or ashamed to be seen, or else of the day,
Would not venture to cross me, tho' just in the way;
But stopp'd, like one shot at, then whisked up a lane:
I'm sure the poor man felt a great deal of pain.
At length came the night, overloaded with fears,
And shew'd us on what we had leaned for five years.
The men who had wished for occasions for blows,
Now suffered themselves to be pulled by the nose.
Sir *Harry* it seems, was more sullen than ever,
And *André* complain'd of much bile on the liver.
The Generals all met, as grave as magicians,
The magii of law, or the sagest physicians:
But all that was done, tho' they sat till near night,
Was to keep at their bottle—and not go to fight.

Pray tell me, what think you of these men in York,
Who formerly cross'd like a bit of dry cork,
When nothing was *near* but a regiment or troop,
As easily drove as a boy drives a hoop;
But when that the rebels come close to their eyes,
Pretend not to see them, tho' thicker than flies;
Let Washington's army do just what they please,
While they in their cholic, would seem at their ease.
For my part, dear sister, I hate all conceit,
You know I love something that's solid to eat.

* * * * * * * * * *

Seest thou, my good sister, where you are, these rogues,
Who fight us to death, without stockings or brogues,
They say a French Marquis commands, my dear girl,
Is it not the same, would have cudgeled an Earl?[1]

* * * * * * * * * *

[1] Lord Carlisle.

But stop with this clatter, what, what do I say?
Here's news that the rebels have all gone away;
At least they have march'd to a place called Fort Lee,
Twelve miles from the Major, and twelve miles from me.[1]

* * * * * * * * * *

From the time that Major André was captured (Sept. 23) until he was executed (Oct. 1), Washington was anxious to spare his life. This could not be done, however, without some suitable substitute. The people were clamorous; but he thought if he could secure Arnold, and offer *him* as a sacrifice, the people would be satisfied. He devised a plan to sound the British General as to his willingness to exchange Arnold for André.

After the conviction of André, Washington sent to Sir Henry Clinton a letter, stating the finding of the court, together with a letter from the prisoner. Captain Aaron Ogden,[2] a worthy officer of the New Jersey line, was selected to bear these dispatches to the enemy's post at Paulus Hoeck. He was requested to call on the Marquis de La Fayette before his departure. The Marquis instructed him to sound the commanding officer at that post (who was —— Ayres) whether Sir Henry Clinton might not be willing to deliver up Arnold in exchange for André. Ogden arrived at Paulus Hoeck on the same evening, September 30, and made the suggestion as if accidentally, in the course of conversation with the officer. He was immediately asked if he had any authority from Washington for such an intimation. "I have no such assurance from General Washington," he replied, "but I am prepared to say that if such a proposition were made, I believe it would be accepted, and Major André set at liberty." Full of hope, the officer crossed the river during the night and communicated the matter to Clinton; but the proposi-

[1] *N. J. Gazette, Sept.* 6, 1780.

[2] Subsequently Governor of New Jersey. He was the father of the late Judge E. B. D. Ogden, who for a number of years presided at the Circuit Court in this county, and the grandfather of Frederick B. Ogden, now of Hoboken.

tion was instantly rejected as incompatible with honor and military principle.[1]

After André's execution Washington matured a plan to seize the person of Arnold and bring him to the Jersey shore. The object was twofold; *first*, to bring the traitor to punishment, and *second*, to clear up suspicions of treachery which rested on one of his generals.[2]

To get a man to carry out the delicate and dangerous enterprise, Major Lee suggested the name of John Champe, of Loudon County, Virginia, a sergeant-major in his command, full of bone and muscle, with a saturnine countenance, grave and thoughtful, full of courage and perseverance. Washington was pleased with the qualifications of the man, and intimated that he should be amply rewarded. The Major pictured to Champe the consequences of success; that he would be hailed as the avenger of the people, and would bring to light new guilt, or relieve the innocent. Champe's objections being finally overcome by the arguments of Major Lee, he entered into the enterprise, on condition that he should be protected if unfortunate in the attempt.

The first difficulty which lay before him was a successful desertion. The patrols in the vicinity were numerous, and occasionally extended southward beyond the Liberty Pole. Besides these there were many irregulars, who sometimes scouted after booty as far south as Paulus Hoeck. To make his desertion apparently genuine, he could not receive any noticeable assistance. The only thing which Major Lee could promise was, in case his departure should be discovered before morning, to delay pursuit as long as practicable.

It was now nearly eleven o'clock in the evening of October 20, 1780. His course would be devious, in order to avoid the patrols, and, comparing his watch with Major Lee's, he begged him to delay pursuit, which he was convinced would take place. The Sergeant returned to camp from his interview with Major Lee, took his cloak, valise and orderly book, drew his horse from the picket, and mounting him, pushed out into the darkness, trusting

[1] *Irving's Washington, iv.*, 148.

[2] St. Clair.

to fortune. Within half an hour Captain Carnes informed Major Lee that one of his patrol had fallen in with a dragoon, who, being challenged, put spurs to his horse and escaped. Lee pretended not to understand what had been said, and the captain was obliged to repeat it. "Who can the fellow be?" said the Major; "a countryman probably." "No," replied the captain, "a dragoon sure; probably one from the army, if not one of our own." Lee ridiculed the idea as quite impossible; for during the whole war but one dragoon had deserted from the legion. The captain withdrew and assembled his squadron. He soon returned. The scoundrel was known, and he was none other than the sergeant-major, who had left with his horse, baggage, arms and orderly book. The captain ordered a party to prepare for pursuit, and then requested the Major's written orders. Lee made numerous inquiries and suggestions during the captain's remarks. Presently the pursuing party was ready. Major Lee directed a change in the commanding officer. He would have particular business for the lieutenant in the morning. Cornet Middleton must command the party. This caused further delay. When the cornet appeared the Major gave him instructions: "Pursue so far as you can with safety Sergeant Champe, who is suspected of deserting to the enemy, and has taken the road leading to Paulus Hoeck. Bring him alive, that he may suffer in the presence of the army; but kill him if he resists, or escapes after being taken." Detaining the cornet yet a few minutes, advising him what course to pursue, enjoining him to look for the enemy, he dismissed him and wished him success.

It was now a few minutes after twelve o'clock, and Champe was over an hour in advance. The pursuing party was occasionally delayed by examining the roads to find the tracks of Champe's horse. This was rendered the more easy, as a shower had fallen soon after Champe's departure. When the day broke Middleton pressed on rapidly. Reaching the summit of the hill north of the "Three Pigeons," he saw the fugitive not more than half a mile in front. At the same time Champe saw his pursuers. This gave new wings to his flight, and a race ensued, like the ride of Tam o' Shanter. From where Union Hill now is there was a short route through the woods to the bridge over Mill Creek. Here Middleton divided his force, some taking the near cut, while the others followed the track of Champe. The fugitive was not forgetful of the short cut, but avoided it, fearing he might meet scouts returning from their nightly expeditions near the enemy. Satisfied that Middleton would attempt to intercept his flight to Paulus Hoeck, he resolved to flee to the British galleys lying in Newark bay, near Brown's ferry. These were there as patrol boats to protect Bergen Neck. Entering the village of Bergen, Champe followed the beaten streets, and took the road leading to Brown's ferry. Here Middleton lost track of him, but hastened on to the bridge over Mill Creek at Prior's mill. Reaching the bridge, he found that the fugitive had slipped through his fingers. Without delay he returned to Bergen, and inquired of the villagers if they had seen a dragoon that morning. They had seen him, but could not tell with certainty whither he went. Middleton then spread his party through the village to find the tracks of Champe's horse. They soon found it, and with renewed vigor started in pursuit. They descried Champe in the distance, and he, with a Parthian look, beheld his pursuers. As he dashed on he prepared himself for the final act. He lashed his valise to his shoulders and threw away unnecessary *impedimenta*. His pursuers were gaining upon him, and by the time he got abreast of the galleys were within two or three hundred yards of him. Then quickly dismounting, he ran across the meadow, plunged into the bay and swam for the boats, calling for help. This was readily given. The British fired upon Middleton, and sent a boat to meet Champe. Thus he was safely within the enemy's lines, and they were fully satisfied of the genuineness of his desertion.

Champe enlisted in Arnold's American Legion. He soon discovered that the suspicions of other officers being connected with Arnold's treason were groundless. After much delay and preparation he sent word to Major Lee to meet him with a party of dragoons at Hoboken on a certain night, when he would deliver up Arnold. The day named arrived. Lee, with three dragoons and three led horses, was at the place appointed. The long, anxious hours after midnight came and went, but brought no Champe, no Arnold. The plans had miscarried. On the preceding day Arnold had moved his headquarters to another part of the city. Poor Champe endured many hardships before he could return to his old comrades. He finally escaped while serving under Lord Cornwallis at Petersburg, Virginia.[1]

In connection with Arnold, it is said that one day Mrs. Tuers, of Bergen, while attending market in New York, went into "Black Sam's" hotel. Sam, under pledges of secrecy as to the source of her information, told her that a conspiracy existed somewhere in the American camp, for he had overheard the British officers talking about it. She told her brother, Cornelius Van Ripen (grandfather of the present Cornelius C.) He went to Hackensack and told General Wayne, who sent the information to Washington. The General offered to reward Van Ripen, but he said, "No, I do not serve my country for money; but I would like, if I am captured, that General Washington would protect me." But a few days afterward the treason of Arnold was discovered.

"On Saturday morning last the Refugee Post at Bergen Point, under command of Captain Thomas Ward, was attacked by a party of rebel infantry and horse, consisting of about 200 men. After receiving a smart fire from the artillery and musketry of the Refugees, assisted by a cannonade from the gallies, they were forced to retreat.

"On the preceding night, as Captain Frederick Hauser, in the Refugee gun-boat, was rowing guard, he met, near Brown's ferry, with a detachment of the rebels in five boats, which it seems were intended for the purpose of making good a retreat for the above mentioned party, in case they should happen to be prevented from retreating by the way of Bergen. Upon being hailed and refusing to give an account of themselves, Captain Hauser immediately fired upon them, when two of the boats struck, in which were made prisoners four of the Continental light infantry; the others on board had jumped ashore and made their escape.

[1] *Lee's Memoirs, ii.*, 159.

One other boat was sunk, having, it is said, one killed and two wounded left on board by the crew who deserted it.

"Mr. Charles Homfray, with two others and a boy belonging to the Refugee party, who had landed some time before the rebels were discovered, were taken by some rebel horse; they were immediately pinioned, and otherwise cruelly treated, according to the usual custom of the rebels, when American Loyalists are so unfortunate as to fall in their hands, in which cruelties they are likely to persevere until a full and spirited retaliation shall take place.

"An inhabitant of Bergen, named Van Waggener, was taken by the Refugees on his return from the rebels. He had gone, after reconnoitering the Refugee Post, to give intelligence of the situation. It is also said that the rebels have carried off Mr. John Phillips, a quiet inhabitant, on a suspicion of his having been friendly to our people."—*N. Y. Gazette and Weekly Messenger*, *Oct.* 16, 1780.

"The rebels on Saturday burnt Colonel William Bayard's New House and Barn at Castile, on the North end of Hoebuck, and destroyed all the forage and timber to be found there to a very large amount."—*N. Y. Mercury*, *Aug.* 28, 1780.

"Generals Washington, La Fayette, Greene and Wayne, with many other officers and large bodies of Rebels, have been in the vicinity of Bergen for some days past. They have taken all the forage from the Inhabitants of that place. Their officers were down to Prior's Mill last Friday, but did not seem inclined to make any attack."—*Same Paper.*[1]

[1] In one of these visits to Bergen, Washington and La Fayette dined under an apple tree in the orchard back of Hartman Van Wagenen's house, close by the Bergen Square. This was blown down by the great gale of Sept. 3, 1821. A pleasing reference was made to this incident when the Marquis visited this country in 1824. On Thursday, the 23d of September in that year, he landed in Jersey City. At Lyon's Hotel he was introduced to Governor Williamson and others. Accompanied by a large retinue, he moved on toward Newark. At the Five Corners the Bergen people had gathered in large numbers to do him honor. He was presented with a superb cane, made of the apple tree under which he and his chief had dined, elegantly mounted with gold, with this inscription: "Shaded the hero and his friend Washington in 1779; presented

"Four Refugees that went over to Secacus last Saturday took three Rebel officers, and brought them to town yesterday morning."—*N. Y. Mercury, Sept.* 18, 1780.

"ALL

"LOYAL REFUGEES

THAT are in want of employment, and can bring proper certificates of their loyalty, and are willing to enter themselves under Captain Thomas Ward, now commanding the important post at Bergen Point, will meet with the greatest encouragement, by applying to Captain HOMFRAY at the sign of the Ship, corner of Fair Street, Broadway."—*Rivington's Gazette, Dec.* 23, 1780.

On the 25th of January, 1781, six or seven tories, under command of Cornelius Hatfield, and known as *Hatfield's party*, perpetrated a great outrage in the execution of Stephen Ball, of Rahway. The unfortunate man had been deluded by a declaration of Sir Henry Clinton, then on Staten Island, that all persons who would bring provisions to the Island should have liberty to sell the same and return unmolested. Ball carried over several quarters of beef, expecting to return undiscovered by his neighbors. Soon after landing on the Island, he was captured by Hatfield, plundered of his beef, and taken before General Patterson. This officer refused to call a court-martial

---

by the Corporation of Bergen in 1824." It was accompanied by the following address from Dominie Cornelison :

"GENERAL : In behalf of my fellow citizens, I bid you a hearty and cordial welcome to the town of Bergen, a place through which you traveled during our revolutionary struggles for liberty and independence. Associated with our illustrious Washington, your example inspired courage and patriotism in the heart of every true American.

"You, sir, left your abode of ease, affluence and happiness, to endure the hardships and privations of the camp. To enumerate your martial deeds is at this time unnecessary ; yet they awaken and call forth our warmest gratitude. As a tribute of esteem and veneration, permit me, sir, to ask the favor of your acceptance of this small token of respect, taken from an apple tree under which you once dined, and which once afforded you a shelter from the piercing rays of noonday ; and, although it possesses no healing virtue, may it still be a support. And may you, sir, after ending a life of usefulness and piety, be admitted into the regions of everlasting joy and felicity."—*Sentinel of Freedom, Sept.* 28, 1824.

to try him, on the ground that he had not committed offence. He was then taken before General Skinner, who also refused to try a man who had brought them relief. Then Hatfield held a mock trial over him, under the pretence that he had injured one of his party. The accounts of his treatment previous to execution greatly differ. The following account of the whole affair is supposed to have been written by the Rev. James Caldwell, "the rousing gospel preacher":

"Then Hetfield and his party robbed Ball of what property he had with him, took him to Bergen Point, and without the form even of a trial, immediately told him he had but ten minutes to live. Ball urged that he only went over with provisions under the declaration; and when he found they were determined to take his life, he begged for a few minutes longer, but his request was refused; but if he had a desire that any person should pray with him, one of their party should officiate. When he was near expiring, James Hetfield, one of the banditti, put a knife in his hand, and swore that he should not go into the other world unarmed. His executioners were, Cornelius Hetfield, John Smith Hetfield, Job Hetfield, James Hetfield, sen., James Hetfield, jr., Elias Mann and Samuel Mann, all of Elizabethtown, and Job Smith of Secaucus.

"Ball's father obtained a flag to get the corpse of his son, but was not suffered to land."[1]

The refugees claimed the following to be a true statement of the case, and which, without doubt, should be taken *cum grano salis*:

"He was taken to Bird's Point, and indulged with a fair hearing and regular trial before a court-martial, consisting of Eleven members appointed for the purpose. Without hesitation he confessed himself to be a spy, and that he came out of the rebel lines under Col. Dayton's pass. It also appeared that Ball had acted a principal part in the late tragedy of Thomas Long's sufferings and death, and that he stripped Long of his boots and

---

[1] *N. Y. Packet, March* 1, 1781.

stockings, when he was wounded. Ball took paper steeped in spirits, and dressed the wounds and then set the paper on fire. Long was then driven a long distance (his toes having been crushed with the butt end of a musket), put into a hog pen and fed on corn. He was then put to death by Ball and others, as a spy. Upon this state of facts he was condemned and executed as a spy."[1]

He is said to have been hung on a small persimmon tree near the tide mill on Constapel's Hoeck. After his death the rope was cut and he fell into his grave. His remains were afterward removed to Newark.

At the close of the war, Cornelius Hatfield fled to Nova Scotia. In 1807, he returned, and was arrested for the crime. He was brought before Judge Pennington on *Habeas Corpus*, and discharged on the 13th of October, 1807, on the ground that, by virtue of the sixth article of the treaty of 1783, he was not answerable.[2]

"A party of rebels came to, and plundered Bergen last Friday."—*N. Y. Mercury, April* 2, 1781.

"Last Friday night a party went from Newark and captured two sloops lying near the Refugee Post on Bergen shore, out of which they took 8 prisoners, who were sent to Morristown."—*N. Y. Packet, Aug.* 30, 1781.

"On the 21st of August, 1780, Captain William Harding with about 40 men of the Refugee post on Bergen Neck, went out as far as Newark, and took four prisoners and about 30 cattle, which he brought to Fort De Lancey."—*Rivington's Gazette, No.* 511.

"Last Wednesday night a party of Ward's plunderers from Bergen Neck, came to the Neighborhood of Hackensack, where they collected a number of cattle, which the inhabitants retook,

---

[1] *N. Y. Mercury,* March 5, 1781. The probability is strong that there is not a word of truth in this attempted justification. Long was a New Jersey tory, who was put to death in 1779.

[2] *Centinel of Freedom, Oct.* 27, 1807. Counsel for the prisoner, Col. Ogden, Mr. Chetwood and I. H. Williamson; for the prosecution, Messrs. McWhorter, Van Arsdale and Halsey.

and killed and wounded several of the miscreants."—*N. J. Journal, Sept.* 5, 1781.

"On Wednesday evening last a party of eleven men under Captain William Harding went from Fort De Lancey on Bergen Neck to Closter, and captured a Rebel Guard of six men, and fifteen cattle, and took them safely to the Fort."—*N. Y. Mercury, Sept.* 17, 1781.

In September, 1781, Prince William Henry, the third son of George III., afterward William IV., then a midshipman under Admiral Digby, arrived in New York. Among the British and tories he was the lion of the day. The Refugees on Bergen Neck, on the first of October, laid at his feet the following submissive address:

"To His Royal Highness Prince William Henry.

"We, his Majesty's dutiful and Loyal Subjects, the Refugees stationed on Bergen Neck, beg leave to address your Royal Highness (through the channel of our commanding officer) on your safe arrival in America. It is impossible for us to express the satisfaction, that is visible in the face of every individual, belonging to our small party, at so distinguished an honor, paid to the loyal inhabitants of this continent, by the arrival of so amiable and distinguished a character as the son of our Royal Sovereign.

"The measures pursued by a designing, base set of men, early in this unnatural contest, obliged us to leave our habitations, and fly for safety to his Majesty's troops; since which we have let our persecutors (who meant our destruction) feel the effects of our resentment; and convinced them that we contended for that, which every man at the risk of his life ought to defend.

"Therefore we flatter ourselves that your Royal Highness is convinced of our sincerity, of our attachment to their Majesties, and the Royal Progeny; (which we are always ready to give fresh proofs of,) praying for that day when rebellion may be crushed, and peace established throughout this continent, and his Majesty's Standard displayed triumphant by land and sea. May Heaven protect your Royal Highness in time of danger, and permit you to return crowned with the laurels of victory to your Royal Parents.

" *Fort De Lancey on Bergen Neck*, 1*st October*, 1781."

This address was presented to the Prince by Major Tom Ward and his officers. Through Admiral Digby, the Prince replied :

"COMMANDANT'S HOUSE,
"*New York*, *Oct.* 3, 1781.

"The humble address of his Majesty's dutiful and loyal Subjects, the Refugees stationed on Bergen Neck, has been received by his Royal Highness.

"His Royal Highness has seen with pleasure the loyal Sentiments contained in the address, and Rear Admiral Digby will take care to make them known to his Majesty.

"ROBERT DIGBY.

" *To the Commanding Officer of the Loyal Refugees stationed on Bergen Neck.*"[1]

"Last Thursday sennight Captain Baker Hendricks with a party of men in whale-boats went down Newark Bay near the Kills, where he boarded and stripped two wood-boats and took one prisoner; and on Thursday night last, he landed a small party of men on Bergen Neck, near the Refugee Post, where he took two prisoners ; and on his return took three noted villains." —*N. J. Journal*, *Dec.* 12, 1781.

"Last Thursday morning a detachment of the Jersey Brigade, under Captain Bowmay, who were joined by a party of Militia, went across the sound on the ice to the Refugee Post on Bergen Neck, where they captured three of the miscreants, one of whom was of a sable hue; they bayonetted the negro, who refused to surrender.[2] No artifice could induce them to sally out ; therefore no other trophies were obtained than those above mentioned." —*N. J. Journal*, *Feb.* 13, 1782.

The following is a tory account of the same affair :

[1] *Rivington's Gazette*, *Oct.* 6, 1781.

[2] Jasper Zabriskie saw this negro three days afterward going over the river to New York, apparently all right.

"On Thursday morning before sunrise, two hundred Rebels from a New Jersey Brigade, attacked Fort De Lancey, commanded by Major Ward. They had meditated the attack for some time and lay for two nights upon their arms. The advanced sentinel, a negro, was bayonetted. They were driven off. They then formed in three columns on the ice, were again attacked and fled."—*N. Y. Mercury, Feb.* 11, 1782.

"FORT DE LANCEY, *March* 31, 1782.

"The night of the 29th instant, a party of rebels came down from Newark and landed at Bergen Neck, took seven prisoners who lodged in houses along the shore. The commanding officer sent a party to intercept them, and coming to the whale-boat almost simultaneously, the party hailed the rebels and were fired upon, and at that time not knowing that they had any of our men along with them, returned the fire, killed two of our own men that were prisoners and wounded two others. One rebel was killed and two mortally wounded."—*Rivington's Gazette, No.* 573.

"*April* 20, 1782.

"We are informed that it was Lieut. John Buskirk of Lieut.-Col. Buskirk's Battalion of the New Jersey volunteers, who went from Staten Island to Second River, and at Schuyler's House, captured Sir James Jay."[1]—*Ibid, No.* 580.

About the first of September, 1782, Fort Delancey on Bergen Neck was evacuated and burned;[2] and on Saturday, October 5, Major Ward with his despised and motley crew of Refugees embarked for Nova Scotia, carrying with them implements of husbandry, one year's provisions, and the undying hatred of all Americans.[3] From this time until the close of the war, Paulus

---

[1] A brother of John Jay, and a member of the State Senate of New York.

[2] *N. J. Journal, Sept.* 11, 1782.

[3] *Ibid, Oct.* 9, 1782. The patriots who had suffered at the hands of their tory neighbors rejoiced at their exile, and in song sneered at their future home:

"Nova Scotia, that cold, barren land,
Where they live upon shell-fish and dig in the sand."

Hoeck was the only foothold which the British had in New Jersey. From this point they continued to forage over the county and raid into adjacent parts.

The enemy evacuated Paulus Hoeck on the 22d day of November, 1783.[1] On the 25th they evacuated New York, and a few days afterward Washington passed through the Hoeck on his way to his home at Mount Vernon. Peace once more smiled upon an afflicted land.

---

[1] *Irving's Washington, iv.*, 438.

CHAPTER VIII.—Duels.

The Duel ground at Weehawken—Duels between Aaron Burr and John B. Church—Goerge I. Eacker and Price—George I. Eacker and Philip Hamilton—John Langstaff and Oliver Waldron—Augustus Smith and Archibald M. Cock—De Witt Clinton and John Swartwout—Richard Riker and Robert Swartwout—Aaron Burr and Alexander Hamilton—Isaac Gouverneur and William H. Maxwell—Benjamin Price and Major Green—Stephen Price and Captain Wilson—Commodore Perry and Captain Heath—William G. Graham and Mr. Barton—Henry Aitken and Thomas Sherman.

Perhaps the most interesting spot in the County of Hudson, around which, in spite of its horrors, fancy loves to linger, is the Duel Ground at Weehawken. Before the iconoclastic hand of enterprise had touched it, the whole region round about was charming beyond description. Just south of the bloody ground was the wild ravine adown which leaped and laughed the Awiehaken.[1] Immediately above was King's Point, or "Highwood," boldly looking down upon the Hudson. From this height still opens as fair, as varied, as beautiful a scene as mortal could wish to behold. The haze-crowned city, the bright, broad, tranquil river; the long reach of waters down to the Narrows and beyond; the vessels at anchor, or flitting around the harbor; misty, blue Staten Island—the Hamels Hooftden of the Dutch—swelling up from the lower bay; the opposite shore lined with a forest of masts, while over and beyond the restless city, sparkles and widens the East River. This beautiful but fatal spot, in the early part of the century, strangers coming to New York were sure to visit. It is now partly destroyed by the construction of the Fort Lee Railroad. Its location was two and a half miles above Hoboken. The rocks here rise almost perpendicularly

---

[1] This creek took its rise in the swampy ground near Guttenbergh, flowed southwardly to Union Hill, thence down to the Hudson. At an early day Nicholas Bayard had a mill on this stream. *Winfield's Land Titles*, 37.

to one hundred and fifty feet above the river. Under these heights, about twenty feet above the water, on a grassy shelf about six feet wide, and eleven paces long, reached by an almost inaccessible flight of steps, was the dark and bloody ground. The old cedar which sheltered the plateau when Hamilton fought was there until about four years ago. The sandstone boulder against which he fell was about the same time removed to the top of the hill, where it now lies. The ground was singularly secluded from inquisitive neighbors and meddlesome officials. With no path leading to it along the river or from the heights, its only approach was by boat. About one-third of a mile below stood a little tavern, where occasionally the combatants would breakfast on their way to the ground. In the early part of this century Captain Deas owned the property, and resided on the hill immediately over the fatal spot. He was a peace man. Whenever he scented a duel, he would hurry to the ground, rush in between the parties, and by his *suaviter in modo* or *fortiter in re*, heal their wounded honor and establish peace.

An account of some of these duels in their order will be interesting to the general reader, who, it cannot be doubted, will regret that the challenged party had not the courage to say of the challenger, what Cæsar said of Anthony:

> "Let the old ruffian know
> I have many other ways to die."

Aaron Burr and John B. Church.

Colonel Burr fought his first duel on the 2d of September, 1799. There was a bit of scandal afloat throughout the State of New York that, for legislative services rendered, the Holland Company had canceled a bond held against Burr for $20,000. Mr. Church,[1] who was a brother-in-law of General Hamilton, and sympathized with that eminent man in his dislike of Burr, spoke at a private table in New York, with much freedom of the

[1] Church lived in Robinson street, N. Y. The funeral of Hamilton was from his house.

existing rumor, and apparent belief in the truth of the charge. This was reported to the victim of the slander.

Condemn the practice of dueling as we may, there are offences against personal reputation for which society has not furnished a remedy. The good name, dearly earned and prized above rubies, may be lost without deserving by the foul breath of the backbiter and slanderer; and where is the remedy? It is not necessary that he render himself open to an action at law; a shrug of the shoulder is sufficient to start on its career the lie that shall bowl down a dozen reputations. Contradict it, do you say? Why, the strongest proof of the total depravity of the human race is found in the fact that nine-tenths—is it put too high?--of the community would believe a lie rather than the truth. Let the slander go, say you; it cannot hurt a solid reputation. Why, the brighest steel may be tarnished with a breath. Upon this subject, one can readily believe that an intelligent man might soon argue himself into a belief that dueling, under certain circumstances, would not be such a bad thing after all. Certainly *one* effectual method of silencing slanderous tongues would be to subject the head in which it rudely wags to the damaging effects of a well-aimed minié.

For this slander Burr sought about the only redress which such a vile crime affords—*he challenged the slanderer.* The challenge was accepted; Mr. Hammond acting as the second of Mr. Church, and Judge Burke of South Carolina as the second of Colonel Burr. The parties, attended by their seconds and a surgeon, met on the duel ground at Weehawken on Monday evening about sunset. Mr. Parton says that connected with this duel was an incident which furnished the town-gossip with a joke and a by-word for many a day. Before leaving home Colonel Burr had been particular to explain to his second that the balls were cast too small for his pistols, and that chamois leather, cut to the proper size, must be greased and put around them to make them fit. Leather and grease were put in the case with the pistols. After the principals had been placed at ten paces apart, Burr noticed his second vainly endeavoring to drive in the ramrod with a stone, and at once suspected that the grease had been forgotten. A moment after, the pistol was handed to him. With that singular coolness which he was wont to exhibit at critical moments, he drew the ramrod, felt the ball, and told the judge it was not home.

"I know it," replied the second, wiping the perspiration from his face. "I forgot to grease the leather; but you see, your man is ready; don't keep him waiting. Just take a crack as it is, and I'll grease the next."

At the word, shots were exchanged, without any other effect than that the ball from Mr. Church's pistol passed through Burr's coat. The pistols were about being reloaded for a second shot, when Mr. Church made an apology which was acceptable to Burr's second, whereupon the principals shook hands, and returned to the city.[1]

Eacker and Price—Eacker and Hamilton.

George I. Eacker was born at Palatine, in the State of New York. At the time of the following event he was twenty-seven years of age, a promising member of the New York Bar, and in politics a sympathizer with Colonel Burr. Price, a friend of Mr. Hamilton, is supposed to have been a son of Stephen Price, lessee of the Park Theatre. Philip Hamilton was the eldest son of Alexander Hamilton, and in the twentieth year of his age. On the 4th of July, 1801, Eacker had pronounced an oration in the city of New York, which was commended by nearly everybody, and would have been by all, only for the party spirit, which at that time was very bitter, and blinded one to every virtue in an opponent. On Friday evening, November 20, 1801, Mr. Eacker, in company with Miss Livingston and others, occupied a box in the Park Theatre. In an adjoining box were young Price and Hamilton. They made some ironical remarks about Eacker's Fourth of July oration, which seemed to be intended for the ear of the young lady. Eacker looked around,

[1] *Parton's Life of Burr,* 240. *Centinel of Freedom, Sept.* 10, 1799.

and saw Price and Hamilton laughing. The following account of what happened between this time and the meeting at Weehawken was written by Mr. Lawrence, a young gentleman who went to the theatre with Mr. Eacker, and accompanied him through every stage of the controversy:

"He took no further notice of their conduct, but joined immediately in conversation with his party, and made use of every means to prevent its being observed by them that he was the subject of ridicule to the gentlemen behind. Immediately preceding the pantomime, the box being full, Messrs. Hamilton and Price, leaving the opposite side of the house, again intruded into the box occupied by Mr. Eacker and his party. At the moment of entrance, they commenced a loud conversation, replete with the most sarcastic remarks upon Mr. Eacker. Their manner was more indecent, if possible, than their conversation. Mr. Eacker himself, thus pointedly the object of contempt and ridicule, and his name being mentioned aloud, could no longer sustain the painful sensation resulting from his situation. He determined to leave the box, and remonstrate with Mr. Hamilton privately, in the lobby. As he stepped into the lobby with his back toward Messrs. Hamilton and Price, covered with agitation and shame to be thus treated, he exclaimed, 'It is too abominable to be publicly insulted by a set of rascals!' 'Who do you call damned rascals?' was the immediate inquiry, repeated again and again. Mr. Eacker felt anxious to avoid a brawl in a theatre, and observed to the gentleman that he lived at No. 50 Wall street, where he was always to be found. 'Your place of residence has nothing to do with it,' was the reply. Upon this, some persons observing an intention, as they supposed, to assault Mr. Eacker, and desirous to prevent a disturbance in the theatre, stepped before the gentlemen, and with difficulty prevented their approaching Mr. Eacker. Mr. Eacker then requested them to make less noise, and proposed retiring to some private place. On the way to the tavern, Messrs. Price and Hamilton peremptorily insisted upon Mr. Eacker's particularizing the person to whom he had applied the appellation of *rascal*. Mr. Eacker demanded of them, '*whether they came into the box on purpose to insult him.*' '*That is nothing to the purpose,*' was the reply. '*We insist upon your particularizing the person you meant to distinguish by the appellation of* rascal.' '*Did you mean to insult me?*' again repeated Mr. Eacker. 'We insist upon a direct answer,' was reiterated. 'Well then, you are both rascals.' Upon leaving the house, Messrs. Price and Hamilton conducted themselves in such a manner as would inevitably, if continued, have drawn the attention of persons in the street. Mr. Eacker said, 'Gentlemen, you had better make less noise; I shall expect to hear from you.' 'That you shall,' was the immediate reply. Mr. Eacker returned to the theatre, and had not been there long before he received a message from Mr. Price, requesting him, in very laconic terms, to appoint his time and place of meeting."—*Am. Citizen & Adv. No.* 529, *vol. ii.*

Mr. Hamilton, on the same Friday night, called on Mr. David S. Jones, who consulted John B. Church, the uncle of young Hamilton. They framed a message to Mr. Eacker, requiring an explanation of the offensive expressions he had used to Hamilton. This was delivered to Eacker about half-past eleven o'clock on Friday night, in the presence of Mr. Lawrence. No explanation was given, but Mr. Eacker said that after the affair with Price was over, he would receive any communication from Hamilton.

On Sunday, November 22, 1801, at twelve o'clock, noon, Eacker and Price, accompanied by their seconds, Mr. Lawrence and James Lynch, met at Weehawken. They exchanged three shots, without effect, when the seconds interposed. The parties, however, wished another shot, and agreed that after that they would shake hands. The fourth shot was had without effect, and a reconciliation ensued, Price remarking that *Eacker was such a damned lath of a fellow that he might shoot all day to no purpose!*

As soon as young Hamilton ascertained that the affair with Price was over, between one and two o'clock on Sunday afternoon, he renewed his communication to Mr. Eacker. On Monday, November 23, 1801, about three o'clock in the afternoon, the parties, accompanied by their seconds, Mr. Cooper, the actor, in behalf of Eacker, and David S. Jones in behalf of Hamilton, met at Weehawken. After the word had been given, a pause of a minute, perhaps more, ensued, before Mr. Eacker discharged his pistol. He had determined to wait for Hamilton's fire, and Hamilton, it is said, reserved his fire, in obedience to the commands of his father. Eacker then leveled his pistol with more accuracy, and at the same instant Hamilton did the same. Eacker fired first, but almost simultaneously with Hamilton. The latter's fire, it is said, was unintentional, and in the air. The ball from Eacker's pistol entered Hamilton's right side, just above the hip, passed through his body, and lodged in his left arm. He was immediately taken over to the city, where he died the next morning at five o'clock.

Eacker died of consumption in 1804, and was buried in St. Paul's churchyard, near Vesey street.

Langstaff and Waldron.—Smith and Cock.

These duels were fought on the 25th of December, 1801, at Weehawken, though the papers of that day speak of Powles Hook. This place and Hoboken were spoken of indiscriminately in the Eacker and Hamilton duel, when we know that it was fought at the regular dueling ground. From the *Daily Advertiser* of Monday, Dec. 28, 1801, the following is taken:

"In consequence of a difference arising between Mr. John Langstaff and Mr. Oliver Waldron, Jun., of this city, they met on Friday afternoon at Powles Hook, accompanied by their seconds, when, after exchanging two shots, the matter was amicably settled; but the seconds, Mr. Augustus Smith and Mr. Archibald M. Cock, having some dispute on account of the ground, they exchanged shots, when the latter received a slight wound in the face." These parties were mere striplings, not over twenty years of age.

On the same day the following leading questions were put to the young duelists in the *Spectator*:

"1st. What was the cause that gave rise to so serious a mode of settling a difference? Is this the new and fashionable way of honor; or why could it not have been settled without exchanging shots?

"2d. What was the difference between the seconds respecting the ground; and did the eager and fighting appetites of the principals insist on fighting without having the ground settled?

"3d. Did you not fight at 7 o'clock in the evening—and was not the night so dark you could not see each other at ten yards' distance? A. W."

From the above it will be noticed that the information respecting the immediate facts and circumstances of the duels were meagre even at the time. It is the same, to a greater or less extent, with all the duels of which an account will be given The reason is that they were in violation of a positive law, although sanctioned and demanded by society. Though under this demand the law was dead, yet it had sufficient terrors to induce the covering up of facts connected with this mode of healing wounded honor.

Clinton and Swartwout.

John Swartwout was a political friend of Colonel Burr, and De Witt Clinton of General Hamilton. Around these last two names seemed to cluster all the political likes and dislikes of that day. In a moment of forgetfulness Mr. Clinton had used certain language concerning Mr. Swartwout, which called forth the following letter:

"New York, 25*th July*, 1802.

"Sir: I am informed that you have lately, in a conversation held at Mr. Ezekiel Robins's, taken very unwarrantable liberties with my character, permitting yourself to use expressions relative to me too gross to be repeated. From your character and standing in society, I presume you will not hesitate to recognize or disavow these charges, and if true, to make me a prompt and suitable reparation.

"I have made my friend Col. Smith acquainted with my feelings and expectations on this subject; at my particular request he does me the honor to present this. He will receive your answer, and act accordingly.

"I have the honor to be, Sir, yours, &c.,

"JOHN SWARTWOUT.

"The Hon. De Witt Clinton, Esq."

Colonel Smith delivered this letter on the morning of the 26th. Mr. Clinton asked what the expressions were to which objection was taken. Colonel Smith replied, *Liar, Scoundrel and Villain.* Mr. Clinton said he recollected having applied the first two to Mr. Swartwout, explained how he came to use them, but refused any apology. The following is his letter:

"NEW YORK, *July* 26, 1802.

"SIR: Having understood that you have, on various occasions and in relation to the controversy respecting Mr. Burr, represented me as being governed by unworthy motives, I have, without hesitation, affixed to such suggestions such epithets as I thought they merited.

"With regard to the conversation that took place at Mr. Robins's, it was predicated upon a full conviction that this system of conduct had been adopted by you. As you have not thought proper to detail, in your letter, the expressions attributed to me, but have referred me to Col. Smith for them, he will in the same way inform you of those which my recollection recognizes.

"I have only to add that any further arrangements you may think proper to make will be attended to by me, with all the promptitude which a regard to the circumstances of the case may require.

"I am, sir, your most obedient servant,

"DE WITT CLINTON.

"John Swartwout, Esq."

On the same (Monday) night Mr. Clinton sent for Richard Riker, who called the next morning and consented to act as Mr. Clinton's friend. Mr. Riker called upon Colonel Smith on Wednesday morning at ten o'clock. They agreed that the "business might be amicably adjusted." Mr. Riker wrote out the following *projet:*

"If Mr. Swartwout will declare that he has not represented Mr. Clinton, in relation to the controversy respecting Mr. Burr, as being governed by unworthy motives, Mr. Clinton will declare that he used the epithets with respect to Mr. Swartwout, *only* in consequence of this supposed imputation, which being disavowed by Mr. Swartwout, he (Mr. Clinton) readily withdraws the epithets complained of, and as a gentleman apologizes for the use of them. These mutual declarations to be made in the presence of Col. Smith and Mr. Riker, and a written statement, signed by Col. Smith and Mr. Riker, to be exchanged."

This proposition was submitted to Mr. Swartwout, and by him rejected, and the following was declared to be the only apology acceptable. It was sent to Mr. Clinton for his signature:

"Having, in the course of a conversation, made use of expressions reflecting on John Swartwout, Esq., I do fully and freely withdraw those expressions as intemperate and unfounded, and request Mr. Swartwout to accept this apology from me for having used them."

Mr. Clinton peremptorily refused to sign anything of this kind, and nothing remained but to settle preliminaries for a meeting of the parties. At one o'clock on Wednesday, July 28, 1802, Colonel Smith and Mr. Riker met at Mr. Little's, on the 29th selected the place of meeting, and on the 30th agreed upon the following

"ARRANGEMENT.

"1. To leave this Island from different points in two boats precisely at 5 o'clock on Saturday P. M., and to proceed to the place proposed. The party first arriving will wait the landing of the other: each boat shall be rowed by four confidential persons *only*, who shall remain in their respective boats until called for. These persons are not to be armed in any manner whatever. There will be but seven persons in each boat, viz., the Principal, his Second, one Surgeon, and four Oarsmen. The Surgeons may attend in silence on the ground.

"2d. The distance between the parties to be ten yards, measured by the seconds, and the positions shall be distinctly marked.

"3d. The seconds shall determine by lot the choice of position.

"4th. The pistols are not to exceed eleven inches in the barrel. They are to be smooth bores, and to be loaded by the seconds in each other's presence, showing a smooth ball.

"5th. The gentlemen will stand with their backs to each other at their respective stations, and in this position shall each receive a pistol, and the seconds having determined by lot who gives the word, he to whom the lot falls shall take his position in the centre, retired from the line of fire, and shall distinctly say: 'Attention, gentlemen—*To the right face*'—upon which they shall face to the right and fire with promptitude; if one fires before the other, the opposite second shall say, 'One, two, three, fire,' and he shall fire.

"6th. The left hand shall not be brought in support of the right arm, nor be placed on the right breast or side.

"7th. If either should be wounded before he has fired, and means to fire, he shall, if he can stand *unsupported*, be entitled to his shot, and not otherwise. If either has fired, is wounded and means to proceed, he shall receive no assistance; his second will only exchange the pistol. If he falls forward the second will repost him.

"8th. At the exchange of pistols correct positions are to be resumed, and the words given as in Article 5.

"9th. A snap or flash to be considered a fire. The pistol must not be recovered.

"10th. Neither party to quit his station without the order or consent of the two seconds.

"R. RIKER,
"W. S. SMITH.

"New York, July 30, 1802."

With such positive and strict rules and regulations did the parties solemnly proceed in their innocent way of adjudicating the difference "'Twixt tweedledum and tweedledee."

At the time agreed upon the parties, accompanied by Doctors John H. Douglass and Isaac Ledyard, left for the Jersey shore. There the seconds tossed up for position and who should give the word. Both were won by Colonel Smith. There is some difference between the seconds as to what occurred after this, and therefore both of their statements are given. Mr. Riker says:

"The parties having their positions, Col. Smith gave the words distinctly, as he did preceding each succeeding fire. They fired without effect. Mr. Clinton then requested me to ask Mr. Swartwout—which I did through Col. Smith—whether he was satisfied, declaring at the same time that he bore him no resentment, and would be willing to meet him on terms of their original friendship. Mr. Swartwout declared he was not satisfied. The pistols were again loaded and delivered to the gentlemen. They turned at the word and fired, as before, without effect. The same declarations were made by Mr. Clinton, and the same question put, the answer being as before. The pistols were a third time loaded, and upon the words, '*Attention, gentlemen,*' being pronounced by Col. Smith, I observed Mr. Swartwout turning, and he was nearly round before Col. Smith had pronounced the words, '*to the right face,*' upon which I said, '*stop.*' He paused a moment, and fired a little before Mr. Clinton. I remonstrated against it immediately after, and requested Col. Smith to inform Mr. Swartwout that it *must not be repeated.* I observed that Mr. Clinton had been shot through the coat, and then said to Mr. Swartwout through Col. Smith, and by request of Mr. Clinton as before, 'Mr. Clinton has no enmity to Mr. Swartwout; he is sorry that this disagreement has happened, and is willing to bury all in oblivion; that he was shooting at a man whom he did not wish to injure.' On asking whether he was satisfied, the answer was no, nor would he be until the apology was made which had been demanded A certificate was then presented to Mr. C. by Col. S. Mr. C. read it, handed it back, saying he would sooner fire all night than ask his pardon. The parties again took their stations, with noticeable coolness. The word was given, the gentlemen fired with more deliberation than usual, Mr. C. rather after Mr. S. His ball took effect, upon which Mr. S. immediately called for another pistol. While the pistols were being reloaded the blood flowed profusely from the wound in Mr. S.'s leg, and he looked pale. His surgeon, Dr. Douglass, went to him, and it is said quietly extracted the ball from the other side of his leg. This was contrary to the 7th article of the code adopted by them, and unbeknown to Mr. Riker. When the parties were again ready, Mr. S.'s looks prompted one of the surgeons to remark, 'Mr. Swartwout requires a surgeon,' whereupon Mr. Riker begged Col. S. to repeat to Mr. S., 'Sir, are you satisfied? Mr. Clinton bears you no resentment. He is sorry for what has passed, and will meet you on the score of original friendship.' Mr. S., standing in his place, replied, 'I am not; it is useless to repeat the question.' Then said Mr. C., 'I beg you all to bear witness, I have no enmity to Mr. Swartwout, and I am compelled to shoot at a man whom I do not wish to hurt; but I will sign no paper —I will not dishonor myself.' The word was then again given, the parties fired, and Mr. C.'s ball again took effect. Mr. S. coolly said he was ready to take another shot. Preparations were being made to load the pistols, when Dr. Ledyard, calling from the bank, said: '*Mr. Clinton, don't fire again; Mr. Swartwout wants our assistance.*' Whereupon Mr. C. stepped toward the bank and asked, 'Will it be right to fire again?' Dr. L. said, 'No, by no means.' Mr. C. then asked Mr. Riker what he ought to do. His second, reflecting a moment, said to Col. S.: 'Mr. Clinton shall not fire again.' Mr. S. was then assisted into the boat, Mr. Riker supporting him on the right side and Dr. Ledyard on the left."

Colonel Smith's statement is as follows:

"The ground being correctly measured and intermediate questions adjusted, the gentlemen took their stations, were each presented with a pistol, and, by order, faced to the right and fired, ineffectually. At the request of Mr. Riker I asked Mr. Swartwout: 'Are you satisfied, sir?' He answered, 'I am not.' The pistols then being exchanged, and their positions resumed by order, the gentlemen faced to the right, and fired a second shot without effect. At the request of Mr. Riker, I again addressed

Mr. Swartwout: 'Are you satisfied, sir?' He answered strongly in the negative. We proceeded, and a third shot was exchanged without injury. At the request of Mr. Riker, I again asked Mr. Swartwout: 'Are you satisfied, sir?' He answered: 'I am not; neither shall I be until that apology is made which I have demanded. Until then we must proceed.' I then presented a paper to Mr. Riker containing the apology demanded for Mr. Clinton's signature, observing that we could not spend our time in conversation; that this paper must be signed or proceed. Mr. Clinton declared he would not sign any paper on that subject; that he had no animosity against Mr. Swartwout; would willingly shake hands, and agree to meet on the score of former friendship.

"Mr. Swartwout insisting on his signature to the apology, and Mr. Clinton declining, they stood at their posts, and fired a fourth shot. Mr. Clinton's ball struck Mr. Swartwout's left leg about five inches below the knee; he stood ready and collected. At the request of Mr. Riker, I again addressed Mr. Swartwout: 'Are you satisfied, sir?' He answered, 'It is useless to repeat the question; my determination is fixed, and I beg we may proceed.' Mr. Clinton repeated that he had no animosity against Mr. Swartwout; was sorry for what had passed; proposed to advance, shake hands, and bury the circumstance in oblivion. During this conversation, Mr. Swartwout's surgeon, kneeling by his side, extracted a ball from the opposite side of his leg.[1] Mr. Swartwout standing erect on his post, and positively declining anything short of an ample apology, they fired the fifth shot, and Mr. Swartwout received the ball in the left leg, about five inches above the ankle; still, however, standing steadily on his post, perfectly composed. At the request of Mr. Riker, I again addressed Mr. Swartwout: 'Are you satisfied, sir?' He forcibly answered, 'I am not, sir; proceed.' Mr. Clinton then quit his station, declined the combat, and declared he would fire no more. Mr. Swartwout expressed himself sur-

[1] While Dr. Douglass was performing this operation, the seconds were at the pistol cases. Colonel Smith turned around and said, "Doctor Douglass, what do you do there, sir? go away, or you will be shot."

prised that Mr. Clinton would neither apologize nor give him the satisfaction required; and addressing me, said, 'What shall I do, my friend?' I answered, 'Mr. Clinton declines making the apology required, refuses taking his position, and positively declares he will fight no more; and his second appearing to acquiesce in the disposition of his principal, there is nothing further left for you *now* but to have your wounds dressed.' The surgeons attended, dressed Mr. Swartwout's wounds, and the gentlemen, in their respective barges, returned to the city."

It was said that after the last shot, and while Mr. Swartwout was sitting on a stone bleeding, Mr. Clinton approached him, offered him his hand, and said, "I am sorry I have hurt you so much." Then turning to Colonel Smith, he said, "I don't want to hurt him, but I wish I had the *principal* here. I will meet him when he pleases." He had reference to Aaron Burr.

Riker and Swartwout.

Richard Riker, at the time Deputy Attorney-General of the State of New York, afterward Recorder of the city, and known as Dickey Riker, and Robert Swartwout, a brother of Samuel, Collector of the Port under General Jackson, fought a duel at Weehawken, on Monday, November 21, 1803. The cause lay in a political quarrel—Riker being a firm adherent of De Witt Clinton, and Swartwout a strong personal and political friend of Colonel Burr. Riker fell at the first fire, from a severe wound in the right leg. The wits who subsequently edited "The Croakers" refer to this combat in the following irreverent lines:

"The Riker, like Bob Acres, stood
Edge-ways upon a field of blood,
The where and wherefore Swartwout knows,
Pulled trigger, as a brave man should,
And shot, God bless them—his own toes."

These two parties were indicted in New York for dueling, November, 1804.

Burr and Hamilton.

At last the two political chieftains of New York are about to meet in mortal combat. Their followers, at intervals for the past five years, had met and fought to settle political and personal differences. Now Weehawken is to witness the last meeting of the rival leaders, and on her rocky shore they part—one

DUEL GROUND.

to his grave, the other to be a fugitive on the earth. The duel was fought on the morning of July 11, 1804. It arose, or rather a pretext for it was found, in what may be called the tattling of one Dr. Charles D. Cooper. For political purposes, he had reported that he "could detail a *still more despicable* opinion which General Hamilton *had expressed* of Mr. Burr." Whatever this silly remark may have meant, it was the cause of the controversy which followed, and which ended in the untimely death of a truly great man.

As soon as this expression of Cooper was brought to Burr's attention, he, ripe for a quarrel with his great rival, called upon General Hamilton for "a prompt and unqualified acknowledgment or denial of the use of any expression which would warrant the assertion of Dr. Cooper," and selected William P. Van Ness as his friend, to deliver his letter. Hamilton replied on the 20th of June, but it is manifest that he could not be held responsible for Dr. Cooper's inferences. On the 21st, Burr rejoined as follows:

"SIR: Your letter of the 20th instant has been this day received. Having considered it attentively, I regret to find in it nothing of that sincerity and delicacy which you profess to value.

"Political opposition can never absolve gentlemen from the necessity of a rigid adherence to the laws of honor and the rules of decorum. I neither claim such privilege nor indulge it in others.

"The common sense of mankind affixes to the epithet adopted by Dr. Cooper the idea of dishonor. It has been publicly applied to me under the sanction of your name. The question is not whether he has understood the meaning of the word, or has used it according to syntax, and with grammatical accuracy; but whether you have authorized this application, either directly or by uttering expressions or opinions derogatory to my honor. The time 'when' is in your own knowledge, but no way material to me, as the calumny has now first been disclosed, so as to become the subject of my notice, and as the effect is present and palpable.

"Your letter has furnished me with new reasons for requiring a definite reply."

Mr. Van Ness delivered this letter. Hamilton told him that he considered it *rude and offensive*, and unless it were recalled, the only answer which it was possible for him to make was that

Mr. Burr must take such steps as he might think proper. Nevertheless, he replied in writing as follows:

"SIR: Your first letter, in a style peremptory, made a demand, in my opinion, unprecedented and unwarrantable. My answer, pointing out the embarrassment, gave you an opportunity to take a less exceptionable course. You have not chosen to do it; but by your last letter received this day, containing expressions *indecorous* and improper, you have increased the difficulties to explanation intrinsically incident to the nature of your application.

"If by a 'definite reply' you mean the direct avowal or disavowal required in your first letter, I have no other answer to give than that which has already been given. If you mean anything different, admitting of greater latitude, it is requisite you should explain."

This letter was delivered to his friend, Judge Nathaniel Pendleton, who had been Aid-de-Camp of General Greene, on the 22d of June, but by reason of certain conversations between him and Mr. Van Ness it was not delivered until the 25th. Before the delivery of this letter Mr. Van Ness had addressed a note to General Hamilton asking him "when and where it would be most convenient to receive a communication." It will be seen, therefore, that Colonel Burr had resolved on extreme measures before General Hamilton's second note was delivered to him.

Pending the negotiations previous to the delivery of the letter of the 22d, Judge Pendleton submitted to Mr. Van Ness the following paper, which shows how far General Hamilton was willing to concede:

"General Hamilton says he cannot imagine to what Dr. Cooper may have alluded, unless it were to a conversation at Mr. Taylor's, in Albany, last winter (at which he and General Hamilton were present). General Hamilton cannot recollect distinctly the particulars of that conversation, so as to undertake to repeat them, without running the risk of varying or omitting what might be deemed important circumstances. The expressions are entirely forgotten, and the specific ideas imperfectly remembered; but to the best of his recollection it consisted of comments on the political principles and views of Colonel Burr, and the results that might be expected from them in the event of his election as Governor, without reference to any particular instance of past conduct or to private character."

After the delivery of Hamilton's second letter, Judge Pendleton submitted another paper, dictated by the same kindly spirit:

"In answer to a letter properly adapted to obtain from General Hamilton a declaration whether he had charged Colonel Burr with any particular instance of dishonorable conduct, or had impeached his private character, either in the conversation alluded to by Dr. Cooper, or in any other particular instance to be specified, he would be able to answer consistently with his honor and the truth in substance, that the conversation to which Dr. Cooper alluded turned wholly on political topics, and did not attribute to Colonel Burr any instance of dishonorable conduct, nor relate to his private character; and in relation to any other language or conversation of General Hamilton which Colonel Burr will specify, a prompt and frank avowal or denial will be given."

These propositions being unacceptable to Colonel Burr, a correspondence between the seconds followed. Finally the formal challenge was given by Burr and accepted by Hamilton. The parties prepared for the meeting, which was to be on the 11th of July. Hamilton executed his will, and signed cogent reasons why he should not fight a duel. His own good judgment, his keen sense of moral right, his obligations to his family, his duty to his country and to the requirements of the law, all united to convince him that he had no right to jeopard his life to the demands of a false sentiment. But louder than all these the public voice called upon him to meet his foe in mortal combat, and he, who had faced death on the battle field, had not the courage to refuse. Burr, on the night of the 10th, wrote several letters—one to his Theodosia, the pride of his heart—and then lay down and slept till morning. Better for him had that sleep been his last—better for him had that morning never dawned. At daybreak a few of his friends gathered around him. Shortly afterward they proceeded from Burr's house, No. 30 Partition, now Fulton street, to the shore, where Burr, Van Ness, Matthew L. Davis and another (probably Swartwout) embarked, and were rowed over to Weehawken.[1] They arrived on the ground about half-past six o'clock, for it had been previously agreed that he should arrive first. Burr and Van Ness, with coats off, were leisurely removing the underbrush from the ground, "so as to make a fair opening," when Hamilton and his second, accompanied by Dr. Hosack, who had been mutually agreed upon as the surgeon, arrived a few minutes before seven o'clock. The principals and their seconds exchanged salutations, and the seconds proceeded with the usual preparations. They measured the distance, ten full paces, then cast lots for the choice of position and to decide who should give the word. The lot in both cases fell to General Hamilton's second, who chose the upper end of the ledge for his principal. The pistols were then loaded in each other's presence and the principals placed, Hamilton looking over the river toward the city, and Burr toward the heights under which they stood. Judge Pendleton gave Hamilton his pistol, and asked:

"Will you have the hair-spring set?"

"*Not this time*," was the quiet reply.

Judge Pendleton then explained to the parties the rules which were to govern them in firing, which were as follows:

> "The parties being placed at their stations, the second who gives the word shall ask them whether they are ready; being answered in the affirmative, he shall say *Present;* after this the parties shall present and fire *when they please.* If one fires before the other, the opposite second shall say, 'One, two, three, fire,' and he shall then fire or lose his fire."

He then asked if they were prepared. Being answered in the affirmative, he gave the word *Present*, as had been agreed on, and both parties presented and fired in succession. The intervening time is not expressed, as the seconds do not precisely agree on that point. The fire of Colonel Burr took effect, and

---

[1] Wilson was one of the rowers.

General Hamilton almost instantly fell, his pistol going off involuntarily. Colonel Burr then advanced toward Hamilton with a manner and gesture which to Judge Pendleton seemed to be expressive of regret,[1] but, without speaking, turned about and withdrew, being urged from the field by his friend, shielded, as it is stated, by an umbrella, with a view to prevent his being recognized by the surgeon and bargemen, who were then approaching. Colonel Burr entered his barge and returned to the city *to breakfast!*

When Hamilton fell his second immediately sprang forward and lifted him to a sitting posture. The ball had struck the second or third false rib, and fractured it about in the middle; it then passed through the liver and diaphragm and lodged in the first or second lumbar vertebra. Dr. Hosack says: "His countenance of death I shall never forget. He had at that instant just strength to say, 'This is a mortal wound, doctor,' when he sank away and became to all appearance lifeless. His pulses were not to be felt, his respiration was entirely suspended, and upon laying my hand upon his heart and perceiving no motion there, I considered him as irrevocably gone. I, however, observed to Mr. Pendleton that the only chance for his reviving was immediately to get him upon the water. We therefore lifted him up and carried him out of the wood to the margin of the bank, where the bargemen aided us in conveying him into the boat, which immediately put off." Before they reached the opposite shore he revived. He survived until the next day about two

---

[1] Burr was considered a good shot, and he is said to have remarked on the afternoon of the same day, by way of apology for firing a little below the breast, that had it not been for smoke or a rising momentary mist, or something of that nature, which intercepted his vision, he should have lodged the ball exactly in the centre of Hamilton's heart. *N. Y. Spectator, July* 28, 1824.

When in England, in 1808, he gave Jeremy Bentham an account of the duel, and said *he was sure of being able to kill him;* and "So," records Bentham, "*I thought it little better than a murder.*" *Sabine on Dueling*, 212. Such was the view held by the grand jury of Bergen county. That body indicted him in November, 1804, for murder. On November 20, 1807, this indictment was quashed by the Supreme Court, on motion of Colonel Ogden. *Centinel of Freedom, Nov.* 24, 1807.

o'clock in the afternoon, when he died, in the forty-eighth year of his age.

Immediately after the duel a question arose as to Hamilton's firing—whether it was intentional or not. The next day Judge Pendleton and a friend went over to the ground to see if they could discover some traces of the course of the ball from Hamilton's pistol. They ascertained that the ball passed through the limb of a cedar tree[1] at an elevation of about twelve and a half feet from the ground, between thirteen and fourteen feet from where Hamilton stood, and about four feet wide of the direct line between him and Colonel Burr on the right side.

A few months after the duel the St. Andrew's Society, of which Hamilton was president, erected a monument to his memory on the ground where he fell. It was surrounded with an iron railing, and while it stood was visited by thousands every summer.

It was intentionally destroyed about the year 1820. The monument seemed to arouse in the people of New York a spirit of emulation. A writer in *The Columbian*, on July 13, 1815, who signed himself "HOBOKEN," wrote of the existence of Hamilton's monument, and said, "It is a subject of complaint to the citizens in the vicinity, and a standing absurdity and outrage on the morals, manners and feelings of society. By the pernicious effect of a conspicuous example, the young and chivalrous are invited to combat and feel a degree of vain glory in measuring ground on the spot where that great man fell from all his glory and usefulness, and furnished a bloody beacon to posterity, which should be at least shrouded from the light of day. Nowadays the boats arrive from your island in broad daylight, the combatants take their stand on each side of the ominous monument, and before the inhabitants can reach the spot the mischief is done, and the *unfortunate* survivors hurried off, too soon to be arrested by the gathering neighborhood. Such is the sensation, I understand, excited by the use of this modern

---

[1] This tree was destroyed when the New York and Fort Lee Railroad was constructed.

Aceldama, that it is not to be expected the pillar will long retain its station, it being considered as a baleful nuisance, not a vestige of which should be suffered to remain on the earth. But for the eminent cause of its origin, I should be almost as willing to have a gallows near my house."

With such a feeling growing in the community, it could not be expected that the monument would long survive. Stansbury, who visited the place August 20, 1821,[1] says, "The monument

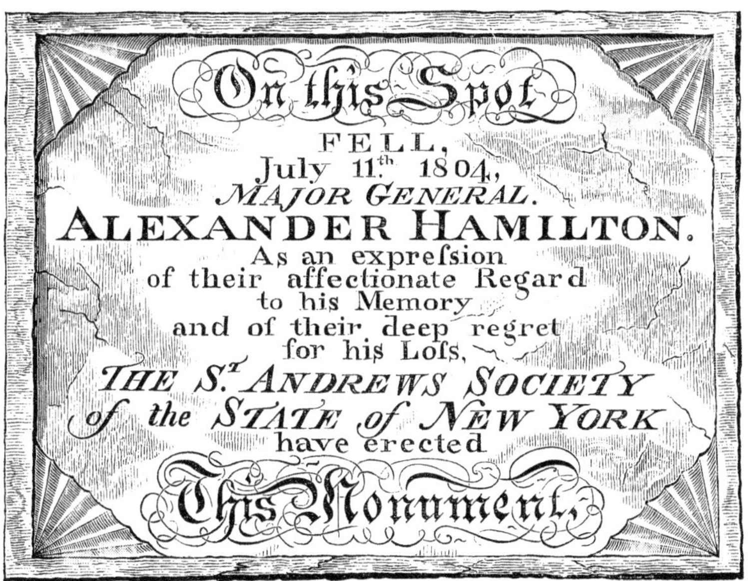

FAC-SIMILE OF THE TABLET IN HAMILTON'S MONUMENT.

that was erected here to the memory of General Hamilton is now taken to pieces by the proprietor of the soil and conveyed to his house, under pretence of its having been too much resorted to for purposes of dueling." From this language it is inferable that the removal was then comparatively recent. Captain James Deas was the owner of the property at the time, and was the person who removed the monument. By some means the slab

[1]*Pedestrian Tour*, 14.

which bore the inscription was taken from Captain Deas's possession. About the year 1833 Mr. Hugh Maxwell, President of the St. Andrew's Society, learned that it had been seen in a junk shop in New York. He traced it up, redeemed it from its ignoble position and presented it to the late James G. King, who about that time had become the owner of the property on which the monument had been erected. The tablet still remains in possession of his family at Highwood. It is thirty-four inches in length by twenty-six and a half inches in width and two and a half inches in thickness.

Gouverneur and Maxwell.

On Monday, July 10, 1815, the New York papers announced the death, "after a short illness," of Isaac Gouverneur, the second son of Nicholas Gouverneur. This death, following a "short illness," was caused by a duel between him and William H. Maxwell on Saturday, the 8th of July, about seven o'clock in the evening. It was fought with pistols, "near the monument of Hamilton, a beacon which should dissuade and deter, like the pillar of salt, from folly and madness, rather than allure, like an *ignis fatuus*, to rashness, error and destruction." George Watts and Doctor Worthington were the seconds in the duel.

Price and Green.

Benjamin Price was a grocer at Rhinebeck, a brother of William M. Price, who lived in Hackensack, and of Stephen Price, of the Park Theatre. Green was a major in the British army, serving in Canada. Price was at the theatre one evening with a beautiful woman, when Green, in an adjoining box, took the liberty of turning around and staring her full in the face. She complained to Price, and, on a repetition of the offence, he turned and seized the nose of the gallant officer full between his finger and thumb and wrung it most effectually. The officer left the theatre, and soon after a knock was heard at the door of Price's box. He opened it, and there stood the officer, who, with a refreshing simplicity, asked Price what he meant by such behaviour, at the same time remarking that he had not meant to insult the lady by what he had done. "Oh, very well," replied Price, "neither did I mean to insult you by what I did." Upon this they shook hands as sworn brothers. Some time after this Green went to Canada to join his regiment. The facts of the affair, however, had reached Canada before him, and were soon the subject of discussion among his comrades. The officers of his regiment brought it to the notice of his brother officers, one of whom, a Captain Wilson, insisted that Green should be sent to Coventry unless he returned to New York and challenged Price. Green, thus goaded, set to work and practiced for five hours a day until he could hit a dollar at ten paces nine times out of ten. He then came to New York and challenged Price. They fought at Weehawken on Sunday, May 12, 1816. Price was killed at the first fire. The ball crashed into his head and the blood streamed from the wound as he fell. Numerous boats lined the shore, a number of spectators viewed the transaction from the neighboring rocks, and a more horrible sight could not have been imagined. The seconds ran off, and Green took a small boat, crossed the river and boarded a vessel in the bay just about to sail for England. The body of Price was found at Weehawken, with a piece of paper attached to his breast, on which were inscribed the following words: "This is Benjamin Price, boarding in Vesey street, New York; take care of him." The body was taken to the city quietly and buried.

As a sequel to the foregoing duel, Millingen, in his *History of Dueling*, relates the following:

"Some years afterwards, Captain Wilson of the British army, whom we have mentioned above, arrived in this city, from England, on his way to Canada, and put up at the Washington Hotel. One day, at dinner, the conversation turned on the death of Benjamin Price, and the manner thereof. Captain Wilson remarked that he had been mainly instrumental in bringing about the duel, and detailed the circumstances connected therewith. This statement was carried immediately to Stephen Price, who was lying ill of the gout, at home: his friends say that he henceforth implicitly obeyed the instructions of the physician, obtained thereby a short cessation of the gout, and was enabled to hobble out of doors, his lower extremities swaddled in flannel. His first course was to seek the Washington Hotel, and his first inquiry was, 'Is Captain Wilson within?' 'He is,' said the waiter. 'Show me to his room,' said Stephen, and he was shown accordingly. He hobbled up stairs with great difficulty, cursing at intervals the gout and the captain with equal vehemence. He at last entered the captain's room, his feet cased in moccassins, and his hand grasping a stick. Captain Wilson rose to receive him, when he said, 'Are you Captain Wilson?' 'That is my name,' replied the gallant captain. 'Then, sir, my name is Stephen Price. You see, sir, I can scarcely put one foot before the other; I am afflicted with the gout. My object in coming here is to insult you. Shall I have to knock you down, or will you consider what I have said a sufficient insult, and act accordingly?' 'No, sir,' replied the captain, smiling, 'I shall consider what you have said quite sufficient, and shall act accordingly. You shall hear from me.'

"In due time, there came a message from the Captain to Stephen Price; time, place and weapons were appointed, and early one morning a barge left New York, in which were seated, face to face, Stephen Price and Captain Wilson, and two friends; they all landed at Bedlow's Island, the principals took their positions, and Captain Wilson fell dead at the first shot. The captain was buried in the vault there, and Price and the two seconds returned to New York; but his friends (Wilson's) thought that he had gone suddenly to Canada, and always thought that he had died suddenly, or had been killed on his way to England to join his regiment."

Perry and Heath.

Oliver H. Perry, the hero of Lake Erie, was post-captain in

the navy of the United States, and John Heath was captain of marines. While on duty in the Mediditerranean, in 1815, a quarrel arose between them. In the moment of excitement Perry struck Heath. A court-martial followed the difficulty, and both were privately reprimanded by Commodore Chauncey, who commanded the American squadron in that sea. After their return to the United States, Heath sent a challenge to Perry. The communication was received in Rhode Island, where the civil authorities would not permit the duello. Commodore Perry, as early as January, had secured the services of Commodore Decatur as his friend, in anticipation of the challenge. On the 10th of October he went to Washington, to give Captain Heath the satisfaction he demanded. The absence of Commodore Decatur rendered it necessary that he should have another friend for a time, that Captain Heath might be informed of his arrival, and for what purpose he had come. This was done, and the following preliminary arrangements agreed upon between Major Hamilton, on the part of Commodore Perry, and Lieutenant Desha on the part of Captain Heath:

" 1st. It is understood that Commodore Perry is to proceed to Philadelphia, or its vicinity, by the route of Baltimore, where he is to remain until the arrival of Captain Heath's friend.

" 2d. That Captain Heath is to proceed by the way of Frederick and York to Philadelphia, and to remain in the suburbs until the arrangements are made for a meeting between himself and Commodore Perry—his name not to be on the stage bills.

" 3d. Lieutenant Desha and Major Hamilton are to meet at Renshaw's, on Wednesday, after the arrival of the Newcastle boat.

" 4th. The meeting between Commodore Perry and Captain Heath is to take place on Saturday morning, or as soon after as practicable.

" *Washington City, Oct.* 12, 1818."

Endorsed on this preliminary arrangement was the following note:

" Captain Perry desires it expressly to be understood, that in according to Captain Heath the personal satisfaction he has demanded, he has been influenced entirely by a sense of what he considers due from him as an atonement to the violated rules of the service, and not by any consideration of the claims which Captain Heath may have for making such a demand, which he totally denies, as such claims have been forfeited by the measures of a public character which Captain Heath has adopted towards him. If, therefore, the civil authority should produce an impossibility of a meeting at the time and place designated, of which he will take every precaution to prevent, he will consider himself absolutely exonerated from any responsibility to Captain Heath, touching their present cause of difference.

"J. Hamilton, Jun.
"(*For Captain Perry*).

"Approved—
R. M. Desha."

In consequence of the foregoing, the parties assembled at Philadelphia, and Major Hamilton then transferred the above memorandum to Commodore Decatur, introducing to him at the same time Lieutenant Desha as the friend of Captain Heath, when the following arrangements were made:

"1st. It is understood that Captain Perry and his friend are to proceed to New York, or its vicinity, where he is to remain until the arrival of Captain Heath, or until the period which is named in this paper for their meeting.

"2d. That Captain Heath, with his friend, are to follow and remain at some convenient point on the Jersey shore, near the city of New York, and to give information after their arrival to Captain Perry's friend, where such arrangements will be made as may be deemed necessary.

"3d. The parties to be on the point specified, and the notification required by the 2d article given, prior to the approaching Monday, the 19th.

"The parties accordingly met at Weehawken on Monday, October 19, 1818, at 12 o'clock. Captain Perry received the fire of Captain Heath without returning it, when Commodore Decatur immediately stepped forward and declared that Commodore Perry had come to the ground with a determination not to return the fire of Captain Heath, in proof of which he read a letter from Commodore Perry to him, which he had written (and which is herewith subjoined), soliciting him to become his friend, and, therefore, he presumed the party aggrieved was satisfied. Captain Heath having expressed his acquiescence in this opinion, and that the injury he had received from Captain Perry was atoned for, the parties returned to the city.

"We do hereby certify the foregoing is a correct statement.

"Stephen Decatur,
"R. M. Desha."

LETTER OF COMMODORE PERRY.

"Washington, *January* 18, 1818.

"My Dear Commodore: You are already acquainted with the unfortunate affair which has taken place between Capt. Heath and myself. Although I consider, from the course he has thought proper to pursue, that I am absolved from all accountability to him, yet, as I did, in a moment of irritation produced by strong provocation, raise my hand against a person honored with a commission, I have determined, upon mature reflection, to give him a meeting should he call on me; declaring, at the same time, that I cannot consent to return his fire, as the meeting, on my part, will be entirely as an atonement for the violated rules of the service. I request, therefore, my dear sir, that you will act as my friend on this occasion.

"Very truly your friend,
"O. H. Perry.

"Com. Stephen Decatur."

Thus fortunately terminated this unfortunate quarrel between these two worthy officers.

Graham and Barton.

William G. Graham was associate editor of the *New York*

Courier and Inquirer, and a native of Catskill. Mr. Barton was a son of the celebrated Dr. Barton, of Philadelphia. The duel was fought at Weehawken on Wednesday, November 28, 1827. It is said that a dispute arose between them while at the card table at a friend's house, in the course of which Graham struck Barton. A challenge was the consequence, Lewis Asbury and W. McLeod acting as seconds, and Doctor R. Pennell as surgeon.

The night before the meeting Mr. Graham wrote the following letter to his associate, Major Noah:

"11 O'CLOCK.

"DEAR SIR: What may be the result of the unhappy *rencontre* which is to take place in the morning between Mr. Barton and myself cannot, of course, be predicted by me. In the supposition that it will be *fatal*, I bid you *farewell*, in the only language that is now left to me. I am perfectly indifferent as to myself, but I trust most earnestly that Mr. Barton (toward whom I have not the faintest enmity of *any kind*) may escape. *I admit that I am in the wrong*—that, by giving him *a blow*, I have forced him into the condition of a challenge; and by not doing what he has he would have blasted his character as a gentleman forever. In common justice I am bound thus to absolve him from all suspicions of unbecoming conduct respecting the challenge. The provocation, though *slight*, was still a provocation which I could not overlook. It is out of the question for me to explain, retract or apologize. I will not hear of any settlement short of some abject and craven submission from him.[1]

"Mr. Barton is a talking man, who dwells very complacently on his own skill as a marksman, on his experience as a duelist, and on his accuracy as a person of *ton*. I pretend to none of these, and therefore must oppose the most inflexible obstinacy. After he is *perfectly satisfied*, I may, perhaps, apologize—that is, in case I am fatally wounded. It is needless for me to say I heartily despise and detest this absurd mode of settling disputes

[1] It is probable that Mr. Graham intended to say, "He will not hear of any settlement short of some abject and craven submission from *me*."

and *salving* the wounds of honor. But what can a poor devil do except bow to the supremacy of custom?

* * * * * * *

"God bless you.

"W. G. GRAHAM."

Here we see a man of fine genius and noble impulses, who, like the talented Hamilton and the gallant Perry, could coolly stand before the cannon's mouth, yet yielded like a child to the omnipotence of public sentiment. How perverted must be that society which, while it condemns dueling, yet shuns and spurns the man who refuses to *accept* or *send* a challenge when he is insulted. And how weak and ineffectual are laws for the prevention of crime, when those crimes are approved by public sentiment.

On the fatal day Graham arose at four o'clock in the morning, and both parties were on the ground at twenty minutes before six o'clock. The principals took their positions, and at the word exchanged shots without effect. Mr. Graham's second proposed that the parties each advance one step. At the second fire Graham said, "*I am shot*—I am a dead man—Barton, I forgive you," and fell. He was immediately conveyed to the boat in waiting. When laid down, the only words he uttered were, "I am in great pain," and died a few minutes afterward. The ball had entered the right side, about two inches from the *umbilicus*, and passed obliquely through the body, injuring in its passage several important organs, and coming out on the left side about four inches from the spine.

The certificate of the cause of death, which Dr. Pennell gave the next day, is quite unique: "I hereby certify that William Graham, aged 34 years, died on the 28th inst. of vulnus."

AITKEN AND SHERMAN.

On Monday, the 19th of October, 1835, Henry Aitken and Thomas Sherman met on the ground at Weehawken. On the Sunday evening previous they had a difficulty in New York respecting a female, which resulted in a challenge on the part of Sherman. This was accepted by Aitken, and ten o'clock on the following morning was fixed upon as the hour to decide the matter in difference. Mutual friends endeavored to reconcile the difficulty, but in vain. On Monday morning they crossed the Hoboken ferry and went to the ground. Before the preliminaries were settled, Andrew Boyd, a constable, arrived and arrested them. They were brought before Squire Paradise, in Jersey City, who committed them to the Hackensack jail to await the action of the grand jury.

On Tuesday P. M., May 16, 1837, a duel was fought at this place between a Spaniard from Guatemala and a Frenchman living in New York, in which the former was slightly wounded. Some pecuniary transaction was the subject of dispute.

Without being able to discover the particulars, I have met the general fact that a duel was here fought at quite a late period, and that one of the parties, named Bird, was shot through the heart, sprang up nearly ten feet, and fell dead.

So far as I can learn, the last duel fought on this ground was on Sept. 28, 1845. Without the knowledge of the principals, the seconds loaded the pistols with cork. The performance was solemnly gone through with as if in mockery of the many tragedies which had there been enacted. The heroes of this *affaire d'honneur* are not known, but with their farce the curtain drops upon the stage at Weehawken. But as we read its sad history may we not quote from Dr. Nott's funeral oration over Hamilton: "Ah! ye tragic shores of Hoboken, crimsoned with the richest blood, I tremble at the crimes you record against us, the annual register of murders which you keep and send up to God! Place of inhuman cruelty! beyond the limits of reason, of duty, and of religion, where man assumes a more barbarous nature and ceases to be man. What poignant, lingering sorrows do thy lawless combats occasion to surviving relatives."

CHAPTER IX.—FERRIES.

Communipaw ferry—Weehawken ferry—Jersey City ferry—Bergen Point ferry—Hoboken ferry—Brown's ferry—Douw's ferry—Pavonia ferry—Budd's ferry—Bull's ferry—De Klynn's ferry—Elizabethtown Point ferry.

THE Common Council of New York have always claimed and occasionally exercised the right of establishing the rates of ferriage. New Jersey has always claimed and frequently exercised the same right. It is not to be supposed, however, that either jurisdiction ever claimed greater authority than to regulate the fare to be demanded on its own side of the river. On the 6th of February, 1799, the State of New Jersey transferred this right to the Board of Chosen Freeholders in the several counties in which the ferries were.[1] The Chosen Freeholders of Bergen, so far as ascertained, never attempted to exercise the power so given to them. But the Chosen Freeholders of Hudson took hold of the subject with more zeal than discretion. The proprietors of the ferries denied their power under the law to establish the rates of fare on ferries not wholly within the county. The contest waxed warmer, until finally an appeal was made to the courts, and then the ferry companies went to the Legislature for relief. That body again took the subject into their own hands, and on the 10th of March, 1853, established the rates of ferriage as they now are.[2]

THE COMMUNIPAW FERRY.

The first ferry legally established on the North River, connecting our shore with Manhattan Island, was the Communipaw ferry.

---

[1] *Paterson's Laws*, 351.

[2] Throughout this chapter, when the lease of a ferry is spoken of, it generally refers to the lease of the slip and ferry privileges on the New York side, by the Common Council of that city.

It was erected in 1661, about the time that the new village of Bergen received its first charter, at the foot of Communipaw avenue. William Jansen was licensed to take charge of it, and so became the first legalized ferryman on the North river.[1] He held the position for about eight years, but it does not seem to have been a peaceable one. On the 22d of December, 1661, at his request, the Governor-General and Council fixed the rates of ferriage, which, it may be taken for granted, Jansen was not slow in demanding.[2] Whetther these rates were exorbitant whether he was too exact in enforcing payment, whether he failed to provide proper accommodations, or whether through the penuriousness of the burghers of Bergen, trouble soon began to thicken around him, and the people sought to get to and from New Amsterdam by some other route. Jansen, under his license, claimed the exclusive right to transport people over the river, and even insisted that the inhabitants could not lawfully ferry themselves over, but must patronize his ferry—the first monopoly in the State of New Jersey. This claim the people resisted, and were clamorous for the right of each one to keep his boat. The authorities took the popular side in the controversy. Tielman Van Vleck, sheriff, and Engelbert Steenhuysen, commissary of Bergen, advised the people that each one had the right to keep his "schuyt," and ferry over whom he pleased. Thus the issue was fairly made. Jansen appeared before the authorities in New Amsterdam and entered his complaint against Tielman Van Vleck and Engelbert Steenhuysen. Upon this complaint they were, on the 28th of December, 1662, commanded to appear before the Governor-General and Council and put in their defence.[3] This they did, and, carrying the war into Africa, they charged that Jansen had not done his duty, and had refused to ferry over certain parties. Jansen replied that he had never refused to ferry over those who would pay.[4] Upon this state of the case judgment seems to

[1] *New Neth. Reg.*, 117. [2] *N. Y. Col. MSS., ix.*, 921.

[3] *Ibid, x., Part i.*, 300.

[4] This original Charon of Communipaw must have learned his rights from the robust son of Erebus and Nox, who would not ferry the shades of the dead over Acheron without the customary obulus.

have been given against both parties, for it was, on the 4th of January, 1663, decided that the sheriff must assist the ferryman "in getting his pay," and that he must do his duty or be dismissed."

Whether Jansen departed this life previous to June, 1669, or whether he was dismissed, is not known, but certain it is that another was chosen in his place, as appears by the following:

"By the Honble Phillip Carteret, Esqr, Gouernor of the Province of Nova Cesarea, or New Jersey, under the Right Honble John Lord Berkeley, &c., &c.

"Whereas the Inhabitants of Bergen and Communipaw have made choice of Pieter Hetfelsen to be their ferryman betweene Communipaw and New Yorke for the constant transporting to and againe their persons, goods and Cattle, for which they have Requested my Lycense, These are therefore to Lycense and appoint the said Pieter Hetfelsen to be the only and constant ferryman between the saide Communipaw and the Citty of New Yorke, for and during the time of three yeares from the day of the date hereof, and to be continued for a longer time, unless ye Inhabitants of the townes aforesaid have any just Exceptions against him. Which said Ferry the said Pieter Hetfelsen is to have and to hold to his own proper use and Benefit, Upon the conditions hereafter mentioned hereby prohibiting all persons whatsoever to transport or Carry over any person, goods, corne or cattle without ye consent or license of the said ferryman upon the penalty of paying to the use of the ferryman aforesaid the sum of tenn shillings sterling for every such default, being first convinced thereof by the Justices or Magistrates of the place, and shall notwithstanding pay to the ferryman the fraight for such persons, corn or cattle as shall be so Illegally transported to the prejudice of the said ferryman, Notwithstanding it shall and may be lawful for any person to keep a canoe or boate of his owne for the transporting and carrying over of such goods, corne and cattle as properly belong unto himselfe and the persons of his own family and no other upon the penalty aforesaid.

[1] *N. Y. Col. MSS, Part ii*, 4.

"Conditions, The ferryman aforesaid is to maintain one good sufficient boat or more for the convenient transporting of all passengers to and again from Communipaw to New York, together with their goods, corne and Cattle at all tymes and on all occasions, but more particularly he is hereby obliged to attend upon the said Inhabitants of Bergen and Communipaw three dayes in the week unless some other Extraordinary Occasions does hinder him, viz.: Mondayes, Wednesdayes and Fridayes, or upon such other dayes as they shall unanimously agree upon, on which dayes the said Inhabitants are to attend with their goods and cattle at the houer and tyme appointed, and punctually to pay and satisfie the said ferryman for his fraight according to these following rates, Whoe is to Recover the same, For case of Delay or Refusall, by ord^{r} of Justice without any charge or forme of process; Always provided that the Gouerno^{r} and his family are to be freed from paying of anything for their persons transporting as aforesaid.

There shall be paid to the ferryman six stuivers a head Wampum for every passenger, - - - -	6 st.
For his fraight Extraordinary at all other tymes iff but one man 4 Guilders in Wampum, but iff by night and unseasonable weather as the parties cann agree,	4 gl.
For every Scheppell of corne 2 stiv. in Wampum, - -	2 stiv.
For $\frac{1}{2}$ a barrell or $\frac{1}{2}$ a fatt of beere 10 stiv. in Wampum, for a whole barrell 20 Stivers for all other goods & Lieg^{rs} in cash proportionable, - - - - -	20 stiv.
For a horse or Mare 4 Gl. in Wampum, - - - -	4 gl.
For a cow 3 guilders, for an ox 4 guilders in Wampum.	
For a hogg or sow 15 Stivers in Wampum, - - -	15 stiv.
For sheep 15 Stivers a head in Wampum, - - -	15 stiv.

"Secondly the ferryman is hereby obliged on all occasions to ferry over any person for the sum of four guilders in wampum excepting what is before excepted.

"Thirdly, the said ferryman is at all tymes and on all occasions for the publicq service when thereunto Required by the Governor or those Authorized by him to carry over any person, letter, packett or message gratis, but if it be upon any business that concernes any particular man's interest, although commanded by the Governor, he is to be satisfied and paid according to the rates above mentioned.

"Given under the seal of the Province the day and year above written.

"June 25, 1669."[1]

Hetfelsen continued to manage the ferry until the 18th of January, 1672, when John Tymensen was commissioned to take charge of it, upon the same conditions, and with power to receive the same fare.

From this latter date no mention is made of this ferry for more than a century. It is probable, however, that it continued in operation until swallowed by its more successful and pretentious rival at Paulus Hoeck. Attention is attracted to it again in 1783. After the war was over and peace declared, but while the British were yet in possession of New York and Paulus Hoeck, an advertisement appeared by which Aaron Longstreet & Co. made it known that "constant attendance was given by the boats at the Ferry Stairs, near the Exchange, at 3 P. M., to bring Passengers to Communipaw, where the Newark Stage" would be ready to convey them to Newark, and thence by "The Excellent New York and Philadelphia Running Machines," in one day to Philadelphia.[2]

When the enemy evacuated Paulus Hoeck, the line of travel turned again in that direction, and the COMMUNIPAW FERRY again slept for nearly another century. When it awoke the old sail boats and periaugers[3] were no more, and it was honored with the finest ferry boats on the Hudson. When the extension of the Central Railroad of New Jersey from Elizabethport to Jersey City was completed, the ferry was revived and now runs from

---

[1] *E. J. Rec. Lib., iii.*, 27. [2] *Rivington's Gazette, August* 20, 1783.

[3] A *periauger* was the old Spanish *pirogue*, which had found its way into Dutch waters. It was pointed at both ends, had two masts, but no bowsprit. When horses and carriages were to be transported they were detached and lifted into the boat.

the Central Railroad depot in Jersey City to the foot of Liberty street in New York.

Names of boats, and when placed upon the ferry.

Central, - - - - - - - -	August 1, 1864.
Communipaw, - - - - - - -	1865.
Elizabeth, - - - - - - - -	June 25, 1867.
Plainfield, - - - - - - - -	June 3, 1869.

Names of Superintendents.

George W. Howe, - - - - -	April, 1863, to 1866.
James J. Winant, - -	October 17, 1866, to October 1, 1872.
Jacob Winant, - - - - - - -	October 1, 1872.

WEEHAWKEN FERRY.

The exact date of the commencement of this ferry is not known. The first record concerning it is an act passed in the third year of the reign of George the First (Jan. 26, 171$\frac{6}{7}$), by which the rates of ferriage were established as follows:

Man and horse to or from *New York*, -	*Eighteen Pence.*
Single Person, - - - - - -	*One Shilling.*
If above three Persons, per piece, - -	*Three Pence.*
Everything per Bushel, - - - - -	*One Penny.*
Hogs, Sheep, &c., per head, - - -	*Two Pence.*
Beef per Quarter, - - - - - -	*Three Pence.*
Barrels, - - - - - - - -	*Four Pence.*
Hogsheads, - - - - - - -	*One Shilling.*
Pipes, - - - - - - - -	*Eighteen Pence.*[1]

The ferry was erected, however, before the year 1700, as appears by the petition of Samuel Bayard, which seems to have been prompted by a desire to destroy an opposition ferry. There is no date to the petition, but Governor Hunter, to whom it is addressed, was not Governor of New York after 1719, and as

[1] *Nevill's Laws, i.,* 60.

the petition alleges that the ferry then had been in operation for upward of twenty years, it is clear that it must have been in operation prior to the date above mentioned.[1] Bayard was then owner of Weehawken.[2] His petition was as follows:

"To His Excellency Robert Hunter, Esq., Capt Generall & Govern^{r} in Chief of the Province of New York, &c., & Vize-Admiral of the same:

"The Humble Petition of Samuel Bayard humbly showeth: That your petitioner having a small parcell of land called Wiehake in Bergen County in the Eastern Division of the Province of Nova Cesarea, most convenient for a ferry of any between New Yorke Island and the southermost clifts of Tappaen and Ahasimes, wch place hath been the accustomed ferry for transportation of passengers, cattle, horses and country produce in these limmits for upward of twenty yearcs, and as such hath been assessed & taxed by the Assembly of the said Province, as by the printed acts to wch your petitioner refers may appear. Notwithstanding seaverall persons and places bounding upon the River within said limmits not assessed or taxed by the Assembly, nor permitted by the Crownes grantes have for some time made it theire Buysenesse to transport passengers, cattle, horses & country produce to and from New Yorke Island at the same rates as the ferry at Wiehake, and do keep and suffer other people haveing no propertys upon the Riverside to keep Boats and Canowes for transportation to and from New Yorke Island to the greate prejudice of the ferry at Wiehake.

"Wherefore your petitioner humbly prayes that y^{r} Exce^{ly} would be pleased to faevour your petitioner with her maj^{tys} grant under the seal of the Province whereby the ferry between the southermost clifts of Tappaen and Ahasimus might be limmited to be keep at said place called Wiehaken, only upon the usuall and accostomed ferridge, and that no person or persons in said limmits haveing a property upon the River might be permitted to transport to or from New Yorke Island any passen-

[1] This petition is bound up between two papers, dated respectively, Sept. 29, and Oct. 19, 1710.

[2] *Winfield's Land Titles*, 38.

gers, horses, cattle or country produce but what properly belongs to themselves, nor suffer any other person whatsoever that have not any property upon the River to keep any vessels for transportation to the prejudice of said ferry at Wiehake. And as in duty bound shall ever pray, &c.

"SAMUEL BAYARD."[1]

Nothing further is heard of the ferry until October 22, 1742, when Francis Covenhoven and Samuel Bayard join in a petition to the Governor and Council of New York for a ferry to "Wehawk."[2] The petition was granted. Until the Hoboken ferry was erected, this was the popular, and, in fact, only regular ferry to New York for the farmers in the upper part of Bergen County, and even for half a century after its powerful rival started upon its career, it continued to be patronized. Its landing place on the Jersey side was at or near the mouth of the Weehawken Creek, just below King's Point.

On the 9th of July, 1788, the privilege of landing on the New York side for the "Weehaack" ferry was granted by the common council to Joseph Smith for three years for £20 per annum.[3] John Stevens being, at that time, owner of the Hoboken ferry, made an effort to secure the control of this ferry, but failed.[4]

On the 5th of August, 1802, Charles and Philip Earle became the lessees for £50 per annum.[5] Shortly after this a "new Weehauk ferry" was put in operation. On the 15th of April, 1805, the "old ferry" was leased to Garret Neefie, and the "new ferry" to Charles Earle, each at £50 per annum.[6] Neefie soon gave up his lease, and Lewis Concklin took charge of the "old ferry."[7] From this time nothing is heard of it until June, 1819, when Charles Watts, of New York, became its lessee. It is then pronounced a "very ancient ferry," grown into disuse by the improvements in Powles Hook and Hoboken

---

[1] *N. Y. Col. MSS.* (*Land Papers*), *v.*, 69.
[2] *N. Y. Records*, *v.*, 51.
[3] *Ibid*, *ix.*, 101.
[4] *Ibid*, *ix.*, 197.
[5] *Ibid*, *xiii.*, 383.
[6] *Ibid*, *xv.*, 176.
[7] *Ibid*, *xv.*, 518.

ferries. Watts took a lease of it for fifteen years from the 1st of May, 1819, on the following terms: For the first five years, rent free; for the second five years, $50, and for the third five years, $200. The landing place on the New York side was to be between the north bounds of the Hoboken ferry lease and Christopher street. On the Jersey side it was to be within one quarter of a mile on each side of "Wehawk." By the terms of the lease, he was bound to keep a "team boat."[1] He found the expense too heavy for the income, and at the expiration of five months abandoned the "team boat." For this the Common Council of New York annulled his lease, and let the ferry to Philip Howe, on condition that he should, on or before the first of May, 1821, put on the ferry two good sail boats, and one horse boat.[2] But the days of sail boats and horse boats had passed. A mightier agent had come and supplanted them. And already, even in so short a time, the "Wehawk" ferry is almost forgotten. It was, however, spoken of as a "present ferry" in the charter of the Paterson and Hudson River Railroad, approved Jan. 21, 1831.

The present *Weehawken Ferry Company* was incorporated March 25, 1852, and the ferry revived on the 1st of January, 1859. Its present landing place on the Jersey side is at Slaugh's Meadow, and on the New York side at Forty-second street. This Company bought of the Union Ferry Company two steamboats, the "Lydia" and "Abbie," used on the East River. The name of the "Lydia" was changed to "Weehawken," and the "Abbie" to "Hackensack." Owing to the navigation laws, however, the old names were soon restored. The "Abbie" was afterward sold and taken to Albany, where it is yet in use as a ferry boat, under the double name of "Abbie" and "Eli Perry," and plies between that city and Greenbush. The "Roslyn" was placed on the ferry in the summer of 1870, and the "Midland" on the 1st of August, 1872.

It is proper in this connection to produce the grant of George

---

[1] *N. Y. Records, xxxviii.*, 267.

[2] *Ibid, xli.*, 249.

the Second to Stephen Bayard in 1752. It covers the ground now used by the ferry. It is as follows:

"George the Second, by the grace of God of Great Britain, France and Ireland, King, Defender of the Faith, &c.: Whereas our loving subject, Stephen Bayard, by his humble petition presented unto Jonathan Belcher, Esqr., Captain-General and Commander-in-Chief of our Province of New Jersey, hath set forth that a ferry over the North River, from the government of New Jersey to the opposite shore, within the Bounds hereafter described, would be of great advantage to his Majesty's subjects who have occasion to go to New York, especially in the winter Season when the Ice renders the Passage from the usual Ferrys very dangerous, and therefore Praying our letters Patent to him, his Heirs and assigns for keeping the said Ferry under such conditions as are usual in like Cases. Know Ye that the taking the Premises into our Royal Consideration, and being desirous to facilitate the Passages of all our loving Subjects over the said North River, and also to encourage the said Stephen Bayard to the Expenses & Trouble he has and may be at for the Public benefit, Have, of our special Grace, certain knowledge and meer motion for us and for our Successors, given, granted, ratified and confirmed, and by these Presents Do give, Grant, Ratify and Confirm unto the said Stephen Bayard, his Heirs and assigns the Sole keeping of the said Ferry over the North River, Beginning at Bergen North line and so along the Shore half a mile below or to the Southward of a Place called the Great Slaugh,[1] Hereby giving and granting exclusive of all others, unto the said Stephen Bayard, his heirs and assigns, our Royal License and Authority to Transport Passengers, Horses, Cattle and Goods over the said North River within the Bounds aforesaid, for so long a time as he, the said Stephen Bayard, his heirs and assigns shall sufficiently attend and keep, or cause to be attended and kept, one or more ferries within the Bounds afores^{d} for the Transporting of Passengers, Horses, Cattle and Goods over the said North River within the Bounds aforesaid. And We by these Presents Do Give,

[1] Once the property of Jacob Slaugh, from whom it received its name.

Grant, ratify and Confirm unto the said Stephen Bayard, his heirs and assigns, Power and Authority to ask, Demand & receive from all and every the Passengers for Transporting or Ferrying over of them, their Horses, Carriages, Cattle and Goods, all Rewards, benefits and advantages whatsoever, as are already Legally established, or hereafter may be within our Province of New Jersey, for performing the Services aforesaid. To HAVE *and* TO HOLD the keeping of the said Ferry or Ferries over the North River within the Bounds aforesaid, with all the benefits, perquisites and advantages whatsoever, unto him, the said Stephen Bayard, his heirs and assigns, to the Sole use, benefit and behoof of the said Stephen Bayard, his heirs and assigns, for so long time as he and they shall well and sufficiently attend and keep, or cause to be attended and kept, the Ferry aforesaid, Yielding and paying therefor yearly and every year during the Term aforesaid unto us, our Heirs and Successors, at the City Hall of Amboy, on every twenty-fifth day of March, the sum of Two Shillings lawful money of America, if the same be lawfully Demanded. IN TESTIMONY whereof we have caused the Great Seal of our said Province to be hereunto affixed, and these our Letters to be made Patent. Witness our Trusty and Well beloved Jonathan Belcher, Esqr., our Captain-General and Commander-in-Chief in and over our Province of Nova Cæsaria or New Jersey in America, Chancellor and Vice Admiral in the same, at the Borough of Elizabeth, in our said Province, the Seventh day of February, in the Twenty-Sixth year of our Reign."

THE JERSEY CITY FERRY

was established June 18, 1764.[1] In the *New York Mercury* of July 2, 1764, we find

"GOOD NEWS FOR THE PUBLIC.

"The long wished for Ferry is now established and kept across the North River, from the Place called Powless's Hook to the

[1] *Dunlap's History of N. Y., ii., cxci.*

City of New York; and boats properly constructed, as well for the Conveniency of Passengers as for the carrying over of Horses and carriages, do now constantly ply from one shore to the other. The landing on the New York Side is fixed at the Dock commonly called Mesier's Dock, and at Powless's Hook is situate nearly opposite to the said Dock, the distance between the two Places being about three Quarters of a Mile, and as the boats may pass and repass, at all Times of the Tide, with almost equal Despatch, it is thought by far the most convenient Place for a Ferry of any yet established, or that can be established, from the Province of New Jersey to the City of New York; and what will give it the Preference by far of all the other ferries in the Winter Season, is that rarely a Day happens but that Boats may pass at this Ferry without being obstructed or endangered by Ice. Constant attendance is given at Powless's Hook by Michael Cornelisse, where the best of Stabling and Pasture is provided for Horses."

It was started as an important part of the new route to Philadelphia *via* Bergen Point and Staten Island. Abraham Mesier and Michael Cornelissen were its founders. They made arrangements with Cornelius Van Vorst for a landing place at Paulus Hook. Cornelissen then built the house afterward known as Major Hunt's tavern. The landing place on the New York side was fixed at Mesier's Dock, at the foot of Cortlandt street. The two periaugers first on the ferry were the "Liberty" and "Property." The projectors of the ferry did not consult the authorities in New York as to the propriety or necessity of the same. Thereupon the Aldermen, on the 10th of September, 1764, appointed a committee to take the opinion of counsel whether the people of "that part of Jersey called Powles Hook have any right of ferriage to and from this city."[1] What the opinion of the counsel was, or that he gave any, or that anything further was done, does not appear. At that time Van Vorst was owner of all the land between the road leading to Bergen on the north, the Hudson River on the east, Communipaw Cove and the Creek of

[1] *N. Y. Records, vi.*, 243.

the Woods on the south and west. The route to Philadelphia by boat to Amboy was about to be superseded by a more certain means of conveyance. Transportation was to be by stage. This must be reached by means of a ferry, and there was no point so convenient for that purpose as Paulus Hoeck. And, what was more to the purpose, Van Vorst saw that it was an enterprise which in the end would pay. The millions who annually pour across that ferry, and the thriving city built on his old farm, more than realize his utmost expectations.

Others were not slow to see what a harvest would be realized from this ferry, and could not forego an attempt to reap it for themselves. Van Vorst's hereditary enemy of the Duke's Farm —Captain Archibald Kennedy—anticipating trouble between Van Vorst and the Common Council of New York, joined one William McAdams in a petition to that body on the third of May, 1765, for an exclusive right of ferry between New York and the Jersey shore. This, if granted, would take the ferry from Paulus Hoeck to Ahasimus, where the Pavonia Ferry now is. Van Vorst was not slow to head off this movement by a counter petition on the 14th of October in the same year. He set forth that he had been to a very considerable expense in erecting his ferry " at a place called Powles Hook, lying in the county of Bergen," and that he was obliged to maintain a causeway half a mile long and a lane nearly twice as long; he therefore desired the board to establish and regulate the ferry on such reasonable terms as would be for the public good. In consideration of the expense he had been put to, he requested the privilege of receiving for some time the benefits of both sides of the ferry.[1] On the 31st of January, 1766, these petitions for an "exclusive grant of the right of ferriage " across to "their respective lands on the Jersey shore" were taken into consideration by the Common Council of New York. That body saw the necessity and advantage to their city of a ferry to the Jersey shore, and appointed a committee to make the best arrangements they could get.[2] To that committee Van Vorst proposed that he would give

[1] *N. Y. Records, vi.*, 286.

[2] *Ibid, vi.*, 306.

to the City of New York £40 a year for seven years, and the corporation should have the power to fix the rates of ferriage; that after said term he would give the corporation a free landing on his side for the purposes of a ferry, *provided* he should have the same privilege of landing in New York. He stated that he had three large and two small boats for the ferry, which he intended to keep in repair and ready for use. He consented that the corporation might decide upon the landing place on the New York side, though he recommended that it should be at the place then used for that purpose. These propositions were accepted, and the landing place fixed at the "ground or pier of Nicholas Roosevelt, Esqr., at the lower end of Thomas street."[1]

It seems, however, that these arrangements were never completed, for on the 23d of March, 1767, the ferry was let at public outcry to Jacob Van Voorhis, a merchant in New York, for £310 per annum for four years from the first of May, 1767.[2] Abraham Mesier, Abraham Russing and Peter Mesier, jr., were at the time, or shortly afterward became associated with Van Voorhis. They soon found that there were other expenses than those of the ferry properly connected with the enterprise. The causeway between Paulus Hoeck and the upland of Ahasimus was occasionally overflowed by the tides. This inconvenienced travelers and diminished the lessee's revenue. He thereupon sought and obtained an abatement of half a year's rent, for the purpose of repairing the causeway.[3] Long before the expiration of his lease he found that his expenses and heavy rent rendered the business unprofitable. He therefore abandoned the lease, and on the first of March, 1771, the ferry was let to Abraham Mesier for three years for the sum of £120 per annum. Thus was saved to the "firm" £180 a year for the balance of the term.[4] The unpaid rent of Van Voorhis was acquitted for the reason that from May 1, 1767, to May 1, 1771, his disbursements and rent paid equaled his receipts. He had lost his labor, and it was thought unjust that he should pay the balance of rent

[1] *N. Y. Records, vi.*, 311.
[2] *Ibid, vi.*, 371.
[3] *Ibid, vi.*, 381, 466.
[4] *Ibid, vii.*, 99.

and thus lose money along with his labor.[1] On the first of March, 1774, Abraham Mesier obtained a new lease of the ferry for three years from the first of May following at a rent of £210 per annum.[2] Shortly afterward Mesier died, and the Hoboken Ferry coming into existence, his executors obtained an abatement of £50 on the last year's rent. The probability is that Mesier's widow remained in charge of the ferry during the war, subject to military control. Soon after the war her name is again connected with the ferry, and in 1786 she petitioned for repairs to the ferry stairs on the New York side.[3] The ferry was now but poorly appreciated. The Legislature of this State had imposed upon it a tax of £50, which had not been paid. The rent had fallen off from £310 a year in 1767 until on the 15th of April, 1789, John Holdron obtained a three years' lease for £50 per annum.[4] But under his management the ferry became so prosperous that at the end of his term in 1792 he was obliged to give £380 a year for a three years' lease, and in addition provide ferry stairs and all other conveniences.[5] Whether this sum was drawn out of him by auction puffers or not is impossible to tell. One thing is certain, he soon found the load too heavy to carry, and called for an abatement of rent. It was agreed on the 5th of May, 1794, that upon his paying £250 the balance of the rent should be remitted. At this rent he held it up to the first of May, 1796.[6] On this date he took a new lease for three years at £300 a year. He agreed (and this is the first regulation looking to the accommodation of the public) to provide two large boats for horses, cattle, carriages, etc., and two row boats for passengers. He also agreed to run the boats from sunrise till 9 o'clock P. M. from May 1st to Oct. 1st, reserving the privilege of charging double ferriage after sunset.[7]

On the 11th of March, 1799, the Common Council of New York City established the following rates of ferriage for this ferry, viz.:

---

[1] *N. Y. Rec*, *vii.*, 244. [2] *Ibid*, *vii.*, 297. [3] *Ibid*, *viii.*, 480.
[4] *Ibid*, *ix.*, 186, 199, 206. [5] *Ibid*, *x.*, 200. [6] *Ibid*, *xi.*, 120, 222.
[7] *Ibid*, *xi.*, 365.

	£	s.	d.
A Passenger, - - - - - -	£0	0	9
A Coach, Chariot, Coachee, or covered Wagon,	0	8	0
A Phaeton, - - - - -	0	5	0
A Chaise or top chair, - - - - -	0	3	6
A Chair, - - - - - -	0	2	6
A Sleigh, - - - - - - -	0	2	6
Horses and Cattle, - - - - -	0	1	9
A Sheep, Calf or Hog, - - - -	0	0	6
A large trunk or chest, - - -	0	1	0
A small do do - - - -	0	0	2
A Pipe or Hogshead of Wine, Spirits or Molasses,	0	6	0
A Barrel of do - - -	0	1	0
A Barrel of Beef, Pork, Flour or Fish, -	0	1	0
Plank of every kind, each, - - -	0	0	1½
Boards do - - -	0	0	1
A side of sole Leather, - - - -	0	0	2
do upper do - - - -	0	0	1
A Raw Hide, - - - - -	0	0	3
Iron, Steel, Lead, &c., per cwt., - -	0	0	6
A Desk, - - - - - - -	0	3	0
A large table, - - - - - -	0	0	9
A small do - - - - - -	0	0	4
A mahogany Chair, - - - -	0	0	2
A common do - - - - - -	0	0	1
Basket or Bag of Fruit of 2 Bushels, - -	0	0	4
Bag of Grain do - - -	0	0	3
Bag of Flour or Meal, - - - - -	0	0	3
A Crate of Earthen Ware, - - -	0	2	0
A Tierce of Earthen Ware, - - -	0	2	0
A Feather Bed, - - - - - -	0	0	6
A Clock Case, - - - - - -	0	1	0
A chest of Tea, - - - - - -	0	2	0
Dye Wood, per cwt., - - - - -	0	0	6
Indigo and Copperas, per cwt., - - -	0	0	6
Gunpowder, per cwt., - - - - -	0	1	0
A large Bale of Cotton, - - - -	0	2	0
An empty Hogshead or Pipe, - - -	0	1	0

An empty Barrel, - - - - - -	£0	0	3
Shad, per hundred, - - - - -	0	2	0
Cabbages, per hundred, - - - - -	0	1	6

And all other articles and things in like proportion.[1]

These rates, in the light of the present day, seem somewhat exorbitant. They appeared the same to the people on this side of the river at that time. How could they exist and pay ferriage on their cabbages at the exorbitant rate of *one shilling and sixpence* per hundred. Rates must come down, or the Knickerbockers must go unfed of cabbage, and pine in want for their *kohl slaugh!* But cabbages beget sixpences, and sooner than such a shining progeny should be untimely cut off, and their ghosts left to haunt the unplanted gardens, the people would make known their grievances. This they did. They held a public meeting, and, in true modern style, passed sundry "Whereases" and "Resolves" upon the subject. Over this meeting Isaac Nichols presided with a dignity becoming the occasion. After the solemn deliberations were ended, good old "Isaac" was chosen to proceed to New York, and there make known their grievances, together with their views expressed "in public meeting assembled." This he did in a becoming manner. It is sad to relate, however, that the whole effort was wasted. Mr. Nichols and the resolutions were duly received, the former bowed out, the latter laid upon the table, and no attention paid to either.

At this time, colored Abraham—Brom for short—the most skillful master of a sail boat in his day, was the man of this ferry.

On the 5th of August, 1802, Holdron took another three years' lease at $2,125 per annum. As usual, in 1803 he sought an abatement of rent, and alleged as a reason that a new ferry had been erected for ten months past, which had injured his business. It is probable that this was Budd's ferry at Ahasimus. If so, Budd had erected his ferry and put it in operation before he asked for permission to land on the New York side, as may be seen by reference to the remarks on that ferry. But his request

[1] *N. Y. Records, xii.*, 458.

was refused. Nevertheless, by renewals of the lease, he held on to the ferry. On the 22d of February, 1808, he took a new lease for two years and nine months.[1]

From the commencement of the ferry up to 1804, Cornelius Van Vorst was its owner, as he was of the adjoining land. On the 2d of February, 1804, he contracted with Anthony Dey to sell Powles Hook and the ferry, subject to a lease which Major David Hunt held, to expire in 1805. Dey received a deed for the same on the 26th of March, 1804. On the 16th of April, 1804, Dey agreed to lease to Hunt the right of ferriage for two years after the 1st of May, 1805. The Major continued in charge of the ferry for a number of years. In 1804 "The Associates of the Jersey Company" were incorporated, when the land and ferry were conveyed to them. After Major Hunt came Joseph Lyon, of Elizabethtown, as ferrymaster. He occupied the old tavern. His stables were in the rear, and to accommodate him the ferry landing was moved from the foot of Grand street (a little west of Hudson), to opposite the gate of his yard between Grand and York streets, so that people coming from New York could signal the hostler to have their carriages ready.

Up to this time the accommodations for the ferry had been a few row boats, each with two oarsmen, with a few spare oars, which the passengers were expected to use if they wished to cross in good time; and a couple of open boats with sails, used when the wind suited, or when it was required to take a horse and carriage over. When the wind was favorable the passage could be made in half an hour, but sometimes three hours were consumed in crossing.

About this time the success of steamboats on the Hudson attracted the attention of Mr. Durand, Elisha Boudinot, General Cummings and others of Newark to the possibility of steam ferry boats. In the autumn of 1809, they subscribed $50,000 to carry the plan into effect. Robert Fulton was requested to construct such a boat as, in his judgment, would answer the pur-

---

[1] *N. Y. Records, xviii.*, 181.

poses of a ferry. Application was then made for a lease of the Jersey City ferry. Immediately a competitor in the person of Daniel French arose. He had obtained a patent for an improvement in the use of steam in propelling boats. Elisha Monell and Levi Kendall claimed that they had an invention which was superior to all others.[1] All of these rival interests strove to get control of this ferry. The Jerseymen incorporated February 7, 1818, in the name of the *York and Jersey Steam Boat Ferry Company* were successful.[2] In March, 1811, they obtained a lease of the ferry, and of the right of landing on the New York side.

In December, 1810, the *New York Evening Post* announced that arrangements had been made with Fulton for the construction of steamboats for this ferry. In May, 1811, two boats were being built by Charles Brown, and were 80 feet in length and 30 feet in width. "One peculiarity is, they never put about." On July 2, 1812, one of them, the "Jersey," was finished, and put in operation, but owing to some needed alteration was taken off for a few days. On Friday, July 17, 1812, it began its regular trips. A writer, on the following day, says: "I crossed the North River yesterday in the Steam Boat with my family in my carriage, without alighting therefrom, in fourteen minutes, with an immense crowd of passengers. I cannot express to you how much the public mind appeared to be gratified at finding so large and so safe a machine going so well. On both shores were thousands of people viewing this pleasing object."[3]

On this occasion a grand entertainment was given at Joseph Lyon's tavern in Jersey City to the Mayor and Common Council of New York and others. The following illustration will give a correct idea of this boat, if the reader will imagine two cigar-shaped floats fastened ten feet apart, with the paddle-wheel working between them.

Fulton's description will explain it fully:

"She is built of two boats, each ten feet beam, eighty feet long

---

[1] *N. Y. Records, xxi.*, 1. [2] *Ibid, xxviii.*, 159.

[3] *Centinel of Freedom, July* 21, 1812.

and five feet deep in the hold; which boats are distant from each other ten feet, confined by strong transverse beam knees and diagonal traces, forming a deck thirty feet wide and eighty feet long

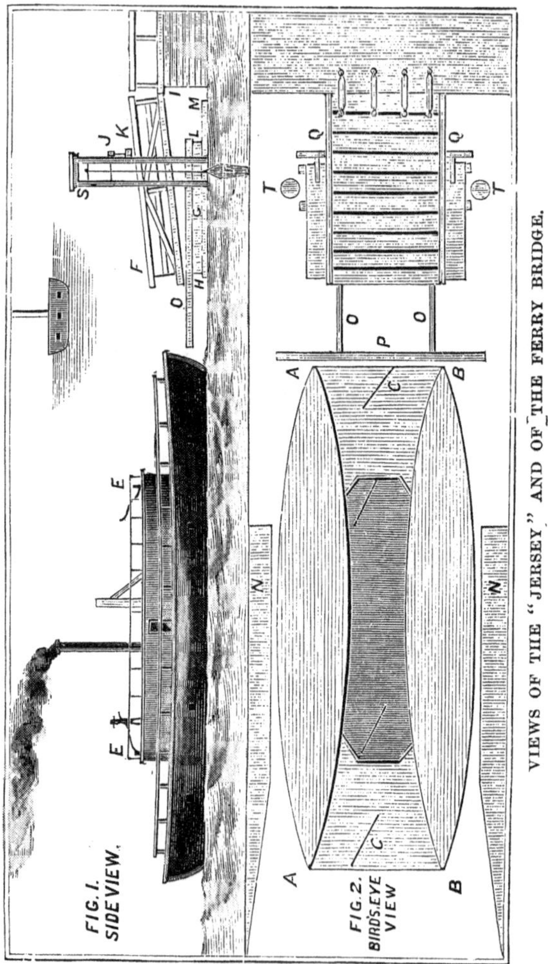

VIEWS OF THE "JERSEY" AND OF THE FERRY BRIDGE.

The propelling water-wheel is placed between the boats to prevent it from injury from ice and shocks on entering or approaching the dock. The whole of the machinery being placed between the two boats, leaves ten feet on the deck of each boat for carriages, horses and cattle, &c., the other, having neat benches and covered with an awning, is for passengers, and there is also a passage and stairway to a neat cabin, which is fifty feet long and five feet clear from the floor to the beams, furnished with benches and provided with a stove in winter. Although the two boats and space between them give thirty feet beam, yet they present sharp bows to the water, and have only the resistance in the water of one boat of twenty feet beam. Both ends being alike, and each having a rudder, she never puts about.

"Of the dock, he says it 'is one hundred and eighty feet long, seventy wide; the bridge is fastened to the middle of the bulkhead. The boat, being only thirty feet wide and the dock seventy, leaves twenty feet vacant on each of her sides; in each of these twenty feet spans and in the water are floating stages, made of pine logs, which lie favorable to the boat for thirty feet, and these run diagonally to the extreme end of the wharves, so that the boat, when coming in, hits within the seventy feet, and the stages guide her direct to the bridge.'"

She was in service for many years, and ended her career as material for the construction of a stable in Greene street built for the elder Isaac Edge.

In 1813 the "York," built on the model of the "Jersey," was completed and placed on the ferry. It is said that these boats were "slow coaches"—that they would ordinarily take an hour and a half to make a trip—that when they met in the river passengers could hold quite a conversation before they got beyond talking distance; in fact they were

"Like fat green turtles fast asleep,
On the still surface of the deep."

They started on their daily duties every morning at sunrise from each side of the river, and ran all day every half hour by "St. Paul's Church clock."[1]

But the experience of the ferry company was similar to that of

---

[1] *Centinel of Freedom, June* 20, 1815.

prior lessees. Up to the 27th of May, 1816, they had made but one dividend of five per cent. For this reason they requested that the Common Council of New York would either purchase the ferry, reduce the rent or increase the rates of ferriage. The only relief obtained was an increase of personal toll to 12½ cents.[1] In those days the fare was collected on the boat during the passage over. On the 1st of May, 1823, the company took a lease of the right of ferry from New York to so much of the Jersey shore as lies between a point "immediately south of Hoboken and a point due west from the Battery Castle." But their experience was not a success. They sank all of their capital, one of their boats blew up in the slip, and the year 1824 found them unable to continue. In September, 1825, they assigned their lease to Francis B. Ogden, Cadwallader D. Colden and Samuel Swartwout. The Common Council of New York consented to the assignment, and gave the assignees a new lease for fifteen years and six months from the first of November, 1825. The lessees were to provide two good steamboats, but in the place of one of these were afterward permitted to use a team boat. They were also to provide the ferry with row boats. They bought and placed on the ferry the "Washington." In October, 1826, Ogden and Swartwout transferred their interest in the lease to Mr. Colden. He failed to make the ferry remunerative, and surrendered it to the owners, "The Associates of the Jersey Company." On the first of January, 1831, the "Associates" leased it to the New Jersey Railroad and Transportation Company for 12½ years. By renewals the latter company continued to hold until 1853, when the lessees bought up the stock of the "Associates," and thus became the owners of the ferry. It continues to be nominally operated under the old lease of the "Associates," and the latter company, which has become a nominal body, nominally receive an annual rent of $18,000 from nominal lessees.

The line to the foot of Desbrosses street was started in 1862. These ferries were transferred to the Pennsylvania Railroad Company in 1871.

---

[1] *N. Y. Records, xxxi.*, 482.

In 1849 the Board of Chosen Freeholders of Hudson County fixed and attempted to force upon the ferry the following:

"RATES OF FERRIAGE TO BE TAKEN BY THE JERSEY CITY FERRY, AS FIXED BY THE BOARD OF CHOSEN FREEHOLDERS OF HUDSON COUNTY.

Every person on foot, above ten years old, - -	3c
Under ten years and above five years old, - -	2
Man and horse or horse only, - - - -	9
Ordinary fourwheeled trucks, loaded, two horses and one person, - - - - - - -	37½
Ordinary fourwheeled trucks, light, two horses and one person, - - - - - - - -	25
Ordinary wagons, or market wagons, including loads of green clover or grass, two horses and one person, -	25
For every additional person, - - - - -	3
Ordinary wagons or market wagons, including loads of green clover or grass, one horse and one person, -	12½
For every additional person, - - - - -	3
A coach, coachee, chariot, barouche, phaeton, pleasure wagon or sleigh with more than one seat, two horses, one person, - - - - - - -	30
For every additional person, - - - -	3
A light pleasure carriage, barouche or pleasure wagon, two horses, one person, - - - - -	25
For every additional person, - - - -	3
A light pleasure carriage, barouche or pleasure wagon, one horse, one person, - - - - - -	18¾
For every additional person, - - - -	3
A cart with driver, one horse, loaded or empty, -	12½
A wagon load of hay or straw, with two horses and one person, - - - - - - -	50
Wagon or cart load of hay or straw, with one horse and one person, - - - - - - -	37½
Any kind of carriage or sleigh, without horse, half price.	
A wheelbarrow and one person, loaded or empty, -	6
A hand cart and one person, loaded or empty, -	8

Cattle, single or in droves—each, - - - -	15c
Calves and hogs, dead or alive, - - - -	3
Sheep, lambs and shoats, dead or alive, - - -	3
Sucking pigs, do, - - - -	2
Raw hides, - - - - - - -	3
Skins, - - - - - - - -	0½
Dry hides, - - - - - - -	1
Bundles of sole and upper leather, per side, - -	1
Bundles of hay, - - - - - - -	9
Paper, per ream, in bundles, - - - -	0½
Wheat, corn and other grain, per bushel, - - -	0½
Oats, green peas and beans, per bushel, - -	1
Potatoes, per bushel, - - - - -	1½
Barrels containing apples and vegetables—each, -	6¼
Boxes of oranges and lemons—each, - - -	5
Baskets containing fruits or vegetables, - -	3
Oysters, per bushel, - - - - -	3
Horse feed, do, - - - - - -	1
Meal, flour or coffee, in bags—each, - - -	3
Large boxes containing live fowls for market—each,	12½
Small boxes and large baskets, containing live fowls, in proportion.	
Salt in bags, per bushel, - - - - -	2
Sugar, per cwt., - - - - - - -	5
Pipe, hogshead of spirits or wine, each, - -	50
When empty, - - - - - - -	8
Tierces of spirits or wine, - - - - -	37½
When empty—each, - - - - - -	6¼
Barrels of spirits or wine—each, - - -	18¾
When empty—each, - - - - - -	3
Hogsheads of molasses or sugar, - - -	37½
When empty, - - - - - - -	6¼
Tierces of molasses or sugar—each, - - - -	25
When empty, do, - - -	5
Barrels of molasses, sugar, beer, beef, pork and oil, -	10
Barrels of flour and lime, - - - - - -	5
When empty, two cents each, except flour barrels, -	1

Baskets of wine, - - - - - - -	$6\frac{1}{4}$
Crate, hogshead, tierce, &c., containing earthenware or glass—each, - - - - - - -	$12\frac{1}{2}$
And when empty, tierce or crate—each, -	4
Large size firkins, do, - -	5
Second do do, - - -	3
Pails of butter, do, - -	1
Cheese, ham, codfish, &c., per cwt., - - -	5
Chests of tea—each, - - - - - -	4
Half chests of tea, do, - - - - - -	2
Tobacco in kegs, do, - - - - - -	4
Churns containing milk, - - - - -	$6\frac{1}{4}$
Iron, steel, lead-paints and other metals, per cwt., -	5
Boxes of window-glass—each, - - - -	2
Boxes of soap and candles—each, - - -	3
Kegs of nails, do, - - - - -	5
Specie in large kegs or boxes—each, - - -	25
For less size, and for every $1,000, - - -	$12\frac{1}{2}$
For fancy chairs—each, - - - - -	2
For common do do, - - - - - -	1
Sofas and pianos—each, - - - - -	25
Bureaus, - - - - - - - -	$12\frac{1}{2}$
Bedsteads, beds, tables, writing desks and small bureaus—each,	$6\frac{1}{4}$
Tool chests, ploughs and corn machines—each, - -	$6\frac{1}{4}$
Stoves and grates, large size, - - - - -	$12\frac{1}{2}$
Small size in proportion.	
Joists and boards—each, - - - - - -	1
Lumber and timber, per thousand feet, - -	$1 00

"And all animals and things not herein enumerated shall be charged proportionably to the foregoing rates. A true copy from the minutes of the Board of Chosen Freeholders of Hudson County, in the State of New Jersey. August 7, 1849.

"H. Van Wagenen, Clerk
"Of the Board of Chosen Freeholders of Hudson County.

"☞ The above Rates are to take effect on and after the 1st day of Sept., 1849."

They were never enforced. The landing place on the New York side is at the foot of Cortlandt street. On the New Jersey side it was at first at the foot of Grand street, about one hundred feet west of Hudson street. It was afterward placed between Grand and York streets, with the slip opening diagonally up the river.[1] Thence it was removed to the foot of York street. On the first of April, 1839, it was changed to the corner of Montgomery and Hudson streets. In 1856 the block east of Hudson street was filled in, and the landing place changed to its present location. On May 5, 1851, the Common Council of New York gave their permission for the Desbrosses street ferry.

The boats on this ferry, since the introduction of steam, have been

Jersey,	1812.
York,[2]	1813.
New Jersey,[3]	
Richard Varick,[4]	November, 1826.
George Washington,[5]	April, 1826.

[1] Between the landing and the hotel was a semi-circular plot, around which the stages would run to unload their passengers. In the centre of this plot was a willow tree, which was sometimes used as a whipping post. Here, as late as 1814, a white-headed old man received thirty-two lashes.

[2] *Colden's Life of Fulton*, 274.

[3] The boiler of this boat exploded while lying in the slip, shortly after her completion, killing a Miss Nelson, who was making her home with the Van Vorst family, while she attended school in New York. Billy West, her pilot, also received injuries from which he afterward died; and a colored man, named Enoch Dorson, was badly scalded, but recovered. The fourth boat, being a failure, was always known as "Tom Vermilye's folly." She was small, with a diminutive engine and boiler, and it is said that in crossing the river she would have to stop to get up steam. She was the cause of much amusement to the river men; and her flues being very small, the story goes that, in order to clean them, they would put a live cat in at the bottom and then build a fire, when the cat would travel through in a lively manner and most effectually clean the flues.

[4] This boat was built for an eight-horse boat, but was changed into a steamer with two engines. It was first designed to name her "General Jackson."

[5] This boat was built for the Catharine street ferry, East river, but purchased for the Jersey City ferry in April, 1826, during the lease of Swartwout & Co. It became the first night boat in June, 1835.

Sussex,	(launched) September 6, 1833.
Essex,	March 31, 1835.
Bergen,[1]	
New Jersey,[2]	May 25, 1836.
Mouse of the Mountain,[3]	
Aresseoh,	1841.
Hudson,	November 12, 1849.
Colden,	October —, 1851.
Philadelphia,[4]	1852.
D. S. Gregory,	June 16, 1853.
John S. Darcy,	1857.
John P. Jackson,[5]	1860.
Jersey City,	1862.
New York,	1863.
Newark,	1864.
New Brunswick,	1866.
Hudson City,	1867.

The ferry masters or agents have been

Michael Cornelisse, from	1764 to 1769.
Verdine Elsworth, from	1769 to 1776.
Major David Hunt, until	1805.
Joseph Lyon,	
C. Rhina, in	1822.
Benjamin Greaves,	
Jonathan B. Jenkins,	
William Woolsey,	

SUPERINTENDENTS.

John Clews,	1833 to 1835.
Darwin F. Rockwell,	1835 to 1845.
Charles A. Woolsey,	1845 to ——.

[1] I have not ascertained when this boat was put upon the ferry. In 1838 it was repaired at a cost of $10,000, and put on as a night boat. It was sold and taken to the Albany and Greenbush ferry March 15, 1847.

[2] The New Jersey, Washington, Sussex, and Essex were sold to the New Jersey Railroad Company January 1, 1839, for $70,000, and the ferry improvements for $18,224.99.

[3] This was a toy steamer, and ran occasionally for passengers only.

[4] Sold to the United States in 1861, and turned into a transport.

[5] Sold to the United States in 1861, and turned into a gunboat.

The Bergen Point Ferry.

On the 15th of September, 1750, Jacob Corsen petitioned the Government of New York for letters patent to erect his ferry, between Staten Island and Bergen Point, into a public ferry, and also for a grant of the soil between high and low water mark within a mile and a half on each side of his land. In answer to his petition he received the King's grant in accordance with his petition, except that he received the right to the shore in front of his own land only.[1] From this petition it is manifest that Corsen had been operating his ferry prior to 1750. Nearly fourteen years afterward it received, in connection with the Paulus Hoeck ferry, the following notice:

"A Ferry is established and kept across the Kill van Kull, and that Boats constantly attend for that Purpose, at a Place belonging to John Beck, and commonly called Mooddses, situate near the Dutch Church on Staten Island, from whence Passengers are transported directly across to Bergen Point, from which place there is a fine Road leading directly to the said Powless's Hook; so that a short, safe, easy and convenient Way is fixed by Means of these two Ferries, for all Travellers passing to the City of New York, from any of the Southern Governments."[2]

From this notice it would seem that this ferry was then for the first time used as a part of the new stage route to Philadelphia and the South. On the 19th of July, 1764, Anthony White sent his petition to Lieutenant-Governor Colden of New York for a ferry or ferries across the "Kill van Corle," from the north side of Staten Island to Bergen Point.[3] In this petition he sets forth that in the twentieth year of the reign of George II. (1747) he had obtained letters patent under the seal of New Jersey granting him the sole right of keeping a ferry across the "Kill van Corle" from Bergen Point to Staten Island. He then petitioned Governor Clinton of New York for a like exclusive right, which he failed to get. His present petition looked

---

[1] *N. Y. Col. MSS., xxi.,* 393. [2] *N. Y. Mercury, July* 2, 1764.
[3] *N. Y. Col. MSS., xcii,* 121; *Winfield's Land Titles,* 136, 141, 144.

toward a monopoly. Whether he was then the owner of Corsen's ferry or whether he was raising an opposition does not appear. He was then the owner of the land where the La Tourette House now stands, and near which the ferry landing then was. Michael Van Tuyl was the proprietor of the ferry in 1765.

As we have seen, the stages on their way to and from Philadelphia passed over this ferry. A serious accident occurred here in 1767. The scow was taking over one of the stages, in which some of the passengers retained their seats. On approaching the shore the stage by some mishap was overturned into the river. By this accident Mrs. Morris and her maid were drowned. She was an actress,[1] and at the time her husband was performing the part of King Henry in Richard III. in the Old Play House in John street, New York.

After the travel to the South was turned to the route which was made over the meadows on or near the present line of the Newark Plank Road, this ferry gradually declined. It was in operation yet in 1786, and in November of that year was assessed by the Legislature of this State the sum of £5. This the owner was unable or not inclined to pay. To persuade him thereto, on the 7th of June, 1787, a supplement was passed which declared that if the proprietor should persevere to keep up the ferry after the first of the following August without taking out a license, for which such assessment was made, he should forfeit and pay £10.

When it suspended operations is not known. Several attempts to resuscitate it have been made, but without success. A horse boat was plying on it between 1840 and 1850, but only for a short time. In 186– a slip was built at the foot of Avenue C on the Kills, and a boat put upon the ferry. It continued in operation for a few months, and was then destroyed by fire. In March, 1868, "The Bergen Point and Staten Island Ferry Company" was incorporated, but never gave any signs of life. On the 15th of June, 1869, Walter H. Frazee attempted to revive it. He placed thereon a small steam yacht called "Jennie."

---

[1] *N Y. Mercury, December* 14, 1767.

After twelve days' experience he was convinced of the unprofitableness of the enterprise and abandoned it. The location is so out of the line of travel that its revival is doubtful.

The Hoboken Ferry.

Early in the year 1774 this ferry was established to connect the corporation dock at the Bear Market in New York with Hoboken. It was leased to H. Tallman for two years at £50 a year.[1] It does not seem to have been put into active operation, however, until May of the following year, as appears from the following notice:

"Cornelius Haring

Begs leave to present his most respectful compliments to the Public, and to inform them that he intends, on Monday, the first of May next, to open the New Established Ferry, from the remarkable pleasant and convenient situate place of William Bayard, Esq., at the King's Arms Inn; from which place all gentlemen Travellers and others who have occasion to cross that ferry will be accommodated with the best of boats, of every kind, suitable to the winds, weather and tides, to convey them from thence to the New Market near the new Corporation Pier at the North River, opposite Vesey Street, in New York, at which place a suitable house will be kept for the reception of travellers passing to and from his house, and will have his boats in good order.

"Said Haring takes this public method to inform all gentlemen travellers and others that he has a most elegant and convenient house, suitable for the purpose, where they will be provided with lodging, eatables and liquors of the best kind; and particular attention will be given to the clean feeding and doing strict justice to all travellers' horses. The elegance of the situation, as well as its affording many amusements, such as fishing and fowling, added to these, its being stocked with the greatest variety of the best English fruits, will make it an agreeable place

[1] *N. Y. Records, vii.*

for the entertainment of large companies; having besides a number of convenient rooms, one of fifty feet in length, by which means (as he will have the best cooks, particularly for the dressing of Turtle and every other dish fit to set before either Gentlemen or Ladies), he hopes to be honored with their company; assuring them there shall be nothing wanting on his part to make it convenient and agreeable, as well to entitle him to the honor of their countenance as custom. And as his boats will always be ready to attend travellers and those Gentlemen and Ladies from the City of New York as well as those of the Province he lives in, at a minute's warning, flatters himself he will make it so convenient that during the summer season such as do not choose to come over to dine may always be provided with tea, &c., &c., pass the afternoon, have the best of fruit the different seasons afford, and return to town again before night, or honor him with their custom longer, as he will be strict with having good beds for the accommodation of Gentlemen and Ladies that are going to any part of the Jersies, Philadelphia or the northern country, and choose to have their horses and carriages brought over that night, and set out early the next morning; or such as are coming from Philadelphia or elsewhere, that choose to stay at his Inn that night, and the next morning go over to the City of New York. He has one of the best wharfs for landing horses and carriages at all times of the tide; and he may say the completest causeway in this country, between the island he lives on and the main ocean.

"☞ The boats are to be distinguished by the name The Hoobook Ferry, painted on the stern."[1]

During the war which shortly followed, this ferry, like its neighbor at Paulus Hoeck, was subject to the control of the army occupying New York. On the 7th of August, 1776, orders were issued from headquarters, in the city, that a subaltern and twenty men should be placed at the Hoebuck ferry to examine the passengers crossing there.[2] This was done to prevent disaffected persons passing into New Jersey, as also to prevent the

---

[1] *Rivington's Gazette, April* 27, 1775. [2] *Am. Archives, 5th Series, i.*, 912.

desertion of the continental troops, which at that time was of frequent occurrence.[1] No mention is made of the ferry from this time until 1784, when John Allen, on the 8th of October, secured a lease of it for three years at a rent of £67 a year.[2] He soon grumbled about the terms, and at his own request was, on the 20th of August, 1785, released from his contract,[3] and Sylvanus Lawrence took the lease for three years at a rent of £37 a year.[4] In June, 1787, he sold out his interest in the ferry to Charles A. Wiessenfels,[5] who, on the 9th of July, 1788, obtained a lease from the city for three years from the 31st of August, 1788, at a rent of £5 a year.[6] This arrangement soon fell through, and the Common Council asked for proposals for this ferry lease. On Wednesday, the 15th of April, 1789, the bids were opened. John Stevens, the owner of Hoboken,[7] offered £10 a year, and was the highest bidder.[8] This is the first time the name of that gentleman appears in connection with this ferry, though there can be no doubt that he was at this time its owner. He held the lease until the 12th of December, 1791, when Joseph Smith obtained it for three years at the rent of £91 a year. This was probably in the interest of Mr. Stevens. By various renewals, Smith held the lease until the 26th of March, 1799, when the same was obtained by Zadock Hedden.[9] In the mean time the ferry had improved, and the rent increased. At this time Elias Haynes was in charge of the ferry on the New York side, and John Town on the Jersey side. Town announced that he spared "no expense to render Hobuckin House and Ferry commodious," and that "he had the best boats on the river."[10]

On the 11th of March, 1799, the Common Council of New York established the following rates of ferriage for "Hobooc-ken:"

A Passenger, - - - - - - - - £0 0 9

[1] *Am. Archives, 5th Series, i.*, 886.
[2] *N. Y. Records, viii.*, 184.
[3] *Ibid, viii.*, 309.
[4] *Ibid, viii.*, 322.
[5] *Ibid, viii.*, 566.
[6] *Ibid, ix.*, 101.
[7] *Winfield's Land Titles*, 40.
[8] *N. Y. Records, ix.*, 199.
[9] *Ibid, xii.*, 470.
[10] *Centinel of Freedom, April* 18, 1798.

	£	s.	d.
A Coach, Chariot, Coachee or covered Wagon, -	£0	8	6
A Phaeton, - - - - - - - - -	0	5	6
A Chaise or top Chair, - - - - - - -	0	3	6
A Chair, - - - - - - - - -	0	2	6
A Sleigh, - - - - - - - - -	0	3	6
Horses and Cattle, - - - - - - -	0	1	9
A Sheep, Calf or Hog, - - - - - -	0	0	6
A large Trunk or Chest, - - - - - -	0	1	3
A small do - - - - - - -	0	0	9
A Bushel of Salt, - - - - - - -	0	0	2½
A Pipe or Hogshead of Wine, Spirits or Molasses,	0	8	0
A Barrel of do - - - -	0	1	0
A Barrel of Beef, Pork, Flour or Fish, - -	0	1	3
Plank of every kind, - - - - - - -	0	0	2
Boards do - - - - - - -	0	0	1
A Side of Sole Leather, - - - - - - -	0	0	2
Do of Upper do - - - - - - -	0	0	1
A Raw Hide, - - - - - - - - -	0	0	3
Iron, Steel, Lead, &c., per cwt., - - - -	0	0	6
A Desk, - - - - - - - - - -	0	3	0
A large Table, - - - - - - - -	0	1	0
A small do - - - - - - - -	0	0	6
A Mahogany Chair, - - - - - - -	0	0	2
A common do - - - - - - -	0	0	1
A Basket or Bag of Fruit of 2 Bushels - -	0	0	4
A Bag of Grain of do - - -	0	0	3
A Crate of Earthenware, - - - - - -	0	2	0
A Tierce of do - - - - - -	0	2	3
A Feather Bed, - - - - - - - -	0	0	6
A Clock Case, - - - - - - - -	0	1	0
A Chest of Tea, - - - - - - - -	0	2	0
Dye Wood, per cwt., - - - - - - -	0	0	6
Gunpowder, per cwt., - - - - - - -	0	1	0
A large Bale of Cotton, - - - - - - -	0	2	0
An empty Hogshead or Pipe, - - - - -	0	1	0
Do do Barrel, - - - - -	0	0	3
Cabbages, per hundred, - - - - - -	0	1	6

Shad, per hundred, - - - - - - - £0 2 0
And all other articles and things in like proportion.[1]

Holden held the lease only for a few months. Experience had taught the Common Council that a promise to pay and the payment of rent for ferry leases were two very different things. To make sure of the rent, they demanded security from Holden. He waxed wroth at the doubt of his honesty which the demand seemed to imply, threw up the lease, and refused to have anything more to do with the ferry.[2] From this time until it was leased to Garret Covenhoven, the ferry was badly managed, and caused much complaint from the people.[3] Covenhoven took it in August, 1802, for three years, at a rent of $250 a year. At the termination of his lease, Peter Voorhis took the lease, at a rent of $350 a year. His management was no more appreciated than that of Covenhoven.[4] Then David Godwin desired to have the ferry, thinking he could meet the demands of the people. Being encouraged by the Bergen Turnpike Company,[5] he succeeded on the 4th of January, 1808, in securing a lease for three years at a rent of $350 a year.[6] During all these years, since the 26th day of July, 1784, John Stevens had been the owner of Hoboken, but remained quiet, with only an occasional remonstrance against the management of the ferry. Now, December 11, 1809, he came forward as the discoverer of a new power in navigation. He claimed to be the first man in the country who had successfully applied steam as a propelling power. At the same time, he claimed to be the proprietor of this ferry, and earnestly remonstrated against the proposition to give to Elisha Boudinot and his associates the exclusive right to ferry by steam between New York and New Jersey. In September, 1810, he asked for a lease of the Hoboken ferry, and promised to place a steamboat thereon.[7] On the 13th of April, 1811, he obtained the lease for the landing on the New York side,[8] and immediately set to work to complete his steam

[1] *N. Y. Records, xii.*, 458. [2] *Ibid, xii.*, 554. [3] *Ibid, xiii.*, 60.
[4] *Ibid, xv.*, 435. [5] *Ibid, xvii.*, 422. [6] *Ibid, xviii.*, 7.
[7] *Ibid, xxii.*, 263. [8] *Ibid, xxxv.*, 331.

ferry-boat. This was completed about the middle of September, 1811, and shortly afterward was made the trial trip of the first steam ferry-boat in the world. At this time a Mr. Godwin, of Hoboken, had charge of the ferry, and he employed the steamboat. It was immediately put into use, and on the 23d of September, 1811, made sixteen trips, with an average of one hundred passengers each trip.[1] At this time, the landing place on the New York side was at the foot of Vesey street. On the 24th of May, 1813, Colonel Stevens secured the lease of the Spring street ferry.[2] On the Vesey (now Barclay) street ferry, he soon abandoned the use of steam, and returned to horse boats as more profitable, and he claimed that this movement "promised to be highly valuable in facilitating the intercourse between New York and the Jersey shore."[3] He continued to operate both the Vesey street and Spring street ferries until January, 1817, when he sold to John, Robert and Samuel Swartwout the exclusive right of ferriage from Hoboken to New York. The Swartwouts proposed to have on the two ferries, by the first of the following May, "two horse boats and other craft for the accommodation of the public."[4] On the 7th of April, 1817, the Common Council consented to the transfer of the ferry leases and an extension thereof for ten years, on condition that the Swartwouts would give to the city $516.25 a year for the Vesey street ferry, and within six months from the first of the following May place thereon "two good horse boats of not less than eight horses to a boat;" and for the Spring street ferry to give $25 a year, and place thereon "as many sail or ferry boats as the corporation may deem proper."[5] About this time the landing on the New York side was changed to Murray street. But that location was found to be too "remote from the market to accommodate the country people," and as Vesey street was "too much covered with carts, &c.," Barclay street was selected as the landing place on the 8th of June, 1818. At this place it has remained ever

[1] *Centinel of Freedom, October* 1, 1811. Mr. Valentine fixes the date of the trial trip, October 11, 1811. *Valentine's Manual,* 1859, 604.

[2] *N. Y. Records, xxxvii.,* 7.

[3] *Ibid, xxxviii.,* 221.

[4] *Ibid, xxxii.,* 109.

[5] *Ibid, xxxii.,* 321.

since. The Swartwouts held these ferries but little over one year. They assigned them to Philip Hone, of New York. The Common Council consented to the transfer. They gave him a lease for twelve years, and permitted him to "substitute a good substantial team boat in the place of a steamboat."[1] About the 1st of March, 1821, an ejectment suit was begun against Hone to take from him the ferry.[2] Before this suit came to trial the parties compromised, and the two ferries reverted to the Stevens family. In May, 1821, John C. and Robert L. Stevens purchased the interest which Hone had in them.[3] They now proposed to place on the Barclay street ferry "a superior steamboat, from ninety to a hundred feet on deck, and forty-two feet beam, built of the best cedar and oak," and promised to put on more than one if necessary. For the Spring street ferry they proposed an eight-horse team boat. The Common Council consented that John C. Stevens should have the lease of the Barclay street ferry for nine years from May 1, 1821, at a rent of $595 a year, and that he and his brother Robert L. should have the Spring street ferry for fourteen years, paying therefor, for the first four years one cent a year; for the next five years $50 a year, and for the next five years, $200 a year. It was further agreed that the Barclay street lease should be extended for five years at a rent of $800 a year.[4] The *Hoboken Steamboat Ferry Company* was incorporated November 3, 1821.

On the 22d of April, 1822, the Messrs. Stevens made a trial trip of the first steamboat placed on the ferry since 1811.[5] This was the "Hoboken." Thereafter it made trips "every hour by St. Paul's Church clock." On the 21st of July, 1823, they received permission to start the Canal street ferry and use steamboats thereon.[6] On the first Friday in September, 1823, the "Pioneer" made its trial trip.[7] In these boats the ladies' cabin was below deck, carpeted and warmed by open fire-places. From 1821 until the present time these ferries have been under the

---

[1] *N. Y. Records, xxxv.*, 331. [2] *Ibid, xlii.*, 249. [3] *Ibid, xliii.*, 7.
[4] *Ibid, xliii.*, 336. [5] *Ibid, xlv.*, 211. [6] *Ibid, xlviii.*, 316.
[7] *Ibid, xlviii.*, 446.

control of the Stevens family or of the Hoboken Land and Improvement Company. The Christopher street ferry was started in July, 1836.

List of boats on the Hoboken Ferry.

Hoboken,	April 22, 1822.
Pioneer,	September, 1823.
Fairy Queen,[1]	April, 1828.
Newark,	April, 1828.
Passaic,[2]	1844.
John Fitch,	1846.
James Rumsey,[3]	1846.
Phœnix,	1851.
James Watt,[4]	1851.
Chancellor Livingston,[5]	1853.
Paterson,	1854.
Hoboken,[6]	1861.
Hoboken,	1863.
Morristown,	1864.
James Rumsey,	1867.
Wiehawken,	1868.
Secaucus,	March 10, 1873.

The Pavonia Ferry.

Standing out boldly on the first page of this ferry's history is an exclusive right of ferriage, the King's Patent for which is as follows:

[1] This boat was rebuilt in 1851, and then named the Phœnix. It was the night boat in the summer of 1856.

[2] This boat was taken from the line to Newark.

[3] Destroyed by fire in 1853 while lying in the Barclay street slip. Her machinery was afterward put in the Paterson.

[4] Destroyed by fire August 2, 1870.

[5] Chartered by the United States Government in 1861 for a transport. It was in the service about one year.

[6] Chartered by the United States Government in 1861 for a transport. It was lost in the Burnside expedition to North Carolina in 1862.

"George the Second, by the grace of God, of Great Britain, France and Ireland, King, Defender of the Faith, &c.

"To all to whom these presents shall come, greeting. Whereas, the convenient, speedy and safe carridge, transportation and conveyance of passengers, horses, goods, wares and merchandizes from one place or one province to another is the life of trade and commerce; and whereas it has been humbly represented unto us by our loving subject Archibald Kennedy, Esquire, one of our Council of the neighboring province of New York, that the County of Bergen is a growing county and yearly increases in its number of inhabitants and productions of all sorts of necessaries, and that it lies the most contiguous to our city of New York, in our said province of New York; and whereas there hath not hitherto been any regular ferry or passage boats, except from our said Jersey shore to our said City of New York, so as to transport or set over any passengers, goods or merchandizes, with any safety or certainty, to the great inconveniency and detriment of all our loving subjects, the inhabitants of both our said provinces. And whereas the said Archibald Kennedy hath proposed and undertaken, though at very great expense and trouble and without any probability of any present advantage, to build a boat or boats, scow or scows, erect a wharf or wharves, and do everything necessary and commodious for the keeping up and employing a regular ferry or ferries, for the transporting of passengers and horses, goods, wares and merchandizes as aforesaid, providing he might obtain our letters patent, granting to him, his heirs and assigns, the sole liberty and privilege of keeping and employing a ferry or ferries, at such place or places, and in such manner and under such provisoes as hereafter mentioned. And we, having always at heart the benefit, ease and safety of all our loving subjects, and being ready and willing to give proper encouragement to all those who shall undertake to contribute to the same, we have thought fit to give and grant, and we do hereby, of our special grace and mere motion, give and grant unto the said Archibald Kennedy, his heirs and assigns, the sole liberty and privilege of keeping, using and employing a ferry or ferries, at a place called Pavonia, alias

Ahasimus, situate on Hudson's, or the North river, in our said province of New Jersey, and at a certain distance on each side of the said place along the shore, that is to say, from the said place called Pavonia or Ahasimus, to the most southerly part of a place called Communipaw, down the said river, and up the said river from the said place, Pavonia or Ahasimus, a quarter of a mile beyond for above Weehawk, for transporting and carrying of passengers, goods, wares and merchandizes, with the liberty of taking and receiving such sum and sums of money, ferriages and hire for the same, as hath been usually taken and received in such cases, or now is, or at any time hereafter shall be legally established or appointed for that purpose. To have and to hold the sole liberty and privilege, ferriages and hire aforesaid, to the said Archibald Kennedy, his heirs and assigns, to the sole and only proper use, benefit and behoof of the said Archibald Kennedy, his heirs and assigns forever. And we do strictly forbid all our loving subjects to carry any passengers, horses, goods, wares or merchandizes, contrary to the liberty and privilege aforesaid, under the pain of our displeasure and the highest penalties the law can inflict, provided always, and these presents are upon this condition and limitation, that the said Archibald Kennedy, with all convenient speed, shall provide a sufficient boat or boats, scow or scows, and sufficient persons or hands for the transporting, carrying and ferrying of passengers, horses, goods, wares and merchandizes as aforesaid, and the same being so provided shall from time to time and at all times hereafter, continue to keep, or cause to be kept such boat or boats, scow or scows, in good and sufficient repair, with good and sufficient persons or hands to give due attendance for the transporting, carrying and ferrying of passengers, horses, goods, wares and merchandizes as aforesaid, according to the true intent and meaning hereof, otherwise this present grant, and every matter and thing contained herein, shall cease, determine and be utterly void to all intents and purposes whatsoever.

"In testimony whereof we have caused these our letters to be made patent and the seal of our province of Nova Cesarea, or New Jersey, to be affixed. Witness our trusty and well-beloved

William Cosby, Esq., Captain-General and Governor-in-Chief in and over our provinces of New Jersey and New York, and territories depending thereon in America, Vice-Admiral of the same, and Colonel in our army, &c. At Fort George, in the city of New York, this Seventh day of January, in the seventh year of our reign, and in the year of our Lord One Thousand Seven Hundred and Thirty-three."[1]

It is quite certain that Captain Kennedy did not fulfill the conditions of the above patent, and so forfeited all the rights intended to be granted thereby. The next notice of this ferry is a petition to the Common Council of New York for a ferry from the "west end of Pearl street" to Harsimus, on the 23d of March, 1753.[2] Nothing came of this movement. On May 3, 1765, Archibald Kennedy and William McAdam made an attempt to secure for themselves the exclusive right of ferriage from New York to the Jersey shore.[3] This was a blow at the Paulus Hoeck ferry, but it fell short. Excepting Budd's ferry, the next that is heard of a ferry from Harsimus is on the 13th of April, 1818, when a number of persons petitioned for a ferry from the foot of Chambers street to Harsimus.[4] Nothing more is heard of this ferry until on the completion of the Bergen Tunnel by the Long Dock Company in 1861. The Erie Railway Company, lessees of the Long Dock Company, revived the Pavonia Ferry.[5] It began business May 1, 1861, with three old boats—*Niagara*, *Onalaska* and *Onala*—from the Brooklyn ferries. The Erie Railway Company have since put upon the ferry the

Pavonia, built in - - - - - - -	1861.
Susquehanna, built in - - - - -	1864.
Delaware, built in - - - - - -	1865.

The Twenty-third street ferry was established in May, 1868.

BOATS.

Jay Gould, built in - - - - - -	1869.
James Fisk, Jr., built in - - - - -	1869.
Erie, built in - - - - - - -	1873.

[1] *Liber C 3 of Deeds* (*Trenton*), 224.
[2] *N. Y. Records, v.*, 329.
[3] *Ibid, vi.*, 269.
[4] *Ibid, xxxv.*, 149.
[5] The *Pavonia Ferry Company* was incorporated February 28, 1849.

BROWN'S FERRY.

The Commissioners who were appointed on the 20th of June, 1765, to lay out a road from Newark to intersect the road leading from Bergen Point to Paulus Hoeck, were authorized to erect ferries over the Passaic and Hackensack rivers, together with all necessary ferry buildings.[1] By the same act the owners of the land where the ferries were to be erected were permitted to operate the same for their own benefit, on condition that they would equip the ferries and keep in repair the causeway over their land. Thomas Brown, of Bergen, was one of the commissioners, and owner of the land on the east bank of the Hackensack where the ferry was erected.[2] From a supplement to said act, passed June 28, 1766,[3] it would seem that the ferry was erected before the latter date. Then arose a dispute between Captain Brown and Garret Newkirk concerning the title to the lands on the east side of the Hackensack, and the right to the ferry. It was decided in favor of the former, and from that time until the Revolution the ferry was known as "Brown's Ferry." For nearly thirty years this was the only thoroughfare between Paulus Hoeck and Newark and the extensive country beyond. It may well be supposed that it did a thriving business with its row boats and scows. A horn hanging to a tree served the traveler to summon the ferryman to his duty and reward.[4] The safety of the ferries over the Passaic and Hackensack rivers was an early care of the Americans in the Revolution. On August 7, 1776, Richard Stockton, a delegate in Congress from New Jersey, sent to the New Jersey State Convention, then in session at Burlington, certain resolutions of Congress requesting the Convention to make such provision for keeping open these ferries as would be effectual. They were accompanied by a Congressional promise to reimburse such expenses to the State. So prompt was the Convention in carrying out the wishes of Congress that on August 9 they passed an ordinance for keeping open the communication between New Jersey and New York by way of these ferries.

---

[1] *Allinson's Laws,* 276.
[2] See the genealogy of the Gautier family.
[3] *Allinson's Laws,* 289.
[4] *Booth's Hist. of N. Y.,* 399.

The preamble of the ordinance declares the ferries poorly equipped and the proprietors negligent. The act took them out of the proprietor's hands and put them in the hands of William Camp and Joseph Hedden until the first of December following. They were to provide four scows to each ferry, supply a sufficient number of hands, and stretch ropes across the rivers. Soldiers were to be ferried over for one-third of the regular rates.[1] After the capture of New York the ferry was suspended. When the war closed the ferries were repaired, and continued in use until the bridges were built on the turnpike. They then fell into disuse until 1805, when they were again repaired. They remained in use until supplanted by the bridges built after the old road across the meadows was made into a plank road.

Douw's Ferry.

This ferry was located at the westerly end of Cherry lane, about 175 feet north of the present bridge of the New Jersey Railroad over the Hackensack river. It was probably set up about the time that Colonel John Schuyler constructed the Belleville turnpike during the French war, and remained in operation until superseded by the bridge erected in 1794. It received its name from John Douw, a friend of Colonel Schuyler. He had formerly operated the ferry over the Passaic at Belleville. The ferry house was on the west side of the Hackensack. Douw used it also as a public house, where he entertained travelers and guests. Bangs says that here, June 27, 1776, by him and Schuyler, "many Decanters of Wine suffered shipwreck, and many Bowles of Grog were poured down. * * Nor was Egg Pop forgot among our Dainties."[2] It was at this ferry that boats had been provided on the night of Lee's attack on Paulus Hoeck to carry over the troops on their retreat. Their delay induced those in charge to believe that the forces had retreated along the hill, and there-

[1] *Am. Archives, 4th Series, vi.*, 1659.

[2] *Proc. N. J. Hist. Soc., viii.*, 122.

fore the boats were taken away. Lee's advance, passing down Cherry Lane, reached the ferry only to find it deserted.

Budd's Ferry.

In the year 1802, Nathaniel Budd, without any license, built or extended a dock in the Harsimus Cove, afterward known as Budd's Dock, and erected a ferry to New York. The western end of this dock was in Eighth street, about the middle of the block east of Provost street, and thence extended southeasterly between one hundred and two hundred feet. The exact date when this ferry was erected is not known; though, from a petition of John Holdron, dated in May, 1803,[1] that the Jersey City Ferry had been injured by a "new ferry" which had been in existence for ten months, the proximate date is ascertained. On the 22d of November, 1802, the Legislature appointed commissioners with power to lay out a road from the "Great Road leading from Newark to Paulus Hook" to Budd's Dock. The act also authorized Budd to erect a ferry from said dock to the city of New York. It would seem from the preamble to the act that he had been operating the ferry for some time, for therein it is said the ferry "hath acquired a great share of public patronage." He had landed on the New York side without the permission or even knowledge of the authorities there; for, in their report on Holdron's petition, on the 16th of May, 1803, the committee expressly say "the corporation was not aware of" any ferry as complained of by Holdron, and they recommended that unauthorized ferries be restrained. Just previous to this report, and immediately after the petition of Holdron, on the 9th of May, 1803, Budd petitioned the Common Council of New York "for liberty to establish a new ferry from the Barclay street wharf across the North River."[2] There seems to be a conflict between this petition and the act of 1802, explained probably by the fact that hitherto he had run it without authority. The request of the petition was refused on the 16th of the same month, for the rea-

---

[1] *Proc. N. J. Hist. Soc.*, *xiii.*, 712.

[2] *Ibid*, *xiii.*, 694.

son that the ferries existing on the North River were then under lease for three years, and it would be improper for the corporation to lease other ferries during that time, and, in the opinion of the committee, "the public interest would not be promoted by erecting another ferry on the North River."[1]

Notwithstanding this, he advertises as follows:

"BUDD'S FERRY.

"The subscriber informs his friends and the public that he has erected a Ferry between Powles Hook and Hobooken Ferries, has also provided good Boats and careful Ferrymen for carrying Passengers, Horses, Cattle, Carriages, Goods, Wares and Merchandize to and from the City of New York, as he hath obtained liberty from the Corporation of New York to land and take off from the same Dock and Ferry Stairs as the Powles Hook Boats do at the foot of Courtland Street, in the City of New York—and also entertainment for them and Horses, and hath erected convenient Stables adjacent to the said Ferry for those who would wish to bring with them their own forage for teams or without.

"Oct. 24, 1803." —*Centinel of Freedom, Oct.* 25, 1803.

There is no record in the minutes of the Common Council of New York, up to 1824, that Budd ever received permission to land his ferry boats on that side of the river; yet, from Holdron's petition, there can be no doubt that his boats were running in 1802, and from the evidence in *Gough vs. Bell*,[2] that "for some years after" 1804, he had a ferry and kept a ferry house.

BULL'S FERRY.

When and by whom this ferry was erected has not been discovered. The name was well known at the time of the Revolution. At that time there lived a family by the name of

[1] *Proctor's N. J. Hist. Soc., xiii.,* 711.

[2] 1 *Zab. Rep.*, 164.

Bull, at the place now known as Bull's Ferry, and the probability is that it took its name from that family, who then owned the land on the Jersey shore and erected the ferry. Nothing particular concerning it is to be found in the *New York Records*. The following named persons have been lessees, and probably managed the ferry, or had an interest in it:

Cornelius Huyler, - - - - - - 1788 to 1792.
Theodorus Brower, - - - - - 1792 " 1805.
Garret Neefie, - - - - - - - - 1805.
Lewis Concklin, - - - - - - - 1806.
Abraham Huyler, - - - - - - - - 1808.

De Klyn's Ferry.

On the 14th of October, 1799, John Towne and Barent De Klyn erected a ferry from the new wharf "south and north" of the State Prison to Hoboken.[1] In March, 1806, the location of it was referred to a committee of the New York Common Council,[2] but nothing more has been learned concerning it.

The following attempts were made to erect other ferries across the North River. There is no evidence, however, that either of them were successful.

On the 19th of May, 1805, Anthony Lispenard and others petitioned the Common Council of New York for "a new Ferry across Hudson River, between De Klyn's Ferry and the Market."[3]

On the 2d of September, 1805, Joseph Watkins and others petitioned for a "new ferry from the Market in Greenwich street," and Gabriel V. Ludlow and others petitioned for a "ferry from the foot of Duane street."[4]

The Elizabethtown Point Ferry.

This ferry is only incidentally connected with Jersey City. About the year 1808, it was purchased by Colonel Aaron Ogden,

[1] *N. Y. Records, xii.*, 548.
[2] *Ibid, xv.*, 518.
[3] *Ibid, xv.*, 328.
[4] *Ibid, xv.*, 349.

and by him leased to John R. and Robert J. Livingston, who owned a monopoly of navigating New York waters by steam. They placed on this ferry the *Raritan*, the first steamer between New York and Elizabethtown Point. It was not long, however, before Colonel Ogden had built, by Cornelius Joralemon, of Belleville, a boat, fourteen feet beam and seventy-five feet keel, in which Daniel Dod, of Mendham, put a twelve-horse engine. It was called the *Sea-Horse*. This boat the Colonel placed on this ferry, but, to avoid seizure under the New York navigation laws, ran her to Jersey City. On the 18th of May, 1813, she was advertised as "an elegant steamboat provided to run between Elizabethtown Point and Paulus Hook; fare four shillings." She made two trips a day. The fare was afterward reduced to three shillings and sixpence. On the 21st of June, 1814, she was advertised to meet the team boat *Substitution*, at Paulus Hook, which would carry the passengers to New York.

"The Bellona, owned by Gibbons, ran from Elizabethtown to Jersey City, fare 12½ cents. In the advertisement was flung to the breeze a banner inscribed with the motto, 'New Jersey must be free.'"—*Sentinel of Freedom, July* 31, 1821.

Powles Hook and Brooklyn.

During the Races at the Union Course on Long Island, in October, 1822, a Brooklyn ferry boat made four trips a day between that city and Jersey City.

CHAPTER X.

History of Jersey City—Paulus Hoeck—Paulus Hoeck race course—Early lotteries—British graveyard—Names of city officials—Consolidation with Van Vorst township—With Bergen and Hudson City—As a port of entry—Water works—Post-office—Bull-baiting — Floating theatre—The old wind mill—History of Bergen—Its officers—History of Harrison—Captain William Sandford—Petersborough—History of Harsimus—West India Company's farm—The Duke's farm—History of Hoboken—Its first occupant—Made into a city—Its officers—History of North Bergen—Secaucus—Three Pigeons—The Frenchman's garden—History of Hudson City—Its officials—Beacon race course—Horses running and time made.

As WILL be seen hereafter, the territory comprised within the county of Hudson includes all the land within the limits of the old township of Bergen, and that part of New Barbadoes Neck now within the bounds of the townships of Harrison and Kearney. This territory has, since the erection of the county, been cut up into several municipalities, a brief sketch of some of which we now propose to give.

JERSEY CITY was incorporated January 28, 1820, but remained a part of the township of Bergen. It was then bounded on the west by a creek and ditch between the lands of the "Associates of the Jersey Company" and Cornelius Van Vorst (Warren street nearly); east by the middle of Hudson's river; north by Harsimus Cove (First street), and south by Communipaw Cove (South street). This territory was the old Paulus Hoeck of the Dutch and Aressick of the Indians. It was sold by the West India Company to Abraham Isaacsen Planck, May 1, 1638, for the sum of four hundred and fifty guilders, calculated at twenty stivers to the guilder.[1] It remained in the Planck family until August 2, 1699, when it was sold to Cornelius Van Vorst for £300, "current money of New York."[2] From this time until

[1] *N. Y. Col. MSS.*, *i.*, 14.

[2] *Winfield's Land Titles*, 45.

1764 it was used as farm land, as most of it continued to be until 1804. In 1764 the ferry was established, and Michael Cornelison built, just north of Grand street, near the water, a low frame house about forty feet in length, with a piazza in front and an extensive Dutch roof which projected over the piazza. In 1800 this house, used as a tavern and ferry house, and several spacious barns and stables and a store house were the only buildings on the Hoeck. Here, when passengers arrived by stage and no boat was at hand to take them to New York, they could get both food and drink. In addition to this, the host would regale them with an inexhaustible fund of anecdote, for he was well acquainted with the world; had seen much of it; had taken part in the War of the Revolution, and was a shrewd observer. Such was the straight, stout, jolly Major David Hunt.

Late in 1800, or early in 1801, a small shanty was put up along the turnpike, a little way from the ferry house, and occupied, as is now supposed, by John Murphy. The portentous sign, OYGH-STORS FOR SALE HEAR, put on the side of the establishment, indicated to the hungry traveler good cheer within and incipient opposition to the sirloins of the Major.[1]

The old tavern, at least as much of it as could be moved, was finally taken to a lot of Colonel Dod, so well known as the veteran post-office man, who for so many years buffeted the storm and ploughed his way through fields of ice in performance of the laudable duty of transporting the United States mail over the river in a row boat!

The Hoeck was made up of a number of sand hills, some of them of considerable height. Around these, and generally along the edge of the upland, Cornelius Van Vorst, in the summer of 1769, made a track for horse racing. It was one mile in length. Here the lovers of fast horses and good sport gathered from the

[1] I find the following in a paper of that date: "The Steer fattened by Major Hunt and killed by Aaron Munn & Co. weighed

The Quarters,	1266
Hide and fat,	260
Total,	1526."

neighboring city and surrounding country, until the Revolution broke out and war put a stop to fun. The first notice met with relating to this course is as follows:

"POWLES HOOK RACES.

"On Monday, the 9th day of October next, will be run for over the New Course at Powles Hook, a Purse of FIFTY POUNDS, New York Currency, by any Horse, Mare or Gelding, not more than three Quarters Blood; and those less than three Quarters Blood to be allowed 5 lb. The best of three 3 Mile Heats; three Years old carrying seven Stone; four Years old seven Stone, eight pounds; five Years old eight Stone, two Pounds; six years old eight stone, eleven Pounds; and aged Horses 9 Stone, seven Pounds, Saddle and Bridle included; Fillies to be allowed three Pounds. Any Horse, &c., running two Heats shall not be obliged to start a third to save his Distance. To run according to the King's Plate Articles.

"Tuesday, the 10th, the beaten Horses to run the best of three Heats for the Stakes.

"Wednesday, the 11th, there will be a Fox Hunt in Bergen Woods,[1] and on Tuesday, the 12th, there will be a Purse of

---

[1] This sport was continued until quite recently. Some are yet living who took part in the chase through Bergen Woods. The following receipt for dinners shows that some of our best citizens belonged to the hunt, and that when the fierce delight of the chase was over they knew how to quiet their overstrained nerves:

"JERSEY CITY, February 18, 1831.

"Gentlemen Fox Chasers,

To Freeman Anderson, Dr.

Colonel Ogden, to	1	Dinner,	$1 00
Doctor Gotier,	"	"	1 00
" Cornelison,	"	"	1 00
Henderson,	"	"	1 00
Hugh McCutcheon,	2	"	2 00
Gilchrist,	1	"	1 00
Mr. Miller,	"	"	1 00
Mr. James,	"	"	1 00
Mr. Freeland,	"	"	1 00

Twenty Pounds, free for any Horse, Mare or Gelding not more than Quarter Blood, Weight for age as above. The Horses, &c., to be shown and entered at the Starting Post, the Saturday before running, between the Hours of 3 and 5 in the afternoon, in presence of the Judges, who will be present, paying 50s. Entrance for each Horse, &c., that starts for the Plate of 50l., and 20s. for every Horse, &c, that starts for the 20l. Plate. Any Dispute that may arise to be determined by a Majority of the Subscribers present.

"No Quarter Blood that ever won the value of 40s. can start for the Purse of 20l.

"Good Crafts will be ready at each Ferry to convey over all Persons who may incline to see the Races; good Stables, with excellent Hay and oats, will be provided for the Horses, and good Accommodations for the Grooms. To start at 2 o'Clock precisely each Day; Certificates of the Ages of the Horses, &c., to be produced at Entrance, from under the hands of the Breeders."[1]

The race came off at the time named. Four horses started for the £50 purse. It was won by Anthony Rutger's horse *Luggs*. Mr. Morris' horse *Partner* had the misfortune to run over a dog. The cur threw the horse and the horse threw the rider, who was very much hurt. Up to the time of this mishap the

---

7	Bottles of	Champaigne, - - - -	14 00
3	"	Port, - - - - - - -	3 00
1	"	Madeira, - - - - - -	2 00
			9)29 00
			3 22½

"April 26, 1831.

"Received by the hands of J. D. Miller three Dollars 22-100 from Doctor Gautier, Dr. Cornelison, David Henderson, Robert Gilchrist and J. D. Miller, respectively, being their quota of amount on the above bill, and acct. in full for the same. FREEMAN ANDERSON."

"Received, Jersey City, December 4th, 1830, of Henry Lyon, Twenty Dollars, in full, for the Use of the Hounds and myself attending the Club of the Jersey Hunt, which is full satisfaction to me.

"$20.00. JOHN BANGHER."

[1] *N. Y. Mercury, August* 14, 1769.

race "in doubtful balance hung," as *Luggs* had won the first heat and *Partner* the second.[1]

The proprietor of the course was anxious to keep the races in good repute. One of the rules was: "No persons to be concerned in a confederacy in running their Horses together or in dividing the Plate."[2] Thus it would appear that it was wholesome for horsemen to be subjected to a little watching even in those days of honesty.

On the 27th of August, 1771, a purse of £100, and on the following day a purse of £50, was run for. For the first purse, Captain De Lancey's chestnut colt *Sultan*, Mr. Perkins' black horse *Steady*, Mr. Dick's gray horse *Vitriol* and Israel Waters' bay mare *Nettle* started. *Nettle* won without difficulty. For the second purse, Whitehead Cornell's horse *Booby*, Armstrong's horse *Hero*, Elsworth's gray colt *Quicksilver*, Butler's bay horse *Bastard*, Timothy Cornell's black horse *Richmond*, Dick's gray horse *Vitriol*, Perkins' black horse *Steady* and Van Horne's gray mare *Dove* started. The race was won by *Booby* in three straight heats, hard running.[3]

On the 31st of May, 1773, a fine race was run with the following result:

	Heats.		
Elsworth's bay horse, *Cyrus*, - - - - - -	5	1	1
Jackson's gray horse, *Quicksilver*, - - - -	1	3	3
Tallman's gray mare, *Dove*, - - - - - -	4	4	2
Wickoff's black horse, *Richmond*, - - - -	3	2	0
Patterson's black horse, *Gimcrack*, - - - -	2	dr	0
Waters' horse, *Valiant* (5 years old), - . -	6	dr	0

On the following day the four-year-olds ran for a purse of £50, with the following result:

Anthony Rutger's bay colt, *Macaroni*,[4] - - -	1	1	0

[1] *N. Y. Mercury, October* 16, 1771. [2] *Ibid, April* 15, 1771.

[3] *Ibid, September* 2, 1771.

[4] This was a beautiful horse. His dam was out of *Ariel*, by *Old Spark*. His sire was *Wildair*, he out of *Old Cade*, and he out of Lord Godolphin's *Arabian*. *Wildair's* dam was *Roxana*, daughter of *Bald Galloway*, and granddaughter of *Old Spark*.

	Heats.		
Patterson's bay mare, *Virgin*, - - - - - -	3	2	0
Waters' brown horse, *Xanthus*, - - - - -	2	3	0
Cornell's bay horse, *Bashaw*, - - . - -	4	4	0[1]

On the 23d of May, 1774, a race was run for a £50 purse, as follows:

Cornell's black horse, *Steady*, - - - -	1	4	3	1
Rutgers' bay horse, *Macaroni*, - - - - -	2	1	2	3
Waters' bay horse, *Auctioneer*, - - - -	5	2	1	2
Elsworth's bay horse, *Cyrus*, - - - - -	3	3	dr	
Jackson's gray horse, *Quicksilver*, - - -	4	5	dr	

At this race the spectators were numerous, the weather fine, the sport excellent, but the most confident in the betting branch were grievously disappointed.[2]

Immediately after the race Elsworth ("Dine" Elsworth, of the Paulus Hoeck Ferry) bought the horse *Macaroni*, and entered him for the race on June 7, at Centre Course, near Philadelphia.[3] Sometimes the programme was changed from a race of blooded horses to a scrub race of Dutch horses, in which the steeds of Bergen and Communipaw had an opportunity to show the metal of their pasture.[4]

These are the particulars of a few of the races run on this course. It was not used during the war, but revived afterward, and continued until the Associates graded down the sand hills and began a new city. A track was then laid out at Harsimus, about where Henderson street crosses the Erie Railway tracks. This was in successful operation in 1808 and 1809.

About a century ago lotteries were much in vogue and very popular. Churches, colleges, schools, roads and prisons were built, and many charitable institutions sustained by them. Paulus Hoeck was a favorite place for this enterprise. The first lottery drawn here was in the summer of 1773. It was noticed as follows:

---

[1] *Rivington's Gazette, June* 3, 1773.

[2] *Ibid, May* 26, 1774.

[3] *Ibid, June* 2, 1774.

[4] *N. Y. Mercury, May* 9, 1774.

"POWLES HOOK CASH LOTTERY.

"SUBJECT to a deduction of 15 per cent. on the Prizes to be given for Purses to be run for at Powles Hook.

1	Prize of	400	Doll. is	400
1	"	200	"	200
2	"	100	"	200
6	"	50	"	300
12	"	25	"	300
31	"	10	"	310
69	"	5	"	345
378	"	$2\frac{1}{2}$	"	945

500 Prizes.
1,000 Blanks.

1,500 Tickets at 2 Dollars each, - - - - 3,000

"The Lottery has two blanks to a prize; will be drawn as soon as full. After the drawing, printed handbills with the fortunate numbers will be distributed among the adventurers, and the prizes regularly paid at Powles Hook."[1]

During the first quarter of this century Yates and McIntyre conducted the lottery business in Jersey City, and in March, 1824, advertised a "Queen's College Literature Lottery."

During the British occupancy of the Hoeck there was a burying ground south of Sussex street and west of Washington street. In this ground many of the enemy were buried, among whom was Major John Smith. Connected with his grave is an interesting fact. The equestrian statue of George III., which was set up in 1770, in the centre of Bowling Green, New York, was torn down on the 9th of July, 1776. It is said to have contained four thousand pounds of lead, covered with gold leaf.[2] The slab upon which the statue was placed now lies in the sidewalk in front of Cornelius Van Vorst's residence, on the south side of Wayne street, near Jersey avenue. It is a coarse marble, and is said to

[1] *Rivington's Gazette, June* 3, 1773.

[2] *Proc. N. J. Hist. Soc., viii.* 125.

have been brought from England. The holes in which three of the hoofs of the leaden charger were fastened are yet to be seen. During the war it was brought to Paulus Hoeck—when, by whom or for what purpose (unless for the purpose to which it was afterward put) is not known. On Friday evening, July 25, 1783, Major John Smith, stationed at Paulus Hoeck, died, and was buried on the following Sunday with military honors.[1] This slab was placed over his grave, with the following inscription engraved upon it:

In Memory of
Major John Smith,
of the
XLIInd or Royal Highland Reg't,
Who died 25 July, 1783,
In the 48th Year of his Age,
This Stone is erected
By the OFFICERS of that Reg't.
His
Bravery, Generosity & Humanity
During an honorable service
of 29 Years
Endeared him to the Soldiers,
To his Acquaintance & Friends.

When this part of Jersey City was graded, Mr. Van Vorst ("Faddy") took the slab to his house in Harsimus, where, from supporting the charger of a king, it became the stepping-stone of a republican. That building was torn down in 1818, when the stone was taken to the residence of his grandson, on the north-east corner of Wayne street and Jersey avenue. It there became a step at the kitchen door. When this building was torn down, in (about) 1854, the slab was placed where it now is. In 1828 an English gentleman offered Mr. Van Vorst five hundred dollars for it.

The Hoeck remained in possession of the Van Vorst family until the 26th of March, 1804, when, with the ferry rights, it was

---

[1] *Rivington's Gazette, July* 30, 1783.

conveyed to Anthony Dey, of New York, for an annuity of six thousand Spanish milled dollars. On the 18th of April, 1804, Dey conveyed it to Abraham Varick, who, on the 20th of the same month, conveyed it to Richard Varick, Jacob Radcliff and Anthony Dey.[1] These three men were the founders of Jersey

[1] The founders of Jersey City were three eminent and successful lawyers. RICHARD VARICK was born in 1752; licensed to practice law, Oct. 22, 1774; appointed Military Secretary-General in June, 1775, with the rank of Captain; in February, 1776, appointed by Congress Deputy Commissary-General of Musters for the northern army, with the rank of Lieutenant-Colonel. He was present at the battles of Stillwater and Saratoga. After Burgoyne's surrender, Colonel Varick was stationed at West Point until after the treason of Arnold, to whose family he was for some time attached as aide-de-camp. Shortly afterward he became a member of Washington's military family, and was by him appointed his Recording Secretary. After the evacuation of the city of New York by the British in 1783, Varick was appointed Recorder of the city, which office he held until 1788. In 1789 he held the office of Attorney-General of the State of New York, and in the same year was appointed Mayor of the city, which office he held for twelve years. He was President of the Cincinnati for nearly thirty years. He died in Jersey City, July 30, 1831.

JACOB RADCLIFF was the eldest son of William Radcliff, a Captain and Brigadier-General of Militia in the Revolution. By profession he was a lawyer; began practice in Poughkeepsie, and was soon raised to the bench of the Supreme Court. He then removed to the city of New York, and in a short time resigned his judicial office and resumed the practice of his profession. He was Mayor of that city in 1810, '15, '16, '17.

ANTHONY DEY was born at Preakness, Bergen County, N. J., in the month of February, 1776. His father, General Richard Dey, and his grandfather, Colonel Tunis Dey, were both of them officers in the Revolutionary army. He was a lineal descendant (the oldest son of the oldest son) of one Derrick Dey, who came to New York city from Holland in 1640, and established a mill and ferry at the foot of Dey street in that city. He resided on Broadway, at the head of that street. The mother of Richard Varick was a Miss Dey, and sister of Anthony Dey's grandfather. At the age of sixteen years Anthony came to the city and studied law in the office of his cousin, Colonel Richard Varick, to whose influence and connection he probably owed his early success in the practice of his profession, for he became a very successful and wealthy lawyer. He was also a very energetic, industrious and persevering man. He made it a rule through life to ignore political preferment, and never held any office, but was, nevertheless, foremost in everything that could be called a public improvement, especially in Bergen County, or that part of it now called Hudson County. He was the owner of large tracts of meadow land lying between the Hackensack and Passaic rivers, and during a long life made their improvement his particular interest and hobby. He was a Director for many years of the New Jersey Rail-

THE FOUNDERS OF JERSEY CITY.

City. They divided their purchase into one thousand shares, and associated other persons with themselves.[1] The whole plot was mapped by Joseph F. Mangin, and the map, dated April 15, 1804, entitled, "A Map of that part of the Town of Jersey commonly called Powles Hook." Anticipating the completion of this map, the owners, on the 12th of April, advertised a sale of lots for the 16th, afterward postponed until the 15th of May. It is probable that this sale was precipitated by the advertisement of John Stevens for a sale of lots in Hoboken. The parties interested now agreed upon a name for their future corporation, and gave notice of an application for an act of incorporation. The required act was passed by the Legislature on the 10th of November, 1804, and the "Associates of the Jersey Company" became not only a body, but a power in the State. For fifteen years, like an *imperium in imperio*, it possessed the government and shaped the destiny of the infant city.[2] To this corporate body Varick, Radcliff and Dey conveyed Paulus Hoeck, Feb. 1, 1805.

The title of the act of incorporation of 1820 reads, "An Act to incorporate the city of Jersey, in the county of Bergen," while the body of the act reads "Jersey City."[3] By this act the "taxable inhabitants" were authorized to elect annually five freeholders to conduct the affairs of the city, and to be known as "The Board of Selectmen of Jersey City." The act named Doctor John Condit, Samuel Cassedy, Joseph Lyon, John K. Goodman and John Seaman as the first board.

---

road, the owner, at one time, of the entire tract of land now known as East Newark, and for many years expended large sums of money in the introduction and improvement of blooded stock, both horses and cattle. He died in 1859, at his residence, in what is now a part of Jersey City, at a good old age.

[1] In noticing this new enterprise, a paper of that date says: "Who knows but that a very few years will make it the emporium of trade and commerce of the State of New Jersey?" *Centinel of Freedom, March* 13, 1804.

[2] By this act of incorporation the Clerk of Bergen County was required to appoint a Deputy Clerk for Powles Hook, to keep the records and record the deeds, &c., in that place. Samuel Cassedy was appointed.

[3] It is said that the Board of Selectmen, who prepared this bill, were desirous to have the place named "The City of Jersey," but it was altered as in the text by the representative of Bergen county.

On the 23d of January, 1829, the corporate name was changed to "The Board of Selectmen and Inhabitants of Jersey City," although the old name "City of Jersey" was still retained in the title.

On the 22d of February, 1838, the name was changed to the "Mayor and Common Council of Jersey City." Up to this time the place had remained a part of the township of Bergen. It now became a separate municipality.

On the 8th of March, 1839, its boundaries were extended westerly along the northerly side of First street to the centre of Grove street, thence southerly into Communipaw bay to the line of South street extended.

On the 18th of March, 1851, the city received a new charter, which extended its boundaries so as to include the township of Van Vorst. The act was not to take effect until a majority of the electors in each municipality voted in favor of annexation. The vote was taken on the 27th of March, with the following result:

Vote in Jersey City.		*Vote in Van Vorst.*	
Whole number of votes,	495	Whole number of votes,	426
"Charter," - -	489	"Charter," - -	377
"No Charter," - -	3	"No Charter," - -	47
Rejected, - - -	3	Rejected, - - -	2

By this charter the city was divided into four wards, each entitled to four aldermen.

On the 28th of February, 1861, the fifth and sixth wards were erected; on the 21st of March, 1867, the seventh ward, and on the 17th of March, 1870, the eighth ward.

From 1820 to 1838, the officers of the "Board of Selectmen" were as follows:

Presidents.	*Clerks.*
Joseph Lyon,[1] 1820–3.	Joseph Kissam, 1820.
William Lyon, 1824.	Philip R. Earle, 1821–4.
Joseph Kissam, 1825.	A. Ogden Dayton, 1825.
George Dummer, 1826–30.	Robert Gilchrist, 1826–8.

[1] Died at Lyon's Farms, March 21, 1829, aged 65.

Presidents.

David C. Colden, 1831–2.
William Glaze, 1833.
John F. Ellis, 1834.
Robert Gilchrist, 1835.
William Glaze, 1836–7.

Clerks.

Peter McMartin, 1829–32.
Peter Bentley, 1833.
Edmund D. Barry, jr., 1834.
William W. Monro, 1835.
Henry D. Holt, 1836–7.

Since 1838, the officers have been :

Mayors.

Dudley S. Gregory, 1838, '39, '41, '58, '59.
Peter McMartin, 1840.
Thomas A. Alexander, 1842.
Peter Bentley, 1843.
Phineas C. Dummer, 1844–7.
Henry J. Taylor, 1848–9.
Robert Gilchrist, 1850–1.
David S. Manners, 1852–6.
Samuel Wescott, 1857.
Cornelius Van Vorst, 1860–1.
John B. Romar, 1862–3.
Orestes Cleveland, 1864–6.
James Gopsill, 1867.
Charles H. O'Neil, 1868, '70–4.[1]
William Clarke, 1869.[2]

Clerks.

Henry D. Holt, 1838, '40–4.
Thomas W. James, 1839.
Edgar B. Wakeman, 1845–7.
John H. Voorhis, 1848–50.
George W. Cassedy, 1850–64.
John E. Scott, 1864 until the present time.

On the 2d of April, 1869, an act was approved providing for a vote by the electors of the several cities and townships in the county, east of the Hackensack river, to decide upon consolidating the several municipalities into one, under the name of Jersey City. The election was held on the 5th of October, with the following result :

[1] In 1868 an act was passed by the Legislature extending the Mayor's term of office to two years. Mr. O'Neil, who had been elected a few days before its passage, refused to hold the office beyond the time for which he had been elected.

[2] Appointed by the Common Council.

	Charter.	*No Charter.*
Jersey City,	2,220	911
Hudson City,	1,320	220
Bergen,	815	108
Hoboken,	176	893
Bayonne,	100	250
Greenville,	24	174
Weehawken,	0	44
Town of Union,	123	105
West Hoboken,	95	256
North Bergen,	80	225
Union Township,	140	65

Thus Jersey City, Bergen and Hudson City became one. On the 17th of March, 1870, the Legislature made provision for the government of the consolidated city. The territory was divided into sixteen wards, the eight wards of Jersey City numbering from one to eight inclusive; the wards of Hudson City, beginning with the first, numbering from nine to twelve inclusive, and the wards of Bergen, beginning with the first, numbering from thirteen to sixteen inclusive. In 1871 the local government was reorganized, the wards abolished and six aldermanic districts erected in their stead, each district being entitled to two aldermen. In 1873, the township of Greenville was annexed to the city by legislative act, and became part of the sixth district.

Captains of the Watch.[1]

Benjamin F. Champney, 1851–2.
John R. Benedict, 1852–3.
Charles J. Farley, 1854.
Thomas B. Kissam, 1854–5.

Chiefs of Day Police.

Hiram H. Fenn, 1854.
Charles J. Farley, 1855.

[1] September 19, 1845, the city watchmen were directed at each hour, from the "setting of the watch until the hour of calling off arrive," to call the hour.

Chiefs of Police.

Thomas B. Kissam, 1856–7.
Benjamin Haines, jr., 1857–8.
Jacob Z. Marinus, 1859–61.
Edward D. Riley, 1862–4.
Patrick Jordan, 1864.
Joseph McManus, 1865–8.
Nathan R. Fowler, 1868–71.
Edward McWilliams, 1871–2.
Benjamin F. Champney, 1873.

Columbia College Scholarship.

On the 13th of July, 1846, the Trustees of Columbia College gave "to the Corporation of Jersey City" the privilege of having one student educated in the college free of charges for tuition. The gift was accepted on the 17th. On the 26th of March, 1847, the Common Council passed "an ordinance concerning the appointment of a student to the scholarship in Columbia College." The following have had the benefit of this scholarship:

William T. Van Riper,	appointed	August 3, 1852.
William R. Hillyer,	"	December 2, 1856.
Charles V. Hillyer,	"	October 4, 1864.
William Holdane,	"	1868.
S. T. S. Henry,	"	June 24, 1872.

Jersey City as a Port of Entry.—By Act of Congress, March 2, 1799, Hudson County was placed within the district of Perth Amboy. This district included all of East Jersey, except such parts as were within the district of Little Egg Harbor.

March 8, 1806, "The town or landing place of Jersey, in the State of New Jersey," was made a port of delivery, within the district of Perth Amboy.

March 2, 1811, the whole county was annexed to the district of New York.

June 30, 1834, the westerly part of the county was annexed to the district of Newark.

From 1811, Colonel Aaron Ogden was Assistant Collector, residing in Jersey City. In 1845 the office was abolished.

Feb. 21, 1863, the whole county was annexed to the district of

New York. This act provided for an Assistant Collector to reside in Jersey City, with power to enter and clear vessels, but subject to such rules and regulations as the Collector of New York might establish. Phineas C. Dummer was appointed.

Feb. 25, 1865, the Assistant Collector was empowered to enroll and license vessels engaged in the coasting trade and fisheries, owned in whole or in part by residents of the Counties of Hudson and Bergen.

WATER WORKS.—The territory east of Bergen Hill, lying but little above tide water, and the most of it salt-meadow, was poorly supplied with water. The yield of the wells was, as a general thing, of an inferior quality. To supply this deficiency quite a business was, at one time, carried on in carting water from the hill, and selling it by the pail from door to door. As the city grew, the necessity for good water became more urgent. As early as March 1, 1839, the "Jersey City and Harsimus Aqueduct Company" was incorporated, with an authorized capital of $40,000, and authority to "search and bore for water" in Jersey City and Bergen, make reservoirs for the collection of water and lay pipes for its distribution through the city. Nothing, however, came from this company.

On the 1st of November, 1847, Clerk & Bacot, City Surveyors, recommended the taking of water from a small reservoir near the New Jersey Railroad, on the west side of the hill. But the supply to be had from that place was too insignificant to merit serious attention.

On the 18th of March, 1851, Edwin A. Stevens, Edward Coles, Dudley S. Gregory, Abraham J. Van Boskerck and John D. Ward were constituted a Board of Water Commissioners to supply the townships of Hoboken and Van Vorst and Jersey City with pure and wholesome water. This Board selected William S. Whitwell, then late of the Boston Water Works, as engineer. He began his labors near Belleville, August 26, 1851.

Besides the plans already referred to several others were suggested to the Commissioners. One was, to dam the Hackensack River near the Newark turnpike bridge and thus keep out the salt water, and pump from above the dam; another, to bring the water from Rockland Lake; and another was to use the western slope of Bergen hill for a gathering ground, and, by a system of underdraining, collect the water at the foot of the slope and then pump it up. Another plan was to bring it from the Passaic river above the falls; another to take it from the Passaic above the Dundee dam; another to take it from the Morris canal on the level between Little Falls and Bloomfield. All these plans were, however, laid aside for the one now in operation. The Commissioners pronounced this the best plan. They had also received a report from Professor Horsford of New Haven, dated November 26, 1851, as to the quality of the water taken from the Passaic at Belleville. The following table exhibited its relative quality when compared with the water supply of other cities:

In one hundred thousand parts in

	Passaic.	Schuyl-kill.	Croton.	Cochit-uate.	Jamaica.	Albany.	Troy.
Solid residue.	12.7500	9.4170	18.7100	5.3400	5.3560	18.4800	11.8600
Inorganic . .	7.8500	7.2938	11.3265	2.9000	3.0560	14.5200	8.2400
Organic	4.9000	2.1232	7.3735	2.4400	2.3000	3.9600	2.6400

The engineer submitted his plan on the 9th of December 1851. On the 25th of the following March legislative authority was given to construct the works. The enterprise was so far completed on the 30th of June, 1854, that water was let into the pipes from Belleville, and on the 15th of August distributed through the city. The cost of the works up to that time was $652,995.73. A grand water celebration was had Oct. 3, 1854.

Connected with the water works a general plan of sewerage was adopted. It was based on the plan of a tidal canal, extending from Communipaw Cove to Harsimus Cove, generally on the line of Mill Creek and Hoboken Creek, which, when filled by the tide, was to be emptied through the sewers at low water. The canal is yet unbuilt, and every year adds to the difficulty and cost of its construction. Besides the benefit to sewerage which it would give to the city, proper locks would open it for navigation, and on its banks would grow up lumber, coal and stone yards, besides foundries and factories. The dullest eye can see the benefits of such an enterprise.

POST OFFICE.—Previous to the establishment of a post office in Jersey City, the residents here received their letters through the post office of New York or Newark. The post office in Jersey City was set up in 1831. The post-masters have been

William Lyon, - -	1831–35	Samuel Bridgart, -	1846–49
William R. Taylor,	1835–37	David Smith, - - -	1849–53
Samuel Bridgart, - -	1837–41	Samuel M. Chambers,	1853–61
David Smith, - -	1841–45	Henry A. Green, - -	1861–
John Ogden (resigned),	1845–46		

BULL-BAITING.—About the year 1825, there was constructed on the south side of Sussex street, between Hudson and Greene streets, a large amphitheatre, capable of seating three thousand people. Here, for about two months, on every Friday, large numbers, mostly from New York, would gather to see the sport afforded by bulls, bears, buffaloes and dogs fighting. The price of admission was fifty cents.

FLOATING THEATRE.—About the year 1842 an attempt was made to introduce upon the Hudson and Connecticut rivers what had proved a profitable enterprise upon the Mississippi—a floating theatre. It was constructed on the hull of a large barge, and would hold an audience of one thousand people. This theatre, in the summer of 1842, had been up the Hudson, and in February, 1843, was brought to Jersey City and moored in the Morris canal basin, in the rear of Judge Lynch's Thatched Cottage Garden, which was on the south side of Essex street, between Washington and Greene streets.[1] The actors, during this "season," were mostly amateurs of Jersey City, well known for wit and humor. The audience, composed of the *élite* of the town, crowded the theatre from "pit to dome." The pieces

[1] Samuel S. Lynch, then late of Castle Garden.

performed were, "The Rent Day," "Three Brothers" and "Bombastes Furioso." The casts in the several plays were as follows:

Rent Day.

Luke Warrington, - - - Mr. William A. Townsend.
Cornelius Crimp, a lawyer, - - - Mr. William Penny.
Old Grasp, - - - - - - - - Mr. John C. Morgan.
Frank, - - - - - - - Mr. Charles A. Heckman.[1]
Bolt, a *roué*, - - - - - - - - Mr. Joseph G. Edge.
Harry Markham, his friend, - - Mr. William Sanderson.
Arnold Headly, - - - - - - - Mr. David Scott.[2]
Mary Warrington, - - - - - - - Mrs. Scoville.
Susan, - - - - - - - - - - - Mrs. Sharpe.

Three Brothers.

Philip, - - - - - - Mr. William A. Townsend.
Reginald, - - - - - - - Mr. John Bruce.
Steward of the Castle, eighty years old, - Mr. William Penny.
Giles, a servant, - - - - - - Mr. David Scott.
Fanny, - - - - - - - - - - - Mrs. Sharpe.

Bombastes Furioso.

King Artaxomines, - - - - - - Mr. David Scott.
General Bombastes, - - - - - Mr. William Penny.
Fresbos, - - - - - - - - - Mr. John Bruce.
Distafina, - - - - - - - - - Mrs. Sharpe.

It is said the parts "were rendered in a manner that actors of a lifetime might have envied." Between the play and farce a song was given by General Edwin R. V. Wright, James S. Gamble and William Penny. Mr. Penny, in order to render the song more effective, borrowed the black tights of the tragedian Townsend. After the song, he found the "heavy man" sitting in the cold, with bare limbs, waiting for his tights. "Ah, my boy," said Penny, "do you hear the applause? how did my

[1] Now General Heckman.

[2] Died Oct. 14, 1870.

song go?" "Oh, curse your song," said the irate tragedian; "give me my tights, I am almost frozen."

The entertainment was repeated in 1845 by the same company, many of whom are well known; some of them have gone behind the scenes, while the others are yet before the foot-lights. The stage manager on the occasion was Gabriel Harrison, afterward manager of the Park Theatre, Brooklyn. The orchestra was composed of residents of Jersey City, the leader being William Robertson, the hardware merchant of Newark avenue, popularly known as "Pop" Robertson. The performance was nominally for the benefit of the poor, but, though the "house" was full at fifty cents a ticket, not a cent found its legitimate destination. It is yet a question among the old patrons of the "Floating Theatre" what became of the funds. Plato might mention the proverb, "One may see a great deal of money carried into Lacedæmon, but one never sees any of it brought out again." On this last occasion the proprietor was subjected to a fine of fifty dollars for exhibiting without license from the city. He attempted to defend under a coasting license from the United States. The hull of the theatre afterward found its way to Coney Island, where, in the summer season, it was used for the more substantial purposes of a restaurant.

Wind Mill.—This old landmark was built in 1815 by Isaac Edge, who for a long time was miller and baker for and distributor of bread to the people of Jersey City. Burmley and Oakes were the contractors and millwrights who built it. It was constructed in all particulars like the mill of Mr. Edge's father in Derbyshire, England. Its location was about seventy-five feet north of Montgomery street and fifty feet east of Greene street. It was a prominent feature on the Jersey shore. At first the fans on the wings were of canvas, but the severe storm of September 3, 1821, tore them to pieces and broke one of the fans. Then Mr. Edge put in iron fans. When the track of the New Jersey Railroad was changed from the south side of Montgomery street to its present location, in 1839, the mill was taken down, its material put on vessels and conveyed to

PAULUS HOECK.

Town Harbor, Long Island, whence it was taken to Mill Hill, in the town of Southold. Here its walls were reared again, and it started anew upon its old career of usefulness. It was there known as *The Great Western Flouring Mill.* At one time a steam engine was put in, but it was soon removed and the old machinery restored. It was in use until between one and two o'clock on Saturday morning, June 25, 1870, when it, with $230 worth of grain, was consumed by fire. R. Villeferr was then owner.

In 1837 there were

Dwellings in Jersey City,	-	213;	in Van Vorst,	- -	106.
Stages and carriages,	" -	22;	" "	- -	9.
Horses,	" -	145;	" "	- -	71.
Cattle,	" -	14;	" "	- -	100.
Dogs,	" -	57;	" "	- -	33.

In 1841, in Jersey City, they were

86 houses.[1]	71 dogs.
9 coaches and stages.	943 vacant lots.
53 chaises and wagons.	206 single men.
16 cattle.	20 merchants.
	829 polls.

Of scholars there were in the

Grammar Department		Primary Department	
Boys, - - -	91;	Boys, - - - - -	73.
Girls, - - - -	33;	Girls, - - - -	56.

In 1842 there were

450 dwellings.	1 bank.
1 lyceum.	5 taverns.
1 classical school.[2]	2 foundries.[3]

[1] I have no doubt that this is an error. It should probably be 386. But thus I find it in a newspaper of the day.

[2] The old academy adjoining St. Matthew's Church was the first schoolhouse on Paulus Hoeck. It was in modern times used for a city prison. About fifty feet west of it was an Indian spring in the olden time.

[3] One of these was Fulton's foundry, located on the corner of Morgan and Greene streets. It was erected in 1812, and managed by Fulton until his death, on the 24th of February, 1815. Here he also erected a dry dock.

40 stores.
1 glass house.[1]
1 pottery.[2]
1 candle factory.
1 firework factory.

THE FIRST CARTMAN in Jersey City was Fortunatus Stone, in 1812.

STREET LAMPS were first used in 1843.

Streets were lighted with gas for the first time on the 4th of December, 1852; one hundred and seventy-four lamps being the number then required. Gas was first used to light houses in Jersey City, Dec. 1, 1852.

THE FIRST VESSEL built expressly for the Jersey City trade was the *Dudley S. Gregory*, launched at Burlington, on the Delaware; made her trial trip on the Hudson, July 11, 1845. She was of 180 tons burden, and cost $8,000.

BERGEN.

The bounds of the township of Bergen were fixed by the grant of Governor Stuyvesant in 1661, confirmed by Governor Carteret in 1668, and reconfirmed by the Charter of Queen Anne in 1714. It then conformed to the lines of the present county east of the Hackensack. By the erection of cities and other townships its territory had been greatly reduced, until on the 24th of March, 1855, its boundaries were the New Jersey Railroad on the north, Mill Creek and the bay on the east, the Morris Canal on the south, and Newark bay and Hackensack river on the west. It was then erected into "the Town of Bergen," with slight powers vested in a board of five councilmen. On the 11th of March, 1862, its charter was amended, its territory divided into three wards (*Columbian, Franklin and Communipaw*), and further

[1] This was established in 1824 by George Dummer and others. Its location is now occupied by the New Jersey Sugar Refining Company.

[2] The original name of this establishment was *The Jersey Porcelain and Earthenware Company*. It was started by George Dummer and others in 1825, for the manufacture of Staffordshire earthenware. Its location was between Morris, Essex and Warren streets.

powers vested in a board of seven councilmen. On the 29th of March, 1866, the charter was still further amended. "The City of Bergen" was incorporated on the 11th of March, 1868, divided into four wards, and the powers of municipal government vested in a Mayor and Council. It was consolidated with Jersey City in 1870.

Mayors.	*Clerks.*
Henry Fitch, 1866.	Henry H. Newkirk, 1866-7.
John U. Cornelison, 1867.	Samuel McBurney, 1868-9.
John Hilton, 1868.	
Stephen D. Harrison, 1869.	

When this was the only municipality between the Hudson and Hackensack rivers its affairs were managed by trustees chosen at first for life, afterward annually by a plurality of voices. At this annual town meeting the freeholders were accustomed to gather and decide questions of general interest which were considered too weighty for the trustees. This meeting was presided over, by a moderator chosen for the purpose. The town clerk was clerk of this meeting.

The township was divided into road districts for the better regulation of the highways, and an overseer appointed for each. They were known by the names of Bergen, Gemonepa, Pemerahpogh, Sekakes, Wehauk, Maisland (now New Durham), Bergen Woods, Bull's Ferry and Bergen Point.

For the accommodation of the people at elections, the polls would be opened in one part of the township for one day and then in another part for one day; *e. g.*, in 1803 the polls were opened at Widow Van Horn's, Bergen Woods, and closed at Peter Stuyvesant's. The latter place was a tavern, on the southwest corner of Bergen and Glenwood avenues. In 1804 the polls opened at the Three Pigeons, and closed at Peter Stuyvesant's; ditto in 1805 and 1806.

Harrison

Township was, by the act creating the county of Hudson, set

off from the township of Lodi. It embraced all of the county lying west of the Hackensack river; also the township of Union, in Bergen county. In 1867 the township of Kearney was set off from the northerly part of it.

The neck of land lying between the Passaic[1] and Hackensack rivers, and extending from their junction to the Boiling Spring (now Rutherfurd Park), was known among the Indians by the name of ***Mighgecticock***. It was estimated to contain 5,308 acres of upland and 10,000 acres of meadow.[2] Captain William Sandford[3] bought it of the Proprietors, July 4, 1668, for £20 sterling yearly, in lieu of the halfpenny per acre quit rent, and on condition that he should settle on the tract six or eight families within three years. On the 20th of the same month, with the consent of the Lords Proprietors, he bought of Tantaqua,[4]

[1] Passaic, Pachsajeck, Pachsaick, Pechiesse, Pishawack, is an Indian word, and signifies "valley;" also called the northwest Kill, to distinguish it from the Hackensack or north Kill. *Long Isl. Hist. Soc.*, *i.*, 156, 266.

[2] *Winfield's Land Titles*, 324.

[3] Captain William Sandford came from the West Indies; resided in Newark in 1675; was member of the Council in the years 1681, '82, '84. In his domestic relations he seems to have loved "not wisely." In a deed to Mrs. Sarah Whartman, dated April 24, 1677, he acknowledges that four of his children were naturally born of her, and yet in his will, dated Jan. 2, 1690, he acknowledges her to be his lawful wife, "formerly Sarah Whartman, while some considerable reasons engaged us to consaile our marriage," and annexes thereto a certificate, which sets forth that the two were married "on board the Pink Susannah, in the river Surinam, March 27, 1667." He requested to be buried on his own plantation, and implored some of his friends "to assist and favour the concerns of a poor Ignorant Widdow and five Innocent Children with their best advice, help and Councill, to preserve them from those Vultures and harpies w[ch] prays on the Carkasses of Widdows and fatten with the Blood of Orphans." He died in 1692. His children were *Nedimah*, married Richard Berry (Constable of Aquackanonck and New Barbadoes in 1695); *Catharine*, married Dr. Van Imburgh; *Peregrine*, married Fytje, daughter of Enoch Michielse Vreeland; *William*, *Grace*, and *Elizabeth* married Captain James Davis.

[4] Tantaqua, known also as Jasper, lived at Hackensack, and was a great friend of the whites. Once, in a time of scarcity of food, he fished for and relieved the necessities of the Dutch. When asked why he was so kind to the whites, he replied: "I have always been inclined from my youth up to do good. I took the fish to them because *Manito* said to me, 'You must take fish to these people,' whispering ever in my ear, 'You must take fish to them.' I had to do it, or Manito would have killed me." *Long Isl. Hist. Soc.*, *i.*, 149.

Tamak, Anaren, Hanyaham, H. Gosque and Ws. Kenarenawack, representatives of the Indians claiming an interest in the same tract, all their right and title. In this deed the tract is described as lying between the "Hackensack and Pasawack" rivers, beginning at the mouth of the said two rivers, then "to goe up Northward into the countrey about seaven Miles till it comes to a certain Brook or Spring now called Sanford's Spring." For their interest he paid to the Indians "170 fathoms of Black wampum, 200 fathoms White wampum, 19 black Coates, 16 Guns, 60 double hands of powder, 10 paire of Breetches, 60 knives, 67 Barrs of Lead, one Anker of Brandy, three half Fats of Beer, Eleven Blankets, 30 Axes, 20 Howes, and two cookes of dozens."[1]

From this time until the division of the province into counties New Barbadoes Neck was under the jurisdiction of Newark.[2] From the latter date until the 21st of January, 1710, it was within the county of Essex.[3] Shortly after this Arent Schuyler purchased a plantation opposite Belleville, and in 1719, through a negro slave, discovered the copper mine. This mine was not worked much in the days of Arent Schuyler, but his son, Colonel John, worked it profitably. The ore was sent to England. In 1753 the first steam engine brought to this country was set up at this mine, at a cost of £3,000 sterling. It was capable of throwing about eighty hogsheads of water per min-

---

[1] Probably "coats of duffels." *Proc. N. J. Hist. Soc., vi.,* 6. Duffels was a coarse cloth.

[2] *Whitehead's East Jersey,* 93.

[3] In 1682 East Jersey was divided into four counties for the "better governing and settling courts in the same." Bergen County contained "all the Set tlements between *Hudson's* River and *Hackensack* River, beginning at *Constables Hook,* and so to extend to the uppermost bound of the Province Northward between the said Rivers." *Leaming and Spicer,* 229. The territory between the Hackensack and Passaic rivers was included in the county of Essex.

In 1693 the counties were divided into townships. The township of Hackensack included all the land in the county of Bergen north of the bounds of the corporation of Bergen. Barbadoes Neck was included in the township of Aquickanick and New Barbadoes in the county of Essex. *Leaming and Spicer,* 329. The bounds of Bergen county were extended on the 21st of January, 1710, so as to include New Barbadoes Neck.

ute.[1] It was destroyed by fire about 1772, and lay in ruins during the Revolution.

The farm opposite Newark owned by Colonel Peter Schuyler was known as Petersborough. It was afterward owned by Archibald Kennedy, who had married Colonel Schuyler's only child. In 1768 he had it in a flourishing condition. It contained 906 acres, 265 of which were covered with timber, 393 under cultivation; the rest was salt meadow. On it was a two-story brick dwelling house, a green house seventy feet long, coach house, stables, barn, overseer's house, cider house, ice and root house, an excellent garden, an orchard capable of yielding two hundred barrels of cider, a large quantity of cedar timber and a shad fishery.[2]

This farm was also graced with a deer park. In 1800 the orchard produced three hundred barrels of cider. There were on the place two dwelling houses, a green house containing a large number of orange, lemon, lime and other West India fruit trees. In the early part of 1802 the land was laid out into ninety building lots of at least one acre each, and advertised as a *New Town.*

At the close of the celebration of the Fourth of July, 1815, the people of the place resolved that they "would henceforth distinguish the small district of country formerly known as Kennedy's Farm, and to the extent of one mile north of the northerly bounds thereof, by the name of 'The Village of Lodi.'"

In the early part of 1776 a company of continental troops was formed on New Barbadoes Neck; Jacobus Jerolamon, *Captain;* Peter Sanford, *First Lieutenant;* Elijah Sanford, *Second Lieutenant;* John Jerolamon, *Ensign.*

The Township of Van Vorst

Was set off from the township of Bergen March 11, 1841. Its

[1] *Whitehead's East Jersey, x.*, 27. Joseph C. Hornblower, father of the late Chief Justice, came with it as engineer.

[2] *Wood's Newark Gazette, December* 28, 1796.

territory included nearly the whole of what was at one time known as Ahasimus. Its name was in honor of the family, which had been so closely identified with its history since 1636. The West India Company's Farm, Van Vorst's patent and a few small patents comprised the whole district. The farm, after tak-

CORNER OF NEWARK AVENUE AND GROVE STREET.

ing out the private grants, included three hundred and eighty-three acres. As this farm has a peculiarly interesting history, some particularity of detail will be pardoned.

In 1636 Cornelis Van Vorst lived here near the water, between Fourth and Fifth streets, in a frame house thatched with reeds.

This house was burned on the 25th of June in that year. After the Company had purchased the interest of Pauw in Pavonia, Ahasimus was reserved for their own use. Van Vorst remained in possession of it until his death, before which event he had put up another house. On the 31st of March, 1639, his widow took a lease of the "Company's bouwerie at Ahasimus" for twenty years, agreeing to build a new frame house and keep those already built in repair.[1] She married Jacob Stoffelsen shortly afterward, and, dying in 1641, left him in possession. He held it as tenant of the Company until February 19, 1647, when he took a lease of it until the 1st of May, 1661. During the war of 1643 he was driven from his home, his buildings burned and the farm laid waste. Shortly before the expiration of his lease he appeared before the Director and Council and said "that he two times had been expelled from there by the savages, all his property burned," and asked for an extension of his lease. This was granted for five years, at a rent of one quarter of the produce; house and buildings at the expiration of his lease to belong to the Company.[2]

In 1655 the buildings were again burned by the Indians and the bouwerie laid waste. In consideration of this fact the farm was granted to him on the 21st of December, 1656, without rent for one year.[3] In the latter part of 1658 a new house was built on the place.[4] In 1661 he obtained a lease for a year,[5] which was renewed in February, 1662.[6] Next door to him lived his step-son, Ide Van Vorst, in a house built shortly after the war of 1655. Van Vorst returned to his home sooner than most of his neighbors, and probably without the sanction of the Government, which now did all in their power to discourage isolated settlements. His position placed him in great risk from the savages, who prowled about watching for an opportunity to strike a blow.[7]

Jacob Stoffelsen, who had married Tryntje, the widow of

[1] *N. Y. Col. MSS., i.*, 92.
[2] *Albany Records, xiv.*, 90.
[3] *N. Y. Col. MSS., viii.*, 313.
[4] *Ibid, viii.*, 1044.
[5] *Ibid, ix.*, 572.
[6] *Ibid, x., part i.*, 40.
[7] *New Amst. Rec., iv.*, 68.

THE VAN VORST HOMESTEAD AT AHASIMUS.
(Henderson and Fourth streets, Jersey City.)

Jacob Walingen Van Hoorn, on the 17th of August, 1657, was in possession of the bouwerie when the country was surrendered to the English in 1664. He remained in possession as the tenant of the West India Company, whose property the farm remained by virtue of the first of the "Articles of Capitulation:" "We consent that the States-General, or West India Company, shall freely injoy all farms and houses (except such as are in the forts), &c."[1] Stoffelsen, being in possession, moved to improve the farm. This being in derogation of the rights of the Lords Proprietors, they served him with the following notice:

"Whereas I am informed that Jacob Stoffelsen Is about the fencing and taking In a Certaine parcell of Land In and about hassemus to the great prejudice of the other Inhabitants there and w^{t}hout any order or Authority from me, these are therefore to Require the said Stoffelsen to forbare the fencing and Manuring of the said Land till farther Order. Given und^{r} my hand the 5th March, 1665. PH. CARTERETT."

This notice was not served. It was burned at the house of Samuel Edsall, and renewed July 18, 1672.

War between England and Holland having been declared, Governor Nicolls, by proclamation in New York on the 15th of June, 1665, "at the ringing of the bell," declared the real and personal property of the Company confiscated to the King.[2] From this time the Duke's governors in New York claimed the same for their master, and leased it in his name. By the treaty of Breda, July 1, 1667, each power was to keep the territory then held. This confirmed New Netherlands to the English. At the time of the surrender only the Van Vorst family, viz., Stoffelsen and wife, Ide Van Vorst and his brother-in-law, Claes Jansen Van Purmerendt, were living at Ahasimus. On the 1st of March, 1667, "in consideration of the Great Paines & Chariges in building as well as clearing and manuring a Good part of the land belonging to the said ffarme," Stoffelsen and wife received from Governor Nicolls a lease of "the bouwerie or ffarme aforesaid wth the Dwelling House, Barnes, Stables, Stalls,"

[1] *O'Cal., N. N., ii.*, 532. [2] *New Amst. Rec.*

etc., from the first day of January, 1667, "during all the terme or termes of ye Naturall life or lives of the said Jacob Stoffel and Trintje his wife or the longest liver of them, Yielding & Paying therefore Yearly and every Yeare duering the said Terme the Sume of two hundred & fifty Guilders sewant, or one & forty Schepels of winter Wheate or the Vallue in other Goods Pay to the Governo^r of this his Royall Highness his Colony or his Order."[1] Stoffelsen died before the expiration of the year, leaving his wife in possession. She married Michael Tades June 17, 1668. Tades died shortly afterward, leaving his widow still in possession. She then married Caspar Steinmets, and with him retained possession of the farm. Acting upon the terms of Governor Nicolls' lease to Stoffelsen and wife, and claiming that it included all the "Land wch he, the said Jacob Stoffells, hath cleared, or which he and Trientje his wife or either of them shall cause to be cleared," Steinmets enclosed some of the land adjoining. In 1671 Governor Carteret ordered him to take down his fence and abandon these lands. With this order he complied. When the Dutch re-established their authority in the country, Ide Van Vorst and his brother-in-law, Claes Jansen Van Purmerendt, protested against Steinmets having any greater privileges than he had under Governor Stuyvesant.[2] Steinmets then asked for a confirmation of the lease of the bouwerie granted to his wife and her former husband by the English government. This was granted, and he obtained a lease on the 12th of April, 1674.[3] This stirred up Van Vorst and Van Purmerendt. They laid their grievances before the authorities in New Orange, charging that the lessee of "the public Bouwerie situate at Ahasymus" was appropriating too large a share of the "valleys and pasture lands." Steinmets was, however, permitted "to fence in all the ungranted valley appertaining to Ahasymus," and Van Vorst and Van Purmerendt to fence in "all the tillage and valley lands belonging to them in lawful property."[4] It will be observed that all the ungranted land at Ahasymus was held to belong to the public bouwerie or West India Company's farm.

[1] *Book of Patents (Albany), ii.*, 177.
[2] *Col. Hist. of N. Y., ii.*, 598.
[3] *Ibid ii.*, 704.
[4] *Ibid, ii.*, 716.

When the English returned, Steinmets was yet in possession. Shortly after Governor Carteret had reorganized the government, he ordered the prosecution of Steinmets, before the court at Bergen, for the rent which he claimed to be due to the Proprietors. This body laid claim to the farm, on the ground that the tract did not pass to the Freeholders of Bergen by the charter of 1668. The people of Bergen insisted that it did so pass, and hence belonged to them, while the Governor of New York claimed it for the Duke on the ground that, by the terms of the surrender to the English, this farm remained the property of the West India Company, and as the same was not confiscated until after the grant to Berkley and Carteret, it could not have passed by that grant. Under this claim for the Duke, Governor Andross, on the 6th of March, 1675, sent George Cook to Bergen to defend the suit which Governor Carteret had instituted against Steinmets.[1] What became of this suit is not known. On the 17th of August, 1678, Governor Andross, "in regard of the long possession of the s[d] Bowery or ffarme by the s[d] Jacob Stoffells" and wife, "together with the good deportment of Casper Stymetts the Survivo[r]," leased to Steinmets the "Certaine Bowery or ffarme at Hassems near Communipon," except what had been granted out of the same by the "Authority of the s[d] Company unto Ide Cornelissen, Claes Jansen, &c.," "for and During the Terme and Time of his Naturall Life and one Entire Yeare after," "*Yielding* and paying therefore yearly and every Yeare the sume of ffoure hundred Guild[rs] Sewant" to the Governor of New York.[2] This lease was repudiated by the authorities in New Jersey, and Steinmets was, on the 25th of October, 1678, again summoned to appear before the court in Bergen, at its next sitting, and show his authority for occupying the farm, and was commanded to pay no more rent in the mean time. He did not obey the summons until the 23d of November, when he gave as an excuse for not appearing sooner, that he could not read the summons, and did not know what it was until the constable told him. On the same day he was directed by Governor Andross

---

[1] *General Entries* (*Albany*), *iv.*, 177. [2] *Book of Patents* (*Albany*), *iv.*, 144

to continue in possession.[1] It is not known that Governor Carteret exercised himself any further about the farm, but in 1683 Samuel Groom, one of the East Jersey Proprietors, demanded rent from Steinmets. Governor Dongan of New York sent him a threatening letter, which effectually silenced this new enemy of the Duke's lessee.

While the Proprietors were thus seeking an acknowledgment of their claim, the people of Bergen were a continuing source of trouble to the Governor of New York, by annoying his tenant and preventing the collection of rent. To avoid further trouble with the "farm at East Jersey belonging to his Majesty," Dongan gave to Judge John Palmer[2] a lease of the reversion for ninety-nine years, "from the feast of St. Michael the Archangel next ensuing after the determination of the estate" of Steinmets. This lease was dated August 13, 1685, and was upon condition that Judge Palmer should pay "as a fine the summ of Sixty pounds to the King, in case hee should not think fit to forgive it, and the rent of twenty shillings p^r^ annum and to defend the title."[3]

Steinmets was now getting old, and his two sons, John and Garret, managed the farm. On the 5th of February, 1686, they bought of Judge Palmer his lease for £50. After the death of their father, in 1702, they divided the farm between them, John taking the southerly half and Garret the northerly half. On the 24th of February, 1708, John Steinmets conveyed all of his property to his wife for life, and, after her death, to the children of his sister Hannah Prior, his nephew, Jacob Prior, to have his interest in the farm. After the death of John Steinmets, his widow married Peter Van Wooglem. These two, with Jacob Prior and Lea, his wife, assigned to David Hnion, *alias* Danielson, the remainder of the term under the Palmer lease for £675. Danielson entered into possession of the southerly half of the farm about 1715, and remained there during the nine years fol-

[1] *General Entries* (*Albany*), *xxxii.*, 78.

[2] Palmer was a member of the Council in East Jersey for several years. *Whitehead's East Jersey*, 96. He was a man of influence.

[3] *Book of Entries* (*Albany*), *vii.*, 170; *Col. Hist. of N. Y.*, *iii.*, 411, 494.

lowing. At this time the only buildings in Harsimus were the house, barn and brewhouse of Danielson; the house, barn and cow-house of Hendrick Claes Kuyper; the house and barn of Ide Van Vorst, and the house, barn and an old house (built in 1658), of Garret Steinmets. All these were quite close together along the shore, now the line of Henderson street, between Second and Fifth streets.

In the early part of the year 1724, Archibald Kennedy, the King's Receiver-General in New York, fixed his eye on the Duke's farm. The title came to him as follows: Robert West, on the 1st and 2d of April, 1684, conveyed his interest in East Jersey to Thomas Cox. Cox conveyed to Sir Eugenius Cameron of Lochiel $\frac{13}{40}$ of his interest of $\frac{1}{24}$ on the 2d and 3d of April, 1685. Sir Eugenius conveyed to Donald Cameron, July 30, 1716, who conveyed to Evan Drummond[1] on the 17th of November, 1721. Drummond conveyed one-half of the unappropriated land of said $\frac{13}{40}$ to James Alexander on the 17th and 18th of July, 1722, and the remaining half on the 5th and 6th of April, 1723. Alexander reconveyed to Drummond 383 acres of unappropriated lands on the 22d and 23d of February, 1725. On the 26th of the same month this amount of land was surveyed to Drummond by the Surveyor-General, "upon a tract of land formerly called the West India Company's Farm." This survey was endorsed with the approval of $\frac{16}{20}$ of the Proprietors. The money for the purchase of the land and the cost of the location was furnished by Kennedy. On the 13th of February, 1724, Drummond executed a declaration of trust[2] that he held the land for the benefit and use of Kennedy. In 1725 Drummond filed a bill in Chancery against Danielson for the possession of that part of the farm occupied by him. Governor Burnet made a decree, according to the prayer in the bill, August 17, 1727. On the 18th of the following month Danielson accepted from Kennedy a lease of the southerly half of the farm until the 1st of the following May.[3] On the 10th of October, 1727, Garret Steinmets, who

[1] Drummond was appointed High Sheriff of Middlesex County in September, 1729.

[2] *Liber F* 2 (*Amboy*), 509.

[3] *Liber H* 2 (*Amboy*), 76.

held the northerly half of the farm under the Palmer lease, surrendered to Kennedy and accepted a lease for life at the rent of *one ear of Indian corn* when demanded, and a proper proportion of the Quit Rents reserved to the Proprietors.[1] His interest in this lease he assigned to Mattys De Mott, February 20, 1729.

On the expiration of Danielson's lease, Kennedy took possession of the southerly half of the farm and began to improve and stock it. In a letter of James Alexander to Governor Hunter, dated May 20, 1731, is the following notice of this farm: "Though there be no place near Inians Ferry,[2] fit for a settlement, to be purchased, yet I beg leave to mention one much better situated and that is the place called Horsamus, over against New York, where you used to meet the Jersey Council.[3] It contains about 400 acres, but out of this there's two small pieces, one of 20 acres and another of 6 acres, belonging to other persons. It has on it a pretty good country house and barn, about 500 apple trees; there's of stock, 27 black cattle, 72 sheep, some horses, hogs and other country stock, all belonging to Mr. Kennedy, which lands, stock and all together he would sell now for £3,000, which is a moderate price when it is considered that the lands thereabouts sell very commonly for £20 per acre."

Garret Steinmets died in 1733. This gave Kennedy possession of the northerly half of the farm. Drummond's will was dated December 13, 1736.[4] Andrew Johnson, his surviving executor, transferred the title to Kennedy, April 24, 1747.[5] Thus his possession was complete, and his title as perfect as the proprietors could make it.[6]

The residents at Harsimus feeling that the farm belonged to the freeholders of the township in common, and that they were kept out of their rights by power rather than justice, gave themselves up to the annoyance of its possessor. Mattys De Mott was especially active. When he was obliged to give up posses-

---

[1] *Liber H 2 (Amboy)*, 77. [2] Now New Brunswick.

[3] The Council met here April 17, 1714. It had been arranged to hold this meeting at Communipaw, but was changed to "Horsimus" by the Governor.

[4] *Book C of Wills (Amboy)*, 140. [5] *Liber F 2 (Amboy)*, 522.

[6] *Winfield's Land Titles*, 132.

sion in 1733, according to the terms of the lease under which he held, he pulled up seventy-one young apple trees. On another occasion, six of Kennedy's best apple trees were girdled; a fine bull, worth £10, was pushed into his well; a stallion, worth £40, pushed into a salt hole and killed, and a steer had a pitchfork stuck into him. De Mott used to threaten to knock out the brains of Kennedy's servants, and Van Vorst would beat his negroes, and on one occasion knocked over Black Peter with a stone, for driving Van Vorst's cows out of Kennedy's cabbage

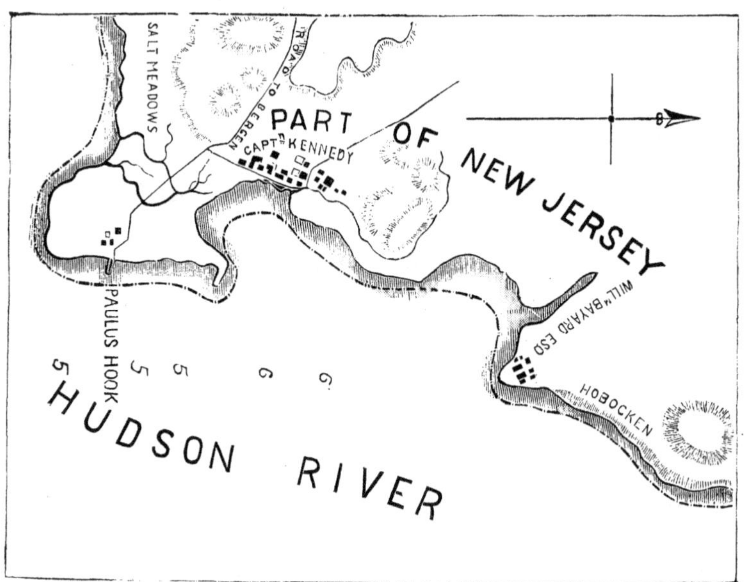

garden. In 1733 Van Vorst committed a trespass upon the farm, that he might be prosecuted, and so have the question of title settled. Kennedy did bring suit, but did not press it to trial. In 1744 the trespass was repeated for a like object, but no suit followed. In 1753 he repeated the experiment. Self respect now forced Kennedy to sue him for trespass. The case was tried at the bar of the Supreme Court at Amboy, in August, 1753. Van Vorst set up his right to enter as a freeholder of the corporation of Bergen. A verdict was rendered in his favor. Things now looked serious for Kennedy. On the 12th of December following, he filed a bill in chancery to restrain Van Vorst from further proceedings, and threatened to appeal to England in case of failure. This threat had more restraining influence on Van Vorst than the injunction. The plain people of Bergen could not think of contending with a crown officer in English courts, and they remained quiet until a successful rebellion destroyed an appeal to the courts of the mother country. Then they renewed the controversy.

In 1776, by permission of the Earl of Casselis (son of Archibald Kennedy, who died June 14, 1763), Thomas McDonald built a small cottage on the farm, and occupied it, with a quarter of an acre of ground adjoining, until his death in 1779. Jacob Brill, as tenant, lived on the farm in 1776. When the continental forces gathered at Paulus Hoeck, they destroyed certain property, for which a claim was rendered as follows:

Ten acres of corn, and three bushels sowing of Buckwheat,	£36	0	0
Six empty hogsheads and one empty pipe,	1	8	0
Sixteen hogs, large and small,	10	0	0

During the Revolution, the British destroyed all the fences and buildings except McDonald's cottage. In 1779 Kennedy[1] re-

[1] Archibald Kennedy (2d) became a captain in the Royal Navy, April 4, 1753. In 1760 he was in command of the *Flamborough* at Lisbon, where he attacked and defeated a French frigate. For this gallant behavior he was put in command of a frigate of thirty-six guns. *N. Y. Mercury, October* 20, 1760. He was afterward in command of the *Blonde*. When the Revolution broke out he was in command of the *Coventry*, lying in New York harbor. To save his extensive estates which he had received by his first wife, he took up a residence on his farm at Petersborough, at present East Newark. But his friendliness to the colonies was suspected. He was arrested and brought before the Council of Safety, January 13, 1778. He was permitted to return home, to appear again in fourteen days. At that time the Council concluded that his residence at East Newark was dangerous to the State, and Ordered, "That he remove within eight days from the date hereof, into the county of Sussex, and there remain within one mile of the Court House at Newton till the further orders of the Board respecting him." On May 7, 1778, the Council released him on his parole

moved from New Jersey, leaving John and Jacob Byre, his tenants, in possession, under the care of Robert Watts, his attorney and brother-in-law. Shortly afterward, William Gray became tenant, and held until 1783. Then came Philip Dowers as tenant for one year, and he was succeeded by one Reid. On the 1st of April, 1784, the Trustees of the corporation of Bergen, desiring to get possession of the farm, induced the widow of McDonald, who was then a tenant upon charity, to remove from the cottage built by her husband. No sooner had she done this than the trustees put Barnt Everson into the cottage as their tenant. This act was followed by a notice published in the *New York Gazetteer and Country Journal*, warning all persons not to purchase or hire any portion of the farm. Watts being informed of these facts, on the 15th of May, 1784, got together materials to build a house on the farm, and was putting up the frame, when the trustees, at the head of a multitude, swooped down upon him, demolished the frame, and carried off the materials in triumph. They then procured about thirty teams, ploughed up a part of the farm and sowed it with buckwheat. For the part he bore in this *coup d'etat*, Daniel Van Ripen was indicted for forcible entry and detainer. He was tried at Hackensack, Chief Justice Brearly presiding, in the October term, 1784, and convicted. The case was taken into the Supreme Court, the verdict set aside, and the indictment quashed in September, 1785. Kennedy also sued Van Ripen and John Dey for the frame and building materials carried off. They justified in the name of the corporation of Bergen. The trustees now opened a cross fire by instituting suits in ejectment against Kennedy's tenants. Kennedy replied by bill for injunction and

---

for his good behavior, and permitted him to return to his farm on New Barbadoes Neck. He succeeded his great grandfather as eleventh Earl of Casselis, in the Scots Peerage. His first wife was the only child of Colonel Peter Schuyler, of New Barbadoes Neck. His second wife was Anne, daughter of John Watts, of New York, whom he married April 27, 1769. He died December 29, 1794, leaving two sons, John and Robert, who, by his will, dated January 19, 1794, inherited all his property in America. In 1803 they made Robert Watts their attorney to sell their lands.

quiet possession, filed on the 8th of September, 1786. After a long contest, Chancellor Patterson dismissed this bill on the 6th of March, 1793. On the 10th of July following, a petition was filed before Governor Howell to open the decree of dismissal, and for a rehearing. This was granted, and the cause reargued on the 11th of February, 1794. On the 20th of the same month, the Chancellor ordered that the trustees should give up possession to Kennedy and then bring an ejectment suit in the Supreme Court, to be tried before a special jury from the county of Somerset, at the bar in Trenton, the verdict to be certified to the Chancellor. Kennedy dying in 1794, Robert Watts was put upon the record in his place on the 26th of April, 1796. The trial began on Thursday, the 25th of February, 1800, and concluded on Saturday evening. On Monday morning a verdict was rendered in favor of the plaintiffs.[1]

Notwithstanding this defeat, Watts held on to the farm. Then the trustees filed a bill asking the Court of Chancery to give effect to the verdict, but before the court decided what should be done, a compromise between the parties was effected, and the trustees were virtually the losers. Both parties disposed of their interest in the farm to John B. Coles,[2] of New York, on the 4th of February, 1804. Kennedy received for his interest $20,000, and Bergen received $14,285.75, out of which were to be paid the expenses of law suits, &c., amounting to $3,057.50.[3] Thus was the magnificent farm of the West India Company, which

---

[1] Aaron Ogden and Mr. McWhorter were the counsel for the plaintiffs, and Richard Stockton and Mr. Lake for the defendant.—*Sentinel of Freedom, March* 11, 1800.

[2] John B. Coles was born on Long Island, December 31, 1760. He married Elizabeth, daughter of Benjamin Underhill, September 22, 1781, and died January 2, 1827. He resided in the city of New York from 1780 until his death. He was Alderman of the First Ward and State Senator.

[3] The items of this bill were as follows:

A. McWhorter's lawyer's bill,	$400 13	
C. Van Vorst for money advanced,	134 27	
Sundry bills in connection with suit,	2,523 10	
		$3,057 50

CASTLE POINT AND THE ELYSIAN FIELDS.

had been the pride of the Indians and the Dutch, frittered away.

> "There onst was two cats in Kilkenny,
> And aich thought there was one cat too many;
> So they quarrelled and fit,
> And they gouged and they bit,
> Till, excepting their nales
> And the tip of their tails,
> Instead of two cats there wasn't any."

The people in Harsimus, prior to the introduction of the Passaic water, depended on wells. Many of these were sunk and kept in repair by assessment on property benefited. Those which had been sunk by individuals prior to 1841 were surrendered to the township.

The first street lamp put up by public authority was on the corner of Grove street and Railroad avenue. This was on the 3d of December, 1845. Lamps were put up only where a majority of the owners of lots lighted petitioned for them.

The following is taken from the *Weekly Post Boy*, January 27, 1746:

"We are credibly informed that some days ago a fish was found dead, ashore, near Horsimus, in New Jersey, opposite the back of this city, having a head nearly resembling that of a man, with hair on it." In a few days the crows carried off the body, except the bones, "which, 'tis said, about the breast and ribs, very much resembled the human anatomy, but as it draws toward the tail, entirely in fish. This strange *phenomenon* has occasioned no small speculation all over that part of the country, as well as in some parts of this city. However, we are told it has since been discovered, or at least thought to be, only a porpoise with his snout cut off!"

Hoboken.

The first white occupant of Hoboken was Hendrick Cornelissen Van Vorst, eldest son of Pauw's Commissary at Ahasimus. When he first occupied this bouwerie is not known, but on the 12th of

March, 1639, he took a lease of it for twenty years from the 1st of January, 1640. In the lease the place is said to have been "heretofore occupied by him." He agreed to give as rent "the $\frac{1}{4}$ part of the crops which God may vouchsafe to the soil, either in sheaves on the field or as shall be considered best, and twelve capons every year," and to deliver back the land unsown.[1] In the summer of 1639 he returned to Holland, and there died. On the 15th of February, 1640, Governor Kieft leased the place to Aert Teunissen Van Putten for twelve years from the 1st of January, 1641. Kieft agreed to erect a small house on the place, and Teunissen agreed to yield as rent "the fourth sheaf with which God Almighty shall favor the field."[2] There is no doubt that the house which Kieft built for Teunissen was the first building in Hoboken. Van Vorst, the former occupant, was unmarried, and most likely lived at his father's in Harsimus.

Teunissen forthwith began to improve his leasehold. He fenced the lands, cleared the fields and erected a brew-house. Thus he became the first brewer within the county, if not within the State. He stocked his bouwerie with twenty-eight head of large cattle, besides various small stock, such as swine, goats, sheep, &c., together with many fruit trees. With a true Dutch farmer's pride, Teunissen continued to improve the place until the war of 1643 broke out, when he, having gone out on a trading expedition, was killed near Sandy Hook.[3] His cattle and other stock were destroyed, his dwelling house, barns and stacks of grain burnt, the brew-house alone remaining.[4] On the 12th of March, 1645, his widow, Susanna Jans, married Sybout Claesen, a house carpenter in New Amsterdam. He shortly afterward claimed a right to the possession of the bouwerie in the name of his wife; but Kieft leased it to Dirck Claesen, from Bremen.[5] This lessee soon abandoned the place, after which it remained unoccupied for some time.

At what time Nicholas Verlet (Varlet, Varleth) came into pos-

---

[1] *N. Y. Col. MSS., i.*, 76.

[2] *Ibid, i.*, 187.

[3] *Valentine's Hist. of N. Y.*, 47.

[4] *Col. Hist. N. Y., i.*, 328.

[5] *Winfield's Land Titles*, 56.

session of the bouwerie is not known, but in March, 1656, he sold the frame of a house at Hoboken to Michiel Jansen, and on the 28th of that month requested of the government six or eight soldiers to aid him in getting it away. But the Indians claiming the frame (except the nails), his request was refused, on the ground that the Indians might commence a fight, which it was feared might become general.[1]

On the return of the planters to their farms in Pavonia, there is no doubt but Verlet came with them. But it was not until the 5th of February, 1663, that he obtained from Stuyvesant a patent for the land. This was confirmed by Governor Carteret on the 12th of May, 1668. Nicholas Bayard (whose widow Verlet had married) was his partner in the Secaucus tract, but it is not known that he was ever interested in Hoboken. On the 19th of June, 1711, however, it came by purchase to the Bayard family,[2] who used it for a summer residence. The farm was worked by tenants, and greatly improved through the liberality of its owners. In 1760 there was on it a garden of five acres filled with a choice collection of English fruit, such as peaches, pears, plums, cherries, nectarines and apricots; a large dwelling house, which Bayard occupied as his summer residence, and another adjoining under the same roof used as a farm-house, with convenient cellars and an "extraordinary kitchen;" out houses, a new smoke house, fowl house, a large stable, with stalls for ten horses on one side, over which was a granary and hay loft, which would hold twenty loads of hay. Upon the farm were thirty milch cows and thirty young cattle, twenty fat hogs, six fat cattle and a pair of oxen. Besides an old orchard capable of producing eighty barrels of cider a year, there were about one thousand young trees, all grafted with the best of fruit. It was considered that scarcely anything in America could equal its convenience for marketing, as in good weather one might "cross, take one time with another, in half an hour."[3]

[1] *N. Y. Col. MSS., vi.*, 347.

[2] *Winfield's Land Titles*, 39, where also see a sketch of Verlet. Although the owner of Hoboken, he lived in Bergen. *Ibid*, 108.

[3] *N. Y. Mercury, December* 8, 1760.

The Bayard mansion was on Castle Point, or "Castile,"[1] and was burned by the patriots on Saturday, the 24th of August, 1780, and the farm laid waste. The owner at this time was William Bayard.[2] This gentleman being a loyalist, his property was confiscated, and, on the 16th of March, 1784, sold to John Stevens. In 1804 the place was laid out upon a map, which was entitled,

[1] *N. Y. Mercury, August* 28, 1780.

[2] William Bayard was associated with Jay, Lewis, etc., the Committee of Fifty Whig sympathizers at the beginning of the war. In 1773 Mr. Quincy, of Massachusetts, in passing on his way from the South, recorded in his journal: "Dined with Col. William Bayard, at his seat on the North River." In 1775 the Massachusetts delegates to the Continental Congress were his guests at the same place. The capture of New York by the British in 1776 induced him to believe that they would succeed in the contest. Hence he forsook the patriot cause and became a loyalist, active and zealous as new converts generally are. The tories in this vicinity were indebted to him for the watch-boats furnished to the Jersey volunteers. *N. Y. Mercury, February* 2, 1778. At the close of the war he went to England, where he lived to be a very old man. He died in 1804, at his seat, Greenwich House, Southampton.

"A Map of the new City Hoboken." On the 20th of March, 1804, Colonel Stevens advertised a four days' sale of eight hundred lots at Hoboken. This sale was to be at public auction, on Monday, April 9, at the Tontine Coffee House, New York; on Tuesday at Hoboken, on Wednesday at the Tontine Coffee House, and on Thursday at Hoboken. Ten per cent. of the purchase price was to be paid within ten days, the balance in four annual payments, the deed to be given on making the first annual payment. David Dixon was the auctioneer. The purchasers were requested to meet at the Tontine on Saturday, the 14th of April, to give names to the streets, each person to have as many votes as he had lots on the streets to be named.

The Hoboken Land and Improvement Company was incorporated February 21, 1838, and the heirs of John Stevens[1] conveyed to it the unsold property, May 6, 1839.

The township of Hoboken was set off from the township of North Bergen on the 1st of March, 1849; organized April 16, 1849. It was incorporated as a city on the 28th of March, 1855, in the name of "the Mayor and Council of the City of Hoboken." The acceptance of the charter was left to the people. The vote thereon was taken on the 29th of March, and stood: "Charter," 337; "No Charter," 185.

Mayors.

Cornelius V. Clickener, 1855-7.
Franklin B. Carpenter, 1857-8, 1859-61.
George W. Morton, 1858-9.
John R. Johnston, 1861-3.
Lorenzo W. Elder, 1863-4.
Charles T. Perry, 1864-5.
Frederick B. Ogden, 1865-7.
Frederick W. Bohnstedt, 1867-9.
Hazen Kimball, 1869-71.
Frederick L. Schmersahl, 1871-3.
Peter McGavisk, 1873.

[1] Colonel John Stevens was the founder of Hoboken. He was born in New York in 1749, and died in 1838. His grandfather, John, was a native of England, and came to New York as one of the law officers of the crown. His father, John, became a resident of New Jersey, and married Elizabeth Alexander. He was at one time Vice-President of the Council. Colonel John married Rachel, daughter of John Cox, of Bloomsburg, N.J. He was for several years Treasurer of the State. His sister married Robert R. Livingston, Chancellor of the State of New York.

Clerks.

Samuel W. Carey, 1855–7.	John Kennedy, 1861–70.
Henry M. Brandis, 1857–8.	Frederick E. Rowald, 1870–2.
Augustus O. Evans, 1858–9.	John R. McCulloch, 1872–
William R. Harrison, 1859–61.	

On the 15th of April, 1814, Samuel Swartwout and his brother Robert purchased a large tract of land at Hoboken. They immediately commenced to reclaim the land by erecting permanent dikes and opening ditches. Part of the land drained came under successful cultivation. About one hundred cows were, in 1819, fed upon these reclaimed marshes, and their milk sent to New York market. Grain of various kinds, and vegetables in abundance, were also raised. In 1819 their funds gave out. They applied to the Corporation of New York for aid. They were not successful, and the project was abandoned.[1]

Water was introduced in October, 1858.

North Bergen.

On the 10th of February, 1843, all that portion of the county lying north of the New Jersey Railroad and the Mill Creek was set off from the township of Bergen, and named the township of North Bergen. It has been, from time to time, despoiled of territory for cities and townships, until at present it is confined to Secaucus and that part of the county lying north of the Paterson plank road and west of Dallytown road. Secaucus is an island, lying between Pinhorne creek and the Hackensack river. It is mentioned in the deed of the Indians to Stuyvesant by the name of Sickakes.[2] On the southerly end of the island is a bold bluff rising out of the salt marsh, known as "Slangen Bergh"[3] and "Snake Hill." It is now owned by the county, and the Alms

[1] *N. Y. Evening Post, July* 24, 1819.

[2] For a minute history of this island, *vide Winfield's Land Titles,* 130.

[3] *Long. Isl. Hist. Soc., i.,* 156. "And is so named on account of the numerous snakes which infest it."

House, Lunatic Asylum and Penitentiary are there. Just north of Snake Hill is an elevated piece of upland, once known as "Mount Pinhorne." This latter place, in all probability, was the residence of Judge Pinhorne. In 1729 the plantation was said to contain "600 acres of timber, 200 cleared land, 1,000 meadow, new house and barn, two orchards of about 1,200 bearing apple trees."[1] Three hundred acres of this plantation now constitute the "Poor House Farm." The purchase of this farm for county purposes was first agitated in November, 1845. It was not, however, until December, 1855, that the Board of Chosen Freeholders resolved to buy it. Several townships and cities had been set off from Bergen, without reserving their right to the farm, so that at this time it was owned by Bergen, North Bergen, Hoboken, and Hudson City. On March 7, 1861, the Legislature named Commissioners from these four municipalities, with power to convey the same to the county. The purchase was completed, and in February, 1862, the title passed to the county at a cost of $12,000. Preparations were immediately made for the erection of the Alms House.[2] James McLoughlin contracted for the carpenter's work at $14,600, and William C. White for the mason work at $12,500. The building was completed in 1863, and the first person received as an inmate was Andrew Donohoe, August 25, 1863. The building now (1873) has accommodation for five hundred inmates. There are in the institution 427 persons, and the cost of maintaining it is $1.71½ per inmate, weekly. Up to November 19, 1873, 2,840 persons had been inmates of the Alms House, whose average age and nationality are as follows:

Total No. of Inmates.	Average age.	Nativity.				Males.	Females.
		Ireland.	England	Germany.	U. S.		
2,840	yrs. m. 30 6	1,154	104	310	1,242	1,700	1,140

[1] *N. Y. Gazette, July* 7, 1729, *and May* 18, 1730.

[2] In the olden time the poor were cared for by selling them to the lowest bidder. The following extract will give a clear idea upon this subject: "At

The contract for the Penitentiary was awarded to Peter Doyle and David Ewling, August 9, 1866, for $83,456. It was completed in 1870, Patrick Warren appointed its first keeper, and Michael Kinney, convicted of breaking and entering and larceny, admitted its first inmate, September 19, 1870. The building has accommodation for 180 persons. On November 19, 1873, ninety-four males and nineteen females were prisoners therein. The following table shows the number of commitments :

PRISONERS COMMITTED TO THE HUDSON COUNTY PENITENTIARY FROM SEPTEMBER 19, 1870, TO NOVEMBER 20, 1873.

What Year.	Total number committed.	Committed.		Committed.		Nativity				Education.		Occupation.		Committed by what Court.		Religion.		
		Males.	Females.	For the first time.	Have been in prison before	Foreign born.	In this country.	Single.	Married.	Read and write.	No education.	Have some trade.	None.	Sessions.	Police Courts.	Catholics.	Protestants.	Jews.
1870	25	22	3	—	2	19	6	13	12	21	4	13	12	25	—	16	9	-
1871	333	258	75	177	156	233	100	201	132	218	115	94	239	75	258	251	81	1
1872	257	196	61	144	113	182	75	170	87	191	66	95	162	77	180	187	70	-
1873	398	310	88	200	198	270	128	257	141	273	125	131	267	78	320	288	107	3
Total	1,013	786	227	521	492	704	309	641	372	703	310	333	680	255	758	742	267	4

The Lunatic Asylum was completed in 1873. The first patients were received March 8, 1873. The building has accommodation for one hundred and forty patients. Since its completion, up to November 19, 1873, one hundred and two patients have been received therein, of whom fifteen have been discharged cured.

New Durham, which up to 1803 was known as the Maisland, lies within this township. In this village is the tavern named "Three Pigeons," a name well known prior to the Revolution.

Here also, near where Macpelah cemetery now is, was the once

Bergen town meeting, December 15th, 1784, at a public Outcry is sold Enoch Earle to the Lowest Bidder for the sum of seven pounds, ten shillings ; the conditions are as follows, the Byer is to find the said Enoch Earle a Good Bed, Washing, Lodging and Victuals and Mending his Close ; the Overseers of the Poor are to find all the New Close and then the said Enoch Earle is to work for the Byer as much as he is able to do until the years End." Until the completion of the present Alms House, the old red building north of the Boonton Branch Railroad was used for that purpose.

celebrated "Frenchman's Garden."[1] Concerning this garden I have met with the following poetic and somewhat sonorous accounts:

"In a wild and romantic situation on Bergen Creek, nearly opposite the City of New York, thirty acres of land were purchased for a garden and fruitery by the unfortunate Louis XVI., who as proprietor became a naturalized citizen by act of the Legislature."[2] This statement of Warden seems to have been based on a notice relating to this garden in the *New Jersey Journal*, June 27, 1787, in which it is said, "Part of this space is at present enclosing with a stone wall, and a universal collection of exotic, as well as domestic plants, trees and flowers, are already begun to be introduced to this elegant spot, which in time must rival, if not excel the most celebrated gardens of Europe. The situation is naturally wild and romantic, between two considerable rivers, in view of the main ocean, the city of New York, the heights of Staten Island and a vast extent of distant mountains on the western side of the landscape." As "tall oaks from little acorns grow," so these exaggerated statements had their origin in the following simple fact. On March 3, 1786, André Michaux, in his petition to the Legislature of this State, set forth that the King of France had commissioned him as his botanist to travel through the United States, that he had power to import from France any tree, plant or vegetable that might be wanting in this country, that he wished to establish near Bergen a botanical garden of about thirty acres, to experiment in agriculture and gardening, and which he intended to stock with French and American plants, as also with plants from all over the world. The Legislature granted his petition, and permitted him *as an alien* to hold not exceeding two hundred acres of land in this State.

He came to this country fortified with a flattering letter of introduction, dated at Vienna, September 3, 1785, from the Marquis de La Fayette to Washington.[3] He was attached to the

---

[1] *Winfield's Land Titles*, 302.

[2] *Warden's History of the United States, ii.*, 53.

[3] *Correspondence of the American Revolution, iv.*, 116.

Jardin des Plants in Paris. He brought with him the gardener, Paul Saunier, who took the title to the ground bought for the garden. The place was stocked with many plants and trees, among which was the Lombard poplar. From this garden this once celebrated tree was spread abroad through the country and pronounced an exotic of priceless value.[1]

Hudson City.

On the 4th of March, 1852, the territory within this city was taken from the township of North Bergen and incorporated as "The Town of Hudson in the County of Hudson." Certain powers were invested in five supervisors, but for all general purposes the place remained a part of the township of North Bergen. On the 11th of April, 1855, it was incorporated "The City of Hudson," with powers of government vested in a Mayor and Common Council. The charter was left to the acceptance or rejection of the people. At an election held on the 12th of April, 1855, a majority of 120 votes was cast for the charter. The Mayor and Common Council were sworn into office by Judge Haines at the court house on the 7th of May. It consolidated with Jersey City in 1870.

Mayors.

Edwin R. V. Wright, 1855.
Garret D. Van Ripen, 1856, '61–8.
Edmund T. Carpenter, 1857–8, '60–1.[2]
Abraham Collerd, 1859.
Benjamin F. Sawyer, 1869.

Clerks.

Alexander Watson, May, 1855 –Sept., 1855.
Thomas Harrison, Sept., 1855 –May, 1856.
Charles J. Roe, May, 1856–May, 1870.

Within the bounds of this city, and partly on the southerly end of the new reservoir, and extending easterly, was the Beacon

[1] *Old New York*, 23.
[2] Died in office in 1861, and was succeeded by Garret D. Van Ripen.

Race Course. It was owned by Cyrus S. Browning, who was here killed by being thrown from his Canadian horse "Hops," November 5, 1845, in a hurdle race. The following list of races over this once popular track will be interesting to "whom it may concern":

Beacon Race Course.

Ajax, Rattler, May 20, 1844; 3 miles; dis., 8:02.
Americus, Ripton, to wagon, Sept. 26, 1842; 2 miles; 5:17, 5:20.
" Dutchman, Ripton, Sept. 21, 1843; 3 miles; 8:04, 8:11, 8:26, 9:40.
" Lady Suffolk, Columbus, June 27, 1844; 3 miles; 7:52½, 8:01.
Amina, Columbus, Doctor (3 dr.), May 9, 1844; 1 mile; 2:37½, 2:38, 2:37.
Awful, Lady Suffolk, Oct. 8, 1838; 2 miles; 5:28, 5:21½.
" Dutchman, to wagon, Oct. 28, 1839; 1 mile; 2:41¼, 2:40, 2:44¾.
Beppo, Independence, June 25, 1843; 1 mile; 2:32¼, 2:31½, 2:33, 2:38, 2:35.
Billy, Seneca Chief, pacers, July 14, 1841; 1 mile; 2:32.
Brandywine, Vernon Maid, Mingo Princess, June 15, 1841; 2 miles; 5:24, 5:24.
Brooklyn Maid, Mingo, Rattler, June 7, 1841; 3 miles; 8:27, 8:24.
" Snaffle, Don Juan, May 5, 1842; 2 miles; 5:22.
Cayuga Chief, Aaron Burr, June 12, 1841; 1 mile; 2:38, 2:38, 2:46, 2:37.
" Washington, Americus, June 19, 1844; 1 mile; 2:35½, 2:35½, 2:40, 2:42, 2:45.
Celeste, Henry, Americus, Oct. 4, 1839; 2 miles; 5:22, 5:32½, 5:26.
Columbus, Ajax, Oct. 21, 1843; 2 miles; 5:24½, 5:32, 5:36.
Confidence, Washington, June 10, 1841; 2 miles; 5:24, 5:28.
" " June 28, 1841; 1 mile; 2:35, 2:37, 2:36.
" Ripton, Awful, Oct. 4, 1841; 2 miles; 5:13, 5:17.
Don Juan, Washington, July 12, 1841; 2 miles; 5:21, 5:39, 5:22½.

Duchess, Cayuga Chief, Pleasure Boy, Sept. 19, 1842 ; 2 miles ; 5:15½, 5:25, 5:35.
" Hector, May 20, 1843 ; 2 miles ; 5:28, 5:22.
" Snaffle, Hector, June 15, 1843 ; 2 miles ; 5:26½, 5:20.
" Lady Suffolk, Oct. 8, 1845 ; 1 mile ; 2:37, 2:35½, 2:35¼, 2:39.

Dutchman, Rattler, Oct. 8, 1838 ; 3 miles ; 7:45½, 7:50, 8:02, 8:24½.
" Rattler (dis.), Oct. 15, 1838 ; 3 miles ; 8.01½.
" Lady Suffolk, April 27, 1839 ; 2 miles ; 5:16, 5:19.
" Awful (dis.), July 4, 1839 ; 3 miles ; 7:41.
" " July 11, 1839 ; 3 miles ; 8:18, 7:59.
" " July 18, 1839 ; 1 mile ; 2:35, 2:32, 2:35.
" against time, Aug. 1, 1839 ; 3 miles ; 7:32½.[1]
" Awful, Oct. 4, 1839 ; 2 miles ; 5:11, 5:16.

---

[1] This remarkable speed and endurance made Dutchman king of the turf, which position he held for thirty-three years. The following is an account of the race as told by Hiram Woodruff himself, who rode Dutchman, in his valuable work on the trotting horse in America :

"The 1st of August came. The course was firm, a large concourse of people were in attendance, and the odds were two to one on Dutchman when we brought him out and stripped him. At six o'clock in the evening he was saddled, and I mounted, feeling fully confident that the feat set would be done with much ease. We were allowed a running horse to keep company, and I had a nice blood-like mare, she being under my brother Isaac. We went off at a moderate jog, gradually increasing the pace, but conversing part of the way at our ease. The mile was accomplished in 2:34½, and Dutchman never was really extended. Now occurred a circumstance which must be related, because it was curious in itself and had its effect on time. Mr. Harrison, the backer of Dutchman, had sent his watch to a friend and was not keeping time of the horses himself as they went round. As we came by the stand some bystander, who had a mistake in timing, told him that the time of the mile was 2:38, which was a losing average. He therefore called out to me as I passed him to go along, and go along I did. Dutchman struck a great pace on the back stretch, and established such a fine stroke that the running mare was no longer able to live with him. My brother Isaac got alarmed and sung out to me that I was going too fast. I replied that I had been told to go along. It was not my conviction that the horse was going too fast even then, for if ever there was one that I could feel of and that felt all over strong and capable of maintaining the rate, Dutchman did then. Nevertheless I took a pull for Isaac, and allowed him to come up and keep company for the balance of the mile. It was per-

Dutchman, Washington, Sept. 29, 1840; 2 miles; 5:17½, 5:17, 5:24.

" Lady Suffolk, Americus, Oct. 5, 1843; 2 miles; 5:19, 5:20, 5:22, 5:29.

Fairy Queen, Cayuga Chief, May 6, 1844; 1 mile; 2:39, 2:39.

" Calhoun, July 8, 1844; 1 mile; 2:34, 2:31.

Greenwich Maid, Dutchman, June 21, 1838; 2 miles; 5:20, 5:22.

Hector, Kate Horn, May 14, 1842; 1 mile; 2:41, 2:41, 2:42, 2:36.

" Snaffle, Pleasure Boy, Sept. 21, 1842; 2 miles; 5:18½, 5:14½.

John C. Calhoun, Fairy Queen, Oct. 31, 1844; 1 mile; 2:32, 2:36.

Lady Clinton, Chancellor, Brooklyn Maid, Brandywine, Buckskin, Hector (1 dis.), Sept. 29, 1841; 1 mile; 2:41, 2:40, 2:41½, 2:41.

Lady Suffolk, Lady Victory, Black Hawk (1 dis.), Cato (1 dis.), Sarah Paff (1 dis.), June 22, 1838; 2 miles; 5:15, 5:17.

" Apollo (1 dis.), April 26, 1839; 2 miles; 5:21.

" Cato (1 dis.), July 3, 1839; 2 miles; 5:39.

" Henry, Celeste, Cato (3 dis.), Oct. 3, 1839; 2 miles; 5:28, 5:28, 5:26.

---

formed in 2:28 very handily. The third mile we kept the same relative positions, Dutchman being under good pull all the way, and able to have left the running mare had he been called upon so to do. The rate was now very even, and it was maintained until we were within about two hundred yards of the stand, when I was notified to check up and come home at a more moderate gait. I therefore crossed the score at a jog-trot, and Dutchman was at a walk within fifteen yards of it. The last mile was 2:30, the whole being 7:32½. Great as this performance was thought at the time, long as it has stood unequaled, and great and deserved as has been and is the fame of those who have endeavored to surpass it, I declare that it is not by any means all that Dutchman could have done that day. I am positive that if I had been called upon to do so, he could have trotted the three miles in 7:27 or better. This is no light opinion of mine, taken up years afterward on inadequate grounds, and when those who might be opposed to it have gone from among us. It was the judgment of those who saw him in the feat, observed him all through and noticed how he finished. It has always been my conviction, and will remain so to my dying day, that Dutchman could have done the last mile in 2:26, and I even hold to the opinion that he could have done it in 2:25. The people who witnessed the race thought so too."

Dutchman's time was beaten by Huntress at Prospect Park Sept. 21, 1872.

Lady Suffolk, Don Juan, Oct. 23, 1839; 2 miles; 5:16, 5:24.
" Aaron Burr, Sept. 21, 1840; 2 miles; 5:22, 5:21, 5:35.
" Ripton, July 6, 1841; 1 mile; 2:35, 2:37½.
" Awful, July 22, 1841; 2 miles; 5:26½, 5:23, 5:24.
" Oneida Chief (1 dis.), July 27, 1841; 2 miles; 5:05.
" Beppo, Independence, July 4, 1843; 1 mile; 2:28½, 2:28, 2:28, 2:29, 2:32.
" Beppo, Oneida Chief, July 12, 1843; 1 mile; 2:26½, 2:27, 2:27.
" Beppo, July 25, 1843; 1 mile; 2:30½, 2:42½, 2:28.
" Confidence, Sept. 14, 1843; 1 mile; 2:38, 2:39, 2:41.
" Americus, Ripton, May 21; 1844; 2 miles; 5:17, 5:19, 5:18.
" Duchess, Washington, Sept. 9, 1844; 1 mile; 2,38, 2:33½, 2:34, 2:37.
" John C. Calhoun, Fairy Queen (4 dis.), Oct. 7, 1844; 1 mile; 2:39, 2:31, 2:28, 2:29, 2:30.
" Moscow, Oct. 13, 1845; 1 mile; 2:34, 2:29½, 2:31, 2:34, 2:36.

Lady Tompkins, Amina, Oct. 17, 1844; 1 mile; 2:37, 2:36, 2:39, 2:38.

Moscow, Reality, Oct. 6, 1845; 1 mile; 2:39½, 2:44.
" Lady Suffolk, Oct. 16, 1845; 1 mile; 2:33½, 2:31½, 2:40, 2:35.

Oneida Chief, Miss Saratoga, June 19, 1838; 2 miles; 5:14, 5:09½.
" Awful, June 17, 1840; 3 miles; 8:17, 8:20½.
" Lady Suffolk, Nov. 1, 1841; 3 miles; 7:50, 8:04.
" " Aug. 14, 1843; 3 miles; 7:44, 7:52.

Rattler, " (3 dis.), July 4, 1838; 2 miles; 5:29, 5:17, 5:40.
" Dutchman, Lady Suffolk (1 dis.), Oct. 1, 1838; 2 miles; 5:17, 5:13½.

Ripton, Brandywine, Don Juan, June 22, 1841; 2 miles; 5:21, 5:14½.
" " Post Boy, Sept. 21, 1841; 2 miles; 5:32, 5:24.
" Quaker, Duchess, Nov. 1, 1841; 2 miles; 5:13, 5,20.

Ripton, Lady Suffolk, Confidence, Aug. 1, 1842; 3 miles; 8:00, 7:56½.
" Americus, Oct. 26, 1842; 3 miles; 8:03, 8:01, 8:04.
" Lady Suffolk, Confidence, May 7, 1842; 2 miles; 5:10¼, 5:12½.
" Americus, May 15, 1843; 3 miles; 7:53, 8:03.
" " May 22, 1843; 2 miles; 5:12, 5:12, 5:17.
" Confidence, June 15, 1844; 1 mile; 2:40, 2:41, 2:38, 2:42½, 2:40.
Sir William, Ajax, Jersey Blue (3 dis.), Oct. 8, 1844; 3 miles; 8:04½, 8:09, 8:06½.
" Hector, Oct. 31, 1844; 2 miles; 5:26, 5:27.
Snaffle, Brooklyn Maid, Hector, Oct. 17, 1842; 2 miles; 5:26, 5:27.
" Rifle, Tom Benton, Sorrel Billy (2 dis.), May 16, 1844; 2 miles; 5:23½, 5:20.
Soldier Bob, Spangle, Cayuga Chief, Awful, Oct. 18, 1843; 1 mile; 2:35½, 2:38, 2:39½, 2:41, 2:46, 2:47.
Unknown, Fairy Queen (1 dis.), Aug. 2, 1844; 1 mile; 2:23.
Volcano, Stranger, Waterman (1 dis.), June 28, 1841; 1 mile; 2:39, 2:31½, 2:34½, 2:38½.
Volcano, Drover, Waterman (1 dis.), Seneca Chief (1 dis.), July 5, 1841; 1 mile; 2:32, 2:35, 2:38.
Washington, Greenwich Maid, Dutchman, Rattler, June 22, 1838; 2 miles; 5:19, 5:17.
" Dutchman, Greenwich Maid, July 4, 1838; 2 miles; 5:22, 5:17.
" Cayuga Chief (2 dis.), Nov. 2, 1840; 2 miles; 5:37, 5:19½.
" Duchess, Rifle, May 23, 1844; 2 miles; 5:17½, 5:20.

The people in the vicinity grew weary of the races and the character of the visitors. It was presented by the grand jury as a "nuisance to the public" in 1845. It was shortly afterward abandoned.

In 186– the Hudson County Agricultural Society, for the purpose of developing a superior species of pumpkin, constructed a race course on Secaucus. It was kept up for some time with great spirit, but after the lapse of two or three years the racing was abandoned. The land belonging to the company was sold to Bishop Bayley, Dec. 14, 1870. It is not yet turned to religious uses. It has in part relapsed to its former condition; perhaps it would be proper to say its last state is worse than the first, for it is now devoted to "scrub" racing, Indian exhibitions and other amusements of an equally inferior character.

Township of Weehawken was set off from the city of Hoboken March 15, 1859.

Township of Union was set off from the township of North Bergen Feb. 28, 1861.

Township of West Hoboken was set off from the township of North Bergen Feb. 28, 1861.

Township of Bayonne was set off from the town of Bergen March 15, 1861, and incorporated as a city March 10, 1869.

Township of Greenville was set off from the town of Bergen March 18, 1863, and consolidated with Jersey City in 1873.

Town of Union was set off from the township of Union March 29, 1864.

Township of Kearney was set off from the township of Harrison March 14, 1867.

Considering the rapid absorption of adjacent territory by Jersey City, it is perhaps proper that the names and location of villages and hamlets, as they have existed and do now exist, should be given for preservation. Beginning at Bergen Point, we go northward.

Centreville is a small village about two miles north of Bergen Point.

Bayonne is a small village about three-quarters of a mile north of Centreville.

Pamrepo is a village in the northerly part of the city of Bayonne, formerly known as Salterville. All of these places are within the city of Bayonne, and the New Jersey Central Railroad Company has a station at each place.

Greenville was a small, poorly constructed village about three miles from the Jersey City ferry, on the old road leading to Bergen Point, settled mostly by Germans. It finally gave its name to a township, which was annexed to Jersey City in 1873.

Claremont was a name given more to a tract of land that was mapped out for sale than to a village. It lies on the heights, north and south of the Newark and New York Railroad.

Lafayette was the name given by the owners of the land to that portion of Jersey City which lies south of the Morris canal, in the vicinity of Pacific and Communipaw avenues.

Centre Hill, like Claremont and Lafayette, was a name which grew out of a land speculation. It is now quite thickly settled. It lies in the upper part of Jersey City, a little south of the Paterson plank road.

West Hoboken is a thriving village, which has given its name to a township. It lies upon the heights, adjoining the north boundary of Jersey City.

Union Hill is quite a large town on the heights, east of the Hackensack plank road, and about two miles north of Hoboken. It was settled and built up almost exclusively by Germans.

New Durham is a small hamlet lying at the northerly foot of Weehawken hill, on the Hackensack plank road.

Guttenberg is a small village on the heights, a little south of Bull's Ferry, settled and built up by Germans. The name was applied to a tract of land mapped for sale. Incorporated March 9, 1859.

West New York lies on the westerly brow of the hill back of Guttenberg.

CHAPTER XI.

Organization of the county—Its officers—Vote for location of Court House—Laying corner stone—Address of Chief Justice Hornblower—Representatives in the Legislature—List of Freeholders—List of Judges.

THE act to set off the county of Hudson from Bergen county passed the Legislature February 22, 1840, by a vote of *twenty-seven* to *twenty-three* in the Assembly, and *nine* to *seven* in the Council. This large negative vote was the result of political considerations. The county then comprised the town of Jersey and townships of Bergen and Harrison. East of the Hackensack its boundaries were identical with the old township of Bergen. West of the Hackensack it included not only the present townships of Harrison and Kearney, but the township of Union in the county of Bergen. This last named township was then included within the township of Harrison, and was set off into Bergen county February 19, 1852.

At a joint meeting of the Legislature, February 27, 1840, the following appointments of county officers were made:

Robert Gilchrist, *Clerk.*

Edmund W. Kingsland, *Surrogate.*

Lewis D. Hardenberg, *Prosecutor of the Pleas.*

Stephen Garretson, Cornelius V. V. Kingsland, *Judges.*

The first term of the County Court began April 14, 1840, at Lyceum Hall, in Grand street, Jersey City.

Joseph C. Hornblower, *Chief Justice, presiding.*

Cornelius Van Winkle, Henry Southmayd, Stephen Garretson, George C. De Kay, *Judges.*

George H. Brinkerhoff, *Sheriff.*

Archer G. Welsh,[1] Abraham Van Winkle, Oliver H. P. Kilburne, Thomas Marinus, *Constables.*

Nathaniel Ellis, *Marshal.*

---

[1] Crier of the Court from this time until October Term, 1870; died November

Grand Jury.

John Lovett, Garret G. Newkirk, John I. Speer, Isaac Q. Underhill, Michael Fisher, Benjamin Mills, John Bunce, Lorenzo Jacquins, Cornelius Van Vorst, Charles F. Durant, Rodman M. Price, John F. Ellis, John Griffith, James Drake, James Devoe, John C. Morgan, Merselis Parks, John Brinkerhoff, Joshua J. Benson, Jacob Vreeland, Jacob D. Van Winkle, John G. Speer,[1] Richard Outwater,[1] William Seeley.[1]

Petit Jurors.

Morris Smith, Jacob M. Vreeland, Henry Van Horn, John Garretson, Nathaniel H. Carpenter, Calvin Tompkins, George De Mott, Charles Gardner, Henry Osborn, James W. Higgins, Daniel Crane, Henry Drayton, John P. Hill, Mindert Vreeland, Albert M. Zabriskie, B. Van Schaick, Garret Ackerman, William C. Kingsland, John G. McLoughlin, Walter Woods, Charles B. C. Bacot, Joseph Danielson, George W. Edge, Joseph Stone, Abraham C. Van Boskerck, Jacob Van Horn, John Gilbert, James Lott, Smith Benedict, Peter Van Horn, James Malone, Joshua Heustis, James Talman, Garret Van Vorst, Dudley S. Gregory, John P. Morgan, Henry Van Embergh, Paul Salter, Garret Newkirk, Arent H. Schuyler.

The courts continued to be held in the Lyceum Hall from that time until September 19, 1843, when the Board of Chosen Freeholders having accepted the "Newkirk House," at the Five Corners, as a Court House, the courts were opened there September 20, 1843. Here the courts were held until March 11, 1845, when the present Court House was completed.

The location of the Court House was a subject of considerable interest to the people. Each district was offered as the desirable spot. The following places were put in nomination:

1. Washington square in Jersey City.

7, 1870. He was succeeded by his nephew, John Wesley Welsh, who yet "cries aloud."

[1] Did not appear.

2. The Public Grounds in Harsimus.
3. Bergen square.
4. Public Grounds in Hoboken.
5. West Hoboken.
6. East Newark.
7. The Five Corners.
8. Near Depot, Paterson Railroad (West End).
9. Bergen Ridge, from road to Communipaw to West Hoboken.
10. Communipaw.
11. Secaucus.
12. Bergen Point.
13. New Durham.
14. Weehawken.

☞ Centre of the county, Poudrette Company, on Hackensack river!

As an inducement to have the Court House located in Jersey City, that municipality offered to donate to the county land worth $10,000 and $8,000 in money.

The vote upon the question was taken June 2, 1840, with the following result:

Vote in Bergen.

For Bergen,	506
Rejected,	2
Whole number of votes,	508

Vote in Jersey City.

For Bergen,	20
" Jersey City,	281
" Harrison,	2
Rejected,	2
Whole No. of votes,	304

Vote in Harrison.

For Bergen,	54
" Jersey City,	2
Whole No. of votes,	56

After the above vote there was much delay in deciding on the locality for the building, and it was not until December 5, 1843, that the contract for the building of the Court House was given to Thomas Thomas, *Carpenter*, and William Brown, *Mason*, for $14,000, which was the lowest bid. Ground was broken for the building May 1, 1844, and the corner stone laid October 17, 1844, with great ceremony. A procession was formed at Drayton's Hotel, at the Five Corners, in the following order:

1. Architect, Superintendent and Builder.
2. Mechanics and laborers employed on the building, about 100 in number.
3. A noble band of music from the U. S. Ship *North Carolina*.
4. Committee of Arrangements.
5. Board of Chosen Freeholders.
6. Clergy.
7. Chief Justice of the State of New Jersey.
8. Members of the Bar.
9. Judges and Justices of the county.
10. Clerk and Surrogate.
11. Sheriff and Constables.
12. Mayor and Common Council of Jersey City.
13. Trustees of the Freeholders Inhabitants of the Township of Bergen.
14. Strangers.
15. Citizens on foot.
16. Citizens on horseback and in carriages.

Prayer by Rev. B. C. Taylor, D.D.; corner-stone laid by John Tonele, jr., Director of the Board of Chosen Freeholders.

In the stone were deposited the newspapers of the day, published in New York, Jersey City, Newark, Trenton, &c., Reports on Education, School Fund and Finances of the State and county, several coins, a parchment roll containing a list of all the county officers, the Governor, State officers, the President of the United States, and other officers of the General Government.

Chief Justice Hornblower made an address, and Rev. Mr. Ballard pronounced the Benediction.

The following is a copy of a paper on file in the clerk's office, which shows the situation of the Court House :

"Latitude and Longitude of Hudson County Court House, North Bergen, New Jersey :

"Latitude, - - -	40°	43′	50″	N.
"Longitude in time, - -	4^h	56^m	14^{sec}	7^t
				3
	14	48	44	1
				5
	74	03	40	5

"West from Greenwich.

"Variation of compass in 1841, 5° 52′.

"W. C. WETMORE,
"U. S. Navy.

"July 7, 1846.'

The first session in the new Court House was opened March 11, 1845, with Prayer by Rev. B. C. Taylor, D.D., and the following address by the Chief Justice :

"*Gentlemen, Members of the Board of Chosen Freeholders, of the Grand Jury, and my Fellow Citizens at large of the County of Hudson :*

"Assembled, as we are, for the first time within this beautiful building, which has been erected by your patriotism and liberality, whose corner stone was laid in prayer, and in prayer fervent, appropriate and eloquent, has just been dedicated to the administration of justice, I feel it my pleasure, my privilege, to address you in words of congratulation as well as in the language of official advice and judicial instruction. Since the frailty, not to say the depravity of our nature, renders it necessary to establish and maintain courts of justice, to settle the rights of individuals, to punish the guilty and protect the innocent, it is desirable and becoming that the public should provide convenient and suitable buildings in which to discharge that high and responsible duty. You, my fellow citizens, have met that demand with a noble and generous spirit. In the erection of this edifice you have manifested your attachment to the institutions of your country, and your readiness to sustain the administrators of public justice in the execution and discharge of their duty. Accept, therefore, I pray you, from me, in behalf of myself and of every member of the court, *and of those who may soon* succeed me and my associates in the seats we now occupy, unfeigned thanks for the convenient and elegant apartments you have provided for the accommodation of courts and their officers. When you first conceived the plan of being erected into a separate county, it met with my approbation and secured my support, from no sinister motive. I remembered the old town of Bergen, when it had very few inhabitants except old-fashioned, honest Dutchmen, and very few houses except those not built for show, but for domestic comfort and convenience; long, low and unpretending in appearance, but durable in materials, and opening upon the streets some two or three hospitable doors, into which the friend and stranger might enter and find a welcome, and from which they might retire and leave a blessing behind them. Hoboken then consisted of little else besides a well-kept public house, and a beautiful retreat from the noise and bustle of the neighboring metropolis. No Jersey City then adorned your shores—nothing but a large, long ferry house, occupied successively by an Ellsworth, a Smith, and a Hunt, with here and there a boatman's or a fisherman's cabin, stood upon the *heap of sand* called Powles' Hook: your settlements were sparse, your occupations agricultural and industrial, and your population small, but healthy, peaceful and honest: you needed, for many years within my recollection, but one physician to administer to your physical necessities, but one man of God to supply your spiritual want, and not even *one lawyer* to satisfy your litigious propensities, for you had none to be satisfied. Peace reigned throughout your borders—simplicity of life and manners and honesty of purpose were the prevailing characteristics of *the good old Dutch*, who almost exclusively occupied the soil of your county in the days of my boyhood. A court at Hackensack and a few Dutch justices at home were all you wanted to punish the few offenders and settle the few lawsuits that troubled you in those days. But, alas! we fear those good old days have gone by, never to return! The rapidly increasing population of our country, the vast improvements in science and the arts, and the enterprising spirit of the age in which we live, have wrought a mighty change within the period even of my memory. The facilities of steamboats and railroad cars, and the increasing spirit of trade and commerce and manufactures and the arts, have brought the good old town of Bergen into contact with the world, cut up her territory into small localities, studded her shores with splendid buildings, turned her farms into pleasure seats, her cabbage ground into pleasure gardens, and her dwelling places into workshops and manufactories. Such, in fact, has been the change in appearance and population of that part of the old county of Bergen which now constitutes the county of Hudson, that I can scarcely retrace the footsteps of my boyhood when, in my visits to friends here or in the city of New York, I used to traverse these hills. When, therefore, you first contemplated the formation of a new county, I favored the object, because I was satisfied that, if not then absolutely necessary, the time was rapidly approaching when the increased number of inhabitants, the diversified character of your population, the rapidly extending trade and commerce with the city of New York and other places, the consequent increase of bargains and contracts, of litigation and of crime, would call for a stronger police, for increased vigilance on the part of magistrates and peace officers, and for a seat of justice nearer your own doors. I rejoiced, therefore, in the consummation of your wishes, and was the more gratified from the reflection that your courts would be held within my judicial district, and thus give me an opportunity of meeting more frequently than I otherwise should with my respected friends and fellow citizens of the county of Hudson. I have long since marked it down in the chronicle of those events, the memory of which I cherish, and which I desire to be transmitted to and remembered by my children, that I had the honor of presiding at the first court ever held in Hudson County. To that I have since been permitted to add the interesting fact that I was privileged to act a conspicuous part in the solemn and imposing ceremony of laying the foundation stone of this edifice, and now shall have the pleasure of adding to this history the gratifying circumstance that I have been spared by a kind Providence to preside at the first court and address the first Grand Jury that ever assembled within these walls. For this privilege I feel thankful, and I invite you all to unite with me in rendering thanksgiving and praise to HIM who is Judge over all, and in whose hands our lives are, that through His kind and protecting care this edifice has been reared from its foundation to its superstructure without any fatal accident or the slightest injury to any of the worthy and industrious mechanics and laborers who have been employed in its erection.

"May the same all-wise and merciful Providence ever preside over the councils and the deliberations of judges and jurors within these walls: may the ermine of justice, by whomsoever it may be worn after we shall have gone to our final account, ever be kept pure and unspotted here, and this sanctuary of justice never be desecrated by bribery or corruption—never be an arena for the indulgence of prejudice, partiality or unhallowed passions of any sort; but may the unadulterated stream of public and private justice ever flow from this sacred hall, and from the pure fountain of eternal truth and righteousness."

The Chief Justice then addressed the Grand Jurors upon their duties.

The following Justices of the Supreme Court have presided over the courts in Hudson County, being regularly assigned to this circuit:

Chief Justice Josiah Hornblower.
" " Henry W. Green.
Associate Justice Elias B. D. Ogden.[1]
" " Joseph D. Bedle.

[1] Died Feb. 24, 1865.

Sheriffs.

George H. Brinkerhoff, 1840, appointed by Joint Meeting; Henry Newkirk, 1840-2; John Garretson, 1843; Abraham Van Winkle, 1844-6; Lorenzo Jaquins, 1847-9; Jacob M. Mer-

JACOB M. MERSELES.

seles,[1] 1850-2; Jasper Garretson, 1853-5; Henry B. Beaty, 1856-8; John M. Francis,[2] 1859-61; Bernard McAnally, 1862-4; Jacob M. Merseles, 1865-6; John H. Midmer,[3] 1867-8; Andrew Mount, 1869-70; John Reinhardt, 1871-4.

[1] Died Jan. 2, 1865. [2] Died June 10, 1873. [3] Died Sept. 17, 1872.

County Clerks.

Robert Gilchrist, - - - - - - - - 1840–65

George W. Cassedy, - 1865–70 | John Kennedy, - - 1870–75

Surrogates.

Edmund W. Kingsland, 1840–55; James O'Neil,[1] 1855–70; Robert McCague, Feb., 1870, present incumbent.

Prosecutors of the Pleas.

Lewis D. Hardenbergh, 1840–5; Isaac W. Scudder, 1845–50; Edwin R. V. Wright, 1850–5; J. Dunn Littell,[1] 1855–60; Isaac W. Scudder, 1860–5; Richard D. McClelland,[1] 1865–8; J. Harvey Lyon, 1868–9; Abram Q. Garretson, 1869–74.

MEMBERS OF THE LEGISLATURE (under the old Constitution).

Council.

Abraham Van Santvoord, 1840; John S. Condit, 1841–2; Edwin R. V. Wright,[2] 1843.

---

[1] Died in office.

[2] Died Jan. 20, 1871.

Assembly.

John S. Condit, 1840; Abraham L. Van Boskerck, 1841-2; Benjamin F. Welsh, 1843.

MEMBERS OF THE LEGISLATURE (under the new Constitution).

Senators.

Richard Outwater, 1845-8; John Tonelc,[1] 1848-50; John Cassedy, 1850-1; Abraham O. Zabriskie,[2] 1851-4; Moses B. Bramhall, 1854-7; Cornelius V. Clickener, 1857-60; Samuel Wescott,[3] 1860-2; Theodore F. Randolph, 1862-6; Charles H. Winfield, 1866-9; Noah D. Taylor, 1869-72; John R. McPherson, 1872-5.

Assembly.

Hartman Van Wagenen, 1845-7; Benjamin F. Welsh, 1848; Oliver S. Strong, 1849; James J. Van Boskerck, 1850; Edmund T. Carpenter, 1851; John Van Vorst, 1852.

1853—John Van Vorst, Edmund T. Carpenter, Joseph W. Hancox.

1854—John Dunn Littell, James S. Davenport, Jacob M. Vreeland.

1855—Albert Augustus Hardenbergh, Clement M. Hancox, Jacob M. Merseles.

1856—John M. Board, Dudley S. Gregory, jr., Jacob M. Merseles.

1857—Robert C. Bacot, Robert Gilchrist, jr., George V. De Mott.

1858—Robert C. Bacot, William Voorhis, Garret Van Horn.

1859—William H. Hemenover, Samuel A. French, Garret Van Horn.

1860—Garret Van Horn, Nathaniel C. Slaight, William H. Peckham.

1861—Franklin B. Carpenter, Theodore F. Randolph, Michael J. Vreeland.

---

[1] Resigned; died Nov. 26, 1852. [2] Died June 27, 1873. [3] Resigned.

1862—Edward D. Riley, George McLoughlin, John B. Perry, Joshua J. Benson, Josiah Conley, Michael J. Vreeland.

1863—James Lynch, George McLoughlin, John B. Perry, Joshua J. Benson, Josiah Conley, Garret D. Van Ripen.

1864—James Lynch, John B. Drayton, John Van Vorst, Joshua J. Benson, Abram W. Duryea, Garret D. Van Ripen.

1865—Delos E. Culver, William L. Broking, John Van Vorst, Leon Abbett, Abram W. Duryea, Hiram Van Buskirk.

1866—Noah D. Taylor, John Ramsey, Obadiah D. Falkenbury, Leon Abbett, Charles F. Ruh, DeWitt C. Morris.

1867—Noah D. Taylor, Hosea F. Clark, Obadiah D. Falkenbury, Augustus O. Evans, John Dwyer, DeWitt C. Morris.

1868—Noah D. Taylor, Hosea F. Clark, John Van Vorst, Augustus O. Evans, John Dwyer, Henry Clay Smith.

1869—Leon Abbett, Sidney B. Bevans, James B. Doremus, Elbridge V. S. Besson, Michael Coogan, Henry Clay Smith.

1870—Leon Abbett, Sidney B. Bevans, James B. Doremus, Herman D. Busch, Abel I. Smith, William Brinkerhoff.

1871—James F. Fielder, John Anness, Herman D. Busch, Michael Coogan, Josiah Hornblower.

1872—George H. Farrier, Dennis Reardon, George S. Plympton, Henry Gaede, Jasper Wandle, James Stevens, John A. O'Neil, Anthony H. Ryder.

1873—George H. Farrier, Dennis Reardon, George S. Plympton, Henry Gaede, Jasper Wandle, Richard C. Washburn, John Lee, Anthony H. Ryder.

1874—Alexander T. McGill, Patrick Sheeran, John D. Carscallen, Alexander McDonnell, Henry Combs, Richard C. Washburn, Rudolph F. Rabe, James K. Selleck.

Board of Chosen Freeholders.

The first meeting of this Board was held May 13, 1840, in Drayton's Hotel, at the Five Corners. The following is a list of the members since the erection of the county. This list also incidentally shows when municipalities were formed or divided into wards.

1840.

BERGEN—Garret Sip, Abel I. Smith. JERSEY CITY—John Griffith, Abraham Van Santvoord. HARRISON—Joseph Budd, William C. Kingsland.

1841.

JERSEY CITY—John Dows, Jonathan Jenkins. VAN VORST—Henry M. Traphagen, David Jones. BERGEN—Garret Sip, Abel I. Smith. HARRISON—Joseph Budd, William C. Kingsland.

1842.

JERSEY CITY—John Dows, Phineas C. Dummer. BERGEN—Cornelius Van Winkle, Edwin R. V. Wright. VAN VORST—David Jones, Henry M. Traphagen. HARRISON—Joseph Budd, William C. Kingsland.

1843.

JERSEY CITY—John Dows,[1] Phineas C. Dummer. BERGEN—William C. Vreeland, Garret G. Newkirk. VAN VORST—Cornelius Van Vorst, Selah Hill. HARRISON—George Kingsland, Peter W. Kipp. NORTH BERGEN—Edwin R. V. Wright, John Tonele, Jr.

1844.

JERSEY CITY—Henry Southmayd, Job Male. BERGEN—William C. Vreeland, Garret G. Newkirk. VAN VORST—Cornelius Van Vorst, Selah Hill. HARRISON—George Kingsland, Peter W. Kipp. NORTH BERGEN—John Tonele, John Van Boskerck.

1845.

JERSEY CITY—Phineas C. Dummer, Joseph W. Morgan. BERGEN—Jacob D. Van Winkle, Jacob Vreeland. VAN VORST—Cornelius Van Vorst, Selah Hill. HARRISON—John S. Condit, George Kingsland. NORTH BERGEN—John Van Boskerck, Daniel Van Ripen.

---

[1] Resigned in Dec., 1843. Henry Southmayd appointed.

1846.

Jersey City—Phineas C. Dummer, Cornelius Kanouse. Bergen—Abraham Becker, Jacob D. Van Winkle. Van Vorst—Cornelius Van Vorst, Henry M. Traphagen. Harrison—John S. Condit, Cornelius C. Jerolemon. North Bergen—John Tonele, Michael Fisher.

1847.

Jersey City—David B. Wakeman, Peter McMartin. Bergen—Abraham Becker, George Thomas. Van Vorst—Erastus Randall, Benjamin Mills. Harrison—John S. Condit, Cornelius C. Jerolemon. North Bergen—John Tonele, Michael Fisher.

1848.

Jersey City—David B. Wakeman, Peter McMartin. Bergen—Garret Sip, Jacob M. Vreeland. Van Vorst—Benjamin Mills, Henry M. Traphagen. Harrison—George Kingsland, Arent H. Schuyler. North Bergen—John J. Newkirk, John Shields.

1849.

Jersey City—David B. Wakeman, James Fleming. Bergen—John Brinkerhoff, Jacob M. Vreeland. Van Vorst—Matthias B. Ward, Henry M. Traphagan. Harrison—George Kingsland, Arent H. Schuyler. North Bergen—James Harrison, John J. Newkirk. Hoboken—Garret Benson, William Hersee.

1850.

Jersey City—David B. Wakeman, John M. Cornelison. Bergen—John Brinkerhoff, Garret Waters. Van Vorst—Matthias B. Ward, John Van Vorst. Harrison—George Kingsland, Arent H. Schuyler. North Bergen—John Shields, John Hague. Hoboken—J. Dunn Littell, Charles T. Perry.

1851.

Jersey City—*First Ward*, George Dummer, R. W. A. Durfee; *Second Ward*, George W. Edge, Robert B. Earle; *Third Ward*, Robert McLoughlin, Henry E. Insley; *Fourth Ward*,

John Van Vorst, John Boyce. BERGEN—John Brinkerhoff, Jasper Garretson. HARRISON—Stephen Kingsland, Thomas Watkins. NORTH BERGEN—Edmund T. Carpenter, Abram W. Duryea. HOBOKEN—Gilliam Van Houten, Denniston B. Wood.

1852.

JERSEY CITY—*First Ward*, George Dummer, Benton B. Grinnell; *Second Ward*, Jacob J. Banta, William Cumming; *Third Ward*, Robert McLoughlin, Henry E. Insley; *Fourth Ward*, John Van Vorst, William Dugan. BERGEN—Mindert Van Horn, Hartman Vreeland. HARRISON—Arent H. Schuyler, Jabez B. Pennington. NORTH BERGEN—Edmund T. Carpenter, Abram W. Duryea. HOBOKEN—Charles Chamberlain, Peter Powless.

1853.

JERSEY CITY—*First Ward*, Minot C. Morgan, David Smith; *Second Ward*, Jacob J. Van Buskirk, Jacob J. Banta; *Third Ward*, Nehemiah Knapp, John S. March; *Fourth Ward*, Clement Hancox, Hervey M. Soule. BERGEN—Hartman Vreeland, Mindert Van Horn. HARRISON—Thomas Lang, Cornelius Shepherd. NORTH BERGEN—Edmund T. Carpenter, Abram W. Duryea. HOBOKEN—Charles Chamberlain, Peter Powless.

1854.

JERSEY CITY—*First Ward*, Minot C. Morgan, David Smith; *Second Ward*, Jacob J. Banta, Samuel A. French; *Third Ward*, Nehemiah Knapp, James Gopsill. *Fourth Ward*, Hervey M. Soule, Jacob B. Schenck. BERGEN—Mindert Van Horn, George Vreeland. HARRISON—Cornelius Shepherd, William S. Ogden. NORTH BERGEN—Edmund T. Carpenter, Abram W. Duryea. HOBOKEN—Benjamin S. Taylor, William C. Arthur.

1855.

JERSEY CITY—*First Ward*, David Henderson, Berryan R. Wakeman; *Second Ward*, Francis Jenkins, Hugh McComb; *Third Ward*, Nehemiah Knapp, Charles M. Holmes; *Fourth*

Ward, Hervey M. Soule, Jacob B. Schenck. BERGEN—Mindert Van Horn, Jacob A. Van Horn. HARRISON—Cornelius Shepherd, William S. Ogden. NORTH BERGEN—John Sturges, Abram W. Duryea. HOBOKEN—*First Ward*, John W. Harny, Louis Huseman; *Second Ward*, Theodore Van Tassel, Ebenezer Montague; *Third Ward*, James H. Dewey, Charles W. Fisher. HUDSON CITY—John H. Platt, Gilliam Van Houten.

1856.

JERSEY CITY—*First Ward*, Minot C. Morgan, Jeremiah Mulford; *Second Ward*, Francis Jenkins, Henry French; *Third Ward*, Charles M. Holmes, George McLoughlin; *Fourth Ward*, Hervey M. Soule, Erastus Randall. BERGEN—Mindert Van Horn, Jacob A. Van Horn. HARRISON—William S. Ogden, Jabez B. Pennington. NORTH BERGEN—Abram W. Duryea, John Sturges. HOBOKEN—*First Ward*, John W. Harny, John Walker; *Second Ward*, David Pollock, Julius G. Garvelle; *Third Ward*, James H. Dewey, William Hersee. HUDSON CITY—John H. Platt, Baily B. Brown.

1857.

JERSEY CITY—*First Ward*, Ai Fitch; *Second Ward*, Henry French; *Third Ward*, George McLoughlin; *Fourth Ward*, John Doyle (in January, 1858, Ephraim Pray). HUDSON CITY—Jacob J. Newkirk. BERGEN—Mindert Van Horn. HARRISON—Hiram Gilbert. NORTH BERGEN—Abram W. Duryea. HOBOKEN—*First Ward*, John Mather; *Second Ward*, Peter J. Powless (in January, 1858, John Dempsey); *Third Ward*, William Hersee.

1858.

JERSEY CITY—*First Ward*, Ai Fitch; *Second Ward*, Alexander Wilson; *Third Ward*, George McLoughlin; *Fourth Ward*, Ephraim Pray. NORTH BERGEN—Abram W. Duryea. HUDSON CITY—Jacob J. Newkirk. HOBOKEN—*First Ward*, John M. Francis; *Second Ward*, William R. Harrison; *Third Ward*, William Hashing. BERGEN—George Vreeland. HARRISON—Hiram W. Davis.

1859.

Jersey City—*First Ward*, Ai Fitch; *Second Ward*, Alexander Wilson; *Third Ward*, James F. Fielder; *Fourth Ward*, Hervey M. Soule. Harrison—Hiram W. Davis. Hudson City—Jacob J. Newkirk. Hoboken—*First Ward*, James Stevenson; *Second Ward*, Louis Kaufman; *Third Ward*, William Hartung. Bergen—George Vreeland. North Bergen—Abram W. Duryea. Weehawken—Denning Duer.

1860.

Jersey City—*First Ward*, Ai Fitch; *Second Ward*, James Lynch; *Third Ward*, James F. Fielder; *Fourth Ward*, Elliston Duncan. Bergen—George Vreeland. Harrison—Hiram W. Davis. Hoboken—*First Ward*, James Stevenson; *Second Ward*, William Hartung; *Third Ward*, James H. Dewey. Hudson City—Charles Luxton. North Bergen—Abram W. Duryea. Weehawken—Denning Duer.

1861.

Jersey City—*First Ward*, Ai Fitch; *Second Ward*, James Lynch; *Third Ward*, John Pringle; *Fourth Ward*, Charles H. O'Neill; *Fifth Ward*, Patrick Reiley; *Sixth Ward*, John Wiseman. Bergen—Hartman Van Wagenen. Bayonne—Albert M. Zabriskie. Hoboken—*First Ward*, James Stevenson; *Second Ward*, Hoyt Sandford; *Third Ward*, James H. Dewey. North Bergen—Abram W. Duryea. Harrison—Hiram W. Davis. Hudson City—Charles Luxton. Weehawken—Denning Duer. Union—Jacob Sweitzer. West Hoboken—Daniel Lake.

1862.

Jersey City—*First Ward*, Ai Fitch; *Second Ward*, James Lynch; *Third Ward*, Patrick H. Nugent; *Fourth Ward*, Charles H. O'Neill; *Fifth Ward*, Patrick Reiley; *Sixth Ward*, Patrick Duff. Hoboken—*First Ward*, James Stevenson; *Second Ward*, Hoyt Sandford; *Third Ward*, James H. Dewey. Bergen—Jacob J. Newkirk. Harrison—Hiram W. Davis.

NORTH BERGEN—Abram W. Duryea. HUDSON CITY—James R. Dey. BAYONNE—Joseph B. Close. UNION—Jacob Sweitzer (in December John Gardner took his place). WEST HOBOKEN—Daniel Lake. WEEHAWKEN—Denning Duer.

1863.

JERSEY CITY—*First Ward*, Francis Stoveken; *Second Ward*, James Lynch; *Third Ward*, Stephen Quaife; *Fourth Ward*, Charles H. O'Neill; *Fifth Ward*, Henry Finck; *Sixth Ward*, John McGuigan. HOBOKEN—*First Ward*, James Stevenson; *Second Ward*, Hoyt Sandford; *Third Ward*, James H. Dewey. HUDSON CITY—George V. DeMott. NORTH BERGEN—Abram W. Duryea. HARRISON—Hiram W. Davis. BERGEN—Abraham Speer. BAYONNE—Peter Vreeland. UNION—Cornelius Van Vorst. WEST HOBOKEN—John Hague. WEEHAWKEN—Denning Duer. GREENVILLE—Henry D. Van Nostrand.

1864.

JERSEY CITY—*First Ward*, Francis Stoveken; *Second Ward*, James Lynch; *Third Ward*, Thomas Gross; *Fourth Ward*, Charles H. O'Neill (resigned in October, Christopher Mills appointed); *Fifth Ward*, John Lowrey; *Sixth Ward*, John McGuigan. HOBOKEN—*First Ward*, James Stevenson; *Second Ward*, James T. Hatfield; *Third Ward*, James H. Dewey. WEEHAWKEN—Denning Duer. BAYONNE—Peter Vreeland. HUDSON CITY—*First Ward*, Herman W. Moller; *Second Ward*, George V. DeMott; *Third Ward*, John M. Wilson; *Fourth Ward*, George Glaubrecht. BERGEN—Cornelius Vreeland (in October Mindert Van Horn took his place). HARRISON—Josiah Conley. NORTH BERGEN—Abram W. Duryea. UNION—John Dwyer. WEST HOBOKEN—John Hague. GREENVILLE—Henry D. Van Nostrand. TOWN OF UNION—John Gardner.

1865.

JERSEY CITY—*First Ward*, Peter Curley; *Second Ward*, James Lynch; *Third Ward*, Thomas Gross; *Fourth Ward*, John H. Smyth; *Fifth Ward*, John Lowrey; *Sixth Ward*,

John McGuigan. HOBOKEN — *First Ward*, Lafayette Tompkins; *Second Ward*, James T. Hatfield; *Third Ward*, James H. Dewey. UNION—Francis Pollock. TOWN OF UNION—John Gardner. NORTH BERGEN—John Sturges. BERGEN—*Columbia Ward*, Jacob J. Newkirk; *Communipaw Ward*, Mindert Van Horn; *Franklin Ward*, Garret Vreeland. HUDSON CITY—*First Ward*, John H. Platt; *Second Ward*, Michael C. Brown; *Third Ward*, John M. Wilson; *Fourth Ward*, George Glaubrecht. HARRISON—Josiah Conley. BAYONNE—De Witt C. Morris. GREENVILLE—Henry D. Van Nostrand. WEST HOBOKEN—John Hague. WEEHAWKEN—Denning Duer.

1866.

JERSEY CITY—*First Ward*, Peter Curley; *Second Ward*, James Lynch; *Third Ward*, N. H. Coykendall; *Fourth Ward*, John H. Smyth; *Fifth Ward*, John Lowrey; *Sixth Ward*, John McGuigan. HUDSON CITY—*First Ward*, John H. Platt; *Second Ward*, Michael C. Brown; *Third Ward*, John M. Wilson; *Fourth Ward*, George Glaubrecht. HOBOKEN—*First Ward*, Solomon Middleton; *Second Ward*, John E. McWhorter; *Third Ward*, James H. Dewey. BERGEN—*First Ward*, Jacob J. Newkirk; *Second Ward*, Edgar B. Wakeman; *Third Ward*, Mindert Van Horn; *Fourth Ward*, Garret Vreeland. BAYONNE—De Witt C. Morris. GREENVILLE—Henry D. Van Nostrand. NORTH BERGEN—John Sturges. HARRISON—Charles L. Gilbert. WEST HOBOKEN—John Hague. UNION—Hugh Mooney. TOWN OF UNION—Frederick Etzold. WEEHAWKEN—Joshua J. Benson.

1867.

JERSEY CITY—*First Ward*, Peter Curley; *Second Ward*, James Lynch; *Third Ward*, N. H. Coykendall; *Fourth Ward*, Adolph Kirsten; *Fifth Ward*, Moses K. Kellum; *Sixth Ward*, John Lennon; *Seventh Ward*, John Fleming. HUDSON CITY—*First Ward*, John H. Platt; *Second Ward*, John W. Smith; *Third Ward*, John W. Wilson; *Fourth Ward*, George Glaubrecht. HOBOKEN—*First Ward*, S. S. Middleton; *Second Ward*, John E. McWhorter; *Third Ward*, James H. Dewey. BERGEN

—*First Ward*, Jacob J. Newkirk; *Second Ward*, John Brinkerhoff; *Third Ward*, Mindert Van Horn; *Fourth Ward*, Samuel A. Besson. HARRISON—Hiram W. Davis. BAYONNE—Henry C. Smith. GREENVILLE—Henry D. Van Nostrand. WEST HOBOKEN—John Hague. NORTH BERGEN—John Sturges. UNION—F. W. Hermann. TOWN OF UNION—Frederick Etzold. WEEHAWKEN—Joshua J. Benson. KEARNEY—William E. Skinner (resigned in October; N. Norris Halstead took his place).

1868.

JERSEY CITY—*First Ward*, Peter Curley; *Second Ward*, James Lynch; *Third Ward*, N. H. Coykendall; *Fourth Ward*, George Warrin; *Fifth Ward*, Patrick Reiley; *Sixth Ward*, John Lennon; *Seventh Ward*, John Fleming. HUDSON CITY—*First Ward*, John H. Platt; *Second Ward*, Clinton W. Conger; *Third Ward*, William E. Benjamin; *Fourth Ward*, James R. Tate. HOBOKEN—*First Ward*, Herman D. Busch; *Second Ward*, John E. McWhorter; *Third Ward*, Timothy Foley. BERGEN—*First Ward*, Cornelius C. Van Ripen; *Second Ward*, John Brinkerhoff; *Third Ward*, Jeremiah B. Cleveland; *Fourth Ward*, Garret Vreeland. HARRISON—Hiram W. Davis. WEST HOBOKEN—Charles Galbraith (in January, 1869, resigned, and William H. Alcorn appointed). NORTH BERGEN—John Sturges. BAYONNE—Henry C. Smith. GREENVILLE—Henry D. Van Nostrand. UNION—Henry Meyer. TOWN OF UNION—Frederick Etzold. WEEHAWKEN—Joshua J. Benson. KEARNEY—N. Norris Halstead.

1869.

JERSEY CITY—*First Ward*, Francis Stoveken; *Second Ward*, John Barry; *Third Ward*, N. H. Coykendall; *Fourth Ward*, George Warrin; *Fifth Ward*, Charles D. Throckmorton; *Sixth Ward*, John Lennon; *Seventh Ward*, Edward Murphy. HUDSON CITY—*First Ward*, John H. Platt; *Second Ward*, John F. Rodefelt; *Third Ward*, John M. Wilson; *Fourth Ward*, James Montgomery. WEST HOBOKEN — William H. Alcorn. UNION—Frederick W. Hermann. WEEHAWKEN—John Frost. Ho-

BOKEN — *First Ward*, Herman D. Busch; *Second Ward*, John E. McWhorter; *Third Ward*, John A. O'Neill; *Fourth Ward*, Michael Healy. BERGEN—*First Ward*, Jacob J. Newkirk; *Second Ward*, John Brinkerhoff; *Third Ward*, Jeremiah B. Cleveland; *Fourth Ward*, Garret Vreeland. HARRISON — Abraham Phelps. NORTH BERGEN — John Sturges. BAYONNE—James W. Trask. GREENVILLE—Henry D. Van Nostrand. TOWN OF UNION—Henry Bridges (resigned in July; John Morgan appointed). KEARNEY—N. Norris Halstead.

1870.

JERSEY CITY—*First Ward*, Michael Doyle; *Second Ward*, John Barry; *Third Ward*, Patrick H. Nugent; *Fourth Ward*, George S. Plympton; *Fifth Ward*, Charles D. Throckmorton; *Sixth Ward*, John Lennon; *Seventh Ward*, Daniel Hartigan; *Eighth Ward*, Andrew J. Ditmar; *Ninth Ward*, John H. Platt; *Tenth Ward*, John F. Rodefelt; *Eleventh Ward*, John M. Wilson; *Twelfth Ward*, James Coyle; *Thirteenth Ward*, Jacob J. Newkirk; *Fourteenth Ward*, John Brinkerhoff; *Fifteenth Ward*, Jeremiah B. Cleveland; *Sixteenth Ward*, Garret Vreeland. HOBOKEN—*First Ward*, Frederick Agatz; *Second Ward*, Richard Burbank; *Third Ward*, John A. O'Neill; *Fourth Ward*, James Kilduff. NORTH BERGEN—John Sturges. HARRISON—Abraham Phelps. BAYONNE—William C. Hamilton. UNION—F. W. Hermann. TOWN OF UNION—John Bernhard. WEST HOBOKEN — William H. Alcorn. WEEHAWKEN — John Frost. GREENVILLE — Henry D. Van Nostrand. KEARNEY—N. Norris Halstead.

1871.

JERSEY CITY—*First Ward*, Matthew Doyle; *Second Ward*, John Barry; *Third Ward*, Patrick H. Nugent; *Fourth Ward*, G. F. Plympton; *Fifth Ward*, C. D. Throckmorton; *Sixth Ward*, John Lennon; *Seventh Ward*, Daniel Hartigan; *Eighth Ward*, Adam J. Ditmar; *Ninth Ward*, John H. Platt; *Tenth Ward*, John F. Rodefelt; *Eleventh Ward*, John M. Wilson; *Twelfth Ward*, James Coyle; *Thirteenth Ward*, Jacob J. Newkirk; *Fourteenth Ward*, John Brinkerhoff; *Fifteenth Ward*,

J. B. Cleveland; *Sixteenth Ward*, Garret Vreeland. HOBOKEN—*First Ward*, Fred. Agatz; *Second Ward*, William Stuhr; *Third Ward*, John A. O'Neill; *Fourth Ward*, James Kilduff. NORTH BERGEN—John Sturges. HARRISON—Abraham Phelps. BAYONNE—William C. Hamilton. UNION—Woltze Kamena. TOWN OF UNION—John Bernhard. WEST HOBOKEN—Alex. N. Sharpe. WEEHAWKEN—Albert B. Dodd. GREENVILLE—H. D. Van Nostrand. KEARNEY—John Boyd, jr.

By the act to reorganize the local government of Jersey City, approved April 4, 1871, the wards in Jersey City were abolished and aldermanic districts erected in their stead, each district being entitled to three chosen freeholders. Candidates were chosen under the old as well as the new law. Those elected under the old law were admitted into the Board; those elected under the new law were excluded. The latter then instituted proceedings in the Supreme Court to compel the Board to admit them to their seats. In this they were successful at the November term, 6 *Vroom's Reports*, 269, and took their seats Dec. 1, 1871, as representatives in the Board from Jersey City:

First District, Wm. B. Rankin, James L. Love, J. R. Parsons; *Second District*, Daniel Hartigan, John Barry, John Lennon; *Third District*, John E. Cronham, H. M. Soule, Wm. R. Clayton; *Fourth District*, Andrew Leicht, Martin Hanley, Charles Kost; *Fifth District*, Jacob J. Newkirk, John Brinkerhoff, Geo. A. Toffey; *Sixth District*, James H. Startup, Garret Vreeland, J. B. Cleveland.

1872.

JERSEY CITY—*First District*, William A. Lewis, Jabez R. Parsons, John H. Garretson; *Second District*, James Harper, Thomas Harmon, Daniel Hartigan; *Third District*, Hervey M. Soule, John E. Cronham, J. C. De La Vergne; *Fourth District*, James Coyle, Martin Hanley, Emil Stiger; *Fifth District*, Jacob J. Newkirk, George Toffey, John Brinkerhoff; *Sixth District*, James H. Startup, Henry D. Van Nostrand, John V. R. Vreeland. HOBOKEN—*First Ward*, William Winges; *Second Ward*,

23

William Stuhr ; *Third Ward*, John R. Wiggins ; *Fourth Ward*, John Gaffney. BAYONNE—William C. Hamilton. HARRISON—John Rohan. NORTH BERGEN—William J. Danielson. WEST HOBOKEN—Daniel Lake. WEEHAWKEN—John Frost. TOWN OF UNION—Jacob Hofmeister. UNION—M. Klein. KEARNEY—N. Norris Halstead.

1873.

JERSEY CITY—*First District*, William A. Lewis, Jabez R. Parsons, John H. Garretson ; *Second District*, David C. Jones, John O'Rourke, Michael O'Grady ; *Third District*, Hervey M. Soule, John E. Cronham, Paul Schober ; *Fourth District*, Jacob Newkirk, Henry Meinken, Emil Stiger ; *Fifth District*, Jacob J. Newkirk, Willard E. Dudley, William Frost ; *Sixth District*, James H. Startup, Henry D. Van Nostrand, John V. R. Vreeland. HOBOKEN—*First Ward*, William Winges ; *Second Ward*, William Stuhr ; *Third Ward*, John R. Wiggins ; *Fourth Ward*, John Gaffney. BAYONNE, William C. Hamilton. HARRISON—John Rohan. NORTH BERGEN—William J. Danielson. WEST HOBOKEN — William Roseman. WEEHAWKEN — John Frost. TOWN OF UNION—Jacob Hofmeister. UNION—F. W. Hermann. KEARNEY—Alexander Jacobus.

Directors of the Board.

Abraham Van Santvoord, 1840.
John Dows, 1841–3.
John Tonele, 1843–4.
John S. Condit, 1845–7.
Garret Sip, 1848.
David B. Wakeman, 1849–50
Robert McLoughlin, 1851–2.
Edmund T. Carpenter, 1853.
William C. Arthur, 1854.
Gilliam Van Houten, 1855.[1]
Abram W. Duryea, 1856–62.
Charles H. O'Neill, 1863–4.

Directors of the Board.

James Lynch, 1864–8.[2]
John Brinkerhoff, 1869, '70, '72.
John A. O'Neil, 1871.
James H. Startup, 1873.

Clerks of the Board.

Hartman Van Wagenen, 1840–54.
Garret I. Van Horn, 1855–64.
Charles J. Roe, 1864–

County Collectors.

Jacob D. Van Winkle, 1840–2.
Edmund W. Kingsland, 1843 until the present time.

---

[1] Killed at the battle of Chancellorsville.

[2] Died June 21, 1869.

Judges of the Common Pleas.

February 27, 1840—John J. Van Buskirk, Cornelius V. V. Kingsland,[1] Stephen Garretson,[1] Peter H. Kipp,[1] Joseph Clark.[1]

November 13, 1840—Richard Outwater.[1]

November 3, 1841—Gilbert Merritt,[1] Richard Outwater.

November 10, 1841—Stephen H. Lutkins.[1]

October 27, 1843—Cornelius Van Winkle,[1] John G. Speer,[1] Michael Saunier,[1] James Striker, James J. McDonald.

November 10, 1843—John Griffith,[1] George C. De Kay,[1] Jabez Wakeman.

March 3, 1847—Stephen Garretson.

March 2, 1848—Thomas A. Alexander.

February 28, 1849—Cornelius Van Winkle.

" John Griffith, *vice* Alexander.

March 6, 1850—George Thomas.

February 21, 1851—Edmund T. Carpenter.[2]

February 6, 1852—Samuel M. Chambers.[2]

" Samuel Browning, *vice* Carpenter.

March 4, 1853—John Griffith.

" Richard Kidney, Jr., *vice* Van Winkle, dec'd.

March 8, 1854—Edmund T. Carpenter.

" Selah Hill, *vice* Chambers (resigned Sept. 20, 1854).

February 8, 1856—Samuel Browning.

February 18, 1856—Edmund Charles.

" Charles Fink, *vice* Browning, dec'd.

March 17, 1859—Jacob M. Merseles.

March 15, 1860—James Pope, *vice* Charles, dec'd.

April 9, 1861—Wm. C. Morris (commissioned by the Governor).

March 5, 1862—Samuel M. Chambers.

March 11, 1863—John Sturges.

April 1, 1863—William C. Morris, *vice* Merseles.

March 2, 1864—Frederick W. Bohnstedt.

---

[1] Judge and Justice.

[2] Resigned.

February 27, 1867—Stephen Quaife (resigned April 1, 1870).
March 11, 1868—John Sturges.
April 9, 1868—Bennington F. Randolph, Law Judge.
March 25, 1869—Frederick W. Bohnstedt.
March 16, 1870—John Brinkerhoff, *vice* Quaife.
1872—James M. Newkirk.
1873—William T. Hoffman, Law Judge.
1873—James Wiggins.

By the apportionment under the census of 1870 Hudson County became a Congressional District, and Isaac W. Scudder was chosen its first representative in 1872.

Hudson County may be credited with the following:

November 8, 1853—Rodman M. Price, elected Governor.
May 1, 1866—Abraham O. Zabriskie, commissioned Chancellor.
June 29, 1869—Robert Gilchrist, appointed Attorney-General.
Jan. 19, 1870—Robert Gilchrist, appointed Attorney-General.

CHAPTER XII.

Roads, traveling facilities and traffic—Banks—Newspapers—Churches and their Pastors—Statistics of population, taxes and crime.

PREVIOUS to the settlement of Philadelphia, in 1682, communication between Manhattan Island and the South river was by water. Occasionally messages were sent overland by means of Indian runners bearing them from tribe to tribe. The first post route seems to have been established about the year 1693. It was yet a long while after this, however, before any road was laid out for through travel.

The first road in the county of Hudson was the one leading from Communipaw to the village of Bergen. This was over the present Communipaw avenue to Palisade avenue, thence northerly along Palisade avenue to Academy street, thence westerly to the village. It was probably laid out in the latter part of the year 1660, by authority. In 1679 it was described as "a fine, broad wagon road."[1]

It was not until September 18, 1765, that Communipaw avenue was extended from the Bergen Point plank road to Bergen avenue, although there was an old private road on nearly the same line, connecting the king's highway with Communipaw avenue.

In 1682, by act of the General Assembly, John Berry, Lawrence Andries (Van Boskerck), Enoch Michielsen (Vreeland), Hans Diedricks, Michael Smith, Hendrick Van Ostrum and Claes Jansen Van Purmerendt were appointed commissioners of highways for Bergen County, with full power to lay out, con-

---

[1] *Long Isl. Hist. Soc.*, *i.*, 155. The old people were accustomed to speak of this road as the "off-fall road." This name was derived from a stream of water which, taking its rise in Tuers' pond, near the intersection of Montgomery street and Palisade avenue, passed southerly, tumbled over a ledge of rock at the intersection of Grand street and Communipaw avenue, and emptied into Sycan's Creek, near the canal bridge.

struct and repair roads at the expense of the county. This was the first "street commission" in the State of New Jersey! In 1694 Gerbrand Claesen was appointed in the place of Van Purmerendt.

On September 9, 1704, the General Assembly "Resolved, That ye Grand Jury of each & every Respective County shall yearly in ye February and March Court, wth ye Approba'ōn of ye Bench, appoint two persons in Each County, precinct, district or Township to lay out all other necessary cross Roads & by Roads wch are to Consist of ye Width of four Rods, & also settle what is proper to be allow'd to those who shall be appointed, for their Service in Laying out ye said Roads."

On the 3d of June, 1718, a road was laid from "Crom-kill to Whehocken" ferry. What place was then known as Crom-kill is not certain, but probably it was the English Neighborhood. The road then laid must be in part the present Hackensack turnpike.

At an early day the dwellers at Harsimus laid out a road by the way of Prior's mill to Bergen. The following return, without date, when compared with the Field Map, will give a general idea of its course, as well as show that some of the residents preferred the war path to a highway: "By ye Surveyors of ye Highways for ye County of Bergen. Application having been made to us by Archibald Kennedy, Esqr., of some hardships & trespasses he meets with from his Neighbor Mattys De Mot for want of particular fences, and We having heard the Allegations of both parties, & having Viewed the Premises, doe order that partition fences be forthwith put up round ye six acres belonging to Mattys De Mot, as it is now marked out by us, ye North Easterly one half to be fenced & Kept up by ye said Archibald Kennedy, and ye South Westerly other half to be fenced and Kept by ye said Mattys De Mot.

"As also that ye Rhoad for ye Use of ye plantations at Pavonia or Ahasimus to ye Mill & Church shall be for ye future to begin at ye North East Corner of ye barn belonging to ye said Archibald Kennedy, and to run through ye said Six Acres one Rodd and a half wide, to be supported and fenced of by said Archibald

Kennedy, where, if he pleases, they may have Swinging Gates, allowing to yᵉ said de Mot So much out of his land as is taken out of yᵉ Six Acres of yᵉ Rhoad, all which we have Determined and Staked out, of which you are to take Notice as you will Answer yᵉ contrary. We have, according to the best of our Judgments, allowed yᵉ said de Mot an Equivalent for yᵉ Rhoad upon yᵉ South Side of his Six Acres out of land belonging to yᵉ said Archibald Kennedy."

On January 12, 1753, the above road was widened to four rods. It came to the shore just south of Kennedy's orchard, at about the corner of Second and Henderson streets, thence passed up by Van Vorst's to a place on Kennedy's land called "Sand Point."

At what time the road from Bergen to Bergen Point was laid it is now difficult to tell. On the 2d of November, 1743, James Alexander, of the Council, reported a bill "for continuing the King's Highway, which leads from Bergen Point to Bergen Town, to some convenient place on Hudson's River, for crossing that River to New York." The bill "passed in the negative." On October 10, 1764, a King's Highway was laid out from Hendrick Sickles' barn to a point opposite the Dutch Church on Staten Island, and the old road was vacated. The reasons for this vacation were that in part it was through a swamp, and if laid along the bay it would be over sandy soil. This road then became a part of the great stage route between New York and Philadelphia. It is probable that this road was not then constructed in such manner as to meet the requirements of travel. On June 28, 1766, an act passed the Legislature providing for a road four rods wide from "the most convenient and suitable Place from the Southwest Point of *Bergen* aforesaid along up *Newark Bay*,"[1] and from thence over to Paulus Hoeck. This road was laid September 12, 1766. The causeway between Harsimus and Paulus Hoeck, at present Newark avenue, was to be "cleared and maintained" by the owner of the ferry.

---

[1] *Allison's Laws*, 288. Originally the road at Bergen Point was on the west side of the "Ferry Lot." It was changed February 17, 1801, to unite this lot with land belonging to the same owner on the west side.

The road from the intersection of Waverly avenue and the New Bergen road to Bergen Point, and recently known as the Bergen Point plank road, from Currie's Woods southwardly, was laid June 29, 1796.

On June 20, 1765, on petition of the people of Morris and Essex counties, an act was passed by the Legislature providing for the construction of a road from "the lower end of the Great Neck belonging to Newark" to the public road leading from Bergen Point to Paulus Hoeck. Nine men were named as *The Trustees of the road and Ferries from Newark to the Road leading from Bergen Point to Paulus Hoeck.* It was soon afterward constructed on the ground now occupied by the Newark plank road,[1] except east of the Hackensack, where it lay further to the south. This part of it was known as *Brown's Ferry Road.* It was vacated April 29, 1799, and the road laid in its present position.

On the 24th of November, 1790, the Legislature provided for locating and building bridges over the Hackensack and Passaic rivers and laying out a road four rods wide from the court house in Newark to Paulus Hoeck. On the meadows the width was afterward changed to six rods. By the act five commissioners were appointed and authorized to raise by lottery £4,000, afterward increased to £27,000, part of which was to aid in completing the road, part in building a bridge over the Raritan and part in providing suitable buildings for the Legislature.

Surveys were then made to ascertain the most practicable route. The map of these surveys, a reduced copy of which is here inserted, is taken from the *New York Magazine, vol. ii.*, 367 (July, 1791), as also the explanations:

"The courses described in the map are the several routes proposed to lead to different stations on the rivers, at one of which it may be judged most advantageous to erect the bridges. The distance from Newark court house to Powles Hook, by the several routes, is as follows:

---

[1] This Company was incorporated as *The Newark Plank Road and Ferry Company*, February 24, 1849.

	Miles.	*Chains.*	*Links.*
No. 1 Camp's Dock Route, - -	9	13	76
No. 2 Hedden's Dock Route, -	7	65	86
No. 3 Beef-Point Route, - -	8	18	41
No. 4 Present Road,	8	59	7
No. 5 " " shortened, -	7	52	6

"The length of causeway required over the meadows is as follows:

	Miles.	*Chains.*	*Links.*
No. 1 Camp's Dock Route, - -	4	1	62
No. 2 Hedden's Dock Route, -	3	55	40
No. 3 Beef-Point Route, -	3	5	42
No. 4 Present Road,	2	26	75
No. 5 " " shortened,	2	44	77

"The breadth and depth of the rivers is as follows:

Hackensack River.

1 At the place where the present ferry is established,

	Feet.	*Inches.*
Breadth, - -	1,448	
Depth at eastern shore,	8	8
" western "	8	11
Greatest Depth in the channel, - -	25	4

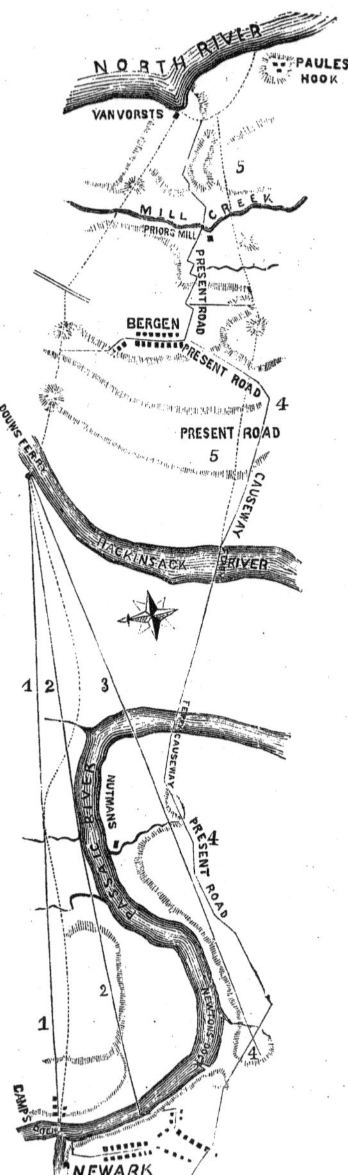

	Feet.	Inches.
2 At the place more northerly, called Douw's Ferry,		
Breadth, - - - - - - - - -	846	
Depth at eastern shore, - - - - - -	19	10
" western " - - - - -	12	
Greatest depth in channel, - - - - -	35	8

Passaic River.

1 At the place where the present ferry is established,		
Breadth, - - - - - - - - -	676	
Depth at eastern shore, - - - - - -	8	6
" western " - - - - -	9	6
Greatest depth in channel, - - - - -	17	
2 At a place more northerly, called Beef-Point,		
Breadth, - - - - - - - - -	799	
Depth at eastern shore, - - - - -	11	
" western " - - - - -	4	5
Greatest depth in channel, - - - - -	13	4
3 At a place more northerly, called Hedden's Dock, in the town of Newark,		
Breadth, - - - - - - - - -	526	
Depth at eastern shore, - - - - -	4	5
" western " - - - - -	10	8
Greatest depth in channel, - - - - -	15	11"

On February 19, 1793, the commissioners contracted with Samuel Ogden and thirty-six others to build the bridges, and gave them a lease thereof for ninety-seven years from Nov. 24, 1792. On March 7, 1797, the stockholders under the lease were incorporated *The Proprietors of the Bridges over the Rivers Passaic and Hackensack.* The bridges were completed in the summer of 1795. The company thenceforth claimed a monopoly of the right to erect bridges over these rivers. Their claim was adjudicated in *The Bridge Co. vs. The Hoboken Land and Improvement Co.*, 13 *N. J. Chancery Reports*, 81, 503.

"The Newark Turnpike Company" was incorporated December 1, 1804. The State took two hundred and fifty shares of the capital stock. The company was authorized to construct a road from the westerly line of the Jersey Associates' land (now Warren street, Jersey City) to the east side of the Hackensack river. It was constructed in 1805. Through Harsimus the company was required to make their road conform to the line of the streets laid down on Coles' Map. This requirement was disregarded, the road laid diagonally across the blocks, and Newark avenue became a permanent nuisance.

The road from the Five Corners to Hoboken Ferry was authorized February 17 and laid April 9, 1794. On the 10th of June following the commissioners were authorized to construct an embankment along the road over the Hoboken meadow, and lay the road six rods wide at the same place. From Central avenue to the brow of the hill the road bore to the east more than now, or took a straight line from the Corners to the hill on the line of the present Hoboken avenue, west of Central avenue. From Central avenue eastward the road was changed to its present position March 30, 1848.

The Bergen Turnpike Company was incorporated November 30, 1802, for the purpose of constructing a road "from the town of Hackensack to Hoboken." It was constructed in 1804, and is known as the Hackensack turnpike.

During the last French war, Colonel John Schuyler constructed the causeway from the upland near Belleville to the Hackensack river at Douw's Ferry, "at a very great expense." It was at first a corduroy road. In April, 1774, an act was approved to enable certain persons to erect and draw a lottery for raising £1,050 to cover this causeway with gravel. The causeway is said to have been made by sailors, whose vessels were blockaded in the harbor of New York. In 1784 Arent J. Schuyler complained that too much of the repair of this causeway fell upon him. Thereupon the Legislature enacted that he should keep in repair the causeway thirty-three chains and thirty-eight links east from the Passaic river, and also the ferry stairs, and that Archibald Kennedy should keep in repair the balance of the causeway to the Hackensack river and the ferry stairs there.

Prior to 1848 all travel from Bergen and the lower part of the county to Paulus Hoeck was around by the Five Corners and Newark avenue, or by the Mill road *via* Prior's mill. Even the residents at Communipaw were obliged to take this roundabout way. But in 1848 Grand street was extended from Jersey City across the meadows.

The foregoing list includes the principal roads in the county of ancient date. There were others, as the Middle road, which was approached through the northwest gate of the village of Bergen, and the Bergen Woods road, which opened into the woods through the northeast gate. There are also the Dallytown and Bull's Ferry roads. But the dates of their laying out or construction have not been ascertained. For convenience in keeping the roads in repair the township was divided into districts, which bore the following names, viz.: Bergen Town, Gomunipa, Pamerpugh, Bergen Point, Wehawk, Maisland, Bull's Ferry, Sekakes, and Bergen Woods.

Traveling Facilities.

In 1764 stages were first "set up" to start from Paulus Hoeck for Philadelphia, *via* Bergen Point and Blazing Star ferries. The vehicle used was a covered Jersey wagon without springs. Three days were consumed in dragging it to Philadelphia. It was modestly called a "Flying Machine!"

In the fall of the same year Sovereign Sybrant gave notice that he had fitted up and completed in the neatest manner a new and genteel stage wagon, which was to set out from Philadelphia on Monday, and get to Trenton that day; the next day to Sybrant's house, "known by the sign of the Roebuck," two miles and a half from Elizabethtown, where, with a good assortment of wines and liquors, and by "Assiduity, Care and Despatch," he hoped for the "Favour and Esteem of the Public." On Wednesday the stage reached "Powless's Hook," by the new post road over Bergen and return to the Roebuck. Thence it would start on Thursday, and reach its destination on Friday.

In 1772 John Mersereau appeared with his "Machines." He left Paulus Hoeck three times a week, and went through to Philadelphia in a day and a half. In 1773 he established a line of stage coaches which left Paulus Hoeck on Tuesday and Friday, "at or before sunrise," and went as far as "Prince-town" the same night. Here they exchanged passengers with the coach from Philadelphia, and returned the next day. Inside passengers paid thirty shillings fare; outside passengers twenty shillings. Each passenger was allowed fourteen pounds of baggage; beyond that weight the charge was two-pence a pound.

In 1769 a new route from Paulus Hoeck to Philadelphia was selected by Joseph Crane and Josiah F. Davenport, *via* Newark, Elizabeth, Boundbrook and the north branch of the Raritan, to Corriell's ferry on the Delaware. They proposed to leave the Hoeck every Tuesday morning by sunrise. Passengers were requested to cross over from New York the night before. The stages met at the South Branch, exchanged passengers and returned.

In 1771 Abraham Skillman started his "Flying Machine" to Philadelphia, *via* Newark, Elizabeth, Woodbridge, New Brunswick, Princeton, Trenton and Bristol. Time, one day and a half; fare, twenty shillings proclamation money; "a good wagon, sober drivers and able horses."

In 1767 Matthias Ward informed the public that he had for some time kept a stage wagon from Newark to "Powlas Hook." Having met with some encouragement, he proposed to make the round trip each day, leaving Newark at sunrise and Paulus Hoeck "sun 2 hours high." All persons might expect the "best Usage at 1*s*. 6 each for coming and going, or 3 Shillings for both."

In 1768 Andrew Van Buskirk gave notice that he would erect a "Stage Wagon" in Hackensack at the New Bridge, to set out for Paulus Hoeck on September 17, to go twice a week; fare, 2*s*. 6*d*. In 1775 he changed the terminus from Paulus Hoeck to Hoboken, and named his vehicle a "Flying Machine."

In the same year and year following, some proprietors adopted the system of having their stages on each side of the Hackensack river, where they would exchange passengers, "which entirely takes off the Inconveniency of detaining Passengers by ferrying of the Wagon over said River."

For some years prior to 1774, Peter Stuyvesant ran a stage from the Hoeck to Brown's ferry, where he met Josiah Crane with a stage from Newark, and exchanged passengers.

In 1770 a stage was run from Morristown to the Hoeck by Daniel and Silas Burnet,and from Hanover in 1775 by Constant Cooper.

In 1775 Abraham Goodwin ran a stage from the Great Falls (Paterson) to the Hoeck twice a week. In May of the same year Thomas Douglas erected his stage to run from Hacketstown once a week, *via* Flanders, Black River, Mendham and Morristown, consuming two days *en route.*

In the same year Verdine Elsworth brought out his "new caravan" between the Hoeck and New Bridge. He informed the public that his horses were "very quiet, and the caravan new and in excellent order."

In 1783 Adam Boyd "established a stage waggon to run between Hackinsack and Hoebuck ferry." He boasted that the roads were very good, his wagon and horses in prime order, and hoped that such a useful institution would be encouraged.

From almost every direction in the interior part of the State stage lines were organized, and all sorts of vehicles started toward Paulus Hoeck to accommodate the public. To such an extent did this system of travel increase, that before the construction of the New Jersey Railroad, as many as twenty regular stages would daily leave the ferry for different parts.

The Morris Canal.—The Morris Canal and Banking Company was incorporated December 31, 1824. Banking privileges were not in the charter. It was authorized to construct a canal from the Delaware to the Passaic. The canal was completed in 1831. On January 28, 1828, authority was given to extend the canal to Hudson's River at or near Jersey City. This extension was completed in 1836. The canal and its appurtenances, with the chartered rights of the company, were sold under a decree of the Court of Chancery, October 21, 1844. By an act of the Legislature, February 9, 1849, the banking privileges were taken from the company. The following table exhibits the extent of the traffic on this canal since the organization of the new company:

Year	Tons.	Year.	Tons.	Year.	Tons.
1845	58,259	1855	553,204	1865	716,587
1846	109,505	1856	563,413	1866	889,220
1847	155,559	1857	536,362	1867	822,741
1848	204,682	1858	554,034	1868	744,412
1849	234,305	1859	638,019	1869	650,200
1850	239,682	1860	707,631	1870	707,572
1851	281,707	1861	619,369	1871	629,044
1852	358,797	1862	612,018	1872	685,191
1853	467,288	1863	718,519		
1854	543,269	1864	723,927		

The Paterson and Hudson River Railroad Company was incorporated January 21, 1831. The road went into operation between Paterson and Aquackanonck (now Passaic) June 22, 1832. The rolling stock at that time consisted of "three splendid and commodious cars, each capable of accommodating thirty passengers," which were drawn by "fleet and gentle horses." It was thought to be a "rapid and delightful mode of traveling." The trial trip over that part of the road was June 7, 1832. It connected with the New Jersey Railroad at West End. The road was leased to the Union Railroad Company September 9, 1852. This lease was assigned to and the road now forms part of the main line of the Erie Railway. Both the lease and assignment were confirmed by the Legislature March 14, 1853.

The New Jersey Railroad and Transportation Company was incorporated March 7, 1832. The first excursion over the road was on September 1, 1834, in the "passenger car Washington," "a splendid and beautiful specimen of workmanship, containing three apartments, besides seats on top." Regular trips began September 15, 1834. Eight trips a day were made. The cars were drawn by horses, stopped at the hotels to receive passengers, and ran from Newark to Jersey City in one hour and a half. At that time, and up to January 1, 1838, when the Bergen cut was completed, the cars were drawn over the hill. The first engine passed over the road from Jersey City to Newark December 2, 1835. "Newark" was the name of this pioneer locomotive. This road consolidated with the Camden and Amboy Railroad, under authority given by the Legislature, February 27, 1867, and the consolidation was leased to the Pennsylvania Railroad Company in 1870.

The following table will show the growth of business upon this road. It is to be regrètted that more complete statistics could not be obtained :

Passengers.

1835	102,359	1860	2,833,113
1836	293,559	1861	2,322,598½
1852	1,592,070	1862	2,394,625
1853	2,170,243	1863	2,989,177½
1854	2,433,715½	1864	3,310,940½
1855	2,164,471	1865	3,684,992½
1856	2,278,913½	1866	3,568,191
1857	2,238,130	1867	2,674,722
1858	2,110,993	1872	5,153,543
1859	2,501,124		

Freight—(tons).

1852	34,656½	1861	99,550
1853	48,167	1862	110,215⅛
1854	56,919¼	1863	167,118
1855	64,049	1864	165,773
1856	68,688	1865	230,280
1857	80,872½	1866	256,534
1858	85,460½	1867	272,168
1859	98,007	1872	324,861[1]
1860	115,653		

The Morris and Essex Railroad Company was incorporated January 29, 1835. At first this was connected with the New Jersey Railroad at Newark. It was extended to Hoboken November 19, 1862, by the completion of the *Newark and Hoboken Railroad;* leased to the Delaware, Lackawanna and Western Railroad Company December 10, 1868.

1 464,087 tons of freight were moved *from* New York in 1872. It is estimated that 30 per cent. of this was taken *via* Amboy.

The following table shows the number of passengers carried over this road from 1853 until it was leased:

1853	238,901½	1861	455,107
1854	267,241	1862	473,205
1855	266,850	1863	590.773
1856	298,922	1864	1,032,973
1857	289,751	1865	1,025,498
1858	245,186	1866	1,066,179
1859	404,936	1867	1,173,398
1860	490,871	1868	1,444,549

The Erie Railway Company was first recognized by the laws of New Jersey March 14, 1853, as the *New York and Erie Railroad Company*, then as the *Erie Railway Company.* After leasing the *Paterson and Hudson River Railroad* and the *Paterson and Ramapo Railroad*, which two roads formed a direct line from Jersey City to Sufferns, Piermont was abandoned as a terminus, and the cars were run to the depot of the New Jersey Railroad Company in Jersey City, until May, 1861. "The Long Dock Company," incorporated February 26, 1856, in the interest of the Erie Railway, completed the Bergen tunnel January 28, 1861. The first passenger train passed through it May 1, 1861. Then the Erie traffic was transferred to its present terminus at the Long Dock.

The Central Railroad of New Jersey for many years terminated at Elizabethport. In 1860 an act was passed authorizing the company to bridge Newark Bay and extend the road to Jersey City. This extension was completed and opened for travel August 1, 1864. Since its termination in this county, its traffic has been as follows:

Year.	Passengers.	Merchandise.	Coal.
1865	928,806	392,650 tons.	1,004,506 tons.
1866	1,083,592	537,010 "	1,289,249 "
1867	1,204,130	566,480 "	1,369,045 "
1868	1,441,992½	659,471 "	1,618,845 "
1869	2,296,864	705,611 "	1,556,052 "
1870	3,291,034	702,529 "	2,052,184 "
1871	3,944,103	990,591 "	1,877,064 "
1872	4,478,513	1,490,689 "	2,228,217 "

TABLE showing the live stock brought to and slaughtered at the Abattoir, Communipaw.

	CATTLE.		HOGS.		SHEEP.	
	Arrived.	Slaughtered.	Arrived.	Slaughtered.	Arrived.	Slaughtered.
1866[1]	4,707	470	65,798	59,333	29,871	11,061
1867	79,829	16,791	456,939	423,512	160,247	143,639
1868	75,226	12,379	500,546	490,319	267,315	266,293
1869	134,229	20,084	453,508	452,335	444,706	438,114
1870	93,257	29,398	404,242	400,282	480,758	470 717
1871	160,487	33,379	514,980	474,737	439,563	395,567
1872	246,323	29,532	701,025	685,614	401,476	400,660
1873[2]	231,138	34,596	709,168	697,712	263,638	262,110
Total....	1,025,196	176,629	3,806,206	3,683,844	2,487,574	2,388,161

Besides the foregoing, this company are bringing over their road to the National Storage Oil Yards about 1,500,000 barrels of petroleum annually.

The Northern Railroad Company of New Jersey was incorporated February 9, 1854; completed October 1, 1859. It was leased to the *Erie Railway Company* in 1869. The following table shows the amount of business done from 1861 to 1869:

Year.	No. of Passengers.	Tons of freight.	Year.	No. of Passengers.	Tons of freight.
1861	131,867½	10,425	1866	450,401	17,687
1862	119,221	12,508	1867	511,882	20,240
1863	142,799½	13,453	1868	541,830	24,054
1864	190,516½	13,230	1869	606,849	29,345
1865	224,568	15,946			

Besides the foregoing, the following named railroads are in active operation, many of them doing a thriving business, viz.:

[1] The Abattoir was opened for business October 17, 1866. Nearly all of the stock brought to this place was carried over the Central Railroad of New Jersey.

[2] The above figures for the year 1873 include receipts up to December 17.

The Newark and New York Railroad, incorporated March 1, 1866; went into active operation August 2, 1869; under the control of the *Central Railroad.* Its terminus is at the depot of the last named company. *The New Jersey Midland Railway*, incorporated March 18, 1867, and *The New York and Oswego Midland Railway*, projected in 1865; incorporated January 1, 1866; construction begun June 29, 1868; first train run over the western end of the road November 5, 1869; first through train, August 18, 1873. *The Jersey City and Albany Railroad*, opened to Tappaen July 30, 1873. The present terminus of these three roads is the Pennsylvania Railroad depot in Jersey City. *The Hackensack and New York Railroad*, incorporated March 14, 1856, completed December 24, 1861, and *The Paterson, Newark and New York Railroad* terminate at the depot of the *Erie Railway Company* in Jersey City. *The Boonton Branch* of *The Morris and Essex Railroad* connects with the main line at the west approach of the Bergen tunnel. *The New York and Fort Lee Railroad*, incorporated March 3, 1862, is completed as far north as Guttenberg; is under lease to the *Erie Railway Company*, and used exclusively for oil, coal, and live stock.

Ocean Steamers.

The *Cunard Line* was the first to terminate in Hudson County. On the 14th of October, 1846, Samuel Cunard communicated to the Common Council of Jersey City the fact that he had made arrangements to bring the ships of that line to Jersey City. He desired their approval, which was given December 20, 1846. The *Hibernia*, Captain Ryrie, arrived in December, 1847, as pioneer of the line. At first the trips were monthly. They have increased until now two ships leave weekly. For some time this line had ships plying between Jersey City and Bermuda and St. Thomas. Besides the Cunard Line there are now the *Hamburgh Line*, the *Bremen Line*, the *White Star Line* and the *Cardiff Line.* The business on these lines has grown to immense proportions. On the Cunard Line alone it amounted in the year 1872 to 94,535 tons of in freight; 143,620 tons of out freight; 32,617 in passengers, and 10,559 out passengers.

BANKS.

On November 13, 1804, *The Newark Banking and Insurance Company* were authorized to establish a branch at Paulus Hoeck, with the consent of the Associates. The State reserved the right to subscribe $50,000 to the stock of this branch bank. This privilege was afterward sold to Colonel Aaron Ogden for $4,000. The branch was established under the name of *The Jersey Bank*, and books opened for subscription January 24, 1805; directors elected April 2, 1805. The bank building, on the southwest corner of Greene and Grand streets, was erected in the summer of 1805. The Legislature laid a tax of one-half of one per cent. on the capital of the Jersey Bank, November 2, 1810. The directors attempted to evade the payment of this tax, and sold their bank building. The sheriff, however, levied upon and sold it at public auction, the State being the purchaser, February 23, 1811. In March, 1811, the directors procured a charter in New York in the name of the *Union Bank;* removed to that city, and began business at No. 17 Wall street, April 11, 1811.

The Jersey Bank (No. 2) was incorporated February 6, 1818, under the name of *The President, Directors and Company of the Jersey Bank;* capital $100,000. The condition of the charter was that the company should purchase of the State the banking house formerly owned by the old *Jersey Bank*, for $5,000. It failed on Thursday, July 6, 1826. This caused a "run" on the *Weehawk* and *Franklin Banks.* On the 24th of November following three commissioners were appointed by the Legislature to inquire into its affairs.

John, Robert and Samuel Swartwout having become the owners of the meadows lying between Hoboken and the hill, and on the Hackensack, and desiring to improve the same, obtained a charter for *The New Jersey Salt Marsh Company*, January 28, 1820, with a capital of $300,000. It received power to "drain, ditch, dyke, embank, cultivate and improve" the marshes. On November 15, 1822, this company were authorized to erect a banking house in Hoboken, and use one-half of their banking capital for banking purposes for fifteen years, in the name of *The Hoboken Banking and Grazing Company.* They forthwith erected the building on the southwest corner of Washington and Second streets. On November 24, 1826, a commission was appointed to examine into its affairs, to inquire if the capital had been subscribed and paid, and whether one-half of the stock had been employed as directed in the act incorporating the *Salt Marsh Company.*

The New Jersey Manufacturing and Banking Company was incorporated December 9, 1823; capital $150,000. It went into operation in March, 1824. On February 4, 1828, the Legislature required it to make a full report of its affairs. It suspended payment in March, 1829, and then the Chancellor enjoined it.

The Franklin Bank of New Jersey was incorporated December 28, 1824; capital $300,000; bonus to the State, $25,000. Its whole capital was subscribed March 22, 1825; directors elected April 8, 1825. It did not live through its appointed time, but suspended in 1826. On the 24th of November in that year commissioners were appointed to examine into its affairs. Proceedings in court were also instituted against it. These were discontinued, and it resumed payment April 2, 1827. It again suspended July 14, 1827. It resumed once more, and was enjoined May 29, 1828. Its charter was repealed February 22, 1843, and so its spasmodic existence ended.

The Weehawk Banking Company was incorporated December 28, 1824; capital, $125,000; bonus to the State, $5,000. On November 30, 1825, the company received authority to change the name to *The Washington Banking Company*, and locate the bank at Hackensack. Its charter was repealed February 22, 1843.

The President and Directors of the New Jersey Protection and Lombard Bank were incorporated December 29, 1824; capital, $400,000; charter limited to twenty-one years; bonus to the State, $25,000. A "run" was made upon the bank November

17, 1825, and on the next day it failed. Its charter was repealed November 23, 1825, and trustees appointed to take charge of its property. Its bills fell to 37½ cents on the dollar.

The more recent banks, some of which endure, while the others had a brief and profitless existence, are as follows:

Name.	Incorporated.
Hudson County Bank,	July 7, 1851.
Mechanics' and Traders' Bank (First Nat.),	1853.
Jersey City Bank (Second Nat.),	June 25, 1856.
Hoboken City Bank,	March 18, 1857.
Marine Bank,	September 21, 1857.
Hudson River Bank,	March 24, 1862.
Bank of America,	July 4, 1862.
City Bank of Jersey City,	September 9, 1862.
United States Stock Bank,	October 17, 1862.
Highland Bank,	December 4, 1862.
North River Bank,	December 10, 1862.
Union Bank,	January 2, 1870.

NEWSPAPERS.

The Bergen County Gazette and Jersey City Advertiser, weekly, was established in 1830 by E. B. Spooner, son of the editor of the *Long Island Star*. It was printed in Hackensack. He soon abandoned the enterprise, and his brother George, afterward of the *Saratoga Whig*, took it in charge. It existed but a few months.

The Bergen County Courier, weekly, was first issued Feb. 1, 1832. It was printed in Jersey City by John Post and Joseph E. Handley. They not only furnished the matter, but printed and distributed the paper. Enterprise and economy were not, however, equal to the occasion, and the paper died Nov. 14, 1832, with the forty-second number. Part of its material went to the outfit of the *Philadelphia Ledger*.

The Jersey City Gazette and Bergen County Courier, semi-weekly, was first issued Feb. 11, 1835, by Robert W. Lang, son of the editor of the *New York Gazette*. The paper was printed at No. 2 Hanover square, New York City, and was burnt out in the great fire of December, 1835.

The Jersey Blue and Bergen County Democrat, weekly, was established in July, 1835; burnt out Aug. 8, 1838. It was published in Hoboken by Childs & Devoe.

The Jersey City Advertiser and Bergen Republican, semi-weekly, was first issued Dec. 2, 1837; Henry D. Holt, editor. It became a weekly Dec. 14, 1838. When Hudson County was set off from Bergen, its name was changed to the *Jersey City and Hudson Republican*. It united with the *Sentinel* in 1848.

The Jersey City Democrat, weekly, was first issued May 14, 1842; M. Cully, editor. It suspended Jan. 15, 1848.

The Morning Sentinel, daily, was first issued Aug. 23, 1845; Mr. Reynolds and Luther A. Pratt, editors. It united with the *Jersey City Advertiser and Hudson Republican* in 1848, and was thence known as the *Sentinel and Advertiser*.

The Daily Evening Sentinel was established in December, 1844; Luther A. and William W. Pratt, Publishers.

The Jersey City Telegraph, semi-weekly, was first issued March 15, 1847: John H. Voorhis, editor. It became a daily; suspended June 25, 1859; John A. Ryerson, editor. Its materials went to the outfit of the *American Standard*.

The Hudson County Union, weekly, was first issued Aug. 12, 1852; A. R. Speer, editor; became a daily Jan. 24, 1854; S. P. Hull and William T. Rodgers, jr., editors; suspended in June, 1854. Its materials went to the outfit of the *Hudson County Democrat*.

The Hoboken Gazette, weekly, was first issued Sept. 12, 1853; Thomas W. Whitley, editor. Became a semi-weekly in Feb., 1855; a daily in Aug., 1855, and suspended in Oct., 1855.

The Hudson County Democrat, weekly, was established in September, 1854; Augustus O. Evans, editor; published in Hoboken; became a daily in 1869.

The Jersey City Courier, weekly, was first issued Aug. 1, 1855; William B. Dunning and H. F. Milligan, editors. In a short time it became a daily; merged with the *Sentinel and*

Advertiser in Jan., 1856; thence known as the *Courier and Advertiser;* suspended in May, 1861. In connection with this paper was a weekly, the *Hudson County Courier and Advertiser;* suspended in 1861.

The City Gazette and Hudson County Chronicle and Cultivator, Thomas W. Whitley, editor, was issued for a short time after the suspension of the *Hoboken Gazette.* When this paper suspended, the same editor, having been elected a justice of the peace, brought out a few numbers of the *Circuit Judge.*

The Hoboken City Standard, weekly, was first issued Oct. 9, 1856; P. M. Reynolds, editor.

The American Standard, daily, arose from the ashes of the *Daily Telegraph*, and was first issued Aug. 8, 1859, by Metz & Brother. John H. Lyon became proprietor Oct. 14, 1859. It is published in Jersey City.

The People's Advocate, daily, was established by John C. Clarke & Co. It was published in Jersey City, and merged in the *Jersey City Times.*

The Jersey City News, weekly, was established in 1854 by Daniel E. Gavitt. It existed about one year.

The Jersey City Herald, weekly, was first issued July 19, 1864, by Hugh McDermott. It merged with the *Hudson City Gazette.*

Jersey City Times, daily, was first issued Sept. 14, 1864; Z. K. Pangborn, editor; changed to a weekly Nov. 8, 1873.

The Evening Journal, daily, was first issued May 2, 1867. It is published in Jersey City by Z. K. Pangborn, Wm. B. Dunning and Joseph A. Dear.

The Hudson City Gazette was established in March, 1867; William D. McGregor, editor. It merged with the *Jersey City Herald.*

Jersey City Chronicle, semi-weekly, was first issued Feb. 14, 1863, by Davidson & Colston; discontinued Aug. 24, 1864, and merged in the *Jersey City Times.*

The Hudson County Volksblatt, weekly, was established in 1868; published in Hudson City by Dietz & Timm.

The Bayonne Herald and Greenville Register, weekly, was

first issued Dec. 25, 1869; Roswell Graves, editor. It is published at Bergen Point.

The Hudson County Journal, weekly (German), was first issued Dec. 19, 1868; published in Hoboken by Rabe & Bayer, now by Bayer and Kaufmann.

Jersey City Herald and Gazette, weekly, was established in 1870 by McDermott & McGregor. It was the result of the merging of the *Jersey City Herald* and *Hudson City Gazette.*

Hudson County Register, weekly, was first issued July 23, 1870, at West Hoboken, by Peter Y. Everett, editor.

Palisade News, weekly, was first issued Aug. 6, 1870, at West Hoboken, by Alfred E. Gregory, editor.

Hudson County Times, weekly, was established in August, 1870; published at Bergen Point by the Times Printing Company of Jersey City, now by Edward Gardner.

Die Wacht am Hudson, weekly, was established in 1871; published in Jersey City by the Hudson County German Publishing Association.

Highland Sentinel, weekly, was first issued March 29, 1873, at West Hoboken; Joseph Paul Bugie, editor.

Hudson County Independent, weekly, was first issued May 3, 1873, at Hoboken, by Augustus O. Evans, editor. It had but a brief existence.

Dispatch, weekly, was established in 1873; published at East Newark by Trelease, Simmonds & Co.

The Evening Palisades, daily, was first issued June 30, 1873, at West Hoboken, by the Palisades Publishing Society.

SKETCHES OF THE CHURCHES IN THE COUNTY.

	BAPTIST.			REFORMED.			EPISCOPAL.		
	No. of churches.	Sittings.	Value of property.	No. of churches.	Sittings.	Value of property.	No. of churches.	Sittings.	Value of property.
1850....	4	1,275	$12,100	5	2,770	$54,000	2	772	$26,000
1860....	6	2,900	60,800	8	4,800	185,000	10	4,150	109,500
1870....	9	3,450		15	8,615		13	4,500	
	METHODIST.			PRESBYTERIAN.			ROMAN CATHOLIC.		
1850....	8	3,150	$37,500	1	1,000	$35,000	1	1,000	$7,500
1860....	11	4,630	85,100	8	4,450	136,000	6	3,500	104,500
1870....	14	6,300		9	5,000		15	9,000	
	GERMAN REFORMED.			LUTHERAN.			SWEDENBORGIAN.		
1850....									
1860....	1	275	$3,000	1	300	$3,000	1	150	$750
1870....									
	UNITARIAN.								
1850....				Total value of property for 1870....$1,849,700					
1860....	1	450	$8,000						
1870....									

The foregoing table is made from the United States Census for the years named.

THE REFORMED (DUTCH) CHURCHES.

The Bergen Reformed Church is the oldest church in the county, and probably the oldest in the State. It was organized about the time, or at least very soon after, the village of Bergen was settled. In December, 1662, the schout and schepens of the village petitioned the Governor-General and Council of New Netherland for a minister, as follows:

"Shew with all reverence the schepens of the village of Bergen, how that they supplicants, having observed and weighed your Honor's fatherly care and direction, the building of churches and schools, they deem it expedient and highly desirable to possess a pious man as minister, who may instruct, edify and learn them to fear God. This would be a desirable object for the community of Bergen and its district; on which the schepens have deemed it proper and highly desirable to propose a similar plan to each individual to inform themselves what sum each of the inhabitants should be willing to contribute, annually, moved by the impulse of a good heart, by pure affection and an ardent love for God's holy and blessed name with the view to obtain a good minister till that time when the Noble Directors of the Privileged West Indian Company, after the custom of this country shall receive the tythes.

"When this was proposed by the schepens, the following persons, goodly minded, declared to be willing to pay annually, which sum of similar voluntary promissors, amounted, as it was calculated nearly to 417 gl. in seawant, however, there are yet among them a few who give to understand that, if the Lord our God did bless them, and their property increased, that then they would perform, in proportion to their abilities, what might be in their power. The second class, by whose names no sums are annexed, contains yet some who are willing, but many very stupid, but as the number of those willing to contribute is the greatest majority, and declare that when a minister should be called, that in such case they would join others to the utmost of their abilities, and whereas the supplicants are not informed if those of Staer Simens[1] are included in it, it is not in the supplicants' power to give a correct account of it, neither can ascertain what they would be willing to contribute. The schepens deem it advisable and highly necessary that the village should be provided with a gospel minister, and therefore they submit it, without hesitation, to your Honor's mature consideration and decision, which then might be communicated to the Lords Patrons with the vessels now ready to sail. Your Honors know with what courage the settling and concentration of the village Bergen

---

[1] I am unable to give any clue to the whereabouts of this place. Wearkimins-Connie was somewhere in this vicinity, but I have not been able to locate it. The two names may refer to the same place.

was undertaken by its inhabitants without any burthen to the Lords Directors. The community, therefore, is of opinion, that this by the patrons shall be taken in consideration to support in their discretion the village of Bergen, and to provide them with a minister during one or two years at their own expense, about which time the country, no doubt, under God's blessing shall have arrived at a higher prosperity, to which then might be added what this liberal minded community would contribute for its assistance.

"Specification of the well intentioned Promissors with the quantity of the promise of each individual."

The following is a copy of the subscription referred to in the body of the petition:

Name	fl.	Name	fl.
Tielman Van Vleck,	fl. 60	Jacob Sergeant,	fl. 8
Michiel Jansen,	25	Arent Laurense,	10
Harman Smeeman,	25	Jan Cornelis,	3
Casper Steynmets,	25	Cornelis Abrahams,	6
Jan Schulten,	25	Claes Pietersen, of Gemenepa,	50
Michiel Tunisen,	6	Geurt Coerten,	13
Dirck Gerritson,	20	Dirck Claeszen,	10
Jan Lubbertsen,	6	Jan Losercht,	6
Jacob Laenderse,	25	Gerrit Gerritsen,	6
Jan d'Engelsman,	6	Claes Arentsen,	8
Paulus Pietersen,	25	Joost Van Linden,	10
William Jansen,	10		
Adriance Post,	20		
Douwe Harmanse,	6		417[1]

At this time, and until 1680, the people used the log school-

[1] *N. Y. Col. MSS.*, *x.*, pt. *i.*, 277, 279, 281. A singular error concerning this subscription has been made by Dr. Taylor in his *Annals of the Classis of Bergen*, 110. Not having seen the original manuscript, but depending on information received from the late J. Romeyn Broadhead, he says: "As early as 1662 * * four hundred and seventeen guilders * * were raised by tax, in the township of Bergen, towards the erection of a church." It was raised, not by *tax*, but by *subscription*; not for the *erection of a church*, but for the *support of a minister*. I am happy to be able to make this correction.

house for a place of worship. This was on the site of the present school-house fronting the square.[1] In the spring of the year 1680, the first church building in Bergen was begun.[2] Willem Day was the builder. Its form was octagonal, with the windows quite high from the ground, probably as much for a protection against the Indians as to prevent the youngsters looking out during the services. The accompanying illustration, enlarged, is taken from the Field Map. It was located in the old graveyard west of Bergen avenue, and south of Vroom street, and was yet standing in 1764.

OCTAGONAL CHURCH, 1680.

In 1773 a new building was placed on the site of the old Octagonal. Over the front door was a stone, with this inscription:

"Kerk Gebouwt in Het Yaer
1680. Her Bouwt in Het
Yaer 1773."

The bricks in the windows and arch over the door were brought from Holland. The corner stone of the present building was laid August 26, 1841. The building was dedicated July 14, 1842.

Previous to the arrival of Rev. Henricus Selyns, Dominie van Nieuwenhuysen did most of the preaching at Bergen—statedly from 1672 to 1680. He preached and administered the Lord's Supper three times a year, for which he received "thirty bushels or fifteen bags of wheat."[3] He preached in Bergen on

---

[1] *Winfield's Land Titles*, 105. [2] *L. I. Hist. Soc.*, *i.*, 157. [3] *Ibid*, *i.*, 158.

week days. He is represented as a thick, corpulent person, with a red and bloated face. There can be no doubt, however, that previous to the services of Van Nieuwenhuysen, Dominies Johannis and Samuel Megapolenses preached in Bergen. The village in its corporate capacity seems to have been responsible for the pay of these clergymen.

BERGEN REFORMED CHURCH, 1773.

Their salaries were not fully paid, and on May 21, 1674, the authorities were informed that there was yet due from the town of Bergen to each of them fl. 100, "for earned salary," which the magistrates were recommended to pay forthwith.[1] On Mr. Selyns' arrival, in 1682, he found at Bergen a new church, and 134 members. He continued the previous arrangement of preaching at Bergen three times a year. He died on Saturday, P M., July 19, 1701.[2] In 1699, Rev. Gualtherius Du Bois became associated with Mr. Selyns, and served the church in

[1] *Col. Hist. of N. Y.*, *ii.*, 722.

[2] *N. Y. Hist. Soc.*, *i.*, 390.

Bergen until September, 1751. He was born in 1671, at Street Kerf, Holland, where his father, Petrus du Bois, was the Dutch pastor. He was educated at the University of Leyden, licensed in 1697, preached until September, 29, 1751, and died on Wednesday, October 9, 1751, in the eighty-first year of his age.[1] The following eloquent tribute to his memory is from the *Weekly Post Boy*, October 14, 1751:

A Gentleman of a spotless Character
and undissembled Goodness;
Amiable in his Temper, and in all Points exemplary:
Of a benevolent Disposition, a diffusive Charity,
and for his engaging Manners,
and for the sanctity of his Morals,
Beloved by all but the Foes of Virtue.
Great was his Knowledge in sacred Literature;
Nor was he ordinarily skill'd in the liberal Sciences:
But for human Prudence, and the Knowledge of Men,
To most superior
and surpassed by none.
Of a catholic Disposition, and a christian Charity,
He never usurp'd the Province of God,
Nor thundered his Anathemas against those of different Sects,
whose lives were irreprehensible.

On controversial Points, and polemic Theology,
often destructive to vital Piety,
He scorn'd to employ his precious Moments:
Yet stripping an Argument of its specious Glare,
He had an admirable Talent to expose
its Disguise and Sophistry.

The awful Majesty, and the Rigour of Religion,
He soften'd by the winning Mildness of his Converse;
And those Virtues which appear stern and forbidding in others,
Shone in him with attractive Beauty,
and ineffable Lustre.

---

[1] *Doc. Hist. of N. Y., iii.*, 537.

His Deportment was grave, venerable and solemn,
yet open, unaffected and familiar.
His Discourses remarkable for a pleasing Variety,
of the Natural and Sublime,
Yet intelligible to the most illiterate :
His style was nervous and emphatic,
Yet neither destitute of flowing Periods,
Nor the Flowers of Rhetoric.

To ecclesiastical Dominion, and spiritual Bondage,
To blind Superstition, and frantic Enthusiasm ;
with every species
of ghostly Tyranny and Priest-craft,
He was a resolute and irreconcileable Foe :
But for primitive Christianity, and the Gospel of Christ
(unadulterate with human Inventions
or the Roguery of Priests),
Together with a Freedom of Enquiry and the Liberty of Man,
A Triumphant Defender.

Unambitious of Power, Affluence, or Honors,
He consecrated his literary Acquirements,
to inculcate Religion
in its Evangelical Purity :
And looking on the glittering Toys of mortal Life
with a wise Indifference,
He laid up Treasures in the Regions above,
Where he now partakes, as the Reward of his Toils,
Pleasures immortal
and everlasting Repose.

By his Doctrine, his Prayers, and his Life,
He liv'd the Blessing and Ornament of his People,
for above the Space of Fifty-two years ;

And longing for Heaven, and for Heaven mature,
He departed this Life with Serenity and Joy,
or rather Acclamation and Triumph ;
Bequeathing to his Church Lamentation and Woe,
And to his Followers a bright and shining Example.

His remains were interr'd in the Old Dutch Church,
where they sleep in Expectation
of a glorious Resurrection.

May his Congregation pass from the Weakness of regretting him,
To the Contemplation of his Virtues;
And rather adorn his Memory with deathless Praises
By imitating his Pattern,
and adopting his Excellencies.

In 1750 Petrus De Wint was chosen Pastor, but turning out to be a rogue, though carrying a shepherd's crook, was not installed.

On June 22, 1753, William Jackson was selected. He then went to Holland, finished his studies, returned, and was installed September 10, 1757. On account of mental infirmities, he was relieved from duty in December, 1789. He died July 25, 1813, and was buried in Bergen.

IN
MEMORY OF
the REV. WILLIAM JACKSON
who departed this life
July 25th, 1813
Aged 81 years
He faithfully fulfilled the pastoral
charge of the united Congregations
of Bergen and Staten Island, for
32 years, until bowed down
under grievous afflictions.
He was esteemed for his piety.
"Be ye followers of them who
through faith and patience inherit
the promises." Heb. 6, 12.

He was an uncompromising whig among the uncertain patriots of Bergen during the trying times of the Revolution. Tradition says that he preached for the Refugees once at Fort Delancey. His text was: *What will ye give me, and I will deliver him unto you? And they covenanted with him for thirty pieces of silver.* Matt. 26, 15. His sermon was a caustic application of the text to his tory hearers—some of them of his own congregation. For this he was arrested and taken before the commanding General in New York. He was asked why he preached against his Majesty. He confessed the fact and justified it as the performance of his duty. He was forgiven and permitted to return home, where he continued to thunder against the enemies of his country. One day old Helmagh Van Houten found fault with the political complexion of his sermon. The dominie replied, "Lord Howe has forgiven me; can't you?"

Rev. John Cornelison became pastor of this church May 26, 1793. Up to this time the preaching had been in Dutch. He died March 20, 1828, and was buried in Bergen.

Commemorative
of the
Rev. John Cornelison, A. M.,
who died
March 20, A. D. 1828,
In the 59th year of his age,
and 35th of his ministry
as Pastor of this church.

In life
Active, amiable, judicious and pious,
He was useful, respected and beloved.
In death
He triumphed, through faith in Jesus,
As the Eternal God.

"Remember them who have spoken unto you the word of God." Heb. 13, 7.

Rev. Benjamin C. Taylor was installed July 24, 1828. Declared by the Classis Emeritus Pastor September 22, 1870.

James L. Ammerman was installed May 7, 1871, and is the present pastor.

Yours very truly
Benjamin C Taylor

The First Reformed Church at Bayonne was organized January 11, 1829, as the Reformed Dutch Church of Bergen Neck. First building was erected in 1828; dedicated January 10, 1829; abandoned February 10, 1867. The second building, the corner stone of which was laid September 4, 1866, was dedicated March 31, 1867. It is on the north corner of Avenue C and Bayonne avenue.

PASTORS.

Rev. Ira C. Boyce, from Sept. 15, 1829, to Jan. 22, 1844.
" James Romeyn, from May 28, 1844, to May 15, 1850.
" Jacob C. Dutcher, from Oct. 8, 1850, to May 25, 1854.
" Aaron L. Stillwell, Oct. 4, 1854; (died) June 24, 1864.
" Theodore W. Wells, from June 22, 1865 to Sept. 4, 1873.

The First Reformed Church of Jersey City was organized December 15, 1825, as *The First Presbyterian Church of Jersey City*. February 16, 1830, the congregation resolved themselves into a Dutch Church. First building was on the site of the present one; the corner stone was laid by Colonel Varick, May 18, 1826. It was moved across the street in 1853, where it became "Park Hall," and was destroyed by fire December 12, 1864. The second building, the corner stone of which was laid September 22, 1853, was dedicated April 5, 1857. It is on the south side of Grand, between Washington and Warren streets.

PASTORS.

Rev. Stephen H. Meeker, from May 9, 1830, to Oct. 20, 1830.
" James R. Talmadge, from Feb. 8, 1831, to Jan. 30, 1833.
" Matthias Lusk, from Nov. 19, 1833, to Oct. 26, 1848.
" John Austin Yates (called), July 31, 1849; (died) Aug. 26, 1849.
" Daniel Lord, from June 16, 1850, to May 5, 1851.
" Alexander W. McClure, from May 19, 1852, to April 18, 1855.
" David H. Riddle, from April 19, 1857, to Dec. 22, 1862.
" Henry M. Scudder, from Dec. 5, 1864, to May 23, 1865.
" George H. Peeke, from Aug. 1, 1865, to Dec. 6, 1869.
" William W. Halloway, jr., June 11, 1871.

The Reformed Church at New Durham was organized April 12, 1843. The building known as "The Grove Church" is located on the west side of the old Dallytown road at Union Hill, "overlooking the region it was appointed to guard." Dedicated September 27, 1847. Enlarged to double its capacity in 1862, at a cost of $12,000. A parsonage is attached.

PASTORS.

Rev. Philip Duryee, of English Neighborhood, acting until 1844.
" William J. R. Taylor, from Oct. 6, 1844, to Sept. 8, 1846.
" William V. V. Mabon, from Oct. 4, 1846.

Second Reformed Church of Jersey City was organized March 15, 1846, as the First Reformed Dutch Church in the Township of Van Vorst. The building is on the south side of Wayne, between Grove and Barrow streets. The corner stone was laid August 24, 1847; building dedicated May 28, 1848.

PASTORS.

Rev. William J. R. Taylor, from Sept. 27, 1846, to Oct. 4, 1849.
" Paul D. Van Cleef, from Dec. 30, 1849.

The First Reformed Church of Hoboken was organized October 27, 1850. The building is on the west side of Hudson, between Fifth and Sixth streets; corner stone laid July 12, 1852; dedicated August 27, 1855.

PASTORS.

Rev. Charles Parker, from April 1, 1855, to Jan. 18, 1858.
" Alexander M. Mann, from March 23, 1858, to March 25, 1861.
" Matthew B. Riddle, from April 15, 1862, to Feb. 26, 1865.
" W. H. Vroom, from June —, 1865, to April —, 1867.
" J. K. Allen, from June 18, 1868, to April 19, 1870.
" Charles D. Buck, from Dec. 21, 1870.

The Third Reformed Church of Jersey City was organized May 7, 1852. The first building—the "Tabernacle," on the southeast corner of Erie and Sixth streets—was dedicated April 16, 1854. The second building is on the corner of Eighth street, and fronting on Hamilton square; corner stone laid September 20, 1859; dedicated May 6, 1860.

PASTORS.

Rev. William J. R. Taylor, from Aug. 19, 1852, to Nov. 14, 1854.
" J. Paschal Strong, from Jan. 21, 1855, to Nov. 25, 1856.
" Calvin Selden, from May 10, 1857, to Oct. 5, 1857.
" Cornelius L. Wells, from June 13, 1858, to March 5, 1863.
" J. Romeyn Berry, from Nov. 25, 1863, to Nov. 1, 1868.
" J. Howard Suydam, from Jan. 31, 1869.

The German Evangelical Church of North Bergen was organized October 4, 1853. The building stands on Columbia street; was dedicated March 28, 1854; enlarged and rebuilt in 1868–9.

PASTORS.

Rev. Leopold Mohn, from August 5, 1855, to April 21, 1857.
" Charles Becker, from Dec. —, 1857, to Sept. 12, 1860.
" John Justin, June 25, 1865.

The Reformed Church of Hudson City was organized December 14, 1853. The congregation worshiped in a room connected with Miss Graves' female seminary. Rev. Aaron Lloyd was missionary from September 15, 1854, to July 19, 1855, and Rev. Frederick L. King from October 16, 1855, to October, 1857. The church was afterward disbanded.

The Reformed Church of Bergen Point was organized May 16, 1854. The building is on the west side of Avenue T, between Second and Third streets; dedicated August 21, 1853.

PASTORS.

Rev. Jacob C. Dutcher, from June 11, 1854, to June 30, 1857.
" Charles Parker, from Feb. 8, 1858, to Dec. 13, 1859.
" Henry W. F. Jones, from August 7, 1860, to ——.

The German Evangelical Church of Jersey City was organized August 17, 1856; occupied Franklin Hall, on the southeast corner of Montgomery and Warren streets; disbanded in May, 1866.

PASTORS.

Rev. C. Doeppenschmidt, from Aug. 17, 1856, to April 14, 1865.
" Charles Meyer, from April —, 1865, to May, 1866.

The Reformed Church of Lafayette was organized May 3, 1863; incorporated June 1, 1863. The building is located on the northwest corner of Communipaw avenue and Pine street; was dedicated November 25, 1866.

PASTOR—Rev. William Rankin Duryee, from July 31, 1864, to ——.

The Second Reformed Church of Hudson City (German) was organized November 6, 1859; served by Rev. C. Doeppenschmidt, as missionary in connection with Jersey City; united with a mission at Washington Village, April 12, 1863, under the care of Rev. Leopold Mohn. The church building is located on Central avenue, near Franklin street. The Pastor of the United Church, Rev. C. Doeppenschmidt, was installed December 11, 1864. Hammond installed July 23, 1871.

Reformed Church of West End was organized November 7, 1869. The chapel stands on the corner of Academy street and Broadway; dedicated November 8, 1868.

Rev. Alexander Shaw was appointed missionary in 1868.
Rev. William H. Van Doren, pastor, installed July 23, 1871.

Reformed Church of Greenville was organized February 19, 1871, and supplied by neighboring ministers until January 19, 1873, when Rev. Alexander H. Young was installed pastor.

Free Reformed Church, Jersey City. The Morgan street (afterward called the Bethel) Sunday School, from which this church sprang, was begun March 1, 1861, under the care of the three Reformed Churches of Jersey City. The first chapel stood on Morgan street. The present one is on the south side of First street, east of Grove, and was dedicated October 2, 1870.

Rev. Alexander Shaw was missionary until October, 1872.

Rev. Andrew J. Park, pastor, installed January 12, 1873.

German Evangelical Church, Hoboken, was organized September 16, 1856. The church building stands on the corner of Garden and Sixth streets.

PASTOR—Rev. Leopold Mohn, from April 21, 1857, to ——.

Reformed Church of Guttenberg was organized November, 1868. The chapel is located on Hudson avenue, and was dedicated in January, 1868. This congregation grew out of a Sunday school established in 1864 by Rev. W. V. V. Mabon, D.D., who, assisted by others, kept up regular preaching until August, 1872, when Rev. Peter B. Crolius was installed pastor.

Central Avenue Reformed Church was organized July 10, 1872. The chapel is on Central avenue, corner of Bowers street; dedicated December 31, 1871. The church was supplied with preaching by neighboring ministers until September, 1872, when Rev. G. H. Pool was installed. He continued until April 21, 1873.

The Third Reformed Church of Bayonne City (German) was organized May 3 and 26, 1872. The church building is located on the corner of Avenue T and Fourth street; corner stone laid October 12, 1873.

Plank Road Chapel.—A Sabbath school was organized in this locality by Rev. W. V. V. Mabon in 1858. In 1866, by the liberality of Mr. James Brown, a chapel was erected. This chapel is connected with the Grove Church, and the services are maintained by the pastor, Rev. W. V. V. Mabon.

EPISCOPAL CHURCHES.

St. Matthew's, Jersey City, was organized August 21, 1808.

The trustees were elected December 8 in the same year. At first the services were held in the "Jersey Academy," built by the town authorities, and completed in February, 1807. The building is located on the north side of Sussex, between Washington and Warren streets; corner stone was laid October 22, 1831; building was consecrated November 26, 1835; destroyed by fire December 4, 1869; rebuilt and opened for service October 15, 1870.

PASTORS.

Rev. Timothy Clowes, from organization until May 1, 1809.
" Edmund D. Barry, from May 5, 1809, to 1816.
" Cave Jones, from 1816 to 1824.
" Edmund D. Barry, from 1824; became rector May 13, 1831; died April 20, 1852.
" A. C. Patterson, assistant pastor from June, 1844, to May 12, 1847.
" Charles Aldis, assistant pastor from July, 1847, to March, 1849.
" James J. Bowden, assistant pastor from June, 1849, to May 4, 1852.
" James J. Bowden, rector from May 4, 1852, to June, 1859.
" J. Brinton Smith,[1] from Nov., 1859, to Dec. 31, 1865.
" William A. Matson, from Sept. 1, 1866, to ——.
" Richard Abercrombie, from Jan. 7, 1872, to ——.

---

[1] RALEIGH, N. C., November 12, 1872.—The coroner's jury rendered a verdict to-day in the case of Rev. Dr. J. Brinton Smith, supposed to have been poisoned by members of his family on the 1st of October: That the deceased, J. Brinton Smith, came to his death on the morning of the 1st day of October, 1872, from the effects of strychnine mixed in a dose of seidlitz powders, administered by Francis L. Mann, and that Mary E. Smith was the custodian of the key of a closet in which was found a vial of said poisonous drug.

Mrs. Mann is the daughter and Mrs. Smith, the wife of deceased. Dr. Smith was an Episcopal clergyman, and President of the Augustine College of this city. The affair has caused great excitement, as all parties held high social position. Mrs. Smith and Mann were committed to the county jail this morning. Applications will be made by counsel for their release on a writ of habeas corpus. The sentiments of the community are divided as to the guilt of the parties. The stomach and brains of deceased were examined by Dr. Genth, of Philadelphia, upon whose professional opinion the jury rendered a verdict.

In 1832 Episcopal services were for the first time held in Hoboken, Rev. William Tryon officiating. For about a year the district schoolhouse was used. Then John and Abraham L. Van Boskerck built a schoolhouse, in which services were held for two or three years.

St. Paul's, Hoboken, was organized March 2, 1835; incorporated March 16, 1835. The first building was on the northwest corner of Hudson and Third streets; corner stone laid May 27, 1836; building consecrated November 1, 1836; enlarged in 1851; sold in 1869. The present building is on the east side of Hudson, between Eighth and Ninth streets. The chapel was opened for service June 12, 1870, and the church September 4, 1870.

PASTORS.

Rev. John M. Ward, from April 4, 1835, to October, 1839.
" C. F. Cruise, to 1844.
" Richard H. Burnham, to July, 1851.
" Van de Wort Bruce, from 1853 to 1866.
" N. Sayre Harris, from 1866.
" — Hartung, from 1873.

Graçe, Jersey City, was organized April 26, 1847, under the care of Rev. A. L. Patterson, missionary for the whole county. The first building was on the west side of Grove street, a little to the north of Newark avenue. This building is now in Morgan street, occupied as an African church. The present building is on the northwest corner of Erie and Second streets; corner stone laid December 6, 1850; building consecrated May 18, 1853.

PASTORS.

Revs. A. L. Patterson, from May 5, 1847, to Sept. 20, 1848; Milo Mahan, from Nov. 26, 1848, to ——; David H. Macurdy; Charles Arey; Spencer M. Rice.

Holy Trinity, late Hudson City, was organized September 10, 1851. The building is on the north side of St. Paul's avenue, a little to the west of Central avenue. The corner stone was laid December 10, 1851; the building was consecrated May 19, 1853.

PASTORS.

Rev. William R. Gries, from 1851 to 1855.
" Norman W. Camp, from May 17, 1855, to 1858.
" Louis L. Noble, from Nov., 1858, to 1872.
" James Chrystal, from July, 1872, to ——.

Trinity, Hoboken, was organized September 16, 1853. At first the services were held in an engine house near the Napoleon Hotel, then called the Town hall. On May 1, 1854, the place of meeting was transferred to Odd Fellows' Hall. The building is on the northeast corner of Washington and Seventh streets. The corner stone was laid December 18, 1855; building completed in November, 1856. Grace chapel, on Seventh street, adjoining the church, was erected and presented to the parish by William P. Wright, as a memorial of his daughter, Grace. It was consecrated November 9, 1856.

PASTORS.

Rev. Norman W. Camp, from Sept. 16, 1853, to Aug. 29, 1855.
" John W. Clark, from Oct. 7, 1855, to May, 1856.
" N. Sayre Harris, from 1856, to Sept., 1865.
" Frederick Fitzgerald, from Sept., 1865, to Aug. 31, 1867.
" Reuben W. Howes, jr., from Dec. 2, 1867, to ——.

Trinity Free, Jersey City, was organized in September, 1854. The first building was on the north side of York, between Grove and Barrow streets; was opened for service June 10, 1855. It is now occupied as a livery stable. It was abandoned by the parish in 1862, and the Unitarian church building, on the southeast corner of Grove and Montgomery streets, secured until 1868, when the church collapsed, and *St. Mark's* entered upon the inheritance.

PASTORS.

Rev. Stephen Douglas, from June, 1854; died Jan. 21, 1857.
" Charles H. Canfield, from 1857 to April, 1859.

Rev. Robert F. Travis, jr., from May, 1859; died Oct. 26, 1866.
" Thomas Coleman, to Aug. 1, 1868.

Christ Church, Bergen, was organized in 1858; incorporated May 21, 1859. The building is on the northeast corner of Claremont avenue and Clerk street, and was consecrated in August, 1867.

PASTORS.

Revs. Orlando Harriman, Charles Ritter, Stephen H. Battin.

Trinity, Bergen Point, was organized in August, 1859. The building is on the southwest corner of Avenue E and Fifth street; consecrated Sept. 4, 1862.

PASTORS.

Rev. Franklin S. Rising, from Aug., 1860, to Jan. 20, 1862.
" Thomas A. Jaggar, from May 1, 1862, to Sept. 26, 1864.
" George Zabriskie Gray, from Feb. 12, 1865, to ——.

St. Paul's, Bergen, was organized August 1, 1860. The chapel, on the north side of Duncan, between Bergen and Grand avenues, was built in the spring of 1861, and opened for service May 20, 1861.

PASTOR—Rev. Fernando C. Putnam, from October, 1860, to the present time.

Grace (late Greenville) was organized January 14, 1864. The first building, on the west side of the old Bergen road, between Danforth and Linden avenues, and formerly a whalebone factory, was opened for service June 12, 1864. The present building, on the corner of Ocean and Pearsall avenues, was opened for service December 25, 1872.

PASTORS.

Rev. William G. Hughes, from Oct. 22, 1864, to Nov. 1, 1867.
" John R. Matthews, from April 20, 1868, to Oct. 20, 1869.
" Frederick M. Gray, ——, to June 29, 1873.

Calvary, Bayonne, was organized March 22, 1867. Occasional services had been held in the neighborhood from August 24, 1859, by Rev. Robert F. Travis, jr., of Jersey City, and Rev. William G. Hughes, of Greenville. In May, 1865, Trinity Parish of Bergen Point assumed charge of the enterprise. It then became known as *St. Bartholomew Mission*. From this time until November 19, 1865, Rev. William G. Hughes had charge of it, and was then succeeded by Rev. Frederick M. Gray. The building is on the southwest side of street, between Avenues C and D; corner-stone laid November 3, 1866; building opened for service June 29, 1867.

PASTORS.

Rev. Frederick M. Gray, from July 30, 1867, to Sept. 6, 1868.
" Samuel G. Appleton, from March 28, 1869, to ——.

St. Paul's, Jersey City, was organized February 14, 1868. The first service was held February 5, 1868, in Luxton's Hall. The building is on the northeast corner of New York avenue and South street; corner stone laid February 19, 1871; building opened for service May 28, 1871.

PASTORS.

Rev. Thomas M. Thorpe, from Feb. 24, 1868, to July 1, 1868.
" William Wardlaw, from Oct. 1, 1868, to Sept. 9, 1872.
" David G. Gunn, from Oct. 10, 1872, to Aug. —, 1873.

St. Mark's, Jersey City, was incorporated December 8, 1868. The building occupied is on the southeast corner of Grove and Montgomery streets, built by the Unitarians in 1856.

PASTORS.

Rev. David H. Macurdy, from March 4, 1869, to April 30, 1871.
" John F. Butterworth, from June, 1871, to ——.

St. John's Free, Jersey City, was organized March 4, 1869, as *Zion Free Church*. The building is on the east side of Palisade avenue, opposite Gardner avenue; ground broken for the foundation November 30, 1870; corner stone laid May 7, 1871; basement opened for service November 25, 1871; building ditto, February 2, 1872.

Pastor—N. S. Rulison, from 1869 to the present time.

St. John's, West Hoboken, was incorporated June 19, 1846. The church building is on the northeast corner of Warren street and Clinton avenue; completed in October, 1849.

Pastors.

Revs. Orlando Harriman; T. M. Thorpe; Wm. T. Jarvis; — Maturen; C. P. Jones; W. C. Cooley, 1870–3; George Chambers, from Nov., 1873, to ——.

East Newark P. E. Church was organized about 1843. The church building is on the corner of Third and Warren streets. The following are a few of the

Pastors:

Rev. Messrs. Myer, Hooper, Webb, Orr, Webb.

St. John's, Bayonne, was organized in 1872; incorporated March 12, 1872. This church was organized as a mission of Trinity, of Bergen Point.

Pastor—Rev. Washington Rodman, from 1872 to the present time.

St. Luke's, Jersey City, was organized in August, 1873. The place of worship is on the corner of South street and Central avenue.

Pastor—Rev. David G. Gunn.

Church of the Atonement, Hoboken, was incorporated May 19, 1866.

Baptist Churches.

The Particular Baptist Church of Jersey City and Harsimus was organized March 11, 1839. The building occupied is yet standing on the west side of Barrow street, between Newark and Railroad avenues.

PASTORS.

Rev. Joseph Houghwout, from 1838 to 1841.
" John O. Edmunds, from 1841 to 1842.
" Arus Haynes, from 1842 to 1844.
" William Smith, from 1844 to 1847.

The Jersey City Baptist Church was organized March 11, 1844.

PASTORS.

Rev. William Rollinson, from May to Nov., 1843.
" Silas C. James, from March to Sept., 1844.
" Joseph M. Morris, from April 1, 1845, to Feb. 26, 1846.
" William Gooding, from Aug. 11, 1846, to Feb. 15, 1847.

The Grand Street Baptist Church, Jersey City, was organized in 1844.

PASTOR—Rev. Arus Haynes, from 1844 to 1847.

The Union Baptist Church, which, by legislative act in 1868, was changed to *The First Baptist Church of Jersey City*, was organized March 1, 1848, out of the material composing the other Baptist churches. The building is on the east side of Grove, between Wayne and Mercer streets. The basement was opened for service April 11, 1852; the building was dedicated July 17, 1853.

PASTORS.

Rev. O. C. Wheeler, from April 6, 1848, to Nov. 21, 1848.
" William Verrinder, from Dec. 1, 1849, to April 1, 1854.
" Wheelock H. Parmly, from Sept. 1, 1854, to ——.

The First Baptist Church of New Durham was organized in 1837. The first building was on the Secaucus road, at the foot of Weehawken hill. The present building is on the east side of the Hackensack turnpike; erected in 1854.

PASTORS—Rev. George F. Hendrickson, Joseph Perry, George

P. Martin, John Gibbs, Wm. Dorman Wright, James A. Metz, John E. Perrine, and Thomas F. Clancy (present pastor).

The First Baptist Church, Hudson City, was organized in 1857. The building is on the west side of Bergen avenue, near the Five Corners.

PASTORS.

Rev. Marvin Eastwood, from 1858 to 1860.
" Rev. Halsey J. Knapp, from 1860 to 1864.
" J. W. Custis, from 1865 to 1867.
" Charles E. Cordo, from 1867 to ——.
" T. R. Howlett, from 1869 to 1872.
" W. B. Harris, from Feb. 6, 1872, to ——.

The Bethesda Baptist Church, Jersey City, was recognized July 11, 1858. The building was located on the north side of Fifth street, between Erie street and Jersey avenue. The church was disbanded in 1863.

PASTORS.

Rev. Mr. Raymond, at the time of recognition.
" Matthew C. Kempsey, from Sept. 30, 1858, to 1860.
" George A. Post, from 1861 to 1863.

The First Baptist Church, Hoboken, was organized in 1845. The first building, on the northeast corner of Washington and Third streets, was sold to the First Presbyterian Church in 1851. The present building is on the northwest corner of Bloomfield and Third streets; dedicated November 4, 1852.

PASTORS.

Revs. Aaron S. Patton; Josiah Hatt, from 1846 to 1855; A. Harris, from 1860 to 1870; — Maull, 1873.

The West Hoboken Baptist Church was organized in 1854. The first building, on the northeast corner of De Mott street and Clinton avenue, was built by John Syms in about 1856. The present building is on the corner of Clinton avenue and Serrell street; begun in 1866; to be dedicated January 15, 1874.

PASTORS.

Rev. C. A. Buckbee, —— James, Robert McGonigle, —— Devan, William Gilkes, 1870, present pastor.

The First Baptist Church, Bergen, was organized Feb. 7, 1859; recognized June 17, 1860. The building is on the northwest corner of Clinton place and Madison avenue. The chapel was dedicated in September, 1860. The corner stone of the building was laid May 8, 1871; the building dedicated March 31, 1872.

PASTORS.

Rev. W. B. Shrope, from Sept., 1859, to Aug., 1860.
" G. W. Pendleton, from Nov., 1860, to Sept., 1862.
" J. S. Ladd, from Oct., 1862, to March, 1864.
" William Rollinson, from Oct., 1865.
" Walter W. Hammond, present pastor.

The North Baptist Church, Jersey City, was organized Sept. 28, 1865. The building is on the east side of Jersey avenue, between Fourth and Fifth streets; dedicated in April, 1867.

PASTOR—Rev. Henry A. Cordo, from Oct. 1, 1866, to Nov. 26, 1871, when he resigned. In 1872 he was recalled, there having been no intermediate pastor.

The First Baptist Church of the Town of Union was organized in 1864; incorporated Jan. 19, 1865. The building, erected in 1866, is on the northeast corner of Bergen Line avenue and Franklin street.

PASTORS—Rev. Washington Wicks, James Metz, Edwin Shaffer, George F. Hendrickson, who resigned in August, 1873.

The German Pilgrim Baptist Church, Hudson City, was incorporated June 1, 1866.

The First German Regular Baptist Church, West Hoboken, was organized in November, 1868; incorporated February 15, 1869. The building at present occupied is in Hoboken avenue, near Clinton avenue. The building of the First Baptist Church will be occupied when that body occupies their new building.

PASTORS.

Revs. C. Frederick Blumenberg, ——— Austermehl, George Knablach, Michael Hüflin.

The Hamilton Park Baptist Church was recognized May 29, 1873.

PASTOR—Rev. Aaron S. Patton.

THE PRESBYTERIAN CHURCHES.

In 1809 a society was organized in Jersey City under the care of Rev. Dr. Miller. In April, 1813, this society obtained the privilege of holding service in the "Jersey Academy," alternating the Sundays with St. Matthew's P. E. Church. A Presbyterian Church was organized December 15, 1825. A frame building was erected on the site of the present First Reformed Church in Grand street. The corner stone was laid by Colonel Richard Varick, May 18, 1826. Rev. James S. Olcott was pastor until 1829. On February 16, 1830, the church, by action of the congregation, dissolved its connection with the Presbyterians, and became the First Reformed Church.

The First Presbyterian Church, Jersey City, was organized April 22, 1844, the services being held in the First Reformed Church. The building is on the northeast corner of Washington and Sussex streets; corner stone laid October 4, 1844; dedicated May 25, 1845. This building was brought from New York city, where it stood on the north side of Wall street. It was known as the "stone-steepled Meeting House;" built in 1718; enlarged in 1768; rebuilt in 1810; destroyed by fire in the fall of 1834, and immediately rebuilt. It was the only church in the city in which Whitfield could obtain a hearing. He preached in it many times. Its size and shape are now what they were prior to its removal to Jersey City, only the basement has been added and the pews and pulpit have been reconstructed.

PASTORS.

Rev. John Johnston, from May 20, 1844, to May 27, 1850.

Rev. Lewis H. Lee, Associate, from Nov. 15, 1848, to Jan., 1850.
" David King,[1] from June 12, 1850, to Oct. 12, 1851.
" Charles K. Imbrie, from Feb. 11, 1852, to present time.

The Second Presbyterian Church, Jersey City, was organized September 9, 1851. The building is on the north side of Third street, between Erie street and Jersey avenue; dedicated January 17, 1858, and, after enlargement, March 21, 1869.

PASTORS.

Rev. Charles Hoover, from June 30, 1852, to 1859.
" George C. Lucas, from May 31, 1860, to 1863.
" James M. Stevenson,[2] from Oct. 15, 1864, to 1871.
" Hiram Eddy, from May 30, 1871, to present time.

The Scotch Presbyterian Church, now known as *The Third Presbyterian Church*, Jersey City, was organized May 29, 1856. At first the old building in Barrow street, between Newark and Railroad avenues, was occupied; then a building in Grove street. In October, 1862, the congregation secured the "Tabernacle," a frame building on the southeast corner of Erie and Fifth streets. A building, nearly completed, is now being erected in Mercer near Varick street.

PASTORS.

Rev. James Petrie, from Nov. 5, 1856, to 1858.
" William Cochrane, from June 7, 1859, to March 28, 1862.
" James Harkness, from Oct. 21, 1862, to present time.

The Third Presbyterian Church, Jersey City, was organized May 13, 1859; Rev. James Cubby, *pastor*. Union Hall, on the southwest corner of Grove and Fourth streets, was, for a while, occupied as a place of worship. Though a "feeble folk," the organization was very zealous in committing *hari-kari*. It was altogether too *militant*. Its existence was turbulent, happily brief, and its *nunc dimittis* applauded by all who believe that a church should lift its members above the level of the hero of Donnybrook Fair.

The Presbyterian Church, Hoboken, was organized June 9,

[1] Died May 15, 1853.

[2] Died October 18, 1871.

1852. A movement for such an organization was made as early as October, 1851, and in November of that year the building of the Baptist Church, on the southwest corner of Washington and Third streets, was purchased. The present building is on the southeast corner of Sixth and Hudson streets; dedicated February 23, 1865.

PASTORS.

Rev. Isaac P. Stryker, from June 11, 1854.
" William H. Babbitt, from 1859 to 1864.
" E. P. Gardner, from 1865 to 1870.
" James Marshall, present pastor.

The First Presbyterian Church, Bergen, was organized October 24, 1855. The building is on the north side of Emory street, between Bergen and Monticello avenues; was dedicated October 28, 1858.

Rev. Edward W. French the only pastor.

Prospect Avenue Presbyterian Church, Jersey City, was organized June 13, 1871, although regular services had been maintained in a hall on Newark avenue from December 11, 1870.

PASTOR—Rev. John Glendenning, from Oct. 26, 1871, to present time.

The First Presbyterian Church, West Hoboken, was organized June 12, 1850. The building is on Clinton avenue; corner stone laid September 4, 1850; dedicated June 25, 1851.

Rev. James C. Egbert, from June 13, 1855, is the first and only pastor.

The Claremont Presbyterian Church, Jersey City, was organized in February, 1868. The building is on the south side of Claremont avenue, between Ocean avenue and Clerk street; corner stone laid August 3, 1869; opened for service December 30, 1869.

PASTORS.

Rev. Samuel W. Duffield, from May 8, 1870.
" J. McNulty, from 1872 to August, 1873.

The Weehawken Presbyterian Church was organized in October, 1868. The church building is located at Weehawken, on the west side of Park avenue extended, and north of Nineteenth street; begun in August, 1870; dedicated in May, 1871.

PASTORS.

Revs. Robert Proudfit; George P. Noble, from Feb., 1870, to April 1, 1871; Robert R. Townsend, from Aug. 1, 1871, to the present time.

The First United Presbyterian Church, Hoboken, was organized November 29, 1854, as *The First Associate Presbyterian Church;* took its present name in 1858, when the union between the *Associate* and the *Associate Reformed* churches was consummated. The church building is on the southeast corner of Bloomfield and Seventh streets; erected 1856; opened for service on the last Sunday in November, 1856.

PASTORS.

Rev. Wm. G. McElhany, from May 10, 1855, to May 20, 1860.[1]
" Samuel C. Marshall, from July 16, 1861, to April 1, 1863.
" Henry Allen, from April 3, 1867, to Dec. 26, 1867.[1]
" Robert Armstrong, from Dec. 2, 1868.

The First United Presbyterian Church, Jersey City, was organized October 15, 1862; incorporated August 1, 1863. The society occupies the old church building in Barrow street, between Newark and Railroad avenues.

PASTORS.

Rev. Robert A. Hill, from Nov. —, 1864, to Nov. —, 1870.
" Thomas W. Pollock, from May 17, 1871, to present time.

The Second United Presbyterian Church, Jersey City, was organized in April, 1871. The building is on Hancock avenue, south of Bowers street.

Rev. Robert Armstrong, first and only pastor.

METHODIST EPISCOPAL CHURCHES.

As early as 1811 an effort was made to establish an M. E. church

[1] Died in charge.

in this county. The appointments were made to "Bergen," which may mean the County of Bergen. They were as follows:

Revs. John Robertson, 1811–12; Daniel Fidler, 1812–13; Joseph Totten, 1813–14; Stephen Martindale, 1814–15; David Best, 1815–16; John Finley, 1816–17; Peter Van Ness, 1817–18; Jos. Sybrand, 1818–19; John Potts, 1819–20; George Banghart, 1820–2; Manning Force, 1822–3; Benjamin Collins, 1823–4; Bartholomew Weed, 1824–26; David Bartine, 1826–27.

At this date the appointments seem to have broken off.

January 20, 1826, Anthony Cathlin, Archer G. Welsh, Hiram L. Meeker, James J. Seaman and Josiah Hornblower certified to their election as trustees of "*The First Methodist Society of the Town and County of Bergen.*" It is probable that this referred to the "Bergen Mission," which afterward revived and became the Simpson Church.

The next effort was at Bergen Neck, where a mission was started, to which appointments were made as follows:

Revs. Thomas G. Stewart, 1831–2; John H. McFarland, 1832–3; John N. Crane, 1833–4; John Nicholson, 1834–5.

This mission terminated in the Bergen Neck (now Mattison) Church.

Trinity M. E. Church, Jersey City, was organized in 1835. The first building was a frame structure, and stood on "legs"—Methodism was more itinerant then than now. The present building is on the south side of York street, between Washington and Warren streets; corner stone laid May 5, 1843; dedicated December 25, 1843.

PASTORS.

Revs. John McClintock, 1835–6; Wesley C. Hudson, 1836–7; Benjamin Day, 1838–9; Charles H. Whitecar, 1839–41; James M. Tuttle, 1841–2; Vincent Shepherd, 1842–4; William Roberts, 1844–6; Francis A. Morrell, 1846–8; Joseph B. Wakely, 1848–50; James M. Tuttle, 1850–51; Israel S. Corbit, 1851–3; James Ayars, 1853–5; Charles H. Whitecar, 1855–7; Isaac W. Wiley,[1]

[1] Mr. Wiley left in August, 1858, and was succeeded by Mr. Monroe for the remainder of the year.

1857–9; Jonathan T. Crane, 1859–60; James Ayars, 1860–1; William P. Corbit, 1861–2; Robert L. Dashiel, 1862–4; Isaac W. Wiley, 1864–5; Samuel Y. Monroe, 1865–6; Hiram Mattison, 1866–8; George H. Whitney,[1] 1868–70; David W. Bartine, 1870–3; John Atkinson, 1873–

The Simpson M. E. Church, Jersey City, was organized in 1841, the first service being held in a schoolhouse near the Five Corners. Previous to 1844 it was known as the "Bergen Mission." The first building was the present police station in Oakland, between Newark and Hoboken avenues. The present building is on the west side of Central avenue, near St. Paul's avenue; basement dedicated in 1857; building dedicated in 1858.

PASTORS.

Revs. Benj. N. Reed, 1839–40; Lewis T. Maps, 1840–41; Wm. M. Burroughs, 1841–2; Abraham T. Palmer, 1842–3; Wm. E. Perry, 1843–4; Aaron E. Ballard, 1844–5; David Graves, 1845–6; John W. Barrett, 1846–7; Garner R. Snyder, 1847–8; Wm. M. Burroughs, 1848–9; F. Robbins, 1849–50; F. S. Hoyt, 1850–1; John Dean, 1851–2; Edwin A. Day, 1852–4; Edward A. Adams, 1854–6; Alex. H. Mead, 1856–8; A. L. Brice, 1858–60; John O. Winner, 1860–2; Thomas H. Smith, 1862–4; Michael E. Ellison, 1864–7; Ralph S. Arnt, 1867–70; Robert B. Lockwood, 1870–3; Wm. Tunison, 1873–

The Mattison M. E. Church, Bayonne, was incorporated June 22, 1844, as *The Bergen Neck Church.* The name was changed by Legislative act, February 26, 1868. The building was erected on the east side of Avenue D, near Twenty-ninth street; corner stone laid in 1854; dedicated in 1855. In 1868 or '69 it was moved to the southwest corner of Oakland avenue and Avenue D.

PASTORS.[2]

Revs. Waters Burrows, 1857–8; James H. Dandy, 1861–3;

---

[1] Mr. Whitney was elected President of the Seminary at Hacketstown in August, 1869.

[2] The Pastors of the Greenville Church were in charge of this church until 1865, except the years 1857–8 and 1861–3. During these three years it attempted to stand alone, but was too feeble.

Stephen K. Russell, 1866–8; Enoch V. King, 1868–9; A. Craig, 1869–70; J. Emory, 1870–1; Abm. J. Palmer, 1871–2; W. L. Hoagland, 1872–4.

St. Paul's M. E. Church, Jersey City, was organized in July, 1848, as the *M. E. Church at Pavonia*. The building is on the north side of Third, between Grove and Erie streets; corner stone laid December 25, 1849; basement opened for service June 30, 1850; dedicated November 27, 1850.

PASTORS.

Revs. Dayton F. Reed, 1849–50; John Parker, 1850–1; Robert Given, 1851–2; George Hughes, 1852–4; Michael E. Ellison, 1854–6; Richard Van Horn, 1856–8; Wm. Tunison, 1858–60; Lewis R. Dunn, 1860–2; Richard Van Horn, 1862–4; Wm. Tunison, 1864–7; Lewis R. Dunn, 1867–70; Charles Larew, 1870–3; Daniel R. Lowrie, 1873–

The Greenville M. E. Church was incorporated July 20, 1845. The building is on the south side of Linden avenue, between Ocean avenue and Bergen road; dedicated January 6, 1846. This society was connected with Bergen until 1851.

PASTORS.

Revs. Waters Burrows, 1851–3; David Waters, 1853–4; Benjamin F. Woolston,[1] 1854–5; Edwin A. Day, 1855–6; William C. Nelson, 1856–7; Waters Burrows, 1857–8; Isaac W. Haff, 1858–60; Thomas E. Gordon, 1860–1; S. L. Baldwin, 1861–2; Richard Johns, 1862–3; William G. Hughes, 1863–4; Bront Slaight, 1864–5; Ambrose S. Compton, 1865–7; Fletcher Lummis, 1867–70; Egbert Clement, 1870–3; Charles R. Barnes, 1873.

The Hoboken M. E. Church was incorporated June 24, 1846. The first building was on the corner of Fourth and Garden streets; corner stone laid October 1, 1846; dedicated April 12, 1848. This was upon property belonging to the city. A new building was erected on the east side of Washington, between Seventh and Eighth streets; corner stone laid October 15, 1869; dedicated February 25, 1872.

---

[1] Mr. Woolston left in September, 1854, and Mr. Day took his place.

PASTORS.

Revs. David Graves, 1846–8; G. R. Snyder, 1848–9; William W. Christine, 1849–50; Michael E. Ellison, 1850–2; Joseph B. Dobbins, 1852–4; Charles S. Coit, 1854–5; Jonathan K. Burr, 1855–7; Joseph K. Knowles, 1857–9; J. O. Rogers, 1859–60; Alexander L. Brice, 1860–2; John O. Winner, 1862–4; Jonathan K. Burr, 1864–7; Michael E. Ellison, 1867–70; William Tunison, 1870–3; Jonathan K. Burr, 1873.

The Hedding M. E. Church, Jersey City, was organized March 20, 1855; incorporated May 10, 1855. The building is on the north side of Montgomery, between Grove and Barrow streets; corner stone laid August 15, 1855; lecture room dedicated January 20, 1856; building dedicated April 11, 1858.

PASTORS.

Revs. Waters Burrows, to April, 1855; Robert B. Yard, 1855–7; William Day, 1857–9; Charles Larew, 1859–61; James R. Bryan, 1861–3; William Day, 1863–6; John Hanlon, 1866–9; James M. Freeman, 1869–72; Robert B. Yard, 1872–4.

The Communipaw M. E. Church was incorporated April 14, 1853. The building is on the south side of Communipaw avenue, near New York bay; corner stone laid June 8, 1854; dedicated October 15, 1854. At the time of this dedication, Rev. T. C. Carman was pastor. He is the only pastor the society ever had exclusively. Since then it has been connected with Greenville, Trinity or Emory.

The Emory M. E. Church, Jersey City, was incorporated July 8, 1862. The first building was on the corner of Mill road and Colden place. It is now occupied by the First Universalist Church. The second building is on the north side of Belmont, between Bergen and Westside avenues; corner stone laid June 18, 1871; dedicated in 1872.

PASTORS.

Revs. Charles E. Winans, 1863–4; John J. Morrow, 1864–7; Daniel R. Lowrie, 1867–70; John Atkinson, 1870–3; S. Van Benschoten, 1873–

The Palisade M. E. Church, Jersey City, was incorporated May 26, 1858. The building is on the west side of Palisade avenue, a little south of the Paterson Plank road.

PASTORS.

Revs. Thomas E. Gordon, 1861–2; Henry M. Simpson, 1862–3; James J. Boswell, 1863–4; James N. Fitzgerald, 1864–7; Benjamin O. Parvin, 1867–70; John S. Porter, 1870–3; George Winson, 1873–

The Centenary M. E. Church, Jersey City, was organized April 17, 1867, incorporated September 27, 1867. The building is on the north side of Pavonia avenue, between Cole and Monmouth streets; corner stone laid September 26, 1870; basement dedicated April 30, 1871. Prior to this latter date, services were held in Union Hall, on the southwest corner of Grove and Fourth streets.

PASTORS.

Revs. David Graves, 1867–8; Hamilton C. McBride, 1868–9; James B. Faulks, 1869–72; Edson W. Burr, 1872–4.

The West End M. E. Church, Jersey City, was organized September 1, 1868. The building is on the east side of Tonele avenue, between St. Paul's and Tuers avenues.

PASTORS.

Revs. Henry M. Simpson, 1869–71; Charles R. Barnes, 1871–3; Thomas H. Jacobus, 1873.

The Lafayette M. E. Church, Jersey City, was incorporated April 21, 1873. The building is on the west side of Pine street, between Communipaw avenue and Lafayette street.

PASTORS.

Revs. W. L. Hoagland, 1869–72; A. H. Tuttle, 1872–3.

The Waverly M. E. Church (Rock Ridge Chapel), Jersey City, was incorporated December 20, 1870. The building is on the corner of Palisade and New York avenues; begun in December, 1870; dedicated November 19, 1871.

PASTORS.

Revs. Henry Baker, 1870–3; Abraham J. Palmer, 1873.

The Janes M. E. Church was incorporated March 10, 1870.

PASTORS.

Revs. Thomas Hall, 1870–3; J. F. Dodd, 1873.

The Porter M. E. Church, Bonnville, in West Hoboken township, was incorporated November 14, 1870. It was a mission, and had no pastor until 1873, when Rev. John Campbell was appointed. The building is on the east side of Bergen Line avenue, and a little south of the Hackensack turnpike; dedicated September 19, 1870.

The Arlington M. E. Church, Kearney. The corner stone of the building was laid (as per newspaper) November 23, 1873.

PASTOR—Rev. Mr. Blaine.

The East Newark Wesley M. E. Church was organized some years ago. A second building is now being erected; corner stone laid July 2, 1873; dedicated January 4, 1874.

PASTOR—Rev. J. L. Hayes.

St. Johanne's M. E. Church; building in Central, near New York avenue.

PASTOR—Rev. C. Brockmeyer.

There are several colored churches in the county of the M. E. persuasion.

ROMAN CATHOLIC CHURCHES.

The Roman Catholics of New Jersey were under the jurisdiction of the diocese of New York until October 30, 1853, when the diocese of New Jersey was created, and James Rosevelt Bayley consecrated bishop.

St. Peter's R. C. Church, Jersey City. The first building erected for this congregation was on the north side of Grand, between Washington and Warren streets; begun in 1831; opened for service in 1837; consecrated in 1839, by Bishop Hughes, assisted by Bishop Fenwick, of Boston. The present building is on the northeast corner of Grand and Van Vorst streets;

J. Kelly

FORMERLY PASTOR OF ST. PETER'S.

corner stone laid in August, 1865; opened for service December 16, 1865. The Jesuit Fathers took possession of this parish April 13, 1871.

PASTORS.

Rev. Fathers Burns, Mohan, Quarter, Rogers, Benney, Reiley, John Kelly, from November 12, 1844, to 1866; Patrick Corrigan, from 1866 to 1871; Victor Baudevin, from 1871.

St. Mary's R. C. Church, Jersey City, dates from April, 1859. The building is on the northeast corner of Erie and Third streets; corner stone laid in June, 1861; consecrated in May, 1863.

PASTOR—Rev. Dominick Senez, from April 1, 1859.

St. Mary's R. C. Church, West Hoboken. The building is on the northeast corner of High street and Clinton avenue; erected in 1851; consecrated November 23, 1851. In this church is a copy of an oil painting of "Our Lady of Mercy," presented by Cardinal Brignole, of Rome, who received it from Paci Typoliti, of Rimini, as an *ex-voto* for his preservation from death.

PASTOR—Rev. Anthony Cauvin, from July, 1851, to April 21, 1861. On this latter date the church was placed in charge of the Passionist Fathers of the Monastery.

St. Mary's R. C. Church, Hoboken. Services were first held in Hoboken in June, 1841, by Father Mohan, of St. Peter's, Jersey City. On December 6, 1844, Rev. John Rogers read mass in Phœnix Hotel, and continued in charge of the enterprise until April 1, 1845. In July, 1851, Rev. Anthony Cauvin took charge of that part of the county which lies north of the Five Corners. The church building is on the corner of Willow and Fifth streets; corner stone laid September 3, 1854; consecrated June 24, 1855. The large painting in this church is a copy of the Madonna of Foligno, by Raphael, executed by order of Charles Felix, King of Sardinia, by him bequeathed to the Duke of Genoa, brother of the King of Italy, and by him presented to Father Cauvin in 1854. It was crowned by Bishop Bayley June 20, 1858. The crown was presented by the Duchess of Genoa. In a side altar repose the "Relics of St. Quietus, Martyr," deposited June 1, 1856; found in the Catacombs January 29, 1849;

presented by Pope Pius IX. The chalice and sanctuary lamp were presented by the Emperor Napoleon III.; the silver ostensorium by Victor Emmanuel, and the painting of the Crucifixion by Henry Hoguet, of New York.

PASTOR—Rev. Anthony Cauvin, from July 1851, to Aug., 1873.

St. Joseph's R. C. Church, Jersey City, was organized as *St. Bridget's* in June, 1856. The first church building was a frame structure on Hopkins avenue, erected in 1856. The second church building was on the southeast corner of Baldwin and Pavonia avenues; corner stone laid in August, 1857; opened for service December 25, 1857; consecrated October 17, 1858. The third church building is on the site of the second; corner stone laid July 19, 1869; basement opened for service June 8, 1871; building consecrated September 14, 1873.

PASTORS—Rev. James Coyle, 1856-7; Aloysius Vanuta, 1857.

St. Mary's Star of the Sea R. C. Church, Bergen Point. The church building was consecrated March 18, 1860.

PASTORS—Fathers Callan, Vincent, Timothy, Neilass and Neiderhauser

St. Patrick's R. C. Church, Jersey City, organized May 1, 1870. The church building is on the northeast corner of Ocean and Bramhall avenues; corner stone laid November 13, 1870; chapel opened for service November 10, 1872.

St. Michael's R. C. Church, Jersey City, was established as *St. Mary's*. The first building was on the southwest corner of Erie and Tenth streets; erected in 1855; opened for service Oct. 21, 1855. The present church building is on the north side of Hamilton square; corner stone laid September 8, 1872; dedicated August 17, 1873.

PASTOR—Father Da Concilio.

St. Boniface R. C. Church, Jersey City, was organized in 1862. The church building is on the north side of First street, between Erie street and Jersey avenue; corner stone laid in June, 1864; basement opened for service in November, 1864.

PASTOR—Rev. Dominick Kraus.

Our Lady of Grace R. C. Church, Jersey City, was incorporated September 20, 1864.

St. Paul's R. C. Church, Greenville, was incorporated October 12, 1864.

Church of the Holy Family, Union Hill, was incorporated February 23, 1869. The church building is on the north side of Jefferson street, between Bergen Wood and Bergen Line avenues.
PASTOR—Rev. Vincent Nagler.

St. Paul's of the Cross R. C. Church, Jersey City, was incorporated September 15, 1867. The church building is on Hancock avenue, near Bowers avenue; corner stone laid in 1870; opened for service in 1871.
PASTOR—Rev. P. Bandinelli.

St. Bridget's R. C. Church, Jersey City. The church building is in Mercer street; consecrated June 5, 1870. A new building is nearly completed.

St. Pius R. C. Church, Hoboken, was incorporated June 9, 1861.
PASTOR—Rev. James J. McGahan.

St. Paul's R. C. Church, Jersey City. The church is on the corner of Manners and Bergen avenues; corner stone laid in May, 1869; basement opened for service January 1, 1870.

St. Paul's German R. C. Church, Hoboken, was organized in October, 1871.
PASTOR—Rev. Angelus Kempen.

St. Joseph's R. C. Church, Guttenberg, was incorporated March 19, 1866.
PASTOR—Rev. Timothy Pacitti.

R. C. Church, East Newark, corner stone laid August 13, 1871.[1]

R. C. Church on Washington avenue, near Van Vorst avenue; corner stone laid in 1869; consecrated October 16, 1870.[1]

---

[1] Of these two churches I have no reliable information.

St. Michael's Monastery, West Hoboken, founded in 1863; corner stone laid July 18, 1864.

Congregational Churches.

The First Congregational Church, Jersey City, was incorporated September 10, 1841. It did not thrive.

The Tabernacle Church, Jersey City, was organized April 14, 1858; incorporated April 13, 1859. The building is on the southeast corner of Henderson and York streets; dedicated in May, 1862. In 1858 services were held in Franklin Hall; in 1861 in the Lyceum in Grand street; from 1861 to 1862 in the Unitarian church on the corner of Montgomery and Grove streets.

Pastors.

Rev. William C. Bartlett in 1858; Rev. John Milton Holmes,[1] from May 23, 1861, to May, 1869; Rev. Giles B. Wilcox, from December 8, 1869, to the present time.

The Second Congregational Church, Jersey City, was organized June 9, 1869; recognized October 13, 1869. The building is on the southwest corner of Summit and St. Paul's avenues; dedicated May 8, 1870.

Pastors.

Rev. Leavitt Bartlett, from June, 1869, to July, 1871; Rev. George Lewis, from August, 1871.

German Churches.

The German Evangelical Lutheran St. Paul's Church, in Harsimus, was incorporated October 24, 1850; Rev. A. Geissenheimer, pastor. Its existence was brief.

The German Evangelical Lutheran St. Matthias Church, Jersey City, was organized in 1860. The society purchased the Bethesda Baptist Church building in 1862.

---

[1] Died September 20, 1871.

PASTORS.

Revs. Carl M. Wassidlo, from November, 1860, to February, 1862; Julius Augustus Bangeroth, from February, 1862, to May 28, 1866; George Ewh, from June 17, 1866, to the present time.

The German Evangelical Lutheran St. Matthias Church, Hoboken, was organized November 23, 1856. The church building is on the southwest corner of Washington and Third streets, purchased of the First Presbyterian Church, April 10, 1864.

PASTOR—Rev. Carl M. Wassidlo, from the organization to the present time.

Immanuel's Church of the Evangelical Association, Union Hill, was organized in 1865; incorporated June 27, 1865. The building is on the west side of New York avenue, between Union and Lewis streets; erected in 1865.

PASTORS.

Revs. Christian Meyer, 1865–7; Adam Gatchel, 1867–9; Gustav Sharp, 1869–70; Nicholas Gable, 1870–3; T. A. Plattenberg, 1873.

Zion Church of the Evangelical Association, Greenville, was organized May 30, 1866. The building is on the south side of Waverly avenue, near Bergen avenue; begun in 1866; completed in 1867. The name was afterward changed to *Evangelical Lutheran Zion Church.*

PASTORS.

Revs. Ryaha, Kuhn, Shuner.

Salem Church of the Evangelical Association, Greenville, was incorporated June 3, 1869. The building is on the west side of Bergen avenue, between Pearsall avenue and Factory lane; erected in 1870.

PASTORS.

Revs. Nicholas Goebel; Emanuel Glazer.

The German Independent Congregation, Hoboken, was incorporated April 3, 1867.

UNITARIANS.

The Unitarian Church, Jersey City, was organized in 1853. The building (now St. Mark's) is on the southeast corner of Grove and Montgomery streets; dedicated September 19, 1855.

PASTOR—Rev. O. B. Frothingham, until 1858. The organization shortly afterward disbanded.

UNIVERSALISTS.

As early as 1852 an attempt was made to organize a church of this faith. Services were held in a schoolhouse near the Five Corners. The effort did not succeed. The attempt was renewed December 10, 1871. This resulted in an organization in January, 1872, which was incorporated as *The First Universalist Church* of Jersey City, March 13, 1872. It purchased the old Emory M. E. Church building on the northeast corner of Mill road and Colden place; opening services October 20, 1872.

POPULATION of Bergen County, including Hudson County:

Year	Population	Year	Population	Year	Population
1729	2,218	1790	12,601	1820	18,178
1737	4,095	1800	15,956	1830	22,412
1745	3,006	1810	16,603		

In 1802 Paulus Hoeck had a population of 13, made up of Major David Hunt and family, John Murphy and wife and Joseph Bryant.

TABLE showing the number of inhabitants in the several cities and townships in Hudson County:

Year.	Jersey City.	Van Vorst Township.	Bergen.	Hudson City.	Hoboken.	Harrison.	North Bergen.	West Hoboken.	Town of Union.	Union.	Bayonne City.	Greenville.	Weehawken.	Kearney.
1829	1,025	....	....	....	....	....	....	....	....	....	....	....	....	....
1837	2,084	923	....	....	....	....	....	....	....	....	....	....	....	....
1840	3,033	1,057	4,211	....	....	1,103	....	....	....	....	....	....	....	....
1843	3,700	1,500	....	....	....	....	....	....	....	....	....	....	....	....
1845	4,258	....	....	....	....	....	....	....	....	....	....	....	....	....
1846	5,418	2,400	....	....	....	....	....	....	....	....	....	....	....	....
1847	5,862	....	....	....	....	....	....	....	....	....	....	....	....	....
1848	5,899	3 601	....	....	....	....	....	....	....	....	....	....	....	....
1849	6,384	....	....	....	....	....	....	....	....	....	....	....	....	....
1850	6,856	4,617	2,758	....	2,668	1,345	3,578	....	....	....	....	....	....	....
1855	21,715	....	4,972	3,322	6,727	1,516	3,571	....	....	....	....	....	....	....
1860	29,226	....	7,429	7,229	9,659	2,556	6,335	....	....	....	....	....	280	....
1865	38,371	....	7,000	13,151	12,976	2,375	2,891	4,232	4,379	....	1,700	1,356	388	....
1870	82,545	....	....	....	20,297	4,129	3,032	4,132	4,640	2,097*	3,834	2,789	597	974

* The abstract of the United States census gives 2,097 as the population of this township in 1870. The census puts it down as 6,737, which is probably an error.

TABLE of Criminal Charges upon which Courts and Juries in Hudson County have acted:

	1840.	1841.	1842.	1843.	1844.	1845.	1846.	1847.	1848.	1849.	1850.	1851.	1852.	1853.	1854.	1855.	1856.
Abduction																	
Abortion																	
Administering Drugs to Procure Abortion																	
Adultery												1					2
Arson			1								2						
Assault with Intent to Rob																	1
Assault and Battery	18	8	7	1	9	10	14	9	14	23	17	28	27	13	54		36
Assault with Intent to Kill	1				1		2				3		4	1			
Assault with Intent to Ravish	1	2							1		1				1		1
Atrocious Assault and Battery								1			5	1			1		
Baratry																	
Breaking and Entering*								2		1		2	2	1			1
Bribery																	
Burglary		1									1	1	2	1			4
Cockfighting																	
Concealing Pregnancy																	
Concealing Birth																	
Conspiracy					1												
Counterfeiting	4				1												6
Cruelty to Animals																	
Cutting Timber															6		
Disorderly House					2		1	1	1	5	2	4	2	9	19		4
Embezzlement												1					
Escape												1					
Exposing Person																	
Extortion																	
False Imprisonment																	
False Pretences							1				2			1	3		2
Forcible Entry																	
Forgery																	2
Fornication						1											1
Fraud																	
Gaming			1														
Having Burglars' Tools																	
Illegal Voting																	
Incest																	
Indecent Assault																	
Infanticide													1				

	1857.	1858.	1859.	1860.	1861.	1862.	1863.	1864.	1865.	1866.	1867.	1868.	1868.†	1869.	1869.	1870.	1870.	1871.	1871.	1872.	1872.	1873.	1873.
Abduction																		1					
Abortion																						3	
Administering Drugs to Procure Abortion																						1	
Adultery		1		2		2		3			2	1			1	2	1	1	3		1		
Arson	1													2		2						1	1
Assault with Intent to Rob																							
Assault and Battery	45	45	33	31	58	44	39	60	37	85	97	72	52	64	53	48	38	71	43	66	77	73	62
Assault with Intent to Kill	3	1		4					1	4	6	6	2	10		5	1	4		2	1	1	1
Assault with Intent to Ravish	2	1	4	3	1					6	2	4	1	1	2	2	1			4		2	1
Atrocious Assault and Battery		3		10	6		4	3	9	7	4	6	1	15	4	16	2	13	13	17	12	24	6
Baratry																						1	
Breaking and Entering*	5	4	6	4	18	14	18	5	13	26	21	13	12	11	38	18	36	20	39	22	23	9	40
Bribery												4											
Burglary	6	11		7								1		1		1							
Cockfighting																						1	
Concealing Pregnancy											1									1			
Concealing Birth						2	1																
Conspiracy								1										2		8		3	
Counterfeiting	9	4	11	4	20	5	7	4	9		2					1	1						
Cruelty to Animals																1		3					1
Cutting Timber		2		1		1						1											
Disorderly House	1	4		2	14	5	1	1	2	8	3	2	1	2	1	1	1	4		2	2	38	
Embezzlement			1	3	1	1	1	1			4	1		2	1	1	5	3	2	4	1	5	2
Escape		1				1										1				1		3	
Exposing Person					1		1	1	1	4				1			4	1	3	1	2		1
Extortion								1				1		36		1				1			
False Imprisonment			1	1	1	2	2	2		1	2	1		3				2		9		2	
False Pretences		1	1	2	2	1		3	3	6	5	7	4	7	5	2		2	1	10	3	5	2
Forcible Entry					1																		
Forgery				1	2		1			11	3	1		2				1		2		2	
Fornication		1			1		1		1	1	1	4	1		1			3		1			
Fraud				1	1		1																
Gaming											1												
Having Burglars' Tools																1		1		3		1	
Illegal Voting						2								1		1				6			
Incest															1								
Indecent Assault							1			1				1	2			4		2		1	
Infanticide																							

Kidknapping																															1									
Larceny	3		2	2	2	4	7	3	7	12	7	11	10	6	28		17	23	32	21	27	18	17	26	37	49	59	58	43	96	39	76	14	76	41	82	38	91	47	104
Lewdness											1																							2					1	
Libel					1								1					1					1						1						2		8		1	
Making False Record																															1									
Malfeasance in Office																												1	2		3		2		1		56		3	
Malicious Mischief	1	1	1			1	1		1				2	3			2	4	2		4	1	1	1	1	1	1	3			2	1	3	2	1	5	2	6	1	7
Manslaughter														2	1					1	2	2				1			2		1	4	5						2	
Misdemeanor			1	2	1									1	13			2	1					2	3		3													
Murder				1	1		1			2	1		3	1	1		1	3			1	2	1	2	2				1				1		2		2		6	
Nuisance	2		1			2	1		1	4	2	2		6	3			2	2	9	4	8	18	11	4	2	6	5	7	2	21	1	3		14		27		6	
Obstructing Railroad																				1			1											1						1
Peddling without License																																		1						
Perjury				1											1		2	1	1		3			7			4	1	2		3		1		2				5	
Picking Pockets			1														2	1	3	2	3	4	7	5	2	2	5	9	5	2	4	8	5	5	3	6	3	9	1	3
Polygamy	1		1									1	3								1				1			2					1	1	2	1			2	
Pound Breach																							1																	
Prison Breach								1		2	1										1	1	4			2	1				1						3			
Prize Fighting																			1			4	2	1	2								2		1					
Rape		3				1	1					2	1				1	1			3		2		1	2	1	4	3		3		5		1				1	
Receiving Stolen Goods				1		1						5							1			2	6	3	5	1	4	4	2		5		3		4		3		5	
Rescue																			1																					
Resisting Officer																																	4	4		3		3	4	3
Riot					1			2	2		3	3						1	1	1		1	1	3	2		3	3			1		2				1			
Robbery														7	2		1	1	1	1		1			1	3	6		5				3		4		4		4	
Selling Liquor on Sunday										18	1	4	4	8	25		5				1	2	2		2	1	5	6				1							6	
Selling Liquor without License	16	22	2	3	6	1	9	21	24	43	9	50	1	3	60		4	4	3			8	2	2				17			1	1								
Selling Lottery Tickets																	17																						1	
Sending Threatening Letters																									1															
Sodomy																											1													
Subornation of Perjury																								2																
Violating Election Law																												1												

* This head includes "breaking with intent" and "entering with intent."

† The Special Sessions was organized in 1868, and this table covers all the cases instituted from that date up to December 1, 1873, and they are to be found in the second column in which the year is repeated.

TABLE showing by Cities and Townships the number of Pupils attending Public Schools, and amount of money received from the State annually:

YEAR.	JERSEY CITY.		BERGEN.		HARRISON.		VAN VORST.		NORTH BERGEN.		HOBOKEN.	
	Pupils.	Received from State.	Pupils.	Received from State.	Pupils.	Received from State.	Pupils.	Received from State.	Pupils.	Received from State.	Pupils.	Received from State.
1840	....	$160 09	....	$345 60	....	$103 30	....	....	....	....	....	....
1841	....	160 09	....	286 92	....	103 30	....	$58 67	....	....	....	....
1842	....	160 09	....	286 92	....	103 30	....	58 67	....	....	....	....
1843	No	report.	....	....	....	....	....	....	....	....	....	....
1844	No	report.	....	....	....	....	....	....	....	....	....	....
1845	No	report.	....	....	....	....	....	....	....	....	....	....
1846	....	138 76	....	119 23	....	135 13	....	71 40	....	$139 19	....	....
1847	....	143 45	....	117 16	....	129 76	....	65 04	....	159 59	....	....
1848	....	147 95	....	120 89	....	114 29	....	67 18	....	164 69	....	....
1849	....	147 92	....	133 21	....	101 99	....	67 18	....	164 70	....	....
1850	....	218 74	....	147 69	....	64 88	....	168 37	....	121 62	....	$98 70
1851	3,436	927 72	885	238 95	359	96 93	consol	idated.	1,119	302 13	606	163 62
1852*	4.208	1,977 76	1,034	490 21	359	168 73	....	....	1,252	588 44	713	335 11
1853*	4 398	1,869 05	1,144	486 10	277	117 72	....	....	1,430	607 75	1,072	455 60
1854*	4.851	1,867 63	1,130	512 05	331	127 43	....	....	1,719	661 81	1,067	410 79
1855*	5,437	1,875 76	1,427	492 31	330	113 85	....	....	1,853	639 28	1,281	441 94
1856*	5.584	1,409 96	1,385	349 70	323	81 55	....	....	1,321	333 54	1,261	318 39
1857*	5,746	1,787 00	1,546	480 80	413	128 43	....	....	1,380	429 18	1.376	427 93
1858*	5.903	1,850 59	1,661	520 72	458	143 58			1,412	442 66	1,415	456 14
1859*	5,959	1,710 23	1,757	504 26	460	132 02			1,442	413 85	1,600	459 20
1860*	6,280	1,679 48	1,829	486 52	488	129 80	UNION.		1,709	454 60	1,800	478 80
1861*	6,862	1,632 47	1,480	352 09	619	147 25	653	155 35	470	111 81	2.237	532 17
1862*	7,816	1,707 79	1,593	348 07	485	105 98	890	194 46	527	115 15	2,221	485 29
1863*	8.192	3,493 88	1,460	622 70	755	321 00	848	361 68	583	248 64	2.031	866 22
1864*	7,891	3,127 96	1,736	687 51	755	299 05	402	159 19	552	218 67	2,227	955 42
1865*	8,042	3,035 85	2,099	765 93	753	284 79	426	160 81	634	239 23	2,227	840 70
1866*	9,778	3,125 04	2,101	671 46	937	299 46	518	165 54	626	200 06	2.803	895 82
1867*	11,027	5,090 93	1,741	803 78	766	353 64	518	339 15	626	289 00	1,275	588 64
1868	11,051	4,793 99	2,300	997 75	814	353 12	569	246 84	699	303 32	2,866	1,243 29
1869	11,822	4,918 25	2,831	1,177 77	974	405 20	637	265 01	704	292 88	4,031	1,679 09
1870	20,165	8,241 27	consol	idated.	1,150	470 00	728	297 53	745	304 48	4,461	1,823 18
1871†	24,552	113,822 03	....	....	1,316	6,100 92	792	3,671 70	850	3,940 60	5,354	24,820 92
1872	24,635	117,525 73	....	....	1,406	6,707 59	852	4,064 62	905	4,317 47	6,037	28,800 61
1873	31,040	145,368 80	....	....	1,504	,043 64	905	4,238 35	931	4,360 10	5,560	26,039 00

Year.	Hudson City.		Bayonne.		West Hoboken.		Greenville.		Town of Union.		Weehawken.		Kearney.	
	Pupils.	Received from State.	Pupils.	Received from State.	Pupils.	Received from State.	Pupils.	Received from State.	Pupils.	Received from State.	Pupils	Received from State	Pupils	Received from State.
1856*	766	$193 41	....	....	....	....	....	....	....	....	..	....	.	....
1857*	972	302 29	....	....	....	....	....	....	....	....	..	....	..	....
1858*	573	179 64	....	....	....	....	....	....	....	....	..	....	..	....
1859*	1,204	345 54	....	....	....	....	....	....	....	....	..	....	..	....
1860*	1,339	356 18	....	....	....	....	....	....	....	....	..	....	..	....
1861*	1,539	366 12	596	$141 78	586	$139 40	....	....	....	....	..	....	..	....
1862*	1,539	335 27	596	130 22	688	150 33	....	....	....	....	..	....	..	....
1863*	1,967	839 32	607	258 88	718	306 22	340	$145 02	....	....	..	....	..	....
1864*	2,722	1,004 44	699	277 94	800	316 80	395	156 55	649	$256 07	..	....	..	....
1865*	2,909	1,098 34	715	269 90	869	327 84	417	156 41	722	272 55	..	$9 32	..	....
1866*	3,476	1,110 92	858	272 20	868	277 40	447	142 86	889	284 12	66	21 08	..	....
1867*	3,468	1,601 10	858	396 12	869	401 20	450	207 76	889	410 44	72	33 24	171	$78 95
1868	4,006	1,937 82	787	341 40	1,117	484 56	533	251 22	1,118	489 89	69	29 93	175	75 92
1869	4,998	2,079 29	903	375 67	1,243	517 01	600	249 62	1,157	481 32	83	34 53	192	79 88
1870	con	solidated.	835	341 00	1,244	508 41	633	238 70	1,280	523 12	71	29 02	184	75 20
1871†	....	....	1,000	4,635 96	1,373	6,365 09	797	3,694 87	1,321	6,124 11	90	417 24	225	1,043 09
1872	....	....	1,082	5,161 89	1,474	7,031 98	950	4,532 15	1,430	6,822 08	110	524 78	265	1,264 23
1873	....	....	1,162	5,441 96	1,604	7,511 98	con	solidated.	1,494	6,996 83	146	683 76	335	1,568 90

* During the years marked thus the payments were made by the State to the county in two instalments.

† In 1871 the apportionment to the county was from the two-mill tax and from the State appropriation of $100,000. The same of the years 1872 and 1873. The apportionment was based upon the number of children between five and eighteen years of age, as per the school census of the preceding year. Under the present law the school year begins on the 1st of September.

TABLE showing assessed valuation of property within the county:

Year	Valuation	Year	Valuation	Year	Valuation
1860	$33,191,925	1865	$54,005,755	1870	$88,670,950
1861	32,319,413	1866	63,833,913	1871	101,049,284
1862	40,698,056	1867	72,360,176	1872	97,478,477
1863	40,218,884	1868	78,849,212	1873	95,064,590
1864	49,837,349	1869	85,133,272		

TABLE showing the bonded indebtedness of the county:

Year	Amount	Year	Amount	Year	Amount
1862	$81,500 00	1866	$1,308,121 87	1870	$1,138,421 87
1863	145,421 87	1867	1,287,121 87	1871	1,133,421 87
1864	140,421 87	1868	1,280,221 87	1872	1,128,000 00
1865	1,182,921 87	1869	1,298,421 87	1873	1,123,000 00

TABLE showing the county and city taxes:

Year.	County.	Jersey City.	Bergen.	Hudson City.	Hoboken.	Bayonne.
1825	....	$100 00	....	....	....	....
1826	....	100 00	....	....	....	....
1827	....	100 00	....	....	....	....
1828	....	100 00	....	....	....	....
1829	....	300 00	....	....	....	....
1830	....	300 00	....	....	....	....
1831	....	300 00	....	....	....	....
1832	....	300 00	....	....	....	....
1833	....	300 00	....	....	....	....
1834	....	300 00	....	....	....	....
1835	....	300 00	....	....	....	....
1836	....	300 00	....	....		....
1837	....	300 00	....	....	....	....
1838	....	2,500 00	....	....	....	....
1839	....	3,165 28	....	....	....	....
1840	$3,000 00	3,186 24	....	....	....	....
1841	3,000 00	3,000 00	....	....	....	....
1842	3,000 00	3,200 00	....	....	....	....
1843	2,000 00	4,500 00	$1,200 00	....	....	....
1844	4,000 00	5,395 13	850 00	....	....	....
1845	4,000 00	6,000 00	850 00	....	....	....
1846	4,000 00	8,300 00	1,150 00	....	....	....
1847	5,000 00	12,000 00	1,275 00	....	....	....
1848	5,000 00	13,500 00	1,650 00	....	....	....
1849	6,000 00	15,000 00	1,490 00	....	$1,625 00	....
1850	6,000 00	15,000 00	3,160 00	....	2,725 00	....
1851	10,000 00	35,000 00	2,650 00	....	2,075 00	....
1852	10,000 00	38,000 00	2,700 00	....	2,850 00	....
1853	20,000 00	55,800 00	3,700 00	....	3,100 00	....
1854	15,000 00	60,800 00	4,000 00	....	3,505 00	....
1855	20,000 00	79,500 00	4,250 00	$7,062 00	11,800 00	....
1856	20,000 00	81,950 00	4,700 00	8,925 00	14,750 00	....
1857	20,000 00	87,250 00	5,500 00	15,188 00	15,700 00	....
1858	20,000 00	88,200 00	6,500 00	13,923 25	16,375 00	....
1859	20,000 00	87,310 00	7,900 00	17,181 00	20,805 00	....
1860	25,000 00	105,788 28	7,925 00	18,575 00	22,012 20	....
1861	30,000 00	94,188 17	6,000 00	16,000 00	23,495 00	....
1862	30,000 00	107,794 28	6,000 00	18,300 00	23,495 00	....
1863	50,000 00	124,752 30	22,000 00	21,260 00	24,495 00	....
1864	60,000 00	194,253 78	26,271 25	40,200 00	33,695 00	....
1865	160,000 00	267,000 00	70,371 08	41,125 00	55,795 00	....
1866	200,000 00	310,220 40	75,902 00	44,500 00	70,516 00	....
1867	270,000 00	404,270 64	81,405 00	58,400 00	103,366 00	....
1868	350,000 00	486,579 43	106,525 00	86,800 00	108,031 00	....
1869	350,000 00	444,997 75	154,141 67	116,450 00	142,543 50	$31,620 00
1870	425,000 00	1,113,111 49			160,035 50	58,906 00
1871	433,000 00	1,103,456 65	Consolidated with Jersey City.		146,155 50	65,003 00
1872	485,000 00	1,445,882 81			131,329 00	69,975 00
1873	500,000 00	1,231,111 20			151,135 00	74,103 62

TABLE showing Hudson County's quota of State tax:*

Year	Amount	Year	Amount	Year	Amount
1840	$410 00	1847	$410 00	1867	$49,351 19
1841	615 00	1861	11,788 08	1868	53,225 58
1842	820 00	1862	63,852 46	1869	54,903 88
1843	820 00	1863	35,724 00	1870	85,135 27
1844	820 00	1864	29,240 00	1871	88,670 95
1845	820 00	1865	38,260 00	1872	101,049 28
1846	820 00	1866	51,914 00	1873	146,217 71

* From 1848 to 1860 inclusive, no State tax was levied.

State school tax paid by the county under the present law—1871, $177,341.90; 1872, $202,008.56; 1873, $194,956.95.

Amount received by the county from the State under the present law—1872, 16,052.88; 1873, $172,034.26; 1874, $193,247.18.

CHAPTER XIII.—GENEALOGIES.

Van Vorst Family—Vreeland Family—Van Winkle Family—Van Wagenen Family—Van Buskirk Family—Van Ripen Family—Van Horn Family—Newkirk Family—Garrabrant Family—Sip Family—Brinkerhoff Family—Schuyler Family—Kingsland Family—Gautier Family—Cadmus Family.

MUCH labor has been expended in writing up the following brief genealogies, and yet the result is confessedly imperfect. All that can be said in its favor is, the author has done the best he could in the face of difficulties and discouragements which need not be described. One who has not undertaken a similar task is not prepared to comprehend how difficult it is to trace out the genealogies of the old Dutch families. There was not among those who originally settled within the limits of this county, more than one family which had a name. That single one was *Van Voorst*, now *Van Vorst;* and even this sat so loosely, by reason of its novelty, that *Ide*, of the second generation, was as often called *Ide Cornelissen*, i. e., *Ide*, the son of *Cornelis*, as *Ide Van Vorst.* Nearly all of the early settlers here were of the peasantry, who came out as farm servants or soldiers in the service of the Dutch West India Company. This class of settlers had no surname, for they had not earned one. They were known from each other of the same name by using

---

Note.—The figures in parentheses (56) point forward to that number in the family name. The figures in brackets [3] point backward to that number in the family name. The figures in parentheses (35) following the second name of parties married refer to the number of that person in his or her respective family name. The figures 1, 2, 3, etc., indicate position in the family genealogy, while the numerals XII. denote the number of the child in the particular family. For illustration:

Enoch [3] had ch.:

21. XII. Joris (56), b. Sept. 25, 1710; m. 2d, Annetje Van Wagenen (35).

This reads as follows: Enoch, who stands third in the Vreeland genealogy, had children, the twelfth of whom stands the twenty-first in the same genealogy; that this son, Joris, had for his second wife Annetje Van Wagenen, who stands thirty-fifth in the genealogy of that family; and that the first child of Joris stands fifty-sixth in the Vreeland genealogy.

Abbreviations.—b., born; m., married; d., died; s., son; dau., daughter; unm., unmarried; ch., child or children; s. p., without issue; bap., baptized; inf., infancy; mos., months; yrs., years; wid., widow; æt., age.

the father's christian name as a surname for themselves. For example, *Jan* had a son named *Michael*. He would be known as *Michael Jansen*, i. e., *Michael*, the son of *Jan*. If *Michael* had a son named *Pieter*, he would be known as *Pieter Michaelson*, i. e., *Pieter*, son of *Michael*. But if the fathers bore the same Christian name, of course the sons would bear the same surname; and thus difficulties and uncertainties were multiplied. In some cases it was not until the second generation that family names were chosen. These were generally (especially those having the prefix "Van") derived from the business, occupation, place of emigration, or some peculiar trait of the founder of the family.

The *Schuyler* and *Gautier* families were not among the earliest settlers. The other families herein mentioned were. As a rule, the bounds of the county and the names of the families limit the extent of the genealogies. Only in a few instances has there been a trespass beyond.

Van Voorst—Van Vorst.

This name is supposed to be derived from a small place in Gelderland, near the river Yssel, called *Voorst*. There was another place in Belgium, in the province of Antwerp, called *Vorst*.

How many of this name came to this country prior to the middle of the seventeenth century is not known. In 1638 a suit was pending before the council in New Amsterdam against Cornelis and Jan Van Vorst.[1] It is quite certain that the second defendant in that suit named was not the son of Cornelis, for he was yet a minor in 1641.[2] In 1639 the West India Company's bouwerie No. 6, on Manhattan, was leased to a Jan Van Voorst, who is probably the one named in the above suit. It is also probable that he was a brother of Cornelis. That he could not have been the son is strengthened by the fact that in 1642 one Garret, son of Jan Van Vorst, was of sufficient age to be employed in the construction of buildings,[3] and to have a family. Jan Geritsen Van Vorst is presumed to have been his son, and quite young when his father was killed. He m. Sara Waldron,

---

[1] *N. Y. Col MSS., iv.*, 11.

[2] *Ibid, iv.*, 89. It is well to bear in mind, however, that under the Dutch law children did not attain their majority until they reached the age of twenty-five years.

[3] *Broadhead, i.*, 347. He was shot by an Indian while thatching a roof near Hackensack.

July 9, 1662; had ch. Johannis, bap. June 29, 1663. This son lived in New York; m. Anneke Hercks, Aug. 26, 1685; had ch. I. Sara, bap. May 24, 1686; II. Herck, bap. Jan. 1, 1688; III. Wyntje, bap. Jan. 19, 1690; IV. Sibout, bap. Aug. 12, 1692; V. Annetje, bap. Sept. 19, 1694.

Cornelis Van Voorst came to this country at an early date. While the Lord of Achtienhoven was yet Patroon of Pavonia, and Walter the Doubter was Director-General of New Netherland, Van Voorst settled at Ahasimus as superintendent of the colonie. The date of his arrival has been set down as 1636. This is probably an error. In *N. Y. Col. MSS.*, i., 127, is a certified copy of a note, dated Sept. 8, 1634, made by Van Voorst in favor of Peter Cock, for the price of two-thirds of a sloop. From this it is inferable that he was in this country at that time. If this be so, it is probable that he returned to Holland in 1635, was appointed by Pauw to superintend his colonie, returned and settled in Pavonia prior to June 25, 1636.[1] His second wife was Vrouwtje Ides. He died in the summer of 1638; she died in March or April, 1641.[2] She was an energetic woman, not easily overcome by difficulties. After the death of her husband she leased the farm at Ahasimus for a term of twenty years, agreeing to pay therefor one quarter of the produce, to build a new frame house, and keep those already built in repair—the Director agreeing to furnish the necessary brick for the chimney.[3] She also hired from the Director-General three ewes and two rams, yielding therefor one-half of the milk and of the increase.[4] In the latter part of the year 1639 she married Jacob Stoffelsen.[5]

---

[1] *N. Y. Hist. Soc. N. S., i.*, 259. [2] *N. Y. Col. MSS., i.*, 238, 241.

[3] *Ibid, i.*, 92. Bricks were brought from Holland at that time.

[4] *Ibid, i.*, 117.

[5] Stoffelsen was born in 1601, *Col. Hist. of N. Y., i.*, 194; came from Zirickzee, the chief city of the island of Schowen, and the oldest city of Zeeland, to this country at an early date. *Powers of Atty. New Amst.*, 39. In 1633 he was "Commissary of Stores," *New Neth. Reg.*, 30, and overseer of the Company's negroes, *N. Y. Col. MSS., i.*, 84; chosen one of the "Twelve" in 1641, *Col. Hist. of N. Y., i.*, 415; one of the "Eight" in 1645; in the same year one of the Directors' Council, *pro hac vice*, to consult on Indian affairs, *New Neth. Reg.*, 15. In 1656 he hired the Company's Bouwerie at Ahasimus, where he continued to reside until his death in 1677. In 1639 he married the widow of Cornelis Van Voorst, and in 1657, being a widower, married Tryntje, the widow of Jacob Walingen Van Hoorn, *Valentine's Manual*, 1861, 648, by whom he had two children, viz., Stoffel and Jacobus. *Ibid*, 1863, 813. In the same year he was admitted to the rights of a small burgher, *New Neth. Reg.*, 183. He was an uneducated man, but greatly respected, and of considerable influence with the Indians. That he was a man of integrity appears from the fact that on the expiration of his term of service he was re-hired at increased wages, the director saying, "No more industrious and faithful workman as overseer could be employed in the Company's service." *Alb. Rec., ii.*, 14.

Immediately after her death dominie Bogardus and Tymen Jansen, as guardians of her children, came forward and claimed her property. An inventory was made April 15, 1641, a copy of which is here inserted for the purpose of showing the personal effects of a well-to-do family in those days:

"Inventory of goods belonging to dame Ides and Jacob Stoffelsen, which, in presence of Everardus Bogardus and Tymen Jansen, guardians of Anna and Ide Van Vorst, surviving children of dame Ides, were found in Pavonia at her house:[1]

3 Jacobuses *a* 12 florins each, - - - - -	fl. 36	
131 Holland shillings, - - - - - - - -	38	
13 Rix dollars *a* 50 stivers, - - - - - - - -	32	10
In double and single stivers, - - - - - -	15	
2 pieces *a* 10½ stivers, - - - - - - - - -	1	1
In English gold, - - - - - - - - -	2	

1 gold hoop ring; 1 silver medal and chain; 1 ditto undergirdle with ring to hang keys; 3 silver spoons; 2 small silver brandy cups; 1 silver goblet; 2 ells black wampum; 2 two-year-old oxen; 3 yearling heifers; 4 old ewes; 2 ewe lambs and 3 rams of this year; 5 cows; 2 mares; 1 yearling stallion; 1 bull and 1 heifer of this year; 4 yearling hogs; 1 boat with its apparel; 1 old yawl; 1 old-fashioned clock; 2 pairs of old stockings; 1 damask furred jacket, half worn; 1 new blue kersey petticoat, unmade; 1 new red bodice; 3 ells of red camlet; 1 white waistcoat; 2 table cloths, colored, of English manufacture; 1 pair of new and one pair of old pattens; 1 black camlet jacket, lined; 1 borst of woolen yarn; 1 pair of damask sleeves, half worn; 1 black coarse camlet jacket; 1 woman's steel gray lined petticoat; 1 black coarse camlet petticoat, lined, half worn; 1 reddish morning gown, not lined; 1 white waistcoat of Harlem stuff; 1 pair of spectacles with case; 1 pair of Spanish leather pattens; 1 new purple apron; 19 cambric caps; 4 linen ditto; 1 half worn red petticoat; 2 old black skirts; 1 old iron gray doublet; 1 new black kersey doublet; 1 fur cap trimmed up with beaver; 1 little black vest with two sleeves; 4 pair of sheets, good and bad; 4 new blue cotton aprons; 9 linen handkerchiefs with lace; 1 do without lace; 2 pillow slips; 3 shifts, half worn; 1 old table cloth; 4 napkins; 5 bear skins; 40 ells of duffels; 2 beds; 4 blankets, old and new; 6 pieces of mink; 10 pewter platters, large and small; 1 pewter basin; 1 tankard and two cups of pewter; 4 tin funnels; 1 little goblet; 2 English salt cellars; 1

[1] *Alb. Rec., i.*, 238, 241.

pewter mug; 1 wooden mortar and pestle; 1½ pewter mutsje;[1] 3 little pewter cups; 1 pewter mustard pot; 1 small tin can with screwed cover; 1 brass warming pan; 2 brass candlesticks; 2 brass snuffers; 2 little brass scales and one balance; 9 pewter plates; 1 iron tongs; 1 iron gridiron; 1 old wagon; 1 good foot plow with 1 coulter; 1 old wheel plow; 2 harrows, 1 with iron and 1 with wooden teeth; 2 pine boxes; 7 copper stove kettles, one partially old among them; 4 milk pails; 1 churn; 6 scythes; 2 new spades; 4 old geese; 2 ganders; 1 iron pan; 2 snaphaunce;[2] 1 broken ditto; 4 pistols; 2 silver spoons; 1 English shilling; 4 old goats; 2 young ditto; 1 yearling sow.

In shillings, double and single stivers & English money, fl.	19	
1 Jacobus *a* - - - - - - - - - - -	12	
17 Rix dollars *a* 50 stivers, - - - - - -	42	10
1 single dollar *a* 30 stivers, - - - - - - -	1	11

"All the preceding is thus found at the house of Jacob Stoffelsen, at Ahasimus, who on his manly troth declares that he has not and does not know of any more chattels than are hereinbefore mentioned belonging to the aforesaid estate.

"Done in Pavonia the 15th April, A° 1641, New Netherland.

"This is the [mark] mark of

"JACOB STOFFELSEN."

Second Generation.

Cornelius had ch.:

2. I. Hendrick, b. in Holland. So far as appears he was the first white person who cultivated the bouwerie at Hoboken. He went to Holland in the summer of 1639, and d. unm. shortly after his arrival there.

3. II. Jan, b. in Holland about 1616. On arriving at his majority in 1641, he took possession of his inheritance,[3] but so far as appears did not reside in this county.

4. III. Annetje, m. Claes Jansen Van Purmerendt, Nov. 11, 1656. In the marriage record she is named "Anneken Cornelissen of Voorst." Her husband was a tobacco planter on Paulus Hoeck. In 1650 she was engaged to be married to Pieter Kock, her father's former partner in the sloop. He was a man of some note, a sergeant in the war of 1643,

[1] A gill measure. [2] Snaphaans, a firelock, fusee. [3] *Alb. Rec.*, *i.*, 270.

and enrolled as a small burgher in 1654. During these happy days many presents were made to her by Pieter. When she was wooed and won by the tobacco planter, Pieter brought suit "in the matter of matrimony" before the Burgomasters and Schepens in New Amsterdam to recover the presents. The suit was pending for more than a year, the record in the mean while having been sent up to their "High and Mighty Lordships, the Director-General and Councillors, to obtain thereon a verdict."[1] The judgment was: "Whereas a certain process has been moved before the court of the city of New Amsterdam by Pieter Kock, single man, a burgher and inhabitant of the said city, as plaintiff at and against Anna Van Vorst, single woman, living at Ahasimus, defendant, respecting a marriage contract or a verbal promise of marriage between the said Pieter Kock and Anna Van Vorst, mutually entered into, and in confirmation thereof certain gifts and presents were made by the plaintiff to the aforesaid defendant, however, it appears by certain documents exhibited by the parties to the defendant and bride of the plaintiff in consequence of certain misgivings is in no way disposed to be married to the said Pieter Kock, and it is also proved by two witnesses on the 24th of December, 1653, testifying that Pieter Kock had given her up with a promise of a written acquittal, therefore the Burgomasters and Schepens of the city having perused the documents exhibited by the parties, and having examined, do by these presents decide that, as the promise of marriage has been made before the Omniscient God, it shall remain in force, so that neither the plaintiff nor the defendant, without the knowledge and approbation of their Lordships, the Magistrates, and the other one of the registered parties shall be permitted to enter matrimony with any other person, whether single man or single woman, provided, however, that all the presents made in confirmation of the marriage contract shall remain in the possession of the defendant,[2] while

[1] *Alb. Rec., v.*, 250.

[2] This was no misfortune to Pieter, for what of his worldly goods the gentle Annetje had not received, a thieving fellow named Marten Van Waert, son-in-law of Abraham Isaacsen Planck, in part appropriated. For this he was sentenced to "be severely scourged with rods in a closed chamber, banished ten years out of this jurisdiction, and further in the costs and *mises* of justice." His father-in-law secured his pardon. *Valentine's Manual*, 1849, 409. On the occasion of his marriage with Susanna Planck, December 4, 1660, Marten attempted to cheat the government out of the excise on a half barrel of beer. Occasionally he "committed great insolence, noise and uproar by night, and at unseasonable hours, as well at Obe's house as in the street; yes, so much that many sprung out of bed, opened doors and windows, not knowing what was going on." He finally came to grief, for "Pieter, the negro," executed sentence upon him. *Ibid*, 1861, 541. A likely heir to Paulus Hoeck!

the parties remain together in good will and contentment with each other, or lawful marriage or until the consent of one another, they shall be exempted from the contract. Furthermore, both the plaintiff and the defendant are condemned equally in the costs of this suit."

This sentence was pronounced May 18, 1654.[1] From it Annetje appealed, but it was confirmed. She united with the church in Bergen, Feb. 19, 1672; d. Jan. 12, 1725; her husband d. Nov. 30, 1688. Their ch. were known by the name of Kuyper.[2]

5. IV. Ide (6) is said to have been the first white male child born and married in New Netherland.[3] In the war of 1643 the "little boy" was captured by the Indians and taken to Tappaen. Captain de Vries and a couple of friendly natives, a few days afterward, went up and ransomed him. He m. Hilletje Jans, of Oldenburgh,[4] Oct. 18, 1652. That he had a good time at his wedding is learned incidentally from the record of a law suit between him and his stepfather about two years afterward. It appears that Stoffelsen had some time previous given a dinner to Captain Geurt Tysen and his friends, and in return the captain had presented Stoffelsen with a negro. Two sheep were required for the entertainment, and these being taken from the common flock, Ide claimed to own one-half of them, and therefore one-half of the negro. Stoffelsen replied that Ide had *two sheep at his wedding*, and these having also come out of the common flock balanced accounts, leaving the negro to him.[5]

He continued to reside at Ahasimus as a farmer, accumulating wealth which was to enable him to become the owner of not an inconsiderable part of the domains of Pauw.[6] He braved the dangers of border life, and exposed his property and family to

[1] *New Amst. Rec.*, i., 463. [2] *Winfield's Land Titles*, 42.
[3] *Valentine's Manual*, 1862, 768.
[4] Oldenburgh was a place of considerable importance in Holstein, on the river Brockaw. It was at one time the capital of the Wagri and Venedi, two warlike nations.
[5] *Ibid*, 1849, 382. *New Amst. Rec.* [6] *Winfield's Land Titles*, 40, 44, 121.

the attack of the stealthy savage rather than abandon his home. During the war of 1655 he took refuge in New Amsterdam, but returned to his farm when peace was established. Yet he was in danger, and occasionally obliged to fly for his life. One day in October, 1659, the Indians came down upon him as he was engaged in dressing some meat near his house. Seizing the meat, he fled to his boat, and pulled across the river to New Amsterdam. The Solons who administered justice in that great city could not wink at such a gross breach of the law, and they solemnly fined him twenty guilders and costs, "for bringing meat to the city without taking out excise license."[1]

In illustration of the strictness with which the laws were enforced in his day, the following is inserted: "Cornelis Aersen, Ide Van Vorst and their servants, complained of, for that their servants raced on Sunday evening after sermon, with horses and wagons, and much noise and singing, from which great damage and disaster might have arisen." Each master was fined three guilders, and they were ordered to watch themselves, so that all dangers and irregularities might be prevented.

His name, Ide, was probably the name of his mother's father, as her name was Ides. His wife survived him, and d. July 18, 1705.

Third Generation.

Ide [5] had ch.:

6. I. Vrouwtje, bap. Aug. 24, 1653; m. Andries Meyer, of New York, Nov. 5, 1671.
7. II. Annetje, b. in 1655; m. John Meyer, of New York, June 13, 1677.
8. III. Cornelius, bap. Aug. 26, 1657; d. in inf.
9. IV. Pietertje, bap. Nov. 9, 1659; m. Merselis Pieterse in 1680; d. Sept. 3, 1744.
10. V. Cornelius (12), bap. July 30, 1662; m. Fitje Gerritse Van Wagenen (4), of Communipaw, April 6, 1685; d. July —, 1753.

---

[1]*New Amst. Rec., iv.,* 68.

11. VI. Joanna, bap. April 16, 1666; m. Jan Adrianse Sip (3), April 22, 1684.

Fourth Generation.

Cornelius [10] had ch.:

12. I. Ide, bap. July 10, 1687; d. Dec. 7, 1689.
13. II. Jannetje, b. June 5, 1688; d. unm.
14. III. Gerrit (23), bap. May 1, 1689; m. Sarah Van Winkle (19), May 22, 1714; he removed to New Barbadoes Neck, near Aquackanonck; his will, dated June 13, 1764, was proved June 15, 1785. Some of his descendants returned, and settled near West Hoboken and Union Hill.
15. IV. Hillegond, b. March 2, 1682; d. Jan. 31, 1710.
16. V. Annetje, bap. Jan. 28, 1694; m. Martin Winne, Dec. 9, 1713.
17. VI. Ide, b. Dec. 4, 1695; d. unm.; VII. Johannis, b. May 7, 1697.
18. VIII. Hendrick, b. Jan. 29, 1699; d. unm.
19. IX. Cornelius (31), b. March 8, 1700; m. Claesje, dau. of Mattys De Mott, Nov. 26, 1726; d. Dec. 5. 1760. He represented Bergen in the 18th Provincial Assembly, in 1751.
20. X. Jacob, b. July 7, 1702. His name does not appear in his father's will, hence it is inferred that he was then dead, s. p.
21. XI. Jannetje, b. March 7, 1704; m. Walter Heyer, Aug. 8, 1723.
22. XII. Maritje, b. May 22, 1706; m. Isaac Hennion, in 1726.

Fifth Generation.

Gerrit [14] had ch.:

23. I. Fitje, m. Gerrebrand Jurrianse Van Ripen (32), Jan. 6, 1742.
24. II. Annetje, m. Frederick Van Ripen (34), Dec. 2, 1742.
25. III. Jenneke, m. Johannis Vreeland.
26. IV. Cornelius (34), m. 1st, Annetje Toers, Dec. —, 1752; 2d, Annatje Outwater, wid. of Abraham Berry, July 2, 1778.
27. V. Waling, b. April 5, 1729; d. in inf.
28. VI. Waling (37), b. March 30, 1731; m. Catrina Van Eydestyn, Sept. —, 1755.
29. VII. Maritje; IX. Hilletje.

30. VIII. Catrina had ch.: I. Catrina, b. Dec. 23, 1754; vader onbekent.

Cornelius [19] had ch.:

31. I. Cornelius (42), b. Nov. 25, 1728; m. Annetje Van Horn (8), April 21, 1753; d. Sept. 30, 1818. He was popularly known as "Faddy;" was one of the wealthiest men in the county, full of fun and practical jokes. He was fond of fast horses, and drove the best team in the vicinity. He established the race course on Paulus Hoeck in 1753, and was the lion of that "Derby." But while he loved the genial side of life, he did not forget its weightier duties. He established the Jersey City ferry in 1764. When the Revolution broke out he took decided ground on the side of his country. At a meeting of the inhabitants of Bergen county, held at Hackensack, June 25, 1774, he was appointed one of a "committee for corresponding with the committees of the other counties in this province, and particularly to meet with the other county committees at New Brunswick, * * * in order to elect delegates to attend a general Congress of Delegates of the *American Colonies*."[1] On June 29, 1776, the Provincial Congress appointed him lieutenant-colonel of the battalion of foot militia in the county of Bergen.[2] It is doubtful, however, if he ever was in actual service. Shortly after the capture of New York by the British, and the fall of Paulus Hoeck, his house at Harsimus was occupied by the officers of a detachment of cavalry. He and his family were crowded into the kitchen.[3] The fact that he continued to reside on his place while in possession of the enemy aroused suspicion that he had become a tory. On Nov. 10, 1776, he was charged before the court with having joined the British. After a thorough investigation he was honorably acquitted.

During this occupancy of his house by the enemy the officers were in the practice, for their own

[1] *Am. Archives, 4th Series, i.*, 450. [2] *Ibid, vi.*, 1633.

[3] Part of this kitchen is yet standing.

amusement, of discharging muskets up the chimney. One day, his mother being sick, he requested them to desist. This they haughtily refused to do. Being a powerful man, he proceeded to vindicate his rights by administering a drubbing to the insolent soldiers. Incarceration in the old sugar house was the consequence of attempting to administer justice *inter arma*. Sir Henry Clinton, then in command at New York, was an old school companion of Van Vorst,[1] and released him with the admonition not to let such a thing happen again. But being impetuous as well as powerful, he was soon in another difficulty—by taking up the cause of a cobbler. An officer refused to pay for the repair of his boots, whereupon Van Vorst satisfied the shoemaker by thrashing the officer. For this he was again locked up in New York, and again discharged with a like admonition.

The presence of the enemy, always offensive to the sturdy patriot, finally became unendurable. They not only lived in his house, but seized his horses and confiscated his cattle. Determined to separate from their company, which he loathed, he took his family to Pompton and there resided with Philip Schuyler. On his return he went to Paulus Hoeck, and lived in the ferry house until the close of the war.

Like his opulent neighbors, "Faddy" was a practical believer in the patriarchal institution, and kept his spacious kitchen well stocked with slaves. Among the number was a character known as "Half Indian Jack," who died at Harsimus February 2, 1831, at the age of 102 years, and was buried on what is now the rear of lot No. 153 Wayne street. Jack ran away from Van Vorst during the Revolutionary war, and became a spy for the British. He was generally in the company of a white spy, named Meyers. Both did their work for pay—Jack for whiskey, Meyers for gold. Meyers deposited his money in a box, which he kept buried. Whenever he was in a condition to add to the deposit, he and Jack would unearth the treasure. When uncovered, Jack would be dismissed, and Meyers buried the money in a different place. The story, as told by Jack, was that, as often as he had helped Meyers dig up the box, he had never seen it buried, nor was it ever buried twice in the same place. At last the patriots entrapped and shot Meyers, but Jack was too wary and escaped. After Meyers' death great efforts were made to discover his treasure. His widow, ever looking for the end of the rainbow where rests the pot of gold, every spring when the

[1] Clinton had probably met Van Vorst at school in the city while his father, Admiral Clinton, was Governor of New York.

ground was soft, would go over what was recently the Fourth and Fifth wards of Jersey City, prospecting with an iron rod, which she pushed into the ground, hoping to strike the box. She never succeeded, though she worked and hoped while she lived. It is possible that the old spy's box of British gold yet lies buried in that part of the city, awaiting its resurrection by the spade of some lucky finder.

Jack pretended among the slaves to be an Indian doctor. He induced them to believe that he was a particular favorite of the devil, and gave them to understand that, unless they helped him to a few pennies, old "clootie" would come for them some day. In time this mode of raising the wind failed Jack, and he was left to suffer from his chronic drought. But, fortunately for him, one day a man came to Jersey City with a horse nineteen hands high. He could be mounted only by means of a ladder, and his foot was like a peck measure. He was put up at Holmes' stable, near the corner of Washington and Montgomery streets. Jack saw the "huge, earth-shaking beast" pass down the avenue. Hastening to the slaves, he reminded them of his frequent warnings that the devil would come for them and how they had disbelieved him; but now he was at hand and had put his horse in Holmes' stable. The poor creatures wondered, yet doubted, and resolved to see for themselves. But when they came to Newark avenue and saw the prints of the horse's feet, they fled in wild dismay. From that day till he died the devil would come at Jack's bidding, coppers were not wanting for his whiskey, and he was prophet and king in Faddy's kitchen.

32. II. John, is said to have been m. and had a family.

33. III. Helena, m. Henry Kingsland. IV. Eleanor.

Sixth Generation.

Cornelius [26] had ch.:

34. I. Arie, b. April 26, 1756; m. Lena Berry, Jan. 5, 1777; removed to the west.

35. II. Gerrit (46), b. Nov. 21, 1758; m. Mary Van Eydestyn, Aug. 5, 1786; d. April 2, 1834.
36. III. Annatje, b. Aug. 25, 1764; d. in inf.

Waling [28] had ch.:
37. I. Gerrit, b. April 30, 1756; d. in inf.
38. II. Sarah, b. April 14, 1761; m. Casparus Van Eydestyn, Feb. 1, 1784.
39. III. Gerrit (51), b. June 22, 1764; m. Elizabeth Bilju, of Staten Island, Aug. 19, 1786.
40. IV. Casparus (54), b. Sept. 3, 1769; m. Margrietje Van Buskirk, June 9, 1799.
41. V. Hendrick (55), m. Annatje Pickston, Dec. 7, 1800.

Cornelius [31] had ch.:
42. I. Johannis (56), b. March 3, 1761; m. Sarah, dau. of Jean François Vashér,[1] June 20, 1816; d. Jan. 13, 1832; she d. Feb. 23, 1851, æt. 64 yrs., 1 mo., 20 days.
43. II. Cornelius (60), b. Sept. 6, 1763; m. Hannah Gilbert.
44. III. Claesje, b. Aug. 31, 1765; d. Oct. 9, 1773.
45. IV. Neeltje, b. Sept. 16, 1768; m. Henry Traphagen, Jan. 25, 1803; d. March 4, 1824.

Seventh Generation.

Gerrit [35] had ch.:
46. I. Ann, b. Feb. 24, 1787; m. Daniel Smith.
47. II. Catharine, b. Oct. 17, 1789; m. John K. Holmes.
48. III. Annatje, b. Nov. 28, 1793; m. Benjamin McCollum.
49. IV. Cornelius (63), b. Dec. 14, 1799; m. Letitia, dau. of James Warner, Jan. 1, 1826.

Gerrit [39] had ch.:
50. I. Waling, m. Maria Kip; had ch.: I. Hendrick and II. Garret, twins, b. Jan. 21, 1814; III. Joanna, b. Dec. 6, 1816; IV. Catharine, b. Sept. 1, 1819; V. Jacob, b. Aug. 28, 1821; VI. John, b. July 25, 1825; VII. Christian, b. Oct. 11, 1828; VIII. William Oscar, b. Nov. 13, 1831.

---

[1] Vashér was a Frenchman. He came to this country during the Revolutionary war; was a surgeon in the fourth New York regiment; an intimate friend of Washington and a member of the Cincinnati. He m. Miss Potter of Madison, N. J. His ch. were, I., Sarah, m. John Van Vorst; II., Eliza; III., Frances, m. Robert Gilchrist, Oct. 1, 1812; her son Robert is now Attorney-General of N. J.; IV., Frank, d. in inf.

THE VAN VORST HOMESTEAD.

(N. E. corner of Wayne street and Jersey avenue.)

51. II. Jacob (67), b. July 17, 1788; m. Christina Everson, Jan. 21, 1809; d. July 4, 1857.
52. III. Gerrit (70), b. June 26, 1790; m. Cynthia Hennion, Dec. 25, 1810; d. March 25, 1852; she b. Dec. 24, 1789; d. Aug. 14, 1852.
53. IV. John, b. Nov. 18, 1795.

Casparus [40] had ch.:

54. I. Catharina, b. April 12, 1800; II. Thomas, b. Sept. 11, 1802.

Hendrick [41] had ch.:

55. I. Catharina, b. Sept. 17, 1801; II. Isaac, b. Aug. 23, 1803; III. Waling, b. Oct. 16, 1805, d. in inf.; IV. Waling, b. Sept. 22, 1806; V. Antje, b. March 7, 1809; VI. Saartje, b. Feb. 12, 1813; VII. Garret, b. March 5, 1821; VIII. Eliza Jane, b. April 7, 1823.

Johannis [42] had ch.:

56. I. Ann Eliza, b. June 2, 1817; m. J. Dickinson Miller, Feb. 19, 1835. He was a prominent lawyer in Jersey City, and, for several years, Alderman.
57. II. Cornelia, b. Nov. 15, 1819; m. Henry Augustus Booraem.
58. III. Sarah Frances, b. Sept. 12, 1820; m., 1st, Charles B. C. Bacot; 2d, Michael Lienau, March 17, 1859.
59. IV. John (73), b. Sept. 25, 1823; m. Emily H., dau. of Peter Bacot, of Charleston S. C., Jan. 10, 1850. He was Alderman of Jersey City and a member of the General Assembly of N. J. for several years

Cornelius [43] had ch.:

60. I. Cornelius (74), b. Aug. 6, 1794; m. 1st, Sarah S., dau. of William Brower, Dec. —, 1816; she d. Aug. 12, 1835; 2d, Antoinette, dau. of Cornelius Roosevelt, Oct. 19, 1836; d. Jan. 23, 1852; she d. Sept. 14, 1849.
61. II. Susanna, b. March 15, 1798; d. March 26, 1815.
62. III. Anna, b. March 26, 1803; m. Joseph Cooper, March 11, 1830; d. Jan. 1, 1865.

Eighth Generation.

Cornelius [49] had ch.:

63. I. Garret, b. Oct. 30, 1826; m. Abigail Hazard; had ch., I. Garret; II. Lena.
64. II. Letitia, b. June 26, 1828; m. Charles W. Ward.
65. III. Cornelius (85), b. May 25, 1830; m. Phebe Jane, dau. of Thomas Gardner.
66. IV. Jane Ann, b. Sept. 18, 1832; m. William H. Tise; d. Dec. 6, 1870.

Jacob [51] had ch.:

67. I. Elizabeth, b. Aug. 4, 1809; m. Henry Spier, Dec. 19, 1830.
68. II. John, b. in 1820; d. in 1824.
69. III. Sarah, b. Feb. 22, 1822; m. Isaac Halenbeck, July 8, 1850.

Gerrit [52] had ch.:

70. I. Elizabeth, b. Nov. 6, 1812; m. Abraham Shotwell.
71. II. David (86), b. Feb. 20, 1823; m. Fanny, dau. of Charles Heritage, June 1, 1851.
72. III. Garret (87), b. June 21, 1826; m., 1st, Sarah, dau. of John Everson; 2d, Mary, dau. of John Spier, Jan. 10, 1861.

John [59] had ch.:

73. I. John, b. Oct. 18, 1850; II. Dickinson M., b. May 15, 1854; III. Eugene C., b. March 2, 1856; IV. Emily H., b. Dec. 1, 1857; V. Sarah, b. Oct. 24, 1860; VI. Henry H., b. Dec. 3, 1865; d. July 14, 1866; VII. Harriet B., b. Feb. 10, 1870; d. July 15, 1870; VIII. Mary S., b. Sept. 11, 1872.

Cornelius [60] had ch.:

74. I. Elizabeth B., b. Nov. 3, 1817; II. Susan, b. Aug. 22, 1819; d. in inf.
75. III. Cornelius (88), b. March 7, 1822; m. Sophia A., dau. of Edward Phillips of Providence, R. I., June 16, 1846. He was Alderman and Mayor of Jersey City for several years.
76. IV. Mary B., b. Feb. 1, 1824; m. William P. Powers, Aug. 14, 1851.
77. V. Susan, b. April 17, 1825; d. in inf.
78. VI. Sarah, b. Feb. 25, 1831; m. Robert Sewell, April 24, 1860.

79. VII. Anna G., b. April 25, 1832; VIII. Juliet, b. Aug. 5, 1834.
80. IX. Julia, b. Oct. 27, 1837.
81. X. Susan, b. March, 30, 1839; m. Louis Dez Armauld, Nov. 17, 1863.
82. XI. Antoinette, b. Nov. 24, 1841; d. in inf.
83. XII. William B., b. Dec. 6, 1842; m. Katie, dau. of S. E. Swain, May 31, 1871; she d. Aug. 31, 1872.
84. XIII. Antoinette, b. Jan. 27, 1846; m. Hugh Toler Booraem, May 14, 1867.

Ninth Generation.

Cornelius [65] had ch.:

85. I. Cornelius; II. Charles; III. Garret Thomas; IV. Harrison; V. Howard; VI. William; VII. William; VIII. Erwin; IX. Letitia.

David [71] had ch.:

86. I. Maria Frances, b. Oct. 7, 1852; II. Garret F., b. Nov. 16, 1854; III. Ella Louisa, b. May 17, 1864.

Garret [72] had ch.:

87. I. Sarah Ann, b. Sept. 18, 1851; II. Cynthia, b. May 19, 1854; III. Garret, b. July 23, 1863; IV. George, b. May 10, 1867.

Cornelius [75] had ch.:

88. I. Mary R.; II. Cornelius P., b. March 29, 1849; III. Edward P., b. Jan. 19, 1852; d. in inf.; IV. Eliza B., b. Jan. 20, 1853.

VREELAND—VREELANDT—FREELAND.

There was in Holland a place named *Vreelandt*, but whether a hamlet, parish or manor has not been ascertained.[1] The family in this county now bearing the name is descended from *Michiel Jansen*, who came from Broeckhuysen (North Brabant).[2] He left Holland October 1, 1636, in the ship Rensselaerwyck,[3] with his wife and two children. He settled at what is now Green-

---

1 *Col. Hist. of N. Y., ii.*, 183.
2 *Valentine's Hist. of N. Y.*, 138.
3 *O'Cal., N. N., i.*, 437.

bush, opposite Albany, as a *boereknecht*, or farm servant.[1] It was not long before he grew weary of agricultural pursuits and the narrow road thereby opened to wealth, and engaged in the fur trade, in which "he made his fortune in two years." Such private speculation being prohibited by law, soon brought him into difficulty with the authorities. He thereupon abandoned his farm, and came to Manhattan. The date of this change is not known, but he was a resident in New Amsterdam November 4, 1644, on which date he empowered Arent Van Curler to settle with Patroon Van Rensselaer all accounts and differences. In 1646 he came over to Communipaw, and settled on the bouwerie owned by Jan Evertsen Bout. In the years 1647, '49 and '50, he represented Pavonia in the Council of "Nine,"[2] and joined his associates in their crusade against Governor Stuyvesant.[3] It was at his house that the journal of Van der Donck was seized, and it was suspected upon information furnished by himself.[4] He was a signer of the application for the first municipal government in New Netherland, July 26, 1649.[5]

The following record of June 15, 1654, shows that he had not yet overcome his reluctance to farming:

"Michiel Jansen, residing at Pavonia, belonging to the jurisdiction of New Amsterdam, appeared before the Court of Burgomasters and Schepens of this city aforesaid, and stated that he intended, for the accommodation of the inhabitants of the place, to brew some beer, and, as it was very inconvenient to give in the same every time, and to procure the excise certificate, wished therefore to make an agreement with the Burgomasters and Schepens about the excise; which being granted to him, the Burgomasters and Schepens have made an agreement with Michiel Jansen for one year, that for all the beer he shall brew and sell at the aforesaid place, he shall pay 50 guilders, each half year the half, and it is hereby allowed to him to sell beer by the small measure also, to persons coming over to that place."[6] Thus he has the honor of being the first licensed tapster in the State of New Jersey.[7]

During the troubles of 1655, the Indians drove him from his home, when, on September 15, they made a raid on Pavonia and killed every man there, except the family of Jansen.[8] From the

---

1 *Col. Hist. of N. Y.*, i., 431.
2 *New Neth. Reg.*, 55.
3 *Col. Hist. of N. Y.*, i., 275.
4 *Ibid*, i., 344.
5 *Valentine's Manual*, 1851, 407.
6 *New Amst. Rec.*, i., 492.
7 Aert Teunissen, of Hoboken, who was killed in 1643, was the first brewer in New Jersey. *Contra Valentine's Manual*, 1860, 612.
8 *Albany Records*, *xiii.*, 327.

dangers and uncertainties of border life at "Gamoenepa," he took refuge on Manhattan, where, because he was an "old man with a heavy family," and had lost his all, he was, November 22, 1655, permitted to keep a tap room.[1] Like many modern tapsters, he soon learned how to keep the letter of the law while he violated its spirit. An ordinance prohibited tapping after bell-ring, and on October 23, 1656, the schout prosecuted Jansen for its violation. The defendant confessed that two soldiers were playing at back-gammon and three sailors waiting for their skipper; denied that he had tapped after bell-ring; admitted that his guests "had their cans by them and got chatting," but shrewdly omitted to state that he had filled their cans against the time when he could not lawfully tap.[2]

For the same reason that he was permitted to tap he received *gratis*, in February, 1656, a lot of ground in the city.[3] On February 21, 1657, he was appointed one of the *Measurers of Lime and Grain*.[4] On April 13, 1657, his name was placed on the roll of small burghers.[5] Much to his credit, he soon grew weary of tap room life, and longed to return to his wheat-producing bouwerie. During the war he had not parted with the title to all the land which he had previously bought of Bout[6] for 8,000 florins.[7] In 1658 he sold part of it to Harman Smeeman.[8] On January 22, 1658, he asked for permission to return to Pavonia, and to be relieved from certain tithes.[9] In September, 1661, he had become a man of "competence,"[10] living on his bouwerie at Gemoenepa. He was one of the first magistrates of the new court at Bergen.[11] In December, 1662, he joined his neighbors in asking the Governor for a minister of the gospel, and for whose support he subscribed twenty-five florins.[12] He died in 1663.

His wife was Fitje Hartmans. In 1679 she was living at "Ghmoenepaen," and had "many grandchildren, all of whom were not unjust." The farm owned by her is marked on the

---

1 *New Amst. Rec., ii.*, 275.
2 *Ibid, ii.*, 603.
3 *N. Y. Col. MSS., vi.*, 269.
4 *New Neth. Reg.*, 116.
5 *Ibid*, 176.
6 *Powers of Attorney, New Amst.*, 152.
7 *Col. Hist. of N. Y., i.*, 432.
8 *New Amst. Rec., iii.*, 29.
9 *N.Y. Col. MSS., viii.*, 649.
10 *Valentine's Manual*, 1863, 569.
11 *New Neth. Reg.*, 100.
12 *N. Y. Col. MSS., x., Part i.*, 277, 279.

field map as lots numbered 14 and 15.[1] The Labadists, in October, 1679, dined with her. An old lady in Brooklyn told them that Fitje came from Cologne. They have left this quaint record concerning her: "We found her a little pious, after the manner of the country, and you could discover that there was something of the Lord in her, but very much covered up and defiled."[2] This is no light testimony to the old lady's religious attainments, considering that it is given by two men who seem to have looked upon all mankind, except that small portion which accepted their own peculiar views, as destined fuel for the everlasting bonfire. She was a member of the Bergen church in 1664; d. September 21, 1697.

Second Generation.

Michiel Jansen had ch.:

1. I. Claas came to this country with his father; m. Annetje Maria Gerbrants, of Norden, April 14, 1657.

2 II. Elias (9), was a carpenter by trade; m. Grietje Jacobs

Van Winckel, of "Hazymus," Aug. 30, 1665; took the oath of allegiance to the king Nov. 22, 1665; was commissioned Associate Judge of the Court of Bergen in 1673, '74, '77 and 1680; ensign in Captain John Berry's company at Bergen, July 15, 1675; was representative in the General Assembly in 1683, '93, '95, '99 and 1708. During the year 1683 he was commissioned one of the Judges of the County of Essex. In March, 1684, he united with his brothers Hartman, Johannis and Cornelis (and others) in the purchase from the Proprietors of "Haquequenunck."[3] They had pre-

[1] *Winfield's Land Titles,* 51.
[2] *Long Isl. Hist. Soc., i.,* 155.
[3] *Taylor's Annals,* 69.

viously purchased the Indian title, and he was an actual resident there in 1683. In 1693 he was appointed to raise revenue for the war between England and France.[1]

3. III. Enoch (10), bap. Oct. 26, 1649; m. 1st, Dircksje Meyers, of Amsterdam, June 20, 1670; she d. Oct. 5, 1688; 2d, Grietje Wessels, wid. of Jan Janse Langedyck, Oct. 23, 1693; she d. Nov. 20, 1697; 3d, Aagtje Van Hooren, Jan. 13, 1704; d. Aug. 17, 1714. He was a member of the General Assembly of the Province in 1675–'88, 1707, '08 and '09.[2] In the last year he was not prompt in his attendance, and the sergeant-at-arms was directed to bring him forthwith before the House. He was commissioned ensign of the militia of Bergen, July 4, 1681; Associate Judge of the Court at Bergen in 1673, '74, '81, '82, and '83; Commissioner of Highways for the County in 1682 and '92; and Assistant Judge of the Bergen Common Pleas, May 22, 1705. He lived on the bluff where the Central Railroad crosses the Morris Canal, near Cavan Point.

4. IV. Hartman (22), bap. Oct. 1, 1651; m. Metje, dau. of Dirck Claase Braecke, in 1672.[3] He was a wheelwright by trade; lived at Rechpokus on part of his wife's inheritance; purchased of Sachem Captahem and Christopher Hoagland (who was the first purchaser, July 15, 1678), 270 acres of land, including "Stoffel's Point" (so named from Hoagland), and an island in the Passaic river near Aquackanonck, named by the Indians *Menehenicke*, by the English "Hartman's Island." In 1693

[1] *Leaming and Spicer*, 335. [2] *Ibid*, 346.

[3] Braecke, or, as he was generally known, Dirck Claesen, was patentee of Cavan Point and Stony Point, having purchased the former place from Egbert Woutersen. He held a lease of Hoboken for a short time about the year 1646, *Col. Hist. of N. Y.*, *i.*, 329; was skipper of the sloop *Union*, from which he was dismissed, April, 20, 1658, for disobedience of orders, *Ibid*, *viii*, 851; and was one of the commissioners to fortify Communipaw in 1663, *New Neth. Reg.*, 159. He d. March 26, 1693; his wife, Neesje Jacobs, d. Dec. 23, 1668. His three daughters m. three brothers, and among them his property was divided.

he was Receiver of Taxes in Bergen;[1] d. Jan. 18, 1707.

5. V. Johannis (35), bap. Oct. 1, 1656; m. Claesje, dau. of Dirck Claase Braecke, May 14, 1682; d. June 26, 1713.

6. VI. Cornelius (44), b. June 3, 1660; m. 1st, Metje, dau. of Dirck Claase Braecke, May 11, 1691; 2d, Lysbet Jacobs, wid., April 17, 1692. On March 17, 1696, he purchased of William Douglas[2] land at Pembrepogh (now Pamrapo, in Bayonne), on which he afterward lived; d. May —, 1727; she d. Aug. 17, 1724.

7. VII. Jannetje, m. Dirck Teunissen Van Vechten, whose father succeeded Michiel Jansen as occupant of the farm at Greenbush, in 1646. He settled on the Raritan, not far from Somerville, and some of his descendants still live thereabouts.

8. VIII. Pryntje, m. Andries Claesen, March 25, 1688; d. April 21, 1711; he d. Aug. 7, 1710, leaving three sons, who became the progenitors of the Andersons in this county. This generation was known indifferently as Vreeland and Michielse. They wrote the name *Michielse*, as *Enoch Michielse*, &c.

Third Generation.

Elias [2] had ch.:

9. I. Michael, bap. April 7, 1666; II. Jacobus, bap. April 8, 1688; III. Fitje, bap. Dec. 25, 1669; m. John Thomas, of Elizabethtown; IV. Trintje, bap. March —, 1672; m. Lourens Van Galen, June 15,

---

[1] *Leaming and Spicer*, 337.

[2] William Douglas (Doeckles, Douckles) lived at Pembrepogh, and was elected to represent Bergen in the General Assembly of N. J., in 1680, but was ruled out of that body *because he was a Roman Catholic, Alb. Rec., xxix*, 116. This is the first, and I believe is the only instance, of such persecution for religious opinions in the State of New Jersey.

1700 (she had five ch. bap. in the Bergen Church); V. Ragel, b. March 8, 1676; VI. Jacob, b. Aug. 9, 1678; m. Antje Lourense Toers, Sept. —, 1703.

Enoch [3] had ch.:

10. I. Elsje, bap. Nov. 12, 1671; m. Edward Earle, jr.,[1] Feb. 13, 1688.
11. II. Catharina, bap. May 15, 1673; m. Aert Albertse, of N. Y., June 26, 1692.
12. III. Michael, bap. Jan. 27, 1675; d. unm. He was *non compos mentis.*
13. IV. Johannis (52), bap. April 7, 1677; m. Maria Berger, June 8, 1701.
14. V. Abraham (53), b. June 22, 1678; m. Margrietje Van Winkle (5), Oct. 28, 1699; his will, dated Dec. 10, 1734, was proved Jan. 8, 1748. He was a member of the church at Aquackanonck in 1725.
15. VI. Fitje, bap. Feb. 28, 1680; m. Peregrine Sanford, of New Barbadoes.
16. VII. Isaac, b. July 4, 1683; m. Tryntje Newkirk (25), March 23, 1706; was a member of the church at Aquackanonck in 1725.
17. VIII. Enoch (55), bap. Aug. 4, 1687; m. Maria St. Leger, Oct. 22, 1709; was commissioned captain in Colonel Parker's regiment in 1724.
18. IX. Benjamin, b. March 6, 1705; d. Oct. 17, 1725.
19. X. Elias, resided at "Pemmerepogh;" d. April 2, 1747, s. p.
20. XI. Jacob, bap. Oct. 18, 1708; d. March 6, 1732, unm.
21. XII. Joris (56), b. Sept. 25, 1710; m. 1st, Annetje Van Winkle; 2d, Annetje Van Wagenen (35), of Aquackanonck; d. June 21, 1795. He owned and resided in the house now owned by the heirs of Captain William Howe, west of Cavan Point. With Rynier Van Giesen, he represented Bergen in the 19th Provincial Assembly of N. J. in 1754.

Hartman [4] had ch.:

---

[1] Earle came from Maryland. On April 24, 1676, he purchased the Secaucus Patent. *Winfield's Land Titles*, 130. He was Commissioner of Revenue in Bergen during the English and French war, *Leaming and Spicer*, 335; constable in 1694-'95, and Assistant Judge of the Bergen Common Pleas in 1705. On July 29, 1702, he purchased of the Indians a tract of land on Rechawack river, in West Jersey, *Proc. of N. J. Hist. Soc., i.*, 198. He was the founder of the Earle family in Bergen and Hudson Counties; d. Dec. 15, 1711. In 1701 Earle, Judge Pinhorne and William Sandford were considered "Persons of y[e] Best Estates in East Jersie."

22. I. Claas, b. April 6, 1675; m. 1st, Annetje, dau. of Hans Harmanse, then of New Utrecht, Long Island, afterward of Constaples Hoeck, May 24, 1697; she d. Nov. 26, 1698, leaving one ch., Hartman, b. March —, 1698, who by his grandfather's will received one-half of the Hoeck; 2d, Elsje Pieters, Aug. 19, 1699. He was a member of the church at Aquackanonck in 1725.

23. II. Aeltje, bap. Oct. 8, 1677.

24. III. Michael, b. Dec. 31, 1678; d. Jan. 14, 1692.

25. IV. Dirck (66), b. April 3, 1681; m. Margrietje Diedricks Banta, of Hackensack, Oct. 20, 1702; resided at Aquackanonck. His will, dated Nov. 8, 1769, was proved Dec. 9, 1773.

26. V. Fitje, b. Feb. 21, 1683; m. Dirck Paulusen of Gemoenepa, Aug. 19, 1699; resided at Aquackanonck.

27. VI. Styntje, b. Feb. 21, 1683.

28. VII. Aagtje, b. Oct. 28, 1684; m. Cornelis Blinkerhoff (8), then of Midwout, L. I., May 24, 1708; d. Feb. 20, 1761.

29. VIII. Dedricksje, b. Nov. 27, 1685.

30. IX. Marietje, b. Nov. 23, 1687; m. Thomas Fredericks, *alias* De Cuyper, April 27, 1711.

31. X. Jannetje, b. July 22, 1691; m. Gerrit Van Ripen (11), June 19, 1718.

32. XI. Michael (67), b. Dec. 26, 1694; m. Elysabet Van Ripen (21), May 30, 1719; d. April 6, 1766.

33. XII. Arriantje, b. July 19, 1698; m. Zacharias Sickles, Nov. 7, 1719; d. Dec. 2, 1731.

34. XIII. Enoch, m. Jannetje Van Blerkum; had ch.: I. Michael, b. May 23, 1730.

Johannis [5] had ch.:

35. I. Michael, b. Sept. 14, 1684; d. Jan. 27, 1710.

36. II. Dirck, bap. Oct. 11, 1686; m. Fitje Dirckse Banta, May —, 1716; was a member of the church at Aquackanonck in 1725.

37. III. Fitje, bap. Oct. 28, 1688; d. Jan. 27, 1710, unm.

38. IV. Enoch, bap. Oct. 28, 1688; m. Mercy ——; among his ch. was Abraham, who lived in Elizabeth, and whose will, dated March 22, 1768, was proved April 6, 1771. In it his ch. are named: Enoch, James, Abraham, Aaron, Hannah, Elizabeth, Rachel, Sarah and Mercy.

39. V. Aagtje, bap. April 22, 1690; m. Cornelis Helmigsen Van Houten, April 19, 1711.
40. VI. Helena, m. Johannis Helmigsen Van Houten, June 17, 1719; d. March 15, 1774.
41. VII. Jannetje, m. Martin Winne, Dec. 21, 1716.
42. VIII. Elias, m. Maritje Van Hooren (5), May 11, 1723; d. April 2, 1748; had ch.: Johannis, b. Aug. 30, 1730; resided at Aquackanonck.
43. IX. Johannis, b. July 1, 1705; m. Antje Diedricks in 1726; d. Feb. 11, 1783; she d. Sept. 19, 1780; had ch.: Johannis, b. July 30, 1731; d. Jan. 25, 1753.
There were several more ch. than those here named; the 13th ch. and 6th dau. was b. July 19, 1698.

Cornelius [6] had ch.:
44. I. Aagtje, b. April 18, 1682; m. Roelof Helmigse Van Houten, April 21, 1701; d. Aug. 14, 1708.
45. II. Fitje, bap. July 22, 1683; m. Laurence Van Buskirk (8), Sept. 18, 1709; d. Oct. 19, 1756.
46. III. Michael, bap. Aug. 2, 1685; d. in inf.
47. IV. Michael, bap. Feb. 23, 1687; d. in inf.
48 V. Jannetje, bap. Nov. 28, 1688; m. Daniel Van Winkle (6), Sept. 3, 1709; d. April 12, 1769.
49. VI. Neeltje, bap. July 23, 1690.
50. VII. Michael (71), b. Sept. 18, 1694; m. Jenneke, dau. of Helmus Van Houten, Oct. 23, 1713.
51. VIII. Metje, b. Oct. 3, 1698.

Fourth Generation.

Johannis [13] had ch.:
52. I. Maria, bap. Nov. 29, 1702; II. Catharina, bap. Nov. 19, 1704; III. Enoch, bap. Jan. 22, 1707; IV. Martinus, bap. April 3, 1709. These were all bap. in N. Y.

Abraham [14] had ch.:
53. I. Enoch, b. March 14, 1700; his will, dated May 14, 1777, proved June 24, 1777, names his wife Rachel and son Daniel, who had a son John.
54. II. Jacob; III. Johannis; IV. Simeon; V. Isaac, d. in 1756; VI. Abraham; VII. Hendrick; VIII. Derrick; IX. Lea; X. Anna. One of these dau. m. Robert Bagley. Simeon m. Rachel ——, and removed to Bergen County. His will, dated

May 29, 1761, was proved Feb. 9, 1765. At its date his wife was *enceinte*.

Enoch [17] had ch.:

55. I. Enoch, bap. Oct. 4, 1710; II. Helena, bap. Jan. 14, 1713; III. Elias, bap. March 4, 1715; IV. Benjamin, bap. Dec. 11, 1717, d. Aug. 26, 1736. These were all bap. in N. Y.

Joris [21] had ch.:

56. I. Aagtje, b. Sept. 18, 1733; m. Helmig Van Houten; marriage bond dated May 4, 1753.

57. II. Enoch, b. Sept. 22, 1737; d. in inf. III. Garret, b. May 17, 1739; d. Jan. 26, 1751.

58. IV. Enoch, b. Feb. 18, 1741; m. Cornelia Kip in 1764; removed to New Barbadoes.

59. V. Jacob, m. Jenneke Cadmus (13); removed to Staten Island.

60. VI. Johannis, b. Sept. 21, 1749; m. Helena Garrabrant (33), June 21, 1778; d. Oct. 27, 1824, s. p.; his only ch., Joris, b. Jan. 10, 1779; d. in inf.

61. VII. Garret (80), b. Nov. 1, 1751; m. Jannetje Cadmus (9); d. Feb. 13, 1825.

62. VIII. Effie, m. 1st, Jacob Van Wagenen (34); 2d, John Vreeland.

63. IX. Lena, b. May 20, 1756; m. Garret Van Ripen (53); d. March 7, 1846.

64. X. Jenneke, b. Dec. 1, 1758; m. 1st, Henry Newkirk (17); 2d, Joseph Van Winkle (46), May 26, 1798; d. June 28, 1847.

65. XI. Annatje, m. Michael Vreeland (78); d. Feb. 23, 1803.

Dirck [25] had ch.;

66. I. Hartman, b. Jan. 24, 1704; II. Rachel, b. July 16, 1707; III. Marritje, b. April 7, 1709; IV. Hester, b. Feb. 25, 1712; V. Dirck, b. Nov. 16, 1716; VI. Johannis, b. Oct. 12, 1719; VII. Antje, b. July 4, 1722. Besides these, his will mentions *Claesje*, *Michael* and *Margrietje*.

Michael [32] had ch.:

67. I. Hartman, m. Marritje Garrabrant (15), Nov. 20, 1739; removed to Wesel, near Aquackanonck; his will, dated Nov. 4, 1776, proved April 14, 1785, names his ch.: I. Michael, II. Cornelius, III. Jennie, IV. Elizabeth, V. Beelitje, b. Jan. 5, 1757.

68. II. Garret, lived at Communipaw; d. Feb. 8, 1784, unm.

69. III. Claas (86), bap. March 30, 1724; m. 1st, Catlyntje Sip (18), May 13, 1757; 2d, Antje, dau. of Stephen Basset, Dec. 13, 1760; d. Feb. 9, 1802; she b. March 29, 1736; d. March 1, 1819. The following is a copy of his bond in this second marriage:

"Know all men by these presents, That We, Nicholas Vreelandt, of the County of Bergen and Province of New Jersey, & Michael Vreelandt, of Essex County & Province af^{d}, are holden and do stand justly indebted unto his Excellency Thomas Boone, Esqr, Governor-in-Chief of New Jersey af^{d}, in the sum of Five Hundred Pounds, of current lawful Money of *New Jersey;* to be paid to his said Excellency, Thomas Boone, Esqr, his Successors or Assigns; For which Payment well and truly, to be made and done, We do bind ourselves, our Heirs, Executors and Administrators, and every of them, jointly & severally, firmly by these presents. Sealed with our Seals; dated this Second Day of December, Annoque Domini One Thousand Seven Hundred and Sixty.

"The condition of this Obligation is such, That whereas the above bounden Nicholas Vreelandt hath obtained License of Marriage for himself of the one Party, and for Nancy Bassett, of Essex County af^{d}, of the other Party; Now, if it shall not hereafter appear that they, the said Nicholas Vreelandt & Nancy Bassett, have any lawful Let or Impediment, of Pre-Contract, Affinity or Consanguinity, to hinder their being joined in the Holy Bands of Matrimony, and afterwards their living together as Man and Wife; then this Obligation to be void, or else to stand and remain in full Force and Virtue.

his
"NICHOLAS X VREELANDT
mark.
"MICHAEL VREELANDT.

"Sealed and Delivered
in the Presence of
"LEWIS OGDEN."

70. IV. Beelitje, b. March 19, 1733; m. Cornelius Sip (16) July 4, 1761; d. Oct. 26, 1789; V. Maritje.

Michael [50] had ch.:

71. I. Metje, b. Dec. 28, 1720; m. Abraham Van Tuyl, Dec. 8, 1738.

72. II. Jannetje, b. Nov. —, 1722; m. Joris Cadmus (6); d. Nov. 12, 1766.

73. III. Cornelius (93), b. Jan. —, 1726; m. Cartrintje Cadmus (5); removed to English Neighborhood.

74. IV. Helmagh (94), b. Feb. 20, 1728; m. 1st, Neeltje Van Horn (7); marriage bond dated April 1, 1752; 2d, Jannetje Sip (20); removed to Staten Island; his ch. returned and settled at Centreville, near Bergen Point.

75. V. Aagtje, b. Feb. 14, 1732; VI. Abraham, b. Aug. 16, 1734.

76. VII. Dirck (97), b. March 11, 1737; m. and removed to English Neighborhood. During the Revolutionary war he was accused of disaffection, and Major Hayes ordered to arrest him, July 11, 1777; he was confined in the jail at Morristown; John Mead became his bail, and he was released Aug. 20, 1778.

77. VIII. Jacob, b. March 11, 1737; removed to Fort Lee.

78. IX. Michael (98), b. June 24, 1739; m. Annatje Vreeland (64); d. Dec. 5, 1804.

79. X. Johannis (102), b. March 2, 1742; m. Keetje Hooglandt, April 29, 1767; d. July 30, 1823; she b. Nov. 13, 1747; d. Sept. 24, 1819.

Fifth Generation.

Garret [61] had ch.:

80. I. Joris, d. Nov. 7, 1786, in inf.

81. II. Jacob (106), b. June 25, 1781; m. Catlyntje Brinkerhoff (37), Jan. 21, 1801; d. in 1866. Previous to his death he removed to Rocky Hill, N. J.

82. III. Annatje, b. Feb. 15, 1784; d. Nov. 14, 1786.

83. IV. George (112), b. July 12, 1787; m. 1st, Catharine Newkirk (31), June 17, 1809; 2d, Maria, dau. of Moses Schoonmaker and wid. of Abraham Collerd, Dec. —, 1857; 3d, Josephine Griffith, Dec. 8, 1872.

84. V. Jannetje, b. March 14, 1790; m. George De Mott, Oct. 1, 1808; d. July 14, 1826.

85. VI. Richard (122), b. July 24, 1792; m. Margaret, dau. of Michael De Mott, Dec. 9, 1815.

Claas [69] had ch.:

86. I. Michael (133), b. July 31, 1758; m. Geertje, dau. of Daniel Sickles, Sept. 16, 1781; d. March 10, 1825; she d. July 2, 1815. By his uncle Garret's will, dated June 16, 1766, proved March 23, 1784, he received land at Aquackanonck.
87. II. Antje, b. Feb. 28, 1762; m. Jurrie Van Ripen, of Slotterdam; marriage bond dated June 20, 1787.
88. III. Elisabet, b. May 30, 1764; m. Cornelius Van Ripen (73); marriage bond dated Jan. 20, 1787; d. April 8, 1788.
89. IV. Sarah, b. Oct. 7, 1766; d. in inf.
90. V. Sally, b. Sept. 14, 1769; m. Jacobus Van Buskirk (38), Dec. 16, 1787; d. Aug. 12, 1832.
91. VI. Beelitje, b. April 17, 1774; m. John Westervelt, of Teaneck.
92. VII. Stephen (142), b. May 31, 1778; m. 1st, Jenneke Vreeland (104), Dec. 16, 1797; 2d, Elizabeth Van Ripen (93), Oct. 14, 1817; 3d, Altje Van Winkle (83), wid. of John Mandeville, Nov. 29, 1828; 4th, Ellen Schoonmaker, of Flatbush, L. I.; she d. Feb. 14, 1849; 5th, Rachel Van Winkle, wid. of Thomas Van Ripen (86); she d. Jan. 29, 1851; 6th, Hannah W. Gross, widow; d. Aug. 31, 1865.

Cornelius [73] had ch.:

93. I. Michael, b. Nov. 24, 1757; II. Dirck, b. May 25, 1760; III. Cornelius, b. Sept. 20, 1762, m. Oct. 5, 1788.

Helmagh [74] had ch.:

94. I. Michael, b. Jan. 14, 1759.

95. II. William (153), m. 1st, Rachel Van Buskirk (37); 2d, Catharine Sickles, wid. of Leonard Johnson, Oct. 12, 1822; d. May 2, 1854, æt. 84 yrs.; she d. June 28, 1847, æt. 58 yrs.

96. III. Cornelius (159), b. in 1769; m. Elizabeth Van Buskirk (36); d. Sept. 2, 1824.

Dirck [76] had ch.:

97. I. Fitje, b. Aug. 16, 1751; II. Metje, b. Oct. 31, 1754; III. Leya, b. Sept. 17, 1758.

Michael [78] had ch.:

Jane Vreeland

98. I. George (167), b. Jan. 31, 1762; m. Jane Brinkerhoff (30), Oct. 21, 1780; d. July 19, 1824.

99. II. Annatje, b. July 19, 1764; m. Jasper Zabriskie, Aug. 17, 1781.

100. III. Jenneke, b. in 1775; m. Dirck Van Ripen (74), Oct. 1792; d. July 1, 1848.

101. IV. John, b. May 1, 1780; m. Aegie Cadmus (15), March 17, 1804; d. April 1, 1832, s. p.

Johannis [79] had ch.:

102. I. Michael (178), b. April 18, 1768; m. Annatje Garrabrant (39), Nov. 5, 1789; d. Nov. 29, 1827.

103. II. Jannetje, b. Oct. 22, 1772; m. Aaron Newkirk (25), Nov. —, 1791; d. June 4, 1830.

104. III. Jenneke, b. Jan. 23, 1774; m. Stephen Vreeland (92), Dec. 16, 1797; d. Aug. 16, 1816.

105. IV. Cornelia, b. in 1782; m. Garret Van Winkle (96), Oct. 3, 1801; d. July 26, 1826.

Sixth Generation.

Jacob [81] had ch.:

106. I. Garret (184), b. Nov. 20, 1801; m. Jane Vreeland (163), Dec. 19, 1822; removed to Rocky Hill.

107. II. Henry (185), b. March 23, 1804; m. Margaret Vreeland (164), Dec 24, 1825; removed to Delaware.

108. III. George (186), b. Aug. 3, 1807; m. Ann Vreeland (259), Dec. 31, 1831; removed to Lisbon, Ill.; d. 1873.

109. IV. John (187), b. Jan. 4, 1810; m. Eliza, dau. of Cornelius Van Ripen, Aug. 18, 1836; removed to Trenton.

110. V. Cornelius (188), b. Aug. 26, 1812; m. 1st, Catharine, dau. of Henry Van Horn, Dec. 25, 1834; she d. March 12, 1842; 2d, Maria, dau. of Henry Vreeland, of Aquackanonck, April 13, 1843; d. Aug. 4, 1848.

111. VI. Jacob, b. Sept. 29, 1817; m. Gitty Vreeland (227), Dec. 20, 1838; removed to Rocky Hill, N. J.

George [83] had ch.:

112. I. Garret (194), b. Oct. 30, 1809; m. Catharine, dau. of Merselis J. Merselis, Feb. 23, 1834.

113. II. Jane, b. April 7, 1812; m. 1st, Andrew Cadmus (30), May 29, 1830; 2d, Oliver P. Smith, Nov. 26, 1835.

114. III. Maria, b. Jan. 28, 1814; m. William Smith, Dec. 14, 1833.

115. IV. George (195), b. Oct. 8, 1816; m. Cathalina Newkirk (64), Feb. 23, 1837.

116. V. Margaret, b. July 28, 1818; m. Merselis M. Parks, Nov. 26, 1835; d. May 25, 1861.

117. VI. Hannah, b. Jan. 10, 1820; m. John Meyers, Feb. 22, 1837.

118. VII. Henry (202), b. Dec. 28, 1821; m. Julia Ann Pharo, June 28, 1846; d. May 15, 1865.

119. VIII. Helen, b. Dec. 22, 1823; m. Jasper Cadmus (49), Dec. 26, 1844.

120. IX. Jacob, b. July 17, 1826; m. 1st, Ellen M., dau. of Moses Schoonmaker, of Rochester, N. Y., Nov. 5, 1857; 2d, Anne, dau. of Henry Rosencamp, July 11, 1867.

121. X. Catharine, b. March 15, 1829; d. Sept. 16, 1832.

Richard [85] had ch.:

122. I. Garret (203), b. Sept. 20, 1816; m. 1st, Elizabeth

dau. of Stephen Terhune, Sept. 27, 1838; she d. July 7, 1858; 2d, Phebe Ellen, dau. of Andrew Rapp, Aug. 23, 1862; she d. Feb. 2, 1868; 3d, Mary Anna Van Ripen (155), March 5, 1869.

123. II. Michael D. M. (205), b. Nov. 21, 1818; m. 1st, Ann, dau. of Henry Van Horn, Nov. 22, 1838; she d. April 20, 1852; 2d, Ann Elizabeth, dau. of Archer G. Welsh, April 1, 1854.

124. III. Richard C. (208), b. Dec. 14, 1820; m. Margaret Ann, dau. of David Demarest, May 27, 1846; removed to Lodi, Bergen Co.

125. IV. Henry (210), b. Oct. 19, 1822; m. Elizabeth Jane, dau. of Charles Musk, Feb. 25, 1852.

126. V. Catherine C., b. May 17, 1825; m. Watts Burrows, M. D.

127. VI. George (212), b. Nov. 3, 1827; m. Susan M. Vreeland (194).

128. VII. John, b. March 23, 1830; m. Jane, dau. of Albert Ackerman, Oct. 12, 1859; had ch.: I. Albert, b. April 19, 1866.

129. VIII. Jane, b. July 11, 1832; d. Dec. 5, 1837.

130. IX. Mary Anna, b. Nov. 11, 1834; d. ——, 1861, unm.

131. X. Jacob B. (213), b. May 11, 1837; m. Kate Ann, dau. of Archer G. Welsh, Dec. 15, 1863.

132. XI. Peter, b. Nov. 24, 1839; d. May 18, 1844.

Michael [86] had ch.:

133. I. Catlyntje, b. Aug. 28, 1782; d. in inf.

134. II. Catlyntje, b. Jan. 9, 1785; m. Henry Van Horn, Dec. 17, 1809; d. March 24, 1848.

135. III. Antje, b. Dec. 14, 1786; m. Jacob D. Van Winkle (84), Dec. 31, 1812; d. Feb. 19, 1866.

136. IV. Nicholas (214), b. Feb. 20, 1789; m. 1st, Annatje, dau. of Edo Winne, March 15, 1814; she b. Nov. 3, 1794, d. July 5, 1832; 2d, Elizabeth, dau. of John Van Ripen, of Wesel, Sept. 21, 1834; d. Dec. 23, 1873.

137. V. Daniel (218), b. Feb. 27, 1791; m. Cornelia Newkirk (46), Jan. 23, 1813; d. Aug. 22, 1867.

138. VI. Garret (225), b. Jan. 31, 1793; m. Jannetje, dau. of Edo Winne, July 21, 1814; d. Oct. 1, 1858; she b. June 8, 1797, d. Sept. 27, 1858.

139. VII. Abraham (231), b. June 27, 1795; m. Annatje Van Ripen (101), Nov. 30, 1816; d. July 23, 1868.

140. VIII. Cornelius M. (241), b. in 1798; m. Catharine Newkirk (48), Nov. 28, 1822; removed to Lisbon, Ill.

141. IX. Geertruy, b. Feb. 23, 1805, d. Oct. —, 1806; X. Guilliam, d. March 30, 1807.

Stephen [92] had ch.:

142. I. Antje, b. Feb. 4, 1799; m. Peter V. B. Vreeland (160), March 16, 1816; d. June 15, 1850.

143. II. Cornelia, b. Nov. 16, 1801; d. May 23, 1802.

144. III. Elizabeth, b. March 28, 1803; d. Feb. 21, 1816.

145. IV. Cornelia, b. July 2, 1806; m. Garret Wauters, Jan. 29, 1825.

146. V. Maria, b. Dec. 10, 1809; m. Peter Van Ripen, of Aquackanonck, Dec. 13, 1828.

147. VI. Isabella, b. Jan 26, 1813; m. Leonard Johnson, Dec. 15, 1832; d. July 21, 1836. She had ch.: I. Gertrude, who m. Theodore F. Morris, M. D., of Jersey City.

148. VII. Eliza, b. Feb. 18, 1816; m. Cornelius Cadmus of Slotterdam.

149. VIII. Nicholas S. (247), b. Nov. 21, 1818; m. Ellen Jane, dau. of Stephen Van Ripen, Oct. 1, 1840.

150. IX. Fanny G., b. Feb. 27, 1821; X. Janet, b. Sept. 2, 1823, d. Sept. 18, 1823.

151. XI. Stephen B. (248), b. Dec. 21, 1824; m. Mary, dau. of Merselis J. Merselis, Dec. 25, 1845.

152. XII. Helen, b. Aug. 18, 1826; d. Sept. —, 1826.

William [95] had ch.:

153. I. Elizabeth, b. Dec. 16, 1794; m. John Cadmus (22), Dec. 3, 1814.

154. II. Margaret, m. Jasper Cadmus, Dec. 17, 1817.

155. III. William (249), b. Dec. 2, 1801; m. Maria Jane, dau. of Cornelius Van Horn, April 25, 1822.

156. IV. Peter V. B. (255), b. Aug. 30, 1811; m. Jane Van Horn (44), Feb. 27, 1840.

157. V. Cornelius, m. Caroline, dau. of James Simonson, June 2, 1838; d. Feb. 13, 1840, æt. 25 yrs., 2 mos., 22 days.

158. VI. Jane Maria, b. Sept. 23, 1823; m. Samuel Meyers of Orange county, N. Y., May 31, 1843; VII. Rachel V. B., b. Oct. 30, 1826.

Cornelius [96] had ch.:

159. I. William C. (259), m. Cornelia Vreeland (180), Nov. 30, 1814; removed to Middlebush, N. J.

160. II. Peter V. B. (262), b. Aug. 27, 1795; m. Antje Vreeland (142), March 16, 1816; d. Dec. 12, 1867.

161. III. Eliza, b. June 18, 1798; m. Stephen Terhune, June 1, 1815; d. March 24, 1848.[1]

162. IV. Cornelius C. (270), b. Nov. 26, 1800; m. Catharine, dau. of John Outwater, Dec. 23, 1824; d. Dec. 17, 1873.

163. V. Jane, m. Garret Vreeland (106), Dec. 19, 1822.

164. VI. Margaret, m. Henry Vreeland (107), Dec. 24, 1825.

165. VII. Rachel, m. Henry J. Mandeville, Dec. 19, 1831.

166. VIII. Ann, m. Michael M. Vreeland (183), May 1, 1830.

George [98] had ch.:

167. I. Michael (274), b. Oct. 31, 1781; m. Aeltje, dau. of Guilliam Outwater, Nov. 30, 1801; d. April 10, 1828; she b. Dec. 11, 1781, d. in 1846.

168. II. Hartman (282), b. March 15, 1784; m. Eliza B.,

ELIZA B. VREELAND. Hartman Vreeland

dau. of Andrew Gautier, Dec. 17, 1808; d. Feb. 6, 1868, s. p., but had adopted his wife's nephew,

---

[1] As to Terhune, *vide Genealogy of the Bergen Family*, 106.

Hartman, son of Garret Van Horn (41), whose name was changed to Vreeland.

169. III. Annetje, b. March 30, 1786; m. Thomas McDonald.

170. IV. Cornelius, b. Feb. 25, 1789; d. Jan. 16, 1813, unm.

171. V. John G. (283), b. Jan. 3, 1792; m. Catharine, dau. of Helmigh Van Houten, Feb. 1, 1817; d. July 17, 1832; she d. Oct. 10, 1849.

172. VI. Claesje, b. Dec. 26, 1794; m. George Van Ripen (71), of Slotterdam, July 23, 1814.

173. VII. Jacob, b. Oct. 11, 1797; d. Dec. 9, 1797.

174. VIII. Henry (287), b. Oct. 11, 1797; m. Lucinda, dau. of Cornelius Jerolamon, May 28, 1820.

175. IX. Jacob, b. July 5, 1800; d. in inf.

176. X. Garret (296), b. June 26, 1803; m. Mary, dau. of Baker Smith, May 15, 1824; d. Feb. 10, 1852.

177. XI. Jacob, b. March 9, 1809; d. Feb. 1, 1811.

Michael [102) had ch.:

178. I. Lybertje, b. Aug. 14, 1790; m. George Cadmus (21), Nov. 14, 1812.

179. II. John M. (301), b. Sept. 30, 1792; m. 1st, Rachel, dau. of Nicholas Mandeville, Nov. 19, 1818; she d. Aug. 23, 1853, æt. 53 yrs., 9 mos., 6 days; 2d, Ellen Schwab; d. July 18, 1864.

180. III. Cornelia, b. Dec. 24, 1794; m. William C. Vreeland (159), Nov. 30, 1814.

181. IV. Annatje, b. March 4, 1797; m. Nicholas C. Prior, Dec. 30, 1818; d. Feb. 6, 1866.

182. V. Myndert (305), b. July 1, 1800; m. 1st, Catharine, dau. of Jasper Cadmus (29), Jan. 18, 1823; 2d, Annatje Van Ripen (110), Nov. 24, 1836; removed to Rocky Hill.

183. VI. Michael (311), b. Dec. 3, 1807; m. Ann Vreeland (166), May 1, 1830; removed to Rocky Hill.

Seventh Generation.

Garret [106] had ch.:

184. I. Jacob, b. Dec. 25, 1828; II. Elizabeth Catharine, b. Nov. 7, 1831; III. Jacob Henry, b. Oct. 11, 1834, d. March 8, 1855; IV. Margaret Amelia, b. Jan. 19, 1836.

Henry [107] had ch.:

185. I. William Henry, b. Nov. 19, 1830; II. Catharine Jane, b. Feb. 3, 1839.

George [108] had ch.:

186. I. Jacob, b. Dec. 11, 1832; II. Cornelia Elizabeth, b. July 23, 1835; III. William Henry, b. Feb. 15, 1838; IV. Catharina, b. Aug. 29, 1842; V. Anna, b. Feb. 10, 1845, m. Jacob M. Van Winkle (163), Feb. 26, 1862; VI. Cornelius, b. Aug. 12, 1849; VII. Martin L., b. Nov. 18, 1852.

John [109] had ch.:

187. I. John Henry, b. Aug. 7, 1839; II. Hannah V. B., b. Nov. 29, 1841; III. Cornelius V. R., b. Dec. 20, 1843.

Cornelius [110] had ch.:

188. I. Jacob, b. Nov. 7, 1836; m. Mary Jane Voorhis, Dec. 29, 1858; removed to Princeton.
189. II. Cathalina, b. March 8, 1838; m. Robert B. Stringham.
190. III. Henry V. H., b. Jan. 1, 1840; removed to Brooklyn.
191. IV. Cornelius, b. May 16, 1844; d. July 25, 1845.
192. V. Amelia Ann, b. Jan. 16, 1846; d. March 15, 1867.
193. VI. Eliza Jane, b. May 13, 1848; m. Theodore R. Cadmus (86), Dec. 31, 1865.

Garret [112] had ch.:

194. I. Susan M., b. Jan. 25, 1840; m. George R. Vreeland (127).

George [115] had ch.:

195. I. Sophia Jane, b. Dec. 7, 1837; m. Andrew Cadmus (71), Oct. 28, 1859.
196. II. Cathalina, b. Aug. 26, 1839; m. Peter S. VanWinkle (157), Dec. 26, 1861.
197. III. George W., b. June 3, 1842; m. Helen G., dau. of Oliver P. Smith, Jan. 15, 1868; had ch.: I. Jennie, d. in inf; II. Catharine.
198. IV. Rachel Emma, b. July 13, 1844.
199. V. Mary Frances, b. Sept. 4, 1847; m. Peter C. Vreeland (353), June 28, 1870.
200. VI. Francis N., b. Sept. 17, 1849; d. in inf.
201. VII. Jefferson, b. Sept. 12, 1851; VIII. Oliver P., b.

Oct. 10, 1853; IX. Ferdinand, b. March 14, 1856.

Henry [118] had ch.:

202. I. Mary C., b. Oct. 21, 1851; II. Julia A., b. Feb. 19, 1854; III. Annie W., b. Aug. 18, 1856; IV. George H., b. Dec. 15, 1859; V. Helen J., b. Dec. 24, 1861; VI. Henry G., b. June 23, 1865.

Garret R. [122] had ch.:

203. I. Eliza Jane, b. Dec. 28, 1839; m. John D. Romaine, Dec. 18, 1860.

204. II. Stephen T., d. in inf.

Michael D. M. [123] had ch.:

205. I. Catharine Jane, b. Nov. 22, 1843; m. John H. Carragan, Sept. —, 1869.

206. II. Peter, b. April 11, 1845; m. Hannah, dau. of Archer G. Welsh, Dec. 14, 1869; had ch.: I. Reuben C., b. May 11, 1872.

207. III. Abraham B., b. Jan. 21, 1848; IV. Margaret Louisa, b. Nov. 22, 1851; V. Lycenia D. M., b. Nov. 11, 1855; VI. Joseph W., b. Nov. 16, 1858; VII. Henry B., b. Dec. 25, 1860, d. Aug. 17, 1867; VIII. William P., b. Aug. 11, 1862; IX. Wallace, b. March 20, 1865; X. Ella, b. March 31, 1867; XI. Matthew, b. April 20, 1870.

Richard C. [124] had ch.:

208. I. James C., b. May 7, 1847; m. Mary Elizabeth, dau. of Henry Norman, of Englewood, Sept. 28, 1870.

209. II. Henry R., b. June 1, 1850; III. David D., b. Oct. 21, 1853; IV. Margaret R., b. June 8, 1856; V. George W., b. Aug. 21, 1858; VI. Lavinia, b. Jan. 1, 1861; VII. William P., b. July 9, 1863.

Henry [125] had ch.:

210. I. Mary Margretta, b. May 26, 1853; m. Garret Van Horn (63), April 22, 1873.

211. II. Kate C., b. July 2, 1855, d. Nov. 3, 1857; III. Emma Elizabeth, b. April 8, 1857; IV. Hamilton, b. March 23, 1859; V. Anna B., b. Feb. 27, 1861; VI. Richard, b. Sept. 21, 1864, d. Oct. 18, 1865;

VII. Charles M., b. Jan. 16, 1867; VIII. Henry, b. March 18, 1870.

George [127] had ch.:

212. I. Catharine Anna, b. Aug. 5, 1862; II. George B., b. Oct. 10, 1870, d. May 21, 1871.

Jacob B. [131] had ch.:

213. Edgar, b. Jan. 4, 1865; II. Lena, b. Dec. 22, 1868; III. Charles Winfield, b. Jan. 26, 1870.

Nicholas [136] had ch.:

214. I. Nicholas, b. Aug. 7, 1816; d. Aug. 14, 1817.
215. II. Nicholas, b. April 3, 1836; d. March 13, 1837.
216. III. John V. R. (320), b. Dec. 3, 1837; m. Anna Maria Newkirk (107), Oct. 16, 1861.
217. IV. Gitty Ann, b. March 14, 1841; m. Samuel D. Tompkins, Jan. 2, 1868.

Daniel [137] had ch.:

218. I. Jane, b. Nov. 15, 1813; m. Cornelius Brinkerhoff (41), Dec. 16, 1830.
219. II. Michael D. (321), b. Jan. 31, 1817; m. Rachel, dau. of John Sturge, Dec. 3, 1835.
220. III. Aaron N. (326), b. Dec. 4, 1819; m. Eliza, dau. of Isaac Pow, Dec. 12, 1844.
221. IV. Gitty S., b. April 17, 1822; m. John B. Welsh, June 29, 1843.
222. V. Cornelius V. R. (330), b. July 24, 1825; m. Susannah Jane, dau. of Henry Smith, Dec. 31, 1849.
223. VI. Nicholas D. (331), b. Feb. 26, 1828; m. Catharine, dau. of John Zabriskie, Sept. 20, 1848.
224. VII. Daniel S., b. Nov. 1, 1831; m. Sarah Catharine, dau. of Thomas Anderson.

Garret [138] had ch.:

225. I. Garret (332), b. Nov. 26, 1814; m. Catharine Van Buskirk (61), Oct. 22, 1834.
226. II. Jane, b. July 9, 1818; d. Sept. 6, 1818.
227. III. Gitty, b. Jan. 7, 1820; m. Jacob J. Vreeland (111), Dec. 20, 1838.
228. IV. Anna Jane, b. Jan. 27, 1822; m. Michael J. Vreeland (301), Dec. 17, 1840.

229. V. Nicholas, b. Feb. 1, 1826; d. Sept. 16, 1847, unm.
230. VI. Abraham, b. June 21, 1835; d. July 29, 1835.

Abraham [139] had ch.:

231. I. Richard, b. Jan. 16, 1818; d. Sept. 3, 1818.
232. II. Michael (340), b. April 3, 1819; m. Rachel Cadmus (48), Jan. 31, 1839; d. March 19, 1849.
233. III. Richard, b. July 29, 1820; m. Eleanor P., dau. of John S. Winner, Dec. 20, 1841; she d. May 17, 1843; had ch.: I. Eleanor P. W., b. April 30, 1843; d. in inf.
234. IV. Abraham (346), b. Jan. 13, 1822; m. Rachel, dau. of John Vreeland (285), Oct. 18, 1845.
235. V. Nicholas, b. Aug. 26, 1825; d. Feb. 13, 1847, unm.
236. VI. Cornelius (347), b. Feb. 16, 1828; m. Mary, dau. of Garret Newkirk (80), Sept. 19, 1849; removed to Wyckoff, Bergen Co.
237. VII. Eliza Jane, b. Oct. 21, 1829; m. Henry N. Van Wagenen (49), May 12, 1849; d. Oct. 22, 1866.
238. VIII. Garret, b. Dec. 22, 1831.
239. IX. Gitty, b. May 21, 1833; m. George Newkirk (54), Dec. 3, 1854.
240. X. Hannah, b. May 20, 1839; m. Garret Vreeland (333), Nov. 3, 1859.

Cornelius M. [140] had ch.:

241. I. Jane N., b. Oct. 28, 1824; m. John Van Pelt.
242. II. Gitty Ann, b. June 9, 1827; m. Abraham Van Ripen, of N. Y., Oct. 1, 1851.
243. III. Caroline, b. Sept. 13, 1829; m. Isaac Van Ripen, of N. Y.
244. IV. Hannah W., b. June 1, 1832; m. Richard C. Van Buskirk (76), Dec. 31, 1849.
245. V. Cornelius, b. July 4, 1834; m. Rebecca Brown.
246. VI. Garret; VII. Cornelia; VIII. Sarah Catharine.

Nicholas S. [149] had ch.:

247. I. Sophia Elizabeth, b. Nov. 23, 1843; II. Stephen, b. March 17, 1846, d. Oct. 31, 1851; III. Ann Maria, b. Jan. 29, 1848, d. April 26, 1851; IV. Benjamin F., b. Nov. 14, 1850, d. April 29, 1854; V. Stephen B., b. Jan. 22, 1853; VI. Ann Helena, b. May 9, 1855; VII. Allie Teresa, b. Dec.

24, 1857; VIII. Jennie, b. Aug. 5, 1863, d. Aug. 15, 1863.

Stephen B. [151] had ch.:

248. I. Elizabeth C., b. Feb. 16, 1847, d. Dec. 28, 1860; II. Susanna, b. May 6, 1851; III. Stephen S., b. Nov. 22, 1854; IV. Fanny G., b. Oct. 17, 1856.

William [155] had ch.:

249. I. William (349), b. Jan. 5, 1823; m. Euphemia B. Vreeland (298), Nov. 26, 1846.
250. II. Cornelius V. H. (350), b. Oct. 27, 1824; m. Rachel Jane, dau. of Nicholas Ackerman, Jan. 27, 1853.
251. III. Sarah, b. Dec. 7, 1826; m. Anthony Dougherty, June 4, 1846; d. Aug. 23, 1855.
252. IV. Ira C. B., b. Nov. 22, 1829; d. Dec. 21, 1858, unm. He and his brother Jacob were drowned in Newark Bay.
253. V. Rachel Catharine, b. April 22, 1832; m. Richard C. Van Ripen (150), May 27, 1852.
254. VI. Jacob C. D., b. Aug. 6, 1835, d. Dec. 21, 1858, unm.

Peter V. B. [156] had ch.:

255. I. Ann R., b. March 11, 1841; d. July 16, 1850.
256. II. Rachel Jane, b. Oct. 13, 1842.
257. III. Cornelius, b. Aug. 21, 1844; m. Alice L., dau. of Alonzo Nutt, Nov. 18, 1868; had ch.: I. Jennie Louise, b. Nov. 2, 1872.
258. IV. Agnes V. H., b. Sept. 6, 1848; V. Anna, b. Dec. 12, 1851; VI. Washington, b. Aug. 13, 1856.

William C. [159] had ch.:

259. I. Ann, b. April 21, 1815; m. George Vreeland (108), Dec. 31, 1831.
260. II. Michael (351); m. Jane D., dau. of Walter Woods, March 7, 1839; removed to Middlebush, N. J.
261. III. Cornelius, b. July 22, 1816; d. July 1, 1828.

Peter V. B. [160] had ch.:

262. I. Cornelius (352), b. June 28, 1821; m. Ann Elizabeth Van Buskirk (64), Dec. 3, 1841.
263. II. Jennet, b. July 31, 1823; m. 1st, Freeman Atkins, Dec. 11, 1840; 2d, ——— Anderson.
264. III. Elizabeth, b. June 10, 1825; m. Nicholas Van Buskirk (56), March 16, 1843.

265. IV. Margaret Ann, b. Aug. 21, 1827; m. Henry C. Post, Nov. 4, 1847.
266. V. Cornelia H., b. Oct. 25, 1829; VI. Mary Jane, b. Feb. 23, 1832.
267. VII. Rachel Aletta, b. March 27, 1834; m. William Elsworth, Jan. 20, 1864; d. March 18, 1869.
268. VIII. Gitty Catharine, b. May 28, 1836; d. Nov. 20, 1839.
269. IX. William P., b. Oct. 15, 1840; d. Sept. 12, 1849.

Cornelius [162] had ch.:
270. I. Cornelius, b. Dec. 6, 1825; d. Jan. 23, 1826.
271. II. Ellen, b. Nov. 26, 1828; d. Aug. 11, 1849, unm.
272. III. Elizabeth V. B., b. Oct. 29, 1834; m. Amos Harrison, March 6, 1852.
273. IV. John O., b. Sept. 27, 1845; m. Maria E., dau. of Geo. Cozine, May 2, 1868; had ch.: I. Ellen, b. Sept. 24, 1869.

Michael [167] had ch.:
274. I. George, b. Jan. 25, 1802; m. Hannah Tise.
275. II. Anna, b. Feb. 17, 1805; m. Teunis Van Pelt, Sept. 21, 1826.
276. III. Gilliam, b. Feb. 19, 1807; d. in inf.
277. IV. Jacob M. (355), b. June 8, 1808; m. Jane, dau. of John Van Clief, May 8, 1830; she b. Oct. 8, 1808.
278. V. Jane, b. Aug. 22, 1810; m. John Housman, Dec. 31, 1829.
279. VI. Matilda, b. Jan. 6, 1813; m. Andrew P. Simonson, June 11, 1831.
280. VII. Cornelius, b. June 25, 1816; m. Susan, dau. of Paul Salter, Sept. 7, 1839; removed to Young America, Ill.
281. VIII. Hartman (364), b. Nov. 8, 1823; m. Seny, dau. of Clayton Cranmer, of Egg Harbor, Jan. 20, 1844.

Hartman [168] had ch. (by adoption):
282. I. Hartman (368), b. Dec. 7, 1826; m. Margaret Cadmus (65), June 1, 1853. *Vide* Van Horn family (41).

John G. [171] had ch.:
283. I. Jane B., b, June 14, 1818; m. Michael Terhune, March 19, 1835.
284. II. Catharine, b. May 14, 1824; m. Jasper Cubberly, June 3, 1840; d. April 2, 1841.

285. III. Rachel, b. March 18, 1827; m. Abraham Vreeland (234), Oct. 18, 1845.
286. IV. Eliza Ann, b. Oct. 19, 1829; m. Michael Vreeland (306), Feb. 2, 1848; d. March 24, 1861.

Henry [174] had ch.:
287. I. Jane, b. Oct. 17, 1821; m. John Salter, Oct. 19, 1839.
288. II. Elizabeth, b. Nov. 28, 1824; m. Cornelius La Tourette, May 29, 1841.
289. III. Cornelius, b. Dec. 24, 1827; m. Catharine Ann, dau. of Israel Decker, June 10, 1857.
290. IV. John, b. May 12, 1830; m. Jane B., dau. of Thomas McDonald, March 27, 1850; had ch.: I. Thomas McD., b. March 1, 1857; d. March 1, 1860.
291. V. George, b. Aug. 17, 1832; m. Eleanor Ann, dau. of John Corsen, of Staten Island, June 27, 1855; had ch.: I. Irwin, b. Dec. 22, 1861.
292. VI. Mary Ann, b. Sept. 6, 1834; d. Feb. 21, 1861, unm.
293. VII. Garret (369), b. Oct. 21, 1836; m. 1st, Isabella Darling, March 2, 1858; 2d, Rebecca Jane, dau. of Stewart H. McFarlane, March 9, 1861.
294. VIII. Hartman, b. Jan. 27, 1839; d. July 22, 1842.
295. IX. Sarah Catharine, b. May 2, 1841; m. Addis Rino, Aug. 12, 1860; d. March 27, 1869.

Garret [176] had ch.:
296. I. Elizabeth, b. April 7, 1825, m. John Post, May —, 1845.
297. II. John, b. July 22, 1826; d. July 28, 1826.
298. III. Euphemia B., b. Aug. 12, 1827; m. William W. Vreeland (249), Nov. 26, 1846.
299. IV. Phebe Ann, b. Sept. 15, 1829; m. David Pollock, Nov. 11, 1869.
300. V. George (370), b. Sept. 6, 1831; m. 1st, Cornelia Vreeland (323), March 24, 1858; 2d, Rachel, dau. of Amos Salter, and wid. of George Malcolm, March 26, 1868.

John M. [179] had ch.:
301. I. Michael J., b. Sept. 3, 1819; m. Anna Jane Vreeland (228), Dec. 17, 1840; removed to Rocky Hill; was a member of the Assembly of N. J., from Hudson County.

302. II. Elizabeth, b. May 14, 1822; m. Winfield Stringham, March 4, 1847.
303. III. Hannah, b. Oct. 19, 1824; m. Garret Bush, Dec. 3, 1846.
304. IV. Nicholas (371), b. April 8, 1827; m. Martha Cadmus (47), Nov. 8, 1848; d. April 20, 1857.

Mindert [182] had ch.:
305. I. Catharine, b. June 12, 1824; d. Oct. 12, 1840.
306. II. Michael, b. Nov. 19, 1826; m. Eliza Ann Vreeland (286), Feb. 2, 1848.
307. III. Hannah, b. Jan. 13, 1829; m. Andrew Van Horn, Feb. 3, 1848.
308. IV. Jasper, b. Aug. 1, 1832; m. Ann Maria, dau. of Teunis Van Pelt, April 5, 1854.
309. V. John, b. Jan. 13, 1834; m. Sophia Van Cleef; removed to Millstone, N. J.
310. VI. Jacob, b. Aug. 2, 1839; m. Louisa, dau. of Jeremiah W. Updyke; removed to Rocky Hill.

Michael [183] had ch.:
311. I. Michael (373), b. Sept. 28, 1831; m. Catherine Sarah, dau. of Jeremiah Skillman, Nov. 18, 1863.
312. II. Elizabeth, b. Oct. 24, 1833; m. Henry H. Brinkerhoff (53), June 6, 1855.
313. III. Cornelius, b. Sept. 8, 1835; d. in inf.
314. IV. William, b. March 19, 1837; d. in inf.
315. V. Cornelius, b. June 1, 1838; m. Emma N., dau. of Wesley Morris, Oct. 8, 1862; had ch.: I. Emma M., b. July 14, 1866.
316. VI. John Henry, b. Oct. 31, 1840; d. Aug. 26, 1841.
317. VII. Mindert, b. Nov. 11, 1842; m. Elizabeth, dau. of Garret Mandeville, Nov. 18, 1866; had ch.: I. Gitty Ann, b. June 24, 1870.
318. VIII. Stephen T., b. July 15, 1846; d. July 6, 1865.
319. IX. Annetta, b. Feb. 26, 1854.

Eighth Generation.

John V. R. [216] had ch.:
320. I. Anna Louisa, b. Aug. 6, 1862; II. John Edwin, b. Sept. 14, 1864; III. Frank, b. Aug. 5, 1870.

Michael D. [219] had ch.:
321. I. Jane P., b. Aug. 21, 1836; d. in inf.

322. II. Abigail P., b. Nov. 13, 1837; m. John G. Wauters, Dec. 13, 1854; previous to her marriage her name was changed to Post, by act of the Legislature.
323. III. Cornelia, b. Oct. 11, 1840; m. George Vreeland (300), March 24, 1858; d. March 26, 1863.
324. IV. Rachel Ann S., b. March 3, 1843; m. George V. N. Van Duyn, Oct. 11, 1871.
325. V. Jane, b. Oct. 26, 1844, d. in inf.; VI. Eunice, b. Oct. 19, 1846, d. Nov. 16, 1863; VII. Daniel, b. Dec. 2, 1848, d. in inf.; VIII. Susan Jane, b. July 1, 1854.

Aaron N. [220] had ch.:

326. I. Sarah Jane, b. July 26, 1845; m. Augustus Jackson.
327. II. Cornelia Ann, b. Jan. 13, 1847; m. Frederick V. L. Voorhis, Feb. 1, 1865.
328. III. Gitty Catharine, b. Jan. 4, 1849; m. Nicholas P. Allen, Aug. 10, 1869.
329. IV. Daniel A., d. Dec. 3, 1870, æt. 18 years 2 mos.; V. Rachel G.; VI. Susan.

Cornelius V. R. [222] had ch.:

330. I. Cornelia Ann; II. Matilda; III. Garret; IV. Cornelius; V. Cornelia.

Nicholas D. [223] had ch.:

331. I. Mary Lavinia, b. Aug. 22, 1850; II. Jane; III. Catharine; IV. John.

Garret [225] had ch.:

332. I. Catharine Jane, b, Oct. 8, 1835; m. Andrew A. Rapp, April 6, 1853.
333. II. Garret (374), b. Dec. 19; 1837; m. Hannah Vreeland (240), Nov. 3, 1859.
334. III. Sarah Arabella, b. Dec. 10, 1840; d. June 16, 1843.
335. IV. Anna Elizabeth, b. July 28, 1843.
336. V. John V. B. (375), b. Sept. 6, 1845; m. 1st, Lilla H., dau. of Ira H. Taylor, April 16, 1868; she d. June 5, 1870; 2d, Mary, sister of his first wife, Jan. 16, 1872.
337. VI. Lawrence M., b. June 21, 1849; d. July 29, 1850.
338. VII. Nicholas G., b. June 21, 1849; m. Catharine Van Wagenen (54), April 12, 1871; had ch.: I. Henry Garret, b. Oct. 4, 1873, d. Dec. 25, 1873.
339. VIII. Edward W., b. Feb. 22, 1855.

Michael [232] had ch.:

340. I. Ann, b. Oct. 29, 1840.

341. II. Abraham, m. Eleanor F., dau. of Abraham Rapp, April 3, 1865.

342. III. Jasper C., b. May 15, 1843; m. 1st, Ellen E., dau. of Henry Mandeville, Nov. 19, 1865; she d. July 16, 1867; 2d, Mary E. Lewis, July 19, 1871; d. Nov. 3, 1873, s. p.

343. IV. Jane, d. Dec. 10, 1845, æt. 10 mos., 18 days.

344. V. Margaret, b. Oct. 5, 1845; m. George Carragan, Aug. 15, 1866.

345. VI. Rachel, b. May 31, 1848.

Abraham [234] had ch.:

346. I. Hartman, b. Dec. 1, 1848; m. Letty J., dau. of John V. H. Clendenny, April 8, 1872; had ch.: I. ——, b. Oct. 20, 1870.

Cornelius [236] had ch.:

347. I. Rachel, b. March 5, 1851; m. John D. Board, Sept. 4, 1872.

348. II. Mary Catharine, b. Jan. 21, 1853; III. Lewis, b. March 19, 1856; IV. Edgar, b. Feb. 11, 1860.

William [249] had ch.:

349. I. Cornelius V. H., b. Sept. 6, 1847; II. Mary Elizabeth, b. March 12, 1849, d. Oct. 25, 1851; III. Garret G., b. April 7, 1850; IV. George, b. March 5, 1853; V. Ira C. B., b. April 28, 1856; VI. Jacob C. D., b. Aug. 29, 1859; VII. William, b. Feb. 2, 1862; VIII. Phebe Ann, b. Dec. 31, 1864; IX. Hartman, b. Oct. 24, 1867.

Cornelius V. H. [250] had ch.:

350. I. William Henry, b. July 14, 1858; II. John Jacob, b. Oct. 14, 1862; III. Bertha Celesta, b. Nov. 11, 1868.

Michael [260] had ch.:

351. I. William, b. Feb. 25, 1840; II. Sarah Ann, b. April 10, 1841; III. Eliza Jane, b. May 23, 1842; IV. Sarah, b. May 1, 1844; V. Eleanor Ann, b. July 20, 1846; VI. Cornelia, b. Dec. 23, 1848; VII. Mary Frances, b. Oct. 15, 1850; VIII. Ruth Almira, b. Feb. 9, 1853; d. Oct. 10, 1854.

Cornelius [262] had ch.:

352. I. John Henry (377), b. Sept. 14, 1844; m. Anne E., dau. of David L. Van Horn, Dec. 24, 1863.

353. II. Peter C., b. March 16, 1847; m. Mary Frances Vreeland (199), June 28, 1870; had ch.: I. George Francis, b. Oct. 30, 1872.

354. III. William P., b. Jan. 1, 1850; IV. Sarah Arabella, b. Dec. 2, 1853.

Jacob M. [277] had ch.:

355. I. Gertrude Ann, b. Dec. 8, 1830; m. 1st, Jasper Garretson, Nov. 6, 1850; 2d, Horace H. Driggs; he d. Feb. 3, 1865.

356. II. Eliza Jane, b. Nov. 8, 1832; m. Henry K. Van Horn, Dec. 25, 1850.

357. III. Michael G., b. May 23, 1835; m. Joanna, dau. of John N. Van Buskirk (98), March 25, 1869.

358. IV. Mary, b. Nov. 30, 1837; m. John Huddleston.

359. V. John, b. Nov. 25, 1839; m. Anna, dau. of Abraham Simmons, Nov. 11, 1863.

360. VI. Sarah, b. Sept. 29, 1842; m. William Hageman.

361. VII. Jacob M., b. Aug. 11, 1844; m. Fanny Richards.

362. VIII. Cornelius, b. March 28, 1847; d. July —, 1850.

363. IX. William Henry, b. March 18, 1850.

Hartman [281] had ch.:

364. I. Ezra C., b. July 23, 1845; d. Sept. 14, 1846.

365. II. Ann Matilda, b. Jan. 20, 1847; m. William Sandford, Oct. 10, 1867.

366. III. Garadata A., b. March 29, 1849; IV. Edwin P., b. Nov. 4, 1851, d. in inf.

367. V. Jane R., b. Aug. 23, 1855; VI. Hartman M., b. Nov. 23, 1858.

Hartman [282] had ch.:

368. I. Crossfield G., b. Oct. 20, 1855; II. Philip E., b. Sept. 27, 1857; III. Richard E., b. Nov. —, 1859.

Garret [293] had ch.:

369. I. Thomas G., b. Feb. 23, 1862; II. Charles S., b. Jan. 14, 1864; III. Madeline, b. June 8, 1866.

George [300] had ch.:

370. I. Rachel Ann, b. March 30, 1859, d. Feb. 25, 1861; II. Garret, b. Oct. 24, 1860.

Nicholas [304] had ch.:

371. I. Rachel Elizabeth, b. Nov. 26, 1850; m. George Henry Cadmus (100), Oct. 20, 1870.

372. II. Catharine Ann, b. June 2, 1853; III. Nicholas, b. April 5, 1857.

Michael [311] had ch.:

373. I. Mary Annetta, b. Feb. 22, 1865; II. Cornelius, b. May 31, 1870.

Ninth Generation.

Garret [333] had ch.:

374. I. Anna Jane, b. Nov, 16, 1861; d. Aug. 4, 1862; II. Edwin, b. Aug. 10, 1864; d. July 26, 1865; III. Garret, b. July 21, 1868; d. Nov. 9, 1871; IV. John H., b. Jan. 16, 1870; V. Charles Henry, b. Sept. 2, 1873; d. Dec. 31, 1873.

John V. B. [336] had ch.:

375. I. John P., b. May 19, 1870; d. July 11, 1870.

John Henry [352] had ch.:

376. I. Anna, b. June 6, 1865; II. Cornelius Peter, b. March 4, 1868; III. Arabella, b. Feb. 10, 1870; IV. David L., b. Sept. 30, 1872.

Van Winckel—Van Winkel—Van Winkle.

This name is derived from *winkel*, a corner, square, shop. *Winkelier* was a shopkeeper. The ancestor was a shop or store-keeper. Its present orthography is comparatively modern. The family settled in Harsimus shortly after their arrival in this country. They came from Middleburgh, the capital of Zealand, one of the United Provinces. The city was on the island Walcheren, about forty miles S.W. of Rotterdam, well built and populous, with a fine harbor and a profitable trade.

I have not ascertained the names of the parents of the three boys and two girls who seem to have made up this family. Their names were Jacob, Waling, Symon, Annetje and Grietje: their patronymic being Jacobse—children of Jacob. Jacob was the founder of the family in the county of Hudson. Waling and Symon were of the company from Bergen who, in 1679, purchased and afterward settled "Haquequenunck," Aquackanonck, now Passaic. They were the founders of the family at that place. The name was formerly written Van Winckel.

1. Jacob (4), m. 1st, Aeltje Daniels, wid., Dec. 15, 1675; she d. June 2, 1692; 2d, Grietje Hendricks Hollinge, March 26, 1695; d. Nov. 20, 1724; she d. Sept. 20, 1732.
2. Waling (14), m. Catharina Michielse, March 15, 1671. His wife was yet living at the date of his will, Nov. 1, 1717.
3. Symon (21), m. Annetje Sip (4), Dec. 15, 1675. His will, dated June 19, 1722, was proved Feb. 24, 1732. His wife was living at the date of the will.

Annetje, m. Johannis Steynmets, Dec. 1, 1676.

Grietje, m. Elias Michielse Vreeland (2), of "Gemoenepa," Aug. 30, 1665.

Second Generation.

Jacob Jacobse [1] had ch.:

4. I. Jacob, b. Sept. 19, 1676; m. Fitje Poulis, March 6, 1703.
5. II. Margrietje, b. Oct. 22, 1678; m. Abraham Vreeland (14), Oct. 28, 1699.
6. III. Daniel (33), b. July 28, 1681; m. 1st, Rachel Straatmaker, May 11, 1707; she d. March 12, 1708; 2d, Jannetje Vreeland (48), Sept. 3, 1709; d. Jan. 10, 1757.
7. IV. Johannis (38), b. June 25, 1686; m. Fitje Hendrickse Banta, April 19, 1713; moved to Belleville.
8. V. Simeon, b. Jan. 22, 1689; m. Jannetje Alger, of Hackensack, May 27, 1710.
9. VI. (Son), b. April 10, 1692; d. in inf.
10. VII. Hendrick (41), b. Jan. 20, 1696; m. Catrintje Waldron, May 26, 1726; d. May 28, 1767.
11. VIII. Trintje, b. Jan. 14, 1697; m. Myndert Gerbrantse (10), May 7, 1715; d. July 21, 1753.
12. IX. Teunis, b. Dec. 21, 1698; d. in inf.
13. X. Samuel, b. Jan. 5, 1705; d. May 2, 1754.

Waling Jacobse [2] had ch.:

14. I. Annetje, m. Hermanus G. Van Wagenen (5), Oct. 6, 1690.

15. II. Jacob, m. Geertruyt Brickers, of Albany, Oct. 30, 1697; had ch.: I. Wyntje.

16. III. Michael, bap. April 27, 1677; d. unm.; his will was dated May 21, 1748.

17. IV. Trintje, bap. March 25, 1680; m. Egbert Sanderse, of Staten Island, Sept. 16, 1709.

18. V. Johannis (47), m. Hillegont Sip (7), Sept. 30, 1710.

19. VI. Sarah, m. Garret Van Vorst (14), May 22, 1714.

20. VII. Abraham, bap. April 22, 1690; his name is not mentioned in his father's will of Nov. 1, 1717.

Symon Jacobse [3] had ch.:

21. I. Margrietje, bap. 1676; m. Martin Winne, Oct. 30, 1697. He was b. in Albany in 1685; d. at Bergen, July 8, 1737. He was the son of Levinus Winne, and founder of the Winner family in Hudson County.

22. II. Jacob, bap. Aug. 9, 1678; a member of the church at Aquackanonck in 1725; m. Jacomyntje Mattheuse Van Nieuwkerck (4), April 21, 1701.

23. III. Johannis (50), b. Aug. 18, 1682; m. Magdalena Spier. His will was dated at Elizabethtown, June 13, 1759.

24. IV. Simon, bap. Aug. 6, 1686; m. 1st, Pryntje Van Giesen; 2d, Antje Pieterse, wid., March 3, 1734; had ch.: I. Jenneke, b. Oct. 9, 1728; II. Helena, b. Feb. 24, 1730.

25. V. Trintje, b. April 2, 1688; m. Isaac E. Vreeland (16), March 23, 1706.

26. VI. Rachel, bap. Oct. —, 1690; m. Johannis Koeiman, of Albany, March 13, 1708.

27. VII. Arie, b. at Constable's Hoeck; m. Annetje, dau. of Tades Michielse, Oct. 27, 1705; had ch.: I. Tades, m. Catharina Bord, Dec. 17, 1736; II. Antje, m. Joris Bord, Jan. 10, 1730.

28. VIII. Aeltje, m. Jurian Tomasse Van Ripen (12), June 12, 1714.

29. IX. Gideon, m. Jannetje Koeiman. In his will, dated Nov. 8, 1764, he names his ch., viz.: I. Annatje, m. Casparus Van Winkle; II. Maritje; III. Ariantje; IV. Lydia, m. Samuel Stivers, and V. Rachel, b. 1727, m. Jedediah Dean.

30. X. Abraham, m. Maritje Van Dyke, of Second River, Jan. —, 1733. In his will, dated April 11, 1743,

he names his ch., viz.: I. Simeon; II. Fransois (who m. 1st, Susanna, dau. of John Forester, Oct. 3, 1777; 2d, Elizabeth Douwe, wid., Feb. 5, 1785; had ch.: I. Abraham, b. Dec. 26, 1779; II. John F., b. Nov. 6, 1781); III. Fitje; IV. Antje; his wife being then *enceinte*.

31. XI. Leah.

32. XII. Marinus, m. Geesje Van Wagenen (7), Sept. 2, 1721; had ch.: I. Annatje, b. Feb. 20, 1730; m. Hendrick G. Van Wagenen (28); II. Margrietje, b. Feb. 7, 1735, m. Michael Vreeland; III. Rachel, m. Jacob Van Wagenen; IV. Jannetje, m. Michael E. Vreeland, Dec. 28, 1755; V. Catrintje, m. Abraham Van Ripen, Nov. 16, 1763. His will, dated May 10, 1762, was proved Sept. 28, 1767.

Third Generation.

Daniel [6] had ch.:

33. I. Metje, b. Dec. 31, 1710.

34. II. Aeltje, b. April 13, 1712; m. Cornelius Van Ripen (27), June 29, 1728; d. July 19, 1776.

35. III. Jannetje, m. Jacob Diedricks, Nov. 26, 1738.

36. IV. Margaret, m. Johannis Van Ripen (28), Sept. 5, 1742; d. Sept. 18, 1754.

37. V. Fitje; VI. Rachel, wife of —— Sickles, and VII. Antje. He also had a son, bap. Dec. 12, 1714; d. in inf.

Johannis [7] had ch.:

38. I. Hendrick, b. March 20, 1714; m. Maritje Jurianse, Aug. 22, 1739; had ch.: I. Jurian, b. April 22, 1740.

39. II. Jacob, b. March —, 1716; III. Johannis, b. July 3, 1719.

40. IV. Agnietje, b. Dec. 16, 1723; V. Daniel, b. Dec. 16, 1723; VI. Aeltje, b. Nov. 25, 1726.

Hendrick [10] had ch.:

41. I. Jacob (59), m. Rachel Commgear, April 8, 1753; d. Dec. 17, 1778; she d. Sept. 18, 1772.

42. II. Joseph, d. in inf., Nov. 22, 1738.

43. III. Daniel (64), b. Jan. 1, 1735; m. Aeltje Van Ripen (54); d. Dec. 19, 1823.

44. IV. Hendrick (67), b. Jan. 23, 1736; m. 1st, Jannetje Brower, May 18, 1759; 2d, Sarah Speer; d. Dec. 19, 1827.

45. V. Johannis, b. May 9, 1739; d. before his father, s. p.
46. VI. Joseph, b. June 4, 1740; m. Jenneke Vreeland (63), wid. of Henry Newkirk (17), May 26, 1798; d. Aug. 4, 1809, s. p.

Johannis [18] had ch.:

47. I. Catrina, m. 1st, Pieter H. Pieterse, Oct 31, 1733; 2d, Johannis G. Post, Oct. 20, 1759.
48. II. Annatje, m. Johannis Sip, Dec. 12, 1744.
49. III. Waling (71), m. Jannetje Van Houten, June 8, 1743. His will, dated May 29, 1774, was proved March 23, 1784.

Johannis [23] had ch.:

50. I. Simeon, m. Annatje Bosch, Oct. 19, 1738, and had ch.: I. Johannis, b. Nov. 7, 1749; II. Benjamin, b. Dec. 1, 1750.
51. II. Alexander, m. Antje Van Winkle, and had ch.: I. Wyntje, b. Sept. 11, 1741; II. Jacob, b. May 1, 1748.
52. III. Jacob, m. Annatje Van Noostrand; d. Aug. 5, 1834, æt. 86 yrs., 4 mos., 24 days; she d. Feb. 18, 1829, æt. 75 yrs., 2 mos.
53. IV. Abraham (80), m. Jacomyntje Newkirk, June 9, 1739; d. Jan. 23, 1796, in his 85th year.
54. V. Marinus (81), m. Maria Evertson, Jan. 15, 1742; d. April 28, 1802, æt. 86 yrs.; she d. June 29, 1820, æt. 102 yrs. He was a private in Major McDonald's company in the French war of 1761.
55. VI. John, who died before his father, leaving issue.
56. VII. Catharine, who m. —— Marsh.
57. VIII. Hannah; IX. Mary; X. Leah; XI. Rachel.
58. XII. Sarah, b. July 14, 1735; m. —— Daly.

Fourth Generation.

Jacob [41] had ch.:

59. I. Daniel (82), b. July 21, 1758; m. Antje, dau. of Johannis Winne, Oct. 26, 1802; d. June 13, 1830; she d. Aug. 25, 1843.
60. II. Abraham (88), m. Antje Clendenny, Sept. 6, 1780; d. Nov. 24, 1823.
61. III. Catrintje, b. June 1, 1763; d. Sept. 8, 1793, unm.
62. IV. Joseph, b. May 18, 1768; d. Jan. 27, 1775.
63. V. Leah, b. Nov. 7, 1770; d. Sept. 18, 1772.

Daniel [43] had ch.:

64. I. Jurriaen (96), b. Feb. 22, 1761; m. Antje Sip (23); d. May 3, 1837.
65. II. Catrintje, b. Jan. 30, 1765; m. Jacob Merselis.
66. III. Hendrick (98), b. Nov. 27, 1774; m. Catlyntje Van Wagenen (51), Jan. 10, 1801; d. Dec. 13, 1848.

Hendrick [44] had ch.:

67. I. Catrina, b. Jan. 26, 1772; II. Raegel, b. March 29, 1775, d. in inf.
68. III. Raegel, b. Feb. 13, 1777; m. Martin Winne, April 1, 1797.
69. IV. Johannis (101), b. Nov. 7, 1778; m. Gertrude, dau. of John Diedricks.
70. V. Jacob H. (107), b. Feb. 20, 1789; m. Mary Smith.

Waling [49] had ch.:

71. I. John (110), m. Eva Kip, Oct. 25, 1747.
72. II. Hillegont, b. Feb. 25, 1749; m. Hendrick Van Wagenen; had ch.: I. Jannetje, b. Dec. 19, 1774; II. Johannis, b. March 2, 1784.
73. III. Jacob, m. Elsie, dau. of Henry Kip; had ch.: I. Waling, who m. 1st, Trintje, dau. of Dirck Paulusen; 2d, Anne Herring, and had ch.: I. Elsie, m. Henry Vreeland; II. Eliza, m. — Richards; III. Jane; IV. Jacob.
74. IV. Cornelius, m.; removed to Paterson; had ch.: I. Christina, m. Adrian Van Houten; II. Jane, m. —Baker.
75. V. Waling (111), b. Sept. 22, 1753; m. Pietertje, dau. of Derrick Van Ripen, Feb. 23, 1783; d. Jan. 17, 1832; she, b. Nov. 16, 1758; d. Jan. 4, 1846.
76. VI. Maritje, b. Sept. 11, 1757; m. 1st, Isaac Housman; 2d, Christian Zabriskie.
77. VII. Helmich (115), b. June 22, 1761; m. Maritje, dau. of Adrian Post, Jan. 24, 1784; d. May 5, 1822; she d. April 13, 1821, æt. 61 yrs., 8 mos., 1 day.

Jacob [52] had ch.:

78. I. Johannis, b. Sept. 1, 1772; II. Jacob, b. Oct. 17, 1774.
79. III. Jannetje, b. March 6, 1782; IV. Isaac, April 30, 1786.

Abraham [53] had ch.:

80. I. Geertruy, b. Feb. 15, 1747; II. Jacob, b. June 9, 1751; III. Simeon, b. Dec. 22, 1756; IV. Helena, b. Feb. 28, 1758.

Marinus [54] had ch.:

81. I. Arie (122), m. Margaret Van Wagenen; d. Dec. 3, 1828, æt. 84 yrs.

Fifth Generation.

Daniel [59] had ch.:

82. I. Cornelius (127), b. Aug. 6, 1783; m. Margrietje Van Ripen (79), Aug. 16, 1807; d. Aug. 4, 1852.
83. II. Aeltje, b. April 11, 1786; m. 1st, John Mandeville, March 29, 1807; he d. March 28, 1815; 2d, Stephen Vreeland (92), Nov. 29, 1828; d. March 4, 1846.
84. III. Jacob D. (135), b. Oct. 8, 1788; m. Antje Vreeland (135), Dec. 31, 1812; d. Dec. 6, 1864.
85. IV. Rachel, b. Jan. 25, 1791; d. Oct. 20, 1821, unm.
86. V. John, b. Jan. 10, 1795; d. Aug, 1, 1801.
87. VI. Daniel, b. May 18, 1798; d. April 23, 1818.

Abraham [60] had ch.:

88. I. Joseph, m. Ann Cubberly, Nov. 23, 1805; d. Nov. 28, 1827, s. p., æt. 46 yrs., 3 mos., 21 days.
89. II. Jacob (141), m. Sarah, dau. of Jasper Cadmus (20), Feb. 7, 1808; d. Sept. 7, 1869, æt. 86 yrs.
90. III. Walter, b. March 26, 1787; m. Phebe Tuers, May 21, 1807; d. Feb. 7, 1868; had ch.: I. Cornelius, b. March 19, 1809.
91. IV. Abraham (142), b. Feb. 18, 1789; m. Mary Gordon.
92. V. Eleanor, b. Feb. 6, 1791; m. 1st, Abraham Tuers, Jan. 29, 1809; 2d, Benjamin F. Welsh; d. Feb. 17, 1859.
93. VI. Rachel, b. July 22, 1793; m. Peter Prine, Feb. 11, 1819.
94. VII. Nancy, b. July 16, 1795; m. 1st, Peter Garrabrant (37), Feb. 15, 1814; 2d, John Metzger.
95. VIII. Catharine, b. Jan. 11, 1798; m. Daniel Welsh, Feb. 13, 1815.

Jurriaen [64] had ch.:

96. I. Garret (143), b. Dec. 16, 1783; m. Cornelia Vreeland (105), Oct. 3, 1801; d. Aug. 30. 1814.
97. II. Daniel, b. May 13, 1787; d. July 3, 1798.

Hendrick D. [66] had ch.:

98. I. Aeltje, b. March 21, 1805; m. John M. Cornelison, M.D., May 22, 1826; d. Dec. 16, 1869.
99. II. Jacob, b. Sept. 27, 1806; d. Aug. 15, 1819.
100. III. Effie, b. Sept. 11, 1818; m. William Thomas.

Johannis [69] had ch.:

101. I. Antje, b. March 2, 1801.
102. II. Hendrick, b. Feb. 26, 1802; removed to Morris County.
103. III. Sally, b. April 27, 1805; d. Dec. 6, 1827, unm.
104. IV. Geertje, b. March 29, 1807; V. John D., b. March 7, 1810.
105. VI. Jacob, b. Feb. 26, 1815; VII. Abraham, b. April 6, 1818.
106. VIII. Rachel, b. July 30, 1820.

Jacob H. [70] had ch.:

107. I. Sarah Ann, b. Feb. 3, 1816; m. Jasper Wandle, May 23, 1833. He was a member of the N. J. General Assembly in 1872–'3.
108. II. Fanny, b. Aug. 5, 1817.
109. III. Gloriana, b. Feb. 20, 1824; m. Charles W. Romain, May 6, 1843.

John [71] had ch.:

110. I. Isaac, bap. Dec. 25, 1753, d. in inf.; II. Catrina, b. May 16, 1759; III. Antje, b. Sept. 15, 1761, d. in inf.; IV. Antje, b. Feb. 6, 1765; V. Isaac, b. Dec. 7, 1767; m. Helena Schoonmaker, Aug. 21, 1796; had ch.: I. Johannis W., b. March 4, 1797; II. Eva, b. Oct. 11, 1772; VI. Waling, b. July 2, 1784; m. Sally Garrabrant; had ch.: I. John; II. Peggy, m. John Jerolamon; III. Jennie, m. Garret Jurianse.

Waling [75] had ch.:

111. I. Waling (148), b. Dec. 30, 1783; m. 1st, Catharina Van Voorhees; she d. April 28, 1826; 2d, Eunice Lingford; d. Sept. 29, 1832.
112. II. Claasje, b. Nov. 25, 1785; m. John M. Ryerse, March 2, 1806.
113. III. Jannetje, b. Oct. 5, 1790; m. John Kip, Dec. 22, 1811.
114. IV. Fitje, b. Jan. 26, 1793; d. Dec. 17, 1793.

Helmich [77] had ch.:

115. I. Waling, b. July 2, 1784; m. Margrietje Ackerman, Sept. 6, 1805; had ch.: I. Helmigh, b. Feb. 6, 1806.

116. II. Geertje, b. Sept. 30, 1786; m. John Sip; d. April 19, 1808.

117. III. Jannetje, b. March 19, 1789; m. Samuel H. Berry.

118. IV. Elizabeth, b. April 7, 1792; d. Aug. 27, 1818.

119. V. Adrian, b. Oct. 4, 1794; d. Oct. 20, 1818, unm.

120. VI. John, b. Aug. 17, 1797; m. Rachel Ann, dau. of Rev. Peter D. Froeligh.

121. VII. Michael (149), b. Oct. 13, 1800; m. Agnes, dau. of Henry I. Kipp, June 20, 1822.

Arie [81] had ch.:

122. I. Marinus, b. Feb. 1, ——; m. Grietje, dau. of Jurie Jurianse; had ch.: I. Jurie, d. unm; II. Mary Ann, m. 1st, John Snyder; 2d, Richard Riker.

123. II. Jacobus (153), b. Feb. 7, 1776; m. 1st, Jannetje Van Winkle, Dec. 25, 1799; 2d, Maria Demarest, March 20, 1834.

124. III. John, b. April 29, 1780, d. in inf.; IV. Helena, b. Jan. 23, 1782.

125. V. John, b. April 30, 1784; m.; had ch.: I. Jacob; II. Benjamin; III. Hannah.

126. VI. Maria, b. Oct. 17, 1793; m. Edo Merselis, Aug. 5, 1829.

Sixth Generation.

Cornelius [82] had ch.:

127. I. Garret V. R. (154), b. Dec. 30, 1807; m. Ann Westervelt; d. Jan. 18, 1857.

128 II. Ann, b. Dec. 24, 1809; m. John G. Van Winkle (144), April 6, 1826.

129. III. John (155), b. July 3, 1812; m. Sarah, dau. of George Tise, Nov. 27, 1834.

130. IV. Daniel, b. April 19, 1817; d. Aug. 31, 1868.

131. V. Cornelius, b. Dec. 25, 1819; d. Oct. 7, 1821.

132. VI. Catharine V. R., b. Jan. 22, 1823; m. —— Chandler.

133. VII. Rachel, b. Jan. 12, 1826; m. Lewis Chandler, Aug. 22, 1848.

134. VIII. Margaret V. R., b. Feb. 12, 1832; m. William Gemmel, Dec. 25, 1850.

Jacob D. [84] had ch.:

135. I. Rachel, b. Dec. 1, 1813; d. Jan. 12, 1815.
136. II. Jacob (156), b. Oct. 6, 1815; m. Maria Sip (30), Nov. 6, 1834.
137. III. Michael (163), b. March 27, 1817; m. Ann Robinson, Oct. —, 1838.
138. IV. Ann W., b. March 7, 1820; m. Peter Sip (31), April 25, 1839.
139. V. Daniel (169), b. June 27, 1822; m. Effie Newkirk (69), June 22, 1847.
140. VI. Gitty, b. Oct. 15, 1823.

Jacob A. [89] had ch.:

141. I. Abraham, b. June 11, 1808; m. Harriet, dau. of Joseph Budd; d. April 2, 1870; had ch.: I. Asa T., b. Oct. 22, 1830; d. Nov. 7, 1834. He was the fourth Sheriff of Hudson County.
II. Catharine, b. Feb. 22, 1810; m. James Holmes, Oct. 6, 1827.
III. Jasper, b. May 24, 1812.
IV. Rachel Ann, b. Feb. 2, 1814; m. 1st, Henry Doremus, Dec. 25, 1832; 2d, Dyer Williams, June 18, 1837.

Abraham [90] had ch.:

142. I. Joseph, b. July 9, 1810; II. Hannah, b. July 29, 1811 III. William G., b. Jan. 27, 1815.

Garret [96] had ch.:

143. I. Daniel G. (170), b. Feb. 14, 1802; m. Rachel, dau. of Jacob P. Roome, April 26, 1824; resides in Plainfield, N. J.
144. II. John G. (180), b. Nov. 25, 1804; m. Ann Van Winkle (128), April 6, 1826; d. Jan. 7, 1846.
145. III. Garret G. (184), b. June 4, 1807; m. Sarah, dau. of Abraham Van Ripen, of Aquackanonck, Dec. 13, 1827.
146. IV. Michael, b. Jan. 16, 1810; d. July 1, 1828.
147. V. Stephen, b. June 15, 1813; d. Sept. 17, 1813.

Waling [111] had ch.:

148. I. Dirck, b. March 28, 1805, d. April 10, 1815; II. Jannetje, b. Sept. 11, 1807, d. May 5, 1824; III.

Sophia, b. Feb. 6, 1810; IV. Nicholas, b. Nov. 17, 1812; V. Richard, b. Oct. 16, 1816; VI. Petrina, b. Nov. 6, 1817; VII. Rachel Ann, b. June 26, 1819; VIII. Clarissa, b. Jan. 14, 1821, d. in inf.; IX. Clarissa, b. June 14, 1823; X. Catharine Jane, b. April 1, 1826; XI. John, b. July 12, 1831.

Michael [121] had ch.:

149. I. Maria, b. Dec. 21, 1822; m. Henry Outwater, May 4, 1843.
150. II. Marinus, b. Dec. 21, 1823; d. in inf.
151. III. Clarissa, b. Nov. 27, 1824; m. Henry H. Jurianse.
152. IV. Wilhelmus, b. Aug. 24, 1828.

Jacobus [123] had ch.:

153. I. Jacob (186), b. May 6, 1802; m. Ann Van Blarcom, June 4, 1823.

Seventh Generation.

Garret V. R. [127] had ch.:

154. I. Maria, b. March 27, 1834; II. Cornelius, b. Dec. 6, 1835.

John [129] had ch.:

155. I. Sarah Jane, b. Aug. 6, 1836; m. Robert P. Percy, Dec. 7, 1858.

Jacob [136] had ch.:

156. I. Elizabeth Ann, b. Oct. 4, 1833; m. Lewis A. Brigham, Nov. 6, 1855.
157. II. Peter S., b. March 16, 1837; m. Cathalina, dau. of George Vreeland (196), Dec. 26, 1861; had ch.: I. George V., b. Sept. 19, 1864.
158. III. Daniel (187), b. Oct. 3, 1839; m. Emma, dau. of William J. B. Smith, Dec. 12, 1861.
159. IV. Garret S., b. Oct. 14, 1841; d. April 6, 1843.
160. V. Margaret Jane, b. March 24, 1844; d. Nov. 28, 1870 unm.
161. VI. Edward, b. Feb. 2, 1846; m. Mary Jane, dau. of Jasper Wandle, Sept. 24, 1868.
162. VII. William C., b. Sept. 13, 1855; d. June 7, 1873.

Michael [137] had ch.:

163. I. Jacob M. (188), b. July 19, 1840; m. Anna Vreeland (186), Feb. 26, 1862.
164. II. Anna Maria, b. Oct. 19, 1841.
165. III. Eliza, b. April 27, 1843; d. May 10, 1843.
166. IV. Edwin, b. Sept. 27, 1844; d. Dec. 16, 1844.
167. V. Gertrude, b. Nov. 16, 1846; m. Henry Fitch.
168. VI. Harriet Eliza, b. June 20, 1848; m. Thomas P. King, June 4, 1873.

Daniel [139] had ch.:

169. I. Alfred, b. June 28, 1848; II. Franklin, b. Sept. 19, 1849, d. Dec. 2, 1866; III. Theodore N., b. Sept. 15, 1851; IV. John Edwin, b. May 10, 1853; V. Clara, b. Jan. 3, 1855, d. Jan. 18, 1856; VI. Howard, b. March 18, 1857, d. July 25, 1857; VII. Anna Gertrude, b. June 10, 1858; VIII. Joseph, b. April 29, 1860, d. March 3, 1861; IX. Adeline Sophia, b. Aug. 9, 1865.

Daniel G. [143] had. ch.:

170. I. Jeremiah (189), b. March 7, 1825; m. 1st, Isabella, dau. of Elisha Runyon, Oct. 23, 1850; 2d, Violet, sister of his first wife, May 11, 1857.
171. II. Susan R., b. Jan. 4, 1827.
172. III. Jacob R. (190), b. Dec. 22, 1828; m. Edith, dau. of Aaron Dunn, Dec. 31, 1863.
173. IV. Peter S., b. Aug. 30, 1831; d. June 1, 1832.
174. V. Cornelia Ann, b. June 26, 1833; m. William C. Conover, May 19, 1859.
175. VI. Nellie, b. Feb. 20, 1836; d. Nov. 12, 1836.
176. VII. Garret, b. Oct. 7, 1837; m. Jennie Jukes, Dec. 12, 1859; had ch.: I. Elizabeth; II. Jennie.
177. VIII. William H., b. Feb. 8, 1840; m. Mary Ann, dau. of Aaron Dunn, Nov. 23, 1864; had ch.: I. William, b. Sept. 9, 1868.
178. IX. John Henry, b. Dec. 4, 1842; m. Adelia S., dau. of Jerome B. Pack, Nov. 13, 1867.
179. X. Daniel, b. Sept. 13, 1845.

John G. [144] had ch.:

180. I. Jeremiah, b. Sept. 5, 1831; d. Sept. 15, 1832.

181. II. Ann S., b. June 27, 1833; m. John A. Van Horn, Jan. 1, 1852.
182. III. Cornelius, b. Feb. 8, 1836; d. Jan. 28, 1837.
183. IV. Garret S., b. Nov. 21, 1837.

Garret G. [145] had ch.:
184. I. Garret, b. July 11, 1831; d. unm.
185. II. Jane S., b. Aug. 28, 1833; m. Henry Duncan.

Jacob [153] had ch.:
186. I. Catharine, b. July 3, 1825; m. Henry Marselus, Nov. 9, 1845.

Eighth Generation.

Daniel [158] had ch.:
187. I. Florence, b. Sept. 28, 1862; II. Grace, b. April 10, 1864, d. Aug. 11, 1864; III. Jessie, b. May 4, 1865; IV. Clara S., b. Jan. 15, 1867, d. Aug. 8, 1867; V. Mary, b. Jan. 7, 1871, d. June 28, 1871; VI. Nellie, b. Dec. 30, 1871.

Jacob M. [163] had ch.:
188. I. Annie Gertrude, b. Dec. 12, 1863; II. Frank, b. Feb. 24, 1865; III. Clara, b. Aug. 14, 1869.

Jeremiah [170] had ch.:
189. I. William, b. Nov. 4, 1858, d. Aug. 6, 1859; II. Charles, b. Oct. 2, 1860; III. Jeremiah, b. Nov. 20, 1862; IV. Francis, b. July 2, 1865; V. Nelson, b. Aug. 9, 1868; VI. Isabella, b. Aug. 11, 1869.

Jacob R. [172] had ch.:
190. I. Edward T., b. Jan. 21, 1865; II. Susan R., b. Jan. 9, 1870.

Van Wageningen—Van Wagenen—Van Wagoner.

This family derives its name from *Wageningen*, an ancient town near the Rhine, about ten miles west of Arnheim, in Gelderland. It stood in marshy ground, was walled, and a place of considerable strength. From this town came Gerrit Gerritsen, with his wife, Annetje Hermanssè, and child Gerrit, then two years old. They arrived at New Amsterdam Dec. 23, 1660, in the ship *Faith*, of which Jan Bestevaer was captain. The fare for the three was 90 florins.[1] He was the founder of the family, which is now spread over Hudson, Bergen, Passaic and Essex Counties. He brought with him a certificate, now in possession of his descendant Hartman, of which the following is a translation :

"We, burgomasters, schepens and counsellors of the city of Wagening, declare by these presents that there appeared before us Hendrick Elissen and Jordiz Spiers, citizens of this city, at the request of Gerrit Gerritsen and Annetje Hermansse, his wife. They have testified and certified, as they do by these presents, that they have good knowledge of the above named Gerrit Gerritsen and Annetje Hermansse, his wife, as to their life and conversation, and that they have always been considered and esteemed as pious and honest people, and that no complaint of any evil or disorderly conduct has ever reached their ears ; on the contrary, they have always led quiet, pious and honest lives, as it becomes pious and honest persons. They especially testify that they govern their family well, and bring up their children in the fear of God, and in all modesty and respectability.

"As the above named persons have resolved to remove and proceed to New Netherland, in order to find greater convenience, they give this attestation, grounded on their knowledge of them, having known them intimately, and having been in continual intercourse with them for many years, living in the same neighborhood.

"In testimony of the truth, we, the burgomasters of the city, have caused the private seal of the city to be hereto affixed.

"Done at Wagening, 27th November, 1660.

"By the ordinance of the same.

"J. AQUELIN."

Soon after his arrival Gerritsen settled in this county, and received several parcels of land.[2] He resided at Communipaw ; d. Oct. 4, 1696; she died Sept. 7, 1696.

Second Generation.

Gerrit Gerritse had ch. :

2. I. Gerrit (9), b. in 1658 ; m. Neesje Pieterse, of Best, in Gelderland, May 11, 1681. He settled at Pembre-

---

[1] *Doc. Hist. of N. Y.*, *iii.*, 55 ; *Alb. Rec.*, *viii.*, 456.

[2] *Winfield's Land Titles*, 120.

pock; was appointed Associate Justice of the Court at Bergen, Aug. 31, 1681, and lieutenant in Gerbrand Claesen's Company, Nov. 10, 1692; d. April 6, 1703; she d. Oct. 9, 1732.

3. II. Jannetje, bap. March 19, 1662.

4. III. Fitje, bap. Dec. 30, 1663; m. Cornelius Van Vorst (10), Nov. 27, 1693; d. May 19, 1734.

5. IV. Hermanus (16), bap. March 10, 1667; m. Annetje Van Winkle (14), and resided at Aquackanonck.

6. V. Aeltje, bap. April 14, 1672; m. Wander Diedricks, Nov. 27, 1693; d. Dec. 22, 1754.

7. VI. Hendrick, bap. Oct. 25, 1675; m. Margrietje Straatmaker, April 3, 1701; removed to Aquackanonck. His will, dated Sept. 9, 1743, was proved Dec. 20, 1758. He had ten ch., viz.: Garret, John, Cornelius, Henry, Abraham, Gesie, m. Marinus Van Winkle (32), Sept. 2, 1721; Antje, wife of Jurrie Pieterse, Jannetje, wife of Adrian Post, Margaret, and Lena, wife of Thomas Jurianse Van Ripen.

8. VII. Johannis (17), b. Jan. 11, 1678; m. Catlyntje Helmigse, Nov. 4, 1703; d. Sept. 30, 1756.

Some of this generation took the name of *Van Wagenen*, while others retained *Gerritsen*, the name of the father, for a family name, which name or its equivalent, *Garretson*, many of them yet retain.

Third Generation.

Gerrit [2] had ch.:

9. I. Elizabeth, b. March 3, 1682; d. Jan. 24, 1707.

10. II. Pieter (25), b. Oct. 4, 1684; m. 1st, Vrouwtje Hesselse, March 26, 1709; 2d, Antje ——. He was born in Hoboken, but at the time of his marriage lived at Pembrepock; afterward removed to Aquackanonck.

11. III. Gerrit (26), bap. March 20, 1687; m. Maritje Gerbrants (8); removed to Aquackanonck; d. Jan. 1, 1737.

12. IV. Annetje, bap. Nov. 13, 1689; m. Johannis Neesje, of Staten Island, Oct. 9, 1710.

13. V. Johannis (27), bap. Feb. 22, 1693; m. Margrietje Sip (9), May 22, 1713.

14. VI. Abraham (28), b. Feb. 2, 1695; m. Rachel Hesselse, March 14, 1717; removed to Aquackanonck.

15. VII. Jacob (30), bap. Nov. 19, 1799; m. Lea Van Ripen (22), May 2, 1719; d. Sept. 23, 1775.

Hermanus [5] had ch.:

16. I. Gerrit (35), m. Annetje Sip (10), Oct. 3, 1713.

Johannis [8] had ch.:

17. I. Aeltje, b. Sept. 6, 1705.
18. II. Helmich (39), b. Feb. 18, 1708; m. Maritje Brinkerhoff (12), Sept. 26, 1736; d. July 19, 1747.
19. III. Gerrit, b. Oct. 7, 1710; d. Aug. 21, 1738.
20. IV. Cornelius, m. 1st, Catrina Sickels, Oct. 17, 1742; 2d, Helena Prior; d. before Sept., 1768. By his father's will he received a farm at "Wenaghke," on which he was living in 1752; had ch.: I. Jacob; II. Annetje, b. Dec. 25, 1750.
21. V. John.
22. VI. Jacob (44), m. Jannetje Van Houten, Oct. 17, 1742.
23. VII. Antje, m. Ide Sip (11), May 23, 1725; d. Jan. 25, 1749.
24. VIII. Jannetje, b. Feb. 22, 1721; m. Hendrick De Mott, Oct. 30, 1740.

Fourth Generation.

Pieter [10] had ch.:

25. I. Gerrit, b. Nov. 7, 1711; II. Elizabeth, b. Aug. 5, 1713; III. Hessel, b. Dec. 11, 1715; m. Catrina Bon, and had ch.: I. Johannis, b. May 27, 1753; II. Hessel, b. Jan. 25, 1760; IV. Peter, b. March 29, 1719; V. Johannis, b. Nov. 14, 1721; VI. Neesje, b. March 11, 1724; VII. Vrouwtje, b. Feb. 6, 1727, m. Jacob Van Winkle; VIII. Lea, and IX. Helena, twins, b. Aug. 10, 1729.

Gerrit [11] had ch.:

26. I. Maritje, b. April 17, 1715; II. Leeja, b. Jan. 8, 1720; III. Gerrebrant, b. Sept. 21, 1723; IV. Neesje, b. April 17, 1728; V. Metje, b. March 2, 1732.

Johannis [13] had ch.:

27. I. Gerrit, b. June 29, 1714; II. Johannis, b. Feb. 27, 1721; III. Cornelius, b. July 2, 1723; m. Claasje Pieterse; had ch.: Claasje, b. April 13, 1755; IV. Ja-

cobus, b. April 27, 1725; V. Hendrick, b. Aug. 17, 1727; m. Catharine Paulussen, Dec. 3, 1747; had ch.: Johannis, b. Nov. 9, 1752; VI. Abraham, b. July 26, 1729; VII. Hermanus, b. March 14, 1731.

Abraham [14] had ch.:

28. I. Hendrick, b. March 5, 1729; m. Annatje Van Winkle (32), Dec. —, 1751; had ch.: I. Garret, b. Jan. 14, 1753; II. Marinus, b. Dec. 19, 1754; III. Abraham, b. Sept. 26, 1762.

29. II. Neesje, b. Sept. 13, 1731.

Jacob [15] had ch.:

30. I. Gerrit, b. May —, 1720; m. Margrietje Van Winkle, April 24, 1746; d. Dec. 4, 1803.

31. II. Neesje, b. Sept. 2, 1724; m. Johannis Van Wagenen (42), Nov. 8, 1750; d. May 24, 1810.

32. III. Johannis, b. March 11, 1727; m. Aeltje Vreeland, Oct. 17, 1748; had ch.: I. Lea, b. Dec. 4, 1759.

33. IV. Beelitje, b. March 11, 1727; m. John Merselis, Aug. 30, 1755.

34. V. Jacob, b. March 8, 1736; m. Aagtje Vreeland (62); d. Jan. 27, 1783; had ch.: I. Annatje, b. Dec. 31, 1757, d. March 20, 1778.

Gerrit [16] had ch.:

35. I. Annetje, b. Sept. 12, 1714; m. Joris E. Vreeland (21); d. Feb. 28, 1782.

36. II. Hermanus (45), b. Feb. 4, 1717; m. Geertruy Van Houten, Dec. 29, 1741.

37. III. Lena, b. Dec. 3, 1720; m. Arent Schuyler (20), Oct. 1, 1741.

38. IV. Catrina, b. Dec. 28, 1722; V. Jenneke, b. Sept. 12, 1725; VI. Johannis.

Helmich [18] had ch.:

39. I. Effie, b. Aug. 9, 1737; II. Catlyntje, b. Dec. 25, 1738.

40. III. Maritje, b. April 7, 1741; m. Jacob Kip, Dec. 4, 1775.

41. IV. Antje, b. April 7, 1741; m. Johannis Diedricks, Dec. 17, 1768.

42. V. Johannis (46), m. Neesje Van Wagenen (31), Nov. 8, 1750; d. March 29, 1797.

43. VI. Jacob, settled at Kinderkemack.

Jacob [22] had ch.:

44. I. Jacobus, bap. March 8, 1736; II. Catlyntje, b. July 23, 1744, d. Aug. 11, 1748; III. Helena, b. April 22, 1747.

Fifth Generation.

Hermanus [36] had ch.:

45. I. Roelof, b. March 17, 1750; II. Johannis, bap. Dec. 14, 1755.

Johannis [42] had ch.:

46. I. Jacob (50), b. Oct. 7, 1751; m. Aegie Brinkerhoff (31); d. June 14, 1839.

47. II. Catlyntje, b. Jan. 2, 1754; m. Garret Van Ripen (60); d. Oct. 27, 1775.

48. III. Lea, b. Dec. 17, 1756; m. Hendrick Brinkerhoff (33), June 19, 1779; d. July 7, 1821.

49. IV. Antje, b. Sept. 26, 1757.

Sixth Generation.

Jacob [46] had ch..

50. I. Claesje, b. March 17, 1778; m. Peter Westervelt, of T'Neck, Oct. 30, 1796.

51. II. Catlyntje, b. Aug. 3, 1782; m. Henry D. Van Winkle (66), Jan. 10, 1801; died July 20, 1847.

52. III. Johannis (54), b. July 27, 1785; m. Ann, dau. of Cornelius Doremus, of New Durham, Dec. 31, 1812; d. Sept. 7, 1827.

53. IV. Hartman, (55), b. Nov. 15, 1790; m. Catharine Newkirk (29), Aug. 16, 1812.

Seventh Generation.

Johannis [52] had ch.:

54. I. Cornelius D., b. Feb. 5, 1814; II. Jacob, b. Sept. 4, 1815; III. Christiana, b. Sept. 20, 1817. This family removed to the city of New York.

Hartman [53] had ch.:

55. I. Effie, b. April 8, 1813; m. Henry P. Kip, jr., of Lodi, Nov. 5, 1835.

56. II. Jane, b. Sept. 28, 1814; m. Edo Sip, of Aquackanonck, Nov. 2, 1833.

57. III. Jacob (59), b. March 31, 1819; m. Jane Van Buskirk (64), Dec. 29, 1842.
58. IV. Henry N. (63), b. Oct. 13, 1823; m. Eliza Jane Vreeland (237), May 12, 1849.

Eighth Generation.

Jacob [57] had ch.:

59. I. Catharine Arabella, b. Oct. 2, 1843; m. John E. Wilson, Dec. 25, 1861.
60. II. Hartman, b. June 28, 1845; d. April 14, 1853.
61. III. Sarah Elizabeth, b. April 16, 1847; m. Alfred Wm. Corbin, Nov. 10, 1869.
62. IV. John V. B., b. May 29, 1849; V. Cornelius; VI. Jane, b. May 14, 1851, d. Sept. 20, 1852; VII. Jacob; VIII. Christian.

Henry N. [58] had ch.:

63. I. Catharine, b. Oct. 7, 1850; m. Nicholas G. Vreeland (338), April 12, 1871.
64. II. Hannah Elizabeth, b. Jan. 14, 1853; III. Hartman, b. Sept. 9, 1858; IV. Eliza Jane V. L., b. Sept. 29, 1866.

VAN BOSKERCK—VAN BUSKIRK—BOSKERK—BUSKIRK.

This name is from *bos* and *kerck*, and with the *van* signifies *from the church in the woods.* The founder of the family in this country was Lourens Andriessen, who sometimes added to his name "Van Boskerck." He came from Holstein, in Denmark,

in the summer of 1655. His name first appears in the records of New Amsterdam June 29, 1656, in a deed for a lot on Broad street. He was then unmarried, and by trade a *turner*,[1] but afterward became a *draper*.[2] Shortly after the settlement of Bergen he purchased the tract of land previously granted to Claas

[1] *New Amst. Rec., ii.,* 523. [2] *Whitehead's East Jersey,* 276.

Carstensen, the Norman, at Minkakwa, recently Greenville.[1] He took the oath of allegiance to the King of Great Britain Nov. 20, 1665. He was a man of more than ordinary ability for the times, and soon acquired great influence among his neighbors. When the country was recaptured by the Dutch, and the people expected a forfeiture of their lands, he and John Berry, Samuel Edsall and William Sandford appeared at Fort Willem Hendrick, Aug. 18, 1673, to request that "their plantations be confirmed in the privileges which they obtained from their previous Patroons."[2] When a contest arose between the town of Bergen and the inhabitants of Minkakwa and Pemrepogh concerning fences and the support of a schoolmaster, he again appeared before the Council to plead the cause of his neighbors.[3] Under the act of Nov. 7, 1668, for the marking of horses and cattle, he was appointed "Recorder and Marker" for Minkakwa, April 6, 1670, and "Marker General" for the town of Bergen, Oct. 8, 1676. On the last named day he was also appointed *Ranger* for Bergen, with power to name deputies "to Range the Woods and bring in all stray horses, mares and cattle." He was commissioned a member of the Bergen Court, Feb. 16, 1677, Feb. 18, 1680, and President of the same Aug. 31, 1681, and President of the County Court Aug. 31, 1682. He was a member of the Governor's Council for a number of years, appointed first, March 18, 1672. To him belongs the honor of holding the first commission to administer "Crowner's quest law" in the county, having been appointed Jan. 18, 1672, to hold an inquest on a child who had died under suspicious circumstances. Jointly with others he purchased, Jan. 6, 1676, a large tract of land, then known as "New Hackensack," upon which he resided as early as 1688. He m. Jannetje Jans, widow of Christian Barentsen,

Sept. 12, 1658. With her he received a fortune, consisting of four sons by her first husband, and about 1,400 florins "heavy money, ten wampum beads for one stiver." They both died in 1694, he surviving her but a few months.

Second Generation.

Lourens Andriessen had ch.:

2. I. Andries, bap. March 3, 1660; was a member of the

[1] *Winfield's Land Titles*, 60. [2] *Col. Hist. of N. Y., ii.*, 576. [3] *Ibid, ii.*, 720.

sixth Provincial Assembly of N. J. in 1710. In 1718 he and Myndert Garrabrant were appointed to enforce the oyster law;[1] d. in 1724.

3. II. Laurens (6), m. Hendrickje Van Derlinde; represented Bergen in the fifth Provincial Assembly in 1709. His will, dated May 8, 1722, was proved June 4, 1724.

4. III. Pieter (8), b. Jan. 1, 1666; m. Trintje, dau. of Hans Harmanse, of Constapel's Hoeck; d. July 21, 1738. She d. Nov. 7, 1736. Through his wife he inherited one-half of the Hoeck, the other half he purchased, and some of his descendants still reside thereon.

5. IV. Thomas, m. Margrietje Hendrickje Van Derlinde; had ch.: I. Johannis, bap. July 1, 1694; II. Abraham bap. March 25, 1700; III. Pieter, bap. Sept. 6, 1702; m. Marytje Van Hoorn, Sept. 1, 1727; IV. Laurens; m. 1st, Sarah Terhune, May 7, 1726; 2d, Hendrickje Van Buskirk, Jan. 27, 1745; V. Andries; VI. Isaac; VII. Michael; VIII. Fitje, m. Andries Arnack; IX. Geertruy, b. March 7, 1715; X. Margrietje, bap. Feb. 17, 1723, m. John Church. His will, dated in Hunterdon County, was proved Oct. 17, 1745.

Laurens and Andries resided at Saddle River before their father's death. In 1668 a monthly court was established at the house of Lourens Andriessen for the accommodation of "the inhabitants of the Out Plantations of the County."[2] This was the first court in the present County of Bergen, if the Hospating tribunal be excepted.

Third Generation.

Laurens [3] had ch.:

6. I. Fitje, m. Arie Banta, July 28, 1712; II. Joost, bap.

---

[1] *Nevill's Laws, i.*, 87.

[2] *Leaming and Spicer*, 304. On a copy of the Charter of Bergen, made in 1681, in the possession of the Van Buskirk family, I found the following agreement. It is not signed, nor is it known who was the father of the girl; but it is interesting as showing—1st. The manner of educating the children of parents in comfortable circumstances. 2d. The kind of compensation—pecunia—in use in the early days of Bergen:

"Agreed with Mrs. Baker that she shall learne my daughter Ellino[r] to read and sew, and make all manner of needle worke, for one whole yeare from the day of the date hereof, being the 12th day of Novemb[r], 1682, and in the meane while the s[d] Mrs. Baker, during the said terme, shall not put her, my s[d] daughter, to any manner of house worke, but to keepe her to her needle worke, and for true performance hereof I am to give the s[d] Mrs. Baker a heaffer of her first calfe, at the time of the Expiration."

in 1695; m. Trintje Martese, and had ch.: Laurens, bap. Sept. 7, 1718, m. Lea Westervelt, Sept. 26, 1739; Martin, bap. Jan. 20, 1723; III. Andrew, m. Jacomyntje Davidse Demarest, Jan. 26, 1717; IV. John, bap. Feb. 26, 1699; m. 1st, Geesje Jurrianse Westervelt, April 1, 1721; 2d, Maritje Van Derlinde, Sept. 13, 1749; had ch.: Antje, bap. Feb. 18, 1722; Laurens, bap. Aug. 6, 1723; V. Jacobus; VI. Jannetje; VII. Benjamin, and

7. VIII. Laurens (16), m. Eva ——. His will, dated Nov. 20, 1773, was proved Feb. 22, 1774.

Pieter [4] had ch.:

8. I. Laurence (18), m. Fitje Vreeland (45), Sept. 18, 1709. He represented Bergen in the 9th–17th (inclusive) Provincial Assemblies; d. Dec. 13, 1752.

9. II. Johannis, bap. Aug. 9, 1696. He and his brother Laurence received by their father's will 600 acres of land near Hackensack.

10. III. Willemtje, m. Abraham Shotwell.

11. IV. Jannetje, m. Cornelius Corsen,[1] of Staten Island.

12. V. Andries (23), m. Margrietje La Grange; d. Aug. 25, 1762; she d. June 3, 1775.

13. VI. Jacobus (25), m. Margaret ——; d. Jan. 3, 1767; she d. Jan. 6, 1774, æt. 70 years.

14. VII. Rachel, m. William Daniels.

15. VIII. Antje, m. Peter Tramolje.

Fourth Generation.

Laurens [7] had ch.:

16. I. Thomas; II. John, m. Theodosia ——; in his will, dated March 3, 1783, proved May 2, 1783, is mentioned the fact that his ch. were dead, leaving ch.; III. Aeltje; IV. Antje; V. Jannetje; VI. Mary; VII. Margaret, and

17. VIII. Abraham (27); will dated Nov. 28, 1788; proved March 6, 1794.

Laurence [8] had ch.:

18. I. Cornelius, m. Beelitje Van Wagenen; d. Sept. 4, 1753; had ch.: I. Cornelius, b. Sept. 15, 1747; d. in inf.

---

[1] Corsen's cousin Cornelius took the name of Vroom, and settled on the Raritan, in Somerset County.

19. II. Metje, m. John Lagrange; d. May 6, 1748.[1]
20. III. Jannetje, m. Jacob Van Horn; d. Jan. 10, 1792.
21. IV. Fitje, m. John Roll, of Staten Island, Oct. 14, 1758.
22. V. Anna, m. Thomas Brown, April 16, 1747; d. Sept. —, 1756.

Andries [12] had ch.:

23. I. Geertje, m. Peter Corsen; d. Jan. 10, 1774; II. Trintje.
24. III. Rachel, m. Barent Van Horn, by whom she had five ch.; d. March 11, 1759.

Jacobus [13] had ch.:

25. I. Peter (35), b. 1732; m. Elizabeth Bogert; d. June 23, 1819; she was b. 1736, d. 1814.
26. II. Johannis (38), b. Nov. 28, 1739; m. Tryntje Van Lone, of Athens, N. Y., Oct. 8, 1762; d. April 5, 1820; she was b. Jan. 13, 1735; d. Nov. 2, 1819.

These two boys were suspected of holding communication with the enemy, July 8, 1776, then on Staten Island. A charge to that effect was made against them, on which they were tried and acquitted.

Fifth Generation.

Abraham [17] had ch.:

27. I. Thomas.
28. II. Cornelius (42), b. June 10, 1743; m. Jane, dau. of David Demarest, of Schraalenberg; d. April 28, 1829; she born June 7, 1749; d. March 28, 1844. Before 1800 he left Bergen County and settled in the present city of Bayonne.
29. III. Helena, m. Cornelius J. Bogert.
30. IV. Margaret, m. Henry Fredericks. She d. before 1788, leaving three ch.: Margaret, Rachel and Henry.
31. V. Jannetje, m. Lawrence Van Buskirk, her cousin. He was Captain in the king's Orange Rangers in the Revolution. At the close of the war he went to Nova Scotia, and d. at Shelburne in 1803, æt. 74 years. His son Abraham was also a Captain in

---

[1] She had a dau. Fitje, who m. 1st, John Mercereau; 2d, Andrew Segort, a mariner, and inherited of her grandfathers property where the depot at Greenville now is.

the Rangers; sailed for Nova Scotia in 1783, and perished at sea, æt. 33 years.[1]

32. VI. Elizabeth, m. Peter Van Buskirk.
33. VII. Rachel, m. Thomas Cooper.
34. VIII. Catharine, m. Thomas Boggs.

Peter [25] had ch.:

35. I. Margaret, m. John Van de Water, of New Barbadoes.
36. II. Elizabeth, b. 1776; m. Cornelius Vreeland (96); d. Oct. 29, 1830.
37. III. Rachel, m. William Vreeland (95).

Johannis [26] had ch.:

38. I. Jacobus (47), b. Sept. 15, 1763; m. Sally Vreeland (90), Dec. 16, 1787; d. Nov. 10, 1823.
39. II. Ann, b. July 23, 1766; m. Lucas Van Buskirk, of Saddle River; d. May 31, 1845.
40. III. Margaret, b. March 3, 1768; m. Derrick Corsen; d. Aug. 4, 1848.
41. IV. Catharine, b. Sept. 24, 1726; m. Peter C. Garrabrant (37), Feb. 1, 1800; d. July 31, 1803.

Sixth Generation.

Cornelius [28] had ch.:

42. I. Abraham (51), m. Elizabeth Cole, May 1, 1805; she d. Feb. 12, 1856.
43. II. David, b. March 10, 1770; m. Mary Garrabrant, of Stonehouse Plains; d. March 22, 1866, s. p.
44. III. Thomas, d. s. p.
45. IV. Cornelius, m. 1st, Peggy Van Horn, Dec. 24, 1800; 2d, Sophia La Tourette; had ch.: I. Thomas, d. s. p.; II. Nicholas; III. Abraham; IV. Cornelius; V. Peter; VI. James.
46. V. James C. (54), b. Jan. 25, 1787; m. Antje Van Buskirk (48), June 28, 1812.

Jacobus [38] had ch.:

47. I. John (62), b. Sept. 27, 1787; m. Beelitje Van Ripen (81), Nov. 20, 1814; d. Dec. 12, 1869.
48. II. Antje, b. March 19, 1790; m. James C. Van Buskirk (46), June 28, 1812; d. Jan. 2, 1868.

---

[1] *Sabine's Loyalists*, ii., 375.

49. III. Jacobus (67), b. Oct. 22, 1791; m. Jane, dau. of Peter C. Garrabrant (45), Dec. 20, 1821; d. July 22, 1856. He was a member of the General Assembly of N. J. in 1848.
50. IV. Nicholas (72), b. Nov. 11, 1792; m. Jane Cadmus (24), Dec. 15, 1814.

Seventh Generation.

Abraham [42] had ch.:
51. I. Cornelius, m. Mary Earle, and had ch.: I. Elizabeth, b. Jan. 5, 1840; II. David, b. Feb. 16, 1841; III. Hannah Jane, b. March 17, 1842; IV. Mary Lavina, b. April 16, 1843; V. Peter, b. July 28, 1844; m. Emeline La Tourette, March 4, 1863.
52. II. Peter, twin brother of Cornelius, d. Dec. 18, 1842.
53. III. Abraham, m. Margaret Ann Witherspoon, March 6, 1862.

James C. [46] had ch.:
54. I. Sarah, b. May 26, 1813; m. Abraham Simonson, Oct. 21, 1837.
55. II. Cornelius (80), b. Jan. 10, 1815; m. Rachel Cadmus (41).
56. III. James (85), b. March 18, 1817; m. Effie Garrabrant (53), Dec. —, 1838.
57. IV. Nicholas (88), b. Aug. 28, 1821; m. Elizabeth Vreeland (264), March 16, 1843.
58. V. Abraham (91), b. Oct. 28, 1828; m. Jane, dau. of Jacob Simonson, June 3, 1852.
59. VI. John, b. July 9, 1830; d. July 14, 1838.
60. VII. Lavina, b. Aug. 17, 1832; d. in inf.
61. VIII. Lavina V., b. Feb. 23, 1834; m. William Cadmus (51), Dec. 3, 1852.

John [47] had ch.:
62. I. Catharine, b. July 13, 1815; m. Garret Vreeland (225), Oct. 23, 1834; d. Jan. 3, 1874.
63. II. Sarah, b. Aug. 16, 1817; m. Henry Newkirk (50), Nov. 7, 1838.
64. III. Jane, b. July 22, 1820; m. Jacob Van Wagenen (57), Dec. 29, 1842.
65. IV. Ann Elizabeth, b. Sept. 28, 1824; m. Cornelius Vreeland (262), Dec. 2, 1841.

66. V. John (92), b. Aug. 30, 1832; m. Mary, dau. of William Elsworth, Nov. 19, 1851.

Jacobus J. [49] had ch.:

67. I. Catharine, b. Oct. 28, 1822; m. John N. Van Buskirk (74), Dec. 27, 1843; d. March 29, 1858.
68. II. Sarah Ann, b. Oct. 28, 1825; m. Jacob A. Van Horn, Aug. 3, 1844.
69. III. John J., b. May 2, 1828; m. Jane, dau. of Egbert Wauters, Dec. 28, 1848.
70. IV. Peter, b. April 2, 1831; d. Oct. 15, 1841.
71. V. Eleanor Jane, b. March 18, 1835.

Nicholas [50] had ch.:

72. I. James (93), b. Sept. 10, 1815; m. Fanny Van Ripen (125), May 18, 1839.
73. II. Jasper (94), b. Oct. 17, 1817; m. 1st, Hannah, dau. of Abraham Post, Dec. 12, 1839; she d. Aug. 4, 1850; 2d, Margaret, dau. of Isaac Dougherty, Feb. 8, 1851.
74. III. John N. (98), b. Aug. 4, 1819; m. Catharine Van Buskirk (67), Dec. 27, 1843.
75. IV. Nicholas (99), b. Feb. 11, 1822; m. Julia Ann Wallace, Dec. 24, 1844; removed to Keyport, N. J.; d. Sept. 26, 1867.
76. V. Sarah Catharine, b. Nov. 23, 1825; m. Henry G. Van Ripen (126), June 1, 1846.
77. VI. Richard C. (100), b. Dec. 29, 1827; m. Hannah Vreeland (244), Dec. 31, 1849; removed to Illinois.
78. VII. Hiram (101), b. Dec. 11, 1830; m. Rachel, dau. of Henry Post, of Saugerties, N. Y., April 2, 1851; was commissioned Major in the 20th N. J. Volunteers in active service, Sept. 6, 1862; afterward promoted to a lieutenant-colonelcy; was a member of the General Assembly.
79. VIII. Andrew (102), b. May 19, 1835; m. Adeline, dau. of Dyer Williams, April 24, 1861; was commissioned Adjutant of the 20th N. J. Volunteers in active service, Sept. 15, 1862.

Eighth Generation.

Cornelius [55] had ch.:

80. I. John C., b. Feb. 1, 1837; m. Catharine Bennett; lives in Newark.

81. II. James, b. Sept. 3, 1839; m. Elizabeth Simonson; lives at Rockaway, L. I.

82. III. Jasper, b. Jan. 5, 1842; m. and lives in Pennsylvania.

83. IV. Cornelius, b. March 12, 1844; m. Phebe Van Duyn; lives in Illinois.

84. V. Martha Jane, b. March 29, 1849, d. in inf.; VI. Peter W., b. June 11, 1851, d. in inf.; VII. Elizabeth, b. Sept. 20, 1853, d. in inf.; VIII. Rachel Anna, b. Nov. 15, 1856.

James [56] had ch.:

85. I. Mindert G. (103), b. Sept. 21, 1839; m. Elizabeth Catharine, dau. of Michael Terhune, March 25, 1858.

86. II. James J., b. Oct. 30, 1841; m. and had ch.: I. Clara; II. Henry; III. Effie.

87. III. Rachel, b. Jan. 29, 1844, d. in inf.; IV. John C., b. June 25, 1850, d. in inf.; V. Benjamin T., b. June 25, 1850; VI. Anna Euphemia, b. Aug. 8, 1852; VII. Mary, b. Aug. 25, 1854; VIII. Charles, b. March 20, 1857; IX. Elizabeth, b. March 1, 1859, d. in inf.

Nicholas [57] had ch.:

88. I. Peter V., b. March 2, 1845; m. Elizabeth Hageman; is a clergyman in the Reformed Church; has ch.: I. Clarence.

89. II. Anna Maria, b. Aug. 2, 1847; m. Ebenezer C. Earle in 1871.

90. III. James Henry, b. Sept. 28, 1849; IV. De Witt, b. April 22, 1858.

Abraham [58] had ch.:

91. I. Jemima Ann, b. April 8, 1853; II. Luther, b. Dec. 16, 1854; III. Maria, b. in 1856; IV. Aaron S., b. July 14, 1860; V. Abraham F., b. April 27, 1869.

John [66] had ch.:

92. I. John W., b. Aug. 27, 1852; II. William E., b. March 20, 1855; III. Edward E., b. Oct. 31, 1856; IV. Margaret M., b. July 28, 1858, d. April 9, 1861; V. Mary Catharine, b. May 6, 1860; VI. Garadata Adelia, b. Dec. 15, 1861; VII. Arabella V. R., b. Nov. 15, 1863; VIII. Jennie A., b. April 28, 1865; IX. Philip E., b. June 5, 1867; X. Eva, b. Jan. 17, 1869.

James [72] had ch.:

93. I. Eliza Jane, b. Feb. 2, 1840, d. April 9, 1844; II. John Henry, b. March 4, 1842, d. May 28, 1862; III. Nicholas, b. Nov. 25, 1844; IV. Garret, b. June 19, 1846, d. Aug. 12, 1846; V. Cornelius, b. May 4, 1849; VI. Fanny, b. April 28, 1854; VII. James, b. Dec. 9, 1859, d. Aug. 15, 1860.

Jasper [73] had ch.:

94. I. Ann Jane, b. Jan. 17, 1841; m. David Kells, May 4, 1861.

95. II. Sarah Catharine, b. Dec. 2, 1842; d. March 18, 1843.

96. III. Ellen Amelia, b. April 28, 1845; m. Jacob Hawrey, Dec. 30, 1861.

97. IV. Frances, b. July 27, 1847, m. Laurence Seeburger; V. James, b. Jan. 29, 1850, d. Aug. 2, 1850; VI. Isaac L., b. Nov. 9, 1851, d. Feb. 24, 1852; VII. Mary Caroline, b. Aug. 25, 1853, m. Joseph Coons, Aug. 12, 1870; VIII. Sarah Catharine, b. April 3, 1858.

John N. [74] had ch.:

98. I. Sarah Catharine, b. Feb. 22, 1844; II. Nicholas, b. April 20, 1845; III. Joanna R., b. Dec. 7, 1846, m. Michael G. Vreeland (357), March 25, 1869; IV. Ellen Lucretia, b. Aug. 12, 1848; V. Cathalina, b. Aug. 10, 1850; VI. Emma, b. Dec. 18, 1851.

Nicholas [75] had ch.:

99. I. Jane C., b. Aug. 27, 1846; II. Henry V. H., b. Nov. 21, 1847.

Richard C. [77] had ch.:

100. I. Hiram, b. Sept. 4, 1851; II. Catharine Jane, b. July 28, 1853; III. Richard C., b. Nov. 7, 1855; IV. William J., bap. April 1, 1862.

Hiram [78] had ch.:

101. I. Rebecca, b. Nov. 30, 1858; II. Jane, b. Sept. 30, 1860; III. Sarah, b. March 23, 1864.

Andrew [79] had ch.:

102. I. Andrew M., b. Oct. 7, 1862; II. Adeline, b. Dec. 4, 1866.

Ninth Generation.

Mindert G. [85] had ch.:

103. I. Edward; II. Laura, b. Jan. 25, 1863; III. Ida.

VAN RIPEN—V. REIPEN—V. REYPEN—V. REIPER—V. REYPER —V. RIPER—V. RYPER.

This name, with its present multitudinous orthography, is derived from the Latin *ripa*, and was the name of a city on the north bank of the river Nibbs, sometimes called Nipsick, or Gram. North Jutland (so called to distinguish it from South Jutland or Schleswig), in Denmark, was divided into four dioceses, the most southwesterly of which, lying along the German Ocean, was called *Ripen*. This diocese was 142 miles in length and 57 miles in width, and was part of Cimbrica Chersonesus of the ancients, where dwelt the warlike Cimbri, who, at one time, invaded the Roman Empire.

The city of Ripen, in the diocese of Ripen, is situated in lat. 55° 36′ north, and lon. 9° 10′ east. Next to Wibourg it is the most ancient town in North Jutland.[1] It once had a commodious harbor and profitable commerce; but the one long since filled up and the other sought different channels. Its cathedral was imposing, built of hewn stone, with a steeple of great height, which served as a landmark for mariners. In the Swedish war of 1645 the city was captured, but recovered by the Danes soon after. From this port, in April, 1663, a vessel named "T'Bonte Koe," *the Spotted Cow*, sailed for New Netherland, with eighty-nine passengers, consisting of men, women and children. Among the number was *Juriaen Tomassen*, a young man of the city of Ripen. About four years after his arrival he m. Pryntje Hermans, May 25, 1667; d. Sept. 12, 1695. Some of his descendants took the name *Juriansе*—now Yereance and Auryansen—while others, taking the name of the city from which their ancestor sailed, became *Van Ripen*.

Second Generation.

Juriaen Tomassen had ch.:

2. I. Tomas (11), bap. June 10, 1668; m. Jannetje, dau. of Jan Straatmaker, June 2, 1691.

3. II. Gerrit (21), bap. June 27, 1670; m. Beelitje, dau. of Dirck Janse Oosten and Elizabeth Cornelis, of Ho-

[1] *Fenning's Geography, ii.,* 123. In Winfield's Land Titles, the name is written *Rypen.* It is thus laid down on a map of Denmark in an old geographical work, published in London during the reign of Queen Anne, the title page of which, of the copy I have, is destroyed. I am now satisfied, from the origin of the word, that the name should be written *Ripen,* and it is thus written in the text and on a map in Fenning. Every other way of writing it is clearly wrong, though sanctioned by generations.

boken, June 6, 1693; d. Sept. 4, 1748; she d. May 20, 1745.

4. III. Aeltje, bap. Dec. 21, 1672.

5. IV. Chrystyntje, bap. Nov. 24, 1677; m. Pieter Gerbrantse (2), Aug. 1, 1698.

6. V. Maritje, bap. April 28, 1680; m. Claas Gerbrantse (3), April 11, 1704.

7. VI. Harman, bap. Oct. 21, 1682; d. in inf.

8. VII. Jan (29), m. Neeltje Gerbrantse (5), April 7, 1702.

9. VIII. Harman (33), b. Dec. 6, 1686; m. 1st, Maritje Fredericks, June 20, 1709; 2d, Judith, dau. of Christopher Steinmets, in 1721; removed to Aquackanonck; his will, dated June 17, 1754, was proved May 14, 1756.

10. IX. Grietje, b. Oct. 5, 1691.

Third Generation.

Tomas [2] had ch.:

11. I. Gerrit (41), b. Feb. 6, 1692; m. Jannetje Vreeland (31), June 19, 1718; his will, dated Feb. 17, 1761, was proved Nov. 23, 1761.

12. II. Juriaen (44), b. June 12, 1693; m. Aeltje Van Winkle (28), June 12, 1714.

13. III. Jan, b. Oct. 8, 1694.

14. IV. Abraham (51), b. April 4, 1696; m. 1st, Elizabeth Hesselse; 2d, Catrintje Andriese, Sept. 13, 1729.

15. V. Isaac, b. Oct. 28, 1697.

16. VI. Jacob (52), b. Oct. 9, 1699; m. Maritje Gerbrants (12), Dec. 17, 1728.

17. VII. Geesje, b. Oct. 4, 1702.

18. VIII. Maritje, b. Oct. 3, 1704; m. Jacob Vreeland, of Belleville, Dec. 21, 1726.

19. IX. Elisabet, b. April 4, 1707.

20. X. Dirck, b. Jan. 25, 1709; m. Pietertje Post, Sept. 28, 1732.

Gerrit [3] had ch.:

21. I. Elizabeth, b. May 29, 1694; m. Michael H. Vreeland (32), May 30, 1719; d. Nov. 18, 1767.

22. II. Lea, b. Sept. 11, 1697; m. Jacob Van Wagenen (15), May 2, 1719; d. Dec. 19, 1775.

23. III. Juriaen (53), b. Aug. 15, 1699; m. Grietje ———; d. July 29, 1739.

24. IV. Garret, b. Dec. 4, 1701; m. Martje Gerbrandse, and had ch.: I. Metje, b. March 2, 1732.
25. V. Dirck, b. Jan. 17, 1704.
26. VI. Aeltje, b. March 29, 1705; d. Sept. 30, 1710.
27. VII. Cornelius (55), b. Oct. 6, 1707; m. Aeltje Van Winkle (34), June 29, 1728; d. Jan. 17, 1771.
28. VIII. Johannis (60), b. June 3, 1710; m. 1st, Sarah, dau. of Henricus Kuyper, Dec. 2, 1740; she d. July 2, 1741; 2d, Margrietje Van Winkle (36), Sept. 5, 1742; d. Aug. 24, 1776.

Jan [8] had ch.:

29. I. Jurrie, b. Jan. 22, 1703; m. Elizabeth Steinmets, Nov. 13, 1730.
30. II. Maritje, b. March 16, 1706.
31. III. Metje, b. July 22, 1711; m. John Vreeland.
32. IV. Gerrebrand (61), b. June 1, 1719; m. Fitje Van Vorst (23), Jan. 6, 1742.

Harman [9] had ch.:

33. I. Juriaen, b. Sept. 12, 1710; m. Helena Van Houten.
34. II. Frederick, b. Feb. 22, 1713; m. 1st, Catrintje Hopper, Oct. 19, 1738; 2d, Annetje Van Vorst (24), Dec. 2, 1742.
35. III. Abraham, b. Jan. 25, 1716; IV. Johannis, b. July 21, 1718.
36. V. Christophel (62), b. Sept. 26, 1722; m. Metje Brouwer, Sept. 28, 1746.
37. VI. Maritje, b. Sept. 14, 1724; VII. Jacob, b. Feb. 8, 1728.
38. VIII. Isaac, b. Sept. 30, 1729; m. Annatje Egbertse; had ch.: Petrus, bap. Nov. 19, 1752.
39. IX. Sarah; X. Jannetje, b. June 11, 1732; XI. Gerrit, b. Nov. 3, 1734.
40. XII. Thomas; XIII. Christina.

Fourth Generation.

Gerrit [11] had ch.:

41. I. Maritje; m. Henry Van Winkle.
42. II. Jannetje; m. Jacob Van Winkle.
43. III. Lea; m. Peter Jacobusse.

Juriaen [12] had ch.:

44. I. Thomas, b. Jan. 7, 1715; m. Lena Van Wagenen, Jan. —, 1741.

45. II. Antje, b. Nov. 4, 1716; m. Martin Ryersen, of N. Y., in 1737.
46. III. Simeon, b. Feb. 8, 1719.
47. IV. Jenneke, b. Dec. 25, 1720; m. Jacob Van Houten, Sept. 6, 1745.
48. V. Abraham, b. Sept. 27, 1722, d. in inf.; VI. Johannis, b. May 7, 1725.
49. VII. Rachel, b. Sept. 4, 1727; VIII. Lea, b. June 14, 1729.
50. IX. Abraham, b. Feb. 12, 1731.

Abraham [14] had ch.:
51. I. Jannetje, b. April 17, 1723; II. Elizabeth, b. Nov. 11, 1726.

Jacob [16] had ch.:
52. I. Catrina, b. Sept. 28, 1729; II. Herpert, b. April 16, 1731; m. Margrietje Berry; had ch.: I. Jacobus, b. Feb. 25, 1765.

Juriaen [23] had ch.:
53. I. Garret (70), m. 1st, Jannetje Diedricks; she d. Oct. 13, 1784; 2d, Lena Vreeland (63).
54. II. Aeltje, m. Daniel Van Winkle (43); III. Beelitje.

Cornelius [27] had ch.:
55. I. Garret, d. s. p. His will was proved May 4, 1795.
56. II. Daniel (72), b. June 26, 1736; m. Elizabeth Terhune, Oct. 13, 1761; d. July 23, 1818; she b. July 15, 1738; d. June 1, 1811. He was a blacksmith by trade, of little education, but of good sterling sense. During the Revolutionary War he was an unyielding patriot. For a short time he was lieutenant in the militia. He was taken prisoner by a tory named Van Wart, and locked up in the old sugar house. When brought before the British officer for examination, his captor and William Bayard, of Hoboken, were present. Van Wart asked him where his rebel coat was. Van Ripen replied, "The coat does not make the man." The officer asked, "What then does?" Putting his hand over his heart, the old patriot replied, "THIS, SIR!" Colonel Bayard desired to have him held a prisoner, but the officer was so pleased with him that he discharged him with the assurance that he would do the same as often as he was arrested. He was

Judge of the Bergen Common Pleas for a number of years after the war. His name appears on many papers and records of his day.

57. III. Beelitje, b. Oct. 10, 1741; m. Johannis Van Horn (10), May 6, 1762; d. Feb. 13, 1826; "Who as it ware fell asleep."

58. IV. Jannetje, bap. April 16, 1745; m. Nicholas Tuers, May 15, 1766.

59. V. Aeltje, b. June 7, 1748; VI. Cornelius, b. Dec. 8, 1750, d. Aug. 13, 1767.

Johannis [28] had ch.:

60. I. Garret (75), b. Feb. 4, 1749; m. 1st, Catlyntje Van Wagenen (47); 2d, Catlyntje Van Ripen (72), March 2, 1779; d. Aug. 31, 1837.

Gerrebrand [32] had ch.:

61. I. Neeltje, b. Oct. 26, 1747; II. Garret, b. April 6, 1753, d. in inf.; III. Garret, b. Jan. 27, 1754; IV. Sarah, b. Feb. 24, 1757.

Christophel [36] had ch.:

62. I. Alexander (82), m. Anneke Brower; d. Aug. 30, 1817.

63. II. Harman, bap. Nov. 25, 1753; d. Aug. 23, 1828.

64. III. Arriantje, b. Jan. 31, 1762; IV. Gerrit, b. Sept. 4, 1764, d. in inf.

65. V. Jurrie (88), b. Feb. 8, 1767; m. Antje Vreeland.

66. VI. Hessel, b. April 12, 1769; VII. Elizabeth, b. Oct. 24, 1770.

67. VIII. Gerrit, b. Nov. 27, 1772, d. in inf.; IX. Neeltje, b. March 13, 1775.

68. X. Jan, b. Oct. 29, 1778; XI. Annatje, b. Dec. 12, 1781.

69. XII. Gerrit, b. Sept. 28, 1786.

Fifth Generation.

Garret [53] had ch..

70. I. Jurrie (89), b. July 20, 1769; m. 1st, Neeltje Van Horn (17), Dec. 18, 1790; 2d, Aegie Diedricks, wid. of Jacob Collard, Sept. 13, 1807; d. April 4, 1826.

71. II. Joris, b. June 3, 1787; m. Clara Vreeland (172), July 23, 1814; removed to Saddle River; had ch.: I. Jane, m. Garret Newkirk (51), Nov. 5, 1840; II.

Cornelius; III. John; IV. George; V. Hartman; VI. Henry, b. Aug. 5, 1835; VII. Ellen; VIII. Eliza; IX. Clarissa, b. Oct. 4, 1840.

Daniel (56] had ch.:

72. I. Catlyntje, b. Sept. 2, 1762; m. Garret Van Ripen (60), May 2, 1779; d. Nov. 14, 1833.
73. II. Cornelius (91), b. May 23, 1767; m. 1st, Elizabeth Vreeland (88); marriage bond dated Jan. 20, 1787; 2d, Vrouwtje, dau. of Garrebrant Gerritsen, of Slotterdam; she d. Sept. 19, 1806; 3d, Aeltje Van Horn (16), wid. of Michael Van Houten, May 31, 1807; d. Jan. 6, 1842.
74. III. Derrick (99), b. Aug. 28, 1772; m. Jenneke Vreeland (100), Oct. —, 1792; d. July 3, 1851.

Garret [60] had ch.:

75. I. Margrietje, b. Oct. 10, 1775; d. July 26, 1776.
76. II. Margrietje, b. Dec. 30, 1780; d. May 31, 1781.
77. III. Catlyntje, b. Nov. 29, 1782; m. Helmich Van Houten, Dec. 7, 1799.
78. IV. Elizabeth, b. July 13, 1785; m. Daniel Van Ripen (91), Sept. 18, 1811; d. Sept. 18, 1852.
79. V. Margrietje, b. Oct. 30, 1788; m. Cornelius Van Winkle (82), Aug. 16, 1807; d. Feb. 23, 1866.
80. VI. Annatje, b. July 12, 1794; m. John G. Van Horn (24), Dec. 19, 1812; d. Dec. 6, 1872.
81. VII. Beelitje, b. Dec. 27, 1797; m. John Van Buskirk (47), Nov. 20, 1814.

Alexander [62] had ch.:

82. I. Christophel (110), m. Gertrude, dau. of John Van Houten, Dec. 27, 1802; d. March 8, 1840, æt. 60 yrs., 1 mo.; she d. Aug. 8, 1860.
83. II. Aeltje, m. John E. Smith, March 27, 1811; d. Oct. 5, 1851.
84. III. Adriana, m. Philip R. Earle, March 6, 1812.
85. IV. Garret (120), m. Hannah Evans, May 28, 1817; she d. Oct. 9, 1824.
86. V. Thomas, m. Rachel Van Winkle, of Aquackanonck; d. June 1, 1849, æt. 69 years.
87. VI. John, d. Sept. 3, 1836, unm.

Jurrie [65] had ch.:

88. I. Simeon, b. Dec. 2, 1789; II. Nicholas, b. Jan. 27, 1792;

III. Stephen, b. July 20, 1793; IV. Antje, b. Jan. 26, 1796.

Sixth Generation.

Jurrie [70] had ch.:

89. I. Antje, d. July 29, 1796.
90. II. Garret (122), b. Oct. 16, 1791; m. Elizabeth Simonson, Jan. 14, 1815; d. Oct. 2, 1833.

Cornelius [73] had ch.:

91. I. Daniel (123), b. March 7, 1788; m. Elizabeth Van Ripen (78), Sept. 18, 1811; d. July 1, 1873.
92. II. Garrabrant, b. Jan. 8, 1793; m. Hannah, dau. of John Van Blarcom; removed to Bergen County.
93. III. Elizabeth, b. April 9, 1794; m. Stephen Vreeland (92), Oct. 14, 1817; d. Dec. 17, 1827.
94. IV. Garret C. (125), b. July 20, 1797; m. Eliza, dau. of Isaac Van Wart, April 28, 1819.
95. V. Helena, b. Sept. 21, 1799; m. Peter Van Winkle, May 20, 1820.
96. VI. Derrick, b. May 22, 1803; m. Margaret, dau. of Thomas Cadmus, Oct. 15, 1825; removed to Passaic County.
97. VII. John, b. May 4, 1808; d. May 14, 1829.
98. VIII. Cornelius C. (129), b. April 8, 1813; m. 1st, Catharine Van Horn (46), May 5, 1832; 2d, Christina C., dau. of Evert Van Alen, Aug. 27, 1835.

Derrick [74] had ch.:

99. I. Michael (135), b. Nov. 8, 1793; m. Cecilia Cadmus (25), Dec. 21, 1816; d. April 22, 1868.
100. II. Elizabeth, b. Nov. 23, 1795; d. Sept. 3, 1796.
101. III. Annatje, b. June 25, 1797; m. Abraham Vreeland (139), Nov. 30, 1816.
102. IV. Elizabeth, b. July 9, 1800; V. Aegie, b. Dec. 19, 1801; d. unm.
103. VI. Daniel R. (144), b. Sept. 7, 1803; m. Jane, dau. of Adrian M. Post, Sept. 7, 1826; d. April 22, 1873.
104. VII. Cornelius R. (150), b. March 27, 1805; m. Mary, dau. of Abraham Sickles, Sept. 15, 1827.
105. VIII. Catharine, b. Sept. 24, 1807; m. Albert Zabriskie, Nov. 7, 1822; d. Dec. 31, 1868; he d. Sept. —, 1872.
106. IX. Jane, b. Dec. 27, 1809; m. Egbert Wauters, Jan. 17, 1828; d. June 14, 1872.

107. X. George, b. Sept. 23, 1811; m. Gitty, dau. of John Outwater, Sept. 13, 1832; d. May 3, 1864, s. p.
108. XI. Helena, b. April 20, 1813; d. May 6, 1813.
109. XII. Aletta, b Oct. 16, 1819; m. John S. Tuttle, Oct. 29, 1840; d. March 29, 1855.

Christophel [82] had ch.:
110. I. Annatje, b. April 10, 1803; m. Mindert Vreeland (182), Nov. 24, 1836.
111. II. Nancy, b. July 23, 1804; m. Martin Tise, Dec. 24, 1829.
112. III. Henry, b. Sept. 12, 1806; m. Catharine, dau. of Jacob Cubberly; d. April 14, 1849, s. p.
113. IV. John, b. July 22, 1808; d. unm.
114. V. Thomas (157), b. Oct. 20, 1810; m. Nancy Parvine, Nov. 30, 1834; d. May 25, 1846.
115. VI. Alexander, b. Nov. 25, 1812; m. Julia Ann Acker, Nov. 15, 1834; d. Dec. 29, 1845; had ch.: Henry and Rosa.
116. VII. Aletta, m. Thomas Wilkes, May 3, 1849.
117. VIII. Elizabeth, b. Nov. 28, 1817; d. unm.
118. IX. Gertrude, b. Sept. 15, 1820; m. Havens Tuttle, Oct. 6, 1836.
119. X. Jane, b. Dec. 28, 1823.

Garret [85] had ch.:
120. I. Ann Elizabeth, b. Feb. 19, 1818; II. Benjamin E., b. May 9, 1820, d. Oct. 7, 1820; III. Harriet E., b. March 29, 1822.
121. IV. Benjamin (158), b. June 23, 1824; m. Nancy, dau. of Benjamin Drake, July 27, 1847.

Seventh Generation.

Garret J. [90] had ch.:
122. I. Eleanor V. H., b. March 10, 1819; m. Edgar R. Harrison, Feb. 4, 1840.

Daniel [91] had ch.:
123. I. Elizabeth Ann, b. April 3, 1822; d. Sept. 3, 1824.
124. II. Garret D. (160), b. Jan. 27, 1826; m. Caroline, dau. of Peter C. Westervelt, of T'Neck.

Garret C. [94] had ch.:
125. I. Frances G., b. Oct. 3, 1820; m. James Van Buskirk (72), May 18, 1839.

126. II. Henry G. (162), b. Aug. 4, 1823; m. Sarah C. Van Buskirk (76), June 1, 1846; d. Jan. 16, 1860.
127. III. Cornelius (163), b. May 27, 1833; m. Mary A., dau. of William Dickinson, Jan. 1, 1853.
128. IV. Isaac Z., b. Nov. 30, 1836; m. Lucy, dau. of William Dickinson, in 1856; d. in Nov., 1868.

Cornelius C.' [98] had ch.:

129. I. John V. H. (164), b. Feb. 27, 1833; m. Margaret Ann, dau. of Jacob Van Ripen, of N. Y., July 2, 1855.
130. II. Catharine V. H., b. Jan. 23, 1836; m. Albert Bogert, Oct. 24, 1867.
131. III. Herman V. A., b. Nov. 2, 1838; d. June 1, 1855.
132. IV. William K., b. Nov. 14, 1840.
133. V. Aletta, b. May 31, 1844; m. Edward P. Buffet, M.D., June 12, 1872; d. Sept. 26, 1873.
134. VI. Anna Deria, b. April 24, 1847; VII. Cornelius, b. March 10, 1852.

Michael [99] had ch.:

135. I. Catharine, b. Sept. 22, 1817; d. Sept. 10, 1819.
136. II. Richard, b. Sept. 25, 1818; d. March 9, 1819.
137. III. Jasper (165), b. Sept. 28, 1820; m. Lucinda Garrabrant; d. Oct. 25, 1849.
138. IV. Jane, b. Jan. 4, 1823; m. John V. H. Clendenny, Oct. 31, 1839.
139. V. Catharine, b. April 25, 1825; m. Adam Rapp, May 13, 1848.
140. VI. Hannah, b. Oct. 22, 1827; m. John J. Rapp, Sept. 9, 1846.
141. VII. Elizabeth, m. James G. Tallman, April 16, 1851.
142. VIII. Sarah, m. Jesse D. Abrams, March 26, 1851.
143. IX. Richard (166), b. Nov. 18, 1839; m. Helen, dau. of Moses Copley, July 10, 1862.

Daniel R. [103] had ch.:

144. I. Eliza, b. July 1, 1826; m. Henry B. Beaty, the eighth sheriff of Hudson County.
145. II. Richard (167), b. Dec. 3, 1829; m. Sarah G., dau. of James Tallman, April 16, 1851.
146. III. Adrian (168), b. Nov. 7, 1832; m. Sarah Jane, dau. of John Van Pelt, of Millstone.
147. IV. John M., b. July 25, 1835; m. Louisa, dau. of John Gurney, March 27, 1860; d. April 27, 1868; had ch.: I. Albert.

148. V. Hannah Jane, b. Aug. 21, 1839; m. Walter Gurney, Jan. 15, 1869.

149. VI. Clara P., b. April 3, 1842, m. John Wallace, Jr., April 13, 1869; VII. Daniel, b. Oct. 21, 1844; VIII. Catharine Euphemia, b. Aug. 22, 1847, d. Aug. 10, 1858; IX. Aletta, b. April 1, 1850.

Cornelius R. [104] had ch.:

150. I. Richard C. (169), b. Dec. 19, 1827; m. Rachel Catharine Vreeland (253), May 27, 1852.

151. II. Abraham, b. March 25, 1829; m. Cornelia, dau. of Jacob Ackerman; removed to Illinois.

152. III. Michael C., b. Dec. 31, 1832; m. Mary Elizabeth, dau. of Jacob Thomas, July 6, 1858; d. Dec. 10, 1870.

153. IV. Matilda Jane, b. May 22, 1836; d. Oct. 23, 1838.

154. V. Cornelius, b. Sept. 19, 1838; d. March 17, 1857.

155. VI. Mary Anna, b. April 6, 1841; m. Garret Vreeland (122), March 5, 1869.

156. VII. Matilda Jane, b. Oct. 14, 1845.

Thomas [114] had ch.:

157. I. Silas; II. John; III. Christopher, b. in 1835; IV. Aletta Jane, b. March 18, 1843, d. Jan. 18, 1847; V. Margaret.

Benjamin [121] had ch.:

158. I. Ann Eliza, b. Nov. 27, 1848; m. Peter B. Steele, Nov. 27, 1866.

159. II. Garret, b. Aug. 1, 1850, d. in inf.; III. Nancy, b. June 5, 1851, d. in inf.; IV. Diedrick, b. July 4, 1852, d. in inf.; V. Archibald P., b. May 3, 1853, d. April 14, 1856; VI. Ida, b. Oct. 1, 1856, d. Nov. 11, 1860; VII. Ansel J., b. April 3, 1858; VIII. Hattie B., b. April 3, 1861, d. July 17, 1862; IX. Edwin A. H., b. Dec. 24, 1866; X. Benjamin, b. May 3, 1869.

Eighth Generation.

Garret D. [124] had ch.:

160. I. Elizabeth, b. Aug. 23, 1849; m. John Henry Bedell, May 26, 1869.

161. II. Peter W., b. Jan. 24, 1852; III. Clarissa, b. June 19, 1854.

Henry G. [126] had ch.:

162. I. Jane, b. March 16, 1848; II. Eliza, m. Florence Griswold; III. Fanny, b. Feb. 23, 1852; IV. Gilbert.

Cornelius [127] had ch.:

163. I. Cornelius, b. Oct., 1855, d. in inf.; II. Fanny G., b. Dec. 17, 1857; III. Lucy Maud, b. Jan. 13, 1860.

John V. H. [129] had ch.:

164. I. John V. H., b. July 14, 1856; II. Edwin, b. June 18, 1859; III. Anna Catharine, b. July 1, 1862.

Jasper [137] had ch.:

165. I. Sarah Elizabeth, b. Dec. 17, 1843; II. Abraham.

Richard [143] had ch.:

166. I. Ira, b. April 13, 1863, d. Sept. 23, 1864; II. William J., b. Sept. 23, 1864, d. Aug. 13, 1865; III. John C., b. Jan. 23, 1866; IV. Edward J., b. July 5, 1868; V. Nellie, b. Sept. 7, 1870; VI. Richard V. and VII. Jennie L., twins, b. July 4, 1873.

Richard [145] had ch.:

167. I. Jennie, b. April 5, 1852; II. Sarah E., b. Dec. 10, 1854, m. John A. Bumsted, May 8, 1873; III. Daniel, b. June 10, 1857; IV. Clara, b. Dec. 5, 1860; V. Mary, b. March 5, 1865; VI. Richard, b. Aug. 20, 1866.

Adrian [146] had ch.:

168. I. Jane, b. Jan. 21, 1861; II. George, b. Nov. 8, 1864; III. John, b. Jan. 15, 1867; IV. Isabella, b. Feb. 27, 1869.

Richard C. [150] had ch.:

169. I. Cornelius, b. July 12, 1853; II. Maria Jane, b. Oct. 12, 1857.

Van Hooren—Van Hoorn—Van Horn.

This name is derived from *Hoorn*, a large, pleasant and rich city, with a convenient port, on the Zuyder Zee, about twenty miles north of Amsterdam. It was surrounded with broad dykes for its security, large pasture grounds for its profit, and fine gardens and walks for its pleasure. Its traffic consisted mostly in butter and cheese, of which large quantities were taken into Spain. The name was written *Hoorn* or *Hooren.* From this place Jan Cornelissen (or John, the son of Cornelius) came to this country. The time of his arrival is not known, but he was in New Amsterdam as early as June, 1645.[1] From a power of attorney, which he executed Oct. 4, 1647,[2] for the purpose of collecting money from his guardian in Holland, it would seem that he came to this country before he arrived at his majority. He was one of the remonstrants against defending the city when attacked by the English in 1664.[3] In October of that year he took the oath of allegiance to the King. Among his children was a son named *Joris*, who m. Maria Rutgers, of Amersfoort, March 11, 1666. At an early period the name was quite common at Hackensack, and I have no doubt that is the place where the family first settled in New Jersey. Joris had eight ch., one of whom, a son, bap. Jan. 5, 1667, received the name of *Rutgers*, in honor of his mother's family.[4] He m. Neeltje, dau. of Diedrick Teunissen Van Vechten, and wid. of Jan Van Derlinden, April 25, 1697. The marriage record speaks of him as a "young man from Hackensack." Van Derlinden resided and owned land in the present city of Bayonne, which was afterward purchased by Van Horn.[5] Her mother was Jannetje, dau. of Michiel Jansen (Vreeland) (7). After his marriage he continued to reside at "Pemmarepocq" until 1711. On the 7th of May in that year he purchased of his wife's uncle, Enoch Vreeland, land at Communipaw, for which he agreed to give *one pepper corn, if demanded!* He then settled there, and the name has become so inseparably linked with the place that the one would seem incomplete without the other. He accumulated a large amount of landed property, including tracts on the Raritan and at Plainfield. He was known as *Rutt*, though he generally wrote his name *Rutgert* Van Hooren,[6] as this fac-simile will show; he d. May 15, 1741.

---

[1] *Valentine's Manual*, 1861, 600. [2] *N. Y. Col. MSS., ii.*, 165.

[3] *Col. Hist. of N. Y., ii.*, 250.

[4] It is due that I should say that the evidence to sustain the above is not so clear and strong as I could wish, but I believe it to be correct.

[5] *Winfield's Land Titles*, 69

[6] As to the proper orthography of *Van Horn*, whether it should be with or without the final *e*, I may say that while both ways of writing it are in use, I

Fourth Generation.

Rutgert had ch.:

2. I. Jannetje, bap. Jan. 30, 1698; m. Diedrick F. Caddemus (Dirck Cadmus), June 10, 1718. Her father gave to her the land in Bayonne still held by the Cadmus family.
3. II. Joris, b. April 2, 1700; d. in inf.
4. III. Jan (7), b. Feb. 3, 1702; m. 1st, Helena Sip (14); 2d, Antje, dau. of Mattys De Mott—marriage bond dated May 2, 1751; d. Dec. 12, 1757.
5. IV. Maritje, b. April 11, 1704; m. Elias Johannissen Vreeland (42), May 11, 1723; d. at Aquackanonck, Sept. 23, 1791.
6. V. Annetje, b. Feb. 6, 1707.

Fifth Generation.

Jan [4] had ch.:

7. I. Neeltje, b. June 28, 1726; m. Helmagh Vreeland (74); marriage bond dated April 1, 1752.
8. II. Annetje, b. March 25, 1729; m. Cornelius Van Vorst (31), April 21, 1753; d. Jan. 20, 1804.
9. III. Jannetje, b. Feb. 28, 1736; m. Cornelius Garrabrant (19), August 10, 1757; d. Nov. 26, 1771.
10. IV. Johannis (13), b. June 8, 1742; m. Beelitje, dau. of Cornelius Van Ripen (57), May 6, 1742; d. Oct. 10, 1786.
11. V. Lena, b. April 20, 1750; m. Rutgert Van Brunt, of Long Island, Dec. 3, 1767.
12. VI. Margrietje, b. March 14, 1752; d. May 14, 1753.

Sixth Generation.

Johannis [10] had ch.:

13. I. Helena, b. April 2, 1763; m. Cornelius Garrabrant (34); d. March 2, 1850.
14. II. Johannis (19), b. March 30, 1765; m. Jannetje, dau. of Cornelius Garrabrant (35); marriage bond dated March 24, 1785; d. Aug. 29, 1843. He was a Member of the General Assembly of New Jersey in 1807.
15. III. Cornelius, b. May 31, 1767; d. July 27, 1776.

---

am entirely satisfied that it should be without the final *e*. There is no authority for its use, and while the name has been reduced from the original, Hoorn, by dropping an *o*, this error cannot justify its further corruption by the addition of an unwarranted final *e*.

16. IV. Aeltje, b. Sept. 7, 1769; m. 1st, Michael Van Houten, Dec. 15, 1793; he d. June 1, 1803; 2d, Cornelius Van Ripen (73), May 31, 1807; d. July 2, 1846.

17. V. Neeltje, b. Dec. 28, 1771; m. Jurrie Van Ripen (70), Dec. 18, 1790; d. Oct. 28, 1801.

18. VI. Garret (24), b. June 28, 1774; m. Trintje, dau. of Mindert Garrabrant (40), July 21, 1795; d. April 7, 1809.

Seventh Generation.

Johannis [14] had ch.:

19. I. John J. (27), b. June 23, 1785; m. Mary, dau. of Jacob Prior, Dec. 27, 1806; she d. Feb. 27, 1858.

20. II. Cornelius (31), b. Feb. 3, 1787; m. Jane, dau. of Cornelius Garrabrant (43), Jan. 21, 1810; d. Feb. 28, 1841.

21. III. Garret (38), b. Sept. 11, 1790; m. 1st, Margaret, dau. of Andrew Gautier, Jan. 5, 1812; she d. Dec. 29, 1828; 2d, Rebecca Sharpley, May 20, 1830; d. Sept. 21, 1838; she d. Sept. 29, 1865, æt. 71 yrs., 5 mos., 13 days.

22. IV. Peter (43), b. March 26, 1793; m. 1st, Ann Ross, June 14, 1817; she was b. Oct. 28, 1799; d. Sept. 18, 1823; 2d, Mary, dau. of John Jerolamon, Oct. 4, 1824; d. Nov. 21, 1841; she was b. Oct. 2, 1804; m. Stephen Terhune, March 6, 1849.

23. V. Daniel, b. March 22, 1795; d. April 24, 1795.

Garret [18] had ch.:

24. I. John G. (46), b. Jan. 25, 1793; m. Hannah Van Ripen (80), Dec. 19, 1812; d. Dec. 1, 1871.

25. II. Mindert (50), b. July 21, 1795; m. Mary, dau. of Abraham Sickles, Oct. 12, 1816; she d. March 4, 1856.

26. III. Beelitje, b. April 25, 1805; d. Sept. 25, 1807.

Eighth Generation.

John J. [19] had ch.:

27. I. Jane, b. June 10, 1810; m. Henry Brinkerhoff (39), Jan. 18, 1827.

28. II. Jacob (52), b. June 8, 1814; m. Harriet, dau. of Richard Outwater, Nov. 17, 1836.

29. III. Sarah, b. Dec. 2, 1818; m. John A. Post, Dec. 11, 1839.
30. IV. John (56), b. May 2, 1826; m. Mary, dau. of R. Newton Post, May 3, 1845.

Cornelius [20] had ch.:

31. I. Cornelius, b. May 9, 1811; d. Aug. 10, 1819.
32. II. John C. (60), b. April 8, 1813; m. Gertrude, dau. of John Ackerman, June 2, 1836.
33. III. Helen, b. Nov. 1, 1815; m. Albert Ackerman, Dec. 3, 1835.
34. IV. Cornelius, b. Oct. 14, 1820; d. Dec. 29, 1822.
35. V. Belina, b. Dec. 14, 1822; m. John Winner, June 28, 1843.
36. VI. Jane, b. April 5, 1826; d. Dec. 14, 1836.
37. VII. Aletta; VIII. Margaret Ann, b. May 10, 1831.

Garret [21] had ch.:

38. I. Eliza, b. March 21, 1816; d. Aug. 21, 1835.
39. II. John G. (66), b. April 4, 1819; m. Ellen Jane, dau. of David Bush, Dec. 3, 1840.
40. III. Stephen C., b. Dec. 9, 1821; d. at sea, July 15, 1842, unm.
41. IV. Hartman V., b. Dec. 7, 1826; m. Margaret Cadmus (65), June 1, 1853. By act of the Legislature his name was changed to *Hartman Vreeland*. His ch. are placed in the genealogy of that family (282).
42. V. Margaret Jane G., b. July 10, 1832; d. Dec. 1, 1851.

Peter [22] had ch.:

43. I. Agnes, b. Nov. 3, 1818; m. Garret Van Horn (50), Nov. 9, 1837.
44. II. Jane, b. Jan. 12, 1821; m. Peter V. B. Vreeland (156), Feb. 27, 1840; d. May 4, 1871.
45. III. John P., b. Jan. 23, 1823; d. Sept. 21, 1823.

John G. [24] had ch.:

46. I. Catharine, b. July 16, 1814; m. Cornelius C. Van Ripen (98), May 6, 1832; d. March 28, 1833.
47. II. Garret, b. April 28, 1820; d. Nov. 28, 1826.
48. III. John J. (67), b. Aug. 4, 1825; m. Cornelia V. R., dau. of Evert Van Alen; d. Sept. 11, 1862.
49. IV. Garret I. (69), b. July 30, 1830; m. Mary, dau. of Abraham Britton, Dec. 25, 1852; d. Nov. 17, 1864. He was for several years clerk of the Board of Chosen Freeholders; also clerk of the town of Bergen.

Mindert [25] had ch.:

50. I. Garret (73), b Sept. 23, 1817; m. Agnes Van Horn (43), Nov. 9, 1837; d. Jan. 25, 1872. He was for several years a member of the General Assembly of New Jersey.

51. II. Mary, b. Feb. 10, 1822; m. Rufus K. Terry, March 19, 1843.

Ninth Generation.

Jacob [28] had ch.:

52. I. John Henry, b. Oct. 7, 1837; d. March 27, 1853.

53. II. Catharine, b. Aug. 16, 1839; m. Albert Augustus Hardenbergh, Nov. 24, 1859.

54. III. Richard O., b. May 30, 1841; d. June 18, 1862, unm.

55. IV. Mary Adelaide, b. Oct. 30, 1853; V. Harriet Eliza, b. Sept. 21, 1856.

John [30] had ch.:

56. I. Eliza, b. Aug. 17, 1846; m. James B. Doremus, Nov. 8, 1866.

57. II. Mary Jane, b. July 25, 1849; d. in inf.

58. III. Mary Jane, b. June 21, 1851; IV. Jacob P., b. July 1, 1854.

59. V. Anna R., b. Dec. 18, 1856; VI. Catharine A., b. July 23, 1862.

John C. [32] had ch.:

60. I. Cornelius, b. July 9, 1838; m. Minnie E., dau. of Thomas Laverty, May 13, 1873.

61. II. Anne Maria, b. Nov. 18, 1840; m. John Henry De Mott, May 22, 1861.

62. III. Jane, b. Nov. 29, 1843; m. Lawrence J. Ackerman, June 27, 1867; d. Sept. 3, 1870.

63. IV. Garret, b. March 9, 1846; m. Mary Margretta Vreeland (210), April 22, 1873.

64. V. Mary Elizabeth, b. July 27, 1849; m. —— Berdan, Nov. 4, 1873.

65. VI. George W., b. Aug. 1, 1852; VII. Julia Gertrude, b. Nov. 8, 1856; VIII. Laura Olivia, b. March 19, 1859.

John G. [39] had ch.:

66. I. Margaret Eliza, b. Dec. 10, 1845; II. David M., b. Oct. 24, 1854.

John J. [48] had ch.:

67. I. Catharine, b. Sept. 3, 1844; m. Abraham W. Colton, of Toledo, Ohio, April 17, 1867.

68. II. Stephen V. A., b. March 4, 1856; III. Frank, b. Nov. —, 1858.

Garret I. [49] had ch.:

69. I. John, b. Dec. 10, 1853; II. Andrew B., b. April 22, 1856; III. William R., b. May 16, 1858; IV. Anna V. R., b. July 15, 1861, d. Sept. 17, 1861; V. Mary Ida, b. Aug. 4, 1862.

Garret [50] had ch.:

70. I. Ann Jane, b. July 3, 1842, d. in inf.; II. Abraham, b. Jan. 14, 1849.

Newkirk—Nieukerke—Van Nieuwkercke.

In the olden time there was a town called *Nykerk*, or Nieukerke, in Friesland, about sixty miles south of Biorenburgh; also Nieuwkerk in Gelderland. It is probable that from this place came *Mattheus Cornelissen Van Nieuwkercke*. The date of his arrival has not been ascertained, but in the ship *Moesman*, April 25, 1669, Geurt Cornelissen Van Nieuwkerck, with his wife, son, twelve years old, and a nursing child, arrived. He was probably of the same family. Mattheus m. 1st, Anna, dau. of Jacob Luby, Dec. 14, 1670; she d. Dec. 20, 1685; 2d, Catrina Poulus, d. May 12, 1705. Her will, dated Sept. 30, 1731, was proved May 7, 1764.

Second Generation.

Mattheus had ch.:

2. I. Geertruyd, b. Sept. 18, 1671.

3. II. Gerritje, bap. July 23, 1673; m. Aelt Jurianse, July 7, 1695.

4. III. Jacomyntje, bap. April 2, 1675; m. Jacob Van Winkle (22), April 21, 1701.

5. IV. Cornelis, bap. March 11, 1680; d. June 7, 1691.

6. V. Jacob, bap. Nov. 21, 1682; m. Sarah Cornelis, May 15, 1707.

7. VI. Jannetje, b. July 8, 1687; d. May 15, 1691; VII. Trintje, b. Dec. 17, 1688.

8. VIII. Jan, b. April 22, 1690; m. Jenneke Bresteede, Nov. 6, 1708.

9. IX. Jannetje, bap. March 17, 1692; m. Garret Diedricks, April 21, 1733.
10. X. Pieter, b. Aug. 26, 1694; m. Trintje Dirckse, July 3, 1726.
11. XI. Gerrit (14), b. Nov. 18, 1696; m. Catrintje, dau. of Hendrick Kuyper, Sept. 5, 1730; d. April 23, 1785; she d. Sept. 12, 1751.
12. XII. Poulus (18), b. Aug. 21, 1699; m. Helena Spier, June 18, 1728; d. Feb. 5, 1763; she d. April 6, 1801.
13. XIII. Cornelis, b. Sept. 3, 1703; m. Lea Marys, wid., of Schraalenburgh, Oct. 18, 1749; d. Sept. 10, 1781, s. p.; she d. March 17, 1757.

Those by the first wife scattered, while those by the second wife remained in the county. By her will their mother gave to these five all of her property.

Third Generation.

Gerrit [11] had ch.:

14. I. Catrintje, b. Aug. 9, 1731; d. Sept. 18, 1759.
15. II. Jenneke, b. April 24, 1737; d. Oct. 4, 1779, unm.
16. III. Mattevis (24), m. Catlyntje, dau. of Arent Toers; d. July 10, 1811.
17. IV. Hendrick (27), b. April 4, 1741; m. Jenneke Vreeland (64); d. July 8, 1795.

Poulus [12] had ch.:

18. I. Catrina, b. May 10, 1729.
19. II. Catlyntje, bap. May 7, 1733.
20. III. Matthew P. (30), b. April 30, 1735; m. Geertje Kock; d. Nov. 12, 1818; she d. Feb. 27, 1828.
21. IV. Barent (31), b. March 12, 1738; m. Antje Toers, April 6, 1765.
22. V. Jannetje, b. May 26, 1740.
23. VI. Jacob (32), m. Fitje Hennion, Feb. 13, 1769; d. June 9, 1818, æt. 75 yrs., 7 mos., 25 days; she b. April 20, 1744; d. Jan. 23, 1808.

Fourth Generation.

Mattevis [16] had ch.:

24. I. Garret (39), b. April 9, 1766; m. Polly Ackerman; d. Aug. 28, 1832.

25. II. Aaron (45), b. Oct. 22, 1768; m. Jannetje Vreeland (103), Nov. —, 1791; d. April 1, 1849.
26. III. Henry, b. June 22, 1771; d. unm.

Hendrick [17] had ch.:
27. I. Garret H., b. Jan. 8, 1781; d. Oct. 21, 1860, unm.
28. II. George (49), b. Nov. 23, 1783; m. Sarah, dau. of Garret Van Derhoof, Feb. 9, 1805; d. Aug. 19, 1861; she b. Aug. 8, 1782; d. Sept. 1, 1861.
29. III. Catrintje, b. Sept. 7, 1791; m. Hartman Van Wagenen (53), Aug. 16, 1812; d. July 25, 1848.

Matthew P. [20] had ch.:
30. I. John M. (55), b. May 18, 1781; m. Maritje Newkirk (37), Feb. 1, 1806; d. March —, 1870.

Barent [21] had ch.:
31. I. Arent, b. Sept. 1, 1768; II. Jannetje, b. Nov. 15, 1777; d. Sept. 17, 1779.

Jacob [23] had ch.:
32. I. Maritje, b. July 18, 1770; d. Aug. 1, 1776.
33. II. Poulus, b. Nov. 25, 1772; d. in inf.
34. III. Poulus, b. April 15, 1776; d. Aug. 27, 1776.
35. IV. Jacob, b. April 28, 1778; d. Dec. 5, 1796.
36. V. Garret (59), b. July 21, 1780; m. Rachel, dau. of George Shepherd, Feb. 22, 1806; d. Aug. 22, 1818; she d. Jan. 16, 1861, æt. 76 yrs., 4 mos., 10 days.
37. VI. Maritje, b. July 13, 1782; m. John M. Newkirk (30), Feb. 1, 1806; d. Sept 24, 1852.
38. VII. John J. (65), b. Oct. 23, 1786; m. Gertrude, dau. of John Collard, May 14, 1814; d. Aug. 15, 1860; she b. June 15, 1788; d. Jan. 23, 1858.

Fifth Generation.

Garret [24] had ch.:
39. I. Catharine, b. Oct. 10, 1788; m. George Vreeland (83), June 17, 1809; d. March 27, 1851.
40. II. Margaret, b. May 22, 1790; m. Garret Sip (26), Nov. 10, 1811.
41. III. Sally, b. June 25, 1793; d. Dec. 9, 1794.
42. IV. Sally, b. Dec. 18, 1796; d. Aug. 15, 1797.
43. V. Henry (70), b. Dec. 16, 1799; m. Eliza Provost, July

24, 1818; d. July 29, 1861. He was the second Sheriff of Hudson County. She b. Sept. 9, 1800; d. Oct. 8, 1858.

44. VI. Garret (79), b. Oct. 17, 1808; m. 1st, Rachel, dau. of Helmigh Van Houten, Oct. 25, 1828; she d. Dec. 1, 1835; 2d, Jane Fowler, wid. of Abraham Tise; she d. Oct. 6, 1849; 3d, Eliza Ann Beaty, Sept. 6, 1851.

Aaron [25] had ch.:

45. I. Catlyntje, b. Nov. 6, 1792; m. Cornelius Van Ripen, of Aquackanonck, Nov. 7, 1813.

46. II. Cornelia, b. Oct. 2, 1794; m. Daniel Vreeland (137), Jan. 23, 1813; d. March 30, 1870.

47. III. Mattevis, b. May 22, 1799; d. Nov. 10, 1799.

48. IV. Catharine, b. May 15, 1807; m. Cornelius M. Vreeland (140), Nov. 28, 1822.

George [28] had ch.:

49. I. Jane, b. Dec. 6, 1805; d. April 19, 1806.

50. II. Henry G. (93), b. Dec. 19, 1808; m. Sarah Van Buskirk (63), Nov. 7, 1838.

51. III. Garret G. (97), b. Sept. 28, 1812; m. Jane Van Ripen (71), of Saddle River, Nov. 5, 1840; d. Feb. 26, 1872.

52. IV. Jane Maria, b. Feb. 17, 1816; m. David Burbank, Jan. 24, 1841.

53. V. Abraham P. (98), b. Dec. 21, 1819; m. Maria Tallman, Sept. 11, 1844.

54. VI. George (99), b. May 8, 1826; m. Gertrude Vreeland (239), Dec. 3, 1854.

John M. [30] had ch.:

55. I. Gertrude, b. Oct. 20, 1810.

56. II. John, b. Oct. 20, 1810; m. Sarah Hedden, Dec. 25, 1834; d. Dec. 28, 1847, s. p.

57. III. Sophia, b. May 31, 1813; d. Feb. 14, 1815.

58. IV. Matthew, b. June 20, 1816; m. Leah Demarest, and resided in Hackensack; d. Aug. —, 1873. His ch. are: I. James D., b. June 8, 1846; II. Maria Catharine, b. Aug. 9, 1850; III. Anne Matilda, b. Dec. 28, 1851.

Garret J. [36] had ch.:

59. I. Jacob (100), b. Nov. 26, 1807; m. Elizabeth, dau. of Siba Brinkerhoff, of Hackensack, May 22, 1830.

60. II. George, b. June 19, 1809; m. Ann, dau. of Isaac Tappan.
61. III. Matthew, b. July 4, 1811; d. May 29, 1812.
62. IV. Sophia, b. Nov. 24, 1812; m. James Provost, Sept. 1, 1832; d. July 11, 1845.
63. V. Garret (106), b. March 18, 1815; m. Jane, dau. of Jacob S. Brinkerhoff.
64. VI. Cathaline, b. March 14, 1817; m. George Vreeland (115), Feb. 23, 1837.

John J. [38] had ch.:

65. I. Jacob (107), b. May 29, 1815; m. Aletta, dau. of Michael Riker, Oct. 24, 1839; she b. March 27, 1820; d. Jan. 14, 1850.
66. II. Abraham (111), b. Oct. 3, 1817; m. Mary Elizabeth, dau. of Abner P. Howell, Oct. 23, 1839.
67. III. Garret J., b. Aug. 29, 1821; d. Aug. 11, 1851, unm.
68. IV. Sophia, b. Sept. 25, 1823; m. Blakely Wilson, Sept. 26, 1842.
69. V. Effie, b. March 23, 1826; m. Daniel Van Winkle (139), June 22, 1847.

Sixth Generation.

Henry [43] had ch.:

70. I. James M., b. June 27, 1819; m. Sarah Jane, dau. of John B. Vreeland, May 27, 1840.
71. II. Henry H. (116), b. March 22, 1823; m. 1st, Margaret, dau. of Job Smith, Sept. 18, 1844; she b. Oct. 11, 1823; d. July 13, 1861; 2d, Anne M. Vermilye, March 22, 1871.
72. III. Mary, b. April 17, 1826; m. George V. De Mott, Feb. 5, 1846; d. Jan. 12, 1858.
73. IV. Garret (119), b. July 23, 1828; m. Catharine, dau. of Henry Ryerson, Sept. 20, 1848.
74. V. John, b. Nov. 10, 1830; m. Antje Boice, Oct. 4, 1854; has ch., and resides in Bridgeport, Conn.
75. VI. Eliza, b. Dec. 10, 1832; m. Francis P. Gautier, Dec. 20, 1860.
76. VII. Cornelius, b. May 20, 1835; d. Oct. 16, 1838.
77. VIII. George V., b. Dec. 1, 1838; d. Feb. 13, 1859, unm.
78. IX. Emma Matilda, m. William H. Bronson, March 27, 1868.

Garret G. [44] had ch.:

79. I. Catharine, b. Feb. 11, 1829; d. Jan. 22, 1830.

80. II. Mary, b. Sept. 1, 1831; m. Cornelius A. Vreeland (236), Sept. 19, 1849.
81. III. Catharine Elizabeth, b. June 30, 1838; m. Reuben Giberson, Dec. 3, 1856.
82. IV. Rachel V. H., b. Sept. 9, 1839; m. George L. Darress.
83. V. Gilbert F., b. Feb. 27, 1841; d. Oct. 21, 1841.
84. VI. Henry Cornelius, b. Feb. 27, 1841; d. Oct. 4, 1842.
85. VII. George V., b. April 1, 1842.
86. VIII. Garret S., b. April 18, 1843; d. July 30, 1843.
87. IX. Sarah Jane, b. Oct. 17, 1844; d. Oct. 29, 1869, unm.
88. X. William Henry, b. Nov. 27, 1845; XI. Margaret S., b. April 8, 1847.
89. XII. Abraham, b. May 15, 1848, d. July 18, 1848; XIII. James S., b. Sept. 9, 1852, m. Elizabeth Terhune, Oct. 29, 1873.
90. XIV. Franklin P., b. Nov. 10, 1853; XV. Laura E., b. Aug. 3, 1855.
91. XVI. Emma Rebecca, b. May 2, 1857; d. Aug. 6, 1860.
92. XVII. Charles Edward, b. Nov. 29, 1863; d. July 18, 1864.

Henry G. [50] had ch.:

93. I. Sarah Catharine, b. Nov. 7, 1835; m. Cornelius W. Van Pelt, Dec. 24, 1855.
94. II. Arabella, b. Nov. 23, 1843; III. John V. B., b. April 11, 1848; d. April 23, 1852.
95. IV. George, b. May 30, 1851; V. John Henry, b. Feb. 3, 1860.
96. VI. Eliza Jane, b. Feb. 3, 1860.

Garret G. [51] had ch.:

97. I. George, b. Sept. 16, 1844; m. Catharine, dau. of George Seebach.

Abraham P. [53] had ch.:

98. I. George W., b. April 29, 1847; II. Eugene T., b. March 17, 1857, d. Oct. 23, 1868.

George [54] had ch.:

99. I. Nicholas V., b. Nov. 23, 1857.

Jacob [59] had ch.:

100. I. Rachel, b. July 16, 1831; m. Jacob M. Merselis, Feb. 13, 1850; d. July 10, 1852.

101. II. Jacob B., b. Dec. 31, 1833; m. Kate M., dau. of Abraham Spear, Oct. 26, 1859; had ch.: I. Jennie, b. ——, 1860.

102. III. Garret, b. Feb. 10, 1836; d. July 17, 1873, unm.

103. IV. Jane Elizabeth, b. Oct. 31, 1838; m. George W. Birdsall, Nov. 10, 1859.

104. V. John Henry (120), b. Feb. 2, 1841; m. Emma C., dau. of Samuel Coe, March 19, 1866.

105. VI. Mary Catharine, b. March 7, 1845, m. Abraham Vanderbeek, Dec. 13, 1866; VII. Abraham, b. Nov. 16, 1847; VIII. William Edward, b. March 6, 1851.

Garret [63] had ch.:

106. I. Sophia, b. Sept. 24, 1856; II. Gertrude, b. Jan. 17, 1859; III. Winfield; IV. Ella; V. Annie; VI. Edward.

Jacob [65] had ch.:

107. I. Anna Maria, b. Sept. 26, 1840; m. John V. R. Vreeland (216), Oct. 16, 1861.

108. II. John William (121), b. Nov. 6, 1842; m. Lavina, dau. of Enoch E. Rino, Oct. 28, 1863.

109. III. Lewis W., b. April 16, 1846; d. July 19, 1847.

110. IV. Lewis, b. May 18, 1848; d. Feb. 27, 1849.

Abraham [66] had ch.:

111. I. Gertrude E., b. June 29, 1841; m. Lewis M. Crosby, Feb. 14, 1861.

112. II. Catharine H., b. Sept. 25, 1843; d. in inf.

113. III. Henry B., b. Aug. 14, 1845; d. in inf.

114. IV. Sophia W., b. Sept. 19, 1847; m. George A. Adams, Nov. 13, 1867.

115. V. Frederick H., b. Oct. 14, 1851; m. Sophia, dau. of John Weeks, July 16, 1871; had ch.: I. Grace, b. July 4, 1872.

Seventh Generation.

Henry H. [71] had ch.:

116. I. Eliza Jane, b. Dec. 28, 1845; m. Frederick W. Stevens, Nov. 2, 1868.

117. II. Phebe Emma, b. Aug. 18, 1847; m. Anthony Daumont, Feb. 24, 1869.

118. III. Sarah Margaret, b. Jan. 6, 1850.

Garret [73] had ch.:

119. I. Henry H., b. Nov. 24, 1853.

John H. [104] had ch.:

120. I. Harry, b. Aug. 19, 1867; II. Arthur, b. Dec. 9, 1869.

John William [108] had ch.:

121. I. Mary Aletta, b. July 8, 1864; II. Anna, b. Aug. 21, 1866, d. in inf.

GARRABRANT—GERBRANDS—GERREBRANDSE.

The founder of this family was Gerbrand Claesen. He was a man of much influence in the early history of Bergen, and held many official positions. He m. Maritje, only dau. of Claes Pietersen Cos, Aug. 25, 1674; d. June 19, 1703; she b. in 1655; d. Oct. —, 1714. Her father was b. in 1619, and came to this country a soldier in the service of the Dutch West India Company. For an assault and battery on Robert Pennoyer he was, Sept. 29, 1644, fined fifty guilders, sentenced "to ride the wooden horse during parade, and to be conveyed thence to prison, or else to go immediately on shipboard and not return on shore, on forfeiture of wages."[1] Previous to January, 1657, he purchased that part of Jan Evertsen Bout's farm which lay northeast of Communipaw avenue for 1,444 florins.[2] At that time, his wife, Neeltje Engels, was dead, leaving Maritje, her only child, then two years old. Michiel Jansen and Egbert Woutersen became her guardians. Being betrothed to Grietje, widow of Claas Teunissen, Cos was required by law to make provision for his child's support. He agreed, not only to support her, but to teach her reading and writing, sewing and some trade, and to give her 200 florins out of her mother's estate. To secure this, he pledged "his person and property, especially his bouwerie at Gemoenepa." *Whoso findeth a wife findeth a good thing* did not hold good in the case of Cos. His Grietje "played the harlot," and finally left him and went to Holland. For this waywardness he was granted a divorce by Governor Carteret, Jan. 20, 1666.

On Jan. 25, 1689, Gerbrand Claesen obtained permission of Governor Leisler to purchase a tract of land at Kigtawangh, now Putnam, in Dutchess County, N. Y. On Dec. 6, 1699, he purchased of George Willocks land at Pequannock, on which many

---

[1] *N. Y. Col. MSS., iv.*, 203.

[2] *New Amst. Rec., iii.*, 143; *Orphans' Court, New Amst. Winfield's Land Titles*, 47.

of his descendants afterward lived. He d. Sept. 21, 1704. His ch., taking his baptismal name, became Gerbrandsen, from which the present name was derived. His brother Arien d. April 9, 1703.

Second Generation.

Gerbrand Claesen had ch.:

2. I. Pieter, bap. April 21, 1675; m. Chrystyntje Jurrianse Van Ripen (5), Aug. 7, 1698.
3. II. Claas (11), b. Aug. 15, 1677; m. Maritje Jurrianse Van Ripen (6), April 11, 1704; removed to Newark.
4. III. Herpert (12), b. Nov. 26, 1679; m. Hillegond Merselis, May 29, 1707.
5. IV. Neeltje, b. Oct. 1, 1684; m. Jan Juriansen Van Ripen (8), April 7, 1702.
6. V. Metje, b. Feb. 23, 1687; m. Dirck Van Sloat, Sept. 9, 1711.
7. VI. Cornelius (15), b. Jan. 23, 1688; m. Jannetje, dau. of Teunis Prior, Nov. 10, 1716; d. Feb. 26, 1774; she d. Nov. 26, 1771.
8. VII. Maritje, bap. Nov. 1, 1693; m. Gerrit G. Van Wagenen, Jr. (11).
9. VIII. Gerrebrand, b. Aug. 9, 1696; d. Sept. 7, 1697.
10. IX. Mindert (22), m. Trintje Jacobse Van Winckel (11), May 7, 1715; d. May 5, 1781.

Third Generation.

Claas [3] had ch.:

11. I. Gerbrants (29), b. Jan 7, 1705; m. Johanna, dau. of Christopher Steinmets.

Herpert [4] had ch.:

12. I. Maritje, b. May 12, 1708; m. Jacob Van Ripen (16), Dec. 17, 1728.
13. II. Abraham (31), m. Maritje Vreeland.
14. III. Petrus, bap. Jan. 31, 1735; m. Elizabeth Gerritse, and had ch.: I. Maritje, b. Feb. 3, 1754.

Cornelius [7] had ch.:

15. I. Maritje, b. Nov. 9, 1717; m. Hartman Vreeland (67), Nov. 20, 1739; d. March 6, 1794.
16. II. Catharina, b. Oct. 15, 1721; m. Hendrick Kuyper; d. July 31, 1801.
17. III. Garrabrant (32), b. Sept. 10, 1723; m. Catharine Speer.

18. IV. Teunis, b. April 8, 1726; removed to Stone House Plains; d. May 15, 1760.
19. V. Cornelius (33), b. Oct. 27, 1728; m. 1st, Jannetje Van Horn (9), Aug. 10, 1757; 2d, Jannetje, dau. of Peter Kip, of Polliflly; d. June 21, 1814. During the occupancy of Paulus Hoeck by the British, he did considerable work for Major Grex.
20. VI. Neeltje, b. June 8, 1733; m. Garret Banta; d. Aug. 3, 1776.
21. VII. Peter, b. July 2, 1737; m. Eleanor Lang, Aug. 14, 1761; d. Jan. 13, 1807.

Mindert [10] had ch:
22. I. Maritje, b. March 9, 1715; m. Hendrick Coeyman, of Belleville, May 5, 1738.
23. II. Jacob, b. June 12, 1717; d. in inf.
24. III. Garrabrant, b. Feb. 15, 1719; m. Maritje, dau. of Martin Winne; d. March 29, 1791, s. p.; she b. March 6, 1730.
25. IV. Grietje, b. Feb. 19, 1721; d. in inf.
26. V. Metje, b. March 30, 1724; d. in inf.
27. VI. Jannetje, b. April 3, 1726; d. in inf.
28. VII. Mindert (39), b. Sept. 1, 1740; m. Elizabeth ———; d. Sept. 20, 1814.

Fourth Generation.

Gerbrants [11] had ch.:
29. I. Christopher (42), b. Nov. 2, 1728; m. Aeltje Jacobusse.
30. II. Maritje, b. March 8, 1731.

Abraham [13] had ch.:
31. I. Jurrie, b. Jan. 26, 1753; II. Derrick, b. Dec. 8, 1755; III. Gerrebrand, b. March 5, 1759; IV. Gerrit, b. May 23, 1761.

Garrabrant [17] had ch.:
32. I. Gerrebrand, b. March 21, 1755; II. Jannetje, b. March 1, 1760; III. Cornelius, b. Feb. 18, 1765.

Cornelius [19] had ch.:
33. I. Helena, b. Dec. 11, 1757; m. John Vreeland (60), June 21, 1778; d. March 17, 1846.
34. II. Cornelius (43), b. Jan. 4, 1762; m. Helena Van Horn (13); d. March 22, 1845.

35. III. Jannetje, b. Sept. 3, 1764; m. John Van Horn (14), April —, 1785; d. April 8, 1854.
36. IV. Neeltje, b. Nov. 28, 1769.
37. V. Peter C. (44), b. Sept. 12, 1779; m. 1st, Catharine Van Buskirk (41), Feb. 1, 1800; 2d, Jane, dau. of Walter Clendenny, Dec. 14, 1805; 3d, Ann Van Winkle (94), Feb. 15, 1814; d. Dec. 24, 1825.
38. VI. Garrabrant, b. Dec. 29, 1786; d. in inf.

Mindert [28] had ch.:

39. I. Hannah, b. May 25, 1769; m. Michael Vreeland (102), Nov. 5, 1789; d. May 1, 1855.
40. II. Trintje, b. May 29, 1773; m. Garret Van Horn (18), July 21, 1795; d. Nov. 7, 1761.
41. III. Mindert (50), m. Aegie Van Houten, Dec. 13, 1800; d. Sept. 3, 1846. She was divorced by act of the Legislature and afterward m. Richard Lyons.

Fifth Generation.

Christopher [29] had ch.:

42. I. Johannis, b. Oct. 11, 1765; II. Lena, b. May 23, 1775; III. Gerrit, b. March 1, 1778; IV. Christophel, b. Oct 3, 1780.

Cornelius [34] had ch.:

43. I. Jannetje, b. March 5, 1788; m. Cornelius Van Horn (20), Jan. 21, 1810.

Peter C. [37] had ch.;

44. I. Cornelius, b. Feb. 8, 1802; d. Feb. 20, 1802.
45. II. Jannetje, b. June 6, 1803; m. Jacobus Van Buskirk (49), Dec. 20, 1821.
46. III. Eleanor, b. Oct. 25, 1807; m. Nicholas Prior, Sept. 20, 1827; d. Nov. 20, 1857; he d. Aug. 9, 1857.
47. IV. Cornelius, b. Sept. 23, 1810; d. May 6, 1841, unm.
48. V. Catharine V. B., b. Sept. 19, 1814; m. Peter C. Westervelt in 1838.
49. VI. Abraham (52), b. May 3, 1819; m. Susanna P. Fielder, Feb. 14, 1847; she d. Sept. 7, 1870, æt. 44 yrs., 3 mos., 12 days.

Mindert [41] had ch.:

50. I. Mindert (53), b. Sept. 29, 1801; m. Rachel, dau. of John Jerolamon, Sept. 26, 1820; d. May 1, 1837.
51. II. John, b. July 1, 1804, d. Aug. 28, 1804.

Sixth Generation.

Abraham [49] had ch.:

52. I. John Henry, b. Jan. 28, 1848, d. Sept. 20, 1854; II. Catharine Ann, b. Feb. 5, 1850; III. Abraham, b. March 2, 1852, d. March 4, 1852; IV. Margaret Adelia, b. June 13, 1853; V. Letitia P., b. March 13, 1855; VI. Peter, b. July 27, 1860; VII. Francis, b. June 22, 1866.

Mindert [50] had ch.:

53. I. Effie V. H., b. March 7, 1822; m. James C. Van Buskirk (56), Dec. —, 1838.
54. II. Mindert, b. May 18, 1825; d. July 29, 1825.
55. III. Mary Elizabeth, b. Dec. 7, 1834; m. Charles G. Sisson, Dec. 24, 1850; d. July 9, 1870.

SIP—SIPPE—SIPP—SIPH.

Claas Arianse Sip was resident in Bergen in 1666. He joined the church there Nov. 13, 1666. He was twice married. The name of his first wife is not known. His second wife was Geertje Aurians, a widow. She survived him, and d. May 17, 1691.

Second Generation.

Claas Arianse Sip had ch.:

2. I. Henricus, m. Annetje Bayard, Nov. 22, 1691.
3. II. Jan Arianse (6), b. May 24, 1662; m. Johanna Van Vorst (11), April 22, 1684; d. Aug. 12, 1729. He was lieutenant in the Bergen militia under Captain John Pinhorne from 1703 to 1711, and afterward captain.
4. III. Antje, m. Symon Jacobse Van Winkle (3), Dec. 15, 1675.
5. IV. Maritje, m. Sibi Opdyke, Oct. 13, 1678.

Third Generation.

Jan [3] had ch.:

6. I. Arie, b. Oct. 25, 1684; m. Gerritje Helmigse, April 19, 1711; removed to Aquackanonck; had ch.: Cornelius, b. May 6, 1730.
7. II. Hillegond, bap. Aug. 28, 1687; m. Johannis Walingse Van Winkle (18), Sept. 30, 1710.
8. III. Ide, bap. Aug. 28, 1687; d. in inf.

9. IV. Margaret, bap. Aug. 17, 1690; m. John Gerritse Van Wagenen (13), May 22, 1713.
10. V. Annetje, bap. Feb. 22, 1693; m. Gerrit H. Van Wagenen (16), Oct. 3, 1713.
11. VI. Ide (15), b. Sept. 3, 1695; m. 1st, Ariantje Cornelissen Cadmus; 2d, Antje Van Wagenen (23), May 23, 1725. He was commissioned lieutenant of the Sixth company of the Bergen militia under Captain Michael C. Vreeland (50), March 13, 1733; d. Feb. 26, 1762.
12. VII. Johannis, b. May 10, 1698; VIII. Cornelius, b. Sept. 27, 1700, d. unm.
13. IX. Abraham, b. April 11, 1704; X. Hendrick, b. Sept. 30, 1706.
14. XI. Lena, bap. Dec. 1, 1708; m. John Van Horn (4); d. May 19, 1750.

Fourth Generation.

Ide [11] had ch.:

15. I. John.
16. II. Cornelius (22), m. Beelitje Vreeland (70), July 4, 1761; d. March 9, 1793.
17. III. Annetje, m. Levinus Winne, Oct. 8, 1749.
18. IV. Catlyntje, b. Aug. 5, 1731; m. Claas Vreeland (69), Nov. 13, 1757; d. Sept. 25, 1759.
19. V. Arriantje, bap. June 2, 1733; m. Ide Marselisse, April 11, 1754.
20. VI. Jannetje, bap. Sept. 30, 1735; m. Helmagh Vreeland (74); d. Sept. 25, 1759.
21. VII. Garret (23), bap. Aug. 21, 1740; m. Jannetje Merselis; d. Oct. 4, 1775; she d. May 24, 1825.

Fifth Generation.

Cornelius [16] had ch.:

22. I. Antje, b. May 20, 1763, d. June 22, 1763; II. Elizabeth, b. May 3, 1764, d. in inf.; III. Ide, b. May 3, 1764, d. in inf.; IV. Ide, b. Jan. 4, 1771, d. in inf.

Garret [21] had ch.:

23. I. Antje, b. Sept. 6, 1764; m. Jeremiah Van Winkle (64); d. March 8, 1848.
24. II. Peter (26), b. Aug. 18, 1767; m. Elizabeth Vreeland, Nov. 1, 1789; d. May 1, 1852; she d. March 1, 1827. He was Judge of the Bergen Common Pleas.

25. III. Jenneke, b. March 12, 1770; m. Cornelius Vreeland, Oct. 5, 1788; d. Dec. 5, 1788.

Sixth Generation.

Peter [24] had ch.:

26. I. Garret (29), b. March 11, 1791; m. Margaret Newkirk (40), Nov. 10, 1811; d. May 6, 1868.
27. II. Maritje, b. Feb. 27, 1795; d. March 25, 1797.
28. III. Richard, b. Aug. 31, 1800; m. Sarah E., dau. of Charles Weyland, Sept. 15, 1856; d. April 10, 1865; had ch.: I. Richard Garret, b. July 2, 1860.

Seventh Generation.

Garret [26] had ch.:

29. I. Jane, b. Oct. 6, 1812.
30. II. Maria, b. Feb. 26, 1814; m. Jacob Van Winkle (136), Nov. 6, 1834.
31. III. Peter (32), b. Nov. 10, 1815; m. Anne Van Winkle (138), April 25, 1839.

Eighth Generation.

Peter [31] had ch.:

32. I. Margaret Ann, b. Aug. 12, 1842; m. Barbarie W. Throckmorton, June 24, 1868.
33. II. Garret, b. Sept. 26, 1844.
34. III. Jacob, b. Jan. 7, 1846; m. Elizabeth Jane, dau. of Benjamin Decker, Nov. 25, 1868.
35. IV. Richard T., b. May 17, 1848; V. Mary Elizabeth, b. April 17, 1851, m. John J. Toffey.
36. VI. Emma Louisa, b. Oct. 2, 1853; m. William V. Toffey, Oct. 29, 1872.

Blenckerhoef—Blinckerhoff—Van Blinckerhoff—Brinkerhoff.

Joris Dircksen Brinckerhoef, the founder of the American branch of this family, came from the county of Drent, or Drenthe, in the United Provinces, and having lived for some time at Flushing, a seaport in Zealand, arrived in this country in 1638. He settled on Staten Island, and entered into a contract with Cornelius Melyn, the owner of the island, to reside there; but owing to the murder of some neighboring planters by the Indians, in 1641,[1] he obtained a release from the contract, Aug. 15, 1641. Then he went to Long Island, and settled in Brooklyn. He m. Susannah Dubbels; d. Jan. 16, 1661.[2]

Second Generation.

Joris had ch.:

2. I. Derrick, was killed by the Indians; d. s. p.
3. II. Hendrick (6), m. Claesie, dau. of Cornelius Boomgaert, and settled near the English Neighborhood. In 1677 he purchased the land on Bergen Hill, on which some of his descendants yet reside.[3] He and his wife were members of the Hackensack Church in 1686.[4]
4. III. Abraham, b. in 1632; lived at Flatlands, Long Island; m. Aeltje, dau. of Jan Stryker, May 20, 1660; d. at Newtown about 1714. His descendants are on Long Island.
5. IV. Aeltje, m. William Van Couvenhoven.

Third Generation.

Hendrick [3] had ch.:

6. I. Geertje, b. Feb. 20, 1670.
7. II. Margrietje, b. June 13, 1671; m. Mattys De Mott, of Kingston, May 6, 1705; united with the Hackensack Church Oct. 5, 1701.
8. III. Cornelius (12), b. in Midwout, L. I.; m. Aegie Vreeland (28), May 24, 1708; d. Sept. 1, 1770, æt. 97 yrs. He was sometimes called Cornelis Hendricksen Van Blinkerhoff; united with the Hackensack Church April 8, 1699.
9. IV. Joris, d. Feb. 5, 1692.
10. V. Derrick (18), united with the Hackensack Church April 8, 1699; m. 1st, Margrita Sibese Banta, Oct. 31, 1702; 2d, Abigail Ackerman, Oct. —, 1733.
11. VI. Jacobus (23), m. Angenitje, dau. of Hendrick Banta, April 17, 1708. Hendrickje, one of his dau., m. Roelof Van Derlinde in 1702; another m. ——— Van Giesen. He and his wife united with the Hackensack Church Jan. 2, 1709.

---

[1] *N. Y. Col. MSS.*, *i.*, 259.
[2] *Annals of Newtown*, 290.
[3] *Winfield's Land Titles*, 50.
[4] *Romeyn's Discourse*, 132.

Fourth Generation.

Cornelius [8] had ch.:

12. I. Maritje, b. Feb. 27, 1709; m. Helmich Van Wagenen (18), Sept. 26, 1736; d. Sept. 23, 1775.
13. II. Claesie, b. Sept. 3, 1710; m. Garret Croese; d. March 21, 1787.
14. III. Geesje, m. Cornelius Bogert; d. May 3, 1783.
15. IV. Hendrick, b. Dec. 13, 1713; d. Aug. 12, 1795, unm.
16. V. Aegie, b. March 23, 1715; m. Abraham Sickles, April 1, 1739; d. Oct. 3, 1802.
17. VI. Hartman (28), m. Claesie Van Houten, Oct. 20, 1744; d. Dec. —, 1798. He resided in the English Neighborhood.

Derrick [10] had ch.:

18. I. Hendrick, bap. Oct. 21, 1705; m. Maritje Westervelt, Nov. 1, 1728.
19. II. Arie, bap. Aug. 29, 1708; m. Margrietje Stegg, Oct. —, 1728.
20. III. Joris, bap. Dec. 13, 1715; d. in inf.
21. IV. Siba, bap. Dec. 13, 1715; m. Beelitje Degrauw, Nov. —, 1744. In the Revolution he sympathized with the British, and was arrested under order of July 11, 1777,[1] but released on taking the oath.
22. V. Joris, b. Aug. 24, 1720.

Jacobus [11] had ch.:

23. I. Hendrick, bap. May 1, 1709; d. in inf.
24. II. Hendrick (34), b. Nov. 1, 1710.
25. III. Joris, b. Oct. 9, 1719; m. Martintje Bogert, Nov. —, 1745; removed to Adams County, Pa.; d. Jan. 3, 1810.
26. IV. Jacob (35), b. Nov. 19, 1721; m. Elizabeth Kip; d. in 1771.
27. V. Maritje, m. Jacobus Huysman, Nov. —, 1741.

Fifth Generation.

Hartman [17] had ch.:

28. I. Cornelius, m. Jannetje Kip; d. Dec. 9, 1772; had ch.: Hendrick, b. Dec. 31, 1770, d. Jan. 8, 1771.
29. II. Eleanor, m. ———, and left two ch.: Claesie, who m.

[1] *Minutes of Council of Safety*, 83, 112.

Christian Burdett, and Rachel, who m. Michael Vreeland.

30. III. Jane, m. George Vreeland (98), Oct. 21, 1780; d. June 2, 1834.

31. IV. Effie, b. June 10, 1751; m. Jacob Van Wagenen (46); d. Jan. 16, 1820.

32. V. John, m. Sally Smith, and had ch.: Hartman, Becky, Philip, Cornelius, John, Claesie and Sarah. He lived at the English Neighborhood.

33. VI. Hendrick (36), b. March 31, 1763; m. Leah Van Wagenen (48), June 19, 1779; d. March 12, 1838.

Hendrick [24] had ch.:

34. I. Jacobus; II. Nicausie; III. George; IV. Hendrick; V. Ann, m. Henry Verbryck.

Jacob [26] had ch.:

35. I. Agnietje, m. Daniel Haring; II. Lucas; III. Annatje, m. John Christie; IV. Jacobus; V. Hendrick; VI. Albert (who had a son, Jacob); VII. George.

Sixth Generation.

Hendrick [33] had ch.:

36. I. Hartman (39), b. April 15, 1781; m. Eleanor, dau. of Walter Clendenny, Nov. 6, 1802; d. July 15, 1832.

37. II. Catlyntje, b. July 13, 1784; m. Jacob Vreeland (81), Jan. 21, 1801.

38. III. Claesie, b. April 8, 1788; m. Henry De Mott, Jan. 25, 1806.

Seventh Generation.

Hartman [36] had ch.:

39. I. Henry (45), b. Aug. 28, 1803; m. Jane Van Horn (27), Jan. 18, 1827; d. Nov. 10, 1858.

40. II. Walter C., b. Aug. 8, 1805; d. March 11, 1813.

41. III. Cornelius (50), b. Aug. 26, 1806; m. Jane Vreeland (218), Dec. 16, 1830; d. June 13, 1850.

42. IV. John V. W. (53), b. Sept. 27, 1812; m. Hannah, dau. of George Tise, Aug. 2, 1832.

43. V. Jannet M., b. Feb. 27, 1818; d. in inf.

44. VI. Leah Ann, b. April 29, 1819; m. Abraham Tuers, Oct. 10, 1844; d. March 18, 1853.

Eighth Generation.

Henry [39] had ch.:

45. I. Mary Jane, b. June 26, 1828; d. May 26, 1834.
46. II. Eleanor, b. Nov. 9, 1830; d. Jan. 28, 1834.
47. III. John Henry, b. Aug. 2, 1834; d. April 11, 1840.
48. IV. Garret V. H. (59), b. July 26, 1839; m. Elizabeth W., dau. of Justus Slater, Dec. 24, 1863.
49. V. Jacob Henry, b. Dec. 14, 1847; d. Aug. 22, 1851.

Cornelius [41] had ch.:

50. I. Cornelia Ann, b. Sept. 16, 1833; d. Aug. 28, 1834.
51. II. Cornelius (60), b. June 10, 1835; m. 1st, Mary Jane, dau. of Abraham J. Rapp, Nov. 15, 1855; she d. Nov. 22, 1855; 2d, Sarah S., dau. of George Perry, Feb. 11, 1857.
52. III. Eleanor C., b. Jan. 26, 1844; m. William H. Speer, Oct. 1, 1862.

John V. W. [42] had ch.:

53. I. Henry H. (61), b. Jan. 6, 1835; m. Elizabeth Vreeland (312), June 6, 1855.
54. II. George, b. Oct. 6, 1836; d. Aug. 20, 1837.
55. III. Abraham, b. May 27, 1839; d. July 1, 1844.
56. IV. Cornelius, b. Aug. 9, 1841; d. June 4, 1842.
57. V. William, b. July 20, 1843; m. Melissa, dau. of Allen Clark, April 15, 1868; had ch.: I. Lillie, b. Nov. 28, 1869.
58. VI. Eleanor Ann, b. Feb. 18, 1845; m. George B. Fielder, April 25, 1865.

Ninth Generation.

Garret V. H. [48] had ch.:

59. I. Henry, b. Sept. 19, 1864; II. Justus S., b. Aug. 30, 1867, d. Dec. 7, 1869.

Cornelius [51] had ch.:

60. I. George T., b. Jan. 24, 1859; II. Cornelius, b. March 1, 1863, d. in inf.

Henry H. [53] had ch.:

61. I. John, b. Oct. 27, 1858; II. Henry, b. May 23, 1865; III. Lois Elizabeth, b. Sept. 18, 1871, d. Jan. 18, 1873.

SCHUYLER—VAN SCHUYLER—SCHUYLAARDT—SCHUILER.

The brothers, Philip Pieterse and David Pieterse Schuyler, were the founders of the family in this country. At first the name was written *Van Schuyler*, derived probably from the place where the family resided in Europe, and then recently adopted as a surname. The place is not to be found in the records of Holland.[1] They came from Amsterdam in 1650, and settled at Fort Orange. David, the younger of the two, m. Catlyntje, dau. of Abraham Isaacsen Planck, the owner of Paulus Hook, Oct. 13, 1657. By her he had five sons—Pieter, Jacobus, Abraham, David and Myndert—who lived to maturity, married, and left families at and near Albany.[2]

Philip Pieterse Schuyler, b. in 1628; m. Margaretta, dau. of Herr Brandt Arent Van Schlectenhorst, of Nieuwkerk, in Gelderland, Dec. 12, 1650. Her father came to this country in 1647 as manager of the colonie of Patroon Van Rensselaer. Schuyler and his wife were respectively twenty-two years old at the time of their marriage. Being now the son-in-law of the Patroon's commissary, he engaged in the fur trade with the Indians, a business prohibited to private persons.[4] In it he soon accumulated wealth. He was a magistrate at Fort Orange in 1656, '57 and '61.[5] On April 6, 1662, he, with others, received permission to plant a village on the Great Esopus.[6] In his will

COAT OF ARMS.[3]

---

[1] *Lossing's Life of Schuyler*, *i.*, 21. [2] *N. Y. Geneal. and Bibliog. Rec.*, *i.* 28.

[3] ESCUTCHEON *argent*, a falcon *sable*, hooded *gules*, beaked and membered *or*, perched upon the sinister hand of the falconer, issued from the dexter side of the shield. The arm clothed *azure*, surmounted by a helmet of steel, standing in profile, open-faced, three bars *or*, lined *gules*, bordered, flowered and studded, *or*, and ornamented with its lambrequins *argent* lined *sable*. CREST—out of a wreath, *argent* and *sable*, a falcon of the shield.

[4] *N. Y. Col. MSS.*, *A.* 138, 140, *xvi.*, 186. [5] *New Neth. Reg.*, 68.

[6] *N. Y. Col. MSS.*, *x.*, *Part* 1, 113.

he is styled "Captain and old commissioner of Albany." He died March 9, 1684, and his wife in 1710.

Second Generation.

Philip Pieterse had ch.:

1. I. Gysbert, b. July 2, 1652; d. before his father, unm.
2. II. Geertruyd, b. Feb. 4, 1654; m. the Right Hon. Stephen Van Cortlandt, Sept. 10, 1671.
3. III. Alyda, b. Feb. 23, 1656; m. 1st, Rev. Nicholas Van Rensselaer, son of the Patroon, Feb. 10, 1675; 2d, Robert Livingston, by whom she had seven children; d. March 27, 1729.
4. IV. Pieter, b. Sept. 17, 1657; m. Maria, dau. of Killian Van Rensselaer, Oct. 25, 1672; d. Feb. 20, 1724. He was the first Mayor of Albany; a member of the Council of New Jersey and New York in 1709, and appointed to command the Indians in the expedition against Canada.
5. V. Brandt, b. Dec. 18, 1659; m. Cornelia Van Cortlandt, July 12, 1682.[1] He became a merchant and settled in New York city. Governor Clinton recommended him to a seat in his Council.[2] He was one of the witnesses to the deed by which Paulus Hoeck was conveyed to Cornelius Van Vorst.[3]
6. VI. Arent (11), b. June 25, 1662; m. 1st, Johanna —— about 1682; 2d, Swan Van Duykhuisen, of Albany; 3d, Maria ——, who was still living at Belleville in 1734.[4] While yet a young man he came to New York city and engaged in mercantile business. In the beginning of the year 1694 he was appointed by Governor Fletcher to visit the Indians at Minisinck. The following is an extract from his report of that visit:

"$169\frac{3}{4}$ y^{e} 3^{d} of Feb.: I departed from New York for East New Jersey, and came that night att Bergen town, where I heired two men and a guide.

"Y^{e} 4th, Sunday Morning. I went from Bergen and travilled ten English miles beyond Hagkkingsack to an Indian place called Peckwes.

"Y^{e} 5th, Monday. From Peckwes North and

---

[1] *Burke's Landed Gentry, ii.*, 1361.
[2] *Col. Hist. of N.Y., vi.*, 465.
[3] *Winfield's Land Titles*, 45.
[4] *Taylor's Annals*, 297.

be West I went about thirty-two miles, snowing and rainy wether.

"Y^{e} 6th, Thusday. I continued my journey to Maggaghkamieck,[1] and from thence to within half a day's Journey to the Minnissinck.

"Y^{e} 7th, Wendsday. About Eleaven a Clock I arrived att the Minnissinck, and there I mett with two ther Sachems and severall other Indians, of whome I enquired after some news, if the French or their Indians had sent for them or been in ye Mennissinck Country. Upon wch they answered that noe French nor any of the French Indians were nor had been in the Mennissinck Country nor there abouts, and did promise y^{t} if ye French should hapen to come y^{t} they heard of it that they would forthwith send a mesinger an give ye Excellency notice thereof. * * * In the afternoon I departed from ye Minnissincks; the 8th, the 9th and 10th of Feb. I travilled and came at Bergen in ye morning, and about noone arrived at New Yorke."[2] As late as May 30, 1709, he was requested by the Governor and Council of New Jersey to summon the Minisinck Sachems to a meeting at Perth Amboy.

On June 6, 1695, he and Anthony Brockholst purchased of the Indians 4,000 acres of land at Pequannock. On Nov. 11, 1695, they purchased the title of the East Jersey Proprietors to the same tract for £100. On May 20, 1697, he received from Governor Fletcher a patent for land in the Minisinck country, called by the Indians Sankhekeneck, *alias* Maghawaem; also a parcel of meadow called Waimsagskmeck, on the river Mennissincks, before a certain island called Menagnock, adjacent to a tract called Maghaghkarnek, containing one thousand acres, at a quit rent of twelve shillings.[3]

At what time he went to New Barbadoes Neck is not known, but in the deed from Edmund Kingsland to him, dated April 20, 1710, he is described as a resident of that place. He paid £330 for the land then bought, but afterward added to his purchase, having accidentally discovered copper on his land. This discovery was made by a negro slave, who, when ploughing, turned up a greenish, heavy stone. He took it to his master, who sent it to England for analyzation. It was found to contain eighty

---

[1] The Indian name of the Neversink, which empties into the Delaware river a short distance south of Port Jervis.

[2] *Col. Hist. of N. Y., iv.*, 98.

[3] *Book of Patents, Albany, vii.*, 71. The location and present names of these places I leave for others to make out.

per cent. of copper. This discovery opened an avenue to wealth, and Mr. Schuyler, desiring to reward the lucky slave, told him to name three things which he most desired, and they should be granted to him. The innocent fellow desired—*First*, that he might remain with his master as long as he lived; *second*, that he might have all the tobacco he could smoke; and *third*, that he might have a dressing gown like his master's, with big brass buttons. The trifling nature of these wants prompted his master to tell him to ask for something that was of value. The old fellow, after mature reflection, filled the measure of his earthly happiness by making his *fourth* request, *that he might have a little more tobacco!* He did not work the mine as extensively as his son John, yet prior to his death he had shipped to the Bristol

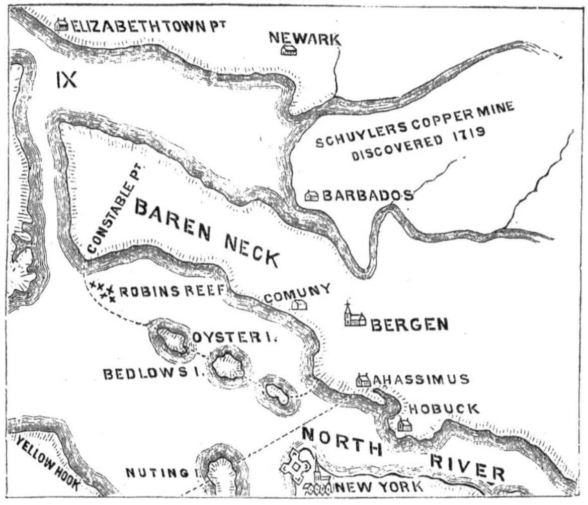

copper and brass works, England, 1,386 tons. In 1761 the mine was leased, an engine brought out from England, and the mine worked for four years. With this engine came Josiah Hornblower, the father of the late Chief Justice, as engineer. In 1765 a workman who had been dismissed set fire to the building, and the engine was destroyed. Until 1793 the engine lay in ruins, and the mine was neglected. Mr. Schuyler's dwelling house, a large stone and brick building, was near the river, a little south of the Belleville road. About three-quarters of a mile east of the house there were, in the days of his son John and grandson Arent, two fine deer parks, stocked with about one hundred and fifty deer.[1]

His will was dated Dec. 17, 1724; codicil dated Oct. 30, 1730. He died about 1730.

7. VII. Sybilla, b. Nov. 12, 1664; d. Dec. 9, 1664.

8. VIII. Philip, b. Feb. 8, 1666; d. s. p.

9. IX. Johannis, b. April 5, 1668; m. Elizabeth Staats, wid. of John Wendell, April —, 1695; d. Feb. 27, 1747; she d. June 3, 1737.

He was an active leader against the French and Indians after the burning of Schenectady in Feb., 1690; was Mayor of Albany from 1703 to 1706, and a Member of the Colonial Assembly from 1705 to 1713.

Among his ch. were *Cornelia; Philip J.*, who was killed by the Indians at Saratoga, Nov. 17, 1745; *Margarita*, "the American Lady," the friend and hostess of Lord Howe, and subsequently of Burgoyne, m. Philip Schuyler, of "the Flats," d. Aug. 28, 1782, æt. 82 yrs., 7 mos., 13 days; *Cathalyna*, b. March 5, 1705, m. Cornelis Cuyler, Dec. 8, 1726. His eldest son, *John*, b. in 1697, m. his cousin Cornelia, dau. of Stephen Van Cortlandt; d. in the fall of 1741, leaving five ch., the eldest of whom was Major-General Philip Schuyler of the Revolution, b. Nov. 22, 1733.

10. X. Margaret, b. Jan. 2, 1672; m. John Collins, of Albany.

Third Generation.

Arent [6] had ch.:

11. I. Philip (19), bap. in 1687; m. Hester, dau. of Isaac Kingsland (3). His will, dated April 9, 1760, was proved Jan. 27, 1764. He received by devise all of his father's interest in the tract of land at Pequannock, which he owned jointly with Samuel Bayard, of Hoboken, and the heirs of Anthony Brockholst. On part of this tract, now known as Pompton, in Passaic County, some of his descendants are yet living. He was a member of the Assembly of New Jersey in 1719, and seems to have had a little "unpleasantness" with William

[1] *Proc. N. J. Hist. Soc., viii.,* 124.

Sandford, a neighbor, and Thomas Van Buskirk, both members from Bergen County, who accused Schuyler of having "drank a health to the damnation of the governor and the justices of the peace."[1] Schuyler denied the charge, and seems to have made good his denial, for he "was acquitted by a solemn vote, and permitted again to take his seat." He held the same position in 1721.

12. II. Olivia, mentioned in her father's will, but dead at that time, leaving issue.

13. III. Casparus, bap. May 5, 1695. He received from his father a deed for land in Burlington, N. J., at Lossa Point or Wingworth's Point. His family continued to reside there for many years. Among his ch. was Arent, who m. Jane ———, and whose will, dated at Burlington, May 7, 1774, was proved Jan. 19, 1780. In it are the names of his ch., viz.: Aaron, John, Ann, Peter, Charles and Abraham.

14. IV. John (31), m. Ann Van Rensselaer, Jan. 1, 1719; his will, dated Dec. 22, 1772, was proved Feb. 12, 1773. He received by his father's will the homestead farm and copper mine on New Barbadoes Neck, a part of which yet remains in the family. Governor Cosby recommended him to a seat in the New Jersey Council, Sept. 5, 1735,[2] to which he was appointed, but resigned in 1746.

15. V. Peter (33), b. about 1710; m. Mary, dau. of John Walter, a man of great wealth, residing on Hanover square in New York City. By his father's will he received seven hundred and sixty acres of land near the Rahway River "in Elizabeth Towne." He was one of the prominent men of his day. When the invasion of Canada was proposed in 1746, he was authorized to recruit, and was then placed in command of the contingent of five hundred men from New Jersey.[3] This force embarked at Amboy, *en route* for Albany, Sept. 3, 1746, and arrived on the 9th.[4] He proceeded as far as the latter place, but owing to the failure of the home government to send forces from England, the ex-

---

1 *Gordon's Hist. of N. J.*, 337.
2 *Col. Hist. of N. Y.*, *vi.*, 36.
3 His commission was dated Sept. 7, 1746.
4 *Nevill's Laws*, *i.*, 332.

Peter Schuyler

pedition was abandoned. His force consisted of five companies, viz.: Captain John Dagworthy's, numbering one hundred and three men; Captain James Parker's, numbering one hundred and one men; Captain Nathaniel Ware's, numbering one hundred and five men; Captain Campbell Stevens', numbering ninety-six men, and Captain Henry Donald's, numbering one hundred and three men. While encamped at Albany his men suffered greatly. On Feb. 26, 1747, he wrote to the authorities in this Province that his men were in want of a surgeon, medicines, shirts, flints, colors, bread and peas. Besides this, unless they were paid, they threatened to leave, with their arms and baggage. In response to these complaints, Governor Hamilton, May 11, 1747, complimented the Colonel on his zeal in his Majesty's service, and assured him that he had that day "ordered two speckled Shirts and one Pair of Shoes for Each man." This was cold comfort, and a mutiny followed. To quiet his men, Colonel Schuyler advanced several thousand pounds out of his own means. This was the cause of bitter complaint on the part of Governor Clinton to the home government,[1] as well as to the Colonel himself.[2] Of this sum so advanced, the General Assembly of New Jersey resolved, Dec. 17, 1747, to refund him £607, 17s., 4d. He afterward marched his regiment to "Saraghtoga" to garrison the fort at that place. Here he was reduced to such extremity for want of provisions that the General Assembly of New York took the matter in hand, Sept. 9, 1747.[3] The war was terminated by the peace of Aix-la-Chapelle in 1748,[4] and Colonel Schuyler returned to his home on the banks of the Passaic. The peace, however, was of short duration. In 1754—two years before war was declared in Europe—hostilities began in America, between the colonies and the French. New Jersey again placed her forces under Colonel Schuyler. His regiment moved up the Mohawk from Schenectady early in July of that year,[5] and reached Oswego on the 20th of that month. But the defeat of Braddock on the 9th of that month exposed the State of New Jersey to the inroads of the savages. To protect the State from the calamity which then threatened, Colonel Schuyler with one-half of his regiment was, in December, with the consent of General Shirley, recalled from the northern frontier.[6] During the winter of 1755–6, he occupied the blockhouses which had been erected on the Delaware, and protected the State from

[1] *Col. Hist. of N. Y., vi.*, 351.
[2] *Ibid, vi*, 363.
[3] *Ibid, vi*, 618.
[4] *Proc. N. J. Hist. Soc., i.*, 52.
[5] *Mass. Hist. Coll.*, 1*st Series, vii.*, 96.
[6] *Gordon's Hist. of N. J.*, 123; *Nevill's Laws, ii.*, 86.

the raids of the Indians. In the spring he returned to the north as colonel, commissary and paymaster of his regiment.[1] He left his home for the seat of war on Friday, March 19. His troops arrived at New York April 12, and set out for Albany the same evening. Owing to vexatious delays at the latter place, he did not reach Oswego until the 1st of July. At this place were three forts, named respectively Oswego, Ontario, and George. The first was a large stone building erected in 1727 to protect a trading post established there in 1722.[2] It was surrounded by a wall flanked with four small bastions, but was commanded from the adjacent heights. To protect this fort, General Shirley, in the autumn of 1755, had constructed the other two.[3] Fort Ontario was on the east side of the Onandaga river, about four hundred and fifty yards from the old fort. Fort George was further down the river and about four hundred and fifty yards west of Fort Oswego.[4] Colonel Mercer was in command of the post and occupied Fort Ontario, and Colonel Schuyler was in Fort Ontario with part of his regiment.

On the 10th of August General Montcalm, with more than five thousand French and Indians, invested the place. He blocked the harbor with two large armed vessels and posted a strong party on the road between Albany and the forts to cut off succor and prevent despatches for reinforcements. On the 12th, at midnight, he opened on Fort Ontario with thirty-two cannon, besides mortars and howitzers. The garrison replied with spirit, but having exhausted their ammunition, spiked the guns and crossed the river to Fort Oswego. On the abandonment of Fort Ontario, three hundred and seventy of Colonel Mercer's men joined Colonel Schuyler, with the view to keep up communication between the two forts. To prevent this, twenty-five hundred of the enemy boldly swam the river on the night of the 13th, and occupied a position to command the route between the two forts. During the same night Montcalm's regulars entered the deserted fort and turned such of the guns as could be made serviceable on fort Oswego, and when the morning dawned opened fire. Colonel Mercer soon fell, and before night the forts were surrendered and fourteen hundred men became prisoners. To please his Indian allies, Montcalm razed the forts, and Oswego became a solitude.

The prisoners and booty—consisting of one hundred and twenty cannon, three hundred boats, six vessels of war, a large

---

[1] *Nevill's Laws, ii.*, 89.

[2] *Holmes' Annals, ii.*, 528.

[3] *Bancroft's Hist. U. S., iv.*, 238.

[4] *Trumbull's Hist. U. S., i.*, 360.

quantity of stores and three chests of money[1]—were taken to Montreal.[2] Among the prisoners were Colonel Schuyler and about half of his regiment.[3] From Montreal he was taken to Quebec.[4] There he remained a prisoner until October, 1757. He was then released on his parol to return in six months,[5] unless a cartel was settled. With a Frenchman and two Indians for guides and companions, he left Quebec on the 12th of October, and passed through the wilderness to fort Edward. He arrived in New York on Saturday afternoon, Nov. 19, 1757. The hero's fame had preceded him, and when night came most of the houses in the city were illuminated, a bonfire was kindled on the common, an elegant entertainment given to him at the King's Arms Tavern, "and the Public in general testified great Joy on his safe Arrival."[6] On Sunday, Nov. 27, 1757, he set out for his home, then called Petersborough,[7] a short distance above Newark, on the easterly bank of the Passaic. Upon his arrival he was saluted with a discharge of thirteen pieces of cannon. The next night he visited Newark in company of several prominent citizens, where he was again saluted with cannon. Bonfires were kindled and houses illuminated "as an Honour due to his great Attachment to the Interest of his country, and uncommon Zeal for his Majesty's Service." An entertainment was given, healths drank, "and a general Joy appeared among all the Inhabitants."[8]

During the first week in January, 1758, he set out for "Trent-town." At "Prince-town" he was met by the people and presented with the following metrical welcome, written by a young lady and addressed

"TO THE HONOURABLE COL. PETER SCHUYLER.

"Dear to each Muse, and to thy Country dear,
Welcome once more to breathe thy native air;
Not half so cheering is the solar Ray,
To the harsh Region of a Winter's Day;
Not half so grateful fanning Breezes rise,
When the hot Dog Star burns the Summer Skies;
Cæsarea's Shore with Acclamation rings,
And, WELCOME SCHUYLER, every Shepherd sings.
See, for thy Brows, the laurel is prepared,
And justly deem'd a Patriot, thy Reward;
E'en future Ages shall enroll thy Name,
In sacred Annals of immortal Fame."[9]

---

[1] *Bancroft's Hist. U. S., iv.*, 238. [2] *Holmes' Annals, ii.*, 70.

[3] The other half of his regiment was placed under the command of Colonel Parker and subsequently captured at Lake George. [4] *N. Y. Post Boy, June* 6, 1757.

[5] *Col. Hist. of N. Y., x.*, 849. [6] *N. Y. Post Boy, Nov.* 21, 1757.

[7] Afterward known as "Kennedy's Farm," then as the "Village of Lodi," now (in part) East Newark. [8] *N. Y. Post Boy, Nov.* 28, 1757.

[9] *N. Y. Mercury, Jan.* 9, 1758.

Wherever he went he was greeted with demonstrations of popular favor. But the days of his parol were rapidly passing and nothing had yet been done relative to the exchange of prisoners. All his efforts to that end were abortive. The King and William Pitt could compliment him for the zeal he had so often shown for the public service, but "saw with concern the disagreeable situation of that Gentleman, from the difficulties that have arisen, with regard to his being exchanged, and though his Maj^ty^ will readily agree to any measures that shall be proper and practicable to obtain the release of so good a subject, yet it is thought, that no steps can be taken here for that purpose, till it is known what answer Monsr Vaudreuil shall have returned to the proposal made to him; and in case that answer should, as Colonel Schuyler apprehends, prove to be negative," why, then, he was assured, no time would be lost to effect in Europe an exchange for him.[1]

As foreshadowed in this sympathetic assurance of the King, Colonel Schuyler was forced to surrender himself. The war was not ended, the term of his parol had long since expired, all efforts for his exchange had failed,[2] and the French commander, the Marquis de Vaudreuil, had repeatedly demanded the return "of the brave old Peter Schuyler of New Jersey."[3] True as brave, the old soldier had given his word, and like Regulus

> Dimovit obstantes propinquos
> Et populum reditus morantem,

and went back to captivity. He left his home about July 1, 1758,[4] Lake George on the 21st, was received by Montcalm at Ticonderoga on the 23d, and by him sent to Montreal.[5] He carried with him full power from General Abercrombie to negotiate an exchange of prisoners. On Nov. 1, 1758, he succeeded in effecting an exchange of himself for Sieur de Noyau, commandant at Fort Frontenac, captured by the English under Colonel Bradstreet, Aug. 27, 1758. He immediately set out upon his return, and arrived at Fort Edward on the 11th, with eighty-eight prisoners, including twenty-six women and twelve children.[6] Some of these he had purchased from the Indians "at a very high price." During his imprisonment he had been of great service to his fellow countrymen, redeeming them from captivity, keeping open house and feeding them at his own table.[7] In these benevolences he expended from his own purse £1,333, 9s., 0½d.,

---

1 *Col. Hist. of N. Y., vii.*, 344.
2 *Ibid, x.*, 711–714.
3 *Proc. N. J. Hist. Soc., i.*, 56; 2 *Dunlap's Hist. of N. Y., Appendix, lxvii.*
4 *Col. Hist. of N. Y., x.*, 772.
5 *Ibid, x.*, 774.
6 *Ibid, x.*, 897.
7 *N. Y. Post Boy, Dec.* 4, 1758

for which he sent in his bill to the Provincial authorities in August, 1758. He also extended his liberality to other prisoners than those of New Jersey. The King refunded to him £211, 8s., 7d., thus expended.[1]

Shortly after his release Colonel Schuyler returned home, but on the opening of the campaign, in the spring of 1759, he again led his Jersey Blues[2] to Canada.[3] He spent the winter of 1759–60 at home,[4] but afterward rejoined the army and entered Montreal as a victor when that city surrendered to the British forces in September, 1760.[5] He died at his home on Sunday, March 7, 1762. A paper of that day said, "He did honor to his country and gave a Noble Example to others: And it will be allowed by all who knew him, that he was a sincere Friend; humane, beneficent and just to all mankind."[6] "He was a brave soldier, of a frank and open behavior, an extensive generosity and unwearied in the service of his country. In person he was tall and hardy, rather rough at first view, yet a little acquaintance discovered a depth of sincerity. In conversation he was above artifice, or the traffic of forms, yet enjoyed friendship with a true relish, and in all relations, what he seemed to be, he was.—*Matthew, vii.*, 20."[7]

16. VI. Adonijah (34), m. Gertrude Van Rensselaer. By his father's will he received two tracts of land at Elizabethtown Point. His will, dated May 20, 1761, was proved May 28, 1762.

17. VII. Eva, m. P. Bayard; d. in 1737.

18. VIII. Cornelia, m. P. De Peyster. By their father's will these two daughters received two lots of ground

---

[1] *Col. Hist. of N. Y., vii.*, 344. Colonel Schuyler kept an account of the money advanced to each soldier, and when, on his return to New Jersey, the soldier received payment, the amount so advanced was deducted. I have now in my possession many of these receipts showing this fact.

[2] A name first applied to the New Jersey troops in the French war of 1747, derived from the color of their uniform. A periodical of that time describes them as "the likeliest well-set men" who ever entered upon a campaign. Their uniform was blue, faced with red, gray stockings and buckskin breeches.—2 *Dunlap's Hist. of N. Y., Appendix, lxvi.*

[3] His commission was dated March 15, 1759. [4] *N. Y. Post Boy, Dec.* 3, 1759.

[5] *Ibid, March* 11, 1762. [6] *Col. Hist. of N. Y., x.*, 776.

[7] *Smith's Hist. of N. J.*, 494.

on Broadway. Eva also received an Indian slave named "Molly," and Cornelia one named "Nanny."

Fourth Generation.

Philip [11] had ch.:

19. I. Johanna, b. Sept. 2, 1713; m. Isaac Kingsland, June 24, 1741.

20. II. Arent, b. Feb. 23, 1715; m. 1st, Helena Van Wagenen (37), of Aquackanonck, Oct. 1, 1741; 2d, Rachel ——; had ch.: I. Philip; II. Adonijah. His will, dated June 8, 1798, was proved Dec. 15, 1806. Major Hayes, July 11, 1777, was ordered to arrest him and lock him up in the Morristown gaol as a disaffected person. He was released Aug. 8, 1777, on taking the oath.[1]

21. III. Isaac, b. April 26, 1716; d. in inf.

22. IV. Philip, b. Dec. 23, 1717; m. and had ch.: Philip and Garret.

23. V. Isaac, b. Sept. 8, 1719; m. and had ch.: Major Schuyler.

24. VI. Elizabeth, b. Feb. 22, 1721; m. Rev. Benjamin Van der Linde; marriage bond dated Nov. 9, 1748.

25. VII. Pieter, b. June 7, 1723; m. Mary ——; d., s. p., Oct. 18, 1808.

26. VIII. Hester, b. April 12, 1725; m. Teunis Dey.

27. IX. Maria, b. Sept. 11, 1727.

28. X. Jenneke, b. Oct. 26, 1728; m. —— Board; resided at Wesel.

29. XI. Johannis, b. June 4, 1730; d. in inf.

30. XII. Casparus, b. Dec. 10, 1735; m. and had one ch., Hester, who m. Gen. William Colfax, of Pompton (license dated Sept. 1, 1783), grandfather of Schuyler Colfax, late Vice-President of the United States.

John [14] had ch.:

31. I. Arent J. (39), b. Oct. —, 1746; m. his cousin, Swan Schuyler (35), Nov. 2, 1772; d. Oct. 28, 1803.

32. II. Mary, b. about 1762; d. unm.[2]

Peter [15] had ch.:

33. I. Catharine, m. Archibald Kennedy, Earl of Casselis. She

---

[1] *Minutes of the Council of Safety*, 83, 114.
[2] *Proc. N. J. Hist. Soc.*, *viii.*, 122.

inherited her parents' property; also the property of her grandfather, John Walter. She was also the heiress of Richard Jones; d. s. p. After her death Kennedy m. Anne, dau. of John Watts and Margaret De Lancey, and great-granddaughter of the Right Hon. Stephen Van Cortlandt and Gertrude Schuyler.

Adonijah [16] had ch.:

34. I. Van Rensselaer; II. Mary.
35. III. Swan, m. Arent Schuyler (31), Nov. 2, 1772; d. May 20, 1801, æt. 60 yrs.
36. IV. John (41), m. Mary Hunter, Feb. 16, 1769; V. Peter.
37. VI. Adonijah. At the age of twelve years he entered the British navy under Captain St. John, rose to a lieutenantcy; m. Susan Shields, of Plymouth, England, where he settled, and where some of his descendants yet remain.
38. VII. Philip, d. s. p. His will, dated Aug. 29, 1795, was proved Sept. 26, 1795.

Fifth Generation.

Arent J. [31] had ch.:

39. I. Ann, d. July 20, 1783, æt. 7 yrs., 8 mos.[1]
40. II. John A. (48), b. April —, 1779; m. 1st, Eliza, dau. of James H. Kipp, in 1800; she d. Nov. 17, 1805; 2d, Catharine, dau. of Robert Van Rensselaer; d. Oct. 12, 1817.

John [36] had ch.:

41. I. Anthony H., d. Aug. 21, 1803, in his 29th yr., unm.
42. II. John R., m. 1st, —— Laberteaux; 2d, Patty Coleman, Jan. 6, 1803; d. s. p.
43. III. Mary, m. John Marley; d. May 31, 1798, in the 26th year of her age, having outlived her husband. The following poetical tribute was annexed to the notice of her death:

---

[1] "The late excessive hot weather has occasioned much sickness in N. J. Mr. Arent Schuyler has experienced it in a high degree; his eldest of two children & five negroes have lately been buried, & the youngest & only remaining child, with 10 negroes, are in so bad a state as their lives have been despaired of." *Rivington's Gazette, July* 30, 1783.

"Does youth, does beauty read these lines?
Does sympathetic tear their breast alarm?
Speak, dead Maria! breathe a strain divine;
E'en from the grave thou shalt have power to charm!
Bid them be chaste, be innocent like thee!
Bid them in duty's sphere as meekly move!
And if as fair, from vanity as free,
As firm in friendship, and as fond in love,
Tell them, though 'tis an awful thing to die!
('Twas e'en to thee), yet the dread path once trod,
Heaven lifts its everlasting portals high,
And bids the pure in heart behold their God."[1]

44. IV. Peter.

45. V. Swan, m. Thomas M. Harvey, of New York, April 16, 1804.

46. VI. Arent, m. Anne Miller, April 15, 1802; had ch.: I. Mary M., m. — Crowninshield, of Mass.; and II. Letitia Caroline, bap. Oct. 7, 1804, m. Geo. Powis; removed to Seneca; d. in 1870.

47. VII. Van Rensselaer; became a sea captain; d. unm.

Sixth Generation.

John A. [40] had ch.:

48. I. Arent Henry (55), b. Nov. 25, 1801; m. Mary Caroline Kingsland (28), April 24, 1828.

49. II. Harriet Ann, bap. Feb. 17, 1803; m. Smith W. Anderson.

50. III. Angelica V. R., d. March, 1864.

51. IV. John A., m. Frances Elizabeth, dau. of Alexander Bleeker, of N.Y.; d. Nov. 21, 1855, in his 44th year.

52. V. Robert V. R., m. Kate M., dau. of Angelo Manchini, Sept. 9, 1851; d. Feb. 19, 1855; had ch.: I. Van Rensselaer, b. July 27, 1852.

53. VI. Jacob R. (65), m. Susanna, dau. of Timothy Edwards, Nov. 18, 1847; she d. Jan. 23, 1870.

54. VII. Catharine Gertrude, m. Henry S. Craig, Oct. 4, 1838.

Seventh Generation.

Arent Henry [48] had ch.:

55. I. Henry K., b. March 5, 1829; m. Ellen, dau. of Anthony P. Valentine, of Spottswood, Dec. 15, 1858; had ch.: I. Arent, b. Sept. 25, 1860; II. Campbell V., b. July 2, 1864.

[1] *Rivington's Gazette, June* 5, 1798.

56. II. John Arent, b. Feb. 19, 1831; m. Kate M., dau. of Angelo Manchini, and wid. of Robert V. R. Schuyler (52), Jan. 14, 1863; d. June 15, 1870; had ch.: I. Sidney S., b. Aug. 25, 1864.
57. III. Smith A., b. Nov. 18, 1832; m. Bessie Kneeland; d. July 26, 1870.
58. IV. Edwin N., b. June 15, 1834; d. Sept. 13, 1835.
59. V. Harriet A., b. Aug. 29, 1836; m. Sidney A. Schiefflin, Sept. 15, 1858.
60. VI. Sarah K., b. June 22, 1838; m. S. Van Cortlandt Van Rensselaer, Oct. 6, 1858.
61. VII. Arent H., b. Aug. 8, 1840; d. Sept. 20, 1863.
62. VIII. Richard K., b. June 24, 1842.
63. IX. Mary Caroline, b. Feb. 16, 1845; d. Aug. 9, 1845.
64. X. Catharine Gertrude, b. Aug. 17, 1846; d. Dec. 16, 1866.

Jacob R. [53] had ch.:

65. I. Sarah E.; II. Rutsen V. R., m. Harriet Augusta, dau. of Andrew D. Mellick, Feb. 4, 1873; III. Catharine V. R.; IV. Susanna E.; V. Edwards O.; VI. Angelica V. R.

Kingsland.

Isaac Kingsland seems to have been the founder of the family of this name, which settled on the east bank of the Passaic river. He was a nephew of Major Nathaniel Kingsland, of the Parish of Christ Church, on the Island of Barbadoes. By his uncle's will he received a large tract of land on New Barbadoes Neck, since then the home of the family. He was a man of some note, and for several years a member of the Council. He had a brother Gustavus, to whom he conveyed a tract of land on the Neck, Dec. 30, 1697. He m. Elizabeth ——, and d. in the early part of the year 1698.

Second Generation.

Isaac had ch.:

2. I. Edmund (4), not yet of age in 1698; m. Mary, dau. of Judge William Pinhorne; marriage license dated Nov. 8, 1703. He was commissioner under the bill of credit act in 1723. His will is dated July 19, 1741.

3. II. John; III. Mary; IV. Hester, m. Philip Schuyler (11); V. Elizabeth; VI. Frances; VII. Isaac.

Third Generation.

Edmund [2] had ch.:

4. I. William (6), b. in 1704; m. Margretta, dau. of Philip Coerten, Dec. 13, 1732; d. Oct. 24, 1770; she d. Sept. 4, 1756. He was appointed Judge of the Bergen Common Pleas, March 8, 1749. Her father was a Huguenot, and came to this country shortly after the revocation of the edict of Nantes.

5. II. John; III. Isaac, m. Elizabeth Dow, wid. of Alexander Gaelt; was Sheriff of Bergen County in 1764; IV. Hester.

Fourth Generation.

William [4] had ch.:

6. I. Elizabeth, b. March 2, 1734; m. Josiah Hornblower. The late Chief Justice Hornblower of New Jersey was their son; d. April 24, 1808.

7. II. Mary, b. Sept. 22, 1737; m. Edmund Leslie.

8. III. Edmund William (11), b. Aug. 17, 1741; m. 1st, Mary, dau. of John Richards; she b. March 20, 1741, d. Oct. 16, 1798; 2d, Sarah Jauncey, Oct. 3, 1801; d. Nov. 8, 1728; she b. Dec. 25, 1748, d. Feb. 9, 1814. Captain John Richards adhered to the British during the revolution, but left his family on New Barbadoes Neck. Hearing that they were sick with the small pox, he attempted to visit them in Jan., 1778. When near Bergen he was captured by a couple of bandits under the guise of patriots. They took him through the woods toward the Three Pigeons. Before they reached that place they attempted to rob him. He resisted, and they shot him. Mr. Kingsland also sympathized with the loyal cause, and left home, it was alleged, to join the enemy, whereupon his wife was sent out of the American lines.

9. IV. Margaret, b. July 2, 1743; m. James Leslie.

10. V. Henry (22), b. June 7, 1745; m. Helena Van Vorst (33); d. May 1, 1828.

Fifth Generation.

Edmund William [8] had ch.:

11. I. William, b. March 20, 1769; m. Margaret Kingsland (23); d. Dec. 3, 1800, s. p.
12. II. John, b. March 20, 1769; m. Eleanor Campbell; d. July 2, 1797; had ch.: I. William S., d. in inf.
13. III. Burnet R. (25), b. Aug. 6, 1771; m. Eliza Smith; d. March 10, 1830.
14. IV. Margaret, b. March 26, 1773; m. 1st, her cousin, William Hornblower; 2d, Charles Trinder.
15. V. Henry W. (28), b. June 4, 1774; m. Sarah, dau. of Joseph Jauncey, July 30, 1803; appointed Judge of the Bergen Common Pleas, Feb. 17, 1819; d. April 8, 1856; she d. Sept. 11, 1858.
16. VI. Richards, b. Nov. 29, 1776; m. Eleanor Campbell, wid. of his brother John; d. s. p.
17. VII. Maria, b. Feb. 21, 1778; d. unm.
18. VIII. Nathaniel, b. April 9, 1779; d. Sept. 9, 1798.
19. IX. Caroline, b. May 9, 1781; m. Peter Reynolds.
20. X. George (32), b. Feb. 9, 1783; m. Frances L. Ten Eyck; d. Oct. 20, 1866.
21. XI. Harriet, b. Feb., 1785; m. William De Forest, Jan. 23, 1814.

Henry [10] had ch.:

22. I. Elizabeth, b. Dec. 10, 1776; d. in inf.
23. II. Margaret, b. Aug. 16, 1779; m. 1st, William Kingsland (11); 2d, George Campbell; III. Anne, m. Pierson Dey; IV. Helena, m. Robert Lee.
24. V. William C. (39), m. Sarah, dau. of William Hervey.

Sixth Generation.

Burnet R. [13] had ch.:

25. I. John S., d. unm.
26. II. Sarah, m. Rodman M. Bartlett, M. D.
27. III. Eleanor, m. 1st, George S. Middlebrook, June 25, 1833; 2d, Stephen P. Britton.

Henry W. [15] had ch.:

28. I. Mary Caroline, b. June 21, 1804; m. Arent H. Schuyler (48), April 24, 1828.
29. II. Sarah Eliza, b. March 14, 1806; m. Charles Adams, March 14, 1838.

30. III. Edmund William, d. May 19, 1825, æt. 17 yrs.
31. IV. Harriet R., b. June 24, 1807; m. Edwin Nesbitt, Sept. 23, 1826.

George [20] had ch.:

32. I. Edmund W. (42), b. May 21, 1816; m. Sarah Ann, dau. of Thomas E. Steele, M. D., Dec. 20, 1838.
33. II. Andrew T., m. Euphemia Lester; d. Nov., 1860; had ch.: I. Fannie.
34. III. Eliza T., m. James E. Camp.
35. IV. Richards, m. Sarah Merrill; had ch.: I. Fannie; II. Minnie; III. Henry B.
36. V. Mary C.
37. VI. George, m. Mary K. Nesbitt; has ch.: I. James E.; II. George; III. Harriet; IV. Sarah; V. Mary.
38. VII. Washington, d. unm.; VIII. Nathaniel, d. unm.; IX. John J., d. unm.

William C. [24] had ch.:

39. I. William H., d. in inf.
40. II. Cornelius V. V. (45), m. Margaret, dau. of John Vreeland.
41. III. Jane Ann, m. Robert Campbell.

Seventh Generation.

Edmund W. [32] had ch.:

42. I. Edmund W., b. Dec. 15, 1839; II. Frances, d. in inf.; III. Mary Eliza, d. in inf.; IV. George, d. in inf.
43. V. George, b. April 19, 1845; m. Angelina B., dau. of James W. Jauncey, March 28, 1866.
44. VI. Thomas Edward S.; VII. Andrew T.; VIII. Frances L.; IX. Mary C.; these four d. in inf.; X. Margaret S., b. March 9, 1852.

Cornelius V. V. [40] had ch.:

45. I. John Henry, d. unm.; II. William C., m. Emma Vreeland; III. Enoch I., m. Lottie Outwater; IV. Sarah W., m. Abraham Ackerman; V. Helena, m. Abraham Garrabrant; VI. James H.

The following Sketch was prepared expressly for the History of Hudson County *by the late John Stagg Gautier, of New York.:*

The Gautier Family.

The progenitor of the Gautier family in New York and New Jersey was a French Huguenot who came to America after the revocation of the Edict of Nantes. By intermarriage a considerable landed estate in Old Bergen County, N. J., came into possession of the family. This property, known as the "Gautier Farm," descended through Capt. Thomas Brown,[1] and consisted

---

[1] Captain Thomas Brown.

The parentage and birthplace of Capt. Brown have never been traced, but tradition asserts that he was born in Bergen County, N. J. (?), his father being of English, and his mother of Dutch descent. He was born in the year 1717, and followed the sea from his youth upward, and soon owned and commanded the vessel he sailed in. During the French wars he was captain of a privateer, and at other periods sailed on trading voyages to the West Indies, etc.

On April 16, 1747, he married Anna, daughter of Lawrence and Feytie Van Buskirk, of Minachquay, in Old Bergen County. By this marriage he had one child, Lawrence Brown, born May 18, 1751. Lawrence Van Buskirk died in the year 1752, and by his will left his extensive estates to his wife for her life, and on her death to his only son Cornelius, subject to certain legacies. This son never married, and as his death preceded his mother's, which took place Sept., 1756, the property, on the decease of the latter, descended to the four daughters of Lawrence Van Buskirk: Anna, wife of Capt. Brown; Jane, wife of Jacob Van Horn; Martha, wife of John Lagrange, and Sophia, wife of ——— Roll. Mrs. Brown being deceased, her portion, being one-quarter of the estate, was inherited by her son Lawrence. On March 23, 1757, Capt. Brown purchased another fourth part from John and Feytie Lagrange, the children of Martha, deceased, thus becoming the owner of one-half of the farm, including the "Old Homestead"

On Jan. 23, 1756, Capt. Brown had married for his second wife Mary Ten Eyck, daughter of Samuel and Mary (Gurney) Ten Eyck, of New York. The issue of this marriage was also but one child, Mary Brown, born Oct. 17, 1756, who, on Oct. 6, 1772, married Andrew Gautier.

On becoming possessor of the farm, Captain Brown (I quote his own words) "proceeded to cultivate and improve the same, and at very great Expense repaired the Old House thereon, which shortly after Was by Accident burned to the Ground, whereby the said Thomas Brown lost upward of one thousand eight hundred pounds.

"That in a convenient Time after the said Thos. Brown built a New House & other Conveniences at a little Distance from the Former which Cost him One thousand pounds, & continued for several years to improve the premises at a very great Expense."

The death of his son Lawrence in August, 1767,* a minor, obliged him to purchase the rights of the three aunts, as the heirs-at-law of his deceased wife, and this was the cause of a long dispute with Jacob Van Horn. This quarrel was a very bitter one, and, after being twice referred to arbitrators, was finally

---

* This is an error; he died July 4, 1767.

of a tract of land situated at old Minachquay (commonly called Pamrapough), now Greenville, about three miles south of Jersey City, and extended from New York to Newark Bay. This property, formerly a portion of the Lawrence Van Buskirk farm,[1] when inherited by Thomas Gautier in 1782, consisted of 406 acres of land, 40 of which were in salt meadows, and the "old homestead," which was erected by Capt. Brown in the year 1760, and is still standing. The engraving of it on another page is a good representation as it appears at the present day, though conveying but a faint idea of what it was while in possession of the Gautier family. The place bore the name of "Retirement Hall," and was celebrated far and wide for its genial hospitality. It passed from the possession of the family in 1829.

The Gautier family in New York are supposed to be descended

---

settled in 1771, when general releases were exchanged. On June 5, 1769, Van Horn advertised the property of Capt. Brown for sale at a public vendue, which actually took place, though the sale was never consummated. The prices the land was sold for at this vendue seem rather curious to our modern views of value, and were as follows:

For woodland near Bergen Point, £11 per acre.

For land near Van Horn's field, £6.10 per acre.

Capt. Brown owned and run the ferry from the western side of his farm on Newark Bay across the Hackensack river, forming a connecting link in the route of travel between New York and Philadelphia. This ferry bore his name, and its location is still pointed out as "Brown's Ferry." In the troubles of the Revolutionary War Capt. Brown espoused the patriot side with warmth and zeal, being one of the notable exceptions in Bergen County. In 1775 he was a member of the Standing Committee of Correspondence for Bergen County, and filled other offices of trust. In 1765 he was trustee of the roads and ferries in the same county, was justice of the peace, etc., etc. In 1757 he was a member of a commission to examine the transports in New York and to report the best plan of fortifying the harbor. He was a large real estate owner in New York city, and was admitted a freeman of the city in the year 1770. He was a man of large wealth, his property being in landed estates, moneys at interest and slaves, besides a large quantity of silver plate.

He possessed great energy of character, strong will, and displayed many traits of inherent talents and abilities. He always held a position of prominence among his neighbors, and was not slow to assert and maintain his rights. He was stricken with paralysis, and after a lingering illness, through which he retained all his faculties except the use of his limbs, he died at the old homestead on the 30th of October, 1782, aged 65 years, and was buried in the Ten Eyck vault, in St. Paul's churchyard, New York city.

Through the marriage of his only surviving child with Andrew Gautier, her children were his heirs-at-law. He, however, executed a will in which, after providing for his wife, he leaves his entire estates to his two grandsons, Thomas and Daniel Gautier. By the death of Daniel in 1791, Thomas became the sole owner of the property.

[1] The property was principally embraced in the original patent from Wm. Kieft, Governor of New Netherlands, to Claes Carstensen Norman, dated March 25, 1647, and confirmed with *additions* to Lawrence Andriese by patent from Gov. Philip Carteret, dated March 26, 1667. The *additions* were portions of the original patents to Barnt Christians and Casper Steymets.

RETIREMENT HALL. ERECTED A. D. 1760.
(*Former homestead of the Gautier Family.*)
JERSEY CITY.

from a Huguenot family of that name, formerly of Saint Blancard, in the Province of Languedoc, France; a noble family and of considerable prominence in the wars of the Huguenots. Jacques Gautier, said to be the first of the name in New York, had two sons, Daniel and François, and several daughters. The family are among the early members of the Huguenot church—*L'Eglise du St. Esprit*—in New York city.

Daniel[2] m., in the Dutch church, N. Y., Sept. 6, 1716, Maria Bogaert, who was bap. in same church July 21, 1689. They had eleven ch.:

I. Maria, b. Dec. 24, 1716; m., March 9, 1743, Daniel Waldron.
II. Magdalen, b. April 4, 1719; m., Sept. 30, 1756, Samuel Foster.
III. Andrew, b. June 4, 1720.
IV. Susanne, b. Sept. 21, 1722; d. an infant.
V. Susanne, b. March 11, 1724.
VI. Hillegond, bap. Aug. 10, 1728; d. an infant.
VII. Elizabeth, b. Dec. 7, 1730; d. an infant.
VIII. Daniel, bap. Feb. 7, 1733.
IX. Hillegond, bap. Jan. 19, 1735; m., Feb. 14, 1760, Jenkin Williams.
X. Elizabeth, bap. Dec. 26, 1736.
XI. Catharine, bap. Aug. 24, 1739; m., July 22, 1762, Christopher Duyckinck.

In the dissensions in the Huguenot church in 1724, caused by a quarrel between two different parties in the church as to the claims of rival ministers, Daniel Gautier sided with the "De Lancey party," as it was called, and upon Gov. Burnet deciding adversely to their claims, left the church. During his lifetime he attended the Dutch church, but his children became members of the English, afterward Episcopal church, in the parish of Trinity.

Andrew[3], m. 1st, Elizabeth Crosfield, an English lady, and sister of Stephen Crosfield, one of the proprietors of Totten and Crosfield's famous Land Patent in the State of New York. They had 4 ch.:

I. Daniel, b. July 12, 1745; d. June 26, 1746. His tombstone is in Trinity churchyard.
II. Elizabeth, m. James Leadbetter, and d. young, s. p.
III. Andrew, b. Dec. 18, 1755.
IV. Daniel, b. Sept. 27, 1759; m., Jan. 11, 1783, Ann Brandon, and had 1 ch.: Andrew. He d. 1786. This

son Andrew, b. Sept. 15, 1783, m., Dec. 12, 1802, Martha Bininger; had two ch.: Thomas and Andrew, who both d. in inf., and he d. Nov. 21, 1806, in Montpellier, France, and is there buried.

Andrew[3] m. 2d, Oct. 23, 1774, Margaret Hastier, dau. of Jean and Elizabeth (Perdrian) Hastier, of one of the early Huguenot families of N. Y. There was no issue by this marriage, and after his death the widow m., Oct. 9, 1783, Andrew Hammersley. Andrew Gautier was a man of some prominence in New York, a large property owner, and held several public offices. He was Assistant Alderman from the Dock Ward from 1765 to 1767, and Alderman from 1768 to '73, and was an ardent loyalist on the breaking out of the revolutionary troubles.[1] He died soon after.

Andrew[4] was educated at King's (now Columbia) College, entering that institution at the early age of fourteen, in 1769, and was designed for the profession of the law, though he never practiced. He m. 1st, Oct. 6, 1772, Mary Brown, only ch. and heiress of Captain Thomas and Mary (Ten Eyck) Brown, of Bergen County, N. J. She was b. at the "Old Homestead," Oct. 17, 1756, being but sixteen years of age at the time of her marriage, while the groom was but seventeen. They had 2 ch.:

I. Thomas, b. June 6, 1774.

II. Daniel, b. Feb. 7, 1776; d. Jan. 7, 1791. The mother d. July 30, 1777.

Andrew[4] m. 2d, Oct. 30, 1784, Hannah Turner, dau. of John and Margaret (Burnton) Turner, and by her had 8 ch.:

I. Eliza Bowater, b. Dec. 17, 1785; m. Dec. 17, 1808, Hartman Vreeland, of Bergen County. She is still living at Pamrapo, and never had issue.[2]

II. Margaret Turner, b. Feb. 17, 1787; m., Jan. 5, 1812, Garret Van Horn, of Bergen Co. She d. Dec. 29, 1828, leaving 4 ch.: Eliza, John Garret, Stephen Crosfield and Hartman Vreeland; the last named was adopted by his aunt, Mrs. Vreeland, and now bears that name.

III. Catharine, b. July 26, 1788; d. unm.

IV. Maria Charlotte, b. Nov. 6, 1789; still living; unm.[3]

---

[1] "Mr. Andrew Gautier, who lately came from New York, appeared before the Council, & was permitted to enter into recognizance to appear at the next Court of Oyer & Terminer held in and for the Co. of Morris." *Minutes of Council of Safety*, 273. C. H. W.

[2] Died Oct. 24, 1872, after the above was written. C. H. W.

[3] Died Oct. 24, 1873, after the above was written. C. H. W.

V. Ann Crosfield, b. Dec. 27, 1793; m. 1st, Edmund Hall; 2d, Dec. 3, 1837, Clark Hewett; living at Watertown, N. Y.; no issue by either husband.
VI. Mary, b. 1795; m. James Cassedy, and lives in Indiana; no issue.
VII. Daniel, b. Oct. 12, 1800.
VIII. Hannah Turner, b. Aug. 20, 1801; m., 1841, John West Mason; d. 1868; no issue.

Thomas[5], b. June 6, 1774, at the "Old Homestead." A lawyer by profession, though not practicing. He m., April 28, 1796, Elizabeth Leavy, dau. of John and Elizabeth (Dickson) Leavy, who was b. June 30, 1775. They had 3 ch., all born at "Retirement Hall."

I. Thomas Brown, b. July 25, 1797.
II. Helen Dickson, b. Feb. 17, 1799; m. Robert French, U. S. A., May 25, 1824, and had 6 ch.: Robert Summerfield, Thomas Gautier, George, Helen, Elizabeth Gautier, and Samuel Gautier. Mrs. French is living, and resides with her son Thomas at Orange, N. J. Dr. French d. Aug. 13, 1835.
III. Samuel Ten Eyck, b. Nov. 10, 1800.

Thomas Gautier d. at his city residence, No. 41 Broad street, Oct. 17, 1802, and was buried in the family vault in Trinity churchyard. His widow survived him many years, and d. in Jersey City, Nov. 15, 1866, in her 92d year. Very many of the inhabitants of Bergen and Jersey City will remember this venerable lady.

Daniel[5], b. Oct. 12, 1800; m., May 3, 1820, Wilhimina McClelland, dau. of William McClelland, of Scotland. He d. in 1821, leaving one child, Daniel William McClelland, b. Feb. 19, 1822, d. Dec. 23, 1848, unm.

Thomas Brown[6], b. July 25, 1797; m. 1st, Oct. 15, 1816, Elizabeth Hornblower, dau. of Dr. Josiah and Anna (Merselis) Hornblower, of Bergen, and had 8 ch.:

I. Mary Brown, b. July 26, 1817; m., April, 1839, David Betts Wakeman, and had 6 ch.: Elizabeth Gautier, Edmund D. Barry, Anna, Jabez J., Sarah, Mary Caroline. She d. in Jersey City, April 5, 1850.
II. Josiah Hornblower, b. Nov. 12, 1818.
III. Thomas, b. July 16, 1820.
IV. Anna Elizabeth, b. March 17, 1822; living; unm.
V. Francis Pantar, b. April 18, 1824.

VI. William Henry, b. Jan. 1, 1826.
VII. Eugene, b. March, 1828; d. Dec. 10, 1848.
VIII. James Robert, b. Nov. 25, 1830.

Mrs. Gautier d. May 28, 1844.

Thomas B. m. 2d, Dec. 23, 1845, Caroline Matilda Taylor, dau. of Daniel and Sarah Maria (Lloyd) Taylor, and had 1 ch.: Helen Dickson. Dr. Gautier d. at his residence in Jersey City, April 11, 1850, and was buried in Greenwood. He was a physician of eminence, a graduate of the College of Physicians and Surgeons in New York in 1823, and received the honorary degree of M. D. from Rutgers College in 1831. He resided and practiced his profession for many years in Bergen.

Samuel Ten Eyck[6], b. Nov. 10, 1800; m., April 19, 1822, Hannah Augusta Stagg, dau. of Abraham and Rachel (Town) Stagg, of New York city, where she was b. April 19, 1803. They had 12 ch.:

I. Samuel Ten Eyck, b. April 13, 1823; d. Aug. 1, 1823.
II. Elizabeth, b. May 23, 1824; d. Aug. 18, 1831.
III. Theodore, b. Jan. 4, 1826; d. Aug. 12, 1831.
IV. Mary Stagg, b. Jan. 1, 1828; d. Aug. 13, 1831.
V. Helen French, b June 2, 1830; d. Aug 11, 1831.
VI. Augusta, b. Jan. 8, 1832; m., June 6, 1854, Edmund Sewell Hamilton; living; no issue.
VII. Julia Adelaide, b. Oct. 9, 1833; m., Oct. 29, 1856, James Bach Kayser; had 5 ch.
VIII. Caroline Virginia, b. Jan. 31, 1836; m. 1st, Dec. 27, 1858, Albert Chesebro, jr., and had 2 ch.; 2d, Nov. 29, 1865, Arnold Nandain, M. D.; had 1 ch.
IX. Robert French, b. Jan. 16, 1838; d. Oct. 20, 1841.
X. John Stagg, b. Nov. 19, 1839.
XI. Henry Clay, b. Oct. 5, 1841; d. Oct. 18, 1842.
XII. Thomas, b. Sept. 8, 1843; d. July 11, 1846.

Mrs. Gautier d. April 13, 1865, at Fordham, N. Y., and is buried in the family vault in Trinity churchyard. Mr. Gautier is still living at Fordham. He was the last owner of the "Gautier Farm," and many of our citizens will remember him as the host of "Retirement Hall," possessing the finest stables and hunting pack in the county.

Josiah Hornblower[7], b. Nov. 12, 1818; m., Dec. 10, 1844, Mary Louisa Gregory, dau. of Hon. Dudley S. and Ann Maria Gregory, of Jersey City, and had 7 ch.: Dudley Gregory, Thomas Brown, Maria Louisa, Josiah Hornblower, Anna Elizabeth, Charles Edward and Clara Sutton.

Dr. Gautier is now a resident of New York. He is a graduate of the University of New York city, and also of its Department of Medicine in 1844. He practiced medicine in Jersey City for some years, attaining a high rank in the profession, but finally abandoned it for more congenial pursuits. He entered into active business in connection with Joseph Dixon, in the crucible works in Jersey City, and afterward became interested in the steel works. He is now the leading partner in the firm of J. H. Gautier & Co. and Gautier, Parker & Co.

Thomas[7], b. July 16, 1820; m., May 16, 1855, Anna Robinson, dau. of Alanson and Sabrina Robinson, of Newark, Illinois, and has 1 ch., Thomas Brown. Resides in Jersey City.

Francis Pantar[7], b. April 18, 1824; m., Dec. 20, 1860, Eliza Newkirk, dau. of Henry and Eliza (Provost) Newkirk, of Bergen, and had 4 ch.: Mary Elizabeth, Annie Louisa, Alice Maud and Frank Henry. He resides in Bergen.

John Stagg[7], b. Nov. 19, 1839; m., Dec. 10, 1862, Abbie Cushman, dau. of Frederick and Sarah J. (Swain) Cushman, of New York. Has 1 ch.: Abbie Cushman, b. March 25, 1864, in N. Y. He resides in New York city.[1]

Cadmus—Codmus—Caddemis.

The first of this family who settled in Hudson County was Dirck, or Diedrick. From the fact that he is sometimes spoken of as Dirck Fredricksen, it is probable that he was a son of Fredrick, who d. Nov. 8, 1745. Dirck m. Jannetje Van Horn (2), June 20, 1718. There was also an Andries Hendricksen Cadmus, who m. Grietje Claesen Kuyper, of Ahasimus, Oct. 22, 1725.

Second Generation.

Dirck had ch.:

1. I. Rutgert, d. Sept. 17, 1746. His body was taken to Tappan for burial. May it not be that the father came from that place?
2. II. Catrintje, d. Oct. 22, 1732.
3. III. Fredrick, m. Saartje Van Winkle, of Wesel, Dec. 9, 1742; removed to Slotterdam; d. Jan. 12, 1753.

---

[1] The author of the above sketch died Oct. 2, 1871. C. H. W.

4. IV. Johannis, d. Sept. 28, 1746; V. Andries, b. Oct. 28, 1733.
5. VI. Neeltje, b. June 23, 1736; VII. Catrintje, b. May 27, 1738; m. Cornelius Vreeland (73).
6. VIII. Joris (7), m. 1st, Jannetje Vreeland (72); 2d, Jenneke Prior; she d. June 29, 1795; he d. April 2, 1781.

Third Generation.

Joris [6] had ch.:
7. I. Jannetje, b. Jan. 7, 1758; d. in inf.
8. II. Jannetje, b. March 17, 1759; m. Garret Vreeland (61).
9. III. Joris (14), b. Oct. 10, 1761; m. Aegie, dau. of Hendrick Fielding, June 22, 1799; d. May 1, 1821.
10. IV. Metje, b. Dec. 22, 1764; m. John Garretson, of Staten Island, Oct. 9, 1781.
11. V. Dirck, b. March 16, 1769; d. unm.
12. VI. Casparus (20), b. Aug. 16, 1770; m. Catlyntje, dau. of John Dodd; d. Sept. 23, 1845; she b. Jan. 27, 1768; d. Oct. 11, 1822.
13. VII. Jenneke, b. July 17, 1773; m. Jacob Vreeland (59).

Fourth Generation.

Joris [8] had ch.:
14. I. Jannetje, b. Feb. —, 1780; m. Andrew Anderson, May 23, 1801.
15. II. Aegie, b. Jan. —, 1784; m. John Vreeland (101), March 17, 1804.
16. III. George (32), b. Aug. 18, 1786; m. Mary, dau. of Cornelius Van Buskirk, March 18, 1808; d. June 1, 1844.
17. IV. Martha, m. John Post; V. Margrietje, b. Sept. 14, 1793; m. Richard McDonald.
18. VI. Catrintje, m. David Brewer, June 22, 1824.
19. VII. Henry, b. Aug. 19, 1796; d. Aug. 3, 1819, unm.

Casparus [12] had ch.:
20. I. Saertje, b. Jan. 9, 1788; m. Jacob A. Van Winkle (89), Feb. 7, 1808; d. May 12, 1862.
21. II. Joris (36), b. Dec. 4, 1789; m. Elizabeth Vreeland (178), Nov. 14, 1812.
22. III. John (41), b. Feb. 21, 1792; m. Elizabeth Vreeland (153), Dec. 3, 1814; d. July 28, 1832.

23. IV. Casparus (48), b. Jan. 13, 1794; m. Margaret Vreeland (154), Dec. 17, 1817; d. Dec. 15, 1854.
24. V. Jannetje, b. Dec. 22, 1795; m. Nicholas Van Buskirk (50), Dec. 15, 1814; d. Oct. 25, 1836.
25. VI. Seelitje, b. Oct. 24, 1797; m. Michael Van Ripen (99), Dec. 21, 1816; d. Feb. 27, 1842.
26. VII. Martha, b. Dec. 7, 1799; m. Nicholas Prior, Dec. 18, 1817; d. May 11, 1826.
27. VIII. Michael (55), b. Oct. 27, 1801; m. Anne Sickles, June 9, 1827; d. Jan. 23, 1870.
28. IX. Richard (62), b. Nov. 22, 1803; m. Cathalina, dau. of Michael De Mott, April 24, 1827; d. Oct. 16, 1873.
29. X. Catharine, b. Jan. 15, 1806; m. Mindert Vreeland (182), Jan. 18, 1823; d. Oct. 22, 1835.
30. XI. Andrew (70), b. March 14, 1808; m. Jane Vreeland (113), May 29, 1830; d. Aug. 27, 1832.
31. XII. Eleanor, b. May 21, 1810; m. Joseph Seguine, of Staten Island, Dec. 24, 1830.

Fifth Generation.

George [16] had ch.:

32. I. Cornelius (72), b. April 18, 1810; m. Rachel, dau. of Paul Vreeland, of Polliflу, Nov. 14, 1833; d. Aug. 9, 1859.
33. II. George (83), b. Aug. 13, 1808; m. Sarah Ann, dau. of William Runyon, Oct. 13, 1832.
34. III. Thomas (92), b. July 5, 1813; m. Julia, dau. of Peter Earle, June 29, 1837.
35. IV. Jane, b. Sept. 16, 1815; m. Jacob Metzger, March 16, 1835.

Joris [21) had ch.:

36. I. Jasper (93), b. Oct. 30, 1813; m. Lavina Van Pelt, May 27, 1835.
37. II. Hannah, m. Jacob Van Name.
38. III. Catharine, m. George Simonson.
39. IV. Eliza, m. —— De Hart, of Staten Island.
40. V. George (94), m. Cornelia Vreeland (186).
VI. Cornelia, m. —— Decker; VII. Jane, m. Henry Huntington.

John [22] had ch.:

41. I. Rachel, b. Sept. 6, 1816; m. Cornelius J. Van Buskirk (55).

42. II. Catharine, b. Nov. 28, 1818; d. Nov. 20, 1835.
43. III. Jasper, b. Oct. 30, 1821; m. Hannah Van Buskirk, March 12, 1846.
44. IV. Elizabeth, b. Dec. 18, 1823; m. Abraham Woods, Dec. 23, 1841.
45. V. William (98), b. Sept. 16, 1826; m. Jane Jerolamon.
46. VI. Richard (99), b. Oct. 26, 1828; m. 1st, Maria Jerolamon; 2d, Frances Simonson.
47. VII. Martha, b. Jan. 13, 1831; m. 1st, Nicholas Vreeland (304), Nov. 8, 1848; 2d, Cornelius Cadmus (72), July 6, 1862.

Casparus [23] had ch.:

48. I. Rachel, b. May 18, 1820; m. Michael A. Vreeland (232), Jan. 31, 1839.
49. II. Jasper (100), b. Feb. 28, 1823; m. Helen Vreeland (119), Dec. 26, 1844.
50. III. Catharine, b. Sept. 20, 1825; d. Nov. 6, 1831.
51. IV. William (102), b. Feb. 6, 1831; m. Lavina Van Buskirk (61), Dec. 3, 1852.
52. V. Peter, b. Oct. 5, 1837; d. June 8, 1840.
53. VI. Sarah Catharine, b. July 15, 1839; m. Abraham Jerolamon, Dec. 30, 1857.
54. VII. Margaret, b. Feb. 11, 1844; m. Alfred S. Chapman, of Conn., Oct. 23, 1866.

Michael [27] had ch.:

55. I. Matilda, b. Sept. 6, 1828; m. William L. Beaumont, Sept. 30, 1848; d. Aug. 28, 1866.
56. II. Jasper, b. Oct. 4, 1830; removed to Illinois.
57. III. Abraham, b. Feb. 4, 1833.
58. IV. John Andrew (103), b. March 2, 1835; m. Sarah C., dau. of Egbert Wauters, Feb. 9, 1865.
59. V. George Edwin, b. Nov. 15, 1838; d. Nov. 21, 1860, unm.
60. VI. Leander, b. March 10, 1842; d. April 13, 1864, unm.
61. VII. Richard, b. Jan. 5, 1845.

Richard [28] had ch.:

62. I. John Henry, b. Aug. 25, 1828; d. March 7, 1831.
63. II. Cathalina, b. Jan. 6, 1830; d. Aug. 2, 1831.
64. III. Mary Elizabeth, b. June 6, 1831; m. John Combs, May 25, 1850.

65. IV. Margaret, b. June 23, 1833; m. Hartman Vreeland (282), June 1, 1853.
66. V. Cathalina, b. Feb. 19, 1835; m. John L. Meade, Nov. 13, 1858.
67. VI. Richard, b. Nov. 1, 1836; d. Aug. 14, 1837.
68. VII. George (104), b. April 12, 1840; m. Cornelia B., dau. of William N. Smith, June 15, 1864.
69. VIII. James R., b. May 1, 1847; m. Catharine Ann, dau. of Andrew Van Horn, Dec. 12, 1872.

Andrew [30] had ch.:

70. I. Jasper (105), b. March 16, 1831; m. Catharine Elizabeth, dau. of James Pharo, Sept. 22, 1850.
71. II. Andrew (106), b. Feb. 20, 1833; m. Sophia Jane Vreeland (195), Oct. 28, 1859.

Sixth Generation.

Cornelius [32] had ch.:

72. I. Cornelius (107), b. March 16, 1835; m. Martha Cadmus (47), wid. of Nicholas Vreeland (304), July 6, 1862.
73. II. Leah Ann, b. Nov. 20, 1836; d. Oct. 21, 1856.
74. III. Henry, b. June 10, 1838; m. Eliza McFarlane, June 5, 1868; had ch.: I. Florence, b. April 28, 1870.
75. IV. Andrew J., b. June 29, 1840; m. Margaret, dau. of William Dunham, of Amboy, April —, 1866; had ch.: I. Alice, b. Feb. 24, 1868.
76. V. Martha, b. Sept. 16, 1841.
77. VI. Maria Jane, b. Dec. 20, 1843; m. 1st, William Taxter, July 3, 1862; he d. April 7, 1865; 2d, William Dexter, May 5, 1868.
78. VII. Alfred M., b. Oct. 8, 1845; d. May 31, 1846.
79. VIII. Margaret Louisa, b. Dec. 31, 1846; d. Sept. 19, 1850.
80. IX. Edward W. H., b. Oct. 8, 1849.
81. X. Emma Louisa, b. May 15, 1851; d. Sept. —, 1851.
82. XI. Emma Louisa, b. Sept. 14, 1852.

George [33] had ch.:

83. I. Sarah Ann, b. Nov. 11, 1833; m. Elias R. Carson.
84. II. George (108), b. Dec. 1, 1835; m. Margaret P., dau. of Richard Runyon, July 3, 1861.
85. III. William R., b. Oct. 7, 1837; d. Oct. 25, 1838.
86. IV. Theodore R. (109), b. Jan. 10, 1839; m. Eliza Jane Vreeland (193), Dec. 31, 1865.

87. V. Allabanner, b. Feb. 1, 1841; m. Catharine Ann Bradley, July 2, 1865.
88. VI. Firman, b. Feb. 12, 1843; m. Julia Chambers.
89. VII. Mary Elizabeth, b. April 4, 1845; d. Aug. 29, 1850.
90. VIII. Amos, b. Jan. 21, 1847.
91. IX. Gertrude, b. May 13, 1849; m. Simpson Braisted.

Thomas [34] had ch.:

92. I. Abby Jane, b. April 12, 1893; II. Hanson, b. June 21, 1842.

Jasper [36] had ch..

93. I. George; II. Elizabeth; III. Gertrude; IV. Louisa; V. David. This family resides in Plainfield, N. J.

George [40] had ch.:

94. I. Annie; II. Laura. This family resides in Lisbon, Ill.

Jasper [43] had ch.:

95. I. Ann Elizabeth, b. Dec. 20, 1846; d. March 22, 1855.
96. II. Charlotta Willhelmina, b. Sept. 14, 1850.
97. III. Sarah Catharine, b. June 15, 1855; IV. Jane Maria, b. Feb. 19, 1857; V. John, bap. Aug. 2, 1862; VI. Lavina, b. April 12, 1865.

William [45] had ch.:

98. I. John Richard, b. Feb. 2, 1850; II. Hiram M., b. March 10, 1852; III. Martha, b. March 17, 1855, d. Sept. 16, 1857; IV. Abraham, b. May 27, 1857, d. July 21, 1861; V. Alida, bap. May 5, 1860.

Richard [46] had ch.:

99. I. Margaret Elizabeth, b. March 7, 1852; II. Elmira, b. Oct. 26, 1854; III. Reuben, bap. April 23, 1859; IV. Priscilla, b. Sept. —, 1861; V. Anna, b. June 13, 1864.

Jasper [49] had ch.:

100. I. George Henry, b. Feb. 12, 1846; m. Rachel Elizabeth Vreeland (371), Oct. 20, 1870.
101. II. Edwin, b. Feb. 23, 1850; III. William, b. Oct. 17, 1851, d. July 7, 1853; IV. Irwin, b. March 11, 1854.

William [51] had ch.:

102. I. John, b. July 7, 1853; II. Margaret Anna, b. March 19, 1856; III. Nelson, b. March 20, 1859.

John Andrew [58] had ch.:

103. I. Egbert W., b. Nov. 13, 1865; II. George; III. John.

George [68] had ch.:

104. I. Henry S., b. April 30, 1865; d. Feb. 2, 1866.

Jasper [70] had ch.:

105. I. James Andrew, b. Oct. 20, 1850, d. July 24, 1856; II. Mary Jane, b. Sept. 26, 1852; III. Julietta, b. Nov. 26, 1854; IV. Agnes Elizabeth, b. Nov. 18, 1856; V. Eleanor Eugenie, b. Feb. 16, 1859; VI. Augustina, b. Nov. 2, 1860; VII. Olivia, b. June 13, 1862; VIII. William Henry, b. Sept. 6, 1863, d. Jan. 17, 1869; IX. Minnie, b. July 29, 1867, d. Dec. 27, 1868; X. Wilhemina, b. Dec. 27, 1868; XI. Georgiana, b. Jan. 13, 1870, d. Sept. 9, 1870; XII. Benjamin F., b. May 12, 1871; XIII. Irene.

Andrew [71] had ch.:

106. I. Anna Frances, b. Dec. 12, 1863; II. Florence.

Cornelius [72] had ch.:

107. I. Asa, b. April 15, 1864; II. Cornelius, b. March 15, 1866.

George [84] had ch.:

108. I. Abraham L., b. June 22, 1865; II. Charles Henry, b. June 20, 1869, d. June 26, 1869; III. Fairy Bell, b. Sept. 20, 1870.

Theodore R. [86] had ch.:

109. I. Cornelius H., b. April 3, 1867; II. Amelia Meora, b. Jan. 3, 1873.

INDEX.

www.ingramcontent.com/pod-product-compliance
Lightning Source LLC
LaVergne TN
LVHW021221110826
845150LV00002B/216

* 9 7 8 1 4 2 5 5 6 4 3 0 8 *